Rhetorical Bodies

Rhetorical Bodies

Edited by

Jack Selzer and Sharon Crowley

THE UNIVERSITY OF WISCONSIN PRESS

The University of Wisconsin Press
2537 Daniels Street
Madison, Wisconsin 53718

3 Henrietta Street
London WC2E 8LU, England

5   4   3   2   1

Printed in the United States of America

Library of Congress Cataloging-in-Publication Data
Rhetorical bodies / edited by Jack Selzer and Sharon Crowley.
    406 pp.   cm.
    Includes bibliographical references and index.
    ISBN 0-299-16470-5 (cloth: alk. paper)
    ISBN 0-299-16474-8 (pbk.: alk. paper)
    1. Rhetoric—Social aspects—United States Congresses.   2. Language and culture—
United States—History Congresses.   3. Materialism Congresses.   I. Selzer, Jack.
II. Crowley, Sharon, 1943– .
P301.5.S63R49   1999
808—dc21   99-14423

Contents

Preface   vii

1. Habeas Corpus: An Introduction   3
   Jack Selzer

2. Contemporary U.S. Memorial Sites as Exemplars of
   Rhetoric's Materiality   16
   Carole Blair

3. Legible Bodies: Nineteenth-Century Women Physicians
   and the Rhetoric of Dissection   58
   Susan Wells

4. Conspicuous Consumption: Cannibal Bodies and
   the Rhetoric of the American West   75
   Christine De Vinne

5. Material of Desire: Bodily Rhetoric in Working Women's
   Poetry at the Bryn Mawr Summer School, 1921–1938   98
   Karyn Hollis

6. Disintegrating Bodies of Knowledge: Historical Material
   and Revisionary Histories of Rhetoric   120
   Wendy B. Sharer

7. Figuring Illiteracy: Rustic Bodies and Unlettered Minds in
   Rural America   143
   Peter Mortensen

8. Material Literacy and Visual Design   171
   Lester Faigley

9. Autobiography after Prozac   202
   John Schilb

10. Materializing Public and Private: The Spatialization of
    Conceptual Categories in Discourses of Abortion   218
    Christina Haas

11. Rhetoric and Technoscience: The Case of Confide   239
    J. Blake Scott

12. Beard   275
    Melissa Jane Hardie

13. Reading Maternity Materially: The Case of Demi Moore   297
    Barbara Dickson

14. Dick Morris, Ideology, and Regulating the Flow of
    Rhetorical Resources   314
    Yameng Liu

15. The Materiality of Coding: Rhetoric, Genetics, and the
    Matter of Life   326
    Celeste Condit

16. Afterword: The Material of Rhetoric   357
    Sharon Crowley

Selected Bibliography on Material Rhetoric   367
Contributors   379
Index   383

Preface

This book is one product of the elaborate collaboration known as the Fifteenth Penn State Conference on Rhetoric and Composition. In July 1997, about 150 scholars from the United States and several other nations, representing a number of disciplines but centered about rhetorical studies, met at Pennsylvania State University to discuss for several days how the material conditions of rhetoric, the material embodiments of rhetoric, and the material configuration of rhetoric's technologies and artifacts shape the ways rhetoric is being practice and theorized at the end of the twentieth century. Those gathered were convinced that the moment was right for a reconsideration of the material situatedness of literate acts, for a rethinking of how rhetorical practices are related to the real conditions of life that give them life, and for a renewed investigation into the rhetoric of material practices themselves. Conferees attempted to articulate the role of rhetoric in the construction and configuration of material bodies, conditions, and artifacts. They also demarcated the theoretical differences and points of intersection that exist within the disparate scholarly discourses which rely on some notion of "the material"—discourses in philosophy, women's studies, literary study, critical theory, American studies, and the interpretive human sciences.

The conference offered scholars an opportunity to try out their ideas in a novel way, thanks to the conferees' resourcefulness and to the opportunities afforded by electronic technology. Those whose proposals were chosen for discussion at the conference submitted drafts of fully developed papers four weeks or more prior to the meeting, and those drafts were then posted on a conference web site where conference participants could read them, at their relative leisure, before the conference began. Conference sessions therefore consisted not of the usual formal reading of short papers, but rather of lengthy, animated, and unusually thoughtful discussions of full-length works in progress that had been completed with an eye toward eventual publication and studied before the sessions began. In addition, during and after the conference, participants communicated with one another at social events, between sessions, and during meals, as well as by means of an electronic listserve. Attending the entire conference was thus somewhat akin to participating in an extended graduate or postgraduate seminar on a specific topic. Participants shared their ideas, critiqued one another's work, and then left town determined to revise their essays into publications that together would make significant progress toward mapping the meanings that today gather about the term "material rhetoric." *Rhetorical Bodies* collects some of those essays into a book that represents the range of work—and the high quality of work—that is possible under the rubric "material rhetoric": we hope that it will speak to the many constituencies that today are considering one or another aspect of the material.

Given the collaborative nature of the conference, there are many people to thank for their help on this book. Locally the collaboration was sustained by the Rhetoric Conference Planning Committee at Penn State, which initiated a substantial dialogue about the conference before it ever began; we are grateful therefore to Don Bialostosky, Steven Browne, Richard Doyle, Margaret Lyday, Ron Maxwell, Marie Secor, Jeff Walker, and Janet Zepernick. Special mention for their efforts in conceiving the event must go to Christina Haas and Jennifer Jackson, who played significant leadership roles in the conference's planning and conception before they each left Penn State for other universities, and to Andrew Alexander and Ann George, who served so conscientiously in many roles as conference assistants. Their efforts are reflected in the pages that follow. The scholars who attended the conference deserve our deepest thanks— not only the people whose work appears here, but also the many others whose essays we were not able to include on account of length or focus (we wanted to be sure to make this into a *book* and not a loose aggregation), or by their own decision, but whose insights, conference contributions, and textual interanimations are quite palpable to us nevertheless. (It has given us special pleasure to see that so many pieces offered at the conference have found publication already; however, each essay in this collection appears here for the first time.) In addition, we are indebted to a great many people at Penn State for making our conference go smoothly, especially Roberta Moore (who planned our arrangements so well as part of her responsibilities in Continuing and Distance Education), Tracey Huston (who handled publicity and arranged for our internet operation), and leaders in the College of Liberal Arts and the Department of English (who lent essential financial support).

For their help in the course of the production of this volume, we especially thank Laura Gurak of the University of Minnesota and Steven Mailloux of the University of California, Irvine for useful comments on an earlier draft of the book; their reviews improved the volume, well, materially. Several anonymous reviewers aided us in the selection of manuscripts. Susan Squier, Richard Doyle, and Christopher Malone made useful contributions to the bibliography, and Linda Selzer offered telling suggestions at so many points and so generously that we cannot begin to credit them all. At the University of Wisconsin Press, Mary Elizabeth Braun and Allen Fitchen offered patience, support, and confidence that we will not soon forget, and we appreciate as well the efforts of those on the production staff who so professionally edited and produced the volume, particularly Jane McGary and Scott Lenz.

Most of all, we appreciate the hard work, cheerfulness, punctuality, scholarly acumen, and eloquence of our contributors, who have together produced, we feel confident, a book that advances the discussion of materiality within rhetorical studies and far beyond it.

Rhetorical Bodies

Jack Selzer

Habeas Corpus
An Introduction

Hold a minute ear to the body.
> Kenneth Burke, letter to Allen Tate
> August 19, 1933

"Be careful what you say / when you make talk with words," warned the speaker of a Carl Sandburg poem addressed to a young child,

> for words are made of syllables
> and syllables, child, are made of air—
> and air is so thin—air is the breath of God—
> air is finer than fire or mist
> finer than water or moonlight,
> finer than spider-webs in the moon,
> finer than water-flowers in the morning.
> ("Little Girl, Be Careful What You Say" 1–9)

Quick switch from profound to silly

Sandburg's simple words and images were chosen for their appeal to a young-ster (he was rarely this bathetic), but within the sentimental metaphors is a se-rious and stereotypical attitude towards language—a conception of language as ephemeral, fleeting, invisible. As something immaterial, in other words. This notion of language as a transparent, insubstantial, neutral medium is still some-thing of a tacit assumption in many quarters—a truism still too often barely worthy of mention, let alone refutation.

bathos

At the same time, especially during this period of social constructionism and a heightened awareness of the power of language to mediate perception, the brute fact of materiality has been shunted a bit to the side. At least in some communities—I'll take up some notable exceptions in a moment—a respect for how reality is constructed by language has mitigated interest in what Maurice Merleau-Ponty called "the lived world." Without essentializing too fervently distinctions between the material and the linguistic, we are nevertheless everywhere aware of the "rhetorical turn" in the sciences and humanities. This turn has helped to make fields from anthropology to zoology increasingly self-conscious about their disciplinary practices, particularly about their language practices, and it has consequently deflected scholarly attention from material realities and toward the way those realities are represented in text. In history, textualized accounts of historical events have come to count as much as the historical events themselves; in anthropology and sociology, cultures have been understood as intangible webs of discourses more than as aggregates of people and things, the substance of tangible realities; in studies of gender and ethnicity, the emphasis has been on constructions of identity through language and other symbol systems; in science, biology and chemistry and physics are now understood as collections of texts as much as they are efforts to engage and describe the physical world through discrete material practices. Things in themselves, consequently, are sometimes being reduced to a function of language: genes, genders, jeans, and genetics have all been reconceived recently through the prism of language. Words have been mattering more than matter.

And yet there are also episodes like the following to consider—episodes that presuppose a somewhat different attitude toward language itself and toward the relationships that abide between language and reality:

> The Baroness Elsa von Freytag-Loringhoven, a protégée of Marcel Duchamp, confounded, fascinated, and frightened the New York artistic avant-garde in the first years following World War I. Some who knew her contend that she literally prepared a "body" of poetry by inscribing original verses on her torso; everyone agrees that her "dress" provoked the traditional lines demarcating the symbolic and the material. She favored unusual colors and habiliments, sported an inverted coal scuttle on her head, and shaved and shellacked her head and painted its two halves in contrasting colors. She applied metal teaballs and other implements to her breasts, while over her nipples she placed two tin tomato cans fastened with a green string tied around her back. She hung between the tins a small bird cage (complete with canary). Her hats were reputedly trimmed with gilded carrots, beets, and other vegetables. William Carlos Williams contended in his *Autobiography* that she once created a sculpture out of chicken guts under glass, and she placed her poems not only on her body but in the most interesting and arresting magazines of her day, notably in the *Little Review*, which carried a photo of her by Man Ray in 1920.[1]

> As he lay dying (or so he thought), John Donne imagined his body as a text being read by his physicians:

> Whilst my physicians by their love are grown
>> Cosmographers, and I their map, who lie
> Flat on this bed, that by them may be shown
>> That this is my south-west discovery
>> Per fretum febris, by these strains to die,
>
> I joy, that in these straits, I see my west;
>> For, though their currents yield return to none,
> What shall my west hurt me? As west and east
>> In all flat maps (and I am one) are one,
>> So death doth touch the resurrection.
>>   ("Hymn to God My God, in My Sickness" 6–15)

The infamous public exhibitions in London and Paris of Saartjie Baartman, the so-called "Hottentot Venus" (her original name has been lost), became a ground for the way sexual differences between "virtuous" European and "corrupt" African women were imaged and inscribed for more than a century. After her death in Paris in 1815, Baartman's body remained on exhibit—incredibly, she remains in storage today in the Musée de l'Homme—with a clear persuasive intent: her corpse was reduced to its sexual organs and then displayed in order to tie her to the orangutan and to the sexual degeneracies associated therewith. This physical synecdoche, of a body reduced horrifically to genitalia that are then used to represent the whole, was soon followed by literal ones as scientists, writers, and artists rushed to figure the alleged voluptuousness, "primitivity," and sexual lasciviousness of the black female by exaggerating the buttocks and other physical features in support of racist premises. Having dissected her, Georges Cuvier, then the greatest anatomist in France, described the Hottentot Venus as "apelike" and "monstrous"; and his famous (infamous?) nineteenth-century American counterpart, Paul Broca, used her to defend his own conclusions on race.[2] In the visual arts, Edouard Manet's *Olympia* and *Nana* assume and perpetuate the values embodied by the Venus, as do Edwin's Long's epic canvas *The Babylonian Marriage Market* (1882) and Picasso's *Olympia* (1902). In literature, the aspect of the Hottentot Venus peers out of Émile Zola's novels *L'Assommoir* (1887) and *Nana* (1880), and shadows the pages of George Eliot's *Daniel Deronda*.

A hundred years ago or so it was conventional for professional baseball teams to employ human mascots, usually to satisfy players' superstitions; they were the precursors of batboys and those cartoon birds and beasts and Phanatics who appear at ball games today. Petey Powers, a street urchin, served as the Cleveland mascot in 1903, and Buck Ewing (perhaps the best player of the nineteenth century) is seated next to a boy mascot in a well-known photo. The notorious bigot Adrian "Cap" Anson,

influential in establishing the color line in professional baseball, employed
what he called a "coon" mascot, one Clarence Duval, for his Chicago White
Stockings; he even took Duval along as his servant during a world tour
sponsored by A. G. Spalding in the winter of 1888–1889. Ty Cobb, the
equally bigoted "Georgia Peach," sponsored "Lil' Rastus" (real name,
Ulysses Harrison) as the Detroit Tigers' good-luck charm in 1909: hitters
would rub his black head for luck before going to the plate. Many mascots
were hunchbacks, their humps serving as the thing to rub for good fortune.
Dwarf hunchbacks were especially appreciated: Louis Van Zelst followed
Connie Mack's Philadelphia A's for many seasons, and the Yankees' batboy
Eddie Bennett appears next to Babe Ruth in photos from the late 1920s. The
most famous such mascot, the misshapen and feebleminded Charlie Faust,
"pitched" the New York Giants to the 1911 and 1912 pennants (or so manager
John McGraw thought) before being bested by Van Zelst in the World Series
and henceforth banished to an asylum, where he died in 1915. Faust is
textualized in Christy Mathewson's magnificent *Pitching in a Pinch* (1912),
and other mascots have appeared in print as well—for instance, in Billy
Boxer's novel for boys *Yale Murphy, the Great Short* (1894), Ring Lardner's
story "You Could Look It Up," and E. L. Doctorow's *Ragtime*. Perhaps the
most extensive verbalization of the mascot hunchback appears in Zane Grey's
The Shortstop (1909), a juvenile novel that features the Horatio Alger-ish star
Chase Alloway and the hunchback he befriends and sponsors, team mascot
Mitti-Maru. In the novel's final episode, Mitti-Maru is installed as the team
manager for the championship game (after the manager loses his wits), leads
his team to a comeback victory, and is hit on the hump by a wayward throw
as the hero completes a game-winning inside-the-park homer.

All of these vignettes suggest others, of course. Mitti-Maru for some reason reminds me of his physical opposites—Arnold Schwarzenegger, Sylvester
Stallone, Mariel Hemingway, and those other buffed bodies who appear in
sports films—or even of the fantastic cyborgs who populate science fiction and
film. The real-life Baroness Elsa von Freytag-Loringhoven resonates with the
calligraphic lovers and other characters in Peter Greenaway's haunting 1996
film *The Pillow Book*, all of whom take literally French feminists' exhortation,
"Write the body!" John Donne's self-analysis of his own torso anticipates the
fascination with the body that is evident in any number of poems today. Saartjie
Baartman speaks on her own behalf in a striking contemporary poem by Elizabeth Alexander that is called "The Venus Hottentot"[3]; from a position on Cuvier's dissecting table, she speaks back to him and to us:

> If he were to let me rise up
> from this table, I'd spirit

> his knives and cut out his black heart,
> seal it with science fluid inside
> a bell jar, place it on a low
> shelf in a white man's museum
> so the whole world could see
> it was shriveled and hard,
> geometric, deformed, unnatural.
>
> (112–20)

Episodes like these have already begun to gather critical commentary about them, as my notes and asides suggest. Recent work in many fields, especially but not exclusively under the impulses of postmodernism and poststructuralism, have come to challenge the centering of subjectivities in the mind and have made the body and the material a focal point of their considerations. Leaders of the women's movement during the 1970s instigated discussions of the body and its ideological deployment, and in the 1970s and 1980s their analyses broadened—often under Marxist imperatives—to account for material conditions. Those discussions persist today in the work of feminists, both French and not so French (e.g., Luce Irigaray and Helene Cixous; Iris Young and Susan Bordo); very recently Judith Butler's work on performativity and the body, wrung out from speech act theory, deconstruction, and phenomenology, has been especially influential. In philosophy, post-Nietzscheans have been puzzling out one or another concept of the human subject and the embodied consciousness ever since Merleau-Ponty developed his version of phenomenology, and Jean-Paul Sartre in a famous passage in *Nausea* imagined one of his characters as drenched in the material: witness Elizabeth Grosz's recent accounts of the representation of women's bodies in texts, Nancy Tuana's problematizations of gender distinctions, and the effort of Gilles Deleuze and Felix Guattari to provide a positive account of the relations between bodily affect and capitalist production. Semioticians for over two decades have been reading bodies and material culture after the example of Roland Barthes's *Mythologies* and *The Fashion System*. Sociologists, anthropologists, and those who work the terrain known as cultural studies (e.g., Dorothy Nelkin, Susan Lindee, Jennifer Terry, and Jacqueline Urla) have been capitalizing for some time on how Michel Foucault defined the body—especially in *Discipline and Punish* (1975)—as a central site for cultural inscription and social regulation, and on how he revealed the regulatory imperatives that underpin material conditions. Historians in the tradition of Foucault have been similarly interested by bodily matters recently; to cite just a few examples, I think of Charlotte Borst's studies of the professionalization of childbirth in the decades before 1920; Robert Proctor's accounts of the mass surveillance and control of human bodies in Nazi Germany; Londa Schiebinger's recovery of the scientific visions of nature that embodied the sexual and racial tensions of the eighteenth century; and a fascinating study by Elizabeth Haiken of how cosmetic surgery has been shaped by the priorities of twentieth-century American culture. Scholars in law and political science (I think in particular of Nancy Fraser, but also of Vikki Bell) are uncovering the ways that discursive practices create, or fail to create, submissive and disciplined human subjects. In science studies, Donna Haraway and Evelyn Fox Keller have wondered over the issue of biological determinism and noticed how science has marked onto bodies (usually women's bodies) figures of inferiority drawn from brain size, skeletal structures, and reproductive organs. In literary criticism, scholars like Katherine Hayles and Susan Squier have exposed those figures in the fiction of this century. Scholars in ethnic and African American studies, in the visual arts, and in queer theory have offered work in the same line: I've already cited Sander Gilman and other contributors to *"Race," Writing, and Difference*, and the work of Eve Kosofsky Sedgwick invigorates the work of several pieces in this collection. Finally, a spate of miscellaneous and often sensational books and articles on individual body parts— buttocks, artificial hearts, noses, skin, breasts, penises, clitorises, feet, hair, and prostheses—have emerged regularly in the 1990s.

This book speaks to all of that prior work and to similar work by many other people. It is an effort to bring rhetorical studies to bear on issues of materiality and, in turn, to contribute a rhetorical perspective to work in other fields that itself has a material perspective or aim. After all, the four vignettes I presented earlier are undeniably rhetorical events of one kind or another. The Baroness presented her physical body as a rhetorical act in order to unsettle the relations between art and life; John Donne literalized a bodily experience into poetry for a devotional aim; the real-life Hottentot Venus and the real-life mascots were living bodies that came to bear ideological freight which writers then translated into text for additional social purposes. All the vignettes are material, embodied events, but they all involve language practices as well. The deployments of language—that undeniable power paradoxically regarded usually as ephemeral, Will-o'-the-wisp—in those vignettes all testify to the fact that language is not really so whimsical, so immaterial, after all. Language and rhetoric have a persistent material aspect that demands acknowledgment, and material realities often (if not always) contain a rhetorical dimension that deserves attention: for language is not the only medium or material that speaks. The factory and assembly line, the prison and the hospital and school, as Marx and Foucault have taught so well, have explicitly coercive functions that rehearse the highly persuasive if less overt ways in which other material realities, cultural practices, and physical bodies shape and persuade. And rhetoric and writing teachers, whether they have read Foucault or not, know all too well how material circumstances—their students' jobs, their institutions' regulations, their colleagues' part-time status, or the specific local imperatives that govern each educational site—speak to their students as forcefully as their own pedagogical advice.

   This recognition of the presence of a material dimension in rhetoric and of the rhetorical dimension in the material is, as I have mentioned, in large measure a consequence of postmodern and poststructural turns in rhetorical thought. As postmoderns have come to challenge the centering of subjectivities in the mind, the body has naturally become a more focal point of rhetorical inquiry. While it is true, as Burke was explaining from the first moments of social constructionism, in his *Permanence and Change* (1935), that people can never get outside the constructions and conventions of discourse, it is also true (as Burke noted in the same book) that neither can we construct ourselves outside the materiality of everyday life: "The universe is not merely the product of our interpretations. For the interpretations themselves must be altered as the universe displays various orders of recalcitrance to them. . . . Our calling has its roots in the biological, and our biological demands are clearly implicit in the universal texture" (256). Nevertheless, material moments of rhetorical action like the ones I have described have largely remained beyond the reach of rhetoricians, who have traditionally (and understandably) been most attentive to oral and written discourses, narrowly conceived. Even though rhetoric has long been concerned with the situatedness of literate acts and the real effects of discourse rather than with ideal possibilities, the relationship of rhetorical events to the material world that sustains and produces them has not often enough been fully elaborated or clearly articulated. True, there have been starts in the direction of a material rhetoric. Celeste Condit, Barbara Biesecker, Cheryl Glenn, Susan Jarratt, Jan Swearingen, and others have concerned themselves with embodiments of the feminine in the rhetorical tradition. Understanding the material conditions surrounding the production and consumption of texts has been the project of Steven Mailloux. The virtual body has come under the scrutiny of Christina Haas, Lester Faigley, and others. A number of rhetoricians, after the example of Judith Butler, are delineating the complex relations that hold between rhetorical force (persuasion) and one or another kind of body, and Carole Blair has been studying the embodiment of public memory.

   Nevertheless, those starts have only been starts, and so this collection of essays attempts to steer rhetoric more firmly in the direction of those elaborations and articulations. It is a sustained meditation on material rhetoric in both senses of the term—a meditation on the material aspects and groundings of language as rhetorical action as it is traditionally conceived, and on the rhetorical nature of material realities, whether they are literate realities or not. Without opposing too firmly the material and the literate, the contributors together consider what it might mean to take very seriously the material conditions that sustain the production, circulation, and consumption of rhetorical power (whether that power is in a text or speech or some other physical form), and the book accordingly sustains two complementary general propositions. First, the contributors insist that material, nonliterate practices and realities—most notably, the body, flesh, blood, and bones, and how all the material trappings of the physical are fashioned by literate practices—should come under rhetorical scrutiny. Second, they demonstrate how literate practices—the speeches and texts that are the traditional staple of rhetoric, as well as the ads and virtual spaces and languages associated with the new media—ought to be understood in the serious light of the material circumstances that sustain or sustained them.

Drawing on and contributing to fields as various as the rhetoric of science, body studies, cultural studies, feminism, historiography, and literacy studies, the following chapters consider and reconsider many terms and issues traditionally employed in rhetorical studies. If the question of materiality has indeed been deferred in rhetoric, why is that so? What barriers have stood in the path of articulating a more material rhetoric? How would a material rhetoric permit us to rethink what is, and what is not, the province of rhetoric? How does a "material" notion of rhetoric contrast with "idealist" notions? What is the fit between particular rhetorical theories and the material, historical events that generated them? In what ways is rhetorical theory tied to the circumstances of physical embodiment? How might the articulation of a material rhetoric force us to reconceive rhetorical entities like "speaker," "writer," "arrangement," and "audience"? What does it mean to speak of "deliberative bodies" or "the body politic"—especially at a time when audiences might be conceived of as porous and contingent, as consisting of multiple, temporary, even conflicting groups? If the concept of "place" (*topos*) has been important in rhetorical affairs, how might that concept be reinvigorated today in material terms, particularly when metaphors of space, place, and geography (e.g., "fields," "domains," "sites," "lines of argument," or "maps") are so pervasive? Should something substitute for the notion of the "material" that has prevailed under the aegis of Marx? If "materialism" now takes us to bodies and to tangible physicality instead of to Marx, what happens to Marxist categories? Just what is so "corporate" about the corporation or about other contemporary sites (civic, academic, commercial) for writing and representation? Where is memory embodied in our cultures, and how is public memory shaped by material practices and structures? How do new literacy technologies, especially electronic ones, affect our understand of rhetoric and literacy? How do those technologies force us to reconceive our notions of text, author, audience, and delivery? How might postmodern notions of materiality and the body affect our understanding of pedagogical practices designed for the "student body"? And how will material rhetorics delineate ethics for a culture confronting material crises in public policy: the politics of race and ethnicity; the issues related to "family values" that revolve around sexual and gender identities; or the choices revolving around reproduction, DNA codings and genome projects, and the spread of disease?

Contributors to this volume do not address all these questions, nor are these all the questions that might be asked. But together the chapters represent the range of work that might be possible—and the range of methodologies that might be brought to bear—on the subject of material rhetoric. Carole Blair begins by "offering some tentative openings" (in her words) to the concept of "material rhetoric" while grounding her points in a sustained rhetorical analysis of five memorial sites in the United States—the Vietnam Veterans Memorial, the AIDS Memorial Quilt, the Civil Rights Memorial, the May 4 Memorial at Kent State University, and the Witch Trials Tercentenary Memorial. Extending what might be considered "text" to physical slate and stone, she offers a method for further studies of landscape and landmark. In chapter 3, Susan Wells inquires into an unusual particular "pleasure of the body"—the satisfaction of dissecting a human cadaver—as that pleasure was enjoyed and then described by nineteenth-century women physicians. Working at the advent of modern therapeutic practices and anatomical studies, and under different ideological frames of reference from those that directed Cuvier's dissections a century earlier, Hannah Longshore and other pioneer graduates of the Women's Medical College of Pennsylvania satisfied an appetite for uncovering the mysteries of the body that they had developed by reading representations of the body in nineteenth-century fiction.

Wells's chapter is the first in a series of reports on and about archival research. Picking up on Wells's renderings of autopsy, Christine De Vinne in chapter 4 offers what she calls a "forensic necropsy." She exhumes and anatomizes the wrenching details of the 1846–1847 Donner Party and its lapse into cannibalism—textualized as it was into letters, diaries, songs, poems, newspaper accounts, interviews, travel books, fictions, advertisements, and other genres—as a nearly inevitable expression of the discourses of territorial expansion that prevailed in the decades before and after the Civil War. In chapter 5, Karyn Hollis accounts for what she found in the records of the Bryn Mawr Summer School for women of the 1920s and 1930s: poems by summer-school students that inscribed working-class conditions, gendered identities, and a tangible sense of how working-class bodies, especially female ones, are disciplined by culture and class. Wendy Sharer in chapter 6 alerts scholars (rhetorical scholars especially) to how authoritative accounts of rhetorical history depend on materials that are currently deteriorating in precarious museum and library collections, and to how political, ideological, and social considerations govern what will persist and what will perish. Sharer's passionate call for action, directed to scholars and scholarly associations, not simply to librarians and administrators, resonates particularly clearly given that her call follows three chapters (and precedes another) that demonstrate what archival research can do for rhetorical studies.

The next four chapters further interrogate the figurings of bodies in texts. In chapter 7 Peter Mortensen, in a manner that parallels the work of Schiebinger and Haraway, assesses how "rustic bodies" were represented as illiterate between 1880 and 1920 in order to evidence their alleged creeping racial degeneracy. Those representations, in fiction, government reports, and popular media, through their resonances with the evolutionary sciences of their day, typically depicted illiteracy as endemic to rural life, and they had the continuing effect of undermining literacy education efforts in rural communities. Lester Faigley in chapter 8 considers the materiality of text itself. He surveys the relation of images and words in texts from antiquity to the World Wide Web—in the process problematizing the grand narrative of alphabetic literacy as a legacy of the Greeks—in order to demonstrate how literacy practices have always had a material dimension, and how that materiality is figured today in electronic media. John Schilb in chapter 9 takes up the "psychological materialities" implied by modern pharmacology. In particular, he wonders (by means of an analysis of several recent memoirs such as Susanna Kaysen's *Girl, Interrupted*, William Styron's *Darkness Visible* and Lauren Slater's "Black Swans") how the invention of Prozac and similar drugs will figure into the rhetorics and "subjects" of autobiography in the future. In chapter 10, Christina Haas shows how texts can be interpreted fruitfully in light of the material conditions that articulate them—in this case, the material conditions attendant on an urban abortion clinic. In the process she interrogates the commonly expressed distinction between "public" and "private" spaces.

Schilb's and Haas's chapters—his because it concerns material bodies, and hers because it turns on a thick ethnographic description of a material site—redirect the collection to an explicit consideration of the rhetoric of the human body and other specific material entities. J. Blake Scott in chapter 11 accounts for the rhetorical materialities associated with the physical assemblage known as the Confide home collection HIV testing system—the testing kit, the supporting documentation, the "needy bodies" that use the system, even the credit cards and phone calls used to pay for the kit. He develops from that account a patient cultural and rhetorical analysis of some of the literate discourses surrounding the product, including hearings and testimony about Confide and advertisements for it, that illuminates how technoscience these days is shaped, mobilized, consumed, and negotiated in different public forums. Melissa Jane Hardie in chapter 12 maps in rhetorical terms the cultural phenomenon of the "beard" (a woman or man who disguises the sexual interest of his or her partner) with reference to its instantiations in persons who bearded for Malcolm Forbes, Rock Hudson, and Liberace. The chapter discloses how the beard functions today in various media as a material signifier operating within complex and contradictory rhetorics of disclosure and orientation. Barbara Dickson's chapter 13 takes up a case representing the pregnant body: Did the photo of a nude, pregnant Demi Moore on the cover of *Vanity Fair* somehow liberate the feminine body, or was it just another case of exploitation of the female form? Dickson considers the matter by saturating the cover in other texts and photos and thinking carefully through the implications of "a material rhetoric."

The book concludes with increasingly theoretical discussions of the questions related to material rhetoric that were opened by Carole Blair. Christina Haas is intrigued by theoretical formulations that have converged about terms like "public" and "private"; Scott and Hardie also extend the theoretical efforts of Nancy Fraser, Eve Sedgwick, and Judith Butler; and Dickson's chapter is motivated primarily by a theoretical interest in what kind of "thing" a material rhetoric is and what it can do. Yameng Liu in chapter 14 offers an analysis of political advisor Dick Morris's role as a rhetor-for-hire during the 1996 presidential campaign, but his real interest is the theoretical issue the case embodies: Can a sophistic rhetor like Morris, a person as tough to defend as Gorgias's Helen, be exonerated on ethical grounds? Is a sophistic rhetoric possible, or even desirable, in today's public sphere? Celeste Condit in chapter 15 explores the tension between the materiality and immateriality of rhetoric through the analogous case of DNA, itself figured as both material and not; she attempts to bridge materiality and idealist notions of language and rhetoric. The ambitious exploration takes her into encounters with contemporary language philosophers and poststructuralists (e.g., Derrida and Foucault), experts in science and science studies (e.g., Richard Lewontin and Evelyn Fox Keller), and rhetorical theorists (e.g., Kenneth Burke and Michael McGee); ultimately she arrives with a use of DNA coding as a model for how material rhetoric might be understood to incorporate both gross physical corporeality and the social and material act of "coding." Finally, Sharon Crowley concludes the book with a reflection on the contents that focuses on the slippery difficulties of mediating between body and identity. She and Condit, as well as the other contributors, offer no small opportunities for further work on the subject, both theoretical and applied. Their aim is to invigorate rhetorical studies with their theoretical and material stories and with their various methodologies and approaches, and to demonstrate concretely what rhetorical studies might offer to others who are interested in corporal works and in the webs of literate renderings that surround them.

That mention of the web brings me full circle. When Carl Sandburg figured language in the poem I quoted to begin this chapter, he used the metaphor of a spider's web because he wished to convey a sense of language's immateriality. But the metaphor can cut another way. In a well-known and eloquent paragraph (at the beginning of chapter 3 of *A Room of One's Own*—"Shakespeare's Sister"), Sandburg's contemporary Virginia Woolf used the same metaphor.

After wondering pointedly about "the conditions in which women lived"—conditions that, she felt, ground the invention of discourse—she too compared writing to "a spider's web, attached ever so lightly perhaps, but still attached to life at all four corners. . . . When the web is pulled askew, hooked up at the edge, torn in the middle, one remembers that these webs are not spun in midair by incorporeal creatures, but are the work of . . . human beings, and are attached to grossly material things, like health and money and the houses we live in" (43–44). Webs of discourse and their anchors in the material, the work of human beings: these are the subjects of *Rhetorical Bodies*.

Notes

1. Freytag-Loringhoven's life is summarized accessibly by Cary Nelson (267–68); Williams's account of her is on pages 164ff. Born Elsa Ploetz in Germany in 1874, she came to the United States about 1910 with her second husband, who abandoned her. In 1913 she married Baron Freiherr Freytag von Loringhoven and resettled in Germany; she removed to New York City about 1920. In 1923 she returned to Germany; she moved to Paris in the mid-1920s, and then died suddenly, perhaps a suicide, in Paris in 1927. Her papers, which include an autobiography and records associating her with Djuna Barnes, are housed in the McKeldin Library, University of Maryland. I also noticed several unusual 1922 letters from her to Joseph Freeman (then editor of *The Liberator*) in the Freeman Papers at Stanford, a fantastic archive of materials related to the American political Left.

2. Gould, *The Mismeasure of Man*, 85–87. My account of the Hottentot Venus and her cultural impact derives from Gould, from Schiebinger (160–72), and especially from Sander Gilman's remarkable "Black Bodies, White Bodies," which also shows how the Hottentot Venus became literalized in works by Freud and Darwin.

3. For drawing my attention to the Hottentot Venus and pointing me to the poem "Venus Hottentot" by Alexander, I thank Linda Selzer.

Works Cited

Alexander, Elizabeth. *The Venus Hottentot*. Charlottesville: University of Virginia Press, 1990.

Barthes, Roland. *The Fashion System*. Berkeley: University of California Press, 1990.

Barthes, Roland. *Mythologies*. Translated by Annette Lavers. New York: Hill and Wang, 1972.

Bell, Vikki. *Interrogating Incest: Feminism, Foucault, and the Law*. London: Routledge, 1993.

Borst, Charlotte. *Catching Babies: The Professionalization of Childbirth, 1870–1920.* Cambridge, Mass.: Harvard University Press, 1995.

Boxer, Billy. *Yale Murphy, the Great Short*. New York: Five Cent Library, 1894.

Burke, Kenneth. *Permanence and Change*. 3d ed. Berkeley: University of California Press, 1984.

Fraser, Nancy. *Unruly Practices: Power, Discourse, and Gender in Contemporary Social Theory*. Minneapolis: University of Minnesota Press, 1989.

Gilman, Sander. "Black Bodies, White Bodies." In *"Race," Writing, and Difference*, edited by Henry Louis Gates, 224–61. Chicago: University of Chicago Press, 1985.

Gould, Stephen Jay. *The Mismeasure of Man*. New York: Norton, 1981.

Grey, Zane. *The Shortstop*. New York: Grosset and Dunlap, 1909.

Grosz, Elizabeth. *Volatile Bodies: Toward a Corporeal Feminism*. Bloomington: Indiana University Press, 1994.

Haiken, Elizabeth. *Venus Envy: A History of Cosmetic Surgery*. Baltimore: Johns Hopkins University Press, 1997.

Hayles, N. Katherine. *Chaos Bound: Orderly Disorder in Contemporary Literature and Science*. Ithaca: Cornell University Press, 1990.

Mathewson, Christy. *Pitching in a Pinch*. New York: Putnam, 1912.

Nelkin, Dorothy, and Susan Lindee. *The DNA Mystique: The Gene as a Cultural Icon*. New York: Freeman, 1995.

Nelson, Cary. *Repression and Recovery: Modern American Poetry and the Politics of Cultural Memory, 1910–1945*. Madison: University of Wisconsin Press, 1989.

Proctor, Robert. *Racial Hygiene: Medicine under the Nazis*. Cambridge, Mass.: Harvard University Press, 1988.

Sandburg, Carl. *The Complete Poems of Carl Sandburg*. Rev. and expanded ed. New York: Harcourt Brace Jovanovich, 1970.

Schiebinger, Londa. *Nature's Body: Gender in the Making of Modern Science*. Boston: Beacon, 1993.

Squier, Susan. *Babies in Bottles: Twentieth-Century Visions of Reproductive Technology*. New Brunswick: Rutgers University Press, 1994.

Terry, Jennifer, and Jacqueline Urla, eds. *Deviant Bodies: Critical Perspectives on Difference in Science and Popular Culture*. Bloomington: Indiana University Press, 1995.

Tuana, Nancy. *The Less Noble Sex: Scientific, Religious, and Philosophical Conceptions of Women's Nature*. Bloomington: Indiana University Press, 1993.

Williams, William Carlos. *The Autobiography of William Carlos Williams*. New York: Random House, 1948.

Woolf, Virginia. *A Room of One's Own*. New York: Harcourt, Brace and World, 1929.

Young, Iris. *Throwing Like a Girl and Other Essays in Feminist Philosophy and Social Theory*. Bloomington: Indiana University Press, 1990.

[handwritten top margin: Could marxist slant improve this?]

[handwritten left margin, vertical: WARSAW MEMORIALS]

2 *Carole Blair*

Contemporary U.S. Memorial Sites as Exemplars of Rhetoric's Materiality

[handwritten: Role of the IDIOM IN Promoting Materiality?]

[handwritten: Does materiality precede Symbolic?]

[handwritten left margin: WINDSOR?]

If we require justification for rethinking rhetoric as material, there is enough in our ordinary idiom. It is not unusual to hear the language of activity or of physicality used to describe rhetoric. Rhetors occupy "ground" and take "stances." They "pose," "posture," or "hold" to an idea. Rhetors "buttress" their arguments and sometimes use "colorful" language to express their ideas. Phrases are "turned" and ideas "taken up." Audience members assume a "position," "feel" a particular emotion, "grasp" an idea, or "see" a point. Minds are "opened" (or "closed") in and by means of rhetoric, and we are sometimes "touched" or "moved" by it. This is all commonplace language, and its very commonness ought to call our attention to it. What it suggests *at least* is that a heuristic of materiality is useful for understanding rhetoric—a practice that Friedrich Nietzsche once described suggestively as a "plastic art" (35).

Yet when we have theorized rhetoric, the "material" or "real" most often has been understood as characteristic of the rhetorical context—the physical setting, or sociocultural environment, of the rhetorical text—rather than of the text itself.[1] There is little doubt that all rhetoric appears within a material context that, at least in part, prompts it, shapes its character, and offers it the opportunity for significance (or oblivion). While those conditions are important, they are not what this chapter is primarily about. Instead, it offers some openings for rethinking rhetoric as itself material, just as substantial and consequential as any element of its setting.[2]

16

Public commemorative art in the United States provides the material for my provisional attempt to rethink rhetoric. It certainly is not the same as the written and oral discourses that more typically draw rhetoricians' attention. Despite the fact that memorials are not encompassed by rhetoric's central domains of written and spoken discourses, they are unquestionably rhetorical, except perhaps under the most narrow object characterizations of rhetoric—for example, as oral speech. Memorials are (centrally) although not exclusively, epideictic; as Neil Michel and I have shown elsewhere, they do the work (often more than the work) that we expect eulogies to do. Precisely because they are different from our usual rhetorical models—speech and writing—these memorials seem useful to consider, because they summon attention to their assiduous materiality. These are structures, for the most part, that remain in our perceptual fields as long as we are nearby. They do not fall into silence like oral speech, nor are they (in most cases) "put away" like the writings that we read and then store in bookshelves out of our way.[3] Because of their recalcitrant "presentness," I believe memorials are particularly revealing for an inquiry into rhetoric's materiality.

I cannot pretend to advance any declarations or fully developed theories about the material character of rhetoric, even working with such strong exemplars. All I can offer are some tentative openings for thinking about it. But even that seems a reasonable start, given the difficulty of the task. We face two significant obstacles in retheorizing (or even thinking about) rhetoric materially. Following a discussion of those two challenges, and relying primarily on the imprints of five contemporary public memorial sites, I will advance some questions that offer some openings for reconsidering rhetoric as material. In doing so, I will discuss similarities and differences among rhetorical media, because degrees, kinds, and consequences of materiality seem to differ significantly, but rather unpredictably, depending in part on whether the "rhetoric" we describe is made of sound, script, or stone.

Challenges To Theorizing a Material Rhetoric

Two challenges immediately present themselves in rethinking rhetoric as material, but the consequence of each is the same: we lack an idiom for referencing talk, writing, or even inscribed stone as material. It has been instructive, and somewhat reassuring, to watch the likes of Michel Foucault, Jean-François Lyotard, and Michel de Certeau grapple with ideas for which they—and we—have no language.[4] Each of them, in very different efforts, has struggled with the lack of a materialist language about discourse. At least as interesting are writers on architecture and landscape who attempt to describe the influence exerted by physical structures and places, often by reaching for the languages of rhetoric and semiotics; these, however, still fail in my view to describe adequately how the places they study do rhetorical work.[5] The challenges that

IDEAS for which we have no language to explain.

these writers have faced, and that we too must confront, are first, the obstinacy of the language of symbolicity in referencing rhetorical texts of any kind, and second, the naturalized, residual effects of liberal humanism in rhetoric.

The Language of Symbolicity

In speaking or writing about a commemorative rhetoric of architecture or sculpture, I take "rhetoric" to be any partisan, meaningful, consequential text, with the term "text" understood broadly as a legible or readable event or object. I am aware of the dangers of definition, and thus I offer this one as conditional; it serves the purpose to the degree that the characterization seems at least reasonable. If we shift our focus further back to question the *source* of the stipulated characteristics—partisanship, meaningfulness, consequence, and even legibility—we must identify what makes these characteristics possible. And perhaps the most basic answer is the materiality of the text. No text *is* a text, nor does it have meaning, influence, political stance, or legibility, in the absence of material form. Rhetoric is not rhetoric until it is uttered, written, or otherwise manifested or given presence. Thus, we might hypothesize as a starting point for theorizing rhetoric that at least one of its basic characteristics (if not the *most* basic) is its materiality.

Materiality, however, has rarely been taken as a starting point or basis for theorizing rhetoric, despite the frequent cues in our language about its material character.[6] In recent memory, rhetoric has been defined by, and theorized according to, its most ephemeral quality: its symbolicity. At least in speech communication's renditions of rhetoric, one does not have far to look for a near consensus about its basic character; it is treated definitively, even exhaustively, as symbolic. For example, enlarging Donald Bryant's classic formulation of rhetoric as the "rationale of informative and suasory discourse" ("Rhetoric"), Douglas Ehninger defined it as "the rationale of symbolic inducement" (3). Richard Johannesen argues that rhetoric is concerned with "the use of verbal and nonverbal symbols by man and his institutions to influence human behavior" (1). Sonja Foss, Karen Foss, and Robert Trapp define it as "the uniquely human ability to use symbols to communicate with one another" (11). Gerard Hauser describes rhetoric as an "*instrumental* use of language," suggesting the entailment of the view that "one person engages another in an exchange of symbols to accomplish some goal." (2). Martin Medhurst and Thomas Benson claim that when critics address how a text functions as rhetoric, they are inquiring about the text "as a symbolic form whose structure and context lead the audience to think, feel, believe, understand, or act in an arguably predictable way" (xx). Although it is not impossible to find a contemporary rhetorician defining rhetoric without reference to symbols, it is at least unusual,[7] whether the rhetorician works in speech communication, in English, or in some other field.

[Why should we describe symbolicity as ephemeral? After all, symbols are articulated (materialized) members of a language system, those elements that combine and recombine in actual utterances or writings. But even if we grant that symbols themselves are material, it is rarely their material manifestation that we attend to; symbols refer us consistently beyond themselves to their referential or meaning domains. The material articulation of the symbol itself seems of no more than vehicular interest, as a means of transport to its *telos*— its meaning. Paradoxically, the symbol is the material element of rhetoric, but the very notion of a "symbol" teaches us to reach outside it for its meaning and to treat that meaning as if it were the real dimension of rhetoric, or at least the most important one. This is not to suggest that it is somehow wrong or incorrect to attend to rhetoric's symbolicity and its capacity to generate meaning; rather, I mean to suggest that it is problematic to treat rhetoric as if it were exclusively or essentially symbolic or meaning-ful. There are some things that rhetoric's symbolicity simply cannot account for. One is its consequence. Even if we were to accomplish the impossible and catalogue the full range of meanings referenced by a symbolic formulation, we would not *therefore* be in any better position than when we began to account for its consequence in use. And if rhetoric is, as I have suggested, defined in part by its potential for consequence, then there is a problem in understanding rhetoric as essentially symbolic. *YES = Cause + effect + intention + use*

That seems to be the difficulty addressed by a number of rhetoricians and communication theorists who have advanced other "units" of analysis to describe rhetorical formulations. The fact that they would sense a need to offer these alternatives at all suggests that there is some flaw in using the heuristic of symbolicity. Karl Wallace suggested in 1970 that we turn to the *speech act* as a way of describing rhetoric that might help us to address its consequence. Michael McGee in 1980 forwarded the concept of the *ideograph*—a language construction that is understood, in part, by its use and its capacity to accrete meanings. Thomas Farrell suggests that we attempt to understand rhetoric as an activity, hence his suggestion that we attend to the *utterance* (148, 152).[8] Finally, John Waite Bowers introduced the *pragmeme* in the mid-1980s in his Speech Communication Association presidential address, insisting that communication's domain is, "in a semiotician's view of the universe, 'pragmatics': the study of the mutual influence between and among people and their signs and symbols" (2). He proposed a program of "pragmemics" as an analogue to phonemics and morphemics in the syntactic and semantic branches of semiotics, and he suggested that issues like power and status "are probably important features for [such] a theory of pragmatics" (3).[9]

These alternatives were offered in different contexts, each with its specific concerns and solutions, but they have this in common: they recognize that rhetoric's potential for consequence is a problem that has been only inadequately addressed. Although none of these authors goes so far as to suggest that symbolicity is at the root of the difficulty, their proposals of other formulations—speech act, ideograph, utterance, or pragmeme—make the case seem plausible. That is, their alternative constructions for understanding instances of rhetorical practice imply that the notion of the symbol is neither adequate to rhetoric nor coterminous with it, and they hint that the heuristic of symbolicity falls short of grasping rhetoric's characteristic of potential consequence.

Symbolicity is also a dubious language for understanding the partisan character of rhetoric. To the extent that we understand politics or partisanship as a symbolic content or as a substance that can be contained in symbols, symbolicity is an adequate model. That is, if we take politics as a genre of rhetoric, symbolicity addresses it effectively. But if we take seriously what Lyotard articulates so elegantly—that politics is not a genre, but "the state of language" (138)—we are again faced with a difficulty in using the heuristic of the symbol. Any language (or other practice) enacts political effects that are not reducible to its resident meanings, as Foucault makes clear in a discussion of governmentality and power:

In itself the exercise of power is not violence; nor is it a consent which, implicitly, is renewable. It is a total structure of actions brought to bear upon possible actions; it incites, it induces, it seduces, it makes easier or more difficult; in the extreme it constrains or forbids absolutely; it is nevertheless always a way of acting upon an acting subject or acting subjects by virtue of their acting or being capable of action. ("The Subject" 220)

Hence, Foucault enjoins that we "distinguish power relations from relationships of communication which transmit information by means of a language, a system of signs, or any other symbolic medium" ("The Subject" 217). His point is that we cannot account for power, even as enacted or enabled by discourse, by resorting to understanding symbols and meanings.

In sum, rhetoricians' excessive reliance on a model of rhetoric as symbolic is simply inadequate to account for some of its most fundamental—arguably, definitive—characteristics: its capacity for consequence, and its partisanship. It is doubtful that such a model can account even for its legibility, but that is open to question and probably the topic for further investigation. What is clear is that the language of symbolicity has become stiflingly dominant in relation to rhetoric; it is treated as our exclusive heuristic, to such a degree that we are rendered virtually aphasic in attempting to deal with rhetoric in other ways. That there *are* other ways—even rudimentary attempts to access the material character of rhetoric—suggests that we make the attempt.[10]

The Residue of Liberal Humanism

If we look back again to the definitions of rhetoric advanced by contemporary theorists, we see their most obvious common feature: their description of rhetoric as symbolic. But another common element finds its way into most of those definitions—the assertion that rhetoric (or symbolizing) is used to accomplish particular ends: "to influence human behavior," "to communicate with one another," or "to accomplish some goal." This is a common enough way of thinking about rhetoric, and it is probably a reasonably accurate description of the motivations people have for engaging in rhetorical practices; however, it describes a motivation rather than an essential or definitive characteristic of rhetoric. Moreover, it creates additional difficulties for rethinking rhetoric as material.

It is almost certain that the goal orientation linked to rhetoric in these definitions is constituted by rhetoric's imbrication throughout the twentieth century with liberal humanism. Certainly, rhetoric's associations with humanism have been multiple and extremely divergent during their phases of historical circulation and recirculation. Generally speaking, however, humanism in the twentieth-century academic world has come to be associated with the impulses that enhance the individual's enlightened freedom and responsibility of action and thought, tempered by a concern for the same freedoms and responsibilities of others. In rhetoric, as in other fields it has touched, humanism has offered its adherents an optimistic but perhaps too comfortable world view. Liberal humanism has enabled and perpetuated a view of rhetorical practice as a (symbolic, meaning-ful) instrument under the control of the rhetor. We use rhetoric *in order to* accomplish goals. We use it for *effect*— or at least, so the story goes. But because the story goes that way, it leads us to attend to particular aspects of rhetoric and not to others. In fact, it seems to have led us to an overemphasis on rhetorical production and an exceptionally narrow understanding of effect. It surely may be granted that rhetorical study in the twentieth century, and perhaps always, has focused on producing rhetorical performances of some kind. It seems equally unproblematic to assent to the proposition that we teach and theorize rhetorical production as goal-oriented, as aiming for some particular outcome (Cherwitz and Theobald-Osborne 52–56). Again, these tendencies are not necessarily wrongheaded, but they are at least incomplete.

Even rhetorical critics, whose own role is reception, return their readers to questions of invention, contextual contingency, and the construction of the rhetorical text far more than they ever deal with what happens to or with a text, once it has been produced. Rarely is consequence taken up as the central focus of our study. When it is addressed at all, it is typically advanced as a reason to study the construction (production values, if you will) of a particular text; and it is frequently understood narrowly as "success" or goal fulfillment. That is, critics typically argue that a particular rhetorical text is worth our attention because it was successful: it achieved the goal of its maker. Such an argument refers us to the goal of the rhetor as if it were the only possible or legitimate measure of effect (Cherwitz and Theobald-Osborne 56).

This is an inordinately narrow view of what happens when rhetorical texts are mobilized. True, rhetoric achieves, fails to achieve, or only partially accomplishes the goals of its maker. But what about the things that happen as a result of texts that lie outside the goal orientation, or even the perceptual field, of a rhetor? Karl Wallace posed the question almost thirty years ago: "Does one distinguish between the effect and the consequence of an act of communication?" (20). Nilsen had already answered the question and diagnosed the problem in the 1950s: "It is the viewing of the social act, the speech, so predominantly from the point of view of the individual—the speaker and his purposes—rather than from the point of view of society and its purposes . . . that has led to much of the conflict and confusion about effects as an object of criticism" (quoted in Medhurst xxix). Even now, consequences beyond the scope of goal fulfillment are rarely, if ever, addressed, despite the fact that even pedestrian, clichéd understandings of motivation (e.g., "The road to Hell is paved with good intentions") suggest that we may be overlooking something significant. Everyone seems to know that rhetoric is not exclusively about production, and more specifically, that it has consequences that exceed goal fulfillment, but hardly anyone seems able or willing to address it as anything else.

That "anything else" surely is located in rhetoric's materiality. Foucault is helpful in diagnosing the silence as anxiety about materiality, describing it as

anxiety as to just what discourse is, when it is manifested materially, as a written or spoken object; but also, uncertainty faced with a transitory existence, destined for oblivion—at any rate, not belonging to us; uncertainty at the suggestion of barely imaginable powers and dangers behind this activity, however humdrum and grey it may seem; uncertainty when we suspect the conflicts, triumphs, injuries, dominations and enslavements that lie behind those words, even when long use has chipped away their rough edges. ("Discourse" 216)

As a result of such anxiety, Foucault argues, societies find ways of dealing with the production of discourse "to avert its powers and dangers . . . [and] to evade its ponderous, awesome materiality" (216). One way to do that is to accept, or at least not to question, the premise that rhetoric's effects are delineated by its maker's goals. It is not an easy assumption to disengage, because there is a certain comfort in it. But rhetoric has material force beyond the goals, intentions, and motivations of its producers, and it is our responsibility as rhetoricians not just to acknowledge that, but to try to understand it. Unfortunately, we do not have much of a language for doing that, as evident in Foucault's (and others') struggles with discussing it.

Understood in the way that Lyotard and Foucault discuss them, partisanship and consequence are nearly indistinguishable. While I see no particular reason to question their linkage, at least in a consideration of materiality, it is important to retain the different emphases they entail. "Potential consequence" broadens the consideration of effect, but it does not imply a particular tilt to the consequences rhetoric may enact, as "partisanship" does. Rhetoric enables some actions and prohibits or at least discourages others; it promotes particular modes of identity and not others. Sometimes this "tilt" is purposeful, and sometimes not. Nonetheless, the narrow study of effect, understood as goal fulfillment, diverts us from the partisan character of rhetoric, except for the constricted arena of ends-means assessments.

How do we begin to theorize materiality, in the face of these obstacles? If the material character of rhetoric is not reducible to its symbolicity, and if materiality implicates us in issues of consequence and partisanship beyond that of the rhetor's goals, where do we begin? Two answers are already available in the question itself. If rhetoric's materiality is not a function of its symbolic constructions of meaning, then we must look elsewhere: we must ask not just what a text means but, more generally, what it does; and we must not understand what it does as adhering strictly to what it was supposed to do. Both these directives open a vast field for us to contemplate, and thus I believe that we can begin most effectively by attending to instances of rhetoric and what they can tell us about their own materiality. In the following section, I attempt to do just that, with the understanding that the attempt is preliminary and provisional.

Openings in Rethinking Rhetoric: Cases of Material Commemorative Rhetorics

Since the Vietnam Veterans Memorial was dedicated in 1982, a remarkable number of public commemorative sites have been proposed in the United States, and a rather large number of those have actually been constructed. The most prominent are those that have evoked the sharpest controversy—for example, the Korean War Veterans Memorial and the recently dedicated Franklin Delano Roosevelt Memorial, both in Washington, D.C. Many more have been built with less overt public conflict, including the U.S. Navy Memorial and the U.S. Law Enforcement Officers Memorial in Washington; the Freedom Forum Journalists Memorial in Arlington, Virginia; the Civil Rights Memorial in Montgomery, Alabama; the Astronauts Memorial at Cape Canaveral, Florida; the May 4 Memorial at Kent State University in Ohio; and the Witch Trials Tercentenary Memorial in Salem, Massachusetts. The NAMES Project AIDS

Memorial Quilt, though not set in a particular place or made of stone or metal, is an immense memorial that has been displayed in various locations around the world. The U.S. World War II Memorial is now under construction in Washington, D.C. This list is far from exhaustive; it represents only a few memorials actually constructed, from among hundreds, perhaps thousands, that have been proposed in the United States since 1982.

The late twentieth-century surge of public memorial building is itself an interesting rhetorical phenomenon, but rather than focus on it macroscopically, I will use five of these contemporary memorial sites individually (and occasionally in relation to one another and others) as resources for understanding rhetoric's materiality. The five that I focus on here—the Vietnam Veterans Memorial, the AIDS Memorial Quilt, the Civil Rights Memorial, Kent State University's May 4 Memorial, and the Witch Trials Tercentenary Memorial—are not necessarily representative of contemporary memorials. I have chosen them not because of what they tell us about their genre, but because of what they propose about the materiality of rhetoric.

Before turning to what they tell us about rhetoric's materiality, we should take a brief tour of the five sites. The Vietnam Veterans Memorial is situated in Constitution Gardens on the West Mall in Washington, D.C., northeast of the Lincoln Memorial. The original structure, dedicated in 1982 and so familiar that I need not illustrate it here, is a chevron of black granite, about 450 feet long, built into a rise. The reflective surface bears the inscribed names of the more than fifty-eight thousand U.S. personnel killed in the Vietnam conflict. The memorial was supplemented in 1984 by a figurative sculpture of three U.S. soldiers and a flagstaff (figure 2.1). It was augmented again in 1993 by the addition of the Vietnam Women's Memorial, another figurative sculpture (figure 2.2)

The NAMES Project began small in 1987, as the idea of Cleve Jones, a San Francisco AIDS activist. His plan was to commemorate each individual who died of AIDS with a four-by-six-foot quilt (approximately the size of a coffin); each quilt was to be made by a friend or loved one of the deceased (figure 2.3). The full AIDS Memorial Quilt has been displayed four times in Washington, D.C., and various portions of it have been displayed in locations throughout the world—in department stores, in high school gymnasiums, and in state capitols. During its more recent visit to Washington in 1996, the Quilt included more than forty thousand individual quilt panels and covered an area reaching from the U.S. Capitol almost to the Washington Monument. Most of the quilts are decorated with the name of the deceased and often incorporate significant symbols of the individual's life.

The Civil Rights Memorial in Montgomery, Alabama, was dedicated in 1989, on the entrance plaza of a new building housing the Southern Poverty Law Center, its commissioning organization (figures 2.4, 2.5, 2.6). The SPLC,

Figure 2.1. *Three Fighting Men*, Vietnam Veterans Memorial (Permission to reprint by Axiom Photo Design)

established by Morris Dees, is a not-for-profit organization that takes on cases of discrimination, usually racially based; the new SPLC headquarters was built following a 1983 Ku Klux Klan firebombing of its former office space. The memorial is composed of two black granite pieces, both water features. The first is a convex, curved wall fronting the SPLC building. Through falling water appears the inscription, ". . . UNTIL JUSTICE ROLLS DOWN LIKE WATERS AND

Figure 2.2. Vietnam Women's Memorial (Permission to reprint by Axiom Photo Design)

RIGHTEOUSNESS LIKE A MIGHTY STREAM. MARTIN LUTHER KING, JR." The other is a circular but off-balance pedestal with water flowing smoothly off the top, with fifty-three inscriptions around the perimeter of the circle. The inscriptions form an annular time line from 1954 to 1968, noting forty racially motivated murders as well as events and advances in the civil rights movement. The first inscription is the *Brown v. Board of Education* decision, and the last is the assassination of Martin Luther King, Jr.

Kent State's May 4 Memorial, dedicated in 1990, marks the events of 4 May

Figure 2.3. A section of the AIDS Memorial Quilt (Permission to reprint by Axiom Photo Design)

1970, when National Guardsmen opened fire during an antiwar demonstration on campus, following President Nixon's 30 April announcement of the invasion of Cambodia. Four students were killed and nine others wounded. The memorial is situated near the site of the shootings, on a wooded, shadowy slope of Blanket Hill. A long bench facing two pylons marks the entrance to the memorial's plaza (figure 2.7). Between the two pylons, in the granite walkway, is the only inscription: "INQUIRE, LEARN, REFLECT." Four polished black granite ground inserts mark a path to four more pylons; both sets of four mark the four student deaths (figure 2.8). A fifth black inset, removed from the focal four, is intended to acknowledge the many other victims of the 4 May events. As an augmentation, 58,171 daffodils were planted on the site, to commemorate each of the U.S. servicepersons killed in Vietnam (figure 2.9).

The Witch Trials Tercentenary Memorial in Salem, Massachusetts, was dedicated in 1992; it marks the events of 1692, when nineteen men and women were hanged and one man crushed to death, following extraordinary witchcraft trials undertaken by a tribunal of questionable legal authority. A weathered stone wall surrounds a small square adjoining the old Salem burial ground, but a sightline is opened to the point where some of the accusers, judges, and other townspeople of the time are interred (figure 2.10). Inside the perimeter of the square are placed twenty cantilevered stone benches, each bearing the name of one of the accused witches, the person's date of death, and the way the death

...UNTIL JUSTICE ROLLS DOWN LIKE WATERS
AND RIGHTEOUSNESS LIKE A MIGHTY STREAM

MARTIN LUTHER KING JR

Figure 2.4. Civil Rights Memorial (Permission to reprint by Axiom Photo Design)

Figure 2.5. Civil Rights Memorial (Permission to reprint by Axiom Photo Design)

Figure 2.6. Civil Rights Pedestal (Permission to reprint by Axiom Photo Design)

Figure 2.7. Entrance to May 4 Memorial, Kent State University (Permission to reprint by Axiom Photo Design)

sentence was carried out (figure 2.11). These death markers are arranged in chronological order. The center of the square is planted with locust trees (Story and Venditti). Inscriptions—protests of innocence made by the accused—appear in the threshold walkway to the square, but they are cut off abruptly by the walls on either side (figure 2.12). Interestingly, another memorial was erected in nearby Danvers—old Salem Village—site of the trials (figure 2.13).[11]

These memorial sites, taken as rhetorical texts, invite us to consider at least five questions that arise from their materiality: (1) What is the significance of the text's material existence? (2) What are the apparatuses and degrees of durability displayed by the text? (3) What are the text's modes or possibilities of reproduction or preservation? (4) What does the text do to (or with, or against) other texts? (5) How does the text act on people? In raising these particular questions, I do not mean to imply that others might be less important; moreover, each of the issues raised by these questions is a complicated one, deserving far more attention than I can give it here. It is my goal, however, not to exhaust this topic but to stimulate further discussion of it, so my hope is that the exemplars will provoke such exploration.

What is the Significance of the Text's Material Existence?

Charles Jencks suggests that "architecture really is a verb, an *action*" (*Language* 104). The same might be said of any rhetorical text. The entry of a text

Figure 2.8. A portion of the May 4 Memorial (Permission to reprint by Axiom Photo Design)

Figure 2.9. May 4 Memorial (*detail*) (Permission to reprint by Axiom Photo Design)

Figure 2.10. Witch Trials Tercentenary Memorial (Permission to reprint by Axiom Photo Design)

Figure 2.11. Witch Trials Tercentenary Memorial (*detail*) (Permission to reprint by Axiom Photo Design)

within a particular context is a move on that context that changes it in some way. Perhaps the best way to think about this notion is to ask what is different as a result of the text's *existence*, as opposed to what might be the case if the text had not appeared at all. Architecture, like natural language use, expresses degrees of significance not just through its symbolic substance but by its very existence. That a memorial to U.S. Vietnam veterans was built at all marked an important change in the U.S. national cultural context. Although the United States had been defeated, the construction—the spare existence—of a memorial to those who had served in the armed forces did at least two things. First, it announced that those who had served their country were worthy of memory, despite the embarrassing military outcome. Second, it marked a place for the veterans and the survivors of the dead (as well as others) to come together to form a community of recognition, grieving, healing, and activism that had been all but missing from the public sphere (Marling and Wetenhall; Ochsner). The AIDS Memorial Quilt has served similar functions more recently, calling stark attention to the grave threat of the epidemic and offering a gathering point for activists and survivors. Both memorials, by their presence, do something closely akin to what has been called the agenda-setting function of televised news; because a topic appears on the news, it is *thereby* deemed newsworthy (McCombs and Shaw). Similarly, when a memorial (or any other text) appears on the landscape, it is thereby deemed—at least by some, and at least for the

Figure 2.12. Witch Trials Tercentenary Memorial entrance (Permission to reprint by Axiom Photo Design)

Figure 2.13. Witch Trials Memorial, Danvers, Massachusetts (Permission to reprint by Axiom Photo Design)

moment—attention-worthy. This is not to say that all such texts actually achieve attention, but rather that their existence marks them with at least a potential for public attention that would not be available in their absence.[12]

The existence of a text may generate other kinds of consequences as well. Some people are worried that the introduction of multiple new memorials on the Mall in Washington, D.C., will diminish the structures' impact, not because of the particularities of their designs or messages, but simply because of overpopulation.[13] Since 1982, the three Vietnam Veterans Memorial structures and the large, complex Korean War Veterans Memorial have been added to the West Mall, and the World War II Memorial will be in place there by the end of the 1990s. The Roosevelt Memorial now augments the Tidal Basin perimeter once left completely to the Jefferson Memorial, and a Black Revolutionary War Patriots Memorial has been approved for a West Mall site as well, should its foundation be able to raise funds to erect it. So acute have been the worries over this tendency to overpopulate commemorative space that the National Commemorative Works Act (P.L. 99–652) was passed in 1986, severely restricting what kinds of memorials may be built in the monumental core of Washington, D.C. The concern that animates this legislation reminds us that texts, simply by their existence, compete with one another for attention. In this instance, the worry is that they will compete to the degree of mutual distraction—a possibility that has analogues with other kinds of discourses, although the distractions in other cases may involve something other than sightlines. In any case, these and other consequences are made possible not by the symbolic gestures of these texts or the goals of their makers, but by their material existence.

What Are the Apparatuses and Degrees of Durability Displayed by the Text?

Even if we take all rhetoric to be characterized by materiality, we must also acknowledge that its materiality varies in both degree and kind, with differential entailments of durability and vulnerability. The kind of material the text is composed of must be a serious consideration. Some texts, by virtue of their constitutive material, are obviously intended to endure; and it seems a natural assumption, if not always a correct one, that such longevity is granted to texts that communities see as more important than others. Granite and bronze are more durable than ink on paper, and paper lasts longer than the moment of oral discourse. It is an interesting paradox of materiality, however, that durable materials may actually render a text more vulnerable. For example, any stone or metal structure, though composed of a hard, lasting substance, is more vulnerable to destruction by hostile forces than is a book or even oral speech. Natural weathering, vandalism, lack of maintenance, and even bulldozing (as we have seen vividly in news accounts from the republics of the former Soviet Union) are more or less constant threats to public memorial sites. The Civil Rights Memorial in Montgomery is patrolled constantly by a security guard, no doubt to protect it against destruction by vandals or hate groups. Some of these threats, of course, have parallels in the cases of other kinds of texts; however, it is difficult to think of a close parallel to bulldozing or weathering in the case of oral speech. About the only threat of actual destruction to an oral text is that its speaker might be shouted down by a "vandalizing" crowd—a possible but rather atypical event. Certainly the mode of preservation may intervene to salvage a speech even if it is overcome by hecklers, but the event of its orality is destroyed nonetheless. Because this is a less likely outcome than either the vandalism or the inevitable physical decay of a public memorial, however, the paradox remains.

The paradox does not, however, entail a perfect correlation between durability of material and vulnerability. Cases vary considerably. The original AIDS Memorial Quilt panels, now just over ten years old, have become so fragile that they will probably not be part of many future displays of the Quilt. Many of the mid-1980s panels were not sewn quilts but were made of simple cotton sheeting, spray-painted with names (see figure 2.3); they are wearing out as a result of travel, cleaning, and exposure to natural elements. In this case, their vulnerability is a direct result of the lack of durable material. They are not unlike rare documents or books that can be reproduced but that lose originary status in the reproduction. Such loss leads directly to a consideration of the third issue.

What Are the Text's Modes or Possibilities
of Reproduction or Preservation?

The link between reproduction of a text and memory is substantial. It seems uncontroversial to suggest that a text and its reproduction constitute different objects or events, yet it is relatively rare that we *practice* a distinction between original and copy, or among different kinds of copies (transcriptions, translations, etc.). What happens when the first of the Quilt's panels disintegrates? The NAMES Project will preserve all panels to the extent possible and reproduce them in photographs and in photo representations on its web site; however, the literal feel of the panels will be lost, as will the rendered work of therapy for survivors that those panels contain. Reproduction is an intervention in the materiality of the text, and it is important to grapple with the degrees and kinds of change wrought by it.

Reproduction has realized a number of possibilities, often democratizing access to texts of various kinds. However, the access offered by reproduction may be very different from interaction with an original or another kind of copy. It is unlikely that reproduction of a novel much changes the nature of the involvement or response of the reader; however, visiting one of the scaled-down, traveling reproductions of the Vietnam Veterans Memorial is an experience distinctly different from visiting the memorial in Washington. Similarly, the photographs accompanying this chapter cannot replicate the experiences of making a memorial a destination, traveling to it, touching it, seeing it, walking through and around it with others, and even hearing its distinctive sounds. The photographs two-dimensionalize and freeze an experience of three dimensions and movement, accommodating a kind of sharing of experience, but only a limited kind.

This is not unlike the problem faced by critics of public address. It is so unusual, in fact, for such critics to deal with events of which they were a part that it is widely remarked when it occurs (Osborn 149–51; Wenzel 167–68). More typically, when critics study oral rhetorical events that are historically completed, they study reproductions—tape or transcript—of an event, which is thus no longer the same event. Even more radically than with a standing memorial, all opportunity to study the original event has evaporated with time. That is a function not of any imperfection of critical procedures or choices, but of materiality. However, the critic who will attend to rhetoric's materiality— whether dealing with rhetoric that is sewn, sculpted, scripted, or spoken— must acknowledge and even work with (instead of struggle against or ignore) the facts of textual reproduction. Sometimes what appears to be the rhetorical text is not *the* rhetorical text, but an altogether different one; and what counts as *the* text is open to question, in any case. Even the bare materiality of a memorial site does not guarantee that it is the same text on a cloudy day as on a sunny one, on a crowded day as when almost deserted, at dawn as at midday. In fact, its capacity to be engaged physically actually determines its extreme mutability.

What Does the Text Do to
(or with, or against) Other Texts?

This is one of the more difficult questions to address because the linkages among texts can be so varied and numerous. In offering examples here, I will address only relationships among memorial sites, and between the memorial sites and their immediate contexts. I recognize that the memorials do work on other kinds of texts as well, and that other kinds of texts do work on them (Blair and Michel); however, because the question is almost unmanageable except in a fully developed critical analysis, I will limit the domain artificially here, for illustrative purposes.

Here are some of the linkages that stand out in attending to these memorials: enabling, appropriating, contextualizing, supplementing, correcting, challenging, competing, and silencing. As I have suggested, the contemporary spate of memorial-building in the United States began after the Vietnam Veterans Memorial was built, and the new commemorative enthusiasm seems to have been inspired by it. Granted, some of the memorials that have been built since—for example, the U.S. Navy Memorial and the Roosevelt Memorial— had been proposed long before the Vietnam Veterans Memorial appeared, but most others had not. In fact, a persuasive case can be made that this famous landmark *enabled*, or at least encouraged, the construction of others (Abramson 679; Blair, Jeppeson, and Pucci 281–82; Haines 18n.).

More significant, perhaps, is the fact that its principal (and at the time unusual) features have been *appropriated* for incorporation into a number of other memorials. These cannot be coded simply as the signature gestures of Maya Lin, the designer of the Vietnam Veterans Memorial and the Civil Rights Memorial, although both these memorials make use of black granite, temporal arrangement of inscribed events, and inscription of names of the dead. Those characteristics have been incorporated in other designs as well. For example, the Witch Trials Tercentenary Memorial uses the names of the convicted "witches" and arranges their representations in chronological order of death. The AIDS Memorial Quilt originated as a naming project; most of the quilt panels carry the name of one or more people the disease has claimed.[14] At the October 1996 display in Washington, D.C., the quilt panels were arranged in a chronology of receipt by the NAMES Project—not quite the same as an arrangement by date of death, but parallel to it. These are not the only memorials to have appropriated various features of the Vietnam Veterans Memorial,[15] but they are not uncharacteristic in this respect. This appropriation has various consequences. One is that each of these newer memorials depends on its audience's familiarity with the syntax of the Vietnam Veterans Memorial. Another is that each more or less explicitly refers to its famous forerunner, possibly even recalling it to the consciousness of visitors and encouraging an intertextual reading (Blair and Michel).

The May 4 Memorial at Kent State University goes a step farther in cementing a relationship to the Vietnam Veterans Memorial. It appropriates the use of black granite for the ground insets leading to the structures representing the four student deaths; that the visitor follows a path of black granite to these structures is a reminder that the deaths at Kent State took place within the context of U.S. involvement in Vietnam (see figure 2.8). The *contextualizing* is even more pronounced with the introduction on the May 4 site of the daffodils planted in memory of those killed in Vietnam. The particular dimensions of this context of linkage to the Vietnam Veterans Memorial and to the U.S. military casualties in Vietnam carries a valence of reconciliation. Here victims of a war protest gone sour and military personnel are placed side by side, not in opposition, as they were often understood to be during the 1960s and 1970s (Morgan 278).

The activity of *supplementing* is an old one at commemorative sites; the practice of decorating graves and other personal memory sites with flowers and intimate tokens is not uncommon. Recently, however, that practice has been transferred to public commemorative sites, beginning with the Vietnam Veterans Memorial. Visitors leave flowers, clothing, letters, and other personal items at the wall every day (figure 2.14); the National Park Service collects the items, and they are stored and cataloged as museum pieces. The custom has become common at other new commemorative sites. Such supplemental commemorations transmute the commemorative site from a completed text to a context for individual, but still public, memory practices.

A different kind of supplemental rhetorical activity has occurred at Kent State University. Over the years since the campus murders, there have been numerous attempts to commemorate the students killed and wounded. A metal sculpture with bullet holes has been left as a marker at the site. A small stone marker was placed first near the location of the shootings (figure 2.15). Two academic programs were dedicated to the memory of the student victims. A student sculpture project was offered as a gift to the university as a memorial, and it still stands on campus. The university's library contains a resource center dedicated to May 4 memory and a commemorative May 4 collection. There is a public commemorative ceremony every year on the anniversary of the killings. And now there is the university's "official" memorial. Although the kinds of supplemental memory work that have gone on at Kent State and at

Figure 2.14. Decorations at the Vietnam Veterans Memorial (Permission to reprint by Axiom Photo Design)

Figure 2.15. Plaque commemorating Kent State shootings, May 4, 1970 (Permission to reprint by Axiom Photo Design)

the Vietnam Veterans Memorial site are very different, they both point to a struggle over memory and its representation, and perhaps also to the inadequacy of any unitary text to mark a contested memory.

The Witch Trials Tercentenary Memorial offers an interesting case of *correcting*, in this case correction of nearby historical geography. For three hundred years there had been no public site recognizing the accused and condemned in the seventeenth-century trials. No one is even sure where Gallows Hill was located, although it is nearly certain that it was in Salem Village, now Danvers. Unmarked, too, were the sites of the remains of those put to death, although it seems probable that their bodies were dumped into anonymous trenches near the site of their deaths. The placement of the memorial adjacent to the old burial ground and with visual access to it seems to rectify the imbalance of scene in some measure. Not only does it mark the deaths publicly, but it also places the markers of those condemned alongside the townspeople who condemned them—those who at the time were considered worthy of community-marked, sacralized burial. Of course, the representations of those put to death for witchcraft remain segregated from the other townspeople's graves, separated from them by a wall. Their difference and removal from the community are maintained, even as they are allowed to re-enter it conditionally.

The effect of correcting other texts may be difficult to separate from another function, that of *challenging* other texts; however, there seem to be different consequences, at least in degree. The Civil Rights Memorial in downtown Montgomery, Alabama, is set in a cityscape awash in symbols of the Confederacy. Prior to its construction, the only prominent structures that marked the civil rights movement in Montgomery were the King Memorial Baptist Church, two blocks away, and some deteriorating historical markers in various locations. By contrast, immediately surrounding the Civil Rights Memorial there are extremely well-maintained and sacralized historical sites dedicated to preserving the public memory of Confederate leaders, soldiers, and solidarity. A sizable portion of the Alabama State Capitol is a dedicated history site; the debate over secession was convened there. Nearby is the "First White House" of the Confederacy, where Jefferson Davis resided for the first few months after secession. The most prominent outdoor sculpture in the downtown area is the Confederate soldiers statue on the Capitol grounds (figure 2.16).

The Civil Rights Memorial is not very large, but it occupies a relatively prominent position geographically with respect to these other history sites. It is also without doubt the most impressive and physically attractive structure in downtown Montgomery. Water features there are nearly nonexistent, and no other structure calls such attention to itself by virtue of the fame of its designer or the costliness of its materials. Although it does not oppose itself explicitly to Montgomery's nineteenth-century preservation sites or address the racism institutionalized in the multiple legacies of the Confederacy, it stands nearly alone as a reminder of the "other," more recent history of Southern and national

Figure 2.16. Confederate Soldiers Monument, Montgomery, Alabama (Permission to reprint by Axiom Photo Design)

racism. It is an interloper in the commemorative context, but it is also readable as a challenge to it.

Texts *compete*, not only for attention by virtue of their existence or proximity, but also on more specific levels of materiality. The two memorials—in Salem and Danvers—commemorating the Salem witch trials offer a useful example. There has been considerable tension historically, sometimes reaching the pitch of hostility, between the two communities. In fact, some historians argue that it was precisely these tensions that set off the paroxysm of accusations, trials, and prosecutions in the 1600s (Boyer and Nissenbaum). As the tercentenary date approached, the two communities again split ranks, and each dedicated its own memorial. Salem's memorial has a higher profile, but Danvers residents point with seeming pride to the fact that theirs was dedicated first.[16] In any case, both towns have benefited in the end; at the least, they are both now ornamented by beautiful commemorative artworks.

Another case of less pointed, but perhaps more unfortunate, competition is that articulated in relation to the planned memorial for the victims of the 1995 Oklahoma City Murrah Federal Building bombing. As Jesse Katz reports, "The project's size and scale and spiritual magnitude is [sic] most commonly compared to that of the Vietnam Veterans Memorial or the U.S. Holocaust Memorial Museum" (A23). Such comparisons inevitably pit sites like the planned Oklahoma City memorial measure for measure *against* the memorials with which they are compared. At the risk of seeming to minimize the great suffering and loss induced by the Oklahoma City bombing, comparisons to Vietnam or to the Holocaust, or to the memorials that mark them in Washington, are absurd at best and crudely self-absorbed at worst. No doubt such competitive renderings are unintended by those making the comparisons, but the effect remains.[17]

The final case I will take up here, *silencing*, has several less restrictive variants that simply make the rendering of other texts more difficult. For example, the AIDS Memorial Quilt has not actually silenced discourses about the "gay plague," but its juxtaposition of representations of deceased two-year-olds, hemophiliacs, and heterosexual women with those of gay men certainly makes such positions difficult to maintain. The most obvious case of actual silencing is the Witch Trials Tercentenary Memorial's lopping off of the inscribed defenses of the accused witches. Of course, this is to be read ironically, as a material manifestation of the court's inability or unwillingness to listen charitably, and it indeed renders a powerful indictment of that failure. There are those who argue, however, that the irony runs deeper. The memorial advocates a spirit of tolerance explicitly, yet the large community of witchcraft practitioners currently residing in Salem maintains that their town is anything but tolerant; the absurd, made-for-tourists representations of witches, witchcraft, and the supernatural in Salem seem to bear them out (figure 2.17). Nonetheless, the presence of the memorial and its explicit aim of tolerance limit the ability of the witches

Figure 2.17. Sign on municipal vehicle, Salem, Massachusetts (Permission to reprint by Axiom Photo Design)

to complain credibly about objectionable attitudes without appearing to be carping. So, they say, they often simply remain silent about what they see as bigotry.[18]

Texts may also serve to silence or limit other texts by means of their own exclusions. This is a troubling issue that might be raised in regard to the Civil Rights Memorial. Its emplotment of civil rights–related deaths and activities leaves out all mention of sacrifices made or actions taken by black nationalist or separatist groups, for example, functionally writing them out of its history. Moreover, the inscriptions that announce historic civil rights successes are represented as actions taken by institutional authority—presidential order, Supreme Court decisions, and paramilitary enforcement. Some argue that such exclusions reinforce conciliatory attitudes and institutional authority (Abramson 707), and silence others by excluding them from rhetorical presence. I am not inclined to read the Civil Rights Memorial this way, but it is a legitimate reading that might limit and exclude particular formulations of racial activism.[19]

How Does the Text Act on Person(s)?

Perhaps the largest "miss" of a symbolic heuristic for rhetoric is its understanding of rhetoric as appealing rather exclusively to the mind of a reader or listener.

Rhetoric of all kinds acts on the whole person—body as well as mind—and often on the person situated in a community of other persons. There are particular physical actions the text demands of us: ways it inserts itself into our attention, and ways of encouraging or discouraging us to act or move, as well as think, in particular directions. The most obvious demands rhetoric makes on the body are the very physical ones required for one to pay attention. Rhetoric, regardless of its medium, is introduced into a space that would be different in its absence. By being introduced, it nominates itself for the attention of potential listeners, readers, or viewers. To read a book, one must physically open it, usually sit down, and gaze at the inscribed words. To attend to a speech is to sit or stand still, usually facing the speaker, and be quiet in order to hear.

Memorials (and other constructed sites) do perhaps even more obvious work on the body. They direct the vision to particular features, and they direct—sometimes even control—the vector, speed, or possibilities of physical movement. Touching them is different from touching a book (except perhaps a rare or deeply significant book), and that touch sometimes yields profound responses. Being prohibited physically from touching them, because they occupy a chained-off space, may be just as important. The point is, though, that rhetoric acts on the whole person, not just on the "hearts and minds" of its audience. Any attempt to theorize rhetoric materially must come to grips with that fuller range of consequence. Again, illustrations from the memorial sites suggest that the material aspect of rhetoric does significant work to shape the character of rhetorical experience.

For one thing, memorial sites are *destinations*.[20] As such, they demand physical labor of a would-be audience member. Some kind of motion is required to go to the sites, and most require mobility to negotiate their spatial dimensions. Memory sites are not the only texts that are treated as destinations, however: people plan their days so that they can finish reading books; they forgo other activities and purchase tickets to hear a speaker; they rush home to see a television show. When we treat texts in such ways, we have already allowed them to affect our material lives as well as our mental activities. Of course, not all texts are granted such status, but it is important to explore the kinds of discursive networks that create such affiliations for some texts, and the consequences of treating particular texts as objects of desire while functionally ignoring others.

There are any number of ways that rhetorical texts may hail or *summon* the person, and some of these means are clearly material. The Civil Rights Memorial asserts itself onto the attention of passersby in two important ways. First, it literally interrupts the path of pedestrians. Its pedestal structure is situated in a plaza that is little more than a broadened sidewalk (see figure 2.5). To walk straight along the vector of the sidewalk is to collide with the structure; thus, it has to be negotiated—a pedestrian has to attend to it to avoid bumping into it. But from there, one must decide whether to stop, look at, walk around, and touch the physical structures of the memorial, or to go out of one's way to avoid doing so. While this first summons transgresses the path of the pedestrian, the second is less aggressive. The presence of water on the site is a lure to visitors in the area. Montgomery's climate is warm and humid, and the sound, sight, and feel of water relieve the dreariness of the heat. Whether one is brought up short while walking or is enticed by the refreshing water, the rhetoric acts on the person to garner attention.

Almost the opposite is true of the Witch Trials Tercentenary Memorial. It imposes on attention so little that sightseers in Salem often pass right by it. The site appears from the outside to be nothing more than a public, shaded rest area with some uncomfortably hard stone benches. However, those who follow their maps to the site or enter it for respite find themselves enrolled in the intolerance of seventeenth-century Salem, because entry means walking on the entreaties of the accused inscribed in the threshold area of the memorial. Some who step on the words are horrified by their own actions as well as by the interrupted nature of the inscribed statements by the walls on either side; others never notice the inscriptions at all, their walks reproducing the Salem townspeople's disregard of the protests of the accused. Even if unwittingly, the directed path into the area enlists visitors in its own rhetoric of displayed intolerance.

These sites also suggest—sometimes *prescribe*—*pathways* for a visitor to traverse, and those pathways influence reception significantly. The most common entry for visitors to the Vietnam Veterans Memorial is from the Lincoln Memorial side. For those who follow that route, the most common pattern is to stop at the *Three Fighting Men* sculpture first. The black wall of names is visible in its entirety from the sculpture's location, and many turn from the statue for that panoramic view of the wall. To gaze on the wall first offers a preparation for the visitor about to enter its space, an experience unavailable to others who enter the site from the east side, opt for the path to the wall first, or miss the path to the sculpture.

The walkway that follows the wall at the Vietnam Veterans Memorial moves the visitor downward as the wall grows in height. The visitor is encompassed bodily by the wall and its inscribed names and is mirrored in its polished surface—visually incorporated by it. There is no alternative to the paved walkway. It is chained in, and pedestrians are prohibited from moving onto the grassy area fronting the wall to gain distance or a longer view. Visitors become increasingly aware of the scale of the wall of names by walking its length. As the visitor turns the corner of the wall's chevron and walks back on an upgrade, the experience seems to come to a close, and for some visitors, the rhetoric of the memorial may end there. There is no sign of any other destination; the second sculpture—the Vietnam Women's Memorial—is barely visible, situated on what appears to be a secondary byway. Most people do find it, usually by following others to it, but often only after their experience of the memorial has been punctuated. The Vietnam Women's Memorial becomes an appendage, experientially separate from the Vietnam Veterans Memorial because of its placement.[21]

Memorial sites, by their very existence, ~~create communal spaces~~, Although it is possible to describe an individual's encounter with a site, it is almost always part of a collective experience.[22] One may seem to be alone with one's thoughts but still be moving among others. That experience of the group's presence is significant, even if not wholly conscious. The 1996 display of the AIDS Memorial Quilt in Washington just *felt* important. Certainly that feeling was overdetermined, but it was created in part by the presence of so many other people; this clearly was an *event*. That collectively inspired feeling was not lost on the display's organizers. One of only a few interruptions in the reading of names of the dead was made to announce that CNN had reported attendance at the weekend display to have reached 2.2 million.

But it is not just the presence of others that lends character to the rhetoric of these sites. Others' actions also help to construct the messages constituted by the memorials' rhetoric. The large AIDS Memorial Quilt displays in Washington generated dozens of spinoff activities—celebrity appearances, candlelight vigils, prayer services, and disruptions of traffic by illegal (but carefully planned) ACT UP marches. Some of the high-impact, memorable moments are the comforting gestures between strangers—the hug, offer of a tissue, or word of condolence. The 1996 Quilt display was not an event that visitors could experience "fully." Because of its magnitude, they took fragments of its rhetoric with them when they left—perhaps the frame of a grieving, anonymous man (figure 2.18), or the chance glimpse of the first U.S. president to see the Quilt, Bill Clinton. In any case, other visitors constitute part of the rhetoric by their presence and activity in the scene.

Although the physical experience of place and communal participation may not be so pronounced in other rhetorical forms, it is by no means absent. Just as the construction of a memorial site offers space for particular (and directed) kinds of activity and contemplation, other rhetorical media do similar kinds of work, if not so obviously. Lisa Flores offers an excellent example in her discussion of the border culture of Chicana feminism and the rhetorical constructions of space:

> While confined geographically as a border culture between the United States and Mexico, Chicana feminists can cross rhetorical borders through the construction of a discursive space or home. By employing a rhetoric of difference . . . Chicana feminists use their creative works as a tool in the discursive construction of a space of their own. (143)

By Flores's analysis, this space is much more than a metaphorical one. It is an actual place to occupy and to act in and from.

Rhetoric's materiality constructs communal space, prescribes pathways, and summons attention, acting on the whole person of the audience. But it also

Figure 2.18. Grieving man at the AIDS Memorial Quilt, 1996 (Permission to reprint by Axiom Photo Design)

allows a rhetorical text to "speak" by its mere existence, to endure by virtue of the durability of its composition, to be preserved by particular modes of reproduction, and to act on other texts. I suspect that its material character allows it to do much more, but it has at least these functions, suggesting that we should attend to its material character far more than we have.

This analysis is limited by the same constraints harbored by any self-consciously inductive attempt to theorize. Even the illustrations offer only examples of rhetoric's material dimension. The scope of the space opened by exploring rhetoric's materiality is untraversable in any brief encounter. But among the many things that I have learned from my experience with these memorial sites—often in spite of my own "educated expectations"—is the fact that they construct valenced reaction and depths of visitor experience that cannot be described, much less explained, in terms of their symbolism or by reference to the intentions of their makers. We have a long trek before we reach the point of even rudimentary understanding of rhetoric's material nature.

I do not mean to deny the significance to rhetoric of its symbolicity or its goal-oriented agents. Its symbolicity and purposefulness are significant, but they are features of rhetoric, not its definitive essence. I am not (quite) certain that materiality is a *more* fundamental characteristic of rhetoric than symbolicity, or than the belief that rhetoric is "made" by goal-oriented users. But I am quite sure that rhetoric's characteristic materiality cannot be reduced to either of those attributes. One of the forgone opportunities of this analysis is a consideration of how the material, symbolic, and purposeful dimensions of rhetoric may interact, interfere, or intersect with one another. For now, though, it is imperative that these three characteristics not be allowed to cede their own functions and that their division of rhetorical labor not be conflated.

Notes

1. When I use the term "real," I wish it were avoidable, because it smacks of a realist philosophical position that I am anxious to eschew. Although there are points of contact between some realist and some materialist positions, the principal difference, in my view, is that materialism is not beholden to a metaphysical defense of a reality independent of perception or interpretation. Materialist positions, instead, typically take "realities" or material phenomena as historically and contextually accreted understandings that assume the status and force of a natural or independent reality; see Silverman and Torode 28–29. The distinction can be made clear by attending to James Hikins's justifications for a realist position vis-à-vis rhetoric: "Because rhetoric is ensconced in the pedestrian world, and because its most direct consequences bear on issues of human conduct and welfare, any theory of rhetoric must eventually land squarely on its feet in the pedestrian world. However esoteric the theorist's view, it must adequately account for what we know about the natural world in which we all reside" (24). Although some materialists might find such a position perfectly acceptable (see McGuire 189–93), a

minor but consequential adjustment is necessary, in my view. Because rhetoric occurs in a pedestrian world and exerts its most important consequences in the realm of human affairs, it seems to me that we must be mindful of the *social* world, which would include the only meaningful characterizations we have available of the "natural world in which we all reside." Whether the physical world has an independent existence is simply a question of very little interest or significance to this brand of materialism—roughly what McGuire would call "social" materialism (193).

2. I undertake this project, even acknowledging the warnings issued by Dana Cloud. This is not the place for a critique of her position. I believe, however, that it is possible to avoid the two extremes she attributes—rightly or wrongly—to some theories of rhetoric as material: that rhetoric "transcend[s] and determine[s] material relations of power (idealism)," or that it "constitute[s] reality and that therefore there are no ontological or epistemological grounds for moral or political critique (relativism)" (158). It seems to me that we can simply argue that rhetoric is one (important, though not exclusive) practice by which realities and relations of power are constituted. I am not certain that any of the theorists Cloud has targeted actually argues for a more excessive position than that, but I will not.

3. There is an exception that I will discuss later, the NAMES Project AIDS Memorial Quilt. Because it is mobile, and portions of it are displayed in various venues and for varying lengths of time, other portions are stored in a warehouse in San Francisco. That is a very unusual case, but I do not mean to dismiss it because it is atypical. Instead, as I will suggest, it seems important to discuss various types of materiality and how they shift with and by means of the kind of material.

4. Although any of their works could be read as dealing with issues relevant to the materiality of rhetoric, those that take up these issues most centrally are de Certeau, *The Practice of Everyday Life*; Foucault, *The Archaeology of Knowledge and The Discourse on Language*; and Lyotard, *The Differend*. All three of these writers, not just these central works, have profoundly influenced this chapter.

5. The most obvious examples, but certainly not the only ones, are Umberto Eco, Charles Jencks, and W. J. T. Mitchell.

6. There are of course exceptions, including Charland, McGee's "A Materialist's Conception," McGuire, and Railsback.

7. One example is Hart's characterization of rhetoric as the "art of using language to help people narrow their choices among specifiable, if not specified, policy options" (4).

8. I disagree with Farrell's assessment of the problem as the use of the term "text." He is correct, I believe, in his view that "text" as a term does imply an inert product. However, his complaints ignore the numerous theorizations of text over the past twenty years, which can hardly change the ordinary sense of the term itself but which do attempt to address the problem of its apparent immobility at a theoretical level.

9. See also Bowers and Bradac, 871–93.

10. Stewart makes the case most explicitly, in suggesting as a conclusion at least worthy of additional study, that "it is an overgeneralization to characterize language as essentially or uniformly representational or symbolic. . . . [The ordinary language philosophers] stress the importance of studying meaning by focusing not on the extralinguistic elements utterances allegedly represent or symbolize, but on the language games that are engaged in or the speech acts that are performed in and by making an ut-

terance" ("Concepts" 132). Although I think there remains a probative issue about whether the result of studying illocutions or performances is an understanding of meaning, rather than of power or politics, the description gets at the distinction between studying language uses of any kind from the point of view of the ephemeral symbolic heuristic versus one that takes up the activity of rhetoric, its partisanship, and its potential for consequence.

More recently, John R. Stewart has intensified his critique of what he calls "the symbol model," arguing for what amounts to a substitution of an ontological understanding of language for an epistemological one. See Stewart, *Language*, and Stewart, ed., *Beyond*. Although Stewart's critique gets at many of the problems of a heuristic of symbolicity, his solution—a re-understanding of language as "articulate contact"—neglects issues of power, precisely those that a materialist position insists on engaging.

11. The Danvers memorial is less publicized and is of local design and construction, but it was actually dedicated before its more famous counterpart in 1992. Information and observations about each of these memorials are based primarily on fieldwork conducted at each site by Neil Michel and me, except as noted. However, I would be remiss not to note the strong, general influence on my thinking about these memorial sites, of Berman, Bodnar, Carr et al., Dickinson, Foote, Fryd, Griswold, Linenthal, Piehler, Schama, Sturken, Mike Wallace, Young, and the collections edited by Linenthal and Engelhardt, Mitchell, and Senie and Webster.

12. The general point here is very similar to one made by Kenneth Foote, that sites of death may be sanctified, rectified, designated, or obliterated. Any of the first three, in my view, are typically different from the fourth. However, even that is not always true, as Foote points out: "A curious feature of obliterated sites I noticed is that, once stigmatized, they stand out as much as sacred spaces" (25). Foote's point is worth noting, but so is his qualification "once stigmatized." Not all sites that evoke public forgetfulness are stigmatized. Moreover, many memorials do not occupy the actual space of the events they represent. In fact, none of the memorials considered here occupies the specific site of tragedy or death. The May 4 Memorial comes closest, but even it occupies a different location on Blanket Hill than did the actual shootings in 1970.

13. See, for example, testimony on S. 2522 and H.R. 4378 (99th Congress, 2d session). Advocates of this legislation, which ultimately became P.L. 99–652, almost universally expressed concern that memorials would get in one another's way, competing for attention among themselves and against the landscaped beauty of the Mall. See also George Will's "Statue Sweepstakes." Will is concerned not only about the presence of too many memorials but also with the particular character of some of them, that is, their symbolic gestures.

14. There are a few quilt panels labeled "anonymous," and some represent only the first name of the deceased. Letters that accompanied some of these contributions to the Quilt suggested that the name was omitted or abbreviated to protect the reputation of the deceased or of his or her survivors. See Ruskin 78–84.

15. The Astronauts Memorial appropriates both the use of black granite and inscriptions of names of the dead. The U.S. Law Enforcement Officers Memorial lists the names of those killed in the line of duty. The U.S. Navy Memorial does not inscribe names but has begun a computerized roster of names of its service personnel. The Ko-

rean War Veterans Memorial replaces names with numbers, although a computerized roster of the dead is planned at that site as well; it appropriates the use of mirror-finished black granite. A large number of state and local Vietnam memorials also incorporate features of the national memorial.

16. Both memorials were dedicated in 1992, but the Danvers work was constructed and dedicated before the Salem site. Reaction of local townspeople is based on my discussions with visitors to the Danvers memorial and with others around the town.

17. Something like historical proportion *must* be maintained in communities like Washington, D.C., that contain numerous, prominent memory sites in close proximity. For example, it is unthinkable that the Vietnam Veterans Memorial could have been of a scale akin to the Lincoln Memorial or even the Jefferson Memorial. Similarly, the World War II Memorial site is relatively close to the Vietnam and Korean War Veterans memorials, and there has been considerable concern expressed that it should represent the scale of World War II reasonably vis-à-vis the two Cold War actions commemorated nearby. Oklahoma City has less experience with such balancing, but it could easily encounter charges of tastelessness or worse if its memorial is perceived as out of all proportion to others in the country that represent tragedies of far more massive scale.

18. This is a very complex issue, especially for an outsider to take up. The interpretation is based on interviews with several residents of Salem who are members of a coven, and on my own observations of other "witch" representations in Salem.

19. I am sympathetic in principle to these arguments, although I think they may be based on a reductive reading of the Civil Rights Memorial. Since reductive or partial readings at memorial sites are actually to be expected on the part of visitors, it may be that those who render these readings have a legitimate cause for concern. However, other features of the memorial, in my view, urge the visitor to see the future of race issues very differently than they have been seen in the past.

20. Some are the endpoints of modern-day pilgrimages, as an audience member at the Penn State conference pointed out. This observation is an important amendment, because it implies the sacralized character of some but not all public commemorative sites.

21. It is arguable that the Vietnam Women's Memorial also sets itself apart from the remainder of the Vietnam Veterans Memorial because of its design features. Whereas the *Three Fighting Men* sculpture refers the visitor by sightline back to the wall (the figures in the statue appear to be gazing at it), there is no such interaction between the Women's Memorial and the wall or between the two statues. See Christopher Knight for a fine commentary on the Women's Memorial; see also Marling and Wetenhall.

22. It is an odd feeling, in fact, to occupy alone what is clearly communal space, whether a commemorative site or some other usually populated place. Having visited a number of these memorial sites late at night or in predawn hours, I know that the experience is radically different than during the day when other people are present.

Works Cited

Abramson, Daniel. "Maya Lin and the 1960s: Monuments, Time Lines, and Minimalism." *Critical Inquiry* 22 (1996): 679–709.

Berman, Marshall. *All That Is Solid Melts into Air: The Experience of Modernity*. New York: Penguin, 1988.

Blair, Carole, Marsha S. Jeppeson, and Enrico Pucci, Jr. "Public Memorializing in Postmodernity: The Vietnam Veterans Memorial as Prototype." *Quarterly Journal of Speech* 77 (1991): 263–88.

Blair, Carole, and Neil Michel. "Commemorating in the Theme Park Zone: Reading the Astronauts Memorial." In *At the Intersection: Cultural Studies and Rhetorical Studies*, edited by Thomas Rosteck, 29–83. New York: Guilford, 1998.

Bodnar, John. *Remaking America: Public Memory, Commemoration, and Patriotism in the Twentieth Century*. Princeton: Princeton University Press, 1992.

Bowers, John Waite. "On the Pragmeme." Presidential Address, Speech Communication Association Convention, 2 November 1984. *Spectra,* January 1985: 2–3.

Bowers, John Waite, and James J. Bradac. "Contemporary Problems in Human Communication Theory." In *Handbook of Rhetorical and Communication Theory*, edited by Carroll C. Arnold and John Waite Bowers, 871–93. Boston: Allyn and Bacon, 1984.

Boyer, Paul, and Stephen Nissenbaum. *Salem Possessed: The Social Origins of Witchcraft*. Cambridge, Mass.: Harvard University Press, 1974.

Bryant, Donald C. "Rhetoric: Its Function and Its Scope." *Quarterly Journal of Speech* 39 (1953): 401–24.

Carr, Stephen, et al. *Public Space*. New York: Cambridge University Press, 1992.

Certeau, Michel de. *The Practice of Everyday Life*. Translated by Steven Rendall. Berkeley: University of California Press, 1984.

Charland, Maurice. "Constitutive Rhetoric: The Case of the Peuple Québecois." *Quarterly Journal of Speech* 73 (1987): 133–50.

Cherwitz, Richard A., and John Theobald-Osborne. "Contemporary Developments in Rhetorical Criticism: A Consideration of the Effects of Rhetoric." In *Speech Communication: Essays to Commemorate the 75th Anniversary of the Speech Communication Association*, edited by Gerald M. Phillips and Julia T. Wood, 52–80. Carbondale: Southern Illinois University Press, 1990.

Cloud, Dana L. "The Materiality of Discourse as Oxymoron: A Challenge to Critical Rhetoric." *Western Journal of Communication* 58 (1994): 141–63.

Dickinson, Greg. "Memories for Sale: Nostalgia and the Construction of Identity in Old Pasadena." *Quarterly Journal of Speech* 83 (1997): 1–27.

Eco, Umberto. "Function and Sign: The Semiotics of Architecture." In *Signs, Symbols, and Architecture*, edited by Geoffrey Broadbent, Richard Bunt, and Charles Jencks, 11–69. New York: John Wiley and Sons, 1980.

Ehninger, Douglas. Introduction. In *Contemporary Rhetoric: A Reader's Coursebook*, edited by Douglas Ehninger, 1–14. Glenview, Ill.: Scott, Foresman, 1972.

Farrell, Thomas B. "On the Disappearance of the Rhetorical Aura." *Western Journal of Communication* 57 (1993): 147–58.

Flores, Lisa A. "Creating Discursive Space through a Rhetoric of Difference: Chicana Feminists Craft a Homeland." *Quarterly Journal of Speech* 82 (1996): 142–56.

Foote, Kenneth E. *Shadowed Ground: America's Landscapes of Violence and Tragedy*. Austin: University of Texas Press, 1997.

Foss, Sonja K., Karen A. Foss, and Robert Trapp. *Contemporary Perspectives on Rhetoric*. Prospect Heights, Ill.: Waveland, 1985.

Foucault, Michel. *The Archaeology of Knowledge and The Discourse on Language.* Translated by A. M. Sheridan Smith. New York: Pantheon, 1972.

Foucault, Michel. "The Discourse on Language." Translated by Rupert Sawyer. Appendix to *The Archaeology of Knowledge and The Discourse on Language*, 215–37.

Foucault, Michel. "The Subject and Power." Afterword to *Michel Foucault: Beyond Structuralism and Hermeneutics*, by Hubert L. Dreyfus and Paul Rabinow, 208–26. 2d ed. Chicago: University of Chicago Press, 1983.

Fryd, Vivien Green. *Art and Empire: The Politics of Ethnicity in the U.S. Capitol, 1815–1860.* New Haven: Yale University Press, 1992.

Griswold, Charles L. "The Vietnam Veterans Memorial and the Washington Mall: Philosophical Thoughts on Political Iconography." *Critical Inquiry* 12 (1986): 688–719.

Haines, Harry W. "'What Kind of War?': An Analysis of the Vietnam Veterans Memorial." *Critical Studies in Mass Communication* 3 (1986): 1–20.

Hart, Roderick P. *Modern Rhetorical Criticism.* Glenview, Ill.: Scott, Foresman/Little, Brown, 1990.

Hauser, Gerard A. *Introduction to Rhetorical Theory.* Prospect Heights, Ill.: Waveland, 1986.

Hikins, James W. "Realism and Its Implications for Rhetorical Theory." In *Rhetoric and Philosophy*, edited by Richard A. Cherwitz, 21–77. Hillsdale, N.J.: Lawrence Erlbaum Associates, 1990.

Jencks, Charles. *The Language of Post-Modern Architecture.* 5th ed. New York: Rizzoli International, 1987.

Jencks, Charles. "Rhetoric and Architecture." *Architectural Association Quarterly* 4 (1972): 4–17.

Johannesen, Richard L. "Editor's Introduction: Some Trends in Contemporary Rhetorical Theory." In *Contemporary Theories of Rhetoric: Selected Readings*, edited by Richard L. Johannesen, 1–6. New York: Harper and Row, 1971.

Katz, Jesse. "A Driving Need for Catharsis." *Los Angeles Times*, 19 April 1997.

Knight, Christopher. "Politics Mars Remembrance." *Sacramento Bee*, 7 November 1993.

Linenthal, Edward T. *Preserving Memory: The Struggle to Create America's Holocaust Museum.* New York: Viking, 1995.

Linenthal, Edward T., and Tom Engelhardt, eds. *History Wars: "The Enola Gay" and Other Battles for the American Past.* New York: Henry Holt, 1996.

Lyotard, Jean-François. *The Differend: Phrases in Dispute.* Translated by Georges van den Abbeele. Minneapolis: University of Minnesota Press, 1988.

Marling, Karal Ann, and John Wetenhall. "The Sexual Politics of Memory: The Vietnam Women's Memorial Project and 'The Wall.'" *Prospects: An Annual of American Cultural Studies* 14 (1989): 341–72.

May 4 Site and Memorial: Inquire, Learn, Reflect. Kent, Ohio: Kent State University, n.d.

McCombs, Maxwell E., and Donald L. Shaw. "The Agenda-Setting Function of Mass Media." *Public Opinion Quarterly* 36 (1972): 176–87.

McGee, Michael Calvin. "The 'Ideograph': A Link Between Rhetoric and Ideology." *Quarterly Journal of Speech* 66 (1980): 1–16.

McGee, Michael Calvin. "A Materialist's Conception of Rhetoric." In *Explorations in Rhetoric: Studies in Honor of Douglas Ehninger*, edited by Ray E. McKerrow, 23–48. Glenview, Ill.: Scott, Foresman, 1982.

McGuire, Michael. "Materialism: Reductionist Dogma or Critical Rhetoric?" In *Rhetoric and Philosophy*, edited by Richard A. Cherwitz, 187–212. Hillsdale, N.J.: Lawrence Erlbaum Associates, 1990.

Medhurst, Martin J. "The Academic Study of Public Address: A Tradition in Transition." In *Landmark Essays on American Public Address*, edited by Martin J. Medhurst, xi–xliii. Davis, Calif.: Hermagoras, 1993.

Medhurst, Martin J., and Thomas W. Benson. "Rhetorical Studies in a Media Age." In *Rhetorical Dimensions in Media: A Critical Casebook*, edited by Martin J. Medhurst and Thomas W. Benson, ix–xxiii. Dubuque, Iowa: Kendall/Hunt, 1984.

Mitchell, W. J. T. Introduction. In *Landscape and Power*, edited by W. J. T. Mitchell. Chicago: University of Chicago Press, 1994.

Mitchell, W. J. T., ed. *Art and the Public Sphere*. Chicago: University of Chicago Press, 1992.

Morgan, Edward P. *The 60s Experience: Hard Lessons about Modern America*. Philadelphia: Temple University Press, 1991.

Nietzsche, Friedrich. "Description of Ancient Rhetoric." In *Friedrich Nietzsche on Rhetoric and Language*, edited and translated by Sander L. Gilman, Carole Blair, and David J. Parent, 3–193. New York: Oxford University Press, 1989.

Nilsen, Thomas R. "Criticism and Social Consequences." *Quarterly Journal of Speech* 42 (1956): 173–78.

Ochsner, Jeffrey Karl. "A Space of Loss: The Vietnam Veterans Memorial." *Journal of Architectural Education* 50 (1997): 56–171.

Osborn, Michael. "'I've Been to the Mountaintop': The Critic as Participant." In *Texts in Context: Critical Dialogues on Significant Episodes in American Political Rhetoric*, edited by Michael C. Leff and Fred J. Kauffeld, 149–66. Davis, Calif.: Hermagoras, 1989.

Piehler, G. Kurt. *Remembering War the American Way*. Washington, D.C.: Smithsonian Institution Press, 1995.

Railsback, Celeste Condit. "Beyond Rhetorical Relativism: A Structural-Material Model of Truth and Objective Reality." *Quarterly Journal of Speech* 69 (1983): 351–63.

Ruskin, Cindy. *The Quilt: Stories From The NAMES Project*. New York: Pocket Books, 1988.

Schama, Simon. *Landscape and Memory*. New York: Alfred A. Knopf, 1995.

Senie, Harriet F., and Sally Webster, eds. *Critical Issues in Public Art: Content, Context, and Controversy*. New York: HarperCollins, 1992.

Silverman, David, and Brian Torode. *The Material Word: Some Theories of Language and Its Limits*. London: Routledge & Kegan Paul, 1980.

Stewart, John R. "Concepts of Language and Meaning: A Comparative Study." *Quarterly Journal of Speech* 58 (1972): 123–33.

Stewart, John R. *Language as Articulate Contact: Toward a Post-Semiotic Philosophy of Communication*. Albany: SUNY Press, 1995.

Stewart, John R., ed. *Beyond the Symbol Model: Reflections on the Representational Nature of Language*. Albany: SUNY Press, 1996.

Story, William, and Arthur Venditti. *The Complete Touring Companion and Historical Guide: The Witchcraft Hysteria of Salem Town and Salem Village in 1692*. Peabody, Mass.: Willart, 1992.

Sturken, Marita. *Tangled Memories: The Vietnam War, the AIDS Epidemic, and the Politics of Remembering*. Berkeley: University of California Press, 1997.

United States. Senate. Subcommittee on Public Lands, Reserved Water and Resource Conservation. *Hearings on Standards for the Establishment of Commemorative Works in the Nation's Capital*. 99th Cong., 2d sess. S 2522 and H.R. 4378. Washington, D.C.: Government Printing Office, 1986.

Wallace, Karl R. *Understanding Discourse: The Speech Act and Rhetorical Action*. Baton Rouge: Louisiana State University Press, 1970.

Wallace, Mike. "Visiting the Past: History Museums in the United States." In *Presenting the Past: Essays on History and the Public*, edited by Susan Porter Benson, Stephen Brier, and Roy Rosenzweig, 378–83. Philadelphia: Temple University Press, 1986.

Wenzel, Joseph W. "'A Dangerous Unselfishness': Martin Luther King, Jr.'s Speech at Memphis, April 3, 1968: A Response to Osborn." In *Texts in Context: Critical Dialogues on Significant Episodes in American Political Rhetoric*, edited by Michael C. Leff and Fred J. Kauffeld, 167–79. Davis, Calif.: Hermagoras, 1989.

Will, George F. "The Statue Sweepstakes." *Newsweek,* 26 August 1991: 64.

Young, James E. *The Texture of Memory: Holocaust Memorials and Meaning*. New Haven: Yale University Press, 1993.

3 *Susan Wells*

Legible Bodies
Nineteenth-Century Women Physicians and the Rhetoric of Dissection

Feminist scholars of science, in particular feminist scholars of medicine, have described the scientific gaze as objectifying, reifying, and quintessentially male: the (male) scientists' gaze penetrates an object, such as Nature, Life, or the Body, which has been constructed a female.[1] Since Bacon, sexual conquest has been a powerful figure in the scientific imaginary; since the pioneering and productive work of Evelyn Fox Keller, feminist students of science have advanced the project of demystifying science's claim to objectivity and gender neutrality by explicating how its imaginary structures are gendered. Nowhere is this truer than in feminist studies of medicine. No scientific discipline intersects more intimately with the lives of the women who write about it, and who also encounter medicine as patients, as caregivers for family members, and as medical workers on various levels; when we write the story of medicine, the story we are writing is in many ways our own. To investigate medicine historically, however, is to encounter another gaze: that of the woman physician, absorbed in the pleasure of doing the scientific work of medicine, and particularly in the pleasure of seeing the interior of the body. This chapter inquires into that pleasure (especially as it is experienced in dissection), considers how it was constructed, and assesses its implications for a material rhetoric.

I take as my starting point the entrance of American women into what was called "regular" medicine in the middle of the nineteenth century. We think of medicine—at least, medicine before managed care—as a difficult, forbidding, lucrative profession, only recently opened to women, effective in managing its affairs and in consolidating its power. Whether or not this image is accurate for contemporary medicine, it cannot easily be read back on the quite different practices of the mid-nineteenth century. Then medical instruction was only loosely articulated with the university system, hospitals were thin on the ground, and licensing was an optional adornment not legally required for the practice of medicine. "Regular" medicine was one of a broad range of therapeutic approaches that included homeopathy, the water cure, electrical treatment, Thompsonianism, and eclecticism; although it was clearly the strongest and best-connected branch of the profession, its hegemony was by no means secure. Most women who practiced medicine in the nineteenth century were educated in women's medical schools, proprietary institutions established in the face of sustained hostility from the regular medical establishment; these institutions produced most of the two thousand women physicians who were practicing in the United States in 1880 (Morantz-Sanchez 92). As the medical profession developed its organizational infrastructure, especially its control of medical education, medicine became even less hospitable to women. The Flexner Report (1910), a program of progressive reform in medical education, established standards for laboratories and clinical experience that few women's institutions could meet. Moreover, the very success of coeducation, particularly after the new Johns Hopkins Medical School admitted women in 1891, decreased women's general access to medical education. Many medical schools agreed to admit women, and the beleaguered women's schools closed or merged with local male institutions; however, women were seldom admitted to co-educational schools at rates higher than 5 percent of an entering cohort, and the ranks of women who had taught at women's medical schools were dispersed into the profession. Ironically, the success of feminist agitation for medical coeducation led to a marked decline in the influence of women physicians: as a group, they would decline in both relative and absolute numbers during the last years of the century and would not regain their presence in the profession until the 1970s (Morantz-Sanchez). Improvements in medical schools—such as the progressive course and systematic clinical education—undoubtedly improved medical practice, benefiting (among others) women patients, but also made medical education long, expensive, and difficult to sustain outside a university setting, thereby restricting women's access to medical knowledge.[2]

In the middle of the nineteenth century, however, none of these conditions held. Women who studied medicine at the Female Medical College of Pennsylvania, later renamed the Woman's Medical College of Pennsylvania, followed substantially the same course as their male counterparts at the Medical Department of the University of Pennsylvania, at Jefferson Medical College, or even at the Homeopathic (Hahnemann) Medical College: they came to school after a year's apprenticeship with a physician; they heard twice, in successive

years, a course of seven lectures; and they wrote a final thesis, the defense of
which was their only examination. This course was often supplemented with
clinical lectures, work in hospital wards and dispensaries, and especially with
dissection (Rosenberg).

Although nineteenth-century medical students were not always required to
dissect complete human bodies, most major medical schools included a dissecting room, which was in many ways the heart of the school. In the absence
of a necessary connection between medical schools and hospitals, the dissecting room was the place where students confronted the material practices of
their future profession. Although a full dissection was optional, medical pupils
were expected to perform autopsies, practice surgical procedures on cadavers,
and dissect "parts." Male students who wanted additional instruction could attend such private institutes as the Philadelphia School of Anatomy, directed by
D. Hayes Agnew, which saw 200 to 250 students a year during the 1850s
(O'Hara 88). Each medical school, whether it was connected with a university
or with a private, proprietary institution, hired a "demonstrator of anatomy" to
secure material and supervise the students.

In some ways, the practice of the dissecting room was not particularly
marked by gender. When Woman's Medical College student Mary Theodora
McGavran visited the Hahnemann dissecting room in 1899, she remarked, "A
mans dissecting room doesn't differ materially from a womans—Ours is a
little larger I think" (Kaiser 233). No evidence that I have found suggests that,
when women medical students dissected, they followed different procedures
from those of male medical students. In women students' accounts of dissection we find many of the same responses that characterize male medical students' narratives: they are frightened or repulsed at first but then grow fascinated by what they learn; sometimes they make jokes about the body they are
dissecting, or imagine it as reanimated. Unlike male students, however, women
students do not seem to have been prone to either practical jokes or sexual humor in the dissecting room.

Earlier in the nineteenth century fledgling women's medical colleges presented dissection carefully, as an acceptably contained practice. When the
Woman's Medical College of Pennsylvania was founded, the construction of
the dissecting room and the appointment of the demonstrator were significant
decisions. The first announcement of the Female Medical College assures readers that "The Anatomical Rooms will be furnished with every convenience and
kept strictly private. They will be under the supervision of the Professor of
Anatomy, *aided by competent female assistants*" (12). The professor of anatomy was initially (and necessarily) male, but as soon as the college graduated its first class, a woman demonstrator was appointed—Hannah Longshore,
sister-in-law of one of the founders of the institution and a dissectionist since
girlhood (Wells). The supervision of the anatomy room soon passed from Han-

nah Longshore, with her suspicious connections to "irregular" medicine, to a more regular and highly trusted graduate; the position was, like that of the clinic assistant, an honor. The demonstrator may have had some difficulty obtaining material; early faculty minutes include a resolution that "the Demonstrator in this College has all the rights and privileges of the most favored Demonstrator in this City and she is authorized to purchase and prepare subjects for Demonstration and present or sell them to the class at her own expense" (Faculty Minutes, 28 October 1850). The faculty and corporators also agreed that the dissecting room should be separate from the school and limited to women. Dead bodies were, of course, a possible source of illness, but the act of dissection was also understood to require privacy—almost secrecy: the book of the body would be opened only in an enclosed space.

And no wonder, given the exigencies of nineteenth-century dissection. Without reliable refrigeration or preservatives, dissection was done as quickly as possible, and only during the winter months. The apparatus for holding and positioning the body was rudimentary, and the scene of dissection could become grotesque. Consider, for example, the following directions for dissection of the (male) perineum:

> To dissect the perineum, the subject should be fixed in the position for lithotomy, that is, the hands should be bound to the soles of the feet, and the knees kept apart. An easier plan is the drawing of the feet upwards by means of a cord passed through a hook in the ceiling. Both of these plans of preparation have for their object the full exposure of the perineum. And as this is a dissection which demands some degree of delicacy and nice manipulation, a strong light should be thrown upon the part. Having fixed the subject, and drawn the scrotum upwards by means of string or hook, carry an incision from the base of the scrotum along the ramus of the pubes and ischium and tuberosity of the ischium, to a point parallel with the apex of the coccyx; then describe a curve over the coccyx to the same point on the opposite side, and continue the incision onwards along the opposite tuberosity, and along the ramus of the ischium and of the pubes, to the opposite side of the scrotum, where the two extremities may be connected by a transverse incision. This incision will completely surround the perineum, following very nearly the outline of its boundaries. Now let the student dissect off the integument carefully from the whole of the included space, and he will expose the fatty cellular structure of the common superficial fascia, which exactly resembles the superficial fascia in every other situation. (Wilson 219)

To contemporary lay eyes, this disposition of the body seems nearly sadistic; it is unlikely, however, that nineteenth-century medical students, especially women medical students, read their anatomy texts as pornographic. The sexual overtones of the language used by nineteenth-century physicians and their patients are quite palpable to us, but they were seldom remarked by contemporaries. Even journalistic critics of medical instruction worried about "indelicacy" and "immodesty" in lectures rather than prurience in the dissecting room. Wilson's dissection of the perineum is clearly intended to impress rather than arouse. The spectacle of the exposed corpse is presented to the presumably male student as a double bind: having exposed and displayed his subject, just as a patient might have been restrained for surgery, the student performed what must have seemed to be a castration. Then he inspected the tissues of the genitals—to find nothing unusual, but only superficial fascia that resemble those of "every other situation." Dissection performed a spectacular exposure of the body in order to assure the student that there was nothing to expose.

The copy of Wilson's *Anatomy* in which this account was printed belonged to Ann Preston, the first dean of the Woman's Medical College and for many years its public voice. She would have read the *Anatomy* when she began medical study at the age of thirty-seven. Her text, properly preserved as a relic of a medical pioneer, bears the marks of her struggle to appropriate the discourse of a scientific education: its flyleaves carry miscellaneous notes, including a list of complementary colors; the anatomical diagrams—though not the diagram of the male reproductive system—are often carefully annotated, with index letters reinscribed in pencil over the structures; and Preston traced over the diagrams that render a complex, three-dimensional body on the engraved surface of the page.[3] The anatomy text, its diagrams, and the dissected body offered students a triangular set of representations. The text carefully translated topography into prose; the act of dissecting demanded that the student arrange physical structures with equal care, demonstrating their relations; and the diagram offered an approximation of the relation between the text and the prepared corpse. The student learned to see the body; she also learned to read the text, and to see the diagram. For Preston, and for her colleagues, the experience of anatomy required new ways of presenting and conveying information. Dissection was enacted as a cultural break, marked by the discovery of a surprising interior: early students at the Woman's Medical College negotiated that break and normalized it for women.

Often their negotiation worked. The act of dissection spoke to the intense desires of women students for a particular experience of the body, and it could be articulated with widespread cultural practices of physiological investigation. The Alumnae Association memorial notice for Ida Richardson, who graduated from the college in 1879, speaks of her conversion to dissection. Richardson had at first resisted the idea of a medical career because she shrank from publicity, but she "finally gave up to what she now believed to be a real heaven-born call." Even after enrolling in the College, she was still doubtful:

Soon after her advent in the college an opportunity offered for commencing dissection, and believing that nothing could be so revolting as that, and a greater test of the strength of her conviction, she determined to try herself thereby, and applied for a part. Even after her request was granted, she still held back until one of the older students tried to convince her that before she really entered upon dissection she should accustom herself to the room and insisted that she go there with her. At first she resisted, but finally yielded, and consented to sit by while the others worked, and read to them from the anatomy in regard to the tissues uncovered in the dissection. Soon after this she began the work for herself, and instead of its weaning her from her chosen course, she forgot the unpleasantness in the marvelous beauty of the hidden tissues of the human frame. Her enthusiasm over dissection was so great that she aroused all the students around her and carried them with her, and became the life of the room. (Alumnae 25)

This student did not manage dissection by acquiring the "necessary inhumanity" that historian Ruth Richardson has identified as the dissectionist's response to "tasks which would, in normal circumstances, be taboo or emotionally repugnant," understandable though that would have been (Richardson 31). Instead, Ida Richardson seems to have experienced something like an aesthetic conversion, an awakening to the perception of the interior spaces of the body as beautiful. Knowledge of the body in the dissecting room is connected to other bodily practices: we read of weaning and arousal, of "life" circulating in that dead room. It was the very privacy of the dissecting room that permitted Richardson's conversion; there, she was remote from the "publicity" she dreaded encountering in a medical career (25).

Many of the early women physicians had been attracted to dissection from girlhood. Hannah Longshore wrote of her girlhood dissections of "such specimens as came into my hands," and the young Mary Putnam Jacobi, another prominent early physician, had had designs on a rat's corpse until, much to her relief, her mother forbade her to touch it (Longshore; Jacobi). For others, dissection was, as it had been for Richardson, a trial of their vocation. As Elizabeth Blackwell was preparing for medical study, one of her fellow teachers gave her a dead cockchafer (a large beetle) "as a first subject for dissection": "I accepted the offer, placed the insect in a shell, held it with a hair-pin, and then tried with my mother-of-pearl handled penknife to cut it open. But the effort to do this was so repugnant that it was some time before I could compel myself to make the necessary incision, which revealed only a little yellowish dust inside" (Blackwell 85). Striking in this account is Blackwell's attempt to perform a "scientific" dissection with the paraphernalia of feminine charm: a shell, a hair-pin, a decorative knife. No wonder she felt queasy. Later, in Philadelphia, Blackwell studied in a private anatomical school, dissecting alone in her room under the direction of a teacher. That teacher

by his thoughtful arrangements enabled me to overcome the natural repulsion to these studies generally felt at the outset. With a tact and delicacy for which I have always felt grateful, he gave me as my first lesson in practical anatomy a demonstration of the human wrist. The beauty of the tendons and exquisite arrangements of this part of the body struck my artistic sense, and appealed to the sentiment of reverence with which this anatomical branch of study was ever afterwards invested in my mind. (Blackwell 59)

If dissection was famously, for Galen, an opening of the body "in order to see deeper or hidden parts" (2.3), for nineteenth-century women opening and viewing could become pleasurable acts. An appetite for the pleasures of sight, particularly of the interior of the body, was widespread among nineteenth-century women, who organized both public and domestic practices of viewing.

That appetite may have been sharpened by a relative scarcity of images, in particular images of the interior of the body. Women patients wished for images that would visually confirm their illness almost as much as they wished for a cure. Sheila Rothman's account of the correspondence among consumptive women in Deborah Vinal's circle during the 1830s recounts Vinal's fantasy of a device that could reveal the mysterious interior of the body: "It is a foolish wish because a vain one, but I *do* wish I could take a peep into Adeline's windpipe, Ellen's lungs and mine, and your *joints* that *ache*" (111). In the absence of any means of seeing the interiors of living bodies—even X-rays were far in the future—dissection was the sole means of directly experiencing those spaces and searching out the causes of illness. Many representations of the body that are readily available to us today were relatively scarce in nineteenth-century culture. We are surrounded with images of cells, membranes, and organs; such events as the Kennedy assassination, the cloning of a sheep, and the discovery of the cause of Alzheimer's disease are explained by photographs and diagrams. We know what a cell looks like; with guidance, we can tell the difference between a healthy cell and a cancerous cell, or between healthy tissue and inflamed tissue. But such images were not so available a century and a half ago. Neither newspapers nor illustrated magazines routinely included images of the interior of the body. Physiology textbooks and anatomical atlases could be illustrated with engravings, lithographs, and mezzotints of dazzling beauty and complexity, but they were not distributed to a broad public market.[4] Even medical journals were very sparsely illustrated. Nor did students produce their own images; even though many nineteenth-century medical students had been raised in a culture that valued vernacular drawing, they seldom made their own sketches of the structures they had seen in lectures or clinics. In the culminating theses produced at the end of the third year of study, many medical students described particular organs, but they never drew these organs; instead, they wrote out laborious topographic descriptions, something like the old technical writing assignment to write a "description of an object."

Although medical images were anything but ubiquitous, they were available, and those who were interested in them found ways to view them. Some images were available for private purchase and inspection. The eclectic physician Edward Bliss Foote not only carried on a lively medical practice through the mail, but, by his own account, he also sold hundreds of thousands of copies of his extremely explicit home medical texts, *Medical Common Sense* (1857–58), *Plain Home Talk* (1869–70), and a book intended for children, *Sammy Tubbs, the Boy Doctor, and "Sponsie," the Troublesome Monkey* (1874). *Sammy Tubbs* included diagrams of the male and female reproductive systems, artfully arranged on two sides of a single page, numbered "180 1/2" and "180 3/4" so that they could be silently razored out by less liberal parents (Sappol 143–44).

Other images were displayed in group situations. Both Hannah Longshore and Ann Preston, early graduates of the Woman's Medical College of Pennsylvania, gave "physiological" lectures; Longshore's introductory lecture was attended by five thousand people (J. Longshore). The lectures were illustrated with diagrams and culminated in the display of a papier-mâché model of the interior of the body. One of the most durable and social of the sites in which women examined such images was the Boston Ladies' Physiological Society.[5] Founded in 1848, the group drew about three hundred women to its weekly meetings during the 1850s. It was one of several such societies in the Boston area, and it continued, with various names and missions, until 1966. Organized initially to sponsor lectures by Dr. Charles P. Bronson, the Ladies' Physiological Society quickly became a repository not only for medical books and diagrams but also for "apparatus," a collection of preserved body parts, models, and charts. The apparatus was entrusted to a designated officer; it was monitored, displayed, maintained, and above all used. Almost the first purchase made by the Society was a skeleton, procured after considerable expense and trouble. Donations, gifts, and further purchases helped the society to assemble an impressive array of anatomical knick-knacks. The writer of the second annual report of the society, in May 1850, observed with satisfaction: "We have added to our Apparatus during the year, by the purchase of a superior Skeleton, a preparation of the upper extremities of a child, showing the skull, thorax, and arms, and a beautiful wax model of a hand, representing Erysipelas [an infection]; we have received a donation of duplicate parts of the Osseous system." To inspect the apparatus was not an act of idle curiosity: it was scientific, maternal, and above all religious. The secretary went on to reflect in the 1850 report:

We have met from week to week, and studied the handiwork of God,—traced His finger in the beautiful workmanship of our bodies—learned the nice relations of the parts to each other, and to the whole, been shown the intricacy and simplicity of this system of body, mind, and soul,—we have seen that all is here governed by fixed laws, as in other parts of God's creation; we have been taught the results of a violation of them, and have learned the law of obedience and harmony in regard to them.

Here, as in the experience of Ida Richardson, the interior of the body is both aesthetically satisfying and a scene of efficacious moral instruction. Study of the body is a simple extension of the study of nature, yielding similar satisfaction and edification. Harriot Hunt, an early (and unlicensed) woman physician, sponsored the formation of a similar society in Worcester in 1843:

Married women—mothers—meeting together to obtain more light regarding their own physical natures; —it seemed a holy thought, and good spirits strengthened it! It ulti-

mated in the formation of a little society composed of some of the members of families
in which I prescribed, and called forth my warmest prayers for its success. (Hunt 161)

The meetings of the Physiological Society were both instructive and social;
the women gathered, heard a lecture, sewed and talked through the afternoon,
and were sometimes joined by their husbands in the evening. In both the
Worcester and Boston societies, the program was eclectic: phrenological heads
were displayed alongside models of skin diseases, and the discussion might
take up the water cure for female diseases or the possibility of "renouncing the
rod" for disciplining children. Sometimes the program included dissection. In
July 1850, Dr. C. W. Gleason, a member of the faculty of the Woman's Medical
College of Pennsylvania, lectured on the eye. His talk was illustrated "with a
natural eye, which was dissected and the diseases of the different humors described." In December 1850, a Dr. Grimes lectured on the brain, "illustrating
his subject by a human brain, (which was passed among the audience,) and several diagrams." The lecture continued over two weeks, "the brain being mi-
nutely described and dissected before the audience," which voted its thanks to
Dr. Grimes and arranged for the preservation of the undissected hemisphere.
Even the "apparatus" could be seen as replicating dissection: when the society
purchased a "collosal ear" in April 1851, the model was described as "capable
of dissection." The practices of the Ladies' Physiological Society reflect a way
of appropriating images of the body and acts of dissection into a surprisingly
flexible separate sphere of womanly domesticity. Dissection, after the first "horrors" were past, could be an uplifting and useful occupation.

I would argue that dissection could become acceptable for women, at least
within reform circles, because it could be modeled on an equally interesting
and absorbing avocation, newly sanctioned for women: the reading of fiction.
Dissection was both metaphorically and metonymically associated with reading. Dr. D. Hayes Agnew, in his 1870 introductory lecture to the Medical Department of the University of Pennsylvania, recommended dissection as "a
charming task" and proclaimed, "The lifeless frame is the greatest of all books.
Turn over its leaves with untiring diligence. You can never know its contents
too well" (24–25). As we have seen, dissection was itself guided by the directions in an anatomy text; a student not lucky enough to have Ida Richardson
reading the text aloud would often keep the anatomy before her as a reference,
so that there was an unusually intimate correspondence between the written
word and the materials of the body that students uncovered. That correspondence helped to mediate the labor of dissection; rather than experiencing it
as *work*, both Richardson and Blackwell (like Longshore, and like Mary Putnam Jacobi in her short story "A Martyr for Science") experienced dissection
as a practice of *seeing*, an opening of the body to the intent gaze. Paradoxically,
dissection was a way of seeing that made the body disappear, as the familiar
organs and structures—the hand, the arm, the belly—gave way to the fascia

(everywhere the same), and then to organs and tissues. Conversely, the act of dissection offered to sight structures that all the students had experienced in their own bodies but had never seen: the heart, the lungs, and the bones that were always available and palpable became, for the first time, visible. The experience of reading fiction similarly dissolved the decorous appearances of social life into episodes of domestic conflict, financial worry, and religious doubts—stories that were everywhere available, the stuff of everyday gossip, but seldom visible.

The family group, listening to a realistic story that offered a representation of daily lives like their own, formed themselves as spectators to the newly elaborated institutions of authorship and entertainment, sitting immobile and absorbed; they had much in common with these avid medical women, gathered in a private room, gazing into a (radically) immobile body which they had in a material sense made to disappear, and working out the correspondences between its structures and a text arranged before them.[6] Moreover, like the literary text, the dissected body was a product of artful arrangement and display, in that medical students prided themselves on their skill in making "preparations" that preserved and clarified the arrangements and relations of organs and structures. Some images and preparations were as durable as literary tropes: the flayed image, or *ecorché*, produced by Ludovico Cigoli from a wax model in about 1600, is still cast and used in anatomical teaching and is praised by Mimi Cazort and her colleagues for its "careful attention to the striation of the muscles" (239). Like the literary text, dissection offered the sensation of a direct contact with nature, mediated by adroit craft.

The dissected body was not only a work of art; it also provided a demonstration of the "laws of health," which were seen by many in mid-century reform circles as secular realizations of religious and moral codes. Like women reading domestic fiction within the setting of the family, women medical students engaged in dissection offered themselves as objects of moral instruction while engaging in a deeply pleasurable activity. The medical student, finding religious lessons in the structures she uncovered, had much in common with the absorbed but edified reader of *The Wide, Wide, World*.[7]

Unlike the literary text, however, the dissected body offered itself as a site of instruction that was both individual and temporally situated: the body, at least potentially, recorded the vicissitudes of one realized and completed life. A reading of the body could demonstrate a case and thereby posthumously vindicate a subject. In one such case, a graduate of the Woman's Medical College wrote to Dean Rachel Bodley in 1886 to arrange for the public dissection of her body after her death (Woman's Medical College, Dean's Files). The dissection would test the graduate's theory about the aftereffects of the oöphorectomy (removal of the ovaries) that had been performed on her. This early woman physician was quite willing to put her medical theory to bodily proof, even after her own death.[8] The correspondent asked that, if dissection supported her theory, her medical history and the results of the investigation be "read before the students of the Woman's College" and later published "for the benefit of science." Dissection was so much a practice of reading that, as in this instance, it could also serve as a practice of writing.

Although it was generally less controversial than women's attendance at mixed clinical lectures, dissection by women could be threatening. In Mark Twain's *The Gilded Age*, the medical student Ruth Bolton is placed in the dissecting room at night with the corpse of an African American man. The corpse is imagined as protesting the indignity of dissection by a woman: "Haven't you yet done with the outcast, persecuted black man, but you must now haul him from his grave, and send even your women to dismember his body?" (148). But Ruth approaches the body with "awe" and "reverence"; her compassionate gaze tempers the rigorous exigencies of science. Much worse encounters between women students and corpses could be imagined: the *Boston Medical and Surgical Journal* of 28 February 1871 ran a story under the heading "Outrage at a Woman's Medical College," reprinted from the *Richmond and Louisville Medical Journal*. It seems that the body of a poor woman had been taken to the Cleveland Woman's Medical College for a post-mortem examination, and the students pledged to give it a decent burial. An Episcopal minister was secured and rites were performed, but "suspicions were aroused" by the lack of a grave in the cemetery:

The coffin was then opened and found to contain billets of wood. The body, the "lady students" had retained for their delectable entertainment! Apart from the revolting and repulsive enormities of such a scandalous transaction, and apart, also, from the abhorrent violations of a sacred pledge, how can any one, in terms sufficiently excoriating, denounce those who would thus deliberately have performed over a mass of wood, the most sacred and solemn rites known to man? Such appalling blasphemy is without precedent and beyond description. ("Outrage" 134)

The writers went on to say that the case demonstrated how a woman who left her sphere was soon "lost to every instinct which brings to her sex its tenderest blessings," and should be punished by other women. Here the vectors of the moralizing scene of dissection have been reversed: the body disappears not because it is revealed but because it has been stolen; dissection is not private but requires a public display, albeit a fraudulent one; and rather than inciting piety, the dissection sponsors blasphemy. Only the absorption, the interest, the "delectable entertainment," are the same.[9]

Whether the woman physician was constructed as a grave-robber, as the object of terror, as herself the object of dissection, or as the rapt and reverent spectator searching the body for evidence of a divine law, the connection between the gaze of the woman and the opened interior of the body is asserted and assumed to be mediated by the woman physician's pleasure in seeing. Writers are surprised by that pleasure, to be sure: if the writing is autobiographical, the writer is surprised by *her own* pleasure. But even though the discourse of nineteenth-century medicine is frankly gendered—and often quite erotic—nobody imagined that a woman who took pleasure in such sights had become male. The gaze she enacted was recuperated in the economy of care and domestic piety; its gender was female. Some women physicians insisted that their agency was not particularly gendered, as in Marie Zakrzewska's counterfactual insistence that "science has no sex" (Vietor 67). We might recuperate their pleasure for contemporary gender theory by arguing that women approached the dissected body in a different, less objectifying way than men; however, all of the tropes I have isolated in the discourse of women physicians can also be found in the discourses of male physicians and medical students. Moreover, such an approach would silence the testimony of women who insisted both that their dissection was indistinguishable from that done by men, and that they were never more womanly than when engaged in this work. I would argue that the activity of medicine, including the potentially threatening activity of dissection, offered nineteenth-century women particular pleasures, that these pleasures connected them with a visual economy associated with the body and its representations, and that the pleasure they took in these activities supported a range of practices—social, hygienic, professional, and scientific—connecting them to "regular" medicine and offering an autonomous sphere of medical activity. We can complicate and historicize our understanding of the medical gaze as essentially male by looking back at this group of rapt and gazing medical women.

In closing, it seems appropriate to ask how this project coheres with the work of constructing a material rhetoric. It is possible that in mapping the work of dissection onto the activity of reading, I have repeated the most reductive structuralist (and poststructuralist) trope, in which an activity is found to be "a language" or "about language." Productive as that trope has been, it is deeply at odds with a project that is more likely to see language as, on some level, a material practice. Dissection, however, is a practice that disrupts many stable binaries: no work is more corporeal; none is more mediated by the abstractions of science. Dissection may be constrained by time and deeply contextualized in a local setting, but its basic tropes of opening and revealing have been stable since Galen. What is revealed, however, is never an unmediated material body: the figurative and textual records of dissections tell us more about the professional practices of anatomists than they do about particular organs and tissues. In the 1850s, in fact, very few dissectionists would have thought in terms of tissues, seeing the body instead as a series of nested organs bathed in mysterious fluids (Rosenberg; Sawday; Warner).

When we think about dissection, then, we imagine an object of inquiry that is both material and stable, and also constructed and signifying. The object, and our attention, hover, suspended together. Such hovering might become a common gesture in the development of a material rhetoric. Material objects and practices can appear as limit cases, demonstrating what is persuasion and what is not: Is force rhetorical? Is wife-battering persuasion? They also appear as suasory practices different in degree, rather than in kind, from the sanctioned force of law, the boundaries of public space, or the habitual constraints of professional practice. A marginal practice, or even a destructive practice from which rhetoric ought to deliver us (*ad bellum purificandum*) re-emerges under analysis as itself constructed through practices of signification. In Aristotle, such objects were to be contained on the borderland of rhetoric—inartistic proofs, including oaths, physical evidence, and testimony given under torture, did not follow the logic of the probable and were not constructed through the rhetor's art. Such evidence was a means of persuasion outside the domain of rhetorical study. But for Aristotle, and still more for Cicero, inartistic proofs were known to be stunningly effective: consider Cicero's discussions of such sensational tactics as the display of wounds, or of one's children. Within the tradition of Aristotle, Cicero, and Quintilian, therefore, the inartistic proof, a point of intersection between the material and the arts of language, was admired and suspected rather than theorized.

Another model of the relation between signifying utterance and material objects can be found in the work of Walter Benjamin, particularly in his provocative early work *One-Way Street* (1928). Benjamin's aphoristic essays compare the body to the house, analyze everyday objects, recount dreams, discuss German inflation, and offer both advice on writing and parodies of advice on writing. Benjamin worries and speculates about the future of writing in a society that had learned other means of inscription; he thought that "the card index [as a business tool] marks the conquest of three-dimensional writing, and so presents an astonishing counterpoint to the three-dimensionality of script in its original form as rune or knot notation" (456). Certain themes recur—dreams, love, children's toys, and the tools and apparatus of writing. The one-way street, as Benjamin constructs it, is not only an emblem of passion but also a place for dancing, and there the hoariest clichés of Marxist materialism—quantity turning to quality, or the inevitability of the collapse of capitalism—leap and spin. *One-Way Street* is also the work of a singular writer, responding to a singular situation: intended for distribution among Benjamin's friends, it is a reverie rather than a rhetoric.

What we can take from this work, perhaps, is its enactment of a possible subject matter for a material rhetoric. Benjamin does not distinguish among works of art, elements of popular culture, literary texts, scientific practices, and the experience of the city street: any cultural artifact or practice is available for an analysis in which the object instructs the writer. The writer makes no totalizing statements but instead arranges a series of moments that open the culture to intelligibility (a series, rather than a succession, because *One-Way Street* frustrates sequential reading). The text presents itself as a record of seduction, as a letter to an absent beloved; the writer's plea for accommodation, for readerly mercy, is available on its surface.

What is missing from *One-Way Street*, however, and central to the project at hand, is a rhetorical understanding of memory as a material practice and a ground of intelligibility. If the classical "offices" of the orator are, under the conditions of modernity, differentiated into many disciplines, practices, and professions, it could be that the rhetorician undertakes (among other things) the work of cultural memory, of the re-animation of discourses and persuasive practices. Like the custodian of the apparatus owned by the Boston Ladies' Physiological Society, the rhetorician offers evidence of the internal structures of common experience, provides a safe space for viewing and working with such evidences, procures new "preparations" as they are needed, and offers an ongoing report on the ways in which such materials are used. This essay is one such "preparation"—the material reinscription of a range of nearly forgotten experiences and practices, an evocation of a pleasure we have inherited and forgotten.

Notes

1. For early feminist studies of science, see Evelyn Fox Keller, *A Feeling for the Organism: The Life and Work of Barbara McClintock*, and her *Reflections on Gender and Science*; and Sandra Harding, *The Science Question in Feminism*. Early studies have been collected in Nancy Tuana, ed., *Feminism and Science*. More recent work is included in Barbara Laslett et al., eds., *Gender and Scientific Authority*. A convenient account of this line of study can be found in Evelyn Fox Keller and Helen Longino, eds., *Feminism and Science*.

2. For accounts of the history of women in nineteenth-century medicine, see Morantz-Sanchez; the documents collected in Apple, ed.; Bonner; and Furst, ed. I should add that the primary research reported in this essay derives from the Archive of Women and Medicine, MCP Hahnemann University, Philadelphia; for their generous support of that research, I am grateful to staff members at the archive.

3. For the development of technologies of representation in anatomical texts of the sixteenth century, see Sawday 133. The convention on keying particular structures in a drawing to a list of named parts, first developed in anatomical texts, required a sophisticated interpretation of the relation between text and picture—between the represented body and the space of the page.

4. For a discussion of the development of anatomical art from the time of Vesalius until the end of the nineteenth century, see Cazort, Kornell, and Roberts.

5. Ladies' Physiological Society of Boston and Vicinity, Secretary's Reports and Board Meetings, vol I. Schlesinger Library, Cambridge, Mass., MC 236. Pages in the reports are not numbered; all quotations in this section are from the secretary's reports.

6. See, for example, Davidson; Hobbs; Kelly.

7. For nineteenth-century reading practices, see Brodhead; Tompkins.

8. Preston said, "Ladies, we should gain nothing by meeting such as these in argument. Prejudices are not amenable to reason. Your business is, not to war with words, but 'to make good' your position 'upon the bodies' of your patients by deeds of healing. . . . The question of the *success* of woman as physician is not now an open one. Her success is already a matter, not of hope or of prophecy, but of history."

9. The phrase "delectable entertainment" suggests an association between dissection and cannibalism. For another example of persistent rumors connecting dissection with cannibalism, see Ruth Richardson's account (221) of workhouse inmates' fears that their daily broth was in fact "Nattomy Soup."

Works Cited

Agnew, D. Hayes, M.D. *Lecture Introductory to the One Hundred and Fifth Course of Instruction in the Medical Department of the University of Pennsylvania, delivered Monday, October 10, 1870*. Philadelphia: published by the class, 1870.

Alumnae Association of the Woman's Medical College of Pennsylvania. "Ida E. Richardson." In *Transactions of the Twenty-Seventh Annual Meeting of the Alumnae Association of the Woman's Medical College of Pennsylvania*, 25–26. Philadelphia: Alumnae Association of The Woman's Medical College of Pennsylvania, 1902.

Apple, Rima, ed. *Women, Health, and Medicine in America: A Historical Handbook*. New York: Garland, 1990.

Benjamin, Walter. *One-Way Street*. In *Selected Writings Volume I: 1913–1926*, edited by Marcus Bullock and Michael W. Jennings, 444–88. Cambridge, Mass.: Harvard University Press, 1996.

Blackwell, Elizabeth. *Pioneer Work in Opening the Medical Profession to Women*. New York: Schocken, 1977.

Bonner, Thomas Neville. *To the Ends of the Earth: Women's Search for Education in Medicine*. Cambridge, Mass.: Harvard University Press, 1992.

Brodhead, Richard. *Cultures of Letters: Scenes of Reading and Writing in Nineteenth-Century America*. Chicago: University of Chicago Press, 1993.

Cazort, Mimi, Monique Kornell, and K. B. Roberts. *The Ingenious Machine of Nature: Four Centuries of Art and Anatomy*. Ottawa: National Gallery of Canada, 1996.

Davidson, Cathy N. *Revolution and the Word: The Rise of the Novel in America*. New York: Oxford University Press, 1986.

Furst, Lilian R., ed. *Women Healers and Physicians: Climbing a Long Hill*. Lexington: University Press of Kentucky, 1997.

Galen. *On the Natural Faculties*. Translated by Arthur John Brock. Cambridge, Mass.: Loeb Classical Library, Harvard University Press, 1952.

Harding, Sandra. *The Science Question in Feminism*. Ithaca: Cornell University Press, 1986.

Hobbs, Catherine, ed. *Nineteenth-Century Women Learn to Write*. Charlottesville: University Press of Virginia, 1995.

Hunt, Harriot Keziah. *Glances and Glimpses: or Fifty Years Social, Including Twenty Years Professional Life*. 1856. Reprint, Boston: Jewett, 1870.

Jacobi, Mary Putnam. "Foreword to the Family." In Jacobi Papers, Schlesinger Library, Cambridge, Mass.

Jacobi, Mary Putnam. "A Martyr for Science." In *Stories and Sketches*, edited by Mary Putnam Jacobi. New York: G. P. Putnam's Sons, 1907.

Kaiser, Robert, Sandra L. Chaff, and Steven J. Peitzman. "A Philadelphia Medical Student of the 1890's: The Diary of Mary Theodora McGavran." *Pennsylvania Magazine of History of Biography* 108.2 (1984): 217–34.

Keller, Evelyn Fox. *A Feeling for the Organism: The Life and Work of Barbara McClintock*. New York: Freeman, 1983.

Keller, Evelyn Fox. *Reflections on Gender and Science*. New Haven: Yale University Press, 1985.

Keller, Evelyn Fox, and Helen Longino, eds. *Feminism and Science*. New York: Oxford University Press, 1996.

Kelley, Mary. *Private Woman, Public Stage: Literary Domesticity in Nineteenth-Century America*. New York: Oxford University Press, 1984.

Ladies' Physiological Society of Boston and Vicinity. Secretary's Reports and Board Meetings, I. Schlesinger Library, Cambridge, Mass., MC 236.

Laslett, Barbara, et al., eds. *Gender and Scientific Authority*. Chicago: University of Chicago Press, 1996.

Longshore, Hannah. Speech. Undated manuscript, with drafts. Archive of Women and Medicine, Philadelphia.

Longshore, Joseph. *Biography of Hannah Longshore*. Undated manuscript notebook, holograph in bound ledger, appended pages. Longshore Papers, Archive of Women and Medicine, Philadelphia.

Morantz-Sanchez, Regina Markell. *Sympathy and Science: Women Physicians in American Medicine*. New York: Oxford University Press, 1985.

O'Hara, Leo J. *An Emerging Profession: Philadelphia Doctors, 1860–1900*. New York: Garland, 1989.

"Outrage at a Woman's Medical College." *Boston Medical and Surgical Journal* 7.8 (23 Feb. 1871): 133–34.

Preston, Ann. *Valedictory Address to the Graduating Class of the Female Medical College of Pennsylvania for the Session of 1857–58*. Philadelphia: published by the class, 1858.

Richardson, Ruth. *Death, Dissection, and the Destitute*. Harmondsworth: Penguin, 1989.

Rosenberg, Charles E. *The Care of Strangers: The Rise of America's Hospital System*. New York: Basic Books, 1987.

Rosenberg, Charles E. "The Therapeutic Revolution: Medicine, Meaning, and Social Change in Nineteenth-Century America." In *The Therapeutic Revolution: Essays in the Social History of American Medicine*, edited by Morris J. Vogel and Charles E. Rosenberg. Philadelphia: University of Pennsylvania Press, 1979.

Rothman, Sheila. *Living in the Shadow of Death: Tuberculosis and the Social Experience of Illness in American History*. New York: Basic Books, 1994.

Sappol, Michael. "Sammy Tubbs and Dr. Hubbs: Anatomical Dissection, Minstrelsy, and the Technology of Self-Making in Postbellum America." *Configurations* 4.2 (1996): 131–84.

Sawday, Jonathan. *The Body Emblazoned: Dissection and the Human Body in Renaissance Culture*. New York: Routledge, 1995.

Tompkins, Jane. *Sensational Designs: The Cultural Work of American Fiction, 1790–1860*. New York: Oxford University Press, 1985.

Tuana, Nancy, ed. *Feminism and Science*. Bloomington: Indiana University Press, 1989.

Twain, Mark, and Charles Dudley Warner. *The Gilded Age: A Tale of Today*. 1873. Reprint, New York: Oxford University Press, 1996.

Vietor, Agnes C. *A Woman's Quest: The Life of Marie E. Sakrzewska, M.D.* New York: Appleton, 1924.

Warner, John Harley. *The Therapeutic Perspective: Medical Practice, Knowledge, and Identity*. Cambridge, Mass.: Harvard University Press, 1986. Reprint, Princeton: Princeton University Press, 1997.

Wells, Susan. "Women Write Science: The Case of Hannah Longshore." *College English* 58.2 (1996): 176–91.

Wilson, Erasmus. *A System of Human Anatomy, General and Special*. Edited by Paul Goddard. Philadelphia: Lea and Blanchard, 1850.

Woman's Medical College of Pennsylvania. Dean's Files. Rachel Bodley, Folder 11, 1886, Acc #291. Archive of Women and Medicine, Philadelphia.

Woman's Medical College of Pennsylvania. Faculty Minutes, I, 1850–64. Archive of Women and Medicine, Philadelphia.

Woman's Medical College of Pennsylvania. First Annual Announcement of the Female Medical College of Pennsylvania for the session of 1850–51. Copy in Archive of Women and Medicine, Philadelphia.

Conspicuous Consumption
Cannibal Bodies and the Rhetoric of the American West

In the spring of 1846, Virginia Reed was a girl of twelve when her family joined a group of emigrants seeking fortune far from their homes in Springfield, Illinois. Ten months and twenty-five hundred miles later, she was a thirteen-year-old whose experiences as member of the Donner Party had marked her for life.

In May 1847, newly recovered from the ordeal of her journey, Virginia wrote a letter to Mary Keyes, a cousin back in Illinois, and sent it on its way with the year's first trading party heading east from Sutter's Fort. "[W]e are all Well at present," she began, but, "My Dear Cousin I am going to write to you about our trubels geting to Callifornia" (Murphy 355).[1] Their problems began, she explained, once the group reached Fort Bridger in what is now Utah and agreed from there to take the barely mapped Hastings Cut-off to California. The new route took them first across the desert south of the Great Salt Lake, on a tortured eighty-mile drive of five waterless days and nights. When their maddened cattle stampeded, the group lost most of their supplies amid arid wastes, still four hundred miles from their destination. Virginia's father, James Reed, was forced to strike out alone for California in the hope of returning with provisions for his family and their companions (356).

But far worse awaited the company. By the time they reached the Sierra Nevada, October was half gone and the autumn rains had turned to snow. Pressing on nonetheless, they were caught one dusk just short of the highest peak; they made plans to cross the next day, then bedded down for the night. But by morning, Virginia recalled, "the snow was so deep we could not go over & we had to go back," forced to dig in by the side of Truckee Lake and "stay thar all winter without Pa" (357). Her letter goes on to describe the meals of boiled bones and chewed hides, the failed attempts at relief, and the cruel necessity of leaving others behind when she finally was able to escape from the mountains with a determined party of snowshoers. Meanwhile, she recounted, her father and a company of rescuers were pushing eastward from Sutter's Fort, forty miles to the west; by the time they reached the snowbound camp, they found a situation so desperate that "some of the compana was eating them that Died" (360). Still, Virginia assured her cousin, the Reed children "had not ate any," and subsequent rescue parties, never without danger, succeeded in carrying out the survivors (360).

"O Mary," exclaimed the young emigrant, "I have not rote you half of the truble we have had but I have rote you anuf to let you now that you dont now what truble is but thank god we have all got throw and the onely family that did not eat human flesh" (360–61). Still, she hastened to add, "We are all very well pleased with Callifornia" (361). After all, she concluded, "it aut to be a beautiful Country to pay us for our trubel giting there" (361).

One of just forty-one people who survived that winter in the Sierras (out of a party twice that number), Virginia Reed was among the first to whisper the secrets of their slopes and thus animate the narrative corpus of the Donner Party. During a decade when nearly fifty thousand settlers would cross the plains before California became U.S. territory and the discovery of gold lured thousands more across the mountains, the Reeds and their companions were not the only party to suffer hardship, nor the only group to require rescue. They were, however, the only party openly to report survival by cannibalism—the one whose identity as "the Donner Party" created a sanctioned, even cherished, locus for the confession of corporeal consumption.

Members of the group, in fact, found themselves defined by the suffering they faced that winter and the means by which they survived it: transgression enacted on bodies of the dead, embedded in memories of the living, inscribed in material texts, and reincarnate in the national imagination. Here the emigrant body collapsed onto the cannibalized body, which bred, inevitably, the narrativized body. To analyze the resulting complex of voices requires first an incursion into the westering culture of nineteenth-century America, and second a close reading of actual records from that winter. Thus I explore in the first half of this chapter the conditions that drove the Donners to cannibalism, as well as the climate of a nation whose apparent fascination with the cannibalism taboo shared a curious homology with its evolution from colonized to colonizer. In the second section, I extend my analysis to the production and reception of two pivotal accounts of 1846–1847: the diary of Patrick Breen from the camp by Truckee Lake; and the efforts of Charles F. McGlashan, thirty years later, to publish in serial form a "correct" account of the Donner Party that would "do exact justice to all parties connected with the history" (MS HOU 52, 53). This chapter, then, attempts a forensic necropsy; I exhume the cannibalized body and probe its abnormalities for evidence of the cannibalizing potential within all discourse. The results not only access intriguing narrative sources but also illuminate key issues of materiality that underlie the production of any text, especially the life-text of autobiography.

Manifestations of a Cannibal Destiny

Certainly the tale of this country's most famous cannibals has titillated generations of Americans, who evince a kind of perverse pride in endless permutations of the Donner story into song, poetry, drama, fiction, and even children's picture-book literature.[2] Beneath an almost benign exterior, this abiding fascination with one band of emigrants hints at a darker sympathy—an allegiance animated by a peculiar ethos of incorporation. If the Donner encampment holds the terror of a primal scene for America, it is partly because the cannibalism of the mountainside embodies on a literal plane the appetitive politics that the country proclaimed as its "manifest destiny." Ultimately, the Donners fascinate—and implicate—America because their confessions adumbrate its national epic.

National myths aside, the facts behind the Donner Party's communal history are quickly told. In the summer of 1846, an irregular band of around eighty hopefuls, all bound for California, collected in Wyoming Territory and elected from among their number one George Donner as leader. Just past the Continental Divide, they committed themselves to a new overland route, the Hastings Cut-off, and on 20 July they struck out southwest of the Great Salt Lake, across the desert and into the mountains. Bad advice, bad trails, and bad luck cost them precious time, so it was late fall before they reached the Sierra. A blinding snowstorm at nightfall on 3 November caught them exhausted, just below the highest pass. With the summit an unreachable three miles away, they had to establish what camp they could on the eastern slope—sixty of them at Truckee Lake, and twenty-one at Alder Creek five miles below. There they faced the winter. By April, when the last occupants of the camp were finally led to Sutter's Fort, forty-two had perished, and it was clear that the living had been sustained by the meat of their dead companions.

The tale that emerged from the mountains in 1847 was polysemic from the start—a sprawling body of discontinuous memory. Conditions in the mountains had split an already splintered party into separate camps, whose further dissolution into irregular escape teams bred widely dissimilar reports. Only fragmentary first-hand experiences were recorded on site, and specifics were difficult to recover from the few textual artifacts that survived the snows:

Breen's diary; a partial journal of James Reed; and, if 1847 newspaper accounts can be believed, the dying verses of one John Denton.[3] Oral histories, by contrast, abounded, and their solicitation as part of recovery efforts further destabilized the narrative. Military involvement in relief efforts proliferated the inscription of rosters, supply lists, and emergency dispatches. Less impartial accounts came from the rescue and salvage teams, who expressed their horror at finding "dislocated and broken bones—skulls, (in some instances sawed asunder with care for the purpose of extracting the brains,)—human skeletons, in short, in every variety of mutilation" (Bryant 263).[4] By June 1847, when an army troop burned the remains of the previous winter and filed a last report, it was obvious that the intimate affairs of a closed community had spread far beyond the confines of Truckee—soon to be Donner—Pass.

Indeed, reports from those directly involved were quickly augmented by second- and third-hand accounts from interpreters eager to enhance a tale McGlashan would call "more thrilling than romance, more terrible than fiction" (*History* 6). Edwin Bryant, a personal friend of James Reed, capitalized on his tour with the 1847 army salvage party in *What I Saw in California* (1848), while Jesse Quinn Thornton began *Oregon and California in 1848* (1849) by detailing his travel with the group during earlier parts of their journey. Likewise, Eliza Farnham regaled readers of *California In Doors and Out* (1850) with stories direct from survivors, who furnished eighty pages of material for her "Narrative of the Emigration of the Donner Party to California, in 1846." Three decades later, McGlashan, owner of the *Truckee Republican*, conceived for himself a similar but grander editorial mission: his 1878 decision to create a serial history of the party launched a correspondence that eventually included twenty-four of the twenty-six members alive at the inception of his project. Inevitably, the admixture of voices heightened the polyvalence of memories from the winter, even for the survivors themselves. Long-lived party members, in fact, continued to revise their own stories and overwrite their companions' well into the twentieth century; successively reinvigorated, the cannibalized/cannibalizing body refused to die.[5]

Scholarly interpretation adds another set of overlays to the Donner palimpsest. Even though historians and sociologists have thoroughly excavated the expedition's records, their statistics preserve only its skeletal outline. W. W. Waggoner's "The Donner Party and Relief Hill" and Donald K. Grayson's "Donner Party Deaths: A Demographic Assessment," although composed sixty years apart, are equally representative of the genre. The former debates the effects of weather and topography on route selection, while the latter casts the entire episode as a classic "case study of demographically mediated natural selection in action" (223).[6] Surprisingly, the party has nearly escaped the notice of America's literary theorists, despite the attention now being paid to autobiographies in general and to frontier diaries in particular. Although Annette Kolodny at least nods to the group in *The Land Before Her: Fantasy and Experience of the American Frontiers, 1630–1860*, only Richard C. Poulsen in "The Donner Party: History, Mythology, and the Existential Voice" attempts a sustained critique, and even so, his analysis addresses the construction of historical rather than personal narrative.

What such studies overlook are the extraordinary first-person accounts that facilitate the rhetorical mediation of a nearly unspeakable ordeal and inscribe it into the literature of the elusive American frontier. Probing the resulting body of narrative proceeds by a three-step process that first confirms the cultural import of the consumption of human flesh, then verifies cannibalism among the Donner emigrants, and finally stakes out the lines of force that link the cannibal body of the mountains to the political appetites of mid-nineteenth-century America.

Cannibalism itself became a subject of study in the nineteenth century, when the emerging discipline of anthropology struggled to mediate between the mores of Western society and the unfamiliar customs of foreign cultures brought under the flags of empire. While early theorists posited for the practice a sort of evolutionary function in a progression from savagery to civilization, later scholars—foremost among them, Claude Lévi-Strauss—have read it under various symbolic schematics.[7] Subject to an elaborate taxonomy, the practice is cross-typed according to the status of the consumed and the motive for consumption. Thus, in terms of meat source, endocannibals consume members of their own group; exocannibals, the bodies of outsiders; and autocannibals, their own flesh. In terms of purpose, dietary cannibalism denotes the practice of eating human flesh for its taste or nutritive value; ritual cannibalism, for liturgical purposes; and survival cannibalism, for the preservation of life under crisis conditions such as those the Donners faced.

Although only the last function has been extensively documented, sociologists had generally assumed the existence of all forms until the publication of William Arens's controversial *The Man-Eating Myth: Anthropology and Anthropophagy* (1979), which undertook an exhaustive review of the literature and charged that it failed to produce a single reliable first-hand account of the consumption of human meat. Nonetheless, Arens noted, xenophobic references to "the cannibal" abounded, leading him to conclude, "The idea of 'others' as cannibals, rather than the act, is the universal phenomenon. The significant question is not why people eat human flesh, but why one group invariably assumes that others do" (139).[8] For Arens, then, cannibalism exists primarily as an ideological phenomenon, and although instances of survival cannibalism remain undisputed, the real matter for study is the cultural fascination with the cannibal body rather than the authentication of past or present practice.

While Arens's iconoclastic argument has stimulated lively debate, it still reinscribes the field's long-standing assertion that "[c]annibalism is never just

about eating" (Sanday 3).[9] Whether real or imagined, cannibalism operates
as a vehicle for crucial body-coded messages that help to define the social order. Linked with parricide and incest, the practice serves as Freud's culture-
founding taboo; isomorphically, the development of selfhood requires development past the cannibalism of the oral stage to individuation founded on an
awareness of the bounded and separate self. Cannibalism, in other words, performs critical gatekeeping functions at the psychosocial borders that distinguish "us" from "them," "me" from "you." Interpreters of culture from Saint
Augustine to Michel Foucault have recognized the power of the trope and noted
the ease with which food modulates into neighboring "appetites" that maintain
the species. Physically, eating coalesces with sexual intercourse as a locus of
desire and bodily union, and with aggression as a site of brutality and domination. Intellectually, it resonates with language, another oral activity whose goals
are communion with and control over the outside world.

The act of incorporation, in fact, subverts the whole field of subject/object,
inside/outside, and self/other binaries. With ingestion, argues Maggie Kilgour,
eater and eaten are rendered "infinitely reversible," and what begins in an
experience of radical alterity collapses into absolute identification (14). Revulsion against human flesh as the definitive "antifood"—the term is Lévi-
Strauss's (206)—derives, then, from a desperate need to deny the permeabil-
ity of the membrane between self and Other. If humankind selects cannibalism
to demarcate particularly freighted boundaries, its special horror seems to lie
in its capacity for the ultimate boundary erasure, as the body of the Other, in-
gested and digested, becomes the body of the self. By compromising the identities of both eater and eaten, cannibalism not only blurs the distinction between human and beast but also helps dismantle the notion of the human body
as repository for the unitary subject.

For the families caught in the mountains, of course, cannibalism was hardly
a matter of ontological debate. Individually and collectively, the emigrants
faced one choice: eat the dead or die themselves. Their recourse to survival cannibalism involved, by definition, an adoption of antinormative behavior despite
full awareness of its stigma. In fact, the eighty-one people (including five nursing infants) forced to winter at Truckee Lake and Alder Creek were at the point
of exhaustion and near starvation even before the first blizzard hit. By the time
of rescue, the trapped families had subsisted for so long on strips torn from
hides and what few field mice they could catch that rescuers were aghast at the
skeletal beings who greeted their arrival. For the fifteen who comprised the escape party known as Forlorn Hope, the danger of starvation was even more immediate.[10] Carrying just six days' rations, they got lost in the trackless passes
and wandered for a month on crude homemade snowshoes. By their tenth day
out, the weaker among them were dying, begging the stronger to consume their

bodies so that some at least might live. Their wisdom prevailed, and seven—
two men and all five women—survived.

The last resort of these determined survivors brought the reality of cannibalism terrifyingly close to the audiences who heard their stories. And while
knowledge of extreme conditions in the mountains undoubtedly prompted pity,
the research of Donald Tuzin suggests that it may have done little to mitigate
disgust. Studying the Arapesh of New Guinea, where soldiers in the Japanese
army of occupation resorted to cannibalism near the end of World War II, Tuzin
demonstrates that survival cannibalism heightens rather than reduces revulsion
in the observer. The notion of cannibalism as a phenomenon of the Other be-
gets, after all, a protective aloofness that consigns the act to another time, another place, another culture. To admit that the universal experience of hunger
can drive someone to cannibalism in the here and now is to render it doubly re-
pellent by reducing the difference between cannibal and noncannibal to a matter of degree and circumstance (65). Thus the Donner stories became more, not
less, awful for the desperation that drove their principals to strip and consume
human flesh.

Where personal horror met cultural taboo in the Donner confessions, then,
the intersection evoked both sympathy and antipathy in their audiences. Certainly any emigrant party crossing the Great Basin confronted the same dangers that overcame the Donners, and that knowledge bred an anxious solidarity
with the unhappy emigration of 1846. The overland route, by all accounts,
tested the emotional, physical, and financial resources of everyone who undertook it. Parties knew that neither careful preparation nor dogged determination
could guarantee safe passage, and news of the Donner story crystallized the
well-founded fears of subsequent emigrants.[11] No matter what trail they took—
and certainly few others ever ventured across Hastings Cut-off—overlanders
after 1847 "were never free of the shadow of that disaster," declares George
Stewart, a twentieth-century Donner historian; from then on, the "memory of
death and cannibalism brooded over the yearly migration as the ultimate horror and the never-relaxed threat" (*Trail* 183).

Indeed, the sensational end of the Donner Party in no way compromised
its representative nature. Rather, Stewart suggests in *Ordeal by Hunger: The
Story of the Donner Party*, the infamous party served as "microcosm of humanity" in nineteenth-century America (13). At the kernel of the group were
the clans from Springfield—two Donner families and the Reeds—as well as
Iowans Patrick and Peggy Breen and their family of seven, various smaller
families, and a number of unattached men, including immigrants from Germany, Belgium, England, and Mexico. A loose aggregate ranging in age from
infancy to sixty-five, the group included not only preliterate children and illiterate adults but also the well-read Lewis Keseberg, fluent in four languages, and

the Massachusetts-bred schoolteacher Tamsen Donner, who planned to open a young ladies' seminary in California. Over all, members of the party conformed closely to the standard profile of mid-century overlanders: independent, literate, somewhat sophisticated, and possessed of sufficient means to undertake a fairly capital-rich venture.[12]

The demographics of mid-nineteenth-century America, then, recommended the Donner group as typical. They became representative not by their individual attributes, and certainly not by the nature of their fate, but by their collective participation in what the American epic viewed as the divinely ordained march of civilization across a waiting continent. The Donner Party's very emigration *from* America cast them in an archetypal American role. Making their way through unmapped wilds, eager for a fresh start in a distant paradise—on land that was neither theirs to take nor their government's to give—they renewed the assault that seventeenth-century Puritans had preached as mission and later generations had canonized as myth. The reality of frontier danger only reinforced the symbolic resonance of the project; uncharted and unsettled, the distant West all the more readily served as focal point for the nation's unrealized hopes. By 1845, when John L. O'Sullivan of the *United States Magazine and Democratic Review* declared extension to the Pacific to be America's "manifest destiny," two centuries of growth—in population and national spirit—had empowered its citizens to "overspread the continent allotted by Providence for the free development of [their] yearly multiplying millions" (5). The country had found in overland emigration, as taxis and trope, a movement peculiarly suited to the personal and cultural ends of the American dream.

Fueled by a residue of financial fallout from the Panic of 1837 and the disturbing reality of a growing urban underclass, thousands of overlanders did turn to the West, the site where, Richard Slotkin observes, "personal good and national greed coincide[d]" (45). Historians estimate that between one-quarter and one-half million emigrants crossed the Great Plains from the 1840s through the 1870s. The primary stimulus for this massive relocation was the land itself, with its implicit promise of health, wealth, and status. Federal policy, fed by a land hunger no less specific than that of the emigrants, encouraged settlement as a means of claiming national title to territory beyond the U.S. borders. Not only did military outposts sustain emigrants along the trail; the War Department established the Topographical Corps of Engineers for the express purpose of surveying and opening land to emigration. Among the corps's earliest efforts were the expeditions of the flamboyant Captain John Charles Frémont, whose reports were published, at the urging of Congress, just in time to stoke the fever of the 1846 emigrants.[13]

Time proved the effectiveness of what Henry Nash Smith terms invasion by "pioneer army," first in Texas, next in Oregon, and finally in California, where

U.S. resident aliens fueled the antagonism that led to the Mexican War (51). The officially declared hostilities, which blazed fitfully from 1846 until 1848, achieved only minimal support across the United States. Unconvinced by rhetoric that proclaimed the liberation of Mexican peoples from European despotism, many citizens—witness Henry David Thoreau's visit to the Concord jail—viewed "Mr. Polk's War" as an act of unprovoked aggression or even conquest.[14] Widespread disapproval did not, however, prevent the war from reviving sagging patriotism and a flagging economy. Moreover, with the 1848 Treaty of Guadalupe Hidalgo, it yielded felicitous territorial results: almost 1.2 million square miles, including not just the contested Texan borderlands but also New Mexico and California, the real if covert objects of the campaign.

The enthusiastic rate at which settlers poured into these territories, both before and after annexation, hid the darker side of what O'Sullivan's rhetoric deemed the "manifest design of Providence in regard to the occupation of this continent" (7). Not only did the zealots of progress mask the aggression that accompanied expansion; they also failed to acknowledge the relationship between the westward impulse and its inevitable result, the erasure of the frontier. In the complex interanimation of politics, economics, and cultural expression, the factors which precipitated that end bound every region of the country to its western shore. Increased birthrates and immigration led to geometric growth in population, felt first in the eastern industrial centers; this growth became a nexus for increased crime, social stratification, and class conflict.[15] When defenders of the American dream fell back on the country's most ancient resource, its land, a favorite device in their rhetoric of regeneration was the Franklin-inspired notion of the frontier as a "safety valve" that would draw surplus bodies from the cities and thus save both urban and rural America. Yet as settlement leapt from the Mississippi to the Pacific, then doubled back to fill in the prairies and mountains, it eliminated the frontier on which America's salvation presumably rested. The standards the Donner Party supposedly championed in 1846 were already on their way to extinction.

Anticipatory nostalgia for America's vanishing pioneer body culminated, in 1890, in the "closing" of the frontier by the U.S. Census Bureau, when it could find no further pockets of territory with a population density of less than two persons per square mile. The results were interpreted for the nation by Frederick Jackson Turner in his 1893 address to the American Historical Society, gathered at Chicago for that year-long tribute to progress, the Columbian Exposition. His reflection was important not only for the narrative of loss it scripted for subsequent discussions, but also for its insistence that the disappearance of the frontier affected all of America, whose uniqueness was for Turner rooted in "democracy born of free land" (83); with the eradication of its wilderness, the nation forfeited the very source of its identity as well as its storehold of natural wealth (88). At risk in 1846, then, were not just the Donner emigrants and their four thousand companions on the trails west, but also the dream that would lure not a few of them to their death.

Scripting and Conscripting the Cannibal Body

Although the rhetoric of triumph or nostalgia might obscure the ravages of political cannibalism, it in no way mediated the effects of the literal act for Donner Party survivors, whose horror is perhaps best understood in the particular. Here Lewis Keseberg, the last member of the party to be rescued, serves as an apt example—if, by all contemporary accounts, the most notorious. Injured and unable to move out with the third relief team, Keseberg was left at camp several weeks after everyone else had departed or perished. When a fourth relief mission finally returned on 19 April, the team found him, as rescuer William O. Fallon reported, "lying down amidst the human bones and beside him a large pan full of liver and lights," with "two kettles of human blood" nearby. According to Fallon's journal, in enforced solitude the man had become particular, even fastidious, about his unfortunate diet. He spurned frozen livestock near his cabin and dismissed unidentified meat lying on a chair with the disclaimer, "'[O]h! it's too dry eating!' the liver and lights were a great deal better, and the brains made good soup!" Of Tamsen Donner, his last living companion, he exclaimed "he [had] eat[en] her body and found her flesh the best he had ever tasted!"

However immoderate was the behavior Fallon attributed to this "Cannibal of the Sierras" (and that is the epithet he earned), a vastly different image emerged when McGlashan convinced the aging Keseberg to relate his story for publication in 1879.[16] "I cannot describe the unutterable repugnance with which I tasted the first mouthful of flesh," he then declared to McGlashan; "[i]t makes my blood curdle to think of it!" (*History* 210). With evident emotion he continued, "[T]o see that loathsome food ever before my eyes was almost too much for human endurance. I am conversant with four different languages . . . yet in all four I do not find words enough to express the horror I experienced during those two months, or what I still feel when memory reverts to the scene" (211).

The striking disparity of tone between the two accounts of this survivor's cannibalism—both purportedly in his own voice—finds several ready explanations, from ambivalence about his actions and the malleability of memory to the difference between the perceptive filters the two recorders brought to their conversations. More to the point, however, is the image Keseberg projects as icon of the Donner Party: the survivor of the mountains become victim in the process of restoration and narration. By reproducing his words, the rescuer-rehabilitators of Keseberg shape his history; biography here overwrites autobiography. The process accomplishes an inscription-conscription that—metaphorically—cannibalizes Keseberg in the very text that preserves him.

While the polyphony of the Donner chorus made it impossible for a single emigrant to speak for the whole, Keseberg's fate at the hands of those who told his story typified the party's collective experience of confession. Bodies consumed in the mountains became not only physical nourishment but also narrative fodder, while the survivors themselves were textually consumed; their narrative products were sold—or stolen—on the open market, and their stories were subsumed into national history. Living and dead alike were absorbed into the plastic textual body through a suspiciously cannibal-like process that transformed personal memory into public property, until the reconstituted remains took on a life of their own.

The literal cannibalism at the heart of this conflation of individual and cultural consumption entailed, without question, radically transgressive behavior, and confessional expression was a source of considerable anxiety for emigrants who found their fare nearly impossible to stomach, and its effect on them nearly impossible to describe. Even though they could and obviously did relate the stark facts of their survival, at another level they doubted the validity of language for communicating such events. Elaine Scarry's perceptive interpretation of physicality in *The Body in Pain: The Making and Unmaking of the World* suggests that the torments of the winter—the ordeal of cannibalism, certainly, but also the extremes of cold, isolation, anxiety, and filth—would render the emigrants' experience essentially unsusceptible to language. Their attempts at narration were blocked, then, not only by the force of taboo but also by what Scarry calls the "unsharability" of pain, its persistent "resistance to language" (4).

In possession of a story whose central action defied language, some survivors invoked hyperbole to convey by superlative what they could ill express at all; others simply conceded the fundamental inadequacy of language. Thus Virginia Reed (later Virginia Murphy) would forever equate that winter with "untold suffering," with pain that "words cannot tell" ("Girl" Oct. 34), with "horrors" that "no pen can describe nor imagination conceive" (28); and Keseberg would exclaim, "[T]o go into details—to relate the minutiae—is too agonizing! I can not do it! Imagination can supply these" (McGlashan, *History* 211).[17] The telling of the untellable underwrote every inscription of the Donner story, embedding the paradoxical assertion of ineffability in the very text.

Narrators' insistence on the inexpressibility of their experience served as a textual marker for the magnitude of their identity displacement from emigrants into cannibals. And although this transformation involved, in every case, the same oral activity, its narrative byproducts issued from dozens of individuals relating a highly personal tale over the course of several decades.[18] Because of the diversity of the narrative, it is important to deal with accounts individually, beginning with those recorded on site as the most immediate reflection of the cannibal experience. The first of these—and the one historians regard as the most reliable—is the journal in which Patrick Breen registered his activities at the Alder Creek camp, in almost daily installments.[19]

Breen's diary opened on Friday, 20 November 1846, with its longest entry, a summary of events from the party's arrival at the pass three weeks earlier. After 102 less expansive passages recorded over the next three and a half months, it closed abruptly with the 1 March entry, which noted, "[T]here has 10 men arrived this morning from Bear Valley with provisions we are to start in two or three days" (16). The text contained, as Poulsen observes, mainly "enumerations of wood, wind, snow, clouds, sun" (113). Here, in the context of imminent starvation, the potential for cannibalism took its place almost matter-of-factly among the other necessary conditions for survival. While the diary served also as the camp's necrology—Breen recorded on 8 February, for example, "Spitzer died last night about 3 o'clock to[day] we will bury him in the snow" (13)—its staccato style reduced the effect of every entry. Thus the 26 February statement, which contained the first direct reference to cannibalism, began with "Froze hard last night today clear & warm" and, with no apparent misgiving, moved on to this:

Mrs Murphy said here yesterday that thought she would commence on Milt. [Milton Elliott, who had died two weeks before] & eat him. I dont [know] that she has done so yet, it is distressing   The Donnos told the California folks that they commence to eat the dead people 4 days ago, if they did not succeed that day or next in finding their cattle then under ten or twelve feet of snow & did not know the spot or near it, I suppose they have done so ere this time. (15)

In his extremity, Breen's concern was with physical necessities, not social prohibitions, and he let circumstances offer their own justification for the narrative he inscribed.[20] His observation was important, moreover, because it unwittingly initiated what later became evident as a pattern in the Donner corpus: he described others' supposed cannibalism rather than his own. The campsite diary ended, in fact, just days before Breen, his wife, and five of their children embarked on the perilous descent from Truckee Lake, in a rescue attempt that would deliver fourteen of seventeen to the safety of Sutter's Fort. En route the company would succumb to famine and cold, and Breen himself would consume human flesh. His diary, then, would require a sequel, which his wife Margaret supplied by telling the tale to Farnham, who in turn provided corroborative material for McGlashan's history. And William Eddy, engaged in the rescue effort, would report Breen's cannibalism in the account he gave out first to other rescuers, then to Thornton, and ultimately to McGlashan as well. Significantly, none of these narrators of transgression delivered an actual confession: Patrick Breen closed his diary before necessity drove him to cannibalism; Margaret Breen and Eddy, at least by their own accounts, abstained from any traffic in human meat. Instead, all three preserved for themselves a distinct, noncannibal identity, even while they invoked close association with flesh-eating companions to substantiate the authenticity of their texts.[21]

The volunteers who risked their lives to save the starving found incontrovertible evidence on which to base their own textual authority. Relief teams confronted the obvious evidence of cannibalism when they reached the Truckee campsites: the ravaged bodies of the dead mutely indicting the living. Thornton, for example, described the scene that greeted rescuers Charles Cady and Nicholas Stone at the late Jacob Donner's tent: one of the party making off with Donner's leg; children feeding on the heart and liver; and, around the fireside, "hair, bones, skulls, and the fragments of half-consumed limbs" (200). As for those who fled the mountains, in the absence of material evidence, their very survival testified to cannibal activity. Forlorn Hope, in particular, was known to have left camp with little over a pound of meat per person; the remnants that reached the settlements thirty days later had obviously subsisted on something other than sheer determination.[22] In the Sierra, there was no need to establish the fact of cannibalism, but there was quite evidently a need to produce this fact as text. Thus, rather than rendering confession superfluous, the ubiquity of evidence became a force for its evocation; survivors needed to supply only the particulars for a tale already conspicuous in outline.

As the story spread from Sutter's Fort to the West Coast, then ricocheted east, the promulgation of their history seemed to evoke in the survivors a kind of confessional urgency. Once the rescue was complete, accounts multiplied, and in them the impulse to divulge the grisliest details seemed scarcely stronger than the narrators' professed reluctance to speak. And although the content of their narratives varied with each author's perspective, all evinced a single overriding intention: exculpation. Without exception, the narrators maintained that their behavior on the trail was an appropriate response to catastrophic conditions. If reports of the winter's mighty ordeal had forced the truth out of them, they faced their audiences as they might a jury of peers, determined to win full acquittal.

Yet guilt inheres in confessional narrative, and it seeps from the Donner Party annals. Denied primacy of place in the accounts of their cannibalism, it found abundant expression elsewhere along the trail. The group's long journey left festering pockets of remorse over actions that violated the tacit code of the West: sixty-eight-year-old Hardkoop was left to die when no one would spare a horse to carry him; an angry Patrick Breen refused water to Eddy's children, near death in the desert; and Mrs. Wolfinger was widowed when her husband disappeared without a trace. James Reed himself was banished—without food and without trial—for the death of John Snyder, and he was unable to clear his name until long after the rescue. Keseberg, less fortunate, spent the rest of his life under suspicion of having murdered Tamsen Donner, either for her flesh or for the considerable fortune she and her husband were said to have carried.[23] And in every case, lasting guilt attended the abandonment of loved ones at the winter camps by those able to escape, despite recognition that their promised return afforded the only hope for rescue of the young, the old, and the weak.

If the emigrants themselves did not emerge from the winter of 1847 with clear consciences, neither did their audiences: in the body of the domestic anthropophage, individual and cultural guilt collided. Five decades later Frederick Jackson Turner would theorize that the frontier defined the nation; mid-nineteenth-century America intuited this, and the identification hinted at a most discomforting recognition. Not only had the Sierran wilderness exhausted the moral and physical resources of its captives—it had also, in a sense, defeated even the survivors; it had driven the standard-bearers of American civilization to savagery.[24] Although the Donners did not, as the Puritans had feared, meet the devil in the wilderness, they at least met their own most bestial selves, and in its pogromic westward sweep the nation to whom the Donners confessed earned complicity in whatever identity they acquired. In their concrete transgression the Donner emigrants helped write the wider culture's narrative of colonizing/cannibalizing in a form that could be told and retold until the victors over physical starvation and the victors over political containment won vindication for, and from, one another.

The degree to which systemic racism accompanied and supported the aims of American appetites was made chillingly apparent in an incident glossed over by the survivors of Forlorn Hope. When Eddy became the chronicler for that snowshoe party, he conceived a hero-studded epic replete with almost eucharistic self-sacrifice: a weakened Charles Stanton slipping off to die alone rather than delay the group; a dying Franklin Graves urging his daughters to use whatever means possible—and his intention was clear—to sustain life; the strongest offering to "cast lots to see who should die, to furnish food for those who survived" (Thornton 134). Despite Eddy's efforts, however, the group's basest secret escaped with them. Among them marched two *vaqueros* who had been sent by Sutter to carry food to the emigrant party. When the snowshoers first resorted to cannibalism, these two had turned aside, revolted by what the others devoured. Days later, after the Mexicans fell dying from exposure and starvation, the Americans conspired to kill them outright in the only confirmed instance of homicidal cannibalism among the entire party. The act was predicated on a neat displacement discernible in the indirection with which Farnham recounted it: "The starving emigrants, who could not slay each other, thought with less scruple of the fate of these" (417). In its neat assimilation into the patterns of guilt without apology and absolution without censure that the Donners' nonhomicidal cannibalism elicited, this commentary exposed the latent prejudice of an audience who saw in it neither irony nor cause for blame.[25]

The eighty-one members of the Donner Party trapped in the mountains were caught not just by the worst winter of the century but also by the moral and political forces that shaped their culture. Certainly the nation did not share the Donners' meat, but it had bred the ideology that sent them west to devour the land. Applauding their courage and determination—even, in extremity, their Yankee resourcefulness—American culture found good cause to exonerate its cannibals. By their sacrifices these citizens had rendered a national service: they had helped tame the West. Their tales proclaimed that emigrants could face the worst and survive; in fact, the weakest—women and children—could survive (a feat Grayson attributes to their lower metabolic rate, but which the popular mind ascribed to less tangible qualities of character [233]). Supplied with this new cast of heroes for its favorite fable, that of fearless pioneers civilizing a savage land, America could continue to deny the effects of its imperial advance across the continent. In the particulars of 1846, the nation would pay in human life the price the Mexican War exacted; it would support in U.S. currency the rescue of the winter camps; it would pledge better roads to carry new emigrants over the mountains; and it would fail to see any kinship between the desperate figure feeding on human carrion and a nation driven to incorporate millions of square miles of foreign territory, to displace or destroy untold numbers of native inhabitants, and to ravage its own resources in the name of progress.[26]

Amid the victorious rhetoric of empire that reigned, the Donner survivors surely won pride of place in their chapter of national history. And while some, understandably, tried to erase all memory of the ordeal or shared their trauma only in private, others discovered that narrativizing the experience offered at least the illusion of dignity and authorial control: to verbalize the memory was, in some measure, to neutralize its pain. Indeed, the more vocal among them came to evince a near obsession with fixing for public record the story of 1846–1847, with telling "what really happened" in the mountains. The results taught an object lesson in rhetorical determinism as these voluble survivors, each in possession of communal yet intensely personal recollections, waged a fierce competition for their narrative keep. Maggotlike, stories swarmed and spread, breeding and feeding on the ever-mutating textual body.

Certainly the kind of narrative consumption to which survivors fell prey became increasingly likely as the popularity of the Donner tales grew. The winter's principals found themselves displaced in a process of mediation founded on the story's polysemic nature, its origin in oral narrative, and of course its sensational appeal. The potential for conscription only intensified in succeeding decades, when attitudes toward the West turned from anticipation to nostalgia. Sympathetic appropriators openly mythologized the Donner Party, elevating members to heroic status according to the standards of the day. By 1871, when Frances H. McDougal composed "The Donner Tragedy" for the *Pacific Rural*

Press of 21 January (where it appeared on the "Home Circle" page just ahead of a column entitled "How to Have a Loving Wife"), the drama shone with sentimental appeal. In Margaret Breen, who had sheltered four other emigrants with her family, McDougal identified a paragon of womanhood: "[The name of Mrs. Breen] should be inscribed in gold lettering on the page of history . . . for she who could give to others what her own children might soon suffer for, deserves . . . the *crown of virtue*." The story bespoke legendary frontier generosity in the ready response of rescuers, well supplied by Captain Sutter. This saga too had its hearty outdoorsmen who, "each with a heavy load on his back, boldly set foot on the trackless mountain," and in Keseberg, of course, the classic outlaw.

Behind such demonizing and eulogizing impulses, the successive transformation of the Donner story revealed the nature of the tale as communal textual possession: what confessions the Donners shared soon ceased to be their own. Especially here, where narration involved dozens of individuals scripting and rescripting a collective history over half a century and more, the winter's survivors could hardly avoid becoming victims of textual consumption. The commodification of the frontier over the same period of time—its reification in everything from postcards and dime novels to "Buffalo Bill" Cody's Wild West Show and Frederic Remington's romantic realism—simply provided a commercial arena for the contest between narrator and audience over the power to shape and control the textual body.

One material result of this competition emerged in 1879, apparently with the most benign of intentions, when McGlashan, as editor of the *Truckee Republican*, decided to compile a full history of the Donner Party. Initiated by an amateur historian in a bid to boost circulation for his newly acquired newspaper, McGlashan's project would ultimately produce a work scholars recognize as a foundational Donner text. What ensued more immediately was a lengthy excursion into investigative reporting that involved thousands of letters, numerous interviews with survivors, a legal battle over rights to the story, and even an archeological dig at the cabin sites. It involved, in addition, a familiar process of cannibalistic incorporation that transformed the confessions of the emigrants into McGlashan's textual property.

Among McGlashan's most willing participants was Eliza Poor Donner Houghton, youngest of the Donner daughters orphaned at Alder Creek. Her correspondence with the editor-historian began on 8 February 1879, when he submitted a request for information regarding her memories of the winter's encampment (MS HOU 52, 53).[27] She replied four days later, cautious, hesitating to contribute until certain that he shared her concern for "having the truth told" and correcting "false impressions" (MS HOU 50). She explained, "My reason for this is, several histories have been published from time, to time, purporting to be true histories of the party; which were not only eroneous, but in many instances grossly exaggerated I am satisfied no one individual can give any thing like a history of the party after [its camp] near Donner lake" (MS HOU 50).

Won over by McGlashan's evident sincerity, Houghton became an enthusiastic contributor to the cumulative history being published in the weekly columns of the *Republican*, with invitations to survivors to suggest any necessary emendations. These repeated appeals elicited ever more detailed responses from correspondents anxious to clarify as if for all time their roles in what McGlashan's advertisements called "the most Thrilling Chapter of Pioneer California History" (*Truckee Republican*). The relationship between these survivor-informants and their editor-confessor evolved with the serialized history, to the point that each came to rely on the other for the symbiotic actualization of needs: they supplied the material, and he was the mouthpiece for that elusive, definitive, "true" history of their ordeal at Donner Lake.

McGlashan's mediation of autobiographical voice effected a curiously aborted process of collaborative authorship. On 17 June, just days before the first bound copies of the text appeared, McGlashan wrote to Houghton, "Please suggest, freely, any changes you would make if you were writing the history all alone instead of having me to assist you" (MS HOU 84). Two days later, when the volumes neared completion, a generous McGlashan wrote again to her:

I have just been reading your—my—our proofs. Suppose I get a reputation as an author—a historian, how much of the honor will belong to me? Here is a chapter appropriated bodily from your pen! In other places there are sweet little phrases, cute sentences, apt expressions which I stole without even saying—"by your leave"? . . . I know you will approve the theft however, because of [your concern for] the subject. (MS HOU 87)

And on 4 July, he wrote jubilantly, "I send you today the beginning and ending of our book" (MS HOU 89). But by 12 July, when he announced, "A very tired mortal is writing you," it was because "[m]y book came out this afternoon and I have since delivered a couple of hundred of them" (MS HOU 90). And five days later, when he reported, "The book is selling very rapidly. Indeed, my most sanguine dreams are more than realized, in a financial point of view," no mention was made of profit-sharing (MS HOU 91).

Luckily Houghton, who had long since made her peace with the Sierra, had by now forged a friendship with the editor from Truckee. Two months before, when her sister and brother-in-law angrily opposed McGlashan's conscription of their history, even seeking a legal injunction against him, she had begged them to reconsider. McGlashan, she wrote, would enable them to "place the acts and memories of their loved ones before the public in a true light"; not only was it their duty to assist him, but it was futile to oppose his efforts, for "[t]he entire vote of the survivors could not stop the publication of the History even if we should desire it" (MS HOU 49).

So confident was Houghton in the trustworthiness of her chosen confessor that when, in 1902, she decided to compile her own reminiscences, the mentor she turned to was McGlashan (MS HOU 142). He generously persevered with her through a long apprenticeship in writing and publishing until he could mark the 1911 appearance of *The Expedition of the Donner Party and Its Tragic Fate* with his warmest congratulations. Of course, Houghton's book, the last full-length account by a Donner survivor, approached no nearer to the "true" history of 1846–1847 than McGlashan's had, but his reflection to her on the process of its composition hinted at the real source of confessional truth: "[Y]our letters to me did educate you as well as help me" (MS HOU 1738).

Thirty years later McGlashan's own editors, George H. Hinkle and Bliss McGlashan Hinkle, became hagiographers and canonized his efforts in explicitly confessional terms. "McGlashan was much more than the mere historian of the Donner party," they declared, "he was its confessor" (xxx). If in eliciting the Donners' stories he also became possessor of their secrets, the power and profit he realized did not come without a price, however; his traffic in their guilt had helped make him complicit in their deeds.

Nor do the readers of any of these tales escape confessional identification with the cannibals whose stories they devour. On a cultural level, the fascinating horror of the Donner saga remains in its ability to literalize a project of commodifying the continental body, cannibalizing its lands and its peoples, confronting the exotic, the extra-national, the radically Other, and consuming it. By their avid consumption of the Donner corpus and their tacit absolution of its cannibal acts, readers vicariously master the unknown beyond their borders and absolve themselves of the auto/exocannibalism America once called its "manifest destiny."

Notes

I acknowledge with gratitude a grant from the Rhetoric and Composition Program of the Department of English at the Ohio State University, whose generosity made this work possible, and the assistance of Peter J. Blodgett, Curator of Western Historical Manuscripts at the Huntington Library, whose expertise lent it invaluable on-site support.

1. Virginia Reed's letter was printed, with editorial corrections, as "Deeply Interesting Letter" in the Springfield *Illinois Journal*, 16 December 1847, making it one of the earliest published accounts of the Donner Party's winter. Although the original eight-page manuscript has been lost, George R. Stewart has reconstructed the text from five extant versions and published it in *Ordeal by Hunger* (355–62). Here and throughout, quotations retain the spelling and punctuation of the sources.

2. Among the more unusual recent adaptations are George Keithley's 254-page epic

poem, *The Donner Party*; Rachel K. Laurgaard's illustrated *Patty Reed's Doll* (newly reprinted), which retold the story for children; the Disney made-for-TV movie *One More Mountain*, with Meredith Baxter; and the theater art of Julie Ince Thompson, who based her performance on Ruth Whitman's poetic re-creation of a lost journal, *Tamsen Donner: A Woman's Journey*. The group has left a distinct mark on California as well: not only have Truckee Lake and Truckee Gap lost their names to the party, but the two campsites, with memorabilia on permanent display, have been preserved at Donner Lake State Park and the aptly if ironically named Donner Picnic Grounds in the Truckee arm of Tahoe National Forest.

3. Breen's diary remains in the collections of the Bancroft Library, and Reed's in the Sutter's Fort Historical Museum in Sacramento. The only record of the poetry Denton is said to have composed just before his death is that published in the *California Star* and reprinted by J. Quinn Thornton in *What I Saw in California*; no original is extant. Tamsen Donner is known to have kept an extensive journal, but nothing of it survived the winter. Published accounts based on journals of William Eddy and rescuer William O. Fallon exist, but it is not clear that the authors composed their reflections while actually engaged in either escape or rescue. Other partial diaries exist, but none for the period during which party members were snowbound.

4. See Hall for assorted records and chronologies detailing everything from the rotations of rescue teams to the reimbursement of John Sutter for such items as seven mules, fifty pounds of dried beef, and eight hundred pounds of flour.

5. By 1936, when Stewart was completing his first edition of *Ordeal by Hunger*, he noted that Isabella Breen MacMahon, the last surviving member of the party, had died on 25 March 1935; as a one-year-old infant in 1847, she would have had no first-hand memories of the winter encampment (286).

6. Grayson's early analysis is consonant with the conclusions recently reached by Stephen A. McCurdy, whose "Epidemiology of Disaster: The Donner Party (1846–1847)" finds "elevated death rates for persons at the extremes of the age distribution" (over age thirty-five or under age six) and a "twofold increased risk" of mortality among males and those traveling outside a family group (341).

7. Lévi-Strauss's structuralism, for example, integrates cannibalism with marriage and kinship into an economy of exchange, while the cultural materialism of Marvin Harris, in *Cannibals and Kings: The Origins of Cultures*, subsumes it into an ecology of production.

8. The heavy political weight born by the "cannibal" epithet lends its own support to Arens's argument. A bastardized form of "Carib," Columbus's designation for the lands and people he encountered on his western voyages, it tacitly equates the xenic with the savage at the same time that it divides the alien from the familiar.

9. Note that Peggy Reeves Sanday, in *Divine Hunger: Cannibalism as a Cultural System*, soundly refutes Arens's conclusions on the basis of her own study of 156 societies that figure in reports of cannibalism. By her count, the data on the 109 for which sufficient evidence is available show that 34 percent yielded information indicating cannibalistic practices (4).

10. I have been unable to determine when or by whom the epithet "Forlorn Hope" was first applied to the snowshoe party, but apparently it was in evidence from the start.

Etymologically, the name is entirely apt; derived from the Dutch *verloren hoop*, literally "lost band," it was a military term applied to those who volunteered to storm an enemy fortification.

11. Nor was the fate of the Donner group unique in the annals of mountain extremity; accounts of disaster and cannibalism peppered the history of the West. Among the more egregious contemporary examples were the 1845 expedition of "Lost Immigrants," whose entrapment in the Cascade Mountains cost nearly twice as many lives as the Donner encampment, and Charles Frémont's 1848 attempt to map the ranges of southwestern Colorado, a failed effort which reproduced the pattern of starvation, cannibalism, and desperate rescue (DeVoto 374–75, 481).

12. For cogent descriptions of mid-century overland emigrants, see Faragher or Schlissel.

13. Lansford Hastings's 1845 publication of *The Emigrants' Guide to Oregon and California* would be the decisive factor in the Donner route. Hastings's ill-founded enthusiasm was tempered by the more practical and realistic *Route across the Rocky Mountains* by Overton Johnson and William H. Winter (which appeared in 1846, but probably too late to have been a major influence on that year's emigration) and the *Route and Distances to Oregon and California* by J. M. Shively, both of which contained invaluable descriptions of terrain and tables of altitudes, temperatures, and distances between key landmarks.

14. Thoreau, of course, was as likely to romanticize American expansion as he was to condemn it, as his paean to the West in "Walking" readily demonstrates.

15. Slotkin argues persuasively, in *The Fatal Environment: The Myth of the Frontier in the Age of Industrialization, 1800–1890*, that class conflict is itself of the essence of American identity—that social stratification has been coterminous with settlement. Displaced first onto racism in the conflict between Puritans and natives, and second onto nature in the conflict between pioneers and the land, this elemental conflict has provided, he suggests, "the building blocks of our dominant historiographical tradition and political ideology" (15).

16. Frances Helen McDougal, writing for the *Pacific Rural Press* in 1871, insists that Keseberg operated an eatery "well known as *Cannibal Tent*" at Sutter's.

17. Nearly half a century after the fact, *Century Illustrated Monthly Magazine* prevailed on Virginia Reed Murphy, then fifty-seven, to publish her story, "Across the Plains with the Donner Party," in the July 1891 issue. Her account was reprinted by *American History Illustrated* as "A Girl with the Donner Party" in its September and October 1986 issues; citations refer to this version.

18. While the common threat of starvation had forced a single choice on its sufferers, the resulting deed was enacted in at least four different sites (two at the original camps, two on the escape routes), and the decision to feed on the dead seems to have been made independently in each situation, without knowledge of other groups' choices.

19. The original, as Frederick J. Teggart describes in his introduction, was written on eight sheets of paper, each folded in half to form a thirty-two-page booklet. Breen carried it with him out of the mountains and then presented it to Sheriff George McKinstry at Sutter's Fort to aid in the official report of the rescue efforts.

20. In observing the relatively late date at which the group entertained cannibalism

as a viable option, McCurdy notes that to break down entrenched inhibitions requires an extended lapse of time, coupled with a high degree of desperation (342).

21. It is interesting to note that while the displacement from first to third person is precisely what Arens argues invalidates historical reports of cannibalism, neither the original nor the mediated Donner accounts seem to have aroused suspicion of fabrication.

22. McGlashan records the quantity of meat carried by the Forlorn Hope in terms the escapees themselves used: enough "to allow each person, three times a day, a piece the size of one's two fingers" (*History* 71).

23. Rather than the altruistic motivation Virginia reported, Snyder's death was the real reason for Reed's October departure, which turned out to be a peculiarly mixed blessing for the party. In retrospect, most emigrants agreed with his assessment that if he had remained with the group, he would have gotten them over the mountains before they were trapped by the snows, yet it was only by his efforts from California to spearhead rescue that many of them were saved.

24. Here Kolodny's discussion of an anxious suspicion on the part of both men and women that the frontier masculinized its women (174) collides forcefully with Grayson's studies confirming the high survival rates among females of the Donner Party (233); the clear inference is that they did not refuse cannibal meat in order to survive.

25. Tellingly, official inscription seems to have erased this story's racial subtext. When Alcalde John Sinclair prepared his summary of the incident, he reported that by the time the snowshoers found the two Mexicans, one was already dead and the other dying: "They raised him up, and offered him some food; he tried to eat, but could not; and only lived about an hour." Only then, in his account, did the Americans consume the Mexicans (Bryant 254).

26. One of the seldom-noted ironies of the Donner disaster is that relief efforts were delayed crucial weeks because any able-bodied male citizens of the western settlements who might have volunteered to undertake rescue were engaged in the war to claim the Pacific Coast for the United States.

27. Many of McGlashan's letters to Houghton are preserved among the hundreds of items in the Houghton files of the Huntington Library. Unlike Houghton, however, McGlashan, to protect confidentiality, shortly before his death systematically destroyed all the Donner Party materials that remained in his possession (Hinkle and Hinkle xxix–xxx). Before that time, Houghton had requested that he return to her whatever of their correspondence remained (MS HOU 141), so some of her letters survive.

Works Cited

Arens, W. *The Man-Eating Myth: Anthropology and Anthropophagy*. New York: Oxford University Press, 1979.

Breen, Patrick. *Diary of Patrick Breen*. Edited by Frederick J. Teggart. Reno, Nev.: Outbooks, 1979.

Bryant, Edwin. *What I Saw in California*. New York: Appleton, 1848.

DeVoto, Bernard. *The Year of Decision: 1846*. Boston: Houghton, 1960.

Fallon, W. O. "Extracts from a Journal Written by a Member of the Party Latest from the California Mountains." *California Star* [San Francisco], 5 June 1847.

Faragher, John Mack. *Women and Men on the Overland Trail*. New Haven: Yale University Press, 1979.

Farnham, Eliza. *California In Doors and Out*. New York: Dix, 1850.

Grayson, Donald K. "Donner Party Deaths: A Demographic Assessment." *Journal of Anthropological Research* 46 (1990): 223–42.

Hall, Carroll D., ed. *Donner Miscellany: 41 Diaries and Documents*. San Francisco: Book Club of California, 1947.

Harris, Marvin. *Cannibals and Kings: The Origins of Culture*. New York: Random House, 1977.

Hastings, Lansford W. *The Emigrants' Guide to Oregon and California*. 1845. Reprint, Princeton: Princeton University Press, 1932.

Hinkle, George H., and Bliss McGlashan Hinkle. Editors' Foreword. In *History of the Donner Party: A Tragedy of the Sierras*, by C. F. McGlashan, vii–xxxi. Stanford: Stanford University Press, 1947.

The History of the Donner Party. Advertisement. *Truckee Republican*, 11 June 1879.

Houghton, Eliza P. Donner. *The Expedition of the Donner Party and Its Tragic Fate*. Chicago: McClurg, 1911.

Houghton, Eliza P. Donner. Letter to Messrs. Crowley and McGlashan. 12 February 1879. MS HOU 50. Huntington Library, San Marino, Calif.

Houghton, Eliza P. Donner. Letter to Benjamin W. Wilder. 20 May 1879. MS HOU 49. Huntington Library, San Marino, Calif.

Johnson, Overton, and William H. Winter. *Route across the Rocky Mountains*. 1846. Reprint, Princeton: Princeton University Press, 1932.

Keithley, George. *The Donner Party*. New York: Braziller, 1972.

Kilgour, Maggie. *From Communion to Cannibalism: An Anatomy of Metaphors of Incorporation*. Princeton: Princeton University Press, 1990.

Kolodny, Annette. *The Land Before Her: Fantasy and Experience of the American Frontiers, 1630–1860*. Chapel Hill: University of North Carolina Press, 1984.

Laurgaard, Rachel K. *Patty Reed's Doll: The Story of the Donner Party*. Fairfield, Calif.: Tomato, 1989.

Lévi-Strauss, Claude. *The Raw and the Cooked*. Translated by John Weightman and Doreen Weightman. New York: Harper, 1969.

McCurdy, Stephen A. "Epidemiology of Disaster: The Donner Party (1846–47)." *Western Journal of Medicine* 160 (1994): 338–42.

McDougal, Frances Helen. "The Donner Tragedy: A Thrilling Chapter in Our Pioneer History." *Pacific Rural Press* [San Francisco], 21 January 1871.

McGlashan, C. F. *History of the Donner Party: A Tragedy of the Sierras*. 1880. Reprint, Stanford: Stanford University Press, 1947.

McGlashan, C. F. Letters to Eliza P. Donner Houghton: 8 Feb. 1879, MS HOU 52, 53; 17 June 1879, MS HOU 84; 19 June 1879, MS HOU 87; 4 July 1879, MS HOU 89; 12 July 1879, MS HOU 90; 17 July 1879, MS HOU 91; 18 Aug. 1898, MS HOU 141; 10 Apr. 1902, MS HOU 142; 14 Dec. 1911, MS HOU 1738. Huntington Library, San Marino, Calif.

Murphy, Virginia Reed. "A Girl with the Donner Party." *American History Illustrated* 21.5 (Sept. 1986): 18–27; 21.6 (Oct. 1986): 24–35.

Murphy, Virginia Reed. Letter of Virginia Reed. In Stewart, *Ordeal*, 355–62.

One More Mountain. Performed by Meredith Baxter. Disney Studios, ABC, WSYX, Columbus, 6 Mar. 1994.

O'Sullivan, John L. "Annexation." *United States Magazine and Democratic Review* 1785 (1845): 5–10.

Poulsen, Richard C. "The Donner Party: History, Mythology, and the Existential Voice." *American Studies in Scandinavia* 16 (1984): 103–16.

Sanday, Peggy Reeves. *Divine Hunger: Cannibalism as a Cultural System.* Cambridge: Cambridge University Press, 1986.

Scarry, Elaine. *The Body in Pain: The Making and Unmaking of the World.* New York: Oxford University Press, 1985.

Schlissel, Lillian. "Frontier Families: Crisis in Ideology." In *The American Self: Myth, Ideology, and Popular Culture*, edited by Sam B. Girgus, 55–65. Albuquerque: University of New Mexico Press, 1981.

Shively, J. M. *Route and Distances to Oregon and California.* Washington, D.C.: Greer, 1846.

Slotkin, Richard. *The Fatal Environment: The Myth of the Frontier in the Age of Industrialization, 1800–1890.* New York: Atheneum, 1985.

Smith, Henry Nash. *Virgin Land: The American West as Symbol and Myth.* New York: Vintage-Random, 1950.

Stewart, George R. *The California Trail: An Epic with Many Heroes.* New York: McGraw, 1962.

Stewart, George R. *Ordeal by Hunger: The Story of the Donner Party.* Boston: Houghton, 1960.

Teggart, Frederick J. Introduction. In *Diary of Patrick Breen*, 3–4. Reno, Nev.: Outbooks, 1979.

Thompson, Julie Ince, perf. *Tamsen Donner: A Woman's Journey.* Music by Evan Harlan. Sullivant Theatre, Ohio State University, Columbus, 4 Nov. 1995.

Thoreau, Henry David. "Walking." In *Writings of Thoreau*, vol. 5, 205–48. Boston: Houghton, 1906.

Thornton, J. Quinn. *Oregon and California in 1848.* Vol. 2. New York: Harper, 1849. Reprint, New York: Arno, 1973.

Turner, Frederick Jackson. "The Significance of the Frontier in American History." In *History, Frontier, and Section: Three Essays by Frederick Jackson Turner*, 59–91. Albuquerque: University of New Mexico Press, 1993.

Tuzin, Donald. "Cannibalism and Arapesh Cosmology: A Wartime Incident with the Japanese." In *The Ethnography of Cannibalism*, edited by Paula Brown and Donald Tuzin, 61–71. Washington, D.C.: Society for Psychological Anthropology, 1983.

Waggoner, W. W. "The Donner Party and Relief Hill." *California Historical Society Quarterly* 10 (1931): 346–52.

Whitman, Ruth. *Tamsen Donner: A Woman's Journey.* Cambridge, Mass.: James, 1977.

5 *Karyn Hollis*

Material of Desire
Bodily Rhetoric in Working Women's Poetry
at the Bryn Mawr Summer School, 1921–1938

[handwritten: 1916 - 1954 ?]

I would like to write a poem,
But I have no words.
My grammar was ladies' waists,
And my schooling skirts.
Anonymous dressmaker quoted in Smith, Opening Vistas

In writing this doubly ironic poem about not being able to write a poem, a student at the Bryn Mawr Summer School subverts discursive rules of class and gender that hinder her creativity. In a further ironic move, she explains the social relations that limit all working-class women. Physically confined to factories for long, painful hours, the women had little time for intellectual pursuits. Their cultural logic or "grammar" had been largely corporeal, based on their physical exploitation for the benefit of a "lady" of another class. The working women felt discursively deprived and unable to write. In their minds, poetry was connected to esteemed literary arts, classical learning, and aesthetic sophistication—all discursive markers of the middle-class and upper-class education they lacked. Yet remarkably, by the end of their Summer School session, many workers were writing poems of a kind that had never been seen before—poems inscribed with working-class and occasionally gendered identities, at times celebratory, at times defiant and demanding. The Summer School's mixture of progressive discursive and material contexts enabled the working women to transgress other contexts that assigned limiting cultural scripts to their gender and class. Poetry was the centerpiece of a liberating writing curriculum which included autobiography, labor drama, report writing, and short fiction. Acting as a discursive bridge, their poetry carried them from the immaterial and ideal world of texts and concepts they studied in class back to the material world which they could describe in terms of the exploitation, poor working conditions, and prejudicial attitudes they wanted to change. This bridging and dialectic—the textual and mental versus the material and corporeal— are especially evident in the bodily motif that pervades the women's poetry. The recovery of this discarded and forgotten discursive "body" of women's work reveals how a pedagogical project can progress from textual to physical context.

A School for Women Workers

This examination of poetry is part of a larger study I am conducting on writing instruction at the Summer School; I have previously described the origins and aims of the institution (Hollis). The Bryn Mawr Summer School was founded as an indirect response to the favorable climate for women's rights and worker education which prevailed during the Progressive Era, but it was more immediately an effort of the National Women's Trade Union League, which in 1916 called on the women's colleges to do more to educate working women. Two feminist educators connected to Bryn Mawr answered this call: M. Carey Thomas, a noted suffragist and president of the college for thirty-five years; and Hilda Worthington Smith, a Bryn Mawr graduate, dean, and director of the Summer School for thirteen years. During its seventeen-year history, approximately fifteen hundred working women, eighty to one hundred each summer, attended the school. Appointed by Thomas to head the school, Smith attracted upper-class and middle-class Bryn Mawr alumnae to the cause of worker education through a flood of promotional publications and presentations.[1] While alumnae committees did most of the recruiting and fund-raising, the school was also assisted by the Industrial Department of the YWCA, the National Women's Trade Union League, labor unions, churches, corporate and private benefactors, and groups of Summer School alumnae.

The Summer School (the first of four resident women workers' colleges established in the 1920s and 1930s) offers a rare example in American history of a successful multi-ethnic alliance among women of the upper, middle, and working classes. Because Summer School policy explicitly called for a diverse student body in terms of trade, geographic region, religion, and eventually race, students were recruited from all over the United States and even from Europe. Scholarships paid for by full-term Bryn Mawr students and alumnae made it possible for "American-born" cotton-mill girls from the South to study alongside immigrant Jewish dressmakers from Eastern Europe or Italian Catholics from the Northeast. Typically, the women were unmarried and under twenty-five. Most had attended school only until the eighth grade. It was policy that half the student body should belong to unions. At their own insistence, the worker-students were given a substantial voice in administrative and curricular matters. The students themselves requested a focus on English composition and literature, economics, and labor studies, with a secondary offering of various combinations of psychology, health education, history, art, drama, physical education, elementary science, astronomy, and music. In 1926 they demanded that African American women be recruited to the Summer School. The diversity among the student body often brought uncomfortable tension and debate, but testimonies from students and faculty indicate that a more sophisticated and tolerant graduate was the result.

Clearly, these working women benefited greatly from their eight-week immersion in liberal arts and labor economics, on a beautiful suburban college campus where, in the words of a student, "the scent of the honeysuckles made us feel that we were in heaven." The Summer School students were offered some of the luxuries their more elite counterparts enjoyed during the fall and spring terms. They were taken on field trips to local museums and factories, honored with teas and luncheons, taught to swim and play tennis, and treated to guest lectures by W. E. B. Dubois, Margaret Sanger, Norman Thomas, Francis Perkins, Harold Laski, Walter Reuther, and Eleanor Roosevelt, as well as many other renowned labor, political, academic, and feminist leaders.

As years passed, students and faculty pushed for a stronger alliance with progressive elements of organized labor. By 1938, the connection to labor had alienated many Bryn Mawr trustees and alumnae. After an incident in which the Summer School was falsely accused of supporting a strike (forbidden in the administrative agreement with the college), it was asked to leave the Bryn Mawr campus. The school then moved to the Smith family estate in upstate New York and continued there as the coeducational Hudson Shore Labor College from 1939 to 1952. Its demise occurred as workers turned to short-term classes offered by unions, to university residential and nonresidential courses, and to university labor education programs to meet their educational needs.

The students at the Summer School enjoyed a richly progressive discursive environment which they appropriated to construct more empowered subjectivities and more satisfying cultural traditions. Public discourse in the 1920s and even more in the 1930s included much pro-worker rhetoric as union demands became public issues and even public policy. The rhetoric of the New Deal often put workers at the center of its stated benefits. Much leftist ideology reached mainstream discourse through the widespread political work of the Communist, Socialist and other leftist political parties. In addition, the perspectives of the progressive and worker education movements were pervasive in the culture of education, especially at the Summer School. The working women therefore found much support in the wider community for the new cultural scripts they were writing. Of course, they also encountered and sometimes wrote against the subtexts of racism, classism, and sexism found in working-class institutions as well as in those of the larger culture.

Summer School faculty placed student experience at the center of the curriculum. They were especially committed to the pedagogical practice of textu-

material ?

alizing that experience, especially through literary genres. Since the turn of the century, mainstream American universities had encouraged their middle-class and upper middle-class students to read and sometimes to write in literary modes, but higher educational opportunities of that kind were rare for the working class until the arrival of the worker education movement in the 1920s. By 1932, more than three hundred worker schools existed in the United States, established by the Women's Trade Union League, labor unions, political groups, and independent labor educators (Orleck 170; see also Nelson). Workers at these schools often wrote creatively in various genres. Firmly convinced of the importance of their educational endeavor, administrators and faculty at the Bryn Mawr Summer School for Women Workers preserved student texts and publications as well as syllabi, lesson plans, and detailed records of curricular meetings and administrative deliberations. Many original application forms also survive, so personal information is available on the people whose poetry I discuss below. After graduating from the Summer School, the women often moved into leadership positions in unions, the YWCA, civic organizations, and churches; indeed, the Summer School became a trend-setter among the worker colleges of the day and left a significant legacy for later generations of women workers, educators, and unionists.

Hilda W. Smith, founding director of the Summer School, reports that "More poetry!" was a constant cry every summer, and that "instructors and tutors do their best to satisfy this desire" (119). The working women were provided with fiction and poetry celebrating the working class and were offered models of textual subjectivities that often called for worker empowerment. The works of many famous poets through the ages were assigned, but poetry celebrating the common people and their right to justice and a better life predominated. Not surprisingly, "high moderns" such as T. S. Eliot and Ezra Pound, with their themes of pessimism, futility, apathy, and degradation, were not valued at the Summer School. By contrast, Walt Whitman's *Leaves of Grass* was common on syllabi and reading lists, along with Carl Sandburg's *Chicago Poems* and *The People, Yes*. Also frequently recommended were Archibald MacLeish's *Land of the Free*, Stephen Vincent Benét's *John Brown's Body*, Upton Sinclair's *The Cry for Justice*, and Marguerite Wilkinson's anthology *New Voices*. African American poetry by Langston Hughes, Countee Cullen, and Stirling Brown was also included (*Suggested Reading List*).

Both faculty and students approached the study of literature from the non-elitist assumption that workers should take part in literary production. Faculty members articulated this view in books, articles, and syllabi. In *Education and the Worker Student*, teacher-directors Jean Carter and Hilda W. Smith gave two reasons for the emphasis on creative writing at the Summer School. First, writing was intended to provide an "emotional outlet" for the woman worker, allowing her to express needs and demands and relieving her of tensions en-

countered at work and in other areas of life (59). Second, writing was important because it provided others with a meaningful glimpse into the life of an industrial worker from an uncommon, first-hand perspective (59–60). In her
book on teaching English to workers, *Mastering the Tools of the Trade*, Carter
suggests to workers that it is their duty to express themselves through poetry or
fiction: "Industrial workers have an unusually rich and unexploited field so far
as novels, plays and poems are concerned" (39).

   Summer School faculty and students were also influenced by the broader
leftist project of building a working-class culture in the United States. In a
"Symposium on Creative Expression" published in a 1935 issue of the *Journal
of Adult Education*, English faculty member William Fincke asserted:

> It would seem logical that the experiences of industrial workers in writing groups es-
> tablished throughout the country might have a significant effect upon our national liter-
> ature. . . . In the beginnings of articulateness among those more close to the borderline
> of survival and those who participate firsthand in processes productive of life's necessi-
> ties, we have the promise of a vastly greater literary perspective. (185)

② Poetry from Women Workers

In their search for "words" and "grammar" to write poetry, women workers at
the Bryn Mawr Summer School created a rhetoric that directed the public gaze
to their exhausting work and located their subjectivity in the public discursive
arena. Since these dressmakers, buttonholers, and hatband stitchers were physically confined to steamy factories, manufacturing objects they could rarely afford, they chose to textualize their bodies in a rhetoric that exposed the oppressive relationships of power, economics, gender, race, and class which plagued
their lives. Fortunately, the Summer School afforded the women workers time
to study their role in the national economy—a role they came to understand as
even more important than that of the upper-class "ladies" whom they served.
Subsequently, through their poetic rhetoric of the body, they were able to speak
their desires for material bounty as well as for intellectual and aesthetic re-
wards. In recovering their poetry, we extend the opportunity begun at Bryn
Mawr for working women to enter the discursive body politic, a space that remains off limits to them even today, and even as they continue to perform many
of the most tedious and exhausting tasks of global capitalist production.

   The pedagogy developed at the Summer School was innovative by all accounts, but the writing instruction was particularly remarkable. The women
wrote copiously at the urging of the predominantly female faculty, whose
student-centered pedagogy helped transform dreams, desires, and fears into
demands. Judging by the amount of poetry they published over the years, the
working women shared the faculty's enthusiasm for the literary arts, especially

poetry. Poetry and fiction-writing was a group activity, but unlike the study of literature and eventually dramatics, creative writing never secured a regular slot in the daytime course schedule. Although a few teachers required students to write poems and narratives in their composition or literature classes, in most instances the creative writers were a self-selected group who met with a faculty sponsor in the evenings, once or twice a week, to exchange and critique poems and stories. From the first summer session in 1921, poetry was included in *Shop and School*, the student publication. From just two poems in that first issue, poetic production increased to 45 poems, or almost half the contents, by 1934. For this study, I examined a total of 185 poems printed in the student publications from 1924 to 1938.[2]

Like much of the poetry they were reading at the Summer School, the student poetry generally fits into what David Perkins has termed the first "modern" phase of American poetry (296). Written in reaction to the Romantic influence and the genteel tradition of the Victorian lyric, this early twentieth-century poetry was "direct and accessible," the speakers were attractive, and the tone affirmative or stoically pessimistic (298). The subject matter was broad and experiential. Many poems of social or political themes celebrated American democracy. The style was frequently colloquial, and the dialect identifiably American; verse was often free (Perkins 306–10; see also Nelson). The women workers' poetic taste departed from the mainstream in at least one respect, however. According to Perkins, in American high schools, colleges, and reading clubs of the 1930s the notion of contemporary poetry was likely to mean the "short, free-verse poems of tender impressionism" such as Sandburg's "Fog" or "Cool Tombs" (297). The poems workers preferred and wrote were more like Sandburg's political poems and his forceful, action-packed impressions of ordinary American life.

The style and themes of the workers' verse remained quite consistent over the years. Slightly more than half the poems are rhyming; the meter is typically free or iambic. Stylistically, the lyric mode predominates; the poems are short, averaging just twenty-one lines. Topics are approached from a "subjective" or personal perspective; only slightly more than one-third of the poems are actually written in first person, however, with about one-third of these directly addressing a second person interlocutor, "you." Fewer still (less than 15 percent) are written from a collective, "we" perspective, the perspective frequently adopted in the workers' autobiographies (Hollis 41). The remainder are written in third person in a mode of commentary, observation, or declaration. The poetry is rhetorical, arousing its audience through stylistic devices such as repetition, sensory imagery, machine rhythms, questions, dialogue, narration, exclamation, and direct address.

Thematically, none of the poetry is confined to the narrow realm of emotive confessionalism, but much of it takes on a reflective, contemplative tone featuring philosophical inquiry, expressions of hope and desire, advice, warnings, and exhortations. At least three-fourths of it could be characterized as "lyrical protest poetry," written to right a wrong, reveal an inequality, or demand justice. In terms of subject matter, about one-third of the poems are about work life. More than half of these concern work with machines, and as I will show, many comment on the machine's relationship to the body. Another major topic is nature, its gifts and revitalizing powers. The next major category includes poems on explicitly political or social issues—poems critical of the rich, poems protesting unemployment and child labor, poems calling for working-class unity, or poems praising the Soviet Union. The value of education is another prominent theme, typically in odes of praise to Bryn Mawr. Of the remaining poems, there are six on the injustice of racism, three on challenges confronting "youth," two character sketches, three prayers for peace and racial harmony, and a couple of desolate descriptions of urban landscapes. No poems explore early family relationships or the writer's personal background, union issues, or strikes—all areas dealt with extensively in the women's autobiographies (Hollis). Romantic or sexual relationships are not broached at all in the poetry, and only rarely in other genres.

3 Poetry of Machines and the Body

The mechanized factory, where women and men worked alongside frighteningly powerful and fast-paced industrial machinery, prompted much poetic discourse at the Summer School. It was here that the Bryn Mawr worker-students felt compelled to write their bodies. In fact, two-thirds of the poems dealing with the workplace make specific mention of workers' bodies. The value of an embodied working-class perspective has been emphasized by Janet Zandy in her anthology of working-class writing, *Liberating Memory*: "The lived experience of working class people encodes a kind of knowledge—especially of the body—that is absent in bourgeois . . . institutions" (2). Similarly, bell hooks writes, "There is a particular knowledge that comes from suffering. It is a way of knowing that is often expressed through the body, what it knows, what has been deeply inscribed on it through experience" (91).

The bodily knowledge disclosed in the working women's poetry rhetoricized their texts in complex, paradoxical, and multifaceted ways. First, the women felt a need to textualize their bodily presence in the factory. Second, they used a rhetoric of struggle to record their fight against owners and machines for control of their bodies. Third, they wrote their bodies as sites of social control as well as sites of individual and collective resistance. In addition, as subjectivities both written by and writing beyond conventional patriarchal dualities, the women asserted that they were more than "mere" bodies; they had inquiring minds, aesthetic ambitions, and creative abilities. And although most of their

poetry was written in solidarity with their white male working-class counterparts, gendered opposition to masculine oppression and racism occasionally
surfaced. Finally, the women encouraged one another to create an alternative
discursive tradition denouncing the injustice of their exploitation and celebrating the working class across differences of gender and race.

The working women frequently called attention to the fact that their jobs
were physically painful and mentally depressing. This discursive rendering of
suffering was assertive in an age when public mention of the body was discour-
aged for women and for the working class more generally, because it named the
site of much class and gender oppression. This poem by Mary Feldman, class
of 1936, exposes capitalism's sacrifice of the worker's body and mind in the
production of relatively insignificant articles of apparel:

Buttons

Remember the old nursery rhyme,
"Buttons, buttons, who's got the button?"
Remember? Yes, such childish play!
It's play no more with buttons. It's work.
Such back-aching, eye-straining work!
Buttons—large buttons—small buttons
White buttons—black buttons—colored buttons
Buttons for shirts—buttons for sweaters—buttons for coats.

Do people think when they buy buttons
Of the fast, steady, monotonous work?
Buttons pouring out of the machine towards
Me on the ever-moving belt!
I stare at buttons, I sort buttons.
All day long. My eyes ache, so, ache!
Buttons, just buttons!

Cultural texts were commonly appropriated by the worker-writers for use in
their poetry. Here Feldman calls on discourse from a more innocent and hap-
pier time to provoke her readers into an awareness of the role of human labor
in the production process. Perhaps she was also familiar with the Marxist concepts of commodity fetishization, surplus value, and alienation, because her
poem seems to illustrate these ideas. In a highly rhetorical style, she employs
textual strategies such as irony, questions, direct address, and exclamations to
condemn the subject position workers occupy in the mechanized industrial
workplace.

The women workers also protested poetically against the ways their bodies
were subjected to the controlling forces of capitalist patriarchy. Feminist interpretations of Michel Foucault's work are useful in understanding this disciplining of the "docile body" for increased utility and efficiency in assigned cultural

tasks. According to Sandra Lee Bartky, "The production of 'docile bodies' requires that an uninterrupted coercion be directed to the very processes of bodily activity . . . ; this 'micro-physics of power' fragments and partitions the body's time, its space and its movements" (quoted in Diamond 62). Indeed, constraints imposed on their time, space, and movement are frequent themes in the women's poetry. An instance is the following poem, written in 1934 by twenty-eight-year-old Adelaide Burgdorf, a part-time stock sorter in a button factory in Rochester, New York. Not a union member, she was recruited to the Summer School through her local YWCA Industrial Club, where she had held numerous offices. Prior to her Bryn Mawr experience, she had attended courses in dramatics, English, economics, and history offered through the Y. Her obvious intellectual ability and curiosity must have made her days at the factory torturous indeed.

doggerel

Factories

Grey walls greet me on all sides,
The roar of motors fills my ears,
And all my eyes can see are fast whirling wheels.
Amid the noise and clashing of wheels,
more speed.
My hands so tired can move no faster.
My eyes droop with weariness,
But I dare not sleep.
I am chained to this huge machine
And it keeps on saying,
more speed.

Can it be that somewhere beyond all this
Bright flowers bloom and birds sing gaily?
Can I find there food for my body
As well as my soul?
Or must I always go on hearing the wheels say,
more speed.

Corporeal representation and transformation are central tropes in this poem: Burgdorf's bodily senses are overwhelmed by the machine which pushes her, and the machine is itself anthropomorphized to represent the embodied owner. When the machine speaks, what is heard is the capitalist's call for "more speed" made material again in Burgdorf's aching hands and eyes. Using conventional cultural dichotomies, Burgdorf presents nature and (woman's) body in opposition to culture and (man's) mind. However, Burgdorf and her fellow poets frequently revalue the culturally maligned half of this dyad. Here she defends the body in its need for repose and praises the natural realm for offering a revitalizing alternative to urban industrialism, thus deconstructing patriarchal meanings.

In the next poem, from 1929, Mary Kosovicz, a twenty-two-year-old textile worker from Rhode Island, describes an incident in which a worker has to fight the machine for control of her body. Kosovicz's application shows that although she left school in the eighth grade, she also had a strong desire to continue learning. Not a union member but educational chair of her local YWCA Industrial Club, she had taken five evening classes at the Y, including Greek mythology, music appreciation, and English literature. She reported having read *Midsummer Night's Dream* and *The American Federationist*, among other works, in the past year.

The Machine

Hello, you big monster.
I'm not afraid of you today.
Yesterday, you played me a dirty trick
By pulling in my hand
And crushing it till I screamed.
You laughed and roared on and on.
Louder and louder, just like a wild lion
Full of joy and that has just caught its prey.
I was helpless.
To fight you would be like fighting wild beasts.
You don't care what you do to me.
Cripple me for life or take it from me.

There is one who can compete with you
And that is Fate in all her glory.
If it wasn't for her,
I wonder where I would be.
When you took the notion, you fierce-looking thing,
That I no longer needed my hand,
Fate stepped in, and said to you,
"You have all the power in this world:
Your gears, your wheels, your huge rollers,
Why! the size of a human being compared to you
Is as great as a mouse compared to him.
This human body doesn't stand a chance with you;
You will go on living and roaring
Long after the human body is dead and buried.
So why should I let you take its life or disable it?"
You paid no heed to that, did you? Of course not.
Remember when you pulled that hand of mine
And how I screamed till I could scream no more?

> Fate heard me and she stepped in,
> Like lightning the power was shut off,
> For what reason, no one knows but I.
> Today, I am not afraid of you.
> I don't hear your terrible noise,
> I hear music, louder and louder.
> Oh, how I wish to dance to you,
> Your roaring wheels and your terrible curse.

Again, the machine here is transmogrified into a monster, a wild lion and a humanlike god similar to those Kosovicz may have studied in her Greek mythology course. She speaks defiantly to the machine that crushed her hand and complains that the "human body doesn't stand a chance with you." Although the human body she has in mind seems to be masculine (the "him" in text), she attributes her rescue to a feminine "Fate," again in accordance with Greek myth. Then "today," likely because of her Bryn Mawr experience, she has courage enough to confront the machine; she is transformed, "not afraid." Her bodily senses are altered. She no longer hears the machine's "terrible noise," but "music, louder and louder." Her new mentality is also embodied in her wish to "dance to you," perhaps as a way of controlling, placating, or domesticating the "roaring wheels" and "terrible curse."

As we see in Kosovicz's poem, although women workers were oppressed through their bodies, they also knew them as means of liberation. In her extension of the work of Foucault, Susan Bordo has pointed out in that "where there is power . . . there is also resistance" (27). Through poetic discourse, the women workers were able to regard their bodies as sites of resistance. Mildred Kuhn clearly had her body's liberating potential in mind when she wrote this poem in 1933:

Lost

> The loud swish, swish of machines
> The stinking, sweating reeking masses,
> Voices loud and harsh echoing in my dull dead brain,
> My body moving, working, slaving, keeping one small spark alive.
> Dimly as tho' miles away, I hear a bell.
> No more swishing,
> No voices loud and harsh,
> Just my body dragging me home.

Although it is through her bodily senses that Kuhn is assaulted by the roar of machines and the sweaty smells on the shop floor, it is also through corporeal sensation that she hears a liberating bell. And it is her body that drags her home to peace and quiet. Writing herself in terms of the familiar mind/body duality, she locates the source of oppression on the mental/immaterial/discursive side of the equation: discursive "voices loud and harsh" echo in her brain. Her body and its materiality, on the other hand, is written in opposition to this oppression. In a deconstruction of patriarchal meanings, she does not accept the conventional masculinist paradigm of valuing the mind over the body. While her brain is "dead," her body keeps "one small spark alive."

In general, the women workers revalued the nature/body side of the masculinist nature/culture duality, affirming the materiality of their bodies and writing in positive terms about physicality and nature. Nevertheless, they lived in a patriarchal culture which stigmatized their women's bodies and devalued or denied their minds, and so they also felt a need to maintain that they were more than bodies, more even than bodies in opposition to machines. This etherealization of the body takes a disturbing turn with respect to African American bodies, as I will note in a moment; but first I want to demonstrate the white women workers' tendency to give equal value and appreciation to both the bodily and the intellectual realms—a tendency that led them beyond an androcentric polarity and dealt a blow to traditional ideologies of white masculinity and femininity. Such a blow is struck in the poetry of Doris Bowman, a twenty-four-year-old Jewish hatmaker, originally from Eastern Europe, who had lived in the United States for eight years when she wrote "Hands" in 1930. Bowman was an officer of the International Cap and Millinery Union and of her local YWCA. Displaying a familiarity with literary classics common among the Jewish students, Bowman had read the following works over the previous year: *The World's Illusion*, *My Life* by Isadora Duncan, *Anna Karenina*, *All Quiet on the Western Front*, *Strange Interlude*, *Red Silence*, and *Mother and Son*. Also recorded on her application was a lecture she attended in Chicago entitled "Is Man a Machine?"—an indication of the prevalence of mechanistic critiques in intellectual and artistic discourse of the day.

Hands

Two hands, bare hands—these are
God's gift to every woman born!
Some hands remain as delicate as flowers,
Shapely, white, unscarred by laboring.
Others grow coarse and rough with use,
Worn with the toil of earning daily bread.
But hands are not symbols of a woman's heart and brain—
The power that moves all hands is very much the same
And once the door of art and learning
Swings wide to those who have found it closed
Their willing minds respond, desires awaken.
They venture through the door with eyes alight,
Eager to grasp the gifts so long denied.

This poem is unusual in its references to gender and class. Not content to have women reduced to mere physical objects or body parts, Bowman insists, "Hands are not symbols of a woman's heart and brain." Using a discourse of equal rights, she proclaims the equality of the "power that moves all hands," implying that women's intellectual capacities are as great as men's. "Hands" also notes class differences among women by calling attention to those women's hands that are "shapely, white, unscarred by laboring." Even more typically, the poem evokes chords of solidarity with working-class men whose hands are also "worn with the toil of earning daily bread" and who long for "the door of art and learning" to swing open. That the solidarity may not extend across race, however, is suggested by the explicit use of the word "white."

(4) Gender and Race in Working-Class Bodies

The textualized bodies in the Bryn Mawr poetry were not often marked by gender, and almost never by race. Of course, in our androcentric culture, an unmarked body is usually considered masculine and white by default—a habit that erases the presence of women and racial minorities. It may be, however, that in some instances the working women's poetry records the disciplining of the working class across gender, if not racial, difference. Lois McNay, for example, argues that formations such as race and class "may work across gender distinctions, breaking down the absolute polarity between the male and the female body" (37). Moreover, in equating masculine and feminine bodies and pointing out the oppressive work conditions both endured, the women were actually writing against the contemporary ideological construction of difference that preferred a notion of women as domestic, weak, and nonworking (Kessler-Harris 57).

In any case, published pieces by African American students are few. I found only one poem by an African American woman in *Shop and School*, and since it did not contain bodily references, I have not included it here.[3] The poem "Ave Maria," however, could be considered typical of white women's poems on the subject of race. This selection, by Kitty LaSota (1938), is meant not to allow the white student to speak for African Americans but to illustrate a representative attitude about race and gender among whites at the school.

Ave Maria

She stood there
And played.
Her whole being
Was immersed
In the beautiful
And enchanting

Melody.
It was Schubert's *Ave Maria*,
There
At the formal opening
Of the school,
Where we are taught
To love, and respect,
And treat one another
As Christ taught.
Speeches were given
By the director,
A gentle and lovely woman,
Beloved by all.
And a colored girl,
Who was lovingly applauded.
No discrimination,
For she is a human being
With a soul
Not unlike your soul
And my soul.

So we sat and listened
Entranced
To a melody
That did honor
The Blessed Virgin
Who was once Flesh and blood
Like us.
And as the young woman played,
Not only on the strings
Of her violin,
But on the strings
Of our hearts
As well,
I wondered why
Girls and women
Who too are flesh and blood
And have souls
Should be treated
Not humanly,
But unjustly,
By employers,
Why Negroes
Should be discriminated against.

God of creation,
Shed light

And create understanding
In the ignorant hearts of men;
Make them aware that we are all
Equal.
That difference lies only
In the color of skin.

The bodily presence of a "colored girl" was noteworthy and celebrated in La-
Sota's poem. But the tragedy of this "liberal" perspective is that the "Negro"
had to be disembodied in order for others to accept her humanity. Thus, LaSota
disparages the materiality of the body in an attempt to devalue the "difference
[that] lies only / In the color of skin." As abolitionists had done a century before, LaSota draws heavily on religious discourse and appropriates conventional dualistic thinking to buttress her argument for racial equality. Because
all humans have immortal souls that are superior to the body, all are worthy of
respect and equal treatment while on Earth. LaSota's frequent allusions to tran-
substantiation, the change from the material into the immaterial, also sustain
her argument. As Christian saints rise from their bodies to a higher state of being, both the singer and her audience are similarly transported. The "colored
girl's" body is left behind, as "her whole being is immersed" in the heavenly
melody. The audience is likewise "entranced" in a beyond-the-body experience
and drawn into the prayer that closes the poem. But in a typical move toward
working-class solidarity, LaSota points out the commonality of feminine experience across race and class because "[white] girls and women / Who too are
flesh and blood / And have souls" are also dehumanized and treated unjustly.
Whether LaSota's vision of solidarity includes men is not clear; it is difficult to
know just how gender-specific is LaSota's comment about the "ignorant hearts
of men."

Although the African American body was allowed only the genocidal cultural script of being erased in order to be accepted, in a few instances white poets thought it acceptable to emphasize their specific bodily knowledge to argue
in favor of their gender and class. In "A Mother's Misery" (by Molly Ferrara,
class of 1934), we have a poignant account, in terms of a woman's corporeal experience, of the troubles experienced by a working-class mother and her family during the Great Depression. Forced to work soon after her baby daughter
was born, the woman in this poem literally embodies the double burden capitalism inflicts on the working mother as she struggles to meet the demands of
both material and bodily production.

A Mother's Misery

Stitch twice and then turn under.
Baby feeling better? Wonder—
Two long seams; now stitch again.

Call the doctor: Yes but then—
Watch your seams now; not too wide.
Oh! for money for help at her side.

Sweat a-dripping from your brow.
You think Mary. I know how.
Maybe Jim has found a job.
Little Nan will cease to sob.
Wonder what I could do and how.
Bronchitis, pneumonia, the grippe?
See what I've done; now rip and stitch.
My it's warm! It's sweltering! Stifling!
Sleeves are done; just put on piping.

Adjust this kerchief, I must, for then
It is sweet nectar nature provides,
But circumstances to you have denied.
Three weeks old! My joy, my pride!
Oh! to hold you to my side,
Tugging gently at my bosom,
Suckling lips, reluctant, loosening.
Little lids slowly lowering;
Slumberman around is hovering.
Then I'd tuck you safe in bed.
I have done just as you said!
Child of mine, oh, to be dead!
God! oh God! Please do not take her.
I can't help if I forsake her.
Every day I toil to earn
Food and clothes for my new-born.

In a machine rhythm of point-counterpoint, Ferrara's internal dialogue textual-
izes the split consciousness that results from mechanized and alienating work.
As her thoughts turn from "Baby feeling better?" to "now stitch again" and
back to "My joy, my pride!" we see the difficulty of her endeavor. Once again
the woman worker complains about the sensory assault inflicted on the corporeal and natural realm by machines. She celebrates the organic domain of which
her body is a part as unsullied and life-sustaining, dispensing the "sweet nectar
nature provides." Supporting this rhetorical strategy of revaluing the natural
realm is the discourse of domesticity, a patriarchal subtext which nevertheless
underscores the injustice of having to work with young children inadequately
cared for at home.

Another Bryn Mawr poem describes class antagonisms among white
women, with the rhetoric of class quite literally inscribed on their bodies. The
poet, Thelma Brown, was an "American born" student from Roanoke, Virginia.
She was thirty years old; she had been an officer of the United Textile Workers

Union, and vice chairman of workers education and president of her YWCA Club. Her 1936 application revealed that she would like to know more about "Trade Unions and Peace," and humorously noted her desire to learn "How to Ask Questions Without Seeming To Be a Red." Several items on her application, however, give the impression that she may have been at least a close sympathizer with leftist projects. She noted that she "had a Pioneer Youth Club" in her community — most likely the local Communist Party-sponsored youth organization. Her reading for the year included the left-leaning publications *The New Republic*, *The Call* (the Socialist Party weekly), *The Daily Worker* (the Communist Party daily), and *The Case for Industrial Organizations*. Brown commented in a postscript that the following poem passed "through my mind as I sat in a conference called at Hollins College for working girls and college girls" (20).

Thoughts

I work, you play.
You have everything.
I have nothing.
Why should I sit here, afraid to take my coat off?
Is it because I smell so strong of acid?
Why don't I take my gloves off?
Is it because my hands are so rough and dirty looking?
Why do I keep my hat on?
Is it because my hair smells like a wet dog?
Acid again. Acid that smells like burning sulphur.
There are fumes of sulphur in Hell.

You daughters of the rich,
You walk so easy and sure of yourselves.
You don't smell at all.
Your hands are well kept.
Your hair shines with cleanliness,
Your eyes are bright and eager looking.
But who makes your sweetness, your cleanliness possible?
Is it not workers like me?
I work, you play,
You have everything.
I have nothing.

Employing the rhetoric of an internal dialogue, Brown is able to accuse and denounce the upper-class students she addresses. Capitalism's injustice is clearly inscribed on her body. She depicts its physical toll graphically in terms of unpleasant smells and dirty hands — results of the hellish work she must do. We are reminded of Foucault's panoptic vision as we note how her poetic persona's self-monitoring inhibits her movements. Because her body is marked as working-class, she refuses to take off her hat, coat, and gloves in front of the upper-class girls. Brown's basic message is Marxist: the exploited labor of the working class makes possible the pampered existence of the capitalist class.

In a similar vein, and in hopes of building a working-class or alternative discursive tradition, Josephine Kiezulas in 1937 reminds her readers of their common labor history—all through discursive interpretations of bodily experience:

Lawrence, Massachusetts

A phantom hope lurks behind its hills.
A voice is heard from a distance.
From mill to mill the echo falls
To all to leave their chains—
The speeded looms and spindles, the bosses' scowl
No voice complains of aching backs.
Our discontent has no meaning
For we are not better than the machines at which we work.

The phantom's name we know so well,
But can we speak it without fear?
The Law says: "Yes"—Our jobs say: "No."
We want our jobs. We need them.
And yet we also need this ghost
To help us live as well as labor.
Bread and work are not alone a full and useful life.
In 1912, '19 and '31 we shouted its name,
And sang of it in soprano and bass
In our picket lines.
And with our whole hearts we yelled
Unionism—Unionism—Unionism.
We yelled so loud that like a shot
It echoed throughout the land.
But the memory of bloodshed and brutality
Has muffled the voices.
You read of us in books and yet wonder
Why we won't accept with open arms—Unionism.
Now this same ghost lurks once more
And beckons to our young who know
So little of their past.
What will come, we know not.
Oh, God, may we but have this favor.
That those who are heaped in riches
Give us the chance to use our might intelligently.
Bread and work are not alone a full and useful life.

Chastising her audience of working women for forgetting their union past in fear, Kiezulas again laments the equation of workers and machines: "We are no better than the machines at which we work." Obviously a fervent union advocate, the poet reminds workers of events that mainstream discourses prefer to erase. Again valuing the material realm, she insists on the materialization of the "ghost" of unionism. From the titular reference to the "Bread and Roses" strike among women textile workers in Lawrence, Massachusetts (also called "The Uprising of the Thirty Thousand," 1909) to the Triangle Shirtwaist fire of 1912 which took the lives of 146 young women workers, Kiezulas tries to reconstruct the discursive record of "bloodshed," "brutality," and victory involved in building the labor movement. We see the same complaints and textual strategies found in the poetry of other women workers as Kiezulas points out the disciplining effect of "speeded looms." We have the same anger at the sensory assault of the factory, the same "aching backs" and "bosses' scowl." The style is dialogic, with voices clamoring for domination and public space: "But can we speak it without fear? The Law says: 'Yes'—Our jobs say: 'No.'" And echoing the refrain of a popular women's labor movement song, "Bread and Roses," the poet declares that workers need more than a decent wage: "Bread and work alone are not a full and useful life." Kiezulas wants workers to "live as well as labor," for to do so requires the militant attitude that Kiezulas calls for, in words reminiscent of Marx's admonition to get rid of "chains." Although the poem is mostly gendered female, in that it recounts the history of women who work at "looms and spindles," a collective "we" narrates and calls for a return to the supposed cross-gendered solidarity of the past, when workers "sang of it [unionism] in soprano and bass."

Conclusion: Agency and Voice in the Bryn Mawr Summer School

The Summer School had its critics from both the left and the right. Each side accused the other of instilling what we may call inappropriate cultural scripts in the minds of the working women. Early in the Summer School's history, many labor unions and leftist political groups voiced suspicions about the motives of the educators. Could an elite institution like Bryn Mawr truly be interested in the future of the working class? Wouldn't the worker students be encouraged to adopt upwardly mobile attitudes and abandon their class identification? On the other side, the Bryn Mawr board of trustees believed the Summer School was too closely connected to a militant labor movement and the political left; the students had even demanded that a Marxist be appointed to the faculty. Finally, when newspapers reported that two faculty members had attended a rally in support of a strike in New Jersey, breaching an earlier agreement forbidding such activity, the trustees withdrew their support for the school. The Summer School was able to continue, eventually as a coeducational labor school, in Smith's family mansion on the Hudson River until it closed in 1954.

Does a "true" working women's voice emerge when women are exposed to a variety of cultural scripts, each vying for their discursive allegiance? It is difficult to assess the "authenticity" of the worker's voices presented here, if one can still talk in such terms. Put more poststructurally, the degree of agency involved in the students' discursive productions is uncertain. The extent to which the students shaped or were shaped by their discursive environment is difficult to assess. Certainly there may have been an element of "teacher pleasing" in their writing. As has been noted, the women were also influenced by discourse from the labor movement, by left-wing political ideologies, by their religious affiliations, and, later, by the rhetoric of the New Deal. Undoubtedly, a "heteroglossic" variety of discourses operated on and through the women workers. At any rate, the poetry examined here was selected for publication in *Shop and School* by an editorial board consisting of students and a faculty advisor, presumably because of its representative or exemplary nature. This, as well as the fact that the poetry was written as an extracurricular endeavor rather than as an assignment, seems to increase its validity as highly authorized discourse.

Unfortunately, the original audience for this poetry was probably small. There were a few anthologies of workers' poetry published over the years by the Affiliated Schools for Women Workers, and these may have gone out to union and YWCA classes. Smith also published a booklet of workers' poetry as a fund-raising project in 1927 (*Workers*). An occasional poem or essay was published in the regular Bryn Mawr undergraduate newspaper. A more personal mode of distribution occurred at the end of the summer, when each Summer School graduate was given her copy of *Shop and School* to take with her to the wider world, where perhaps it was read by family members and acquaintances in church or union. But in spite of its small audience, the publishing and exchange of poetry must have been rewarding to the women in a number of ways: through it they registered and validated their complaints, feelings, and desires; they created images of better lives and healthier bodies; they built collective solidarity; they issued inspirational calls to action; and they boosted morale and found the courage and conviction they needed to fight for justice on the shop floor and the picket line. Through their poetry, the working women constructed stronger public and private voices for themselves and began to envision a worker's movement and culture that would make their lives easier and that would satisfy many of their most profound desires.

Notes

1. Much of the background information on the Summer School comes from Hilda Worthington Smith's 1929 book describing its early success, *Women Workers at the*

Bryn Mawr Summer School. My account is also based on records of the school's administrative and curricular activities, which Smith and subsequent directors carefully preserved. These records, as well as student publications, application forms, course syllabi, and committee minutes, are found in archival collections at Bryn Mawr, Rutgers, Cornell, and the University of Wisconsin. In addition, I received much inspiration and information from Rita Heller's definitive dissertation on the school, as well as from a film she produced, *Women of Summer*, which depicts the history of the school and a moving 1984 reunion of many Summer School faculty and students.

2. Concerted efforts to locate the copyright holders of the poems reprinted in this chapter were unsuccessful.

3. This poem will be included in a future article on creative writing at the Summer School.

Works Cited

Bordo, Susan R. "The Body and the Reproduction of Femininity: A Feminist Appropriation of Foucault." In *Gender/Body/Knowledge: Feminist Reconstructions of Being and Knowing*, edited by Alison M. Jaggar and Susan R. Bordo, 1–33. New Brunswick: Rutgers University Press, 1989.

Bowman, Doris. "Hands." *Shop and School*, 15. Bryn Mawr, Pa.: Bryn Mawr Summer School for Women Workers, 1930.

Brown, Thelma. "Thoughts." In *Shop and School*, 48. Bryn Mawr, Pa.: Bryn Mawr Summer School for Women Workers, 1936.

Burgdorf, Adelaide. "Factories." In *Shop and School*, 21. Bryn Mawr, Pa.: Bryn Mawr Summer School for Women Workers, 1934.

Carter, Jean. *Mastering the Tools of the Trade: Suggestive Material for Experimental Use in the Teaching of English in Workers' Classes*. New York: Affiliated Schools for Workers, 1932.

Carter, Jean. *This America: A Study of Literature Interpreting the Development of American Civilization*. New York: Affiliated Schools for Workers, 1933.

Carter, Jean, and Hilda W. Smith. *Education and the Worker Student: A Book About Workers' Education Based upon the Experience of Teachers and Students*. New York: Affiliated Schools for Workers, 1934.

Diamond, Irene, and Lee Quinby. *Feminism and Foucault*. Boston: Northeastern University Press, 1988.

Feldman, Mary. "Buttons." In *Shop and School*, 5. Bryn Mawr, Pa.: Bryn Mawr Summer School for Women Workers, 1924.

Ferrara, Molly. "A Mother's Misery." In *Shop and School*, 56. Bryn Mawr, Pa.: Bryn Mawr Summer School for Women Workers, 1934.

Fincke, William Mann. "The Place of Literature in Workers' Education." *Affiliated Schools Scrapbook* 1 (1936): 10–12.

Fincke, William Mann. "Written Words." *Journal of Adult Education,* 1935: 179–82.

Hapke, Laura. *Daughters of the Great Depression: Women, Work and Fiction in the American 1930s*. Athens and London: University of Georgia Press, 1995.

Hollis, Karyn L. "Autobiographical Writing at the Bryn Mawr Summer School for Women Workers." *College Composition and Communication* 45 (1994): 31–60.

hooks, bell. *Teaching to Transgress*. New York: Routledge, 1994.

Kessler-Harris, Alice. *A Woman's Wage: Historical Meanings and Social Consequences*. Lexington: University of Kentucky Press, 1990.

Kiezulas, Josephine. "Lawrence, Massachusetts." In *Shop and School*, 10. Bryn Mawr, Pa.: Bryn Mawr Summer School for Women Workers, 1937.

Kosovicz, Mary. "The Machine." In *Shop and School*, 44. Bryn Mawr, Pa.: Bryn Mawr Summer School for Women Workers, 1929.

Kuhn, Mildred. "Lost." *Shop and School*, 43. Bryn Mawr, Pa.: Bryn Mawr Summer School for Women Workers, 1933.

LaSota, Kitty. "Ave Maria." In *Shop and School*, 41. Bryn Mawr, Pa.: Bryn Mawr Summer School for Women Workers, 1938.

McNay, Lois. *Foucault and Feminism: Power, Gender and the Self*. Boston: Northeastern University Press, 1992.

Nelson, Cary. *Repression and Recovery: Modern American Poetry and the Poetics of Cultural Memory, 1910–1945*. Madison: University of Wisconsin Press, 1989.

Orleck, Annelise. *Common Sense and a Little Fire: Women and Working-Class Politics in the United States, 1900–1965*. Chapel Hill: University of North Carolina Press, 1995.

Perkins, David. *A History of Modern Poetry: From the 1890s to the High Modernist Mode*. Cambridge, Mass.: Harvard University Press, 1976.

Sayre, Henry M. "American Vernacular: Objectivism, Precisionism, and the Aesthetics of the Machine." *Twentieth Century Literature* 35 (1989): 310–42.

Smith, Hilda Worthington. Foreword. In *The Workers Look at the Stars*, edited by Hilda Worthington Smith, 3–4. New York: Vineyard Shore Workers School, 1927.

Smith, Hilda Worthington. *Opening Vistas in Workers' Education: An Autobiography of Hilda Worthington Smith*. Washington, D.C.: privately published, 1978.

Smith, Hilda Worthington. *Women Workers at the Bryn Mawr Summer School*. New York: Affiliated Schools for Women Workers in Industry and American Association for Adult Education, 1929.

Suggested Reading List. Bryn Mawr, Pa.: Bryn Mawr Summer School for Women Workers, 1937.

Suggested Reading List: Novels, Plays, Biographies, Poetry Dealing with Social and Economic Problems. New York: Affiliated Schools for Workers, 1933.

Susman, Walter I. *Culture as History: The Transformation of American Society in the Twentieth Century*. New York: Pantheon, 1973.

6 *Wendy B. Sharer*

Disintegrating Bodies of Knowledge
Historical Material and Revisionary Histories of Rhetoric

The new historians must realize that the desire for historical truth is
never disinterested. They must acknowledge that they themselves are
involved in a rhetorical enterprise, relying on the rules of a specific
rhetoric inscribed with a particular ideology—a version of what
exists, what is good, and what is possible.
> James Berlin, "Revisionary History: The Dialectical Method"

Moreover, the act of writing history on the part of the historian is one
of power. It allows him/her to select materials to include in history as
well as those to exclude.
> Carole Blair, "Refiguring Systems of Rhetoric"

History-writing inevitably involves culturally influenced processes of selection
and rejection on the part of the writer, whether or not she is consciously aware
of her involvement in those processes and the power inherent in her decision to
write a historical account. Those who would revise or, in Carole Blair's term,
refigure histories of rhetoric ought implicitly or explicitly to acknowledge this
power, and they ought to reveal the narrative choices of previous historians by
naming the omissions and filling the gaps of existing historical accounts. The
power to identify what is missing from existing chronicles of rhetoric, however,
does not reside only with the writers of such histories; it also depends on powerful evaluative practices that are occurring beyond traditional boundaries of
scholarship. Decisions about historical relevance within the field of rhetoric
and composition are predicated on prior determinations of what is historically
relevant source material. To appropriate James Berlin's terms, historical versions of "what is good" depend on "what exists," or specifically what *materially* exists as sources for histories, and on "what is possible" for revisionist historians of rhetoric to do with what exists. Writing a historical account is, as
Blair explains, "an act of power"; nevertheless, this act of power derives from
previous acts of power that configure the physical and material conditions of
historical research.

I recall first realizing the importance of these previous acts of power in the
course of my own research. An employee at the circulation desk of a major re-

search library brought out a dozen or so dilapidated handbooks and club histories published by women's organizations in the 1930s, which I had requested from the library's remote storage facility. As she brought the rubber-banded, yellowed texts over to the counter, she seemed shocked by the materials I planned to examine. "Requests for materials from the annex—so *many*?! Sorry about the rubber bands; we don't send these to the bindery," she apologized as one of the many bands snapped and the cover and first few pages of a club-woman's handbook fell to the floor. If not these crumbling texts, then what does go to the bindery?

Questions about the material availability of resources for revisionist histories cannot, unfortunately, end with ponderings about the repair of deteriorating texts. Researchers must also consider how materials come to be in collections in the first place. What is selected for inclusion in collections reflects and often perpetuates existing notions of what is valuable. Sandra Spanier, who has conducted extensive archival research on the American writer Kay Boyle and who is editing Boyle's collected letters, points out that locating much of that correspondence required a good deal of travel because Boyle sold many of the letters she received to dealers and archives. Because she corresponded with well-known writers, Boyle, whose own prolific writing rarely yielded her more than a precarious income, was at least able to profit by selling their letters (Spanier). But what has become of letters and other documents composed by those not quite so famous? Many such materials are of course overlooked, discarded, or maintained precariously in private residences. When my eighty-seven-year-old grandmother, Naomi Steward, died recently, I obtained boxes of records pertaining to her tenure as president of the Bethlehem, Pennsylvania, Y-Dames (a women's club operating through the YWCA). Had I not asked my mother to look for these records as she and others prepared my grandmother's home for sale, I doubt that they would have survived. Anne Ruggles Gere relates similar tales of women who maintained club records in their homes. These records, according to Gere, are often kept in attic firetraps where, like the squirrel-mutilated records of the Cleveland Questers Study Club that I recently examined, they are prey to the appetites of insects and rodents. Scholars' awareness of the existence of such records depends on word of mouth, and the security of placing these materials in archives comes only when acquaintances or relatives of the record-holders donate them. Collecting facilities cannot regularly offer financial incentives for potential donors, nor can they promise to catalog and care for the material traces of lesser-known individuals and groups.

Even if material has been selected for preservation, material acts of power still shape the body of evidence available to historians. Traditional cataloging and indexing practices, for example, can obscure potentially valuable materials. When Gere was doing research for her recent comprehensive study of women's clubs in the late nineteenth and early twentieth centuries, she often found locating materials difficult because "women's clubs don't fall neatly into a category, so sometimes papers were under individual women's names (or their husband's names) and sometimes under a club name" (Gere, correspondence). Even what many archival researchers identify as the joys and successes of archival research—the unexpected finds and unexplored material—actually reflect the difficulty of locating materials. Cheryl Glenn has explained how, after searching through the drawers of the autograph file in a university archive, she discovered a letter written by Princess Elizabeth in a tissue-paper-filled box with a pink ribbon still fastened around it, as if it had not been opened since before the library acquired it early in this century. How many other works by individual women and groups of women remain obscured by organizing practices that group historical materials by date or by individual (an individual who is often male)?

Preservation relies on identification, and for the archival or library researcher, the ability to identify sources that merit further study originates in finding aids and indices; yet for materials to be included in such finding aides, they must first be deemed important. The process of locating and valuing disparate types of historical materials demands much of revisionist history-writers. As Carole Blair discusses in this volume, rhetorical practices such as public commemorative art confound traditional notions of rhetorical texts. Even certain textual materials within academic institutions have escaped consideration as rhetorical practices. In the preface to his recent anthology charting the development of composition in the late nineteenth and early twentieth centuries, John Brereton comments on the disparity of conditions among archival collections of composition course materials: "University archives have large quantities of student essays, course syllabi, lecture notes, and teaching materials. . . . Untold numbers of student papers sit in American college and university archives. These repositories vary widely from superb facilities . . . to a dreary basement . . . to a back room full of uncataloged boxes" (xv). Perhaps with further work like Brereton's, some of these previously unexamined and uncatalogued materials in dreary basements will be organized, indexed, and stored in climate-controlled rooms for future research.

The theoretical motives behind revising histories merit the extensive discussion they now receive; yet, as the chapters in this volume by Susan Wells and Christine De Vinne demonstrate vividly, it is also important to consider the presence and accessibility of historical materials from which revisionist histories can be constructed. Historians of rhetoric should be aware of threats to archival and library resources because these sources hold potential for future revisionary histories of rhetoric. Concern about versions of the past means that revisionist historians have an obligation to seek out and advocate the preservation of material traces of the past when those traces are threatened by disintegration and discard. I do not mean to suggest that, through such preservation, historians can establish a definitive collection of historical versions, but I believe that rich, beneficial alternatives to the canonical rhetorical traditions are at great risk.

Reconsidering Materials of the Past: The Historiographic Context

During the 1990s, historians of rhetoric have moved away from grand narratives that rely on the Great Men of the rhetorical canon. Instead of sweeping stories of a sturdy past, many scholars instead offer more localized, contextualized accounts of rhetoric and rhetorical practice. Rather than establishing and filling broad historical categories, Sharon Crowley explains, rhetoricians need a "constructionist historiography" that "prefers difference to identity; it reads the particulars of history rather than its general sweeps; and it situates historical events in cultural constructs that may seem exotic and/or foreign to today's readers" (16). Expressing similar desires for historical contextualizing, several feminist scholars criticize the rhetorical tradition because it has focused on a Cartesian model of the rhetor. Barbara Biesecker attributes the difficulty of feminist rewritings of the history of rhetoric to the powerful influence of individualism and the paradigm of individual achievement in academia. This elevation of the individual use of language privileges an autonomous author-creator and divorces rhetorical practices from social contexts. Such models of achievement also impede feminist attempts to revise the history of rhetoric. As Biesecker explains:

Already entailed in the valorization of the individual is a mechanics of exclusion that fences out a vast array of collective rhetorical practices to which there belongs no proper name. The exaltation of individual rhetorical action is secured by way of the devaluing of collective rhetorical practices which, one cannot fail to note, have been the most common form of women's intervention in the public sphere. (144)

Revising histories and building alternative narratives bear on the present. The ability to identify and describe alternative practices, Berlin has suggested, can provide direction for current subversion: "Our search for alterity, for rhetorics other than the familiar, can reveal to us alternative possibilities in conceiving discursive practices and their power formations" (118). Similarly, Patricia Bizzell has argued that excluded areas and practices ought to serve as the historical bases on which "to frame arguments redefining the whole notion of rhetoric in order to include . . . work by women" (51). Opportunities for feminist research in the history of rhetoric thus originate in "places not previously studied" that contain evidence of practices "that would not have been traditionally considered as rhetoric" (51). However, researchers cannot locate such places if material traces of them no longer exist. The precarious material existence of sources through which to reconsider the rhetorical tradition now poses a more immediate threat to our abilities to rewrite histories of rhetoric than do the institutional attitudes criticized by Biesecker, Bizzell, and other feminist historians.

As a participant in a 1997 forum on the politics of historiography, Linda Ferreira-Buckley stressed the importance of archival work. She argued that in their enthusiasm for theorizing the writing of history, historians of rhetoric have come to neglect primary materials: "Ten years ago our histories were undertheorized; today I fear they are under-researched" ("Octolog" 28). Using archives and other primary sources, however, is only part of the problem for our future research. The historian must also examine the practices that determine the active inclusion of certain materials in archives and library collections, and the exclusion of other materials. Are there critical sources neglected in remote storage facilities, or on rarely visited library shelves, or even beyond the academy in private attics? In addition to examining the opportunities for archival research and its potential benefits for future histories of rhetoric, researchers should consider both the materiality of the objects from which we might derive "new" knowledge, and the physical construction of collections containing these bodies of knowledge. We cannot afford to ignore the various material processes—acquisition, appraisal, collection management, description, indexing, preservation, oxidation, and deaccession—that affect the corpus of historical records on which we may be able to construct diverse and subversive narratives to challenge previous, exclusionary historical accounts of rhetoric.

The Preservation Challenge:
Disintegration and Discard of Historical Material

As university enrollment and the publication of new materials increased dramatically just after World War II, research collections in scholarly libraries also grew exponentially. With ample budgets during the late 1960s, many libraries expanded in an effort to house the increasing resource material. But despite providing space for 163 million additional volumes, the "library building boom from 1967–1974" did not produce facilities adequate to house the nearly 166 million new volumes that appeared during the same period (Paquette 4). Not only are published volumes overflowing library facilities, so are archival records; and there are inadequate resources to organize, describe, index, and preserve those records as well. The increase in information has placed an immense burden on the space and time of libraries and their staffs, necessitating the reduction of archival materials and other collections.

Beyond their space problems, libraries face what the Harvard University Library Task Group calls "The Preservation Challenge" (10). The sheer number of books is only one factor complicating the maintenance of items in research collections. The age and rapid deterioration of many older sources mean that there is not enough time to preserve all useful sources before they disintegrate beyond repair. Decisions must be made about which sources to preserve, which to discard, and which to relegate to what librarian Ross Atkinson calls "planned deterioration" (350)—or what I call, in less euphemistic terms, "accepted loss." Particularly endangered are materials from the middle of the nineteenth century, but recuperation of twentieth-century material is equally important because these records, "especially after the Second World War, are being lost in the gigantic mass of contemporary documents and in the elusive maze of modern information technology" (Cox 2). These twentieth-century materials are past or near the end of their estimated fifty-year shelf life (Matthews 230).

How extensive is the problem facing libraries and the researchers who depend on those libraries? According to a 1991 report by the Harvard University Library Task Group, "It is estimated that the number of [rapidly deteriorating] books in the nation's libraries is more than 80 million." Also at risk are "2.5 billion pages in archives [as well as] . . . photographs, prints, slides, tapes, etc., etc." (10–11). As early as the 1970s, the Library of Congress estimated that approximately six million volumes—about 40 percent of its collections—were too brittle to be used by patrons (Matthews 230). According to Mirjam Foot, director of collections and preservation at the British Library, preservation problems challenge libraries worldwide. At a recent forum at the University of Texas, Foot reported that as early as 1975, "of the six million printed books [in the British Library's London Humanities Collection] about 750,000 needed conservation work or rebinding; of the 80,000 manuscripts, 14,000 needed conservation, and 80,000 volumes of the total of 440,000 Oriental manuscripts and printed books also needed rebinding and/or repair" ("Part One" 3).

The preservation challenge also confronts acquisitions specialists who in part determine the fate of the uncountable historical records and documents now outside libraries or repository facilities. Even if the owners of these records recognize their potential worth to researchers, they may have a difficult time getting a library or repository to accept them, because space and financial constraints prevent the collecting facility from caring for additional records. Even if a gift is accepted, its records and documents may remain uncataloged and thus unexplored.

Specialists in rhetoric who wish to help librarians and archivists respond to the preservation challenge need to consider several questions. First, how do archivists and librarians deal with such enormous amounts of threatened material? In response to overcrowding in their stacks, they have developed management strategies to determine which records and volumes should be available for future use, and which should be removed from the stacks and either placed in remote storage facilities or eliminated completely. Once a librarian or archivist has decided to preserve an item, she has to select a means of long-term preservation—microfilm, microfiche, digitization, or conservation (i.e., repair); published materials can be replaced with a new copy if still in print, or with a better-conditioned copy if not. These options entail substantial expenditure. With this in mind, the National Endowment for the Humanities in the late 1980s designed a program to save the texts of 3.3 million titles, approximately one-third of the titles held in American libraries. Even if funding for this nationwide preservation effort continues—a prospect at best uncertain—more money will be needed to preserve additional resources that scholars and researchers consider valuable. As the Task Group explains, "Funding is needed from private sources and from the university's resources as well as from the federal government" (46). In even the best scenario, materials must be prioritized for preservation, and many will be lost.

Second, how do archivists and librarians determine priorities in archival acquisition and collection preservation? Answers to this question do not point to an objective decision-making process but to a hierarchy of social and cultural values. Exploring the reasons for the accepted deterioration and deaccession of certain library and archival items, Brien Brothman reminds us that materials become waste only when we judge them to be waste: "Social communities create and destroy value. Rubbish does not have an objective, autonomous existence. Dirt and rubbish are products of socially determined exclusion, which provide clues about social values. Furthermore, they, as much as what we save, mirror a hierarchy of categories of social value" (81). As the Harvard Task Group admits, some materials are saved because of the political power of their advocates: "One body of material might be filmed because an individual librarian is a successful fund raiser or because a scholar has a particular passion for a subject. . . . Some material will be filmed because it is at strong institutions; other records will be lost because they are in small or moribund ones" (11). In other words, the political savvy of a given faculty or staff member and the prestige or financial standing of a repository can determine which materials exist to inform future histories.

Appraisal of a source's worth and its selection for preservation also mirror social and cultural values, because both rely on information about frequency of circulation and popularity among users. Use by patrons or researchers is of utmost importance in determining both what kinds of records an archival facility will purchase or accept and which titles a library will retain. Librarians and collection staff emphasize the centrality of circulation records in determining what to preserve: "The most reliable predictor of later use is past use" (Willard 25). If records indicate that certain archival collections receive more attention than others, the institution will fund the acquisition and preservation of similar and related materials. If circulation records indicate a volume is not used, it becomes a likely candidate for remote storage (Paquette 10). The move to storage may perpetuate the lack of use: a stored item is no longer an obvious or integral part of a library's active collection. As materials move farther from view and from regular consultation, they become prime candidates for "planned deterioration." They are also particularly susceptible to deterioration, because they tend to be older materials with less obvious relevance for researchers, and because they are more likely to escape the notice of library preservation staff. Furthermore, these volumes already suffer from brittleness, oxidation of their acidic paper, and crumbling bindings barely held together by dried glue.

The types of use to which scholars put historical materials also determine what will remain available. In the academic library, for example, disciplinary attitudes toward older information influence which collections stay. Collections management specialists guide their decisions with queries like "How does a field refer to its older literature? Does it make only a perfunctory reference, or does it really draw upon the content of the precursors to advance its own case? Are earlier works evaluated for their own worth, or as representative phenomena?" (Harvard Task Group 41). These specialists also base decisions on their assessments of the "primariness" of the material. Primariness, the Harvard Task Group explains, refers to the "materials of social movements, political parties, the literature of non-elites, the tracts of fringe religious groups [and all other] sources for future study . . . —particularly those hitherto unused— that fuel new directions in scholarship" (38–39). Holdings are valued according to the research they may edify; the difficulty lies in identifying which source material contains this edifying potential.

Another important criterion for preservation is rarity or uniqueness. The numbers of copies owned by U.S. libraries determines, to some degree, which records and volumes will be preserved. In the case of published titles, specialists in collections management observe their "three Cs"—cooperation, communication, and collaboration—so that one or two copies of an endangered source will be preserved. Although archival records are not duplicated at different institutions, a similar axis of cooperation and collaboration is central to archival deaccession. Because not all archival records can possibly be saved, archivists and preservation specialists attempt to preserve a variety of records while still maintaining manageable quantities of material. The disposal of records or volumes, Gerald Ham writes, "should take place in an interinstitutional context to assure that archivists do not all throw out the same kinds of collections" (139).

The Access Challenge: Locating Materials for Histories

In addition to encountering disintegration and discard, the revisionist historian looking for alternative historical records quickly comes up against a rather restrictive and Foucauldian "order of things" within archival collections. The principles by which archival sources are collected and organized can pose challenges for the historian, particularly if she hopes to find resources about previously (or currently) marginalized groups. The gathering of archival materials into collections, Ham suggests, "helps to establish their *bona fides* as legitimate collections" (quoted in Brothman 82). The legitimating gestures of current archival practice also involve value-organizing practices. Archivists group records according to *provenance* and *original order*. Provenance suggests "that records should be kept according to the person, organization, office, or administrative entity that created them" (Dearstyne 129). Similarly, archivists organize records on the premise of "original order," which "holds that records should be kept in the order in which they were created or that was imposed on them by the person, organization, or institutions that created or assembled them" (Dearstyne 130). What impact do these principles have on researchers' investigations? Does organizing and describing archival collections in this way best reflect the needs of researchers, or might it obscure important interconnections among originators of records and across chronological order? Ordering material by such principles, Brothman explains, "simplifies reality. . . . [I]t produces a version among other possible versions of the information universe" (84). Thus, even before Berlin's "new historian" can produce her version of history, acts of power have created a version of the material traces of history.

Description and indexing practices also establish and perpetuate cultural and social values by allowing only certain materials to become visible to researchers, while obscuring others. Cataloging materials in databases and publicizing collections through periodicals and promotional fliers influence the scope of material available for revisionist histories. If materials are not indexed in a readily available database, or if the presence of valuable individual records is not reflected in collection descriptions, the materials obviously will have less influence on historical accounts. The cultural and social values informing collection description and indexing become even more apparent when one considers which material resources are widely known. Most scholars are probably familiar with the "major" research and archival collections related to their specialties, but what about materials that have not been publicized by collecting agencies? Here the financial foundation of historical research also becomes apparent. What about facilities that do not have the resources to publicize their holdings? How can they establish resources if no one knows about the holdings, and hence no one uses them? Writing and distributing descriptions of collections, then, actually creates value in the materials. Before a historian can produce "a version of what exists, what is good, and what is possible," numerous others have already constructed versions as they identify, organize, describe, and publicize primary materials.

Responding to Preservation and Access Challenges:
The Involvement Imperative

Given the extent of the preservation challenge, the Harvard Task Group urges the users of resources not to remain passive:

Something other than enhancement, expansion, and additional funding is required. A fully conscious intentionality and clear focus on long-range goals, a greater sophistication about the types of material and their varying uses, a lack of dogmatism, a willingness to explore all approaches, a readiness to face difficult choices . . . are also among the requirements of the preservation program of the 1990s. . . . It is crucial that faculty participate. (quoted in George 1)

Yet despite numerous calls for involvement and support, scholars still seem reluctant to participate in preservation decisions. Patricia Battin, president of the private, nonprofit Commission on Preservation and Access, attributes this reluctance to a lack of understanding among scholars about the extent of damage to historical sources:

Unless scholars happen upon a badly decayed volume in the ordinary course of research, they are unlikely to have given much thought to the physical condition of the collection and are likely to be unaware of its slow but steady march to oblivion. Even a direct encounter with crumbling pages is likely to be treated as an isolated, chance phenomenon, not an epidemic. (quoted in George 1)

An important move toward scholarly involvement began in 1994 when the Commission on Preservation and Access assembled committees of scholars to assess collection and archival materials in their respective disciplines. After surveying collection conditions, the committees explored strategies for further involvement on the part of researchers and scholars from across the academy. The Modern Language and Literature committee's work, however, illustrates the confusion and apathy about preservation and access issues in English departments. As part of their search for scholarly input, the committee published a request for suggestions about what should be preserved in the *MLA Newsletter*, which reaches about thirty thousand U.S. members. The survey depressingly resulted in "only a handful" of responses (George 8).

In spite of the lack of feedback, the committee came up with some guidelines, though they are problematically vague—more like general concerns rather than the specific instructions librarians and archivists need. For example, the committee recommends that "Ancillary materials must also be preserved. This principle is based on the assumption that it is impossible to be sure now what works will seem essential to research, teaching, and for reading in the future" (quoted in George 8). The call for this immense breadth of materials to be preserved is essentially a self-protecting move. Gerald George, the compiler of the report, suggests there is

> an understandable reluctance of scholars to make choices because of the unpredictability of research needs. Scholars are loath to say "this book will be more useful for future research than that one," because the history of their fields shows that writers and subjects that seem inconsequential to scholars in one era may become of great interest in the next. . . . Moreover, discovery and serendipity may lead to lines of inquiry unforeseen. (12)

The increasing interdisciplinarity of departments like English also makes it difficult to state definitive or truly helpful guidelines about what to retain. As the committee's report concludes, "Research and pedagogy in modern language and literature cannot take place without materials in history, popular culture, newspapers, magazines, graphic materials, and so on, materials that are not traditionally thought to be literature at all" (quoted in George 8). With these very general recommendations, how are preservation specialists, collection managers, or archivists to determine what to keep and what to discard? Before considering how scholars in composition and rhetoric might respond to this question, I want to emphasize the importance of scholarly inquiry into preservation issues by providing a detailed example of the kinds of materials that are currently at risk.

Texts of Women's Associations:
An Example of What May Be Lost, and Why

Several scholars, notably Anne Ruggles Gere, Karen J. Blair, and Anne Firor Scott, concentrate their historical work on the study of women's organizations during the nineteenth and early twentieth centuries. But what happened to these organizations after suffrage? Recent feminist historical scholarship has begun to challenge the historical assumption that the vote dramatically changed women's involvement in politics and public discourse. Kristi Andersen, for example, argues that women's organizations shifted their purposes after 1920 but remained central throughout the decade, particularly in determining the fate of "Progressive" legislation: "Many new women's associations, which arose or expanded to fill in the void left by the conclusion of suffrage work and the disappearance of the NAWSA [National American Woman Suffrage Association], worked hard to promote a variety of Progressive measures in Congress in the 1920s" (155). Through this extension of association and organization work, women continued and even expanded their collaborative practices of public discourse.

Other feminist historians have stressed the continuation of women's participation in organization-based politics after suffrage. As Nancy Cott explains,

"The Nineteenth Amendment is the most obvious benchmark in the history of women in politics in the United States, but it is a problematic one. . . . Concentrating on suffrage and the electoral arena means viewing women's politics [and, I would add, their participation in public discourse] through the conventional lens where male behavior sets the norm" (153). Traditionally, Cott writes, narratives of feminism and women's activism in America claim that "after the achievement of the vote, the large coalition movement among women disintegrated; now insiders rather than outsiders, women (ironically) lost influence within the political process" (154). Cott and several other feminist historians undermine these narratives of decline by positing a greater continuity in women's political activism and efficacy, particularly through women's continued involvement in voluntary associations.[1]

The rhetorical practices of these groups—including the General Federation of Women's Clubs, the National Women's Trade Union League, the Women's International League for Peace and Freedom, and many more—have been identified as the origin of lobbying and interest-group politics. Rather than selecting their own candidates, women's organizations applied pressure politics, rallying for specific bills and sending petitions, resolutions, and correspondence to governing bodies. As Cott explains, the nationwide activities of the YWCA, despite its original religious mission, exemplify the involvement of women's associations in civic betterment in the 1930s:

In 1926 the YWCA stopped requiring that members be Protestant Christians, and membership grew; by 1930 the organization boasted over 600,000 members. . . . [T]he YWCA industrial clubs educated and helped organize both black and white women workers in southern textile mills and brought them to testify before legislatures about industrial conditions. (163)

A brief sampling of the achievements of women's organizations after suffrage includes the founding of approximately 80 percent of public libraries in the country by 1942 (Milligan and Milligan 214); the establishment of scholarship funds for undergraduate and graduate study by women; the education of women voters on voting procedures and candidates' stances; the construction of community houses where working women and rural women could congregate for classes and activities; the passage of anti-lynching and food safety inspection laws in many states; and the development of low-cost housing and job training for women in many communities. Even into the conservative 1950s, women's organizations brought millions of American women of diverse religious, ethnic, and class backgrounds into public life and discourse. Figures in organization manuals and club guides published during the 1950s indicate that between twenty and thirty million American women participated in "at least 200,000 such clubs" (Avery and Nye 5).

Throughout the middle decades of the twentieth century, women's organizations also greatly influenced local politics. This demands greater, coordinated research, but a brief example from a 1951 pamphlet-length study of women's organizations (Johnson and Golding)—which I obtained from Penn State's remote storage facility—illustrates the coordinated efforts and the discursive practices such organizations employed to alter their communities.

In the early 1940s, twelve days after a train wreck claimed seventy-nine lives, various women's organizations in Nassau County, New York, established a collaborative forum to address the safety of local rail travel. Following extensive study of the causes and possible prevention of the crash, and after hearing testimony from relatives of the accident victims and from railroad experts, representatives from several hundred women's organizations drafted demands for specific corrective measures, including the installation of automatic safety devices and flashing stoplights on the rear of standing trains. Club members distributed these resolutions to government and railroad officials, who soon approved and implemented them (Johnson and Golding 4). The power of collaboration did not stop with this emergency meeting. The intergroup clearinghouse, calling itself the Woman's Forum of Nassau County, became a permanent and active feature in the community life of Long Island as it carried out the mission its members established with their constitution: "to unite the community for education, health, public affairs, peace, human relations, and democracy, . . . to conduct a year-round intergroup adult education program in order to develop informed opinion on vital problems, . . . to meet the needs of the sponsoring organizations and to coordinate their activities for their mutual benefit and for that of the community" (quoted in Johnson and Golding 12). The Forum's increasing numbers reflect its success: in 1944 it comprised thirty-three organizations; by the end of 1950, more than five hundred, with a collective membership exceeding eighty-five thousand women.

Other studies and actions of the Woman's Forum centered around a poor section of Freeport, New York, called Bennington Park. Forum women visited the area to study its deplorable housing, transportation, and sanitation. They then drafted letters criticizing the property-owners in the area for their neglect and for voting down legislation that would have made slum clearance possible. The Forum sent stories to local newspapers and presented their findings in a detailed report to leading citizens, including the mayor and the village board of trustees. The mayor responded by establishing a housing authority in the area and assigning a committee to oversee the construction of new low-rent housing in Bennington Park. This community action in Long Island mirrored the work of numerous other women's associations in other localities.[2]

Despite their achievements during the early and middle decades of the twentieth century, such women's organizations are in danger of being overlooked by scholars interested in the history of rhetoric, partly because historians have established the period from suffrage to the 1960s as a time of decline. This devaluation also results from the resistant rhetoric of "official," male-controlled public discourse at the time. Critiques of women's associations were prevalent in the popular press throughout the first half of the century. Particularly derogatory were popular comic representations of women's meetings in the pages of national publications like the *New Yorker*, which regularly depicted women's organizations discussing inconsequential issues like their "'favorite-bird' poll" (quoted in Peffer 94). The minimizing of the work done by women's organizations did not come only from men: women also wrote flippant narratives of club activities. In her 1942 study of women's clubs, Helen Hayes Peffer offers—alongside assertions that women's clubs were an important factor in American life at the time—a rather diminishing presentation of what women's clubs actually did. She reprints several cartoons (by a woman) from the *New Yorker*, and she details in condescending language the struggles she has witnessed among clubwomen. Peffer attributes these disagreements to "the dangerous stimulant of a public platform, which brings out the worst in some females" (99). Following the widely held cultural belief that women should be demure rather than hold strong opinions on public affairs, women involved with associations sometimes minimized the importance of their public discourse.

Further examination of the handbooks and public-relations documents of women's organizations from the 1930s, 1940s, and 1950s might provide valuable insights into how women in these organizations negotiated their roles in the face of an oppressive cultural climate. Study of records and publications might reveal how women's organizations worked both with and against local male-dominated political structures. How did these women respond to and adjust their rhetoric to the mostly male law-making bodies that were frequently their audiences? How did they temper their activism as a result of the sexist environment in which they operated (for example, through the rhetoric of "municipal housekeeping")? How did they both reinforce and counter popular stereotypes like those painfully illustrated in the *New Yorker* cartoons?

Preservation of association records and their further consideration with such questions in mind might help counter practices of "essentialist historians" who "naively write the narratives of historical figures so that their behavior accords with contemporary cultural constructions, eliding behavior or beliefs that do not" (Crowley 14–15). The desires to produce a heroic category of women rhetoricians to challenge the male-dominated tradition of rhetorical genius reflects what John Schilb calls "our unfortunate zeal for classification. . . . That is, we attempt to map a whole field of study by dividing it into neat, distinct parts, often assigning them varying degrees of worth" (129). While these female categories open up the playing field of rhetorical history, the practice of "rescuing" women rhetors from the past should not ignore women rhetors who were influenced by and participated within spheres of communication traditionally defined as male. Such critical, non-essentialist historical accounts will depend on the preservation of the records, handbooks, and other materials that present a positive, active picture of women's associations, as well as the popular presentations that minimize their activities.

Further damaging the preservation chances of the records and published accounts relating to women's organizations in the first half of the twentieth century is their often local focus. Understandably, national or international phenomena are easier to identify and perhaps more deserving of research attention, but a reluctance to study rigorously local practices with local impacts means missing a great deal of material with an immense cumulative impact. The accomplishments of these organizations rarely altered national policy radically, but the results of their practices in places like Nassau County merit extended attention. Focusing on local communities might reveal significant, effective alternative literacy practices at work in these organizations. Nevertheless, much of their potential to complement and problematize traditional histories remains unexplored.

Meeting minutes, handbooks, and resolutions or correspondence to local and national officials may also have been overlooked because the content appears practical and the structure is often standardized. As a result, they are frequently judged intellectually unworthy of preservation. This judgment, however, misses the larger sphere of meaning in which these documents operate and circulate. As James O'Toole has asked specialists in archival profession: "Are there cases in which records contain practical information, but in which the real significance is larger and more symbolic? . . . When is the act of record making more important than the record that is made?" (238). The symbolic activities of sharing reports, drafting resolutions and letters, keeping meeting minutes, writing charters and constitutions, and keeping detailed yearbooks may not provide us with "original" content, but the research significance of these literacy activities in their historically specific contexts might greatly increase once we explore their role as symbolic rhetorical acts of power.

Preservation and Access: What Can We Do?

What, then, can scholars in rhetorical studies do to help ensure the availability and accessibility of archival materials for future scholars? Most important, scholars in all fields need to take seriously Mirjam Foot's assertion, "Decisions on what to preserve are not the prerogative of librarians and conservation experts, they are equally the responsibility of scholars and users" ("Part Three" 6). Our first responsibility is to provide specific suggestions about what to acquire and what to preserve. The administrative structure of academic libraries requires such specifics: at many institutions "subject selectors," library staff members responsible for guiding acquisition decisions, "are assigned a sub-ject/discipline area(s) in which they select and maintain a particular collection" (Wilson and Edelman 195). Funding for acquisitions and maintenance is simi-larly distributed among discipline-based collections. Thus, selectors generally group collections and allocate funds along department lines. It is therefore par-ticularly urgent that researchers in rhetoric and composition voice their inter-ests, which may differ substantially from the interests of other English depart-ment members.

Furthermore, as the breadth of research interests in this volume demon-strates, studies in rhetoric incorporate materials from many disciplines. Hence, the materials scholars in rhetoric require for research do not fall neatly into discipline-bounded acquisition policies. As Paul Metz and Bela Foltin write, "Because the very basis of allocation is by subject or department, whole areas of knowledge which fall outside the scope of traditional disciplines are ig-nored. . . . An additional problem with subject or disciplinary approaches is that of defining the fields so that emerging or interdisciplinary areas are cov-ered" (34). Volumes held in the library but considered public or popular rather than academic also vanish under this paradigm of selection. The academic re-search library can restrict the purview of its users by omitting materials—like women's organizations' handbooks—that do not fit into a disciplinary cate-gory. More clearly articulating our diverse research interests, especially those that cross disciplines or extend outside the academy, may keep research mate-rials from being counted among the missing.

Concern about preservation of historical materials and access to them should not end with the academic library but should extend to local historical repositories, if we truly want to concentrate on the "particulars of history" or to write in a way "that situates historical events in cultural constructs" (Crow-ley 16). Local historical societies and municipal libraries often retain records detailing the activities of people and groups important in the history of the com-munity. The collecting policies of these smaller libraries and historical soci-eties, as Bruce Dearstyne notes, "are often vague and general. . . . [They] may collect almost any types of historical records from within their localities or re-gions" (31). Researchers might help to clarify what specific materials need to be preserved within these broad collections, particularly because smaller col-lection facilities and institutional archives make preservation decisions under greater duress than do larger, more profitable academic libraries. The Wiscon-sin State Historical Records Advisory Board laments the schism between the two types of collection facilities:

There is a stark contrast between the few major archival institutions—the "haves"—and the many minor ones—the "have nots." Not only do the "haves" hold most of the records, but they have most of the expertise and practically all of the staff. . . . In the scores of smaller repositories and institutional archives, record preservation functions are at best minimal and rudimentary; often they are nonexistent. (quoted in Dearstyne 51)

Any assistance from scholars and researchers would be greatly appreciated by the "have nots."

Scholars in rhetoric also need to contribute directly to the work of organizations like the Commission on Preservation and Access. Its Modern Language and Literature Committee included eight respected scholars from English departments across the country; however, it did not include a well-known scholar whose primary interest is in rhetoric.[3] This indicates the need for rhetoricians to get involved. We might begin by expanding our list of special-interest caucuses at conferences to include more discussion of library and archival preservation.[4] Through national committees, scholars might further assist libraries by coordinating primary materials findings and making suggestions for preservation and acquisition of archival materials. Librarians and archivists might be invited to participate regularly in our conferences and to contribute to our publications. Within individual institutions, faculty might also request workshops and demonstrations to familiarize themselves and their students with archival research and with finding aids. I am suggesting, fundamentally, that we expand our professional responsibilities into realms previously marked off as the territory of library and information science. The preservation challenge dictates that researchers in all fields become directly involved in the material selection and preservation of our research materials. We cannot afford to leave these choices and decisions to others, if only because those others simply do not have enough time or resources to perform the tasks we have expected of them.

To facilitate the location and subsequent use of materials, publishing practices might also change so that bibliographies and bibliographic essays receive more professional appreciation. Published, widely circulated bibliographies of once-forgotten materials relevant to rhetoric might alleviate some of the exclusion induced by traditional description and indexing procedures. For instance, in the area of women's organizations in the nineteenth and twentieth centuries, historian Karen J. Blair has produced an invaluable bibliography of more than six hundred published records; in addition to drawing attention to these previously obscured resources, it might serve as the basis for future bibliographic work designed to bring more important resources back into circulation. In many other areas of potential interest to scholars in rhetoric, however, no such historian and bibliographer has emerged. Even if scholars in other disciplines assume these bibliographic responsibilities, history-writers in our field cannot be sure that they will identify the materials that we might value; for example, instructions for forming groups and determining meeting procedures might prove quite useful to a researcher interested in rhetorical features of organizational activity. Bringing genre preferences to the attention of archivists and collections management specialists can displace assumptions about what constitutes valuable research material. Elaborating the forms and genres behind histories of rhetoric undermines restrictive assumptions like this one, expressed in a recent guide to preservation of historical records:

> Researchers usually seek information on a particular topic; the pertinence of the information is of greater concern than documentation on the creating entity. . . . Records that are concise and compact but that have much information to offer are likely to be better candidates for permanent preservation than bulky records with sketchy information. (Dearstyne 116–17)

People with research interests in rhetoric frequently contradict this claim because they focus not only on what is communicated, but also on ways of communicating. A document that has little informational content can contain much informational value in its structure, genre, and function.

Scholarly journals might also serve as bibliographic organs, providing space for articles about recent acquisitions at institutions. In addition to helping researchers, bibliographic work publicizes underused, undervalued, and potentially endangered records. We need to bear part of the burden of publicity, because funding and time constraints limit the publicity that repositories can provide for their materials. A recent study of archival practices in California, for example, revealed that "more than 80 percent [of archives] do not report new accessions to scholarly journals or other sources where they would be seen by researchers" (Dearstyne 53). Fortunately for my own area of interest, in 1994 May Lee Tom of the Schlesinger Library began compiling information about archival resources for the study of American women's organizations. The directory resulting from her survey, while somewhat sketchy in coverage (only eighty institutions responded) and in its individual entries (which list only the names of the organizations for which each responding archive maintains records, or from which they accept gifts), will probably lead to more extensive bibliographic work.

Like bibliographies of library collections, descriptions of holdings will be more helpful and specific if scholars in rhetoric share reviews and descriptions. The cataloging and descriptive principles of archival practice do not necessarily reflect our research interests, particularly those in previously marginalized groups. According to librarian Diane Beattie, "Archival information about these hidden or marginalized groups can often only be located in archival records created by others [outside the field of archival studies]. Because traditional archival descriptive practices are heavily biased towards describing the creators of records at the expense of describing their subject or content, records of these groups are not easily retrievable" (84–85). Compiling our own bibliographies of archival holdings would give researchers access to useful records and might keep relevant materials in the available body of knowledge.

We should also demonstrate clearly how scholars in our field use historical materials, and we should inform librarians of any significant changes in focus that the discipline undergoes. Louis Willard's conviction that "[t]he most reliable predictor of later use is past use" (25) should be disturbing because it can so easily reify a canon and perpetuate the disciplinary status quo. This rigidification of academic boundaries is ideological and, perhaps more important, physical: it materializes in the form of works preserved. Susan Jarratt's call to "resist the curricular impetus toward coherence" (205) thus has material consequences; it allows for an open-ended, diverse range of interests and research materials in the field. The increased use of noncanonical texts from the past may bring such texts back into circulation and hence to the attention of preservation specialists and archivists.

Furthermore, scholars can continue to look outside academic collections and other archival facilities to locate material traces of what Thomas Miller calls "community literacies" (*Formation* 7). Such research confronts the material gaps in academic libraries and other collecting facilities. What about texts and records not acquired by libraries or archives that, as a result, are not part of the currently recognizable or defined past? Perceiving and redrawing the boundaries of the histories of rhetoric involve recognizing and exploring material exclusions.

Convincing archivists or directors of acquisition to accept or seek out records they once excluded is no easy task. These professionals must carefully consider whether their budgets allow them to locate, acquire, and preserve more material. Thus researchers might consider involving themselves in acquisitions by locating records of "community literacies." I had the pleasure of locating such records recently, when I met a woman who had been active with the student YWCA at Penn State from the 1930s until the late 1980s. She was moving from her home to a small apartment, and had I and another graduate student not asked about her materials, she would have discarded several folders of records dating back to the 1930s. In such cases, provided we have room and can spare an airtight box, we might offer to take materials ourselves. I am not suggesting that we all start extensive home archives without outside support; this would not be responsible. But it is responsible to preserve such materials temporarily until a permanent collection can care for them.

Finally, methods of research—both those used and those taught—might be altered to accommodate better the material conditions of historical sources. Graduate programs in composition and rhetoric should encourage a variety of research interests and should include more training in archival and library research. Students of rhetoric and composition should be encouraged to read texts

outside the traditional, individual-centered canon, including samples of rhetorical practice from particular, historically located communities; the chapters by
Wells and De Vinne in this book offer instructive examples of the benefits.
Placing such examples in anthologies and offering historically specific examples of public discourse in graduate seminars or survey courses might further direct attention to disappearing resources. Beyond shifting attention toward these resources, we should also expand training in how to find and use
them. Such training is important not only for graduate students, but for everyone interested in the history of rhetoric and composition. As Miller argues, "If
historical scholarship is to contribute to our interest in the social construction
of discourse, we need to explore new ways of making historically oriented
courses relevant to the study of rhetoric and composition. . . . How can composition specialists study writing as a social process if they do not know how
to research the history of social practices?" ("Teaching the Histories" 71). If
scholars are not aware of potentials for research in older library holdings, our
histories, as Ferreira-Buckley fears, may go under-researched.

For scholars of classical rhetoric, recuperation of texts is no longer possible.
Takis Poulakos explains that revisionist historians of classical rhetoric can construct alternative histories only by rereading a limited number of extant items:
"What makes recuperation problematic in this case is not theory but history—
especially the kind of history that was either never recorded at all or was once
part of a record now irretrievably lost" (59). Historians writing revisionist accounts in the absence of textual bodies from the past face the task of rereading
what has been preserved in order to locate silences within those texts. To avoid
similar or even worse material limitations, historians of all the ages of rhetoric
must become involved in material preservation. Certainly there will always be
silences. Nevertheless, revisionist historians can more effectively undermine
dominant discourses and expose silencing moves if they preserve ample material documentation of the existence and activity of supposedly silenced groups.
With these implications in mind, we should heed the warnings of conferees at
a recent international symposium sponsored by the Commission on Preservation and Access: "At minimum, scholars must take responsibility for developing a personal, informed interest in preservation and for carrying the message
of preservation into the chambers of power" (Commission on Preservation and
Access 8).

Notes

1. In addition to clubs and organizations interested in social reform, numerous
women's groups were less concerned with the welfare of others than with their own entertainment or hobbies. I do not mean to suggest that women's associations universally
embraced ideals of community involvement and civic philanthropy, but these motives
did inform a great deal of their public discourse both before and after suffrage.

2. Several articles and book-length historical studies of the achievements of various organizations have been published recently. A brief sample includes the works cited by Cott, Deutsch, Foster, Schackel, Scott, Ware, and Watts.

3. Committee members were Emory Elliot of the University of California, Riverside; Henry Louis Gates, then at Duke University; Elaine Marks of the University of Wisconsin–Madison; J. Hillis Miller of the University of California, Irvine; W. J. T. Mitchell of the University of Chicago; Rainer Nagele of Johns Hopkins; Annabel Patterson of Duke; and Catherine R. Stimpson of Rutgers.

4. The 1999 Conference on College Composition and Communication (CCCC) meeting about the development of a National Archive of Composition and Rhetoric is a welcome step in this direction.

Works Cited

Andersen, Kristi. *After Suffrage: Women in Partisan and Electoral Politics before the New Deal.* Chicago: University of Chicago Press, 1996.

Atkinson, Ross. "Selection for Preservation: A Materialistic Approach." *Library Resources and Technical Services* 30 (October/December 1986): 341–53.

Avery, Helen, and Frank Nye. *The Clubwoman's Book.* New York: Henry Holt, 1954.

Beattie, Diane. "Retrieving the Irretrievable: Providing Access to 'Hidden Groups' in Archives." *Reference Librarian* 56 (1997): 83–94.

Berlin, James. "Revisionary Histories of Rhetoric: Politics, Power, and Plurality." In *Writing Histories of Rhetoric,* edited by Victor Vitanza, 112–27. Carbondale: Southern Illinois University Press, 1994.

Berlin, James. "Revisionary History: The Dialectical Method." In *Rethinking the History of Rhetoric,* edited by Takis Poulakos, 135–51. Boulder: Westview Press, 1993.

Biesecker, Barbara. "Coming to Terms with Recent Attempts to Write Women into the History of Rhetoric." *Philosophy and Rhetoric* 12 (1992): 140–61.

Bizzell, Patricia. "Opportunities for Feminist Research in the History of Rhetoric." *Rhetoric Review* 11 (Fall 1992): 50–58.

Blair, Carole. "Refiguring Systems of Rhetoric." *Pre/Text* 12 (1991): 180–89.

Blair, Karen J. *The History of American Women's Voluntary Organizations, 1810–1960: A Guide to Sources.* Boston: G. K. Hall, 1989.

Brereton, John C. Preface. In *The Origins of Composition Studies in the American College, 1875–1925,* edited by John C. Brereton. Pittsburgh: University of Pittsburgh Press, 1996.

Brothman, Brien. "Orders of Value: Probing the Theoretical Terms of Archival Practice." *Archivaria* 32 (Summer 1991): 78–99.

Commission on Preservation and Access. *Preserving the Intellectual Heritage: Report of the Belagio Conference.* Belagio, Italy, 7–10 June 1993. Washington, D.C.: Commission on Preservation and Access, 1993.

Cott, Nancy F. "Across the Great Divide: Women in Politics before and after 1920." In *Women, Politics, and Change,* edited by Louise A. Tilly and Patricia Gurin, 153–76. New York: Russell Sage Foundation, 1990.

Cox, Richard. *American Archival Analysis: The Recent Development of the Archival Profession in the United States.* Metuchen, N.J.: Scarecrow Press, 1990.

Crowley, Sharon. "Let Me Get This Straight." In *Writing Histories of Rhetoric*, edited by Victor Vitanza, 128–38. Carbondale: Southern Illinois University Press, 1994.

Dearstyne, Bruce W. *The Archival Enterprise: Modern Archival Principles, Practices, and Management Techniques*. Chicago: American Library Association, 1993.

Deutsch, Sarah. "Learning to Talk More Like a Man: Boston Women's Class-Bridging Organizations, 1870–1940." *American Historical Review* 97 (1992): 379–404.

Foot, Mirjam. "Preservation Policy, Dilemmas, Needs: A British Library Perspective, Part One." *Conservation Administration News* 58/59 (July/October 1994): 1–6.

Foot, Mirjam. "Preservation Policy, Dilemmas, Needs: A British Library Perspective, Part Three." *Conservation Administration News* 61 (April 1995): 5–8.

Foster, Carrie A. *The Women and the Warriors: The US Section of the Women's International League for Peace and Freedom, 1915–1946*. Syracuse: Syracuse University Press, 1995.

George, Gerald. "Difficult Choices: How Can Scholars Help Save Endangered Research Resources? A Report to the Commission on Preservation and Access." Washington, D.C.: Commission on Preservation and Access, 1995.

Gere, Anne Ruggles. Electronic mail correspondence. 2 October 1997.

Gere, Anne Ruggles. *Intimate Practices: Literacy and Cultural Work in US Women's Clubs, 1880–1920*. Champaign: University of Illinois Press, 1997.

Gere, Anne Ruggles. *Writing Groups: History, Theory and Implications*. Carbondale: Southern Illinois University Press, 1987.

Glenn, Cheryl. Personal interview. 16 October 1997.

Ham, Gerald. "Archival Choices: Managing the Historical Record in an Age of Abundance." In *Archival Choices*, edited by Nancy E. Peace, 133–47. Lexington, Mass.: Lexington Books, 1984.

Jarratt, Susan. "Speaking to the Past: Feminist Historiography in Rhetoric." *Pre/Text* 11 (1990): 190–209.

Johnson, Dallas, and Elizabeth Bass Golding. *Don't Underestimate Woman Power: A Blueprint for Group Interaction*. Public Affairs Pamphlet no. 171. New York: Public Affairs Committee, 1951.

Matthews, Graham. "Surveying Collections: The Importance of Condition Assessment for Preservation Management." *Journal of Librarianship and Information Science* 27 (1995): 227–35.

Metz, Paul, and Bela Foltin, Jr. "A Social History of Madness—or, Who's Buying This Round? Anticipating and Avoiding Gaps in Collection Development." *College and Research Libraries* 51 (1990): 33–39.

Miller, Thomas. *The Formation of College English: Rhetoric and Belles Lettres in the British Cultural Provinces*. Pittsburgh: University of Pittsburgh Press, 1997.

Miller, Thomas. "Teaching the Histories of Rhetoric as Social Praxis." *Rhetoric Review* 12 (1993): 70–82.

Milligan, Lucy R., and Harold V. Milligan. *The Clubmember's Handbook*. New York: New Home Library, 1942.

Monro, Kate M., and Isabel S. Monro. *The Clubwoman's Manual*. New York: Macmillan, 1957.

"Octolog II: The (Continuing) Politics of Historiography." *Rhetoric Review* 16 (1997): 22–44.

O'Toole, James M. "The Symbolic Significance of Archives." *American Archivist* 56 (1993): 234–55.

Paquette, Judith. "What Goes to the Storage Facility: Options and Consequences." In *The Great Divide: Challenges in Remote Storage*, edited by James A. Kennedy and Gloria Stockton, 3–16. Chicago: American Library Association, 1991.

Peffer, Helen Hayes. *Madam Chairman, Members, and Guests*. New York: Macmillan, 1942.

Poulakos, Takis. "Human Agency in the History of Rhetoric: Gorgias's Encomium of Helen." In *Writing Histories of Rhetoric*, edited by Victor Vitanza, 59–80. Carbondale: Southern Illinois University Press, 1994.

Report of the Harvard University Library Task Group. *Harvard Library Bulletin* 2.2 (1991).

Schackel, Sandra. *Social Housekeepers: Women Shaping Public Policy in New Mexico 1920–1940*. Albuquerque: University of New Mexico Press, 1992.

Schilb, John. "Future Historiographies of Rhetoric and the Present Age of Anxiety." In *Writing Histories of Rhetoric*, edited by Victor Vitanza, 128–38. Carbondale: Southern Illinois University Press, 1994.

Scott, Anne Firor. *Natural Allies*. Chicago: University of Chicago Press, 1991.

Spanier, Sandra Whipple. Personal interview. 16 October 1997.

Tom, May Lee. *Directory of Repositories Collecting Manuscripts of Women's Organizations*. Cambridge, Mass.: Schlesinger Library, 1994.

Ware, Susan. *Beyond Suffrage: Women in the New Deal*. Cambridge, Mass.: Harvard University Press, 1981.

Ware, Susan. *Holding Their Own: American Women in the 1930s*. Boston: Twayne, 1992.

Watts, Margit Misangyi. *High Tea at Halekuni: Feminist Theory and American Clubwomen*. New York: Carlson Publishing, 1993.

Willard, Louis Charles. "Brittle Books: What Order of Preservation?" *Microform Review* 20 (1991): 24–26.

Wilson, Myoung Chung, and Hendrik Edelman. "Collection Development in an Interdisciplinary Context." *Journal of Academic Librarianship* 2 (1996): 194–200.

7 *Peter Mortensen*

Figuring Illiteracy
Rustic Bodies and Unlettered Minds in Rural America

[handwritten: IDEOLOGY?
Social Science VIEW?
HISTORY?]

[handwritten: 'disabled' classification]

Well over five million adult illiterates were enumerated in the federal census of 1910. The majority of them were white and living in rural areas. In its official report on this finding, the U.S. Bureau of Education conjured a terrible vision:

> In double line of march, at intervals of 3 feet, these 5,516,163 illiterate persons would extend over a distance of 1,567 miles—more than twice the distance from Washington City to Jacksonville, Fla. . . . A mighty army is this, with their banners of blackness and darkness inscribed with the legends of illiteracy, ignorance, weakness, helplessness, and hopelessness—too large for the safety of our democratic institutions, for the highest good of society, and for the greatest degree of material prosperity. (7)

Thus embodied, illiteracy was imagined to have enough mass and momentum to doom American prospects in the new century. What, then, must be done? "To wait for a generation of illiterate men, women, and children to die is a slow *[handwritten: wow!]* and painful process," the writer lamented. Therefore, the Bureau proposed a more timely solution: "Teach these grown-ups, in schools organized especially for them, to read and write, and possibly something more" (28). In this way, once-undisciplined bodies could be brought under the civilizing influence of freshly literate minds. Not a new idea, to be sure, but popular and powerful—then and now.

But what if the illiterate body could not be so influenced? What if it had such minimal intellectual capacity that literacy could not take hold? This was precisely the fear behind a new vision of illiteracy that emerged early in the twentieth century: one that figured the inability to read and write as a symptom of creeping racial degeneration. This relationship between illiteracy (as well as alcoholism, pauperism, and illegitimacy) and degeneracy was unsurprising to the white social scientists who discerned it in the African American and European immigrant communities they studied at the turn of the century. They were alarmed, however, by their discovery of degeneration in white native-born rural populations, particularly because the moral and economic boundaries separating city from country were growing steadily more porous.

The scenarios imagined in these observations stake out the major positions taken on adult illiteracy in North America in the twentieth century. Either illiteracy is a transient deficit that temporarily bars one from independent participation in building culture and economy, or it is a permanent disability that necessitates an unending reliance on the fruits of others' cultural and economic labors. If temporary, adult illiteracy is remediable, usually with the help of volunteers; if permanent, the underlying problems that manifest illiteracy must be contained by professionals whose expertise empowers them to control bodies deemed defective. My aim in this chapter is to examine these competing figurations of adult illiteracy as they appeared in popular novels, scholarly treatises, government reports, and magazine articles between 1880 and 1920. I argue that each figuration was rooted in a distinct strand of evolutionary science: to believe that illiteracy was remediable implied that racial degeneration had environmental causes that could be ameliorated; to believe in the permanence of adult illiteracy implied that racial degeneration was an inherent, irreversible process that operated within the confines of the body. Yet despite diverging opinions on the origins and consequences of adult illiteracy, there was consensus on one thing—its location. Illiteracy was held to be endemic to rural life, and its persistence there at the turn of the century was thought to be hampering the agricultural modernization needed to support the rising demands of city dwellers. This insistence on situating the unlettered in rustic bodies, I contend, continues even today to influence our ways of knowing and responding to adult illiteracy. It is the rhetorical force behind this influence that I examine in this chapter.[1]

The Revolt from the Village

In popular literature, "the revolt from the village," as *Nation* critic Carl Van Doren termed it (407), began with Edgar Watson Howe's *The Story of a Country Town* (1883); it was complete four decades later with the arrival of Sinclair Lewis's *Main Street* (1920).[2] Howe's story cut forcefully against the grain of local-color fiction that featured genteel, sentimental portraits of rural life. Where the local colorists found refuge from the immorality of urban capital, Howe found unbearable oppression of (and by) unlettered minds. Says his narrator, the editor of a country weekly:

Civilized morality of literacy
ONG

The only remarkable thing I ever did in my life—I may as well mention it here, and be
rid of it—was to learn to read letters when I was five years old, and as the ability to read
even print was by no means a common accomplishment in Fairview, this circumstance
gave me great notoriety. I no doubt learned to read from curiosity as to what the books
and papers scattered about were for, as no one took the pains to teach me, for I remember that they were all greatly surprised when I began to spell words, and pronounce
them, and I am certain I was never encouraged in it. (12)

In Howe's day the link between morality and literacy was commonplace in the
American imagination. Since colonial times literacy had been prerequisite to
Christian piety; in the new republic, it was essential to secular faith in democratic freedom. Howe believed that if Gilded Age corruption among the citified
masses suggested that literate morality endured only in the countryside, it was
his responsibility to speak from experience and report otherwise.[3]

Because this pairing of literacy and morality would have been cherished by
Howe's nineteenth-century readers—as it is by many today—Fairview's illiteracy is a plausible motivation for the shabby behavior of its inhabitants. Lest
readers doubt the truth of Howe's account, he repeats it in his 1929 autobiography, this time casting himself as the young man who astonished antebellum
Fairview, Missouri, with his literate abilities (*Plain People* 17–18). Yet however cramped the moral life of rural Missouri was in Howe's 1850s youth, illiteracy was hardly more prevalent there than it was elsewhere in the nation before the turn of the century.[4]

It may well have been unusual for a five-year-old country boy to read and
write in 1850, but the likelihood of Howe's peers growing up completely illiterate was slim: nearly three-quarters of Missourians aged five to fourteen attended school in 1860, and in that year more than 85 percent of adults (twenty
and older) reported that they could read and write.[5] Moreover, in the twenty
years between Howe's living in Fairview and his reconstructing it fictionally,
the adult illiteracy rate in Missouri dropped dramatically to a little more than
9 percent, just slightly above the national average. The schooling of Howe's
generation and the mortality of his elders had profoundly changed the rural
landscape he wrote about in *Country Town*. But the realism Howe sought—
and that his mentors William Dean Howells and Mark Twain applauded—
demanded an unreal but useful representation of illiteracy to signify the impov-
erishment of country life (see Simpson).

Howe did not invent this useful representation. He inherited it from generations of Northern writers who invoked illiteracy to explain Southern resistance to abolition before the Civil War and opposition to Reconstruction thereafter. After the 1840 federal census, it was possible to quantify the degree to
which white native illiteracy in the South exceeded that of the North.[6] Drawing
on these numbers, public figures as diverse as Horace Mann and Hinton Helper   Who?
blamed illiteracy—and, thus, corrupted democracy—for accelerating the nation's career toward disunion. Both Mann and Helper (along with many others)

argued that the catastrophe of civil strife might be averted if, through federal intervention, the mass of poor white Southerners could be made to read and write: in their enlightenment they would recognize the folly of slavery.

As Howe demonstrates, by the 1880s it was possible to spread the stigma of illiteracy to areas beyond the rural South, and to succeed in doing so in the face of empirical evidence to the contrary. In many ways Howe's denigration of Plains illiteracy follows the Southern script: it came at a time when waves of political upheaval threatened an emergent nationalism he favored. Howe contended that farmers were dupes for letting themselves become pawns of Populist reformers. Stressing this point, Howe's narrator in *Country Town* colors a prominent Farmers Alliance organizer as the most dishonest of men, willing to exploit the farmer while confiding that "he is no more oppressed than other men, except as his ignorance makes it possible" (203). Embedded in this cynical confidence is the implication that only a commitment to literacy, not politics, will raise farmers from poverty by sparing them the manipulations of both unscrupulous businessmen and demagogic anti-business activists.

It is one thing to name illiteracy as the cause of a grave social ill—slavery, poverty—and then to call for its eradication as the remedy. It is quite another to explain in functional detail how that eradication ought to proceed. Although it was beyond the scope of Howe's narrative, many of his readers would have known of the most common proposal for eradicating illiteracy: national aid to state education. The year after *Country Town* was published, a U.S. Bureau of Education circular reported on the unacceptable numbers of "white youths" in all sections who "were in many instances beyond all chance of instruction" (Warren 19). In an appendix to the report, the progressive educational reformer J. L. M. Curry put a fine point on the government's bureaucratic discourse. "The life of the Republic is one desperate and prolonged struggle against ignorance," he wrote, "and the States are impotent in the encounter." To win this "death struggle with ignorance," the federal government must be permitted to aid states in providing more, and more effective, schooling for American youth. Only then could the "demagogues" and "corrupt schemers" Howe lamented be prevented from turning succeeding generations of illiterate voters into "the instrument of caprice, or revenge, or bribery" (91–93). And only then could individuals, like the farmers, free themselves from what kept them poor. But for a host of reasons—well documented in histories of education—the particular intervention Curry called for was far off; not until well into the twentieth century did the federal government become directly involved in primary and secondary education.[7]

Ironically, it was not illiteracy's connection to poverty, but rather prosperity that drew the national government into local educational affairs, if only indirectly. The rural Plains states, like their Southern neighbors, had been relatively poor through the turn of the century, at least by metropolitan standards, but around 1900 the farm economy took a turn upward. Rising food prices put many farmers and other rural dwellers on a solid financial footing. Yet what was good for the farmer was not good for urban industrial growth. More expensive food drove up factory wages and thereby diminished company profits (Danbom, *Born in the Country* 161–84).

Urban elites blamed this wage inflation on farmers: their underproduction of food elevated food prices and thus the cost of labor. A conventional analysis, as Howe might have rendered it, would have cast this problem in moral terms. Underproductive farmers are indolent, and they are indolent because they are illiterate. Make them literate, and they will do right by harvesting all the food needed to sustain urban industrial growth. This analysis, however, failed to account for an intriguing byproduct of increased rural literacy—farm leaving. It was perceived that literacy awakened rural folk to the seeming advantages of urban and suburban life and so lured them off the farms where their labor was most needed. Clearly, a more nuanced approach to rural illiteracy was called for, and it came by way of redefining the relationship between illiteracy and underproduction. Rather than proposing indolence—a moral judgment—as the middle term, inefficiency—a scientific explanation—was offered. For a worker to be efficient, whether in farm or factory, required *some* literacy, but by no means a full measure of it. Thus, intervention aimed at promoting a limited literacy—or put another way, at maintaining a certain degree of illiteracy—emerged as a workable strategy by which industrial interests could gain some measure of control over agricultural production and food prices.[8]

The complexity of the price-production problem spurred a multifaceted, often incoherent search for solutions. Evidence of this confusion can be seen in a spate of articles circulated in the U.S. Department of Agriculture's *Yearbook*s after 1900. In one article, for example, illiteracy is eliminated as a cause of agricultural inefficiency in tones resonant with a sense of American racial superiority and imperialist destiny:

The bulk of agricultural products are still wrung from the soil by main strength and awkwardness. Indian ryots, Chinese coolies, and Egyptian fellaheen, comprising more than half of the agricultural labor of the world, continue to farm by traditional methods; and the peasants of Europe are little better off. The clog to their progress has not been a lack of books; it has been the lack of elementary education; the lack not merely of a habit of reading, but of knowing how to read at all.

But in this country the first great step has been taken; most farmers are readers. (Greathouse 492; see also Bailey)

Yet just two years later another *Yearbook* article argued that if "the number of illiterate farmers must be at least 800,000, and the illiterate agricultural population must aggregate 3,000,000," then

it will thus be seen that illiteracy is one of the great obstacles to the progress of agriculture in the United States. This inert mass of absolute ignorance constitutes not only a menace to our social and political institutions, but it prevents the introduction of better crops, better methods of cultivation, and better farm machinery in many sections. In these regions, even if intelligent farm managers are available, their efforts to improve agriculture are largely defeated by the stupidity of the only farm laborers who can be procured to perform the necessary routine operations. (True 135)

For A. C. True, author of the latter article, if agriculture is to progress as industry had done—if inexpensive food is to be available to keep industrial growth going—then the "obstacle" of illiteracy must be removed. Yet even if farmers are made literate, their farmhands, because of their illiteracy, will defeat measures to run farms with scientific efficiency. But educating farmhands would put them, like their employers, at risk for leaving the farm for the comparative ease of factory work.

True and his colleagues disagree about the significance of illiteracy both because they are not working from a common set of assumptions about rural difficulties, and because they are not in any kind of dialogue aimed at resolving their differences. Lacking consensus, or a conversation that could lead to it, their views simply reflect the competing political interests that drove farm policy at the turn of the century. From a *Yearbook* reader's point of view, this lack of consensus probably mattered little anyway. Among the half-million farmers receiving each *Yearbook*, there would have been few who were looking for an overarching theory that could explain (and explain what to do about) rural illiteracy, The *Yearbook* was rather like any other periodical that reached farmers through the post: nothing about it created the expectation that a unified perspective should prevail from issue to issue, or even from article to article.[9]

Still, if a singular vision of rural illiteracy did not concern farmers themselves, it was of real interest to the academic professionals who desired to invent the very theories and arguments missing from the *Yearbook*.[10] Take, for example, the question of what to do with the farmhands identified by True as an "inert mass of absolute ignorance." In the fledgling *American Journal of Sociology*, Frank Blackmar of the University of Kansas stipulates that "farm hands are, many of them, substantial boys from neighboring families," but he maintains that many others

form a group of irregular workers of a vile nature. The lack of variety in life, the little time to be devoted to books and papers, and the destruction of all taste for the same bring the mind to a low status. Their spare time on the farm and when out of employment is spent telling obscene stories, in which perpetual lying is necessary to keep up a variety in the conversation, and the use of vile language is habitual. All this tends to weakness of mind and the decline of bodily vigor and health. The youth who is so unfortunate as to listen to all this, and to be associated with such characters, is in danger of having his imagination polluted and his standard of life degraded. The crowd that gathers at the corner grocery may be of a different type from the city hoodlum, and less dangerous in some ways, but as a type of social degeneration it is little above imbecility itself. ("Smoky Pilgrims" 488–89)

Like Howe, Blackmar argues that there is nothing inherently redemptive about country life in the age of industrial capitalism, and like True, he is particularly concerned about the prospects of farm progress in the face of illiteracy and ignorance. But he pushes his concern further still: illiteracy and aliteracy threaten to precipitate "social degeneration" that leaves farmhands in a condition "little above imbecility."

Blackmar's analysis of degenerate farmhands prefaces his case study of the "Smoky Pilgrims," a Kansas family whose living conditions betray decades of degeneration—degeneration, he worries, that could spread in susceptible populations throughout the rural countryside. For the Smoky Pilgrims and other degenerate men and women, Blackmar recommends that "breaking up of the family group, steady enforced employment until the habits of life are changed and become fixed, are indispensable means of permanent improvement" ("Smoky Pilgrims" 500).[11] There is no implication that anything but manual labor will help the adults. But this labor will not benefit degenerates themselves, Blackmar explains. Rather, the benefits accrue only to society at large:

The arts of civilization must begin from the foundation. The warp and the woof of the whole fabric must be constructed. Their desires for a better life are not sufficiently persistent to make a foundation for individual and social reform. How difficult the task to create new desires in the minds of people of this nature! Considered in themselves, from the standpoint of individual improvement, they seem scarcely worth saving. But from social considerations it is necessary to save such people, that society may be perpetuated. The principle of social evolution is to make the strong stronger that the purposes of social life may be conserved, but to do this the weak must be cared for or they will eventually destroy or counteract the efforts of the strong. (500)

From this it might be concluded that Blackmar, in the tradition of so-called eugenic family studies, does not see literacy as a remedy for illiteracy. Rather, illiteracy, among other signs of degeneration, justifies professional intervention in the form of cutting family ties and imposing hard work. These are strategies of containment, not rehabilitation. The best that can be hoped for, Blackmar intimates, is halting the Pilgrims' genetic line before its defects spread further through the rural population. But Blackmar complicates his findings by suggesting that "since this investigation began there are some marks of improvement in the children of this group. They have attended school more regularly and seem inclined to be free from thieving" (500). While it appears, then, that literacy has no favorable influence on degenerate adults, it can reverse the effects of degeneration in the young.[12]

Blackmar's equivocation on the implications of illiteracy captures something of the conflicting arguments about human intelligence that had evolved since the mid-nineteenth-century arrival of Darwinian thought in America. Specifically, what appears to blur Blackmar's conclusion is the question of whether (and which) characteristics acquired by one individual can be inherited by that individual's offspring. The general thrust of Blackmar's argument supports a neo-Darwinian argument that heredity is all, and that environmental influences shape nothing in succeeding generations. His reservation about the Pilgrim children, however, reveals an interest in neo-Lamarckian thought, which stressed that organisms adapt to their circumstances, then incorporate those adaptations into their "congenital endowment." Neo-Lamarckianism, which lost credibility in biology with the rise of neo-Darwinian experimentalism at the turn of the century, remained credible among many sociologists; without the notion that environment could enhance the intellect, it would have been difficult to build the nascent science of sociology as a professional academic pursuit. That is, if society were formed fully by biological determinants, sociology could only *describe* what another sciences could *analyze* and *explain* (Cravens 35–38).[13]

Howe's *Country Town* was still popular at the turn of the century, and so were the traditional ideas about rural illiteracy he espoused. But Blackmar's "Smoky Pilgrims" and the multiple versions of hereditary theory with which he struggled were also gaining currency. More and more, public discussions of illiteracy departed from simple assessments of an individual's spiritual and secular morality. Instead, such discussions were integrated into broader conversations about the fitness and prospects of individuals grouped according to accepted social and biological categories—class and race chief among them. As such, representations of illiteracy, amplified by various social-scientific discourses, grew to have profound and lasting consequences for those deemed illiterate.

Perhaps these consequences are best known in the case of southern Appalachia, long a region associated with illiteracy. Appalachian men and women found themselves at the turn of the century subjected to an array of efforts aimed at explaining and improving their living conditions. Most of these efforts were predicated on the belief that, in neo-Lamarckian fashion, social degeneration might be reversed within a generation, given the acquisition of reading and writing skills. And because Appalachians were theorized to be direct descendants of the hardy Anglo-Saxon stock who supposedly settled the region, making the mountaineers literate was viewed as prerequisite to producing a new generation of pioneers—a people driven to push the frontiers of empire beyond the nation's western shores.[14]

There was another side to this argument for Anglo-American racial superiority, and it was grounded in fear of immigration. How could Americans build a great nation, Blackmar and others wondered, if white, native-born Americans fell to a degeneracy that was not, as the neo-Lamarckians contended, reversible with literacy training? The situation called for a rethinking—a refiguration—of illiteracy as a symptom of an embodied defect that had to be managed with the utmost scientific care. Nowhere was this refiguration accomplished more conspicuously than in the Pine Barrens of southern New Jersey.

2 Rural Illiteracy Made Indelible

In 1922 *The Nation* commissioned Edmund Wilson, Jr., then just twenty-seven, to contribute an essay on his native New Jersey to a series profiling each of the states. With the acerbic wit that would later characterize his best literary criticism, Wilson lamented that the Garden State was reduced to being a "slave of two cities," New York and Philadelphia (243). Among the very few places whose "local flavor" (245) had not been lost to metropolitan hegemony, Wilson found most intriguing

the settlement of poor white trash or "pine rats" which infests the southern pines. . . . Scattered about the edges of this desert are found rudimentary communities of men who manage to live in a perpetual state of indolence and destitution. Without lawyer, doctor, or clergy, in the crudest of timber shacks, devoured daily by fleas, mosquitoes, sand-ticks, and gigantic flies, they ask nothing of the world but to be allowed to deteriorate in peace. They have practically nothing except gin that civilization can supply. They are interrupted only by sociologists who find them a useful laboratory of degeneracy. (246)

ideology

The sociologists Wilson refers to were no doubt researchers affiliated with the Training School at Vineland, situated at the edge of the Pine Barrens. The school, to quote its motto, was "devoted to the interests of those whose minds have not developed normally" (Doll iii). Founded in 1906, the school's laboratory emerged in the 1910s and 1920s as an important site of research on human intelligence, with emphasis on abnormal psychology and eugenic techniques for regulating supposedly defective populations. Wilson could sneer at "destitution" in the Pines for precisely the same reason the Vineland staff could solicit philanthropic dollars to do research there: for more than a century, the place had been identified with illiteracy. For many of these years, metropolitans scorned Pineland illiteracy simply because it allegedly spawned immorality and poverty. But the Vineland scientists saw something else in illiteracy: symptoms of heritable, irreversible defectiveness that imperiled a vibrant Anglo-American nation.[15]

By the turn of the nineteenth century, illiteracy already stigmatized the Pine Barrens. In Charles Brockden Brown's *Arthur Mervyn* (1799, 1800), Arthur's infamous stepmother, Betty Lawrence, is sketched as "a wild girl from the pine-forests of New Jersey" with a "mind totally unlettered, and . . . morals defective in that point in which female excellence is supposed chiefly to consist" (18). This public indictment of illiteracy and immorality in the Pines foreshadows decades of private accounts which registered the same finding. Most vivid among them are the journals and reports of Princeton seminarians who

spent their summers attempting to spread Presbyterianism among the rural un-
churched of southern New Jersey. Some of the earliest missionary records, such
as a journal kept in 1826 by William S. Potts, make repeated reference to men
and women who appear unable to read, and who therefore are unable to attain
Christian salvation through the study of holy scripture. During one day's journey through the Pines, Potts encounters "a family able to read a little," but
only "in the same careless way" as others he had met during the previous nine
days of his journey (Smoot 70). Later he encounters a free African American
couple who, claiming to be Universalists, express suspicion of literacy by rejecting the New Testament as the product of "*high learned people*, who wanted
to make poor people believe any thing and every thing." Potts's dismissive
judgment of the pair: "Neither the man nor his wife were able to read" (75).
Throughout his journal Potts figures illiteracy as a spiritual stumbling block for
the unsaved *and* himself: if people could just read the Bible, then he could be
about the good work saving souls. Although he makes an implicit connection
between illiteracy and damnation, he is careful not to forge a link between illiteracy and low intelligence; indeed, he writes specifically of "a lad of uncommon smartness, though unable to read" who serves well as his guide (71). Illiteracy is thus rendered as a failure of moral, not intellectual, dimensions—a
failure with greater implications for the day of reckoning than for daily life in
the Pines.

As missionary work in the Pines became more professional under the aegis
of the American Tract Society, the discourse on illiteracy there began to change.
Mission reports from 1843 and 1844 register a perspective on the relationship
between literacy and intelligence quite unlike that of Potts. Consider, for example, reports filed by two young men in the summer of 1844. David William
Eakins remarks on widespread family illiteracy—"It was no unusual thing to
meet with whole families, not a single member of which could read" (New Jersey 49)—and he notes further that in at least one settlement he found "very
little if any taste for reading" (52) among the inhabitants. Samuel McCulloh
goes a step farther in his charge that illiteracy has become an intergenerational
affliction: "It is for the condition of such as these ignorant & depraved as they
mostly are, that the Christian heart should deeply feel, & indeed yearn over
them. Without schools within their reach, or the disposition to profit by them if
they had them, they had grown up generation after generation, three fourths of
them unable to read a sentence" (63–64). By 1844, then, literacy is no longer
imagined to be merely *absent* from the Pines; there is a sense that there is an
aversion to it there, and that over successive generations this aversion has intensified the depravity in which the irreligious dwell (see also Nord).

The sensational accounts set down by Princeton seminarians and American
Tract Society colporteurs were essentially private in their day, and so they only
hint at more widely held beliefs about Pineland illiteracy. Nonetheless, the ac-

counts are consonant with claims made somewhat later by one W. F. Mayer in an 1859 *Atlantic Monthly* essay excoriating Pine residents as "completely besotted and brutish in their ignorance" (566). With illiteracy and immorality rampant, Mayer writes, it is little wonder that "they are incapable of obtaining an honest living, and have supported themselves, from a time which may be called immemorial, by practising petty larceny on an organized plan." But Mayer differs from the missionary commentators in one respect. The theology students complained that illiteracy led to immorality that had consequences in afterlife. Mayer relocates these consequences in the material world, and he suggests that illiteracy encourages Pines residents to resist integration into a thriving regional economy. Because of this resistance, this inability to make community, Mayer concludes, the Pine "Rat must follow the Indian,—must fade like breath from a window-pane in winter!" (568). *Ouch*

Needless to say, the people of the Pine Barrens did not immediately fade from existence, but the notion that they might persisted. In an 1882 novel by John Darby, pseudonym for the pioneering Philadelphia oral surgeon James Gerretson, the Jersey pine forest is the site of an experiment aimed at proving that intelligence is all that is needed successfully to farm the area's acid soil. *Brushland*'s narrator, a city doctor, drains a plot of Pines swampland and commences to farm it, his only obstacle being the inability to secure the helping hand of a Pines native smart enough to realize the value of his project. The narrator struggles with his own beliefs about Pines residents: the "prig" in him *Novel* chastises an ignorant neighbor for his illiterate speech, while the part of him that "is with the simple" understands how hard it must be to see the farming potential in the thicketed parcel he has purchased (108, 62). With little assistance, the doctor finally manages to produce a handsome crop, and his satisfaction is so complete that he wonders why impoverished Philadelphians do not colonize the hidden riches of the Pine Barrens. He concludes that the "illiterate laborer" in the city, like "the farmer's son" in the Pines, has not the "wit" to "raise his eye above the sixpence which conceals the dollar beyond" (178). In other words, poor illiterates make choices that keep them poor because they lack the intelligence to do otherwise.

Over the course of the nineteenth century, then, metropolitans' understanding of illiteracy in the rural Pine Barrens passed through roughly three phases. In the first two, illiteracy was connected with immorality, initially as an impediment to attaining Christian salvation and later as the cause of uncivil and impoverished life on Earth. Such interpretations vary little from those held against rural America more generally, as Howe's case against illiterates in *Country Town* illustrates. In the third phase, however—the phase represented by Garretson's *Brushland*—there is an interpretive shift of subtle but significant proportions. Garretson posits illiteracy as symptomatic of defective intelligence, and intelligence as essential to success in life. Phrased this way, Garretson's formulation appears little different from the proposition implicit in turn-of-the-century writing about rural illiteracy elsewhere, especially in the South. But Garretson's narrator hints that mental defect cannot be remedied by the removal of illiteracy. Thereby Garretson signals a way of thinking about rural illiteracy not contemplated by the Southern anti-illiteracy crusaders: a way defined by professional scientists rather than by volunteer educators, a way funded by industrial philanthropists rather than modestly by local charitable organizations.

Though hardly a best-selling author—his handmade theory of illiteracy and intelligence reached only thousands—Garretson was far from alone in his view that something was permanently amiss in the Pine Barrens, and that illiteracy was just the most obvious aspect of it. There were others who would tell the story of "Piney" degeneracy, coloring it not with the aesthetics of literary realism but with the logic of a new human science, abnormal psychology. The laboratory of the Training School at Vineland, on the edge of the Pines, became an intellectual center for this science, and Henry Herbert Goddard and Elizabeth S. Kite some of its foremost exponents.

The Vineland laboratory gained national notice in 1912 when Macmillan published *The Kallikak Family: A Study in the Heredity of Feeble-Mindedness*. In this book Goddard presents what he claims to be the first compelling evidence proving that feeble-mindedness—the "scientific" name for what Garretson detected in the Pines—was heritable. A startling discovery, to be sure, but not half so alarming as Goddard's discovery of a "high grade" feeble-minded population, dubbed morons, whose mental defects were evident only to those, like Goddard and his staff, trained to detect them.[16] With hundreds of supposed mental defectives close at hand, the staff at Vineland sought to advance the research of Blackmar and other scientists interested in the heritable nature of human intelligence. In doing so Goddard continued the tradition of searching family backgrounds for instances of defect, augmenting the method by developing an instrument for reliably measuring intelligence. His adaptation of French researchers Alfred Binet and Theodore Simon's intelligence scales enabled Goddard to diagnose three distinct types of feeble-mindedness: the idiot, the imbecile, and the moron. The Vineland staff became most interested in high-grade imbeciles and morons because, according to Goddard, the mental defects inherent in these types were not easily diagnosed. Certain imbeciles and almost all morons could pass as normal in the general population; passing as normal, they would undoubtedly procreate, bringing into the world yet another generation beset by mental inadequacy.

For Goddard, feeble-mindedness was present in those whose "mentality" or mental age was markedly less than their physical age. The "arrested development" that would open such a gap was easily documented in failure to progress in the use of language, especially reading and writing. Here Goddard closely follows Binet and Simon, who argue (in a text translated by Vineland staffer Elizabeth Kite) that if one is in doubt as to the intellectual level of an imbecile, if one supposes, for instance, that he could reply to questions but that he does not reply because of a rebellious character, it would often be sufficient to slip a pencil into his hand and to let him write, in order to judge. Someone, perhaps Richelieu, said "With two lines of a man's writing one could have him hung." We willingly add, with a line of writing we can establish the intellectual level even among those who do not know how to write. (46)

Thus, for those whose behavior and appearance were not symptomatic of feeble-mindedness, an assessment of literacy—and the finding of illiteracy or low literacy—could confirm an otherwise problematic diagnosis.

Goddard and his associates were certain that feeble-mindedness was hereditary, which meant that the illiteracy or low literate ability observed in one generation would likely pass to the next. This notion was popularized in the Kallikak family study, which takes as its primary subject twenty-two-year-old Deborah Kallikak, who had entered the Vineland institution in 1897 at age eight. In her thirteenth year at the school, her teachers reported that she could "write a well-worded story, but has to have more than half the words spelled for her" (*Kallikak Family* 6). Several years after that, Vineland officials came to the consensus that Deborah could still write "fairly" but was a "poor reader" (7). This unsatisfactory literacy, combined with a general lack of progress in school, convinced Goddard that Deborah was "a typical illustration of the mentality of a high-grade feeble-minded person, the moron, the delinquent, the kind of girl or woman that fills our reformatories" (11). Goddard laments the fact that many such girls also populate the public schools, where "rather good-looking, bright in appearance, with many attractive ways, the teacher clings to the hope, indeed insists, that such a girl will come out all right. Our work with Deborah convinces us that such hopes are delusions" (11–12). Generalizing from Deborah's case, Goddard suggests that illiteracy or low literacy among adults does not indicate missed opportunities in school, but rather the sort of "mental defect" that renders morons "incapable of mastering abstractions." Thus morons "never learn to read sufficiently well to make reading pleasurable or of practical use to them" (55). As a result, illiterate and low literate morons become either indolent and dependent, or criminal.

Deborah's condition, Goddard argues, owes much to a lineage of feeble-mindedness stretching back generations to the American Revolution. What makes Deborah's case extraordinary, though, is that her Revolutionary-era progenitor, Martin Kallikak, Sr., had initiated two family lines, one legitimate (through marriage with a "respectable girl of good family," a Quaker woman), and the other not (through an affair with a nameless "feeble-minded girl") (29). Deborah, descended from the illegitimate union, bears the marks of feeble-mindedness not found in the legitimate branch of the Kallikak family tree— "a family of good English blood of the middle class" (50). Thus it is certain, Goddard insists, that "feeble-mindedness is hereditary and transmitted as

Peter Mortensen

surely as any other character" (117). And because the feeble-minded, given to
sexual immorality, "are multiplying at twice the rate of the general population,"
Goddard recommends "segregation through colonization" to protect the normally intelligent population from destruction (71, 117).[17]

What is not established in the Kallikak study is the mechanism by which
feeble-mindedness is inherited. Not two years later, in 1914, Goddard published the answer in *Feeble-Mindedness: Its Causes and Consequences*: intelligence "*acts like a unit character*" following the "Mendelian law of inheri-
tance," much like eye or hair color (556). He arrives at this conclusion after
surveying the case studies of hundreds of persons institutionalized at Vineland
since childhood, many of them, it turns out, from rural backgrounds. Prominent
in most of these cases are notations about literacy—notations crucial to up-
holding the given assessment of diminished mentality. The most striking commentary on literacy applies to men and women classified as morons and high-
grade imbeciles. Take the case of twenty-five-year-old Mary N., for example.
Goddard reproduces in facsimile the fluent letter Mary wrote to Santa Claus in
1911. Her effort is judged appropriate to a ten-year-old, an assessment Goddard
defends by stressing that she can do no better after sixteen years of instruction
in letter-writing. Mary's obvious literacy, which Goddard casts as evidence of
near-illiteracy, is simply part of what enables her to deceive "the very elect as
to her capacity" (93). According to Goddard, "In Institution life she is happy
and useful. Unprotected she would be degraded, degenerate and the mother of
defectives" (94). But for an imbecile such as fourteen-year-old Horace C., there
is no possibility of deception through false literacy. Barely able to copy a sentence written by his teacher, his effort "is typical feeble-minded writing" (162).
This despite the facts that Horace, a boy likely raised in the nearby Pine Barrens, had no formal schooling before arriving at Vineland at age seven, and that
the writing sample in question was taken after only a few years of rudimentary
literacy instruction.[18]

What most agitates Goddard is his belief that as many as four hundred thousand feeble-minded persons, many of them undetected morons, are at large in
the United States in 1914. He confesses that his staff is "bewildered at the thot
of segregating them all" into isolated colonies. Goddard proposes, as an alternative, that "if we cannot remove the mental defective from society to a colony,
we can at least colonize him where he is" (582). On these reservations, populated predominately by morons and imbeciles, the feeble-minded will be protected from the mistreatment that can make them vicious, licentious threats to
society. Especially with morons, mental testing will be used to establish what
schooling, if any, should be attempted. For instance, in the case of a young man
whose mentality is that of a ten-year-old boy, "We will teach him in school only
those things that a ten year old child can learn. This will leave him with a minimum of the three R's and a maximum of manual and industrial training" (583).

Such would be the fate of the colonized feeble-minded: their *inability* to read and write, taken as *incapacity* to read and write, would justify the imposition of a curriculum aimed at sustaining illiteracy, or something close to it.

Just where actual enclaves of feeble-minded persons might be colonized remains untold in *Feeble-Mindedness*. Clearly, the territory ideal for colonization would be a place where family histories could be readily obtained, and where these histories would point—like the imbecile Horace C.'s case—back to Anglo-American racial stock gone bad. An obvious choice, given its century-long reputation of illiteracy and careless living, was the laboratory's own back yard, the New Jersey Pine Barrens. Good evidence that Goddard and his associates considered the Pines for this purpose appears in an account of the "Piney" people published in a widely circulated 1913 number of *The Survey*, a popular magazine of public policy. The article's author, Elizabeth Kite, was the assistant to Goddard who conducted most of the field research for *The Kallikak Family* and, under Goddard's direction, translated Binet and Simon's *Intelligence of the Feeble-Minded*. She was also among three field workers who researched the hundreds of cases Goddard presented in *Feeble-Mindedness*.

Kite tells a story that reinterprets Pineland social history in terms of a race-conscious theory of heredity. In this reinterpretation she departs from the popular view that illiteracy among rural native whites merely represented a moment of arrested development—development that could be set in motion again with schooling. Kite, following Goddard's lead, makes a different assumption about the nature of heredity, concluding that feeble-minded Anglo-American degenerates lack the mental constitution to be restored to normalcy. Thus an anti-illiteracy campaign like those being conducted by volunteers in some Southern states would surely fail in the Pines. What is called for instead, as Goddard argues in his technical publications, is a professional effort to colonize and contain feeble-minded persons wherever they "naturally" concentrate. Working from this premise, Kite adds an infamous chapter to the already well-known story of unlettered life in the Pines: she explains that the cause of illiteracy there is feeble-mindedness, and feeble-mindedness can be cured only by imposing clinical measures to prevent Pines residents from mingling their feeble-minded gene plasm with the normal plasm of those outside the Pines. Lest readers think the problems Kite documents are peculiar to the Pines, she stresses, "What is true of the Pines is true, with local variations, of all outlying districts" around the nation ("The 'Pineys'" 40; see also Kite, *Research Work*).

For Kite's claims about hereditary feeble-mindedness to hold, she must establish that the Pines environment is not responsible for degeneracy within the "distinct people" there, many of whose families "can be traced back directly to where they branch from excellent families, often of sturdy English stock" (7). This she does in two brief case studies. The first refers to a "Yankee agent" who in the 1850s developed techniques to cultivate the cranberries native to the

Pines (9). As the agent was experimenting with bog farming, he "put up warning signs bidding the natives keep off, which signs they very naturally ignored, since none were able to read" (10). Because of this illiteracy, the agent was forced to make a more dramatic gesture: he faked a murder near the bog. Only then did Pine residents keep their distance, although Kite speculates that they would have anyway because "the real Piney has no inclination to labor, submitting to every privation in order to avoid it" (10). Kite's second case against environmental influence is even more damning. She narrates the arrival of "Italian Mike," who cleared twenty-five acres of land and established a farm that provided fresh fruits and vegetables to customers miles away in the city. Kite remarks that "'Mike' has never had the advantage of schooling for himself . . . but his alert mind has had time amidst the stress of his active life to acquire the essentials of the three 'R's' so that he is by no means an illiterate man." The immigrant's "progressive mentality" enables him to claim literacy even in the absence of schools, much to the shame of a neighboring family whose adult members do little work and whose unschooled children have been institutionalized for antisocial behavior (11). Both cases remind us of Garretson's claim that a healthy and intelligent man from the city can do quite well by exploiting what ignorant Pines natives cannot—the great untapped wealth of the rural landscape.

With environment ruled out as the cause of "Piney" degeneracy, illiteracy can no longer be considered subject to remediation. Instead, as with the inmates at the Vineland School, illiteracy betrays an inability to become literate—an inability with far-reaching consequences. Kite seeks to document these consequences by tracing the family trees of several clans she encountered in the Pines. She is particularly intrigued with a man nicknamed "Old Iz," clearly mentally deficient in her estimation, but possessed of a "shrewdness, an ability to take care of himself that is characteristic of his class and is very misleading." Although conditions in the field make it impossible to test the mental age of "Old Iz," Kite discovers that she can learn all about the man's mentality by examining his sister's daughter and son-in-law (13).

Kite locates the sister's daughter, Beckie, who has just been captured after escaping from the county house, where she had been placed after arrest for abandoning her children. Kite's interrogation begins with inquiry about Beckie's literacy:

> "Were you ever at school, Beckie?"
> "Yes, but I didn't get no learnin'; been awful sorry since."
> "Can't you read or write?"
> "No."
> "Why couldn't you learn?"
> "Didn't seem as though there was anything in my head could take it." (13, 38)

Subsequent mental testing fixes Beckie's mental age at between eight or nine. Contrasting this assessment with her physical age of twenty-three, Kite confirms the woman's designation as a moron. Beckie puts her own illiteracy in perspective: it is not for lack of opportunity that she can neither read nor write; instead, the lack of "anything in my head [that] could take it" is responsible.

More intriguing still is Ford, a thirty-year-old man set to marry Beckie's youngest sister, May. While May is "following rapidly in Beckie's footsteps," there is something "normal" about Ford "that suggested good blood" (38). But appearances can be deceiving, Kite informs readers. After "precise tests," she determines Ford's mentality to be that of a nine-year-old child. And like Beckie, "he could neither read nor write," though "evidently for a different reason." That reason: Ford has never been to school. Still, Kite holds out no hope that belated schooling in literacy might improve Ford's intellect. From all scientific indications, Ford will forever remain "kind-hearted and gentle," yet unable to "grasp an abstract idea nor hold two ideas together to compare or relate them." This condition leaves Ford "strictly honest" given his own understanding of things, but a "most atrocious liar" from a normal adult's perspective (39).

It is Kite's contention that people like Beckie and Ford could do considerable damage to the "enlightened community" living near the Pines. Setting aside the question of whether or not a "Piney" is "capable of receiving sufficient education to make of him a desirable citizen," Kite worries about the "lowered moral tone" that marks all encounters with outsiders. So it becomes all the more important to "set about clearing up these 'backdoors of our civilization' and so to save from the worst form of contagion what remains of moral health in our rising generation" (40).

Kite reminds readers, as Goddard did, that the rising generation worth safeguarding resides in the city and its suburbs, and that what most threatens this precious generation lives in the country. This distinction between urban and rural space formed the essential geography of feeble-mindedness for the better part of the decade before World War I. But as Goddard, Kite, and others grew more certain that feeble-mindedness was fixed in the body, their attention shifted from external contexts to internal mechanisms. Goddard's *Psychology of the Normal and Subnormal*, a textbook published in 1919, completes this transition. Goddard's previous treatments of illiteracy detailed the (typically rural) environmental conditions that to the layman—and to the teacher—appeared responsible for the inability to read and write, only to show how the expert diagnosis of high-grade feeble-mindedness proved a better explanation. But in *Psychology*, with the influence of environment on literacy discounted, Goddard prefaces his discussion of illiteracy with sweeping claims about human neurology and cognition. The result is to bypass case studies—no Beckie and Ford are necessary—and to issue a general pronouncement about the futility of teaching the feeble-minded, or at least most of them, how to read and write.

Based on Training School research, Goddard recommends that of those diagnosed feeble-minded, only high-grade morons be taught to read and write. He warns, though, that "very few ever make any real use of such accomplishments afterwards" (303). In light of this, Goddard asks readers to bear in mind that if moron adults are not likely to use reading and writing skills "to any real advantage," it *is* likely that literacy will put them at disadvantage because "here as everywhere else a little knowledge may easily prove to be a dangerous thing" (307–8). Thus, instead of wasting time on reading instruction—and on teaching writing, which is "in even a worse state"—"we may give with a clear conscience our time to things that for him are much more worth while!" So goes Goddard's rationale for withholding literacy from—for forcing illiteracy on— hundreds of thousands of adults who exhibited the barely visible signs of feeble-mindedness as preliterate children (308).[19]

In 1928, less than ten years after *Psychology* appeared, Goddard abandoned the idea that feeble-mindedness was heritable as a unit trait. Further, he conceded that it was careless to label as morons all adults who tested at a mental age of twelve. Still more, Goddard reversed his stand on educating morons: although such an education had not yet been perfected, one was conceivable ("Feeblemindedness" 220). "When we get an education that is entirely right," he insists, "there will be no morons who cannot manage themselves and their affairs and compete in the struggle for existence" (224). And if suited to this struggle, Goddard concludes, "the feeble-minded . . . do not generally need to be segregated in institutions" (225). For her part, Kite, in a 1940 interview, expresses regret that her work on feeble-mindedness in the New Jersey Pine Barrens had humiliated the region's inhabitants. "I have no language in which I can express my admiration for the Pines and the people who live there," she said, with irony doubtless unintended (quoted in Halpert 12).[20]

Recent research on life in the Pine Barrens at the turn of the century challenges many of the stereotypes out of which Kite constructed her polemic for segregation of the region. John Sinton shows that throughout the nineteenth century, literacy rates there outpaced those of surrounding areas and the rest of the nation. This suggests that Presbyterian missionaries in the Pines probably exaggerated the frequency of adult illiteracy they encountered, possibly as a way of expressing frustration with the unbending Methodism that census documents indicate was prevalent there. By the turn of the century, illiteracy rates had fallen in the Pines, as they had throughout the nation. Contributing to this decline were good schools and stable homes that flourished within a flexible agricultural economy. But, as elsewhere, a modest agricultural economy did not empower the people of the Pines to resist misrepresentation by Goddard and Kite. Goddard and Kite exercised the power of literacy, amplified by scholarly expertise, to create the subjects they needed to build a professional institution that had a lasting effect on the way Americans perceive literacy and its relationship to intelligence (Sinton and Masino 181; see also D. Cohen; and Moonsammy, Cohen, and Williams).

Altering the Figures

From a conventional *historical* perspective, a way of knowing illiteracy is peculiar to a particular moment in time. It took an unusual confluence of circumstances for Goddard and Kite to shape their ideas about an unlettered rural populace into the exemplary cases of racial degeneracy for which they became known. It might be argued that when these ideas lost currency, the ways of knowing illiteracy embedded within them were lost too. But from a *cultural* perspective, ways of knowing illiteracy—or, for that matter, any construct that intersects both the social and material worlds—are never entirely lost. They fragment, and once fragmented, they circulate tacitly through channels of public and private discourse, until they are recombined into new complexes of knowledge that can again be ascribed cultural authority. This process of recombination and reauthorization is evident in recent discussions of illiteracy in the New Jersey Pine Barrens. And crucially, although these discussions direct public attention toward illiteracy in rural America, they have discernible consequences for our understanding of illiteracy in metropolitan settings as well.

Consider the case of essayist John McPhee. One summer in the mid-1960s, more than a century after Princeton seminarians had scoured the Pine Barrens for lost souls, McPhee, also of Princeton, ventured into the piney woods. He searched there not for souls but for stories. What he found he crafted into a 1967 *New Yorker* essay, which a year later appeared as *The Pine Barrens*, a slim volume that, like all of McPhee's books, has yet to go out of print ("An Album" 121). Excerpts from *The Pine Barrens* have been anthologized widely and appear in *The John McPhee Reader*, a text used since 1976 in countless university-level advanced writing courses.

In the essay's third section, "The Separate World," McPhee takes up Kite's and Goddard's work in the Pines, holding it and them responsible for "a stigma that has never worn off" (*Pine Barrens* 53). Yet having made this judgment, McPhee is surprisingly gentle in his critique of the Vineland researchers. While he finds their conclusions faulty and their generalizations irresponsible, he is willing to grant that in the declining Pineland economy of the late nineteenth century,

some of the people slid into illiteracy, and a number slid further than that. Marriages were pretty casual in the pines late in the nineteenth century and early in the twentieth. . . . To varying degrees, there was a relatively high incidence in the pines of what in the terms of the era was called degeneracy, feeblemindedness, or mental deficiency. (47–48)

Something *was* amiss in the Pines, even if Kite and Goddard had failed to understand it. In reaching this conclusion, McPhee accepts the claim that illiteracy rates ran high in the Pines around 1900, that a low moral tone prevailed there, and that certain Pines residents lacked the mental capacity of "normal" metropolitans. Whether illiteracy was the cause or an effect of this immorality and mental deficiency, McPhee does not say; he leaves it to readers to make the most plausible connections.

And what connections might readers make? William Howarth provides one answer in his introduction to a *Pine Barrens* excerpt in the *McPhee Reader*. Howarth simply repeats the racial truisms advanced by Vineland researchers decades before: "The region is both an archetype and another country; a place so at variance with modern norms that it breeds perfect descendants of America's original stock, 'pineys' like Jim Leek: 'There ain't nobody bothers you here. You can be alone. I'm just a woods boy. I wouldn't want to live in a town'" (53). The nonstandard, "illiterate" speech, the desire for isolation, the descent from honorable "stock"—all are elements of what Kite and Goddard taught metropolitan Americans about the people of the Pine Barrens. It is ironic, then, that McPhee finds it "surprising" that "people in New Jersey today seem to think that the Pine Barrens are dark backlands inhabited by hostile and semi-literate people who would as soon shoot an outsider as look at him" (*Pine Barrens* 53). In light of what he writes, how could they think otherwise?

As we near the end of the twentieth century, the rural landscape of McPhee's Pine Barrens contrasts starkly with other representations of the American countryside. In the Pines, illiteracy is aberrant and isolated, nearly eliminated. Elsewhere, in various mass-mediated representations, rural illiteracy has transcended its origins in the countryside to envelop the city and the nation. So either the essential qualities of rural illiteracy have almost vanished, or they are ubiquitous. Either way, this fixation on the rural has serious implications for contemporary discussions of illiteracy.

Let me close by pointing to the rural fixation evident in E. D. Hirsch's *Cultural Literacy* and Herrnstein and Murray's *The Bell Curve*. Both books offer the "fact" of adult illiteracy as backing for the claim that metropolitan culture must be reorganized to endure, and both books locate the blueprint for this reorganization in an agrarian past—specifically, a Jeffersonian one (see Ellis 3–23). Hirsch finds appealing Jefferson's plan to provide, at public expense, a rigorous education in common subjects for all citizens of the republic. Herrnstein and Murray invoke a somewhat different Jefferson—one who favors a sustainable community in which citizens carry out those duties to which, in all ways, they are best suited. In either Jeffersonian future, illiteracy ceases to be a problem. In Hirsch's future, illiteracy simply does not exist; in Herrnstein and Murray's it exists, but illiterates willingly pursue occupations appropriate to their limited—though not necessarily debilitating—mental capacities (Hirsch 12–13; Herrnstein and Murray 530–31, 540).

Surely it is not the supposed moral and economic poverty of illiterate country life to which Hirsch and Herrnstein and Murray make their contemporary appeals. But that, as we have seen, is how popular and powerful commentators once characterized the agrarian past from which we inherit our contemporary ways of knowing—and not knowing—adult illiteracy. In path-breaking historical work on North American literacy, Harvey Graff identifies as myth the notion that, at least in the nineteenth century, acquisition of reading and writing skills led inevitably to social advancement (*Literacy Myth*). My conclusion, ironically resonant with Graff's, is that *il*literacy enabled the social advancement of those willing to use it as the conceptual capital central to their turn-of-the-century charitable and professional enterprises. Gleaning the fields of rustic illiteracy has left a legacy no less devastating to rural livelihood than blight or drought. As Hirsch and Herrnstein and Murray demonstrate, that legacy—inaccurate as it was and is—still animates what passes for informed debate on literacy and intelligence in American culture.[21]

Notes

I am grateful to Janet Carey Eldred and Scott Hendrix for helpful comments on rural illiteracy. And many thanks to Jennifer Workman Pitcock and Ronald Pitcock for expert research assistance.

1. There is no shortage of excellent scholarship examining rhetorical relationships between literacy practices and their cultural meanings, but there is less work that explains how *illiteracy* comes to have meaning in literate culture, and what the material consequences of such meaning might be. Denny Taylor and J. Elspeth Stuckey have shown in separate studies how, in contemporary America, the official designation of illiteracy is a rhetorical act that often limits personal liberties. Carolyn Marvin, in research on anthropodermic bibliopegy, has theorized how this limiting of liberty disciplines not abstract personages but rather actual bodies. She argues that "those with access to powerful literate currencies learn to conceal their bodies" such that the literate "body is less socially visible in the practices and products of literacy than the more visible but less socially esteemed body of illiteracy" (130–31). It is my interest in this chapter to emphasize how rhetorical figurations of adult illiteracy lead to the regulation of real bodies when it is perceived that remediation is not a plausible solution.

2. Van Doren's mention of Howe gives some indication of his enduring popularity. On Van Doren's role in the soaring influence of *The Nation* among the intellectual elite, see Tebbel and Zuckerman 204.

3. For discussions of literacy as prerequisite to piety and citizenship in early America, see Cremin, *American Education: The National Experience*; Graff, *Legacies* 248–57; Lockridge; Monaghan, "Literacy"; Monaghan, "Family Literacy"; Davidson; Gilmore; and Heath. For an overview of perspectives from the late nineteenth century on, see Kaestle et al.

4. For biographical detail on Howe's childhood in Harrison County, Missouri, see Pickett 5–12. For statistics on population, literacy, and schooling in Harrison County,

see United States, Department of the Interior, Bureau of the Census, *Population* 286, and *Statistics* 507–8.

5. Soltow and Stevens found that intergenerational illiteracy of the sort Howe claimed to know was sustained only in places where population sparseness, economic desperation, and geographic isolation worked against the establishment of schools or school attendance. Howe's Missouri and Kansas were rural, to be sure, but not without population density and mobility. According to Soltow and Stevens's hypothesis, children of Howe's generation would probably transcend their parents' illiteracy (184–88).

6. See M. Anderson 26–31, and P. Cohen; see also B. Anderson 163–85.

7. "The federal government did not become extensively involved in education before World War II" (Cremin, *American Education: The Metropolitan Experience* 229).

8. Ultimately, limiting farmers' literacy meant narrowing their understanding of the consequences of industrializing farm production. And, as Wendell Berry has pointed out in numerous books and essays, industrializing farm production makes farmers dependent on an industrial economy over which they can exert little control. On metropolitans' views of the appropriate life and literacy for rural dwellers, see Danbom, *The Resisted Revolution*; on farmers' resistance to such metropolitan views, see Scott 37–63, 170–89. For commentary on the tensions between industry and agriculture during the years of farm prosperity, see Danbom, *Born in the Country* 132–84. For important revisions and extensions of Raymond Williams's groundbreaking work on urban-rural axes of difference, see Creed and Ching. And for inquiry into what happens when these spatial axes are mapped onto race and class, see Bunce, and Wray and Newitz.

9. The preface to the 1897 *Yearbook* tells readers that the secretary of agriculture wished the publication to "be of such a popular character and of such value to practical agriculture as to justify the enormous edition issued by Congress"—506,000 copies distributed through the offices of senators, representatives, and the Agriculture Department (Hill 3). That volume of distribution compares favorably with the circulation of much popular fiction at the turn of the century.

10. After 1900, work on "the rural problem" began migrating from government to the university. For example, Congress commissioned leading academics in the area of rural life to report on conditions in the country. In their 1910 final report, the commissioners stressed the urgency of reforming country life because "the people"—presumably metropolitans like themselves—"realize that the incubus of ignorance and inertia is so heavy and so widespread as to constitute a national danger, and that it should be removed as rapidly as possible" (*Report* 124–25). Likewise, the sociologist John Gillette implicated illiteracy and aliteracy as central to "social stagnation and social poverty" in the country. Such stagnation and poverty result from "a lack of intellectual stimulus and ferment" because "reading has not been cultivated as a source of pleasure and a means of larger information" (8). Gillette's essay led off a special issue of the *Annals of the American Academy of Political and Social Science* on "Country Life." For an overview of the Country Life Movement and its leaders' investment in a "redirected" rural education, see Bowers 4–5, 39; and Danbom, "Rural Education."

11. Coincidentally, Blackmar's Pilgrims lived in the university town of Lawrence, Kansas, not fifty miles away from Atchison, where Howe composed his *Country Town*. And like the impoverished creatures in *Country Town*, Blackmar's subjects came west from Indiana. Years later, Blackmar completed a survey of Lawrence in which he passes

over mention of the degenerate Pilgrims and their ilk. Instead, he laments that the presumably highly literate white men and women of the university town limit themselves to one or two children per family. Of this low fertility Blackmar comments, "Race suicide is not a future peril, but a present menace. Lawrence is not contributing its share to the future American stock" (*Lawrence Social Survey* 17).

12. For an excellent overview of family studies such as Blackmar's, see Rafter, *White Trash* 1–31.

13. For an overview of how evolutionary thought came to influence debates about eugenics and intelligence, see Degler 32–55. The classic treatise on the cultural side of this subject is that of Hofstadter. For an apt critique and revision of Hofstadter's views, see Bannister, *Social Darwinism* and *Sociology and Scientism*.

14. For an elegant summary of the various racisms that permeated American culture at the turn of the century and their relation to rural politics, see Saxton 349–77. Kaplan and Michaels helpfully place these racisms in the context of American imperialism. For an overview of historical treatments of Appalachia, see Billings, Pudup, and Waller; for specific commentary on representations of illiteracy in the Southern mountains, see Mortensen.

15. For an early history of the laboratory, see Johnstone. Recently James Trent has examined how work at Vineland sparked anxieties about the "menace of the feebleminded" (131–83), and Nicole Hahn Rafter has detailed how Vineland research contributed to the definition of the "criminal imbecile" (*Creating Born Criminals* 133–48). It is important to note that the Vineland research effort depended on philanthropic giving to support some of its work. For example, Samuel Fels, president of Fels and Company, manufacturer of Naptha soap, contributed significantly to the school's laboratory (Smith 44–45).

16. In addition to being widely reviewed, research on the Kallikaks was played up in popular periodicals. See, for example, "The Kallikak Family"; and Goddard, "The Kallikak Family." Of course, Goddard and the Vineland staff were not the only prominent researchers in abnormal psychology and eugenics interested in rural populations; see Davenport.

17. Goddard preferred institutionalization to sterilization because the health consequences of sterilization were unknown, and because sexual sterility might not curtail sexual activity and would do nothing to halt the emergence of criminal behavior.

18. In many of the case histories Goddard presents, a mother's alcohol abuse is mentioned, but causal connections between the abuse and a child's perceived mentality are never fully drawn—in part because there was no extant discourse in which such a connection would make sense. See Dorris for a lay discussion of the emergence of fetal alcohol syndrome as a credible diagnosis.

19. For a sample of the literacy research Goddard refers to, see Lindley. As an example of moronic writing, Goddard includes a photograph captioned, "High Grade Moron, and a sample of his work. Notice the hyphen (partly concealed by a brace) between the separated parts of 'Scho-ol.' Who has not had similar experiences with supposedly normal workmen?" (*Psychology* 190).

20. See Gould 172–74, for an argument that only at this point did Goddard understand how Binet intended his examinations to be used.

21. But there are other voices and other representations—as there always have

been—faint though they may be. For example, there is the steady voice of Jonathan Kozol, whose concerns about fairly representing urban illiteracies dates back to *Prisoners of Silence* (1980) and *Illiterate America* (1985). More important, there are the essays and memoirs of men and women who became literate as adults: see, for example, Prete and Strong's *Literate America Emerging: Seventeen New Readers Speak Out*. And there are powerful new fictional representations of urban illiteracy, such as Sapphire's *Push*.

Works Cited

Anderson, Benedict. *Imagined Communities*. 2d ed. New York: Verso, 1991.

Anderson, Margo J. *The American Census: A Social History*. New Haven: Yale University Press, 1988.

Bailey, Liberty Hyde, comp. *Farmers' Reading Courses*. USDA Farmers' Bulletin no. 109. Washington, D.C.: Government Printing Office, 1900.

Bannister, Robert C. *Social Darwinism: Science and Myth in Anglo-American Social Thought*. Philadelphia: Temple University Press, 1979.

Bannister, Robert C. *Sociology and Scientism: The American Quest for Objectivity, 1880–1940*. Chapel Hill: University of North Carolina Press, 1987.

Berry, Wendell. *The Unsettling of America: Culture and Agriculture*. 3d ed. San Francisco: Sierra Club Books, 1996.

Billings, Dwight B., Mary Beth Pudup, and Altina L. Waller. "Taking Exception with Exceptionalism: The Emergence and Transformation of Historical Studies of Appalachia." In *Appalachia in the Making: The Mountain South in the Nineteenth Century*, edited by Mary Beth Pudup, Dwight B. Billings, and Altina L. Waller, 1–24. Chapel Hill: University of North Carolina Press, 1995.

Binet, Alfred, and Th. Simon. *The Intelligence of the Feeble-Minded*. Translated by Elizabeth S. Kite. Baltimore: Williams and Wilkins, 1916.

Blackmar, Frank W. *Lawrence Social Survey*. Topeka: Kansas State Printing Plant, 1917.

Blackmar, Frank W. "The Smoky Pilgrims." *American Journal of Sociology* 2 (1897): 485–500.

Bowers, William L. *The Country Life Movement in America, 1900–1920*. Port Washington, N.Y.: Kennikat, 1974.

Brown, Charles Brockden. *Arthur Mervyn; or, Memoirs of the Year 1793*. Vol. 1. 1799. Reprint, Port Washington, N.Y.: Kennikat, 1963.

Bunce, Michael. *The Countryside Ideal: Anglo-American Images of Landscape*. London: Routledge, 1994.

Cohen, David Steven. "The Origin of the Pineys: Local Historians and the Legend." In *Folklife Annual 1995: A Publication of the American Folklife Center at the Library of Congress*, 40–59. Washington, D.C.: Government Printing Office, 1985.

Cohen, Patricia Cline. *A Calculating People: The Spread of Numeracy in Early America*. Chicago: University of Chicago Press, 1982.

Cravens, Hamilton. *The Triumph of Evolution: American Scientists and the Heredity-Environment Controversy, 1900–1941*. Philadelphia: University of Pennsylvania Press, 1978.

Creed, Gerald W., and Barbara Ching. "Recognizing Rusticity: Identity and the Power of Place." In *Knowing Your Place: Rural Identity and Cultural Hierarchy*, edited by Barbara Ching and Gerald W. Creed, 1–38. New York: Routledge, 1997.

Cremin, Lawrence A. *American Education: The Metropolitan Experience, 1876–1980.* New York: Harper and Row, 1988.

Cremin, Lawrence A. *American Education: The National Experience, 1783–1876.* New York: Harper and Row, 1980.

Curry, J. L. M. "National Aid to Education." In *Circulars of Information of the Bureau of Education*, no. 3–1884, 89–99. Washington, D.C.: Government Printing Office, 1884.

Danbom, David B. *Born in the Country: A History of Rural America.* Baltimore: Johns Hopkins University Press, 1995.

Danbom, David B. *The Resisted Revolution: Urban America and the Industrialization of Agriculture, 1900–1930.* Ames: Iowa State University Press, 1979.

Danbom, David B. "Rural Education Reform and the Country Life Movement, 1900–1920." *Agricultural History* 53 (1979): 462–74.

Darby, John [James Edmund Garretson]. *Brushland.* Philadelphia: Lippincott, 1882.

Davenport, C. B. "The Nams: The Feeble-Minded Country Dwellers." *Survey* 27 (2 March 1912): 1844–45.

Davidson, Cathy N. *Revolution and the Word: The Rise of the Novel in America.* New York: Oxford University Press, 1986.

Degler, Carl N. *In Search of Human Nature: The Decline and Revival of Darwinism in American Social Thought.* New York: Oxford University Press, 1991.

Doll, Edgar A., ed. *Twenty-Five Years: A Memorial Volume in Commemoration of the Twenty-Fifth Anniversary of the Vineland Laboratory, 1906–1931.* Vineland, N.J.: The Training School, 1932.

Dorris, Michael. *The Broken Cord.* 1989. New York: HarperPerennial, 1990.

Ellis, Joseph J. *American Sphinx: The Character of Thomas Jefferson.* New York: Knopf, 1997.

Gillette, John. "Conditions and Needs of Country Life." *Annals of the American Academy of Political and Social Science* 40 (1912): 3–11.

Gilmore, William J. *Reading Becomes a Necessity of Life: Material and Cultural Life in Rural New England, 1780–1835.* Knoxville: University of Tennessee Press, 1989.

Goddard, Henry H. *Feeble-Mindedness: Its Causes and Consequences.* New York: Macmillan, 1916.

Goddard, Henry H. "Feeblemindedness: A Question of Definition." *Proceedings and Addresses of the American Association for the Study of the Feeble-Minded* 32 (1928): 219–27.

Goddard, Henry H. "The Kallikak Family." *Hearst's Magazine* 23 (February 1913): 329–31.

Goddard, Henry H. *The Kallikak Family: A Study in the Heredity of Feeble-Mindedness.* New York: Macmillan, 1912.

Goddard, Henry H. *Psychology of the Normal and Subnormal.* New York: Dodd, Mead, 1919.

Gould, Stephen Jay. *The Mismeasure of Man.* New York: Norton, 1981.

Graff, Harvey J. *The Legacies of Literacy: Continuities and Contradictions in Western Culture and Society.* Bloomington: Indiana University Press, 1987.

Graff, Harvey J. *The Literacy Myth: Cultural Integration and Social Structure in the Nineteenth Century.* New Brunswick, N.J.: Transaction, 1991.

Greathouse, Charles H. "Development of Agricultural Libraries." In *Yearbook of the United States Department of Agriculture, 1899,* 491–512. Washington, D.C.: Government Printing Office, 1900.

Halpert, Herbert Norman. "Folktales and Legends from the New Jersey Pines: A Collection and a Study." Ph.D. dissertation, Indiana University, 1947.

Heath, Shirley Brice. "Toward an Ethnohistory of Writing in American Education." In *Writing: The Nature, Development, and Teaching of Written Communication,* edited by Marcia Farr Whiteman, vol. 1, 25–45. Hillsdale, N.J.: Lawrence Erlbaum, 1981.

Helper, Hinton Rowan. *The Impending Crisis of the South: How to Meet It.* 1857. Reprint, edited by George M. Fredrickson, Cambridge, Mass.: Harvard University Press, 1968.

Herrnstein, Richard J., and Charles Murray. *The Bell Curve: Intelligence and Class Structure in American Life.* New York: Free Press, 1994.

Hill, George William. Preface. In *Yearbook of the United States Department of Agriculture, 1897,* 3–4. Washington, D.C.: Government Printing Office, 1898.

Hirsch, E. D., Jr. *Cultural Literacy: What Every American Needs to Know.* Boston: Houghton Mifflin, 1987.

Hofstadter, Richard. *Social Darwinism in American Thought, 1860–1915.* Philadelphia: University of Pennsylvania Press, 1944.

Howarth, William L., ed. *The John McPhee Reader.* 1976. Reprint, New York: Noonday-Farrar, Straus, and Giroux, 1991.

Howe, E. W. *Plain People.* New York: Dodd, Mead, 1929.

Howe, E. W. *The Story of a Country Town.* 1883. Reprint, Cambridge, Mass.: Harvard University Press, 1961.

Johnstone, E. R. "The Institution as a Laboratory." In Doll, 3–15.

Kaestle, Carl F., et al. *Literacy in the United States: Readers and Reading since 1880.* New Haven: Yale University Press, 1991.

"The Kallikak Family." *Popular Science* 82 (April 1913): 415–16.

Kaplan, Amy. Introduction. In *Cultures of United States Imperialism,* edited by Amy Kaplan and Donald E. Pease, 3–21. Durham: Duke University Press, 1993.

Kite, Elizabeth S. "The 'Pineys': Today Morons; Yesterday Colonial Outcasts, 'Disowned' Friends, Land Pirates, Hessians, Tory Refugees, Revellers from Joseph Bonaparte's Court at Bordentown, and Other Sowers of Wild Oats." *Survey* 31 (4 Oct. 1913): 7–13, 38–40.

Kite, Elizabeth S. *Research Work in New Jersey.* N.p.: New Jersey Department of Charities and Corrections, 1913.

Kozol, Jonathan. *Illiterate America.* Garden City, N.J.: Anchor-Doubleday, 1985.

Kozol, Jonathan. *Prisoners of Silence: Breaking the Bonds of Adult Illiteracy in the United States.* New York: Continuum, 1980.

Lindley, Martha. "The Reading Ability of Feeble-Minded Children." *Training School Bulletin* 14 (1917): 90–94.

Lockridge, Kenneth A. *Literacy in Colonial New England: An Enquiry into the Social Context of Literacy in the Early Modern West*. New York: Norton, 1974.

Mann, Horace. *An Oration Delivered before the Authorities of the City of Boston, July 4, 1842*. Boston: Eastburn, 1842.

Marvin, Carolyn. "The Body of the Text: Literacy's Corporeal Constant." *Quarterly Journal of Speech* 80 (1994): 129–49.

Mayer, W. F. "In the Pines." *Atlantic Monthly* 3 (May 1859): 560–69.

McPhee, John. "An Album Quilt." *Creative Nonfiction* 8 (1997): 105–22.

McPhee, John. *The Pine Barrens*. 1968. Reprint, New York: Noonday-Farrar, Straus and Giroux, 1988.

Michaels, Walter Benn. "Anti-Imperial Americanism." In *Cultures of United States Imperialism*, edited by Amy Kaplan and Donald E. Pease, 365–91. Durham: Duke University Press, 1993.

Monaghan, E. Jennifer. "Family Literacy in Early 18th-Century Boston: Cotton Mather and His Children." *Reading Research Quarterly* 26 (1991): 342–70.

Monaghan, E. Jennifer. "Literacy Instruction and Gender in Colonial New England." In *Reading in America: Literature and Social History*, edited by Cathy N. Davidson, 53–80. Baltimore: Johns Hopkins University Press, 1989.

Moonsammy, Rita Zorn, David Steven Cohen, and Lorraine E. Williams. Introduction. In *Pinelands Folklife*, edited by Rita Zorn Moonsammy, David Steven Cohen, and Lorraine E. Williams, 1–11. New Brunswick: Rutgers University Press, 1987.

Mortensen, Peter. "Representations of Literacy and Region: Narrating 'Another America.'" In *Pedagogy in the Age of Politics: Writing and Reading (in) the Academy*, edited by Patricia A. Sullivan and Donna J. Qualley, 100–20. Urbana, Ill.: National Council of Teachers of English, 1994.

New Jersey Historical Records Survey Project. *Colporteur Reports to the American Tract Society, 1841–1846*. Newark: Historical Records Survey, 1940.

Nord, David Paul. "Religious Reading and Readers in Antebellum America." *Journal of the Early Republic* 15 (1995): 241–72.

Pickett, Calder M. *Ed Howe: Country Town Philosopher*. Lawrence: University Press of Kansas, 1968.

Prete, Barbara, and Gary E. Strong, eds. *Literate America Emerging: Seventeen New Readers Speak Out*. Sacramento: California State Library Foundation, 1991.

Rafter, Nicole Hahn. *Creating Born Criminals*. Urbana: University of Illinois Press, 1997.

Rafter, Nicole Hahn, ed. *White Trash: The Eugenic Family Studies, 1877–1919*. Boston: Northeastern University Press, 1988.

Report of the Commission on Country Life. New York: Sturgis and Walton, 1911.

Sapphire. *Push*. New York: Knopf, 1996.

Saxton, Alexander. *The Rise and Fall of the White Republic: Class Politics and Mass Culture in Nineteenth-Century America*. London: Verso, 1990.

Scott, Roy V. *The Reluctant Farmer: The Rise of Agricultural Extension to 1914*. Urbana: University of Illinois Press, 1970.

Simpson, Claude M. Introduction. In *The Story of a Country Town*, by E. W. Howe, vii–xxvii. Reprint, Cambridge, Mass.: Harvard University Press, 1961.

Sinton, John W., and Geraldine Masino. "A Barren Landscape, A Stable Society: People and Resources of the Pine Barrens in the Nineteenth Century." In *Natural and Cultural Resources of the New Jersey Pine Barrens: Inputs and Research Needs for Planning*, edited by John W. Sinton, 168–91. Pomona, N.J.: Stockton State College, 1978.

Smith, J. David. *Minds Made Feeble: The Myth and Legacy of the Kallikaks*. Rockville, Md.: Aspen, 1985.

Smoot, Joseph G. "Journal of William S. Potts: A Mission in the Pines of New Jersey in 1826." *New Jersey History* 106 (1988): 61–85.

Soltow, Lee, and Edward Stevens. *The Rise of Literacy and the Common School in the United States: A Socioeconomic Analysis to 1870*. Chicago: University of Chicago Press, 1981.

Stuckey, J. Elspeth. *The Violence of Literacy*. Portsmouth, N.H.: Boynton/Cook-Heinemann, 1991.

Taylor, Denny. *Toxic Literacies: Exposing the Injustice of Bureaucratic Texts*. Portsmouth, N.H.: Heinemann, 1996.

Tebbel, John, and Mary Ellen Zuckerman. *The Magazine in America, 1741–1990*. New York: Oxford University Press, 1991.

Trent, James W., Jr. *Inventing the Feeble Mind: A History of Mental Retardation in the United States*. Berkeley: University of California Press, 1994.

True, A. C. "Some Problems of the Rural Common School." In *Yearbook of the United States Department of Agriculture, 1901*, 133–54. Washington, D.C.: Government Printing Office, 1902.

United States. Department of Interior. Bureau of Education. *Illiteracy in the United States and an Experiment for Its Elimination*. Bulletin 20. Washington, D.C.: Government Printing Office, 1913.

United States. Department of the Interior. Bureau of the Census. *Population of the United States in 1860*. Washington, D.C.: Government Printing Office, 1864.

United States. Department of the Interior. Bureau of the Census. *Statistics of the United States . . . in 1860*. Washington, D.C.: Government Printing Office, 1866.

Van Doren, Carl. "Contemporary American Novelists." *Nation* 113 (1921): 407–12.

Warren, Charles. "Illiteracy in the United States in 1870 and 1880." In *Circulars of Information of the Bureau of Education*, no. 3–1884, 7–20. Washington, D.C.: Government Printing Office, 1884.

Wilson, Edmund, Jr. "New Jersey: The Slave of Two Cities." In *These United States: Portraits of America from the 1920s*, edited by Daniel H. Borus, 243–48. Ithaca: Cornell University Press, 1992.

Wray, Matt, and Annalee Newitz, eds. *White Trash: Race and Class in America*. New York: Routledge, 1997.

8 *Lester Faigley*

Material Literacy and Visual Design

Phaedrus Media is a typical web site these days, especially in a university town like Austin, Texas. It advertises a new, technology-related small business, probably run out of someone's home. It offers examples of work in a portfolio; if you click on "portfolio," you jump to another index page that offers a choice among "graphics," "bleed" (for bleeding edge technology), and "Java" prototypes and demos. If you then click on "graphics," you get a catalog of thumbnail graphics, which can be enlarged. After you enlarge a few of the abstract graphics, some of which are animated, you might wonder what the point *is*, so you click back to the previous screen and look at the words beside the thumbnails:

genesis jellyfish
Created in: Painter 4
Notes: genesis jellyfish. I don't know what it means but the image is
    kind of cool. That's why I animated it. It was animated in Painter,
    too. (Painter has very nice animation and rotoscoping tools)

Soon you begin to suspect that the web site is the creation of an adolescent, and you're right. Phaedrus Media is the web site of Ben Syverson, who was fifteen when he built it.

Among his peers Ben Syverson is exceptional, but he is hardly unique. Thousands of teen-agers now have personal web pages, many of which display the multimedia capabilities of the World Wide Web. The web sites of two young women from Community High in Ann Arbor, Michigan, are more typical teen-

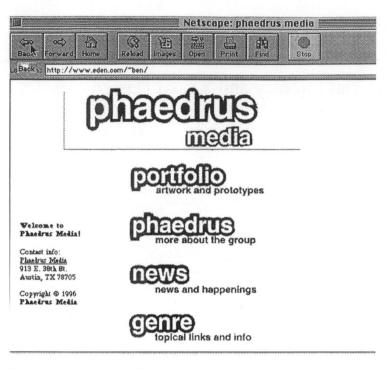

Figure 8.1. Phaedrus Media. Web site no longer available.

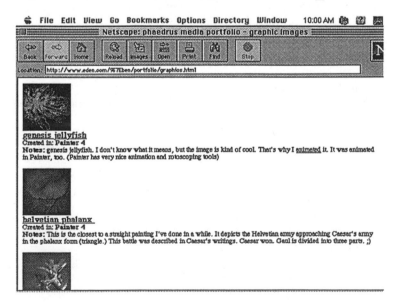

Figure 8.2. Phaedrus Media Portfolio. Web site no longer available.

Figure 8.3. Jessica Draper's "Llanarth's Lair." Web site no longer available.

Figure 8.4. Time Warner's Pathfinder. Web site: http://pathfinder.com.

ager's personal pages. Seventeen-year-old Jessica Draper has a web site called "llanarth's lair," with the title illuminated by flashing multicolors, making the letters appear to move across the page. If you scroll down her page, you find text which announces that her dog "rules," as well as a long clickable list of what she finds cool, including e-mail. Another student, Kate Levy, has a home page that announces, "This is Kate Levy's site. I am Kate. My homepage uses frames. If you can't handle this, I'm sorry." At the bottom is a blinking message that requires concentration and several seconds to read. It says: "Blink tags are annoying. interesting, huh? I think so. But not really . . . oh well . . . maybe someday I'll understand you. O if things never change, I won't. Of course things do . . . change is good . . . someday everything will change. INCLUDING YOU!!!"

I find these sites remarkable for a number of reasons, not the least of which is the considerable design talent of these teen-agers; compare, for example, Time Warner's Pathfinder site, which is the work of professionals and cost many thousands of dollars to produce. But far more interesting is the way these sites intersect with three long historical trajectories: the development of writing systems, going back at least fifty-five hundred years; the development of images, going back at least to cave paintings thirty thousand years ago; and the development of capitalism, variously dated but at least a few centuries old. Other chapters in this volume discuss how the body emerged as the central problematic for material rhetoric in the 1990s, following from the obsession with the body evident in much postmodern theory. My chapter concerns another aspect of material rhetoric—the materiality of literacy. Later in the chapter I turn to the relationship of material literacy with the problematic of the body, but I first investigate the concept of material literacy. Why I should even want to discuss the materiality of literacy is not obvious, because, as Carol Blair points out in her chapter, a literate act assumes an object, a text that can be read. Yet it was precisely that object that one of the ideals of Enlightenment rationality—the ideal of the transparent text—sought to erase. It took decades of critical and empirical studies to convince scholars that texts are not transparent and that reading and writing are situated acts, but the ideal of the transparent text still persists in perceptions of literacy held by much of the public.

The ideal of the transparent text entails several other presuppositions. Foremost is that "true" literacy is limited to the abstract representation of sounds— a presupposition that subordinates syllabic and logographic writing systems and banishes pictograms and images to the status of illiteracy. Scholars of the history of literacy have shown us how much cultural baggage the conceptions of literacy have carried (see especially Peter Mortensen's chapter in this volume). A loathing for mass-produced images is part of that cultural baggage. Barbara Maria Stafford has examined how current attitudes toward images were formed in eighteenth-century England when educated people began associating images with ignorance, illiteracy, and deceit (110). These attitudes followed from the Protestant mission of defeating the "mindless" auditory, visual, and olfactory credulity of Catholicism with the power of reason expressed in print. In the nineteenth century, these prejudices began running squarely against an increasingly shared world culture of images made possible by new technologies. The crisis these new technologies caused for the prevailing concept of literacy is expressed in a poem by William Wordsworth, signed in 1846, commenting on the mass publication of illustrated books and newspapers following the appearance of the *Illustrated London News* in 1842:

> DISCOURSE was deemed Man's noblest attribute,
> And written words the glory of his hand;
> Then followed Printing with enlarged command
> For thought—dominion vast and absolute
> For spreading truth, and making love expand.
> Now prose and verse sunk into disrepute
> Must lacquey a dumb Art that best can suit
> The taste of this once-intellectual Land.
> A backward movement surely have we here,
> From manhood—back to childhood; for the age—
> Back towards caverned life's first rude career.
> Avaunt this vile abuse of pictured page!
> Must eyes be all in all, the tongue and ear
> Nothing? Heaven keep us from a lower stage!

Wordsworth's lament has been uttered again and again in the century and a half since his poem "Illustrated Books and Newspapers" was written. Each new popular image technology has brought accompanying cries that "dumb Art" has captured the reading public of "this once-intellectual Land" and caused "a backward movement surely."

Lately the World Wide Web, the most powerful publishing technology ever created to distribute both words and images, has provoked an eruption of jeremiads about how the Web is destroying literacy as we conceive of it in the academy. We hear that critical thinking and reflection, a sense of order, dialectical interaction, logical relations in texts, depth of analysis, trails of sources, and the reform mission of public discourse are all going to be lost. Even those who take a more balanced view fear that the multimedia capability of the Web will undermine or overwhelm the power of prose. Jay David Bolter writes, "The new media . . . threaten to drain contemporary prose of its rhetorical possibilities. Popular prose responds with a desire to emulate computer graphics. Academic and other specialized forms respond by a retreat into jargon or willful anachronism" (270). The coming of the Web, however, does not have to be viewed as a loss to literacy. Images and words have long coexisted on the printed page and in manuscripts, but relatively few people possessed the resources to exploit the rhetorical potential of images combined with words. My argument in this chapter is that literacy has *always* been a material, multimedia construct, even though we only now are becoming aware of this multidimensionality and ma-

teriality because computer technologies have made it possible for many people
to produce and publish multimedia presentations.

The Paradox of the Alphabetic Literacy Narrative

The reasons that we have not acknowledged this multidimensionality and materiality have much to do with the influence of the grand narrative of alphabetic
literacy. Based on a dichotomy between the oral and the visual, the grand narrative is often identified with the work of Harold Innis, Jack Goody, Walter
Ong, and Eric Havelock.[1] This reduction of their wide-ranging scholarship,
however, is misleading. The grand narrative of alphabetic literacy is actually an
accumulation of ideas about language and culture that began to take shape in
the eighteenth century. In recent years it has been popularized in books such as
Robert Logan's *The Alphabet Effect*, complete with explanations of why the invention of the alphabet led to the superiority of northern Europe. Logan writes:

> Many of the seminal ideas in Western science, mathematics, jurisprudence, politics,
> economics, social organization, and religion are intrinsically linked with the phonetic
> alphabet. . . . Of all mankind's inventions, with the possible exception of language itself,
> nothing has proved more useful or led to more innovations than the alphabet. (17–18)

According to the grand narrative, not only the rise of science but also the development of democracy, the celebration of the individual, the establishment
of Protestantism, the codification of law, and the spread of capitalism resulted
from a shift from an oral bias to a written bias for conveying information and
ideas. This shift is claimed to have facilitated abstract thinking and deductive
logic.

The narrative of alphabetic literacy assumes the existence of an evolution
from pictographs to modern writing systems. This theory was first advanced by
William Warburton, the future bishop of Gloucester, in his 1738 book *Divine
Legation of Moses*. From his study of Egyptian, Chinese, and Aztec manuscripts, Warburton hypothesized that all scripts evolved from narrative draw-
ings. His theory was widely diffused by Diderot and d'Alembert's *Encyclopédie* and remained definitive for over two centuries (Schmandt-Besserat 4).
Even though twentieth-century archeologists have amassed a great deal of evidence to the contrary, the pictograph theory is still repeated in popular accounts
of the origins of writing (e.g., Claiborne; Gelb). Logan follows the underlying
assumption of the pictographic theory in arguing that "the absence of Western-
style abstractions and classification schemes in Chinese culture is related to
the differences in writing systems" (47). In a chart of cultural patterns (49), he
makes the following comparisons:

EAST	WEST
Ideograms	Alphabet
Right-brain oriented	Left-brain oriented

		E of R
Nonlinear	Linear	*Literacy*
Acoustical	Visual	
Analogical	Logical	
Inductive	Deductive	
Concrete	Abstract	
Mystical	Causal	
Intuitive	Rational	

Logan concludes, "The lack of abstraction in the writing system reflects itself throughout Chinese thought and discourages the development of abstract notions of codified law, monotheism, abstract science, and deductive logic" (58). For those who endorse the narrative of alphabetic literacy, China provides the example of what happens to a culture whose writing system fails to evolve—to "progress."

The two crux points in the narrative of alphabetic literacy occur with the inventions of the modern alphabet in classical Greece and of Gutenberg's printing press in the mid-fifteenth century. Singling out the contribution of the Greeks to the alphabet at first seems a curious move because systems of writing as abstract signs existed long before Greek civilization. Greeks living in Phoenicia simply adapted the twenty-two Phoenician consonant characters to represent the Greek language; they converted a few of the consonants to vowels and added a few signs—phi, chi, psi, ksi, and omega—which were either borrowed, modified, or independently created. The earliest known alphabetic Greek inscription dates from about 730 B.C.E., and the earliest surviving commercial documents in Greek come two hundred years later. The Greek alphabet was subsequently transmitted to Latin via the Etruscans, who lived in central Italy from about the seventh through the first centuries B.C.E. Until nearly the end of the fifth century, the Euboean alphabet was used in Greece; hence it was the script the Etruscans imported, and the one that later became the basis for the Roman alphabet. Had the Etruscans borrowed the later Ionian alphabet instead, modern European and Greek scripts would now have a much closer resemblance.

The mutation known as the Greek alphabet, then, came relatively late in the history of writing. The earliest written texts appeared many centuries earlier in Mesopotamia with the development of the first urban centers around 3500 to 3100 B.C.E. We base our knowledge of the earliest writing on a collection of about fifteen hundred texts preserved on clay tablets, produced by the Sumerians, who in the middle of the fourth millennium became dominant in southern Mesopotamia. Although the content of many of these texts remains enigmatic, most apparently are administrative records of economic transactions, bearing official seals. Writing was one of the inventions that made civilization possible. It allowed kings to send instructions to far-off administrators and to collect taxes. It allowed merchants to order goods and bill customers. It allowed farmers to buy, sell, and lease land. But even though we know a great deal about the functions of writing in early civilization, the precise origins of writing have remained mysterious. The repertory of signs on the earliest tablets is surprisingly large—more than two thousand words at minimum. Furthermore, the great majority of these signs are abstract. My colleague at the University of Texas, Denise Schmandt-Besserat, believes that the small clay tokens commonly found at archeological sites in the Middle East are an important clue to the origins of writing. These tokens, which come in several shapes and extend over a long time span from the ninth to the second millennia B.C.E., were handmodeled out of clay; they are widely distributed over a region extending from Khartoum in the Sudan, to mainland Greece, to sites east of the Caspian Sea. Until a decade ago, however, archeologists had few guesses about what the tokens were used for.

Schmandt-Besserat thinks that the tokens were an early recording system. Many of the tokens are contained inside bullae, which have to be broken open to discover their contents. One bulla, found at Nuzi in the 1920s and dating from about the sixteenth century B.C.E., throws light on what the tokens might have been used for. It contained forty-nine small tokens, but more important, it also bore a lengthy cuneiform inscription on the outside. The translation is

Figure 8.5. Tokens with various geometric shapes have been recurrently found in great numbers throughout the Middle East at archaeological sites dating from 8500–1500 B.C.E. (Photograph by Denise Schmandt-Besserat, Pergamon Museum, Berlin, Germany)

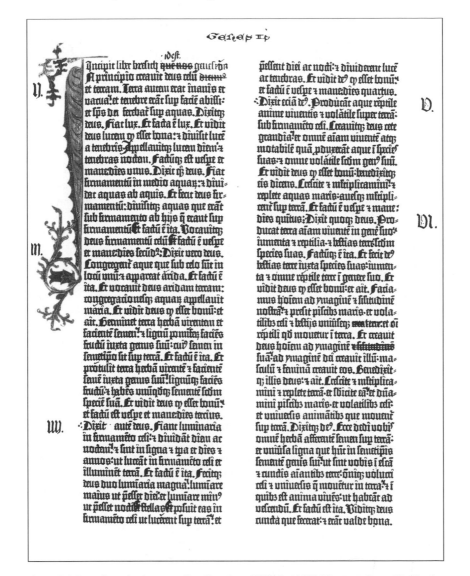

Figure 8.6. Page from the forty-two-line Gutenberg Bible, ca. 1455 (Photograph provided by the Harry Ransom Humanities Research Center, the University of Texas at Austin)

'twenty-one ewes, six female lambs, eight adult rams, four male lambs, six female goats, one male goat, three female kids,' and the seal of the shepherd. These numbers add up to forty-nine, leaving little doubt that the tokens were counters representing the herd. Tokens, then, were very likely invented in response to another technology—agriculture—and advances in agriculture that created surpluses. Suppose one farmer had a bumper crop of grain, and his neighbor had a herd of pregnant but hungry sheep. The second farmer might have used tokens to promise the first farmer a certain number of lambs the next spring in return for a load of grain. To ensure that the number delivered was the one they agreed on, the tokens were sealed in a bulla. In this way tokens functioned like a modern bill of lading.

The crux of Schmandt-Besserat's theory, however, is the way that three-dimensional material tokens led to two-dimensional symbols. Again, consider the example of the farmer with a grain surplus, eager to make futures trades for livestock and other goods. As this proto-agribusinessman wheeled and dealed his way up and down the Tigris and Euphrates, the bullae on his shelves piled up. After a while he couldn't recall exactly how many sheep and goats he was going to acquire in the spring, because the tokens were sealed in the bullae. Schmandt-Besserat thinks that some clever trader began impressing symbols of the tokens on the outside of the bullae to indicate what they contained. Eventually the convenience of noting the number of tokens on the surface of the bullae supplanted the system of tokens altogether. Schmandt-Besserat also hypothesizes that many of the tokens represent numerical signs rather than individual objects. Consequently, it appears, two-dimensional writing began not by representing reality through pictographs but by representing in two dimensions the previous recording system. If Schmandt-Besserat is correct, her theory helps to explain why the first tablets contain a surprisingly large percentage of symbols, why these symbols are abstract, and why they apparently were standardized at a very early date. Even if she is not correct, the unearthing of large numbers of archaic texts dating from the fourth millennium B.C.E., and their subsequent deciphering, dispute the assumption that writing evolved from pictures. True pictograms are actually relatively rare in the earliest Sumerian texts, representing "plow," "chariot," and "sledge." By 3000 B.C.E. the Sumerians had considerably reduced the number of signs and had developed the cuneiform script, which mixes phonetic signs and ideograms. Throughout the history of writing in the West, we find such mixed systems; indeed, we have only to look at the top row of a keyboard to find words represented by single symbols: @, #, $, %, &.

The paradox of the narrative of alphabetic literacy lies in its claim of a cognitive divide between oral and visual cultures. In order to make this claim, one has to ignore a great deal about how information and ideas are stored and transmitted. The essential shortcoming in the narrative lies in its desire to provide a simple explanation of cultural differences by theorizing that writing systems shape cultures. The history of writing suggests just the opposite: cultures freely borrow and adapt systems for information storage when the need arises. Thus, in its claim for the primacy of the visual, the narrative of alphabetic literacy effaces not only the material tools used in writing (as Christina Haas has noted), but also the element of visual cognition.

The second great moment in the grand narrative of alphabetic literacy is the invention of the printing press. Robert Logan writes:

With the printing press we finally encounter a technology whose impact on the use of the alphabet is so great that it must be ranked in importance with the alphabet itself. For not only did the printing press greatly multiply access to alphabetic texts, it also, through the regularity it introduced, transformed the way in which the alphabetic text was placed on the page and was perceived by its readers. (177)

The issue of perception is essential to the narrative of alphabetic literacy. Logan and others claim that print magnified the changes brought about by the introduction of the alphabet. Because scribes often used variant spellings and irregular punctuation, readers of hand-copied texts often had to speak the texts in order to interpret them. Print brought regularity to spelling and the conventions of punctuation, enabling rapid, silent reading. Logan quotes Harold Innis, who maintains that "the discovery of printing in the middle of the fifteenth century implied the beginning of a return to a type of civilization dominated by the eye rather than the ear" (186). But like the argument on the effects of alphabetic literacy on Greek culture, the concept of the visual in print literacy is severely truncated. With the regularity of uniform type, Logan argues, the "printed medium became transparent and hence its effects more abstract" (193). The ideal of print literacy is the conduit metaphor, by which ideas flow directly from the mind of the author to the mind of the reader. Thus, again the argument for the turn to the visual paradoxically means the effacement of the visual.

The development of the Phoenician alphabet and its subsequent adaptation by the Greeks are largely a subject of speculation, but we know a great deal about the development and distribution of the printing press. The central figure is Johannes Gensfleich, known as Gutenberg from the name of the family estate—*Zu Guten Bergen*, "the good mountain." For many years scholars have debated Gutenberg's role in the invention of printing. Much of what we know about him comes from the legal records of Strasbourg and Mainz, where lawsuits in 1439 and 1455 make claims for loans and partnerships related to Gutenberg's invention. Gutenberg was a goldsmith by trade, and his innovations came in the replica casting of movable metal type, uniform in size, and in the mixing of an oil-based ink that would adhere to type. The result was a book with very high technical and aesthetic quality—with regular lines, justified margins, and beautiful type design.

There is little doubt that Gutenberg made major technical achievements in printing, but many questions remain. To what extent was he a synthesizer of traditions of printing that had preceded him by centuries, rather than an originator of printing? And how influential was the printing press in the major cultural and economic changes that were taking place during the Renaissance? Major scholarly controversies have centered on these questions, which are too complex to rehearse fully here. In brief, Gutenberg inherited two technologies that originated in China: paper and block printing. The process of making paper was invented in China by 200 C.E., following an even older technology of producing a paperlike material from the bark of mulberry trees. A battle in Central Asia, fought in 751 C.E. between Arab-led armies and Chinese armies, eventually led to the transmission of paper technology to Europe. Captured Chinese paperworkers established paper workshops in Samarkand and later in Baghdad (al-Hassan and Hill 191). A paper and book industry then flourished in Baghdad and spread to other parts of the Islamic world, including Morocco and Spain. When Toledo was captured by Christian forces in 1085, Europe gained both access to the knowledge in paper books and the technology to make them. The papermakers of Baghdad also learned how to harness water power for the labor-intensive process of pounding fibers into pulp. In the thirteenth century, a paper industry grew up in Italy using water power; it spread to France in the fourteenth century and throughout western Europe in the fifteenth. The book historian Henri-Jean Martin observes, "The importance of this movement can hardly be exaggerated. Before paper became available, the hides of a veritable herd of young animals were required to make a single *in-folio* volume" (210).

Along with paper, the Chinese developed several technologies for reproduction of images. A history of the Sui dynasty (581–617), written in the seventh century, describes Taoist priests who printed charms as cures for illnesses. During the eighth century the Chinese had mastered block printing, which allowed images to be combined with text. During the eleventh century, they used movable type made of baked clay, and both Chinese and Koreans may have been printing with movable metal type as early as the twelfth century. The extent to which these technologies were known in Europe is still debated, but various kinds of wood-block printing were already practiced in Europe by the time Gutenberg began experimenting with his press. Engraved wood blocks were employed primarily to print religious images, but blocks were also used to print textiles, playing cards, pamphlets, tabletops, and secular images (Martin 212). Gutenberg also benefited from new technologies of metalworking, an industry that was flourishing in Europe, with metals being extracted in large quantities to meet a strong demand. Metallurgists learned new techniques of making alloys and casting metal copies; Gutenberg himself had a background in minting coins and manufacturing mirrors. From a larger perspective, therefore, Gutenberg's achievements represent a stage in the evolution of a series of linked technologies rather than a distinct breakthrough.[2]

The second and much more extensive controversy has been the debate over the historical impacts of printing. The expansion of the printing industry in the fifteenth century was phenomenal. By 1501, at least ten million copies (possibly double that number) of an estimated twenty-seven to thirty-five thousand publications had been printed. Like answering machines, VCRs, and e-mail in the late twentieth-century, printed books spread quickly through the emergent middle class. Logan claims that the printing press "unleash[ed] a powerful new force that completely transformed Western civilization, leaving in its wake the Renaissance, the rise of science, the Reformation, individualism, democracy, nationalism, the systematic exploitation of technology, and the Industrial Revolution—in short, the modern world" (183). The extravagance of Logan's claim is underscored by the facts that the Renaissance had been in progress in Italy for over a century, while the Industrial Revolution lay two or three centuries ahead.

Nevertheless, there were notable short-term impacts of printing, and one of the most important was the use of print by religious reformers to disseminate the translated Bible and their religious views. Martin Luther believed that all Christians should read from the Gospels daily in their own languages, and he advocated schooling so that children could read the scriptures before age ten. But even with the success of the Reformation, the great majority of books published during this first century of print were in Latin. Latin remained the language of international scholarship, and its decline was slow. During the Counter-Reformation, the Jesuits established schools that rivaled the Protestant ones, and they actively published Latin titles. Even after the energy of the Counter-Reformation was spent, the dominance of Latin lingered. Some of the best records of early books come from the catalogues of the Frankfurt Fair, where new books were announced to Europe. Not until the 1680s did more German than Latin books appear (Febvre and Martin 232).

Furthermore, there is little evidence that the practices of literacy changed radically with the appearance of printed books. Roger Chartier notes, "In the sixteenth and seventeenth centuries the reading style implicit in a text, literary or not, was still often an oralization of the text, and the 'reader' was an implicit auditor of a read discourse" (9). Thus the great cognitive achievement alleged for print literacy—silent reading—occurred long after printed books became dominant. Similar claims have been made for the impact of print on science but are not borne out by the historical record. Logan writes that "the rapid dissemination of information and knowledge to a mass audience was one of the essential elements in the use of modern science" (194), but what was in fact disseminated in the early decades of printing was hardly scientific by modern standards. (The most popular "scientific" subject was astrology.) Febvre and Martin observe that early books did not contribute much to scientific theory, though they did draw attention to new technical advances in architecture, agriculture, and machinery. Febvre and Martin conclude that printing brought about no sudden or radical cultural transformation; this is hardly surprising, since booksellers were interested in making a profit and thus looked for books that would sell in the largest numbers (260).

Those who argue for a strong impact of print on science, such as Elizabeth

Eisenstein, point out that the visually dependent sciences of botany, zoology, and anatomy flourished after accurate print images replaced scribal images that became intolerably degraded in copying. Copperplate engravings, which later became important in printing, in the middle of the fifteenth century, about the same time as Gutenberg's press. For the sciences, engraving was as important a technology as movable type.

Logan credits alphabetic literacy with creating an environment where images and diagrams thrive. At no point is his version of the rise of alphabetic literacy more confused. Illustrations had a long tradition in manuscripts, and they came to early books as woodcuts. Printers quickly learned to place wood blocks beside type and to print such a sheet with one pull of the press bar. Just two decades after Gutenberg's forty-two-line Bible, printers of the 1470s produced a library of illustrated books, including *The Golden Legend*, *The History of the Destruction of Troy*, Aesop's fables, and works by Boccaccio and Petrarch (Martin 229). Great artists worked as illustrators; the wood engravings of Albrecht Dürer, including his *Apocalypse* (1498), *Great Passion* (1498–1501), and *Life of the Virgin* (1502–1510), were issued first as prints and later in bound volumes. In the early 1500s emblem books came into vogue; the *Iconologie* of Caesare Ripa, published in 1539, is a dictionary of visual signs, describing the symbols for the virtues, vices, wisdom, justice, and other qualities. Both Protestants and Catholics used printed images for propaganda.

The forces allied with print during the fifteenth, sixteenth, and seventeenth centuries are ambiguous, and distinctions between cause and effect are problematic. Much of what is claimed for print by the proponents of alphabetic literacy is in fact the heritage of Enlightenment rationality. If the cognitive effects of literacy are as profound as some proponents have claimed (for example, Jack Goody and Ian Watt maintain that Aristotle's syllogistic reasoning was made possible by writing), then these effects should be manifest in the nineteenth and twentieth centuries, by which time the spread of mass literacy and the proliferation of cheap printed texts should have extended the benefits of print literacy.

The assumption of a cognitive gulf created by alphabetic literacy was effectively challenged by Sylvia Scribner and Michael Cole, who studied the Vai of Liberia, a people who had developed literacy apart from schooling. Scribner and Cole found that while literacy produces differences in certain contexts, in the important dimension of logical thinking, literates and illiterates do not differ in performance; many of the abilities claimed especially for literates could be attributed to schooling. Scribner and Cole pointed the way for new concepts of literacy as pluralistic and socially situated. That the narrow view of literacy as alphabetic literacy has dominated so long into the twentieth century stems directly from the limited tools most people had for producing texts. Beginning in the nineteenth century, people were exposed to many mass-produced images, and in the twentieth century to broadcast audio and video, but until very recently most people had little opportunity to produce and distribute images, audio, or video themselves. With the advent of the World Wide Web in the mid-1990s, technologies of the visual can no longer be denied.

Technologies of the Visual

In an often-quoted passage in *Ways of Seeing*, John Berger observes:

The visual arts have always existed within a certain preserve; originally this preserve was magical or sacred. But it was also physical: it was the place, the cave, the building, in which, or for which, the work was made. The experience of art, which at first was the experience of ritual, was set apart from the rest of life—precisely in order to be able to exercise power over it. Later the preserve of art became a social one. It entered the culture of the ruling class, whilst physically it was set apart and isolated in their palaces and houses. During all this history the authority of art was inseparable from the particular authority of the preserve.

What the modern means of reproduction have done is to destroy the authority of art and to remove it—or, rather, to remove its images which they reproduce—from any preserve. For the first time ever, images of art have become ephemeral, ubiquitous, insubstantial, available, valueless, free. They surround us in the same way as a language surrounds us. They have entered the mainstream of life over which they no longer, in themselves, have power. (89)

Although Berger is discussing great art, his distrust of mass-produced images— both explicit and implicit in this passage—is widely held. Berger is indebted to Walter Benjamin here, but the overall argument has been embraced by both conservative and radical social critics. The assumption is that outside cloistered art, images lack the capacity to encourage deep reflection, serious thought, or even the creation of identity. Instead, they play on the emotions, encourage stereotypes, and at best merely record reality—even though the recording of reality is hardly a simple process.

The recording of reality was a focal problem in Gutenberg's productive years in the mid-fifteenth century. Some of the great masterpieces of the Italian Renaissance, including Botticelli's *Primavera*, were painted on commission from the Medici and other patrons within twenty years of the printing of the forty-two-line Bible. We know from theoretical treatises by painters such as Cennino and Alberti at the beginning of the fifteenth century that they took as their goals the imitation of natural objects, and above all the illusion of three-dimensional space. The masters of the Italian Renaissance succeeded in establishing a dominant though often challenged ideal of literal naturalism that would not be completely overturned until the advent of photography brought painting into crisis.

Berger decries the way great art loses authority when it is mass-reproduced, but we often hear this thesis extended to a claim that we now live in a culture based on images that is somehow different from our past. This claim is one of the great misperceptions of the alphabetic literacy narrative. Preliterate peoples fashioned many everyday images. We know best only the pieces with most skilled craftsmanship, because they are the ones represented in museums. Less frequently exhibited are thousands of everyday objects from prehistoric and historic cultures. Every known culture, past and present, has a language of images. The primary difference, as Berger points out, is the means of reproduction. The rapid expansion of technologies of reproduction in the nineteenth century brought the modern era of the image. Most accounts of the book discuss the development of the steam press around 1814 and of the rotary press in 1847—both of which increased production from about three hundred hand-pressed sheets a day to more than twelve thousand sections—and that of linotype in 1885, a process that automated composition and replaced the handwork of routine typesetting. Along with woodpulp paper, which came about 1875, these technologies made mass media possible. Less noted in histories of printing is the rapid improvement in engraving that occurred during the nineteenth century. Wood engravings, which had been replaced by copper, were brought back to illustrate newspapers. In 1804 the *Times* of London began to feature illustrations. Unlike earlier wood engravings, which were carved with knives, the new generation of wood engravers used the more precise burin. Steel engravings were also introduced by the 1830s, and the overall quality of all engravings increased dramatically by the 1850s. In the United States, *Frank Leslie's Illustrated Newspaper* began in 1855, and the more famous *Harper's Weekly* in 1857. Both covered the Civil War extensively and featured the work of outstanding artists, including Alfred Waud and Winslow Homer.

More accurate engravings brought the desire for even more true-to-life images. As early as the Renaissance, artists aspired to reproduce exactly what they saw. In 1519 Leonardo da Vinci described the camera obscura, and many other artists experimented with it to explore problems of perspective, but it was not until the nineteenth century that a technology developed to fix images. The daguerreotype, presented to the Académie des Sciences in Paris in 1839, quickly became a medium of popular portraiture. By 1851 the wet-plate process made photography widely available. With their heavy, clumsy equipment, photographers began to document the world around them. Within a few years the uses of photography proliferated, extending from art and ethnographic recording to postcards and pornography. In 1889 the first inexpensive Kodak cameras were marketed, made possible by George Eastman's invention of flexible roll film, and by the turn of the century many Americans were pasting photographs into family albums. Photographs also became widely distributed consumer objects through the popularity of stereo viewers, introduced at the 1851 Great Exhibition in London's Crystal Palace, to the delight of Queen Victoria. In 1856 twin-lens cameras made stereo viewers a long-running consumer fad. From 1860 to 1920, millions of stereo viewers were manufactured and sold; they gave the illusion of three-dimensional solidity, an effect that neither engraving nor painting could achieve.[3] For the first time a visual medium produced the illusion of actually seeing the object itself, conflating the image with reality. The new visual technologies of the photograph and stereoscope were deeply implicated in the expansion of industrial capitalism and colonialism: once the world was made visible, it became appropriable and transformable.

The spread of photographs, postcards, and comics in the last decades of the nineteenth century, along with the continuing proliferation of posters, illustrated books, and illustrated newspapers, brought predictable conservative responses (see Harris). Pictures were accused of offering an overly simplified view of the world, a view that lacked interpretation. Furthermore, photographs could be staged and retouched to give misleading views of reality. Stronger accusations were leveled against the new genre of the comic strip, which began in 1895 when a staff illustrator, Richard Felton Outcault, working for Joseph Pulitzer's *World*, published a one-panel cartoon called "Down Hogan's Alley," featuring a gap-toothed, bald little boy in a long frock. Shortly after, the *World's* printers were experimenting with colored ink and ran a test yellow on the boy's frock. Thus was born "The Yellow Kid," credited as the first comic strip; many others shortly followed. Comics were alleged to corrupt the morals and manners of youth.

Despite these warnings, the invasion of images accelerated. In the twentieth century, image technologies have diversified to an extent that makes even a quick sketch impossible. The trajectory of bringing more and better images into printed texts led to the publication in 1936 of *Life*, the first mass-market picture magazine.[4] Even more transformative image technologies had been launched by the time *Life* appeared. Beginning with Eadweard Muybridge's 1877 photographic experiment to prove that galloping horses lift all four hooves off the ground at once, innovations in the photography of movement made motion pictures possible, and the commercial potential was quickly recognized. In the first decade of the twentieth century in Europe and the United States, film companies were created, special theaters were built, and very profitable distribution networks were established. By 1910, twenty-six million Americans were going to the movies at nickelodeon theaters every week (Merritt 86). Television became technically feasible in 1931, and the BBC began broadcasting televised programs in 1936. In the United States following World War II, television grew in a way that predicted the speed of the Internet: the number of sets in use passed one million in 1949 and ten million just two years later; by 1959, fifty million television sets were being watched in the United States. With the development of telecommunications and computer technologies, the potential of television was convincingly demonstrated in 1969 in live broadcasts from the surface of the moon. Less spectacular but no less influential has been the expansion of video and audio recording and production technologies to reach mass markets. The majority of American households now have answering machines and VCRs, and many have computers, video cameras, fax machines, synthesizers, and sophisticated audio equipment. The most powerful combination of these technologies is the World Wide Web, which possesses a massive capacity for distributing images and is already a means for distributing audio and video.

The progression of computer-generated images in motion pictures gives us a sense of where we are headed. The first major studio film to use computer graphics was *Futureworld*, a 1976 science fiction thriller that computer-mapped the head of Peter Fonda on a monitor. Many people think that the battle scenes in *Star Wars* were created with computer graphics, but actually they were made with small scale models. The first film to use computer graphics to advance a plot line was *Tron* (1982), with about twenty minutes of the movie produced by computers. *Tron*, however, was a box office flop, and it was not until the 1990s, with films like *Terminator 2*, that the commercial potential of computer graphics in films was realized. In 1995 Disney's *Toy Story* became the first film with every frame generated by computers. Digital humans are now used in dangerous movie stunts formerly performed by people. The era of the virtual actor—the "vactor" or "synthespian"—cannot be far in the future. Craig Barrett, the chief operating officer at Intel, predicts that very soon the technology of the $75,000 workstation that produced *Jurassic Park* will cost about $2,000 ("Intel View"). He foresees that personal computers in the year 2011 will use a chip that has as many as a billion transistors, compared with about eight million in today's most advanced chip. The web sites of Ben Syverson, Jessica Draper, and Kate Levy only hint at what might be just around the corner.

Literacy as Design

Even after a century and a half of saturation with mass-market image technologies, the heritage of alphabetic literacy from the Enlightenment still dominates within the academy and in literacy instruction. The totemization of alphabetic literacy and the denial of the materiality of literacy have had the attendant effect of treating images as trivial, transitory, and manipulative. Visual thinking remains excluded from the mainstream literacy curriculum in the schools, and it is taught only in specialized courses in college, in disciplines such as architecture and art history. When, in the early 1960s, one of the first designers of three-dimensional computer graphics, Lawrence G. Roberts, looked for scholarship on perspectival imaging, he found a dearth of work in the twentieth century; instead, he had to refer to German geometry textbooks from the early nineteenth century to find a mathematics of perspective.

Perhaps because images are ubiquitous, we in the academy have paid little attention to how they work. But an even stronger reason may be that images have been so thoroughly appropriated by advertising. No aspect of our culture is more despised from the viewpoint of the academic humanities than advertising, the discursive Anti-Christ that does everything the tradition of academic literacy detests: it persuades with images; it acts on the emotions; it bends and stretches language; it employs humor and parody; it cannot always be explained; and it is anonymous. To parade the usual statistics, we see more than three thousand ads a day, and today's teenagers will probably spend a decade of their lives watching ads; but this is only stating the obvious (Twitchell 2). It is now difficult to find any public space free of advertising or to listen to or watch any public medium, including the public channels, without encountering ads. The state of Iowa sells advertising in its income tax booklet. Universities have cashed in by selling sponsorship of sports teams to shoe manufacturers, signing exclusive deals with soft-drink companies, and selling rights to their own images. Penn State football jerseys, which used to be distinctive for their lack of adornment, now display the Nike logo.

Advertising is a 158 billion-dollar business in the United States and has grown to around 200 billion dollars in the rest of the world, with Western-style advertising quickly expanding into emerging markets like China and Vietnam. Nonetheless, the academic response to advertising continues to be to ignore it, to accuse it of deception, and to dismiss it as trash. The basic criticisms of advertising remain the same: either by outright deception or, more insidiously, by creating wants and desires that otherwise would not exist, advertising causes people to purchase goods they have no wish to purchase. Herbert Marcuse is representative in arguing that advertising creates false needs that perpetuate misery and injustice: "Most of the prevailing needs to relax, to have fun, to behave and consume to accordance with the advertisements, to love and hate what others love and hate, belong to this category of false needs" (5). Certainly there is a long list of products consumed today for which markets barely existed before advertising—cosmetics, deodorants, soft drinks, credit cards, household cleaning products, cigarettes, bottled water, insurance, state lotteries, mouthwash, and most over-the-counter medicines. The usual account of advertising is that it depends on an irrational connection between the product and an object of desire. Throughout most of this century, print ads and later broadcast ads depended on a narrative of the object of desire being attained through purchase of the product. Most often the promise was one of sexual success, either in attracting a partner or in keeping one. The right choice of chewing gum or mouthwash got the partner; the right choice of coffee kept him interested.

Mass media ads of today, however, depend far less on narrative coherence for their appeal. By the late 1980s, advertisers realized that the old tactics would not work for an audience oversaturated with advertising and overly cynical. Thus the emphasis in advertising for a number of products shifted from story to style as advertisers became increasingly self-referential, recirculating images drawn from the cultural landscape, most often from media representations. This mode of advertising—lifting images and meanings from one

"Drink provokes the desire but takes away the
performance"
--William Shakespeare

Figure 8.7. Absolute Impotence. Web site: http://www.adbusters.org.

context and placing them in another—resists the simple analysis of attaching a product to an object of desire. Instead, advertisers enact a conversation of images with their audiences. Advertisers are both manipulators and manipulated, because they must interject their product into an ongoing system of signs. Their effect depends on extending a set of cultural associations.

Since many of those associations are charted on bodies, it is no accident that cultural critics have had to explore the consequences of advertising on bodies in terms other than the creation of false needs (one such exploration is J. Blake Scott's chapter in this book). At no time before in advanced nations have so many people of different genders, ethnicities, age groups, and social classes participated in the altering of their bodies through transplants, implants, augmentations, lifts, and tucks, along with intense regimens of exercise and dieting. Clearly advertising is participating in a much larger cultural discourse in which fat is viewed as ugly and aging as repulsive, but more important, in which personal empowerment is expressed in terms of controlling one's body image. Thus human agency can be summed up in Nike's slogan, "Just Do It!" The problem for scholars criticizing the effects of consumerism and advocating change is how to get their students to interrogate the chains of assumptions in the rhetoric of personal empowerment.

An alternative approach to responding to ads comes from a Canadian media activist group, the Media Foundation, which challenges the advertising it considers harmful by subverting it. The Media Foundation publishes an ad-free magazine, *Adbusters*, and it supports the Adbusters web site, both of which take on specific advertising campaigns with clever spoofs. The group's president, former advertising man Kalle Lasn, explains Adbusters' mission: "I don't have any problem with advertising. I love advertising. We are into selling ideas, not products. We're social marketers, not product marketers. To me, that is a whole different kettle of fish" (Lewis). At the top of the Adbusters' sabotage list have been alcohol and cigarette ads. Because ads are in the public domain, their copyright status is questionable, and Adbusters has pushed that question. One target has been Absolut vodka. "Absolut Impotence," shows an empty, shriveling bottle with a caption quoting Shakespeare: "Drink provokes the desire but takes away the performance." In February 1992, Absolut threatened to sue Adbusters, but Absolut quickly backed it down when it recognized that the suit would lead to a public debate about protecting advertisers who sell dangerous products.

A more difficult challenge for Adbusters is posed by ads that fetishize glamor. Adbusters has launched a spoof campaign against one of the most exploitive marketers, Calvin Klein, using the gray-scale tones its ads are famous for. Adbusters produced a thirty-second spot that points to the connection between eating disorders and the worship of the adolescent body in fashion images. The commercial begins with a soft-focus image of a thin, naked woman,

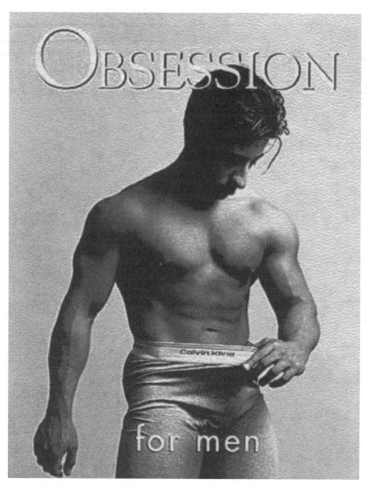

Figure 8.8. Obsession for men. Web site: http://www.adbusters.org.

accompanied by a voice-over saying, "Obsession, fascination, fetish." The writhing woman appears to be in slow-motion ecstasy until we realize that she is vomiting into a toilet bowl. The voice says, "Why do nine out of ten women feel dissatisfied with some aspect of their bodies? The beauty industry is the beast." Several women's groups joined Adbusters in purchasing four spots for the CBC show *Fashion File*, and they attempted to buy airspace on CNN's *Style with Elsa Klensch*. Both networks refused to run Adbusters' uncommercial.[5]

Even though Adbusters' uncommercial was censored by the networks, it and other uncommercials have been viewed by many people via the World Wide Web. The Adbusters' URL is frequently mentioned in lists of favorite web sites

Figure 8.9. Obsession for women. Web site: http://www.adbusters.org.

in newspapers and on individuals' home pages. It offers a critique of the visual iconography of the perfect body and the "Just Do It" rhetoric of personal empowerment embedded that iconography. Adbusters seeks to redefine agency by "trickle-up" activism. The "Culture Jammers Toolbox" section of the site gives production advice on how to introduce noise into focus groups, compose alternative print ads, make television spots, buy television time, and subvert billboards with spray-painted modifications.

The "Culture Jammers Toolbox" says nothing about making web sites, but the Web has become the primary medium for grass-roots media activism. Among the tens of thousands of web sites of individuals are many pages devoted to media criticism and parodies of advertising. This activism has come at a time when the Internet has become the battleground for the deregulated corporate giants, where control of the coaxial cable and fiber-optic conduits represents only a small part of the potential fortunes to be made from an array of services carried through the pipe: advertising, credit cards, banking, entertainment, news, and sales of other products. Given the corporate vision of the Internet as the ultimate Home Shopping Network, is there reason to expect anything other than a more accelerated, more international, and much more profitable global consumer culture?

The Web and Material Matters

In spite of all the talk about the Internet as cyberspace and a virtual world, the materiality of the Internet as a medium is unavoidable. You sit in front of a machine that has to be turned on and connected to the net. And if you want to access the resources of the World Wide Web, you need at least a 28.8 kilobytes-per-second modem and a computer with enough memory to support the current versions of Netscape Navigator or Internet Explorer. Kate Levy puts it bluntly: "My homepage uses frames. If you can't handle this, I'm sorry." In the United States, not every neighborhood has access to a local server, and in the rest of the world, almost the entire continent of Africa outside South Africa is not on line. At present the Internet continues the one-way flow of information from the First to the Third World. Can the Internet become a factor in promoting a two-way flow between the margins and the center?

One of the groups least likely to become a significant presence on the World Wide Web is the Ejército Zapatista de Liberación Nacional, whose members rose in rebellion in Mexico on New Year's Day, 1994, the day the North American Free Trade Agreement went into effect. The Zapatistas are primarily indigenous people from the Lacandón mountain jungles of Chiapas, Mexico's southernmost state, bordering on Guatemala. They take their name from Emiliano Zapata, hero of the Mexican Revolution, who was the champion of land reform and indigenous peoples in the south of Mexico. Estimates of the Zapatista forces vary, but the high-end guess of the number of well-armed troops is only three thousand.

The Zapatista uprising took the Mexican government by surprise. When Luis Donaldo Colosio was unveiled on 28 November 1993 as the presidential candidate of Mexico's governing Institutional Revolutionary Party (PRI), the policies of President Carlos Salinas, in his last year of a six-year term, appeared to be firmly in place. The signing of the North American Free Trade Agreement

(NAFTA) cemented Salinas's free-market economic policy, and opposition on the right and left was not attracting wide popularity. Colosio seemed to be the ideal candidate to continue Salinas's modernization policy. But on 1 January, the day NAFTA went into effect, the smooth road of Colosio's ascendancy suddenly developed a deep rut. The Zapatistas, unsuccessful in their previous efforts to address the misery of the people in Chiapas, called on Article 39 of the Mexican Constitution, which states that "the people have, at all times, the inalienable right to alter or modify the form of their government." They seized four towns in Chiapas, including San Cristóbal de las Casas.

In other years, the news of the uprising would have been suppressed in Mexico and little noticed abroad. Most people in the United States have never heard of Chiapas and probably would have overlooked a brief report in the back pages of a newspaper, just as they paid little attention to the concurrent massacres of people in East Timor. But the Zapatistas had two great allies: their timing, and their innovative use of communications technologies. The Zapatistas faxed their Declaration of War to newspapers, to radio and television stations, and to the international press. They represented themselves as the heirs to the long struggle for social justice in Mexico—the legacy of Emiliano Zapata and the Mexican Revolution of 1810. On the second day of the uprising, they held theatrical press conferences at which men, women, and children wore black ski masks. They invited reporters from the major international papers, including *Der Spiegel*, *Le Figaro* and the *New York Times*, the independent Mexican dailies *La Journada* and *El Financiero*, and European television crews, but they refused access for the pro-government Mexican media (Gómez-Peña 91). The primary spokesperson for the Zapatistas, Subcomandante Marcos, was photographed with a pipe sticking out of his mask and a Zapata-style bandolero with shotgun shells that didn't match the rifle slung over his shoulder. The Zapatista media campaign within Mexico was enormously successful, forcing the government to declare a cease-fire on 9 February. On the day of the cease-fire, more than one hundred thousand people in Mexico City marched in support of the Zapatistas. A month later, the hand-picked PRI candidate, Colosio, was assassinated after expressing sympathy for the Zapatistas. By the end of the year, the Mexican economy had crashed with a huge flight of capital out of the country, and former president Salinas had fled into exile.

The Zapatistas effectively used the Internet for an ongoing alternative commentary on politics in Mexico. They critiqued NAFTA and the Mexican government's treatment of indigenous peoples, and they disputed the modernist view of peasant communities as isolated, backward, societies that should be relegated to the past as quickly as possible. They have explained why it is important to have a viable and sustainable peasant agriculture if the rain forests of Chiapas and the cultures of its Mayan peoples are to be preserved. The Zapatistas have been greatly assisted by academics in Mexico and the United States, who have created distribution sites and translated communiqués. On-line discussion lists concerning Chiapas were formed in Mexico and in the United States, and a web site, "¡Ya Basta!," was begun in spring 1994 by Justin Paulson, then an undergraduate student at Swarthmore. The web site has become much publicized through articles in magazines and newspapers, including the *Guardian* (U.K.) and *Reforma* (Mexico). In April 1995, the Mexican foreign minister, José Angel Gurría, declared that the uprising in Chiapas is a "guerra de tinta y de Internet" ("a war of ink and of the Internet").

The cleverness of the Zapatistas in distributing images has been one of the keys to their success. Subcomandante Marcos even created a cartoon

Figure 8.10. Subcomandante Marcos, spokesperson for the Zapatistas. Web site no longer available.

Figure 8.11. Venustiano Carranza, Casa del Popolo, July 1996 (Photograph by Massimo Boldrini). Web site no longer available.

character, a loquacious beetle named Don Durito, who skillfully avoids being stepped on. To reach sympathetic people in advanced nations, the Zapatistas have taken advantage of the graphic power of the Web to issue many images of themselves, which portray both their revolutionary struggle and the daily lives of indigenous people. Without those images, I doubt that the numerous web sites around the world that support the Zapatistas would be quite so prominent. The Zapatistas, with a little help from their friends, have shown how the disempowered can also engage in cross-marketing if they understand the material effects of visual literacy. After nearly five years of intermittent peace talks, the Mexican government still has not granted the people of Chiapas the right of self-government. But if the Zapatistas have failed thus far to win a just settlement, the government likewise has failed to restore credibility in its ability to lead the people of Mexico, and violent uprisings of other groups have occurred in Guerrero and other states. The Zapatista rebellion exposed quickly the sense that the only people in Mexico who would benefit from NAFTA would be the urban elites in the North and in Mexico City, while the indigenous peoples and the poor would suffer even greater marginalization.

The Zapatistas also offer an important lesson in material literacy. In the face of claims that computer-mediated language and images have broken with the past and have lost reference to the perceived world, the Zapatistas have shown that although language and images are increasingly self-referential, they still have material consequences. The example of Chiapas demonstrates that people are still adapting new technologies of literacy for their own purposes, that literacy can still be used to promote social justice, and that history, including the history of literacy, indeed still continues.

history still continues

Notes

1. For critiques of the oral-literate dichotomy, see Brandt; Daniell; and Street.

2. In this respect, the achievement of Gutenberg compares with that of James Watt, who is often credited with inventing the steam engine. In 1765 Watt repaired an existing steam engine designed by Thomas Newcome and made a minor modification that allowed the engine to pump water more efficiently out of coal mines. Watt thereby became wealthy as a manufacturer of steam-driven mine pumps. The gearing system that allowed the steam engine to be used to power factories, making possible the Industrial Revolution, was invented sixteen years later by one of Watt's employees, William Murdock.

3. The research on vision that led to the development of the stereoscope was done in the 1820s and 1830s, thus preceding the development of photography. See Crary 116–36.

4. The first issue of *Life* sold out all 250,000 copies on its first day of release, and soon a million and a half copies a week went into American homes. *Life* was preceded by European periodicals that used glossy paper, making possible a photographic realism unavailable in newspapers. *Life*, however, was unique in allowing photographs to

tell its stories, relying on the visual literacy of its readers. It was also the first magazine to generate the majority of its revenue from advertising, which also depended on photographs. Its success relied on the ambiguity of the title—that the images in the magazine are not about life, they *are* life (Berger, *About Looking* 50).

5. Adbusters also attempted to buy time on CNN, ABC, NBC, and CBS for a spot declaring the day after Thanksgiving "Buy Nothing Day." The spot opens with an image of a bloated pink plastic pig, wiggling and grinning. The voice-over says, "The average North American consumes five times more than a Mexican, ten times more than a Chinese person, and thirty times more than a person from India." Then the spot cuts to a bulldozer piling up a mountain of trash in a landfill. The voice continues, "We are the most voracious consumers in the world. . . . Give it a rest. November 29 is Buy Nothing Day." CNN ran the ad once, but the other major networks refused it. Richard Gitter, NBC's vice president of advertising standards and program compliance, says that NBC does not air controversial ads. Gitter continued with more candor, "This action was taken in self-interest. It was a spot telling people, in effect, to ignore our advertisers" (Oldenburg).

Works Cited

"Adbusters Culture Jammers Headquarters." 3 October 1997. http://www. adbusters.org/ (3 Nov. 1997).

Berger, John. *About Looking*. New York: Pantheon, 1980.

Berger, John. *Ways of Seeing*. New York: Viking, 1973.

Bolter, Jay David. "Ekphrasis, Virtual Reality, and the Future of Writing." In *The Future of the Book*, edited by Geoffrey Nunberg, 253–72. Berkeley: University of California Press, 1996.

Bordo, Susan R. *Twilight Zones: The Hidden Life of Cultural Images from Plato to O.J.* Berkeley: University of California Press, 1997.

Brandt, Deborah. *Literacy as Involvement: The Acts of Writers, Readers, and Texts*. Carbondale: Southern Illinois University Press, 1990.

Chartier, Roger. *The Order of Books: Readers, Authors and Libraries in Europe between the Fourteenth and Eighteenth Centuries*. Translated by Lydia G. Cochrane. Cambridge: Polity, 1994.

Claiborne, Robert. *The Birth of Writing*. Alexandria, Va.: Time-Life Books, 1974.

Crary, Jonathan. *Techniques of the Observer: On Vision and Modernity in the Nineteenth Century*. Cambridge, Mass.: MIT Press, 1990.

Daniell, Beth. "Against the Great Leap Theory of Literacy." *PRE/TEXT* 7 (1986): 181–93.

Diderot, Denis, and Jean le Rond d'Alembert. *Encyclopédie*. Vol. 5. Paris: Briasson, David, Le Breton, Durand, 1755.

Draper, Jessica. "llanarth's lair." http://chs-web.neb.net/~llanarth/ (15 May 1997).

Eisenstein, Elizabeth L. *The Printing Press as an Agent of Change: Communications and Cultural Transformations in Early Modern Europe*. Cambridge: Cambridge University Press, 1979.

Febvre, Lucien, and Henri-Jean Martin. *The Coming of the Book: The Impact of Printing, 1450–1800*. Translated by David Gerard. London: NLB, 1976.

Gelb, Ignace J. *A Study of Writing*. Chicago: University of Chicago Press, 1974.

Gómez-Peña, Guillermo. "The Subcomandante of Performance." In *First World, Ha Ha Ha! The Zapatista Challenge*, edited by Elaine Katzenberger, 89–96. San Francisco: City Lights, 1995.

Goody, Jack. *The Domestication of the Savage Mind*. Cambridge: Cambridge University Press, 1977.

Goody, Jack, and Ian P. Watt. "The Consequences of Literacy." *Comparative Studies in Society and History* 5 (1963): 304–45.

Haas, Christina. *Writing Technology: Studies on the Materiality of Literacy*. Mahway, N.J.: Lawrence Erlbaum, 1996.

Harris, Neal. "Pictorial Perils: The Rise of American Illustration." In *Cultural Excursions: Marketing Appetites and Cultural Tastes in Modern America*, by Neal Harris, 337–48. Chicago: University of Chicago Press, 1990.

Hassan, Ahmad Y. al-, and Donald R. Hill. *Islamic Technology: An Illustrated History*. Cambridge: Cambridge University Press, 1986.

Havelock, Eric. *The Literate Revolution in Greece and Its Cultural Consequences*. Princeton: Princeton University Press, 1982.

Innis, Harold. *The Bias of Communication*. Toronto: University of Toronto Press, 1951.

"The Intel View Of Future PC's." *New York Times*, 23 April 1997.

Levy, Kate. "Freedom of speech, good to the last drop." http://chsweb.neb.net/ ~katelevy/ (15 May 1997).

Lewis, Peter. "Site-Seeing—Adbusters." *Seattle Times*, 8 June 1997.

Logan, Robert K. *The Alphabet Effect: The Impact of the Phonetic Alphabet on the Development of Western Civilization*. New York: William Morrow, 1986.

Marcuse, Herbert. *One Dimensional Man: Studies in the Ideology of Advanced Industrial Society*. Boston: Beacon, 1964.

Martin, Henri-Jean. *The History and Power of Writing*. Translated by Lydia G. Cochrane. Chicago: University of Chicago Press, 1994.

Merritt, Russell. "Nickelodeon Theaters, 1905–1914: Building an Audience for the Movies." In *The American Film Industry*, edited by Tino Balio, 83–102. Rev. ed. Madison: University of Wisconsin Press, 1985.

Oldenburg, Don. "No-Shop Option; Campaign to Change 'Thanksgiving' Friday." *Washington Post*, 28 November 1996.

Ong, Walter J. *Orality and Literacy: The Technologizing of the Word*. New York: Methuen, 1982.

Paulson, Justin. "¡Ya Basta!" 20 October 1997. http://www.ezln.org (4 November 1997).

Roberts, Lawrence G. *Machine Perception of Three-Dimensional Solids*. Lexington, Mass.: MIT Lincoln Laboratory TR 315, 1963.

Schmandt-Besserat, Denise. *Before Writing*. Vol. 1. *From Counting to Cuneiform*. Austin: University of Texas Press, 1992.

Scribner, Sylvia, and Michael Cole. *The Psychology of Literacy*. Cambridge, Mass.: Harvard University Press, 1981.

Stafford, Barbara Marie. *Good Looking: Essays on the Virtue of Images*. Cambridge, Mass.: MIT Press, 1996.

Street, Brian V. *Social Literacies: Critical Approaches to Literacy in Development, Ethnography and Education*. London: Longman, 1995.

Syverson, Ben. "Phaedrus Media." 20 May 1997. http://www.eden.com/~ben/ (3 November 1997).

Time, Inc. "Time Warner's Pathfinder!" 15 May 1997. http://pathfinder.com/ (15 May 1997).

Twitchell, James B. *Adcult USA: The Triumph of Advertising in American Culture.* New York: Columbia University Press, 1996.

Warburton, William. *Divine Legation of Moses.* London: Fletcher Gyles, 1738.

Wordsworth, William. "Illustrated Books and Newspapers." In *The Poetical Works of William Wordsworth*, edited by William Knight, vol. 8, 174–75. London: Macmillan, 1896.

9 *John Schilb*

Autobiography after Prozac

In 1993 Susanna Kaysen published *Girl, Interrupted*, a best-selling memoir of her year-long stay as a mental patient in Boston's McLean Hospital when she was eighteen years old. In brief but telling chapters, Kaysen chronicles life on her ward, especially her own life. Occasionally she ponders developments in medicine, psychology, and other fields in the years since she was hospitalized. Toward the end of the book, she comments specifically on a trend in neuroscience:

A lot of mind . . . is turning out to be brain. A memory is a particular pattern of cellular changes on particular spots in our heads. A mood is a compound of neurotransmitters. Too much acetylcholine, not enough serotonin, and you've got a depression. (137)

Kaysen doesn't urge that this biochemical discourse be rejected. Regretting that "the analysts are writing about a country they call Mind and the neuroscientists are reporting from a country they call Brain" (142), she implies that these two groups should converse more. Yet if her memoir is beholden to either of their discourses, it is the discourse of Mind. Whenever she describes her personal moods, she avoids describing them as "compounds of neurotransmitters." More often, she uses not the rarefied vocabulary of laboratories and scientific journals but the kind of talk ordinary people have used in discussing mental conditions. Probably her memoir would have been altogether different, if in ways we cannot determine, had she embraced maxims like "Too much acetylcholine, not enough serotonin, and you've got a depression."

Nonetheless, such language has spread with the emergence of psychological materialism as a way of thought. I am not sure who coined the term "psychological materialism," but in a 1997 letter to the *Washington Post*, the psychiatrist Peter Kramer wrote as if it was now part of his profession's vernacular. Kramer brought up the term as he defended his 1993 book *Listening to Prozac*, which takes a generally positive view of that drug. In his letter, he did not exactly define "psychological materialism," but he did associate it with studies of how cells, neurotransmitters, serotonin, and other features of the body affect human thinking.

Repeatedly, research on the subject of psychological materialism has indicated that our minds are strongly influenced by physiological events in the "country" of "Brain." The links have not been firmly pinpointed; as research, psychological materialism is still work in progress. Nevertheless, it has already acquired great intellectual cachet. Even the general public has grown comfortable about referring to serotonin when discussing what causes stress. The public is more aware, though, of the drugs that psychological materialism has produced. A lot of us are not just listening to Prozac but also taking it. First marketed by the Eli Lilly Company in 1987, it has become this country's seventh most often prescribed medication. As Elizabeth Wurtzel indicates with the title of her own widely read memoir, the United States can now be called "Prozac Nation."

Here, I am not out to praise Prozac or to condemn it. Quite simply, I think it can be good for some people and bad for others. What I want to do here is to consider how its present widespread use may affect autobiographical rhetoric. The drug itself, the research that produced it, and the studies following in its wake may all lead to new accounts of selfhood. What exactly might autobiography look like after Prozac, in the age of psychological materialism?

This is a complicated question. Still, I want to complicate it even more by noting that psychological materialism is not the only materialism ever proposed. Throughout history there have been numerous materialisms, and moreover, they have often competed with one another. At the Penn State conference on material rhetoric, many papers dealt with psychological materialism in one way or another, even if they didn't call it that. As the chapters in this book attest, several other writers focused on materialisms akin to the psychological; I think in particular of Celeste Condit's chapter on genetic science. These chapters were interesting, and they taught me a great deal, yet I was dismayed that only a small number of materialisms got extensive treatment. There was one in particular that I thought should have been considered more; were he still alive, it would quite likely have been brought up at the meeting by the composition historian and theorist James Berlin. As I sat listening to others talk, I could imagine him brusquely asking them all the same thing: "What about *historical materialism?*"

To define "historical materialism" in all its possible range and complexity would require many volumes. Here I simply use the term to denote both Marxist and neo-Marxist thought. In various ways, these schools have been at odds, and they have suffered internal conflicts as well. Both, however, assume that economic conditions and cultural circumstances greatly and fundamentally affect human lives. What I am calling historical materialism focuses on more than on individual brains or bodies; it insists on situating selves within societies, and it is especially concerned with how capitalist societies enforce dominance and subordination. At the same time, historical materialism is not just a mode of analysis. It actively tries to bring about a better world.

Why did the conference participants slight *this* kind of materialism? I can think of several reasons. With the demise of Communist rule in the Soviet Union and its former satellites, the credibility of leftist thought has eroded. In addition, its perennial attention to social class has threatened to marginalize other key variables, such as gender, race, sexuality, and culture. To be fair, however, many leftists have now widened their concerns. Though still attending to class, they do not dwell on it alone but rather view human life as shaped by various elements. Furthermore, the relative absence of historical materialism at the Penn State conference fits academic tradition. Although conservatives like Roger Kimball, Lynn Cheney, and John Ellis find this form of materialism all too present in higher education, American universities have never afforded it real status. I would even argue, as I suspect Berlin would, that rhetoric and composition have been distinctly unfriendly to Marxist and neo-Marxist views. The field's basic agenda has been ameliorative and reformist. Far from aiming to transform existing social structures, it has tried to help the individual self produce discourse within them.

Nevertheless, historical materialism deserves to be treated by all fields as more than a relic. True, today capitalism seems to be triumphing worldwide, but its current ubiquity should drive people to consult a body of work that has long studied, theorized, and judged it. I am not calling for historical materialism to be accepted uncritically. Among other things, its utopian component has to be rethought. Nor do I think this kind of materialism can be easily applied, for more than ever, capitalism's complex, rapid dynamics are hard to grasp and address, as even hard-core Marxists like Frederic Jameson readily admit. (After all, these processes involve the far-flung and speedy circulation of commodities, firms, and data.) Genetic mapping of the individual body seems more feasible than cognitive mapping (Jameson's name for the task of tracing and transforming class relations in the new world order), but historical materialism can still be as insightful and efficacious as any other materialism, including the psychological kind that Kramer invokes.

In the next section, I will consider what psychological materialism implies for autobiography; in particular, I will refer to Prozac, using Peter Kramer's book on it as a guide. Following that, I will look at autobiography in the age of

Prozac by drawing on historical materialism. Next, referring to both materialisms, I will examine the rhetoric of a specific autobiographical essay by a Prozac user. In conclusion, I will return to both materialisms and suggest yet another way of connecting them.

Psychological Materialism

To begin considering what autobiography might look like after Prozac, let us turn first to Kramer's book, a report of what he has learned about Prozac after prescribing it for several of his patients. Kramer in the end assumes that Prozac will turn out to be "on balance a progressive force" (272), but he is sometimes ambivalent and sometimes downright uneasy about trends it has prompted or may prompt. Moreover, he admits that neuroscientists are still rather ignorant about how the brain works, let alone how drugs like Prozac affect it.

In his own spirit of tentative exploration, Kramer also suggests several ways that Prozac can influence people's notion of self. He reports seeing numerous instances in which it has dramatically changed patients' personalities, often abruptly: "You take it to treat a symptom, and it transforms your sense of self" (222). He notes, too, that it has given quite a few of his patients a new sense of security, which in turn has enabled them to explore their pasts in analytic sessions. Kramer is apparently concerned, however, that with the success of Prozac and similar drugs, society will come to see character traits as biological mechanisms that can, if necessary, be "fixed" (in both senses of the word) one by one. He also worries that people will increasingly tend to disclaim responsibility for their behavior. Furthermore, he fears that they may overlook the role that experience plays in shaping their identity.

Kramer also points to issues of self-definition that the era of Prozac has produced but not resolved. Among other things, he observes that if a person who shows obsessive-compulsive behavior responds well to Prozac, this may or may not mean that the person should be categorized as suffering from obsessive-compulsive disorder (OCD). To clarify this point, Kramer notes, "If someone develops a pill that makes people less gullible, we will see gullibility as a biological predisposition" (189). Of course, such an explanation of gullibility may be premature or even wrong; nevertheless, it may lead gullible people to describe themselves as essentially and genetically gullible. A similar self-description may result when a person with obsessive-compulsive tendencies finds Prozac alleviating them.

Kramer observes that another issue arises with neuroscientists' increased interest in theories of "kindling." Basically, these theories hold that when people experience psychological trauma, unhealthy dispositions can become "hardwired" into them. These dispositions, in effect, emerge from a memory latent in their body and can be activated by some event. If theories of kindling prove credible, Kramer notes, psychiatrists may prescribe drugs like Prozac even for mild depression, fearing that a full-scale crisis might otherwise erupt. I would add that if you assume that memories slumber within your body, waiting to be revived, your autobiography might differ greatly from self-accounts that rely on conscious recollection.

For the most part, Kramer seems delighted with the changes of personality that his Prozac patients undergo. Still, he wonders how such transformations will affect the traditional belief in a persisting core identity. Referring to one particular patient who changed quite a lot, Kramer poses a question that students of autobiography should also ponder: "How [are] we to reconcile what Prozac did for Tess with our notion of the continuous, autobiographical human self?" (14). Of course, plenty of Americans have thought, like Jay Gatsby, that they could reinvent themselves. In fact, this belief has often been seen as a central plank in our national ideology; thus Prozac can be called a very American drug. Moreover, not every autobiographical book depicts the self as "continuous." Kaysen's is a case in point, as the word "interrupted" in her title suggests. Her book features numerous interruptions or discontinuities: she depicts her year at McLean as an interlude in her life; her short chapters hop from subject to subject, not lingering on any particular one; she plays her hospital records off against her more personal reflections on herself; and she reports how staff members and patients intruded on her privacy. Ultimately, Kaysen's focus on interruptions ironically has the effect of continuity, and they become a unifying thread of her book. Besides, even a fantasy of self-reinvention can serve to hold one's life together. More important, Kramer seems right when he suggests that many people feel as if key aspects of themselves do or should endure.

Ironically again, the Eli Lilly company has supported this conviction in its advertising of Prozac. Consider the ad for the drug that appeared in the 18 August 1997 issue of *People* magazine. Its text referred to depression not as a person's chronic state but rather as a mere interlude in an otherwise happy life. One page of the ad featured a gray picture of rain clouds, signifying the sudden onset of depression; the facing page featured the sun and blue skies, signifying that Prozac dispels an internal storm and restores one's essentially temperate climate. Underscoring the association of Prozac with recovery of self was a slogan at the bottom of the second page: "Welcome back." The ad's emphasis on restoration was at odds with the issue's cover story, "Hollywood's Split Parade," which chronicled an epidemic of celebrity divorces and break-ups; most of the people featured in *People* hardly seem models of a stable, unified existence, but Lilly's ad implies that users of Prozac can achieve this goal. Yet because it is so glib, the ad can easily be seen as a ploy—a transparent attempt to distract readers from the possibility Kramer raises: that Prozac may significantly alter the self.

Suppose that one takes Prozac and finds that certain aspects of his or her identity in fact persist. Even so, psychological materialism throws into question which of these aspects are biochemical. Probably many Prozac users start to ponder how selfhood is related to physiology. Because the drug has become much used as well as much discussed, probably even people *not* taking it are beginning to ask the same thing. Again, scientists are still working to answer another version of the classic mind-body problem. For them, mysteries persist. Meanwhile, more and more autobiographies will probably bring up the mind-body problem *and* offer solutions to it, no matter how tentative their answers must be.

Historical Materialism

If we look at Prozac through the lenses of historical materialism, the Lilly ad still intrigues us. It reminds us that Prozac and similar drugs are products of capitalism, developed and marketed by companies bent on profit. Not that this reminder is blazingly clear—only when we reach the bottom of the ad's second page do we come across the word "Lilly," in minuscule lettering in the right-hand corner.[1] Of course, this reticence about the company's name is a marketing strategy: readers may be more willing to try Prozac if they believe it is purely the product of science.

In an incisive critique of the ad, Erik Parens notes another move it makes. He points out that the ad encourages people to use Prozac for what may be understandable, short-term "situational" depression: "The reader learns that being depressed isn't just feeling down; if you've gotten divorced or lost somebody in your family and you're feeling sad, maybe you have a 'real illness'" (C2). As Parens suggests, Lilly and other manufacturers of psychotropic drugs do more than push their products as remedies; they are also engaged in persuading people to identify themselves as sick. Sometimes that is a wise diagnosis, but at other times it is not. In any case, the companies' existence depends on people seeing themselves as possible consumers of psychopharmacology, and for this to happen, presumably they must see their malaise as disease.

Ads are not the only means of fostering such identification. A remark by Elizabeth Wurtzel indicates another way in which it comes about. In her memoir *Prozac Nation*, Wurtzel recalls that being treated with Prozac led to her being labeled depressive, rather than the other way around. "This is strictly Marxian psychopharmacology," she jokes, "where the material—or rather, pharmaceutical—means determine the way an individual's case history is interpreted" (301). Although she ultimately emphasizes the word "pharmaceutical," my guess is that Wurtzel isn't using the words "Marxian" and "material" simply as brief decoys. I think she is reminding us that pharmaceutical companies *are* material forces, and capitalist ones, pushing certain self-definitions for profit. I suspect that she is gesturing specifically toward the neo-Marxian theory of reification. Espoused most notably by Georg Lukacs, it holds that in a commodified, class-structured society, people feel driven to assume fixed, abstract identities. In the process, they fail to confront social forces operating in and on their lives.

When people get depressed, these social forces may be the main cause, or at least as important a cause as biochemistry is. For example, much research shows that social class can be a factor in depression. Focusing on studies of women, Sharon Lerner notes that "depressive symptoms are consistently higher among less educated and poorer women" (60). Lerner's article was published in a 1997 issue of *Ms.* as part of a special section on psychotropic drugs. In effect, the magazine was emphasizing that depression often relates to gender too. Notwithstanding the visibility of William Styron's memoir *Darkness Visible*, many more women than men are diagnosed as depressive and take drugs such as Prozac. Various explanations for this disparity have been proposed. Recently, for instance, a Canadian research team reported finding significantly lower levels of serotonin in women than in men. Yet even if their finding is confirmed by future studies, surely more than biochemistry is at work when vastly greater numbers of women than men visit psychiatrists and get prescriptions from them. No doubt the power hierarchies, economic arrangements, and gender ideologies of a patriarchal society influence this phenomenon, if in ways that have yet to be precisely delineated. Thus, when a woman sets out to write about her mental difficulties, she has to decide whether and how to link them to society's treatment of her gender. (Actually, the same holds for men, although in their case they would presumably be reflecting on their own socialization as males.) To be sure, gender need not be the sole focus of these accounts; they would probably be more insightful and interesting if they considered gender's interactions with class, race, and other variables.

From a historical materialist perspective, it is also important to consider the ways insurance companies and managed care organizations promote the use of Prozac. To maximize their profits, both kinds of enterprises now force psychiatric hospitals like McLean to release patients quickly rather than providing them with long-term therapy. If Susanna Kaysen were admitted to McLean today, she and the hospital would face much pressure to end her stay within a couple of weeks; only if she were wealthy could she now remain a whole year. In their 1994 book *Under Observation: Life Inside the McLean Psychiatric Hospital*, McLean doctor Alexander Vuckovic and his coauthor Lisa Berger report that "the average number of days a patient stayed at McLean plummeted from 81 days in 1988 to 24 days in late 1992" (22). In fact, by the spring of 1993, "that stay was twenty-two days," and by spring 1994, "that stay had dropped to thirteen days" (xiv). There is no evidence that patients at McLean have become more resilient over the years and are genuinely able to re-enter the world more swiftly. Instead, many of them are being driven out by this country's profit-oriented health care system. A situation like this encourages doctors and patients to rely on psychotropic drugs as an alternative, if limited, form of treatment. If they cannot hospitalize, they are more apt to medicalize.

Insurance and managed care are also likely to play a role in determining who prescribes Prozac. Summarizing a survey done by Scott-Levin, a consulting firm, Parens reports that "Prozac is now prescribed less often by psychiatrists than by primary-care physicians—doctors who aren't specialists in the distinction between clinical and non-clinical mental health conditions" (C2). Although Parens does not say so, I suspect that a big reason behind this trend is the financial arrangements that many primary-care physicians have with insurance companies and HMOs. Increasingly, these doctors are reluctant to send their patients to any specialists, including psychiatrists, because they stand to lose money if they exceed a certain number of referrals.

At the same time, and as Blake Scott notes elsewhere in this book, this country's health care system has the effect of *denying* many people access to drugs like Prozac. These drugs are expensive; if you do not have much money, and if you do not have insurance, then it will probably be out of your reach. I have yet to read the autobiography of an unemployed or working-class person on Prozac. As with much else, economic conditions determine who can afford to make a product a central part of his or her life.

These conditions also figure in the production and distribution of autobiographies written by users of Prozac. Such books are becoming hot commodities themselves. As many cultural commentators have remarked, the publishing industry is currently going through a "memoir boom," with an emphasis on books about psychologically dysfunctional individuals or families. The commercial success of Kramer's *Listening to Prozac*, Styron's *Darkness Visible*, Wurtzel's *Prozac Nation*, and Kay Redfield Jamison's *An Unquiet Mind* shows that there is a ready market for personal accounts of depression and of the drugs prescribed for it. Furthermore, the thematic concerns and rhetorical strategies of such books may influence future writers in this genre, especially if publishers solicit autobiographies that imitate what has already sold well.

Lauren Slater's Angels

These meditations lead me to a consideration of one specific memoir, Lauren Slater's essay "Black Swans." Slater is the author of the well-received book *Welcome to My Country*, in which she recalls her experiences as a therapist and as a psychiatric patient herself. "Black Swans" is a later essay, first published in *Missouri Review* and then included in *The Best American Essays 1997*. It focuses on the obsessive-compulsive tendencies that Slater began suffering in her mid-twenties. She found that she could not concentrate. She ended up taking Prozac for her problem and evidently stayed on the drug at least until she wrote these works. As we try to develop methods of analyzing autobiographies deal-ing with Prozac—especially methods that are avowedly "materialist" in vari-ous senses of the word—several aspects of Slater's essay are worth noting.

Being diagnosed with obsessive-compulsive disorder (OCD) has apparently led Slater to look back on her life for earlier signs of it, as if OCD were a theme she had failed to spot in interpreting her life so far. She points out:

> For a long time my life was difficult but not impossible. Both in my childhood and my adulthood I'd suffered from various psychiatric ailments—depressions especially—but none of these were as surreal and absurd as the obsessive-compulsive disorder that one day presented itself. Until I was twenty-five or so, I don't think I could have been really diagnosed with OCD, although my memory of the angels indicates I had tenden-cies in that direction. (30)

The "memory of the angels" that Slater refers to is the opening scene of her es-say. Specifically, she recalls her seven- or eight-year-old self desperately trying to make perfect angels in the snow in front of her house. Starting with this rec-ollection is appropriate because, chronologically, the angels episode came be-fore the full-blown emergence of her problem and the diagnosis she received. Yet those later events are apparently what led Slater to look back in the first place and to discover significance in her angel-making. To use a Freudian term, the scene with the angels seems to have become for her a "deferred memory"—a memory activated and reinterpreted by her in the light of subsequent devel-opments. Of course, this is a typical feature of autobiographies; many writers of such works engage in retrospective analysis provoked and shaped by more recent occurrences. However, Kramer's discussion of kindling and Wurtzel's remark about Marxian psychopharmacology also seem relevant here. Once an autobiographer is diagnosed with OCD and given a drug such as Prozac, she is apt to wonder whether her body harbors a covert history, a set of hidden mem-ories, that she is only beginning to glimpse.

Historical materialism also seems applicable to Slater's account of her in-troduction to Prozac. Like Elizabeth Wurtzel, she first learned of it from a doc-tor at Kaysen's old haunt, McLean Hospital. At the time, McLean was partici-pating in Prozac's first clinical tests. As she describes the moment when her doctor at McLean first mentioned Prozac to her, Slater calls our attention to various items that were in his office:

> "The clock is ruining my concentration," I think and turn toward it. The numbers on its face are not numbers but tiny painted pills, green and white. A chime hangs down, with another capsule, probably a capsule replica, swinging from the end of it. Back. Forth. Back. Back.
>
> The pads of paper on Vukovic's desk are all edged in green and white, with the word "Prozac" scripted across the bottom. The pen has "Prozac" embossed in tiny letters. He asks me about my symptoms for a few minutes, and then uses the Prozac pen to write out a prescription. (36)

Slater's evocation of this scene is not a full-fledged exercise in Marxist psychopharmacology, to use Wurtzel's term; however, her emphasis on commodities associated with Prozac—I am tempted to call them Prozac tchotchkes—reminds us that Prozac itself is a commodity, produced and marketed by a particular firm.

Nonetheless, much of Slater's essay reflects on psychological materialism. Throughout it, she clearly makes an effort to resolve the "Mind vs. Brain" conflict to which Kaysen alludes. For Slater, this effort involves grappling with a vocabulary that seems coldly physiological—even inhuman. At one point, she says, "I have always believed in the mind as an entity that at once subsumes the body and radiates beyond it, and therefore in need of interventions surpassing the mere technical; interventions that whisper to mystery, stroke the soul" (35). Slater proclaims this credo as she recalls one of the first treatments she underwent for OCD. Obeying a doctor who practiced cognitive therapy, she recorded herself repeatedly saying "I can't concentrate" and then constantly listened to the tape on a Walkman. Her expressed interest in "surpassing the mere technical" is also consistent with the uneasiness she apparently felt when she started taking Prozac:

I had swallowed a pill designed through technology, and in doing so, I was discovering myself embedded in an animal world. I was a purely chemical being, mood and personality seeping through serotonin. We are all taught to believe it's true, but how strange to feel that supposed truth bubbling right in your own tweaked brainpan. Who was I, all skin and worm; all herd? For the next few weeks, these thoughts accompanied me, these slow, simmering misgivings. In dreams, beasts roamed the rafters of my bones, and my bones were twined with wire, teeth tiny silicone chips. (39)

Slater goes on to report that the drug eventually brought her bliss. Ultimately, though, the effect waned. At this turning point, she notes, she learned to cultivate inner resources, "a private space" (44) that made her less dependent on Prozac for tranquility. She indicates that she abandoned the idea that "whatever was wrong with me had a simplistic chemical cause," preferring to think that illness contained "creative possibilities" (43).

Slater does not altogether reject a psychopharmacological frame of reference in describing her change of philosophy. She conjectures that "our brains are broader than we ever thought. Perhaps the brain, because of its wound, has been forced into some kink of creativity we can neither see nor explain. This is what the doctors didn't tell me about illness: that an answer to illness is not necessarily cure, but an ambivalent compensation" (45). Thus, Slater can be seen as finding some value in theories of Mind and in theories of Brain, resisting temptations to privilege either.

Of great significance is the kind of diction that Slater employs throughout her essay. As is obvious from the passages I have quoted, Slater is a lyrical autobiographer, fond of describing her experiences in a style conventionally regarded as poetic or literary. She recalls that after her Prozac-prescribing doctor said her condition was a "disease," she thought that "the treatment I'm receiving, with its insistence upon cure . . . means the abolition of hurt instead of its transformation" (37). Ultimately, she points out, she learned that Prozac was not an outright cure for her. At the same time, she implies that she is now dedicating herself to the "transformation" of hurt.

Traditionally, art has been seen as one mode of such transformation. Moreover, this is a view that Slater seems to uphold by writing her memoir in the first place, and by designing it so artfully. Her chief device for organizing her text is the image of the white angels, the products of her childhood attempt to create art. Much of the essay develops this image. On the day she first had trouble concentrating, she recalls, she took repeated doses of a Valium-like medication, and as she fell asleep she saw "the shadow of a bird in a tree, and it had angel wings" (31). Obviously the green and white of Prozac, colors reiterated by the other Lilly products in her doctor's office, serve as a counterpoint to the sheer whiteness of the angels. Later, Slater recalls that her roommate seemed an "angel" to her because he tried to relieve the headaches that Prozac initially induced (37). Slater conspicuously returns to the angel motif at the conclusion of her essay. There, thinking of children whose brains have managed to readjust after being operated on, she envisions their tendrils "joining left and right, building webbed wings and rickety bridges, sending out messengers with critical information, like the earliest angels who descended from the sky with news and challenge, wrestling with us in nighttime deserts, straining our thighs, stretching our bodies in pain, no doubt, until our skin took on new shapes" (46). With this ending, Slater clearly finds in her childhood experience of angels an image that can organize her whole essay and, in a sense, her whole life. Furthermore, when she relates angels to other children and alludes to the biblical story of Jacob's wrestling match with an angel, she broadens the relevance of her story about sheer personal crisis and Prozac. Indeed, she seems to identify her own difficulties, hopes, and inner resources with those of humanity at large.

Earlier, in the climax of her essay, Slater sets up a striking contrast between the white snow angels of her youth and a vision she had as an adult. This climax takes place at the moment when the contentment that Prozac had brought her waned. She recalls that she was in the process of mourning its loss when she encountered swans on a moonlit pond. Because they were in silhouette, she writes, they looked black, even though they must have been white. The dichotomy she establishes between black surface and white reality implies that hope can be found in the midst of sorrow. Indeed, Slater reports that this vision had a healing effect on her: "I had been quieted for a bit; doors in me had opened; elegance had entered" (44). Then she immediately alludes again to angels, using that image to affirm the sense of peace the swans gave her. Specifically, she embraces Freud's notion of the superego, which she chooses to see as "the angel in the self who rises above an ego under siege, or a medicated mind, to experience the world from a narrow but occasionally gratifying ledge" (44).

I have spent some time here on Slater's references to angels because the image enables her not only to craft her essay, but also to reinforce the idea that she was a would-be artist even in childhood. Now consider once more her references to "transformation," to "elegance," to cultivating "a private space," and to settling for "ambivalent compensation." Together with the references to angels, all these words are redolent of esthetic theory, especially as it has been defined by those who see art as a counterpoint to the messy, spiritless economics and politics of bourgeois society. Just as Kant supposed the esthetic to be a realm wonderfully mediating between different kinds of reason, so Slater favors an esthetic vocabulary as she attempts to navigate the chasm between discourses of Mind and Brain.

Historical materialism has, however, long been suspicious of Kantian esthetics. Its complaint has been that Kant and his followers have acknowledged insufficiently the economic conditions that shape art's content and form, as well as those affecting how art is produced, distributed, and received. There are two moments in Slater's memoir when she seems so intent on achieving a classical esthetic effect that she herself neglects social inequities. Interestingly, both moments can be seen as typical of the essay, which commonly attends to journeys and often depicts them as both physical and psychological. By using the journey motif at the two moments I will discuss, Slater demonstrates that even autobiographers in the age of Prozac may follow some old conventions. Mainly, though, I want to point out what her references to journeying ignore.

Early in the essay there comes a moment when Slater seems to let her esthetic ambitions thwart any impulse she may have had to explore differences in social status. Describing the high she had come to experience on Prozac, she writes:

My mind was lubed, thoughts slipping through so easily, words bursting into bloom. I was reminded of being a girl, on the island of Barbados where we once vacationed. My father took me to a banquet beneath a tropical Basian sky. Greased black men slithered under low poles, their liquid bodies bending to meet the world. Torches flared, and on a long table before me steamed food of every variety. *A feast*, my father said, *all the good things in life*. Yes, that was what Prozac was first like for me—all the good things in life—roasted ham, delicate grilled fish, lemon halves wrapped in yellow waxed paper, fat plums floating in jars. (40)

Later parts of the essay cast an ironic light on Slater's association of Prozac with "all the good things in life." She reports that its potency eventually flagged, and that she found herself wanting a degree of freedom from it. Yet at no point does she encourage her reader to criticize the rosy picture she evokes of her childhood visit to Barbados.

Nevertheless, it is important to consider who gets to make physical journeys in the first place, and what specific circumstances enable them to travel. Only families with ample money are able to make jaunts from the United States to Barbados and enjoy the revels Slater evokes. Moreover, Slater's flashback has racial implications. Her fond recollection of the "Greased black men" whose "liquid bodies" were "bending to meet the world" bears a close affinity to the primitivist visions white artists have long concocted. By associating the men with items in a feast, she even suggests that they too were something to be consumed.[2] To be fair, Slater may be more sensitive than she lets on here; perhaps she was trying to re-create the naive egoism of her childhood self, or the sheer bliss of an adult enjoying her first Prozac high. In looking back on these two selves, however, Slater as essayist could have done more to identify the power relations that made her feast possible.

A view starkly different from Slater's is developed in June Jordan's autobiographical essay "Report from the Bahamas." Compare Jordan's opening paragraph with Slater's scene:

I am staying in a hotel that calls itself The Sheraton British Colonial. One of the photographs advertising the place displays a middle-aged Black man in a waiter's tuxedo, smiling. What intrigues me most about the picture is just this: while the Black man bears a tray full of "colorful" drinks above his left shoulder, both of his feet, shoes, and trouserlegs, up ten inches above his ankles, stand in the also "colorful" Caribbean salt water. He is so delighted to serve you that he will wade into the water to bring you Banana Daiquiris while you float! More precisely, he will wade into the water, fully clothed, oblivious to the ruin of his shoes, his trousers, his health, and he will do it with a smile. (424–25)

Far from delighting in a black islander's willingness to serve her, Jordan is bitterly ironic. As the essay proceeds, she is continually uneasy about the visit she made to the Bahamas, repeatedly acknowledging that she was better off than the natives. Obviously, her perspective is greatly influenced by her own racial identity: unlike Slater, she is black herself. Yet Jordan also acknowledges class, noting that her middle-class status did much to divide her from the black islanders she met. Unlike Slater, she seems determined to analyze various social barriers.

Slater's other troubling use of the journey motif occurs when she recalls suddenly feeling bad again after she had been on Prozac for a while. This reversal took place in Appalachia, where she had gone "to collect oral histories of mountain women" (41). Note how she introduces us to this setting: "A gun hung over the door. In the oven I saw a roasted bird covered with flies. In the bathroom, a fat girl stooped over herself without bothering to shut the door, and pulled a red rag from between her legs" (41). Here Slater seems to be writing her own version of *Tobacco Road*. This impression is soon reinforced by her description of the specific event that traumatized her:

In one swift and seamless move, Lonny reached down to grab a bird [a chicken]. His fist closed in on its throat while all the crows cawed and the beasts in my bones brayed away. He laid the chicken down on a stump, raised an ax, and cut. The body did its dance. I watched the severing, how swiftly connections melt, how deep and black is space. Blood spilled.

I ran inside. I was far from a phone or friend. Maybe I was reminded of some pre-verbal terror: the surgeon's knife, the violet umbilical cord. Or maybe the mountain altitudes had thrown my chemistry off. I don't really know why, or how. (42)

This passage is disquieting because Slater seems unwilling to consider how her social class background may have influenced her reaction. Perhaps many others besides her would be appalled by the milieu and customs of these Appalachian people, but surely her being from a different class worked against her becoming the sympathetic, Agee-like observer she aspired to be. To a great extent, her trauma seems to be the collapse of bourgeois ethnographic fantasy. Again, to be fair, Slater may have assumed that her reader would reach exactly this conclusion without her having to spell it out. Still, her emphasis on her individual horror is disconcerting. It leaves me wishing that her essay had been more dialectical, playing off her lyrical testimony against sustained remarks by the mountain women she had set out to interview. The scene with the swans, which occurred soon after and near the family's dwelling, is artfully evoked and poignant, but the Yeatsian resonance that Slater gives the scene jars with the family's poverty. Once more, she brackets her class differences from them as she turns to emphasizing her own inward recovery.

In faulting Slater's handling of these two episodes, I realize that I may be accused of political correctness. Historical materialists often are. For the most part, though, I find her essay compelling, beautifully wrought, and thoughtful, especially as an exploration of issues raised by psychological materialism. Many historical materialists, I think, would see it as skirting other important issues. Yet if I call attention to those, I do so in part because I want to remind myself of something. Although I often like memoirs that employ literary or esthetic styles, I need to remember that such a register may be politically short-sighted even as it is emotionally engaging.

A Speculative Coda

I could have focused on other cases of autobiography after Prozac, but I trust that my extended discussion of Slater's has shown how psychological materialism *and* historical materialism can help us analyze such discourse and perhaps even produce it. I know, however, that I have not discussed the ways in which historical materialism can illuminate the science of Prozac: the conditions and assumptions influencing scientists at they study the brain, develop psychotropic drugs, and describe their research to the public. I have avoided this subject mostly because it is so vast, as indicated by the mushrooming field known as science studies.

Still, I would like to close by offering one conjecture about the relationship between contemporary neuroscience and the larger world of late capitalism. Prozac belongs to a group of drugs officially known as selective serotonin re-uptake inhibitors (SSRIs). The following paragraph, taken from *Ms.*'s "Prozac Fact Sheet," is a typical explanation of what SSRIs do:

SSRIs work by increasing the amount of serotonin in your brain. Serotonin, a compound that carries messages between nerve cells and is thought to control mood, is usually re-absorbed by the cell that created it or otherwise destroyed. SSSRIs block the process that eliminates used serotonin, leaving more in the brain for future use. Older genera-tions of antidepressants worked in similar fashion, but were less discriminating in the neurotransmitters they affected, were more toxic than SSSRIs, and left patients with a multitude of side effects like dry mouth, heart abnormalities, memory impairment, and blurred vision. (Moore 65)

I focus on this text not because it is distinctive but, again, because scientists and other people have often explained Prozac this way. Note that the body is de-scribed as a place where "messages" circulate. Much talk and writing about Prozac evokes the body as an information system, but apparently it is a system in which data can be "destroyed" unless there are interventions to prevent loss. As a form of intervention, SSRIs are better than their predecessors because they discriminate more while doing less harm to the self's health. In particular, they do not threaten things like heart, memory, and vision.

Some readers may take this account as yet one more sign that computers have taken over the world, deeply affecting how we perceive everything else. A computer, like the brain, circulates messages and discriminates among them, while computer users fear that vital data will be lost. But the paragraph can also be taken as reflecting the way the whole global economy now operates. In this economy, information circulates *among* computers as well as *within* them. Furthermore, companies increasingly seek to discriminate, if only in the sense that they want to identify and accommodate specific categories of consumers. If you're at your local pharmacy to buy your latest dose of Prozac, a mere glance at the store's magazine rack will show you that periodicals are more specialized than ever, geared to particular marketing niches. Contemporary capitalism en-courages talk of "generations" because it sees profit in getting even members of the same family to think of themselves as belonging to different consumer groups. At the same time, many workers in the new global economy fear that they have only a limited supply of energy and thus seek ways of conserving what they have. They fear as well that in the world of downsizing, outsourcing, frenzied e-mailing, and abrupt relocation of companies, their lives will become not only dry, not only toxic (metaphorically and literally), but also bereft of heart, memory, and vision. Neuroscience's image of the inner body, therefore, may actually be the image many of us hold of late capitalism.

If there is any merit in the analogies I have just drawn, psychological materialists and historical materialists have many subjects to discuss with each other. Autobiography is just one.

Notes

1. The company's name also appears on the third page of the ad, which is devoted to technical data about Prozac and its potential side effects. Again, however, the identification of the company is in small lettering in the bottom right corner.
2. I thank my colleague Jane Donawerth for this observation.

Works Cited

Berger, Lisa, and Alexander Vuckovic. *Under Observation: Life Inside the McLean Psychiatric Hospital.* New York: Penguin, 1994.

Jameson, Fredric. *Postmodernism, or the Cultural Logic of Late Capitalism.* Durham: Duke University Press, 1991.

Jamison, Kay Redfield. *An Unquiet Mind.* New York: Knopf, 1995.

Jordan, June. "Report from the Bahamas." In *Constellations: A Contextual Reader for Writers*, edited by John Schilb, Elizabeth Flynn, and John Clifford, 424–32. New York: HarperCollins, 1992.

Kaysen, Susanna. *Girl, Interrupted.* New York: Random House, 1993.

Kramer, Peter D. Letter. *Washington Post.* 18 May 1997.

Kramer, Peter D. *Listening to Prozac.* New York: Viking, 1993.

Lerner, Sharon. "Chemical Reaction." *Ms.* 8.1 (July/August 1997): 57–61.

Moore, Celia. "Prozac Fact Sheet." *Ms.* 8.1 (July/August 1997): 61.

Parens, Erik. "The Problem with Mixing Drugs and Ads." *Washington Post*, 26 October 1997.

Slater, Lauren. "Black Swans." *Missouri Review* 19 (1996): 29–46. Reprinted in *Best American Essays 1997*, edited by Ian Frazier, 144–61. Boston: Houghton Mifflin, 1997.

Slater, Lauren. *Welcome to My Country.* New York: Random House, 1996.

Styron, William. *Darkness Visible.* New York: Random House, 1990.

Wurtzel, Elizabeth. *Prozac Nation.* 1994. New York: Riverhead, 1995.

10 *Christina Haas*

Materializing Public and Private
The Spatialization of Conceptual Categories in Discourses of Abortion

Foucault - Act outplays Language.

beyond Linguistic meaning.

Jean Bethke Elshtain, in *Public Man, Private Woman: Women in Social and Political Thought*, has commented on the way that the casual, everyday use of the terms *public* and *private* has belied their complex, intertwined relationship. One particular difficulty in distinguishing conceptually between public and private, of course, is that each term has myriad meanings. Seyla Benhabib, for instance, identifies three distinct meanings of the term *private* as moral or religious conscience, as a set of economic liberties, and as the intimate sphere that pertains to the household and daily life. Nancy Fraser identifies four meanings for *public*—state-related, accessible to all, of interest to everyone, and pertaining to the common good—and she notes that each of these meanings of "public" invokes a corresponding sense of *private*. Jeff Weintraub and Krishan Kumar claim that distinctions between public and private are rooted in sociohistorical as well as theoretical differences. For example, mainstream economists may label the market economy "private" and government administration "public," while for Marxist feminists, it is the market economy that is "public" and in opposition to the "private" family. Timothy Dykstal identifies the dyadic structure of public/private as corresponding to other conceptual dyads, among them duty/rights, distribution/production, state/individual, and economic/domestic. The title of Elshtain's volume suggests another—male/female.

Distinguishing between public and private in everyday practice is no easier than distinguishing them conceptually. In both cases the distinction turns out to be slippery and elusive. The purpose of this chapter is to explore how one textual artifact situated in everyday practice participates in the conceptual ambiguities attendant on the public/private dyad. The artifact that is the focus of my exploration is a legal document, the Permanent Injunction issued the Court of Common Pleas in Dorset County, Ohio, and posted on the front door of an abortion clinic, Women's Choice Services (WCS).[1] In attempting to understand the Permanent Injunction, I examine it from three perspectives. After a brief description of the Permanent Injunction and WCS, my first section illustrates how the use of a particular methodology helped me identify the Permanent Injunction as a critically important literate artifact; it then presents an analysis of qualitative data from WCS and shows how the Permanent Injunction functions within the particular historical and material circumstances in which it is embedded.[2] My second section looks at the ways that three prominent social theorists—Hannah Arendt, Jürgen Habermas, and Nancy Fraser—have conceptualized the public/private dyad, and it suggests how those conceptualizations can help us understand the power of the Permanent Injunction. The third section looks at the Permanent Injunction in light of the way the public/private dyad is operationalized in Supreme Court rulings on privacy, particularly those involving cases of reproductive freedom. Taken together, these analyses suggest that the "spatialization" of public and private is pervasive both in conceptual treatments and in everyday practice. That is, a spatial metaphor—signaled by nouns such as *sphere*, *realm*, *zone*, and *space*—is typically invoked to anchor and ground the slippery constructs of "public" and "private." I conclude the chapter with some suggestions about how the analyses of the Permanent Injunction can also help to illuminate the cultural power of the public/private dyad itself.

The Permanent Injunction and Women's Choice Services: Brief Descriptions

Although the 1994 Permanent Injunction is placed prominently (at eye level on the main entrance of the clinic), it is torn and faded, and the nearly one hundred women and men who walk through the front door of the clinic each day seem not to notice it. The first page states that the Plaintiff (WCS) and the Defendants (representatives of three specific local anti-abortion groups) "have entered into an agreement in the granting of this Permanent Injunction, which the Court hereby accepts as its order." The Permanent Injunction expressly prohibits the Defendants from trespassing on the premises, including the building itself and the sidewalks immediately in front of it; from blocking access to or egress from the clinic by workers, physicians, or patients; from engaging in acts of violence, harassment, or abuse; from threatening physical harm or suggesting the presence of such harm; and from picketing at the home of the Plaintiff. The Per-

manent Injunction states that "nothing in this Permanent Injunction shall pro-
hibit peaceful, non-defamatory picketing," and it goes on to describe the nature
of this legal picketing, including the specific number of protesters (eight) and
the material spaces they may occupy around the clinic.

Women's Choice Services is situated in a medium-sized Midwestern city, on
a busy corner of Virginia Avenue, a well-traveled thoroughfare that runs almost
the entire length of the city. Virginia intersects suburbs and upscale malls at
its outer edges, but WCS is quite near the center of the city, in a working-class,
mostly African American neighborhood. Inside the glass door on which the
Permanent Injunction is posted is a small waiting room. Thirty chairs, a television, four tables, and two magazine stands make the room seem cramped even
when it is empty. On busy days the room is often near capacity, full of patients
as well as their friends and family members.

On the opposite side of the waiting room from the entrance is a small slid-
ing, two-way glass window that permits the staff to look out but does not allow
those in the waiting room to look in. This window is almost always kept locked.
On either side of the window are doors, also kept locked from the inside. Directly behind the glass window and the two doors is the area clinic personnel
call "the front," a small eight-by-fifteen-foot work area which functions as both
a reception area and a nurses' station. At the center back of this work area is the
door for the clinic director's small office. A counter with telephones, office supplies, a computer, and stacks of documents runs underneath the glass window
between the two doors, and on the opposite wall, next to the door to the director's office, is a wall of hanging folders containing patients' charts for the current and previous calendar years. A small desk, with typewriter and phone, occupies the space on the other side of the director's office door. The walls of this
area are covered with numerous posted documents, including directions for
traveling to WCS via several routes (directions that personnel read when directing patients to the clinic by phone); charts with fee schedules, also used when
staff members are "working the phones"; OSHA regulations; greeting cards
from medical suppliers and former patients; a photocopied "patient's bill of
rights"; and a list of procedures for maintaining clinic security and worker
safety.

"The front" (including the work area and nurses' station, and the clinic director's office) is in many ways the center of the WCS operation. It is a heavily
congested area, with at least two or three people—sometimes as many as seven
or eight—occupying space there. Two, three, or more medical assistants are
often at work in the eight-by-fifteen-foot area; the RNs and doctor on duty often spend time there; and since doors to the waiting room open from this area
as well, all patients pass through it several times. In addition to being heavily
trafficked, "the front" functions as a centralized location for the text-mediated
work of the clinic: it is in this area that most texts are produced, used, and stored.

Almost two-thirds of the women served by the clinic are white, and a little more than one-third are African American. About a quarter of all women served receive reduced rates because of their economic circumstances. Ideally, each patient visits the clinic three times: for initial counseling with a physician (mandated by state law), for the abortion, and for a follow-up exam about two weeks after "the procedure," as the abortion is referred to by clinic personnel. However, between 15 and 20 percent of the patients have their physician counseling over the telephone, and about 25 percent do not return for their follow-up exams. The clinic employs six female medical professionals: a full-time licensed practical nurse (LPN), two full-time medical assistants, three part-time medical assistants, and two part-time registered nurses (RNs). In addition, two male physicians work at the clinic: the Asian American who owns the clinic, and his Haitian-born colleague.

I studied WCS and its activities, focusing on the work of clinic staff and their use of written and printed artifacts (including the Permanent Injunction), from July 1995 through September 1996, in conjunction with the Center for Research in Workplace Literacy at Kent State University.[3]

The Permanent Injunction in Context: Analysis of Site-Specific Data

For my study of WCS, I used the "grounded theory approach" (GTA), a qualitative, field-based methodology developed initially by Barry Glaser and Anselm Strauss to study the work of medical professionals (Glaser and Strauss; Strauss; Strauss and Corbin). The goal of the GTA according to Strauss and Corbin, is the development of "grounded theory"—theory that is inductively derived from systematic study, over time, of a specific human activity or practice. Theoretical categories emerge from the data (in this case, written artifacts, field observation notes, and interviews) and are then "dimensionalized" through recurring comparison with one another. The researcher then returns to existing data, or gathers more data, in an attempt to build a powerful theory of the phenomenon under study; this theory is "grounded" to data in specific, identifiable ways. Data, analysis, and theory are reciprocally related to one another, and the researcher engages iteratively in data collection, analysis, and theory-building.

Although I do not present a detailed analysis of the entire study in this chapter, an example of the way I used the GTA may be useful. Because I was interested initially in the role of texts in the work of the clinic, I began by cataloging all the printed and written texts used regularly there.[4] From this set of documents several category dimensions emerged. For example, the documents came be categorized by *formal features* (e.g., brochures, forms, charts, or signs), by *source* (e.g., clinic staff, patient, American Medical Association, or county court), by *use* (e.g., convey information, gather information, restrict movement, indicate acceptance, or provide a record), by *means of produc-tion* (e.g., handwritten, professionally printed, photocopied, typewritten, or computer-generated), by *accessibility* (e.g., available to everyone, available to staff and patients, or available to staff only), by *actions* taken on it (e.g., read, signed, and filed; not read, but signed; written, read, and filed; written but not read; or distributed and discarded), by *location* (e.g., posted on walls of wait-ing rooms, offices, or hallways; stacked on desks, counters, or shelves; or filed in drawers or in hanging files). Next, through what Strauss and Corbin call "constant comparison," I examined relationships among these categories, iden-tifying ways in which, for example, the means of production was related to the document's author or source, or to actions taken on the text. For instance, pro-fessionally printed documents almost always came from outside sources such as the state, the American Medical Association (AMA), or the National Abor-tion Rights Action League (NARAL), but often little was done with these docu-ments: they were distributed but not read, like pamphlets produced by the state, or they were made available to all but not actively distributed, like the stack of NARAL documents on the waiting-room counter.

One particularly useful outcome of "dimensionalizing" and establishing relationships among categories was that this analysis helped to reveal "out-liers" or "mismatches," texts or artifacts that fell outside the regular patterns of relationships between categories. The Permanent Injunction on the door of WCS was one such outlier. This text is unlike other signed documents in that it is posted; it is unlike other posted documents in that it does not look like a "sign" (it is not enlarged or enhanced in any way for readability); and it is un-like other posted documents in that, although it is posted in perhaps the most prominent location in the clinic, it is not in fact accessible, because it is taped to the door so that only the first of six pages are visible. While the Permanent Injunction is interesting for a number of reasons, GTA provides an inductively derived rationale for its examination which is based on a global understanding of the clinic and its everyday practices, particularly as they are revealed through documents and artifacts.

At the same time that I collected, cataloged, categorized, and compared doc-uments, I conducted interviews with clinic personnel about their individual and collective work at the clinic, and the goals of that work.[5] For these interviews I used methods adapted from the work of James Spradley; I found these partic-ularly useful in that they are explicitly designed to elicit informants' under-standings of their culture in their own terms.[6] The interviews were conducted primarily with the clinic director, a full-time medical assistant, and a full-time LPN, but doctors, RNs, and part-time staff were also interviewed. From inter-view notes and transcripts, I identified five major goals that guided the work of clinic staff: (1) *providing patient care*, including both medical care and emo-tional care; (2) *managing the clinic's operation*, including its daily financial and its logistical operations; (3) *protecting against violence*; (4) *providing political information* to women on abortion and abortion rights; and (5) *enforcing state and local abortion laws*. The first two goals—patient care and clinic management—I termed "accepted" goals of clinic personnel; actions directed toward these goals were things staff members wanted to do and things that they felt prepared by their training to do. The other three goals—protecting against violence, enforcing laws and regulations, and providing political information—I termed "ambivalent" goals. Although clinic staff viewed actions deriving from these kinds of goals as necessary, often these were not actions that workers wanted to do or felt trained to do. Often these kinds of actions—locking the door, for instance, to protect against potential violence, or distributing certain kinds of printed literature mandated by state law—were imposed on staff from outside.

In keeping with the goal of the GTA to account systematically for greater amounts of data from multiple sources within an emerging, inductively based, theoretical framework, I also identified relationships between these goals and the categorization of documents I have described. Clearly, many of the goals identified by clinic personnel are accomplished primarily through the creation, use, distribution, circulation, and storage of specific documents. This is particularly true of the "accepted" goals of patient care and clinic management, and most of the documents used every day are used to accomplish these main goals. Such documents include medical charts kept on each patient, information sheets on procedures, forms detailing results of laboratory work, records of payments, proof of Aid to Dependent Children (ADC) status, and printed instructions for staff members conducting phone counseling. Furthermore, most of the documents used in the accomplishment of these accepted goals were documents created, used, and stored "in house" (written and/or filled out at the clinic by clinic staff and used and stored at the clinic).

However, in regard to goals about which clinic staff were ambivalent or even outwardly resistant (such as enforcing abortion laws and regulations, providing political information, and protecting against violence), the documents do less to accomplish goals than they do to manage conflicting goals or to circumvent resisted goals. Again, the Permanent Injunction provides an example. This document is not used in work directed toward the two main goals of the clinic, which are understood by clinic personnel to be patient care and clinic management. Rather, its purpose (according to the clinic's director, who posted it) is to keep protesters from interfering with the work of the clinic and to keep personnel and patients safe. Moreover, the Permanent Injunction is not a document created "in house." It is imported from the legal world of the county court, written and signed by a judge who has never visited the clinic, and enforced by the implicit presence of a police force that presumably can and will intervene.

The Permanent Injunction, then, is a document created in and imported from the "public" world of the law courts to manage "public protest." At the same time, it protects the free enterprise of the "privately held" business of WCS and the "private" decision-making of women who choose to have abortions there. In fact, there are several meanings of both *public* and *private* at work in the single text posted on the door of the abortion clinic. The Permanent Injunction is of course a legal document and thus carries the sense of *public* that denotes state or government administration. In addition, the Permanent Injunction invokes *public* in the sense of common concerns and accessibility. That is, the document makes clear that public protest *per se* is not prohibited. At the same time, the Permanent Injunction protects the free enterprise of a private business, expressly prohibiting the Defendants from "blocking of access to and egress from the Plaintiff's place of business." Also at work is the sense of *private* as individual decision-making, specifically the individual reproductive right to abortion as protected by state and federal law.

The Permanent Injunction mediates these multiple meanings of *public* and *private*—and the conflicting concerns of participants, including the Plaintiff's staff and patients, and protesters associated with the Defendants—by sharply delineating the private work of the clinic from the public protest that takes place outside it. This delineation is specified in a fundamentally material way. There are spaces (certain sidewalks and the parking lot) where protest is allowed, and other spaces (the interior of the clinic beyond the glass door, the homes of physicians and staff, and the bodies of patients and staff) that are protected from the presence of protesters and their hostile (even violence-invoking) language and actions. All these spaces are clearly and specifically laid out in the Permanent Injunction. The Permanent Injunction also controls the physical actions of protesters: no more than eight may be present at any one time; no more than four may be on any one sidewalk; the protesters may not utter threats or verbal abuse; and they may not "create a single band of picketers." In short, despite— or possibly because of—the multiplicity of notions of *public* and *private* that are operative at this site (and presumably at most abortion clinics), the legal definitions of *public* and *private* are sharply specified.

This spatial delineation of public and private seems to work, at least according to WCS staff. While "it's still hell coming in here on Saturday mornings," as one RN said, the workers at the clinic indicated that the posting of the injunction made them feel safer: it reduced the threat of the protesters, if only by making them more distant physically. The protesters, too, understood the Permanent Injunction as limiting their ability to enter the clinic and to get close to patients.[7] Interestingly, none of the protesters or nurses whom I interviewed had read the injunction, although the clinic physicians had, and one medical assistant said she thought she may once have read it. In fact, the Permanent Injunction was very difficult to read: it was taped onto the door so as to make pages two through five inaccessible, and the front page was weathered and torn.

Nevertheless, the clinic workers I interviewed claimed that they "knew what it said."

The analysis of qualitative data gathered at WCS (artifacts, observations, and interviews) shows that the Permanent Injunction lays out a spatial distinction between public and private. That is, certain specific spaces are designated as "public" (including parking lots and some sidewalks) and therefore both accessible to protesters and open for protest activities while at the same time; other spaces (the interior of the clinic, the homes of the physicians, and the physical bodies of patients and staff) are deemed "private" and therefore protected. Note, however, that the Permanent Injunction does more than delineate the spatial distinction between public and private: it enforces that distinction as well. In the words of clinic personnel, the Permanent Injunction "works": it keeps the activity of protest and both the bodies and verbalizations of protesters away from and outside the material enclave of the clinic and its personnel. If at other times the boundaries between an individual and others can become murky and problematical (as Christine De Vinne's chapter in this book indicates, for example), in this instance the injunction serves to create an enforceable, material distinction.

In order to provide further context for understanding the function and power of the Permanent Injunction, I now turn to an examination of some of the discourse of the public/private distinction—in particular, to influential texts that have "theorized" public, private, or both.[8] First I want to examine a body of literature in social and political theory (Arendt, Habermas, and Fraser) that has primarily treated the concept of "public"; second, I will look at the discourse of the U.S. Supreme Court (manifest under the authorship of several different justices) as it has both theorized and operationalized "privacy" in the context of reproductive decision-making. In both cases, I argue that these discourses gain some of their cogency through the use of powerful metaphors—in particular, metaphors of physical and material space—as they attempt to anchor the elusive concepts of public and private. At the same time, however, these discourses appear to go beyond the metaphoric to make claims not only about the conceptual realities of public and private but also about their status as empirical realities in the material and social world.

The Spatialization of "Public"
by Arendt, Habermas, and Fraser

Hannah Arendt, Jürgen Habermas, and Nancy Fraser each are interested primarily in theorizing the concept of "public" and in using that concept to argue either for a particular historical interpretation, or for a certain set of political possibilities. In this section I suggest that, despite differences in their political and historical projects, Arendt, Habermas, and Fraser all employ the metaphor of "space" to describe the concept of "public" and to make historically based empirical claims for the "reality" of public spaces.

Much of Arendt's work, especially *The Human Condition*, has been read as a series of tracts against modernism. Certainly the modern does not fare well in comparisons, both implicit and explicit, between the political world of an-cient Athens and the complex and disturbing post–World War II realities to which Arendt responds so deeply. One of these comparisons concerns the lo-cation of political action, the action that Arendt believes defines "the human condition." As conceptualized by Arendt, political action in ancient Greece took place in the public space of the *polis*. Citizens emerged from the "shad-owy interior of the household"—the world of slaves and women, labor and necessity—to an open, free public space.[9] The *polis* was not merely distinct from the household, it was organized in direct opposition to it. The "rise of the social" meant that issues and processes like economics, work, and intimacy emerged from the household (where they properly belonged) to interpose them-selves between the private sphere and the political state. Arendt sees this trans-formation as one in which a true public space of "action" deteriorates into a pseudospace of mere behavior. It is extremely difficult, Arendt writes in *The Human Condition*, for us (as moderns) to

> understand the decisive division between the public and private *realms*, between the *sphere* of the *polis* and the *sphere* of the household and family, and finally, between ac-tivities [like political discourse] related to a common world and those related to the maintenance of life, a *division* upon which all ancient political thought *rested*. (28; em-phasis added)[10]

Note that Arendt's conceptions of these politico-historical processes are al-together spatial: the words *realm* and *sphere* characterize both public and pri-vate spaces; the world of the private is an interior space from which issues emerge; public discourse happens in the free and open space of the *polis*; a di-vision *rests*. These are images of spaces, spatial objects, and objects moving through space. Seyla Benhabib has noted this "topographical figure of speech" (77) throughout Arendt's work, and it certainly lends evocative power to this passage.

However, the spatial delineation of public from private that Arendt proposes is not merely a trope or figure. Her descriptions point specifically to the histor-ical reality of a political world that seems to have been quite literally (if prob-ably incompletely) spatialized. In other words, Arendt does not just theorize distinct spaces of *polis* and *oikos* (household); she posits them as historical facts. Her discussion of public and private is couched in the past tense, sug-gesting its basis in historical circumstances, and her documented sources in-clude the philosophical, dramatic, and legal discourses of the day (as well as Roman commentaries on them). In sum, Arendt's argument about public and private is a conceptual one, but also a historical-empirical one in which she urges the historical reality of distinct, mutually exclusive spaces of public action, on one hand, and privacy, intimacy, and "necessity" on the other.

Habermas's *The Structural Transformation of the Public Sphere: An Inquiry into a Category of Bourgeois Society* responds, at least in part, to some of the same twentieth-century circumstances that Arendt seeks to understand, but his solution is much different. Rather than attempting to recapture some lost or uncorrupted sense of *public*, Habermas wants to trace a historical process: the emergence and subsequent debasement of a "public sphere," a third space that arose between the state and private individuals in early modern Europe.[11] This public sphere is a space constituted by private citizens putting reason to use. This reason is primarily discursive, and the discourse is primarily critical: private citizens leave their businesses and homes to come together in the coffeehouse or the salon to debate, argue, articulate, and eventually enact a radically new relationship between themselves and the state.

Habermas—like Arendt—conceptualizes the difficult distinction between public and private in fundamentally material ways. Here is a familiar passage from early in *Structural Transformation*:

Because, on the one hand, the society now *confronting* the state clearly *separated* a private *domain* from public authority and because, on the other hand, it turned the reproduction of life into something *transcending* the *confines* of private domestic authority and becoming a subject of public interest, that *zone* of continuous administrative *contact* became "critical" also in the sense that it provoked the critical judgment of a public making use of its reason. (24; emphasis added)

There are no fewer than seven words or phrases here that directly invoke spatial relationships and the spatial delineation of private and public. In effect, the private domain gives rise to a public one which is suspended or grounded between the private realm and the state, drawing sustenance from the private domain while confronting and redefining the state. But the spaces for this public activity are more than metaphoric: the salons and coffeehouses, and the critical conversations (first about literature and later about politics) that take place within them, have historical and empirical reality for Habermas. In the "Author's Preface" to *Structural Transformation*, Habermas discusses his methodology, calling the public sphere "a historical category" and contrasting his project in historiography with the more deductive methodology that he calls "sociological" (xviii). Again, not only does the language of *Structural Transformation* invoke spatial metaphors; in addition, Habermas's argument rests on his establishing a certain historical and empirical validity for his account of what happened in those eighteenth-century coffeehouses.

Fraser, in "Rethinking the Public Sphere: A Contribution to the Critique of Actually Existing Democracy," addresses two inherent problems in the Haber-

masian model of "public sphere." First, despite early disclaimers, Habermas
tends to identify the bourgeois public sphere as *the* public sphere, singular and
presumably overarching. A second, related problem that Fraser recognizes in
Habermas's account is an implicit liberal assumption built into his model: that
difference can be flattened and, indeed, must be bracketed both in political discourse and in subsequent political action. Taken together, these shortcomings
lead Fraser to a central question: If the contemporary post-bourgeois political
world requires a model of public that is multiply conceived and that accounts
for rather than brackets difference, does the Habermasian notion of "public
sphere" retain any utility or validity? She answers in the affirmative, claiming in fact that "no attempt to understand the limits of actually existing late-
capitalist democracy can succeed without in some way or another making use
of . . . [the idea of the public sphere]" (57).[12]

Despite this strong claim, Fraser takes seriously the exclusions built into
Habermas's model and his apparent naiveté about those exclusions. In her sum-
mation of problems in the Habermasian notion of public sphere, Fraser draws
on the same metaphors of space initially used by Habermas to delineate that
sphere:

It is not possible to *insulate* special discursive *arenas* from the effects of societal inequality. . . . These effects will be exacerbated where there is only a single, *comprehensive* public *sphere*. In that case, members of subordinated groups would have no *arenas*
for deliberation among themselves about their needs, objectives, and strategies. They
would have no *venues* in which to undertake communicative processes that were not, as
it were *under* the supervision of dominant groups. (66; emphasis added)

Particularly important for Fraser's radical reclamation of the Habermasian public sphere is the notion of "subaltern counterpublics." These are "parallel discursive arenas" where members of subordinated groups meet to create and circulate "counterdiscourses." Not only does the name of these arenas, "subaltern
counterpublics," suggest a spatial dimension, but the work done in these new
political arenas is described in spatial and material terms:

The point is that in *stratified* societies, *subaltern* counterpublics have a dual character.
On the one hand, they function as *spaces* of *withdrawal* and regroupment; on the other
hand, they also function as *bases* and training *grounds* for agitational activities directed
toward *wider* publics. It is precisely in the dialectic *between* these two functions that
their emancipatory potential *resides*. (68; emphasis added)

For Fraser, the subaltern counterpublic is an empirical reality as well as a conceptual category. She identifies existing counterpublics, both historical and
contemporary, and she suggests that they grow and thrive in particular places:
feminist bookstores, festivals and local meeting places, academic programs and
conferences, self-managed workplaces, day-care centers, and residential com-

munities. (Some discourse practices of feminist subaltern counterpublics are documented in Fraser's *Unruly Practices*.)

Whatever their philosophical and ideological differences, Arendt, Habermas, and Fraser suggest that certain kinds of material spaces are preconditions, or at least supporting conditions, for the kind of political discourses in which each is interested. For Arendt, it is the clear delineation of the public *polis* from the shadowy household that makes possible the high-minded, pure political discourse of the Greek city-state. The sharp delineation of these spaces (along with the invisibility of the intimate sphere) is vital for the conduct of the agonistic political discourse idealized by Arendt. For Habermas, the case is slightly different—but no less spatialized. While Arendt is concerned with the delineation of public and private and the separation of these two, Habermas is interested in the emergence during the eighteenth century of a new space between the two. Private people came together as a public, says Habermas, and then "soon claimed the public sphere . . . against the public authorities themselves (27)." The public sphere, then, is a precondition—a space that is already in place, if you will—and it gives rise as the distinctly critical public discourse with which Habermas is most concerned. Fraser, concerned with the critique of existing political forums and feminist-based alternatives to them, sees the creating and nurturing of "subaltern counterpublics" as centrally important. In these spaces, the counter-discourses would develop and circulate, a process vital to Fraser's project of imagining and building truly egalitarian, participatory democracies.[13]

The root metaphor for conceptualizing public and private in the work of these three very different theorists is *space*—not process, or force, or commodity, or any of the other ways that this distinction might be conceived of, but space. The public is a space, a sphere, an arena; the private is a realm, a zone, an area. In sharply delineating public and private spaces, the "author" of the Permanent Injunction invokes a metaphor that, however complex and fraught it may be, has a great deal of cultural currency. And, just as Arendt, Habermas, and Fraser acknowledge the historical and empirical reality of various public spaces, the Permanent Injunction "works" by specifically delineating actual spaces for public activities (protest) and private activities (inside the clinic, on the sidewalks approaching the clinic, in workers' homes).

The Spatialization of Privacy
in Supreme Court Rulings on Abortion

The conceptual spatialization of the public/private dyad is powerful and apparently robust. Based in historical circumstances (ancient Athens, eighteenth-century France, contemporary U.S. society), it appears to work at a conceptual level which extends beyond historical particulars. One of the historical contexts in which the spatialization of the public/private dyad continues to operate is a discursive arena directly relevant to the Permanent Injunction on the door of WCS: Supreme Court rulings on reproductive freedom, and on the right to privacy more generally.

Supreme Court rulings on privacy generally, and on reproductive freedom particularly, have treated "privacy" spatially, in much the same way that social theorists have treated "public." Supreme Court rulings are especially powerful speech acts in American society, and they must be translated immediately into a concrete set of practices. Because of the need for concrete guidance in putting the Court's decisions into practice, the texts of the rulings pertaining to the right to privacy have over the past thirty years increasingly treated "privacy" as an actual, material construct. The history of these rulings is the story of an increasing spatialization of the concept of privacy.[14]

Interestingly, the U.S. Constitution does not explicitly protect a right to privacy. Arguments about this right are usually made in two ways and draw on two different constitutional precedents. Drawing on the Fourth Amendment's protection against "unreasonable searches and seizures," courts have upheld the protection of personal property from government seizure and the rights of citizens to be presented with warrants before they must allow themselves, their homes, or their vehicles to be searched. Because the Fourth Amendment protects citizens from physical searches and their property from government seizure, what is protected by the Fourth Amendment is a "right of private property," not a right to personal decision-making or what Justice Louis Brandeis called "the right to be let alone."[15]

For these kinds of protections, the Supreme Court has drawn on the due process clause of the Fourteenth Amendment, which protects citizens from being deprived of "life, liberty, or property without due process of law." Beginning in the early twentieth century, the Court made a number of rulings—including ones supporting parents' rights to make decisions about their children's education—that in effect interpreted the word "liberty" as freedom of movement. By a series of logical extensions (described more fully by Alderman and Kennedy), this "liberty" came to be interpreted by the courts as a right to private decision-making free from government interference. Over the past thirty years the Court has gradually extended this right of personal decision-making—from freedom to marry whom one chooses, to freedom to use contraception, to freedom to obtain an abortion. In contrast to the Fourth Amendment, which directly and explicitly protects citizens' privacy of property and persons, the due process clause of the Fourteenth Amendment is less directly—and consequently more controversially—linked to privacy rights.

The history of Supreme Court rulings pertaining to citizens' rights to make intimate personal decisions, such as decisions about childbearing, free from government interference, suggests that privacy as personal decision-making has increasingly been conceptualized spatially. In *Griswold v. Connecticut* (1965), the Court upheld couples' rights to use contraception; in the majority opinion, Justice William O. Douglas wrote that the spirit and structure of the Bill of Rights creates a "zone of privacy" which protects aspects of personal and family life (485). Seven years later, in *Eisenstadt v. Baird*, the Court again described privacy in spatial terms, writing that "the right to privacy is the right of the individual to be free from unwarranted government intrusion" (453)— an intrusion, based on the Latin root "to thrust," being a forceful entering. In the landmark *Roe v. Wade* decision (1973), the Court again established the right to privacy as a material space. Supporting the majority opinion, Justice Harry Blackmun wrote, "The right to privacy is broad enough to encompass a woman's decision whether or not to terminate her pregnancy" (152).[16] Note not only the adjective *broad*, which implies a literal space, but also the verb *encompass*, meaning to circle, to enclose, to envelop—all alluding to privacy as an actual, material object.

As the political makeup of the Court changed during the 1980s, the right to privacy as decision-making concerning one's own body became more contested; and as it became more contested, conceptualizing privacy as space became more pronounced. In *Webster v. Reproductive Health Services* (1989), the Supreme Court upheld a lower court's decision that severely restricted the right to personal decision-making about reproduction, though not overturning *Roe* completely. Writing eloquently in the dissent, Justice Blackmun maintained that the Constitution establishes the "moral fact that a person belongs to himself [or herself] and not to others nor to society as a whole" (549). Blackmun went on to elaborate, further conceptualizing privacy in decidedly spatial terms:

In a Nation that cherishes liberty, the ability of a woman to control the biological operation of her body must *fall within* that limited *sphere* of individual autonomy that *lies beyond* the will or power of any transient majority. This court stands as the ultimate guarantor of that *zone* of privacy. (558; emphasis added)

Three years later, in *Casey v. Planned Parenthood*, Justice Sandra Day O'Connor joined her voice to that of Blackmun and earlier justices in conceptualizing privacy as a space. Writing the joint opinion in *Casey*, O'Connor maintained, "It is a promise of the Constitution that there is a *realm* of personal liberty which the government may not *enter*" (2,805; emphasis added). In overruling some aspects of *Roe*, the Court, through O'Connor, represents the law itself as a material object, maintaining that only laws that proved a "substantial obstacle" to women's exercising their right to choose were unconstitutional (2,820).

Until the mid-1990s, the Court's conceptualizing of privacy as a space remained just that: conceptual. However, in the face of mounting violence at abortion clinics, the Court has increasingly spatialized privacy in literal ways. The right to privacy (including reproductive freedom) is now pitted against First Amendment rights to free speech, and the result is that the Court must make operational just what it has meant for three decades by the phrase *zone of privacy*. Accordingly, in *Madsen v. Women's Health Center* (1994), the Supreme Court upheld a thirty-six-foot buffer zone around clinic entrances, but it struck down a three-hundred-foot buffer zone around the homes of doctors and other clinic workers (2,528–30). Early in 1997, in *Schenk et al. v. Pro Choice Network of Western New York*, the Court upheld a fifteen-foot buffer zone around clinic entrances and a patient's right to ask others to "cease and desist" from so-called "sidewalk counseling" within that zone. Struck down was a fifteen-foot "floating bubble" around clinic patients and workers.[17] Privacy— defined in this case as the right to reproductive freedom—has been legally established not just conceptually and metaphorically, but literally and materially. "Privacy" is a space at least fifteen feet wide, but less than three hundred; its shape is a rectangular area in front of clinic entrances, not a bubble around individual persons.

This brief review of Supreme Court rulings on privacy, and specifically on reproductive freedom, suggests that the delineation of public from private in spatial terms is a kind of material practice. That is, the distinction between public and private in spatial terms works not only in theory but also in practice. It is a truism in many humanistic disciplines that "discourse constructs reality," but seldom can such construction be taken so literally: the text of the *Schenk* ruling establishes that "privacy" (in some circumstances, at least) is a literal, actual, material space at least fifteen feet wide.

The Supreme Court rulings, understood in broad historical context, lend credence to Bryan Turner's claim that under circumstances of great political anxiety and confusion, there arises a cultural obsession with the material and the bodily (2–6). As notions of public and private become more contested and emotionally laden in practice (as they have in the case of abortion in U.S. society in the late twentieth century), the legal discourse surrounding them becomes more concrete and literal. A similar trend is noted by the Harvard law professor Morton Horwitz, who suggests that three factors—the emergence of the market as a central legitimating institution in the early nineteenth century, disillusionment with rapid industrialization around 1900, and reaction to threats of totalitarianism during the 1930s and 1940s—led to attempts by legislatures and courts to delineate the public from the private as precisely as possible.

Nonetheless, constructing privacy as literal space will remain problematic. There are already test cases and appeals being prepared to force the Justices to be even more precise in establishing the physical dimensions of material "zones of privacy," and because the right to privacy is linked tenuously to the Constitution, these appeals are likely to continue. Part of the difficulty is that the right to privacy is more abstract and conceptual than other rights, such as the right to bear arms or the right to keep one's possessions free from unreasonable seizure. Certainly it is easier at talk about personal property (whether weaponry or real estate) than it is to talk about the freedom to be "let alone" (in Judge Brandeis's words), partly because personal property is more salient and tangible. The desire of an individual to be "let alone" is strongly tied to the ebodied, spatially oriented existence of that individual—an existence that, though indisputable, is extremely difficult to articulate. Elaine Scarry, in *The Body in Pain*, suggests that "the relative ease or difficulty with which any given phenomenon can be *verbally* represented influences the ease or difficulty with which that phenomenon comes to be *politically* represented" (12; emphasis in original). It may be that the increasing literalization of the spatial metaphor and the increasing materialization of privacy are reactions to the Court's difficulties in verbally and politically representing this important but elusive right.

Final Remarks

In sum, what is the relationship between the particular situated document examined here—the Permanent Injunction on the door of WCS—and the cultural power of the public/private dyad?

Like any conceptual construct, the public/private dyad oversimplifies. And, like other common dichotomies, it can be and has been used to perpetuate or enforce insidious political distinctions. It may appear to some that the concept of "public" is so masculinized as to be useless, if not dangerous. One feminist counter to this view is Fraser's in "Rethinking the Public Sphere," as I have noted. Another is provided by the examination of the Permanent Injunction *in situ* and the theoretical and legal discourse surrounding it. In practice, "public" and "private" are made material together and simultaneously. It is impossible to invoke one of the pair without at least implicitly invoking the other. This suggests that it is also impossible to discard "public" (as masculinized and exclusionary) without putting at risk the concept of "private" as well. Nonetheless, the concept of "private," as Jean Cohen argues in "Rethinking Privacy," is critical not only for feminism but also for other liberatory or democratizing projects. Women's and men's decisional autonomy, bodily integrity, and inviolate personalities all require a fundamental right to privacy—a right that is not expressly protected by the Constitution but one that is widely understood in practice. Indeed, Jean Cohen argues that the concept of a right to privacy can and should "replace property as the symbolic principle around which the key complex of personal civil rights are articulated" (162).

Indeed, the "everyday feminists" who work at WCS (that is, women who enact feminist projects without necessarily articulating feminist positions) welcome and even embrace the spatial delineation of public from private manifest in the Permanent Injunction. The injunction protects them, reassures them, and helps them "get about their business." Furthermore, as the public/private dyad is rethought conceptually and reworked in practice, it is important to remember that at the present historical moment, a variety of political discourses (positioned on *both* sides of the abortion question) are continuing to delineate public from private in literal, material, and powerful ways.

Examined together, this site-specific document and the larger conceptual categories it invokes illuminate one another: the Permanent Injunction draws on and makes material the conceptual distinction between public and private, and in doing so it rehearses the distinction and reinforces its power. At the same time, the conceptual distinction functions to manage some of the conflicts—between goals, between specific individuals, or between political positions and ethical beliefs—that occur in the daily practice of abortion provision at WCS. The Permanent Injunction, like other powerful cultural texts, mediates between the world of words and the lived world of human experiences, experiences as human as those enacted on a daily basis at WCS: engaging in meaningful labor, making decisions about one's future, and putting beliefs into collective and concrete action.

Notes

I am grateful to the Research and Graduate Studies Office at Kent State University for a university research leave; to Kerrie Haskamp Farkas for research assistance; to participants at the 1997 Penn State Rhetoric Conference, especially the editors of this volume, for lively conversations and thoughtful comments; to Susan Wells and Steve Witte for their close readings, challenges, and encouragement; and especially to the women and men of WCS, for their time, patience, and honesty with me, and for their everyday courage. Earlier versions of this paper were given at the 1997 meeting of the Society for Critical Exchange at Case Western Reserve University, and at the 1997 Conference on College Composition and Communication in Chicago.

1. At the request of the physician who owns WCS and the women who work there, names and identifying details of all sites and participants have been changed.

2. My study did not examine discourses of the abortion debate—that is, the agonistic, often powerfully persuasive discourse practices of pro-life and pro-choice groups. Rather, my inquiry has focused on a specific group of individuals, primarily women, who do the "work" of abortion on a daily basis. For treatments of the "official" discourse of the abortion debate, see Bracher; Condit; and Luker.

3. While our research on workplace literacy is in its early stages, some CRWL-sponsored projects have been reported by Bracewell and Witte; Dunmire; Greenwood; Haas, "Cultural Tools" and "Embodied Practice"; and Witte, "Practice" and "Investigating Literacy."

4. I determined that a text or document was used "regularly" if I observed it being used (read, written, distributed, referred to, filled out, filed, etc.) more than once on any

full day I was at the clinic, or if a staff member (usually the WCS director or a medical assistant) told me that the text was used daily or regularly. The category of "regular use" was robust and reliable: every staff member I interviewed identified virtually the same set of documents (about 54 of them) as those in regular use, and my observations of use matched the staff members' reports almost as closely. Excluded from the cataloging were texts (such as waiting-room magazines and exit signs) that have a generic use within our culture or that were not produced or used in the "work" of the clinic as that work was defined by clinic personnel.

5. In work sponsored by the Center for Research on Workplace Literacy (of which this study of WCS is a part), my colleagues and I have used cultural-historical psychology (Cole; Vygotsky, "Instrumental Method" and "Thought") and activity theory (Leont'ev, Wertsch) to understand the nature of literacy as it functions in "activity systems" within particular historical and cultural contexts. These activity systems are comprised of goals-directed actions and operations (Leont'ev), and they are mediated by tools (including artifacts), as well by communities, rules, and divisions of labor (Engeström; Cole and Engeström).

6. My adaptations of Spradley's techniques had to do primarily with the conditions under which I interviewed informants. Most of the interviews were conducted opportunistically, when there was a lull in clinic activity or when staff went on break; some were conducted in the context of specific incidents, including patient interactions or the use of specific documents, that I had just observed. The interviews Spradley describes tend to be more extended and formal.

7. The language of the Permanent Injunction is ambiguous and vague in a number of ways. For instance, "threats" and "verbal abuse" are prohibited but not defined. However, protesters seem not to have not challenged these ambiguities, or they have not challenged them blatantly enough to discomfort clinic staff.

8. The literature on the public/private distinction, its origins, utility, applications, and viability, is vast; a review of it is beyond the scope of this chapter. In addition to texts discussed or cited in this section, important treatments of the public/private dyad are included in Calhoun; Robbins; and Weintraub and Kumar.

9. For Arendt, political action is ipso facto rhetoric or persuasive speech, for "to be political, to live in a *polis*, meant that everything was decided through words and persuasion and not through force and violence" (26). Barbarians and members of households (presumably women and slaves), on the other hand, were persuaded by violence.

10. The invocation of spatial metaphors to explain or describe "public" is pervasive in Arendt, as it is in Habermas and Fraser. In each case, the passages cited demonstrate the authors' reliance on the language of spatialization, as well as being important passages in the original texts.

11. An important part of Habermas's project is to "reclaim" the notion of "public sphere" for contemporary social and political practice, but as numerous commentators have pointed out, the strongest sections of *Structural Transformation* are the descriptions of the public sphere itself, not how it might be reclaimed (Calhoun; Fraser, "Rethinking").

12. Note that it is not just democratic processes and practices that require a "public sphere"; the act of critique, with which Fraser is very concerned, requires it as well.

13. The spatial construction of public and private has important implications for the

way "public discourse" is both conceived and practiced. A discussion of some of these implications, and their grounding in field research at WCS and in a city government, appears in a working paper I have coauthored with Kerrie Haskamp Farkas, titled "The Relationship of Public Space and Public Discourse in Social Theory and in Everyday Practice."

14. My account of Supreme Court rulings on privacy and reproductive freedom has benefited from my reading of Alderman and Kennedy, Friedman, Milbauer, and Tushnet, although none of these specifically discusses the use of "space" in defining and delineating privacy. It should also be noted that, in addition to a "right to privacy," *Roe v. Wade* and many of the challenges to it elaborated other important legal questions, including, perhaps most critically, the notion of "personhood."

15. The quote is from Justice Brandeis's 1928 dissenting opinion in *Olmstead v. United States*, p. 478. In my discussion of Supreme Court rulings, I will indicate parenthetically page numbers from which quotes are drawn. The cases themselves are listed alphabetically after Works Cited.

16. The *Roe v. Wade* ruling did not so much "make abortion legal" as assert that the states may not interfere with a woman's securing of an abortion. At the time of *Roe*, many states had already legalized abortion. It is also worth noting that throughout much of the nineteenth century, abortions were legal in the United States and, apparently, were widespread among all social classes (see Luker; Mohr).

17. The *Schenk* case was, at the time I wrote this, not yet bound in the *Supreme Court Reporter*, the official transcript of the Court's decisions. For this case, I have cited the majority opinion excerpted the day after the decision in the *New York Times*, 20 February 1997.

Works Cited

Alderman, Ellen, and Caroline Kennedy. *The Right to Privacy*. New York: Alfred Knopf, 1995.

Arendt, Hannah. *The Human Condition*. Chicago: University of Chicago Press, 1958.

Benhabib, Seyla. "Models of Public Space: Hannah Arendt, the Liberal Tradition, and Jürgen Habermas." In *Habermas and the Public Sphere*, edited by Craig Calhoun, 73–98. Cambridge, Mass.: MIT Press, 1993.

Bracewell, Robert, and Stephen Witte. "Implications of Activity, Practice, and Semiotic Theory for Cognitive Constructs of Writing." Paper presented at the Annual Convention of the American Educational Research Association, Chicago, 1997.

Bracher, Mark. "Anti-Abortionist Discourse." In *Lacan, Discourse, and Social Change: A Psychoanalytic Cultural Criticism*, by Mark Bracher, 103–18. Ithaca: Cornell University Press, 1993.

Calhoun, Craig, ed. *Habermas and the Public Sphere*. Cambridge, Mass.: MIT Press, 1993.

Cohen, Jean. "Rethinking Privacy: The Abortion Controversy." In *Public and Private in Thought and Practice: Perspectives on a Grand Dichotomy*, edited by Jeff Weintraub and Krishan Kumar, 133–65. Chicago: University of Chicago Press, 1997.

Cole, Michael, and Yrjo Engestrom. "A Cultural-Historical Approach to Distributed

Cognition." In *Distributed Cognitions*, edited by Gavriel Salomon, 1–46. Cambridge: Cambridge University Press, 1996.

Condit, Celeste. *Decoding Abortion Rhetoric: Communicating Social Change*. Urbana: University of Illinois Press, 1990.

Dunmire, Patricia. "Negotiating Professional and Political Restrictions: The Case of the Nurse Practitioner." Paper presented at the Penn State Conference on Rhetoric and Composition, State College, Pa., 1997.

Dykstal, Timothy. "Introduction: The Intersections of the Public and the Private Spheres in Early Modern England." *Prose Studies* 18 (1995): 22–40.

Elshtain, Jean Bethke. *Public Man, Private Woman: Women in Social and Political Thought*. Princeton: Princeton University Press, 1981.

Engestrom, Yrjo. "Developmental Studies of Work as a Testbench of Activity Theory: The Case of Primary Care Medical Practice." In *Understanding Practice: Perspectives on Activity and Context*, edited by Seth Chaiklin and Jean Lave, 64–103. Cambridge: Cambridge University Press, 1993.

Fraser, Nancy. "Rethinking the Public Sphere: A Contribution to the Critique of Actually Existing Democracy." *Social Text* 25/26 (1990): 56–80.

Fraser, Nancy. *Unruly Practices: Power, Discourse, and Gender in Contemporary Social Theory*. Minneapolis: University of Minnesota Press, 1989.

Friedman, Leon. Introduction. In *The Supreme Court Confronts Abortion*, edited by Leon Friedman, 3–21. New York: Farrar, Straus, and Giroux, 1993.

Glaser, Barry, and Anselm Strauss. *The Discovery of Grounded Theory: Strategies for Qualitative Research*. Chicago: Aldine, 1967.

Greenwood, Claudia. "Observing the Mediating and Constructive Functions of Literacy in a Social Service Agency." Paper presented at the Cultures of Writing Conference, Society for Critical Exchange, Cleveland, Ohio, 1997.

Haas, Christina. "Cultural Tools as Psychological Tools: Mediational Means and the Embodied Nature of Writing." Paper presented at the Annual Convention of the American Educational Research Association, Chicago, 1997.

Haas, Christina. "Writing as Embodied Practice: Toward a Theory of Technologies in Literacy." Paper presented at the English Department Colloquium, Ohio State University, Columbus, 1997.

Habermas, Jürgen. *The Structural Transformation of the Public Sphere: An Inquiry into a Category of Bourgeois Society*. Translated by Thomas Burger. Cambridge, Mass.: MIT Press, 1989.

Horwitz, Morton J. "The History of the Public/Private Distinction." *University of Pennsylvania Law Review* 130 (1982): 1,423–28.

Leont'ev, A. N. *Activity, Consciousness, and Personality*. Translated by M. J. Hall. Englewood Cliffs, N.J.: Prentice-Hall, 1978.

Leont'ev, A. N. "The Problem of Activity in Psychology." In *The Concept of Activity in Soviet Psychology*, edited by James Wertsch, 37–71. Armonk, N.Y.: M. E. Sharpe, 1981.

Luker, Kristen. *Abortion and the Politics of Motherhood*. Berkeley: University of California Press, 1984.

Milbauer, Barbara. *The Law Giveth: Legal Aspects of the Abortion Controversy*. New York: Atheneum, 1983.

Mohr, James. *Abortion in America: The Origins and Evolution of National Policy*. New York: Oxford University Press, 1978.

Robbins, Bruce, ed. *The Phantom Public Sphere*. Minneapolis: University of Minnesota Press, 1993.

Scarry, Elaine. *The Body in Pain: The Making and Unmaking of the World*. New York: Oxford University Press, 1985.

Spradley, James. *The Ethnographic Interview*. New York: Holt, 1979.

Strauss, Anselm. *Qualitative Analysis for Social Scientists*. New York: Cambridge University Press, 1987.

Strauss, Anselm, and Juliet Corbin. *Basics of Qualitative Research: Grounded Theory Procedures and Techniques*. Newbury Park, Calif.: Sage, 1990.

Turner, Bryan S. *The Body and Society*. 2d ed. London: Sage, 1996.

Tushnet, Mark. "The Supreme Court on Abortion: A Survey." In *Abortion, Medicine, and the Law*, edited by J. Douglas Butler and David Walbert, 161–76. New York: Facts on File.

Vygotsky, Lev S. "The Instrumental Method in Psychology." In *The Concept of Activity in Soviet Psychology*, edited by James Wertsch, 134–43. Armonk, N.Y.: M. E. Sharpe, 1981.

Vygotsky, Lev S. *Thought and Language*. Edited and translated by Alex Kozulin. Cambridge, Mass.: MIT Press, 1986.

Weintraub, Jeff, and Krishan Kumar, eds. *Public and Private in Thought and Practice*. Chicago: University of Chicago Press, 1997.

Wells, Susan. "Rogue Cops and Health Care: What do We Want from Public Writing?" *College Composition and Communication* 47 (1996): 325–41.

Wertsch, James. *Vygotsky and the Social Formation of Mind*. Cambridge, Mass.: Harvard University Press, 1985.

Witte, Stephen. "Between Some Rocks and Some Soft Places: Practice, Activity, Semiotic." Paper presented at the First Biennial Thomas R. Watson Conference, Louisville, Ky., 1996.

Witte, Stephen. "Toward a Theoretical Framework for Investigating Literacy." Paper presented at the Annual Convention of the International Research Association, Atlanta, Ga., 1997.

Supreme Court Decisions Cited

Eisenstadt v. Baird, 405 U.S. 440–472 (1972).

Griswold v. State of Connecticut, 381 U.S. 480–531 (1965).

Madsen v. Women's Health Center, Inc., 114 S.Ct. 2,516–2,551 (1994).

Planned Parenthood v. Casey, 505 U.S. 833–1,002 (1992).

Roe v. Wade, 410 U.S. 116–179 (1973).

Schenk et al. v. Pro-Choice Network of Western New York et al. (1997).

Webster v. Reproductive Health Services, 492 U.S. 490–572 (1989).

11 *J. Blake Scott*

Rhetoric and Technoscience
The Case of Confide

On 3 July 1997, the pharmaceutical manufacturer Johnson & Johnson announced that it was pulling from the market (on account of low sales) its home collection HIV test kit named Confide, marking the end of the product's short marketing life and its longer, tangled history. Confide had been approved by the Food and Drug Administration about a year earlier, on 14 May 1996, after a decade-long controversy about extending HIV testing into the "private," "nonscientific" sphere of the home. The history of Confide, and of home collection HIV testing more generally, offers a rich opportunity for studying what Bruno Latour calls "technoscience"—all the cultural elements tied to science and technology in the making or in action, before the science and technology get black-boxed or made to appear clean, coherent, and ready-made (174–75, 130–31). In this chapter, a rhetorical and cultural analysis of the discourse surrounding Confide and home collection HIV testing, I approach Confide not as a finished black box, but as a messy set of rhetorical and cultural practices.

The product Confide could more precisely be defined as a home *collection* HIV antibody *system* rather than as a simple, self-contained HIV or AIDS test kit, as it has been frequently called.[1] Unlike a home performance test, which gives users immediate results (for example, a home pregnancy kit), a home collection testing system involves collecting a blood sample at home and then sending it to a laboratory to be tested. In the case of Confide, a user first obtained the test kit by purchasing it at a pharmacy or health clinic, ordering it

with a credit card over the Internet, or ordering it with a credit card by calling
1–800–THE–TEST. Confide sold for thirty to forty dollars at a pharmacy, and
forty dollars plus shipping if ordered through the mail; in the latter case it arrived at the user's address in a "discreet" brown box with no identifying information. The kit itself, a small white box that opened up (figure 11.1), contained
the following elements: an informational booklet about HIV/AIDS written by
former Surgeon General C. Everett Koop (this constituted the "pre-test counseling"); instructions; lancets, a sterile wipe, Band-aids, and containers for dis-
posing of used lancets, a test card for the blood samples; a personal identification card with the user's unique identification number for anonymous access
of test results; and a prepaid, preaddressed mailer. Materials were described in
English and Spanish. After the user read the informational booklet and, following the instructions, took the blood sample, she or he sent the sample off to the
laboratory in the mailer. After seven days the user could get the results by calling an 800 number between 8:30 A.M. and 8:00 P.M., Monday through Friday.
If the user's test was non-reactive or negative, she or he would most likely be
connected to a recorded message (in such a case, this message would constitute
the "post-test counseling"). If the user's test was positive, she or he would be
connected to a trained counselor who would discuss the results and refer the
user to local resources, using the Center for Disease Control's (CDC) computerized nationwide database of HIV/AIDS organizations. The small number of
users with indeterminate or inconclusive results would be encouraged to re-
test. Confide and similar home collection test kits, then, are complex systems
that involve a number of steps and depend on a number of technologies, including telephones, computers, the Postal Service, laboratories, a centralized results center, written documents, and possibly credit cards. To adopt one of Latour's descriptions, Confide is a machine or an assemblage rather than a single,
simple tool (129).

In Foucauldian terms, Confide could also be called a new and improved
disciplinary technology. Confide and other home collection tests extend and
transform the disciplinary power of HIV antibody testing into new sites and
practices, further spreading what Foucault calls the "centres of observation"
throughout the social body (*Discipline* 212). While Latour might describe
home collection testing as a network of human actors and resources, Foucault
might describe it as a circuit of biopower—the power to regulate the subjuga-
tion of bodies and the control of populations (Foucault, *History* 140; see also
Grosz 152). Thus, this chapter amounts to a case study of an instance of technoscience as biopower, a consideration of how technoscience is shaped, transformed, mobilized, and negotiated in different public forums. I offer first a
chronological overview of the controversy over home collection testing approval that exposes the cultural networks and rhetorics that made the product
Confide possible. Next, I provide more detailed rhetorical analysis of public

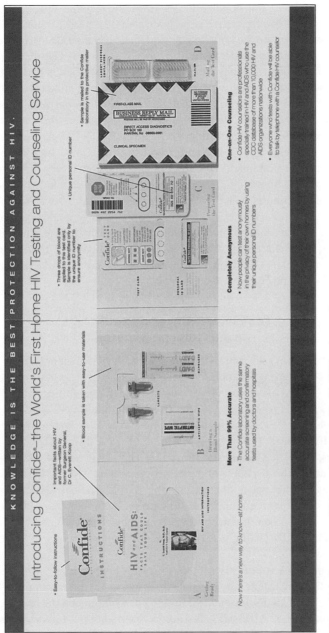

Figure 11.1. Components of Johnson & Johnson's Confide HIV testing service

241

health, biomedical, and popular media texts about home testing, critiquing problematic and often reductive arguments about the need for home HIV testing technoscience, and the knowledge and effects it is assumed to produce. My analysis, which draws on the work of rhetoricians such as Carolyn Miller and cultural critics such as Nancy Fraser, focuses on how science and technology are figured and used in rhetoric about home HIV testing, and on how this rhetoric, as an exercise of power, interpellates and employs particular constructs of "needy" bodies. My analysis then moves to a consideration of post–FDA-approval discourse on home testing, in the forms of television, print, and web-page advertisements for Confide and Home Access Express (the second home collection test); I find this to be a discourse posited on a very different set of bodies than those figured in the approval controversy. I conclude by anatomizing some of the cultural effects—including material effects on actual bodies—that home collection HIV testing and its discourses have made possible: using Foucault, I indicate some of the ways home testing functions as a new disciplinary technology that enables the extension and diffusion of HIV testing into new cultural contexts, including some that permit home testing discourse to influence sexual practices.

The Confide Approval Controversy
and Its Cultural Networks

The story of home collection HIV testing began in 1986, when the FDA learned that a small company intended to develop and market an over-the-counter, mail-in test kit for the use of a layperson in a nonclinical setting. Shortly thereafter, University Hospital Laboratories (UHL) submitted a pre-market-approval application to the FDA for its home collection testing system, misleadingly named AIDS Check. (The testing system does not test for AIDS, but for HIV antibodies, and is not diagnostic for AIDS. This conflation of HIV and AIDS was common in the discourse of the controversy.[2]) In 1988 the FDA responded to UHL and other test applicants, stating that it would consider only tests designed for use by recognized health care professionals (e.g., physicians or nurses) in official health care settings (e.g., physician's offices, hospitals, or clinics). Thus, HIV testing was off limits, for the time being, to laypeople in the home.

While the FDA steadfastly refused to review applications for home collection tests, the new technology began to be discussed in different public forums. In March 1989, U.S. Representative Ron Wyden summoned the hearing "Risks and Implications of AIDS-HIV Testing in Nontraditional Laboratories and in the Home," which featured testimony from FDA Commissioner Frank Young and UHL head Elliot Millenson, the developer of the test. The primary *stasis* question framing the disagreement at this hearing was evaluative—Is home collection testing safe and effective?—and the primary evaluative criteria had to do with the technical efficacy (accuracy and reliability) and the safety of the new, state-of-the-art tests. As its title suggests, the hearing was framed by what I call the "scales *topos*"—the balancing or weighing of potential benefits against risks and costs; this is a liberal *topos* that implies an objective, fair stance. Although Wyden hinted that home testing might be viable in the future, he drew on what Lawrence Prelli has called the "objective" scientific *topoi* of skepticism and disinterestedness in concluding that home testing was not ready for approval (United States Congress 11). Wyden and most of the health care officials advocated a skeptical, cautious approach to home testing, one driven by the standards of "good medicine" and "good science" rather than by the marketplace (2). "We simply need more scientific data about this new technology," speakers representing the FDA and the American Psychological Association (APA) in effect stated. Wyden and Dr. Peter Hawley of the Whitman Walker Clinic argued that home tests were driven more by profit than by science. In addition to the *topos* of skepticism, Wyden and others deployed a rhetoric of control: the control of biotechnology and the public's use of it. Wyden and Young both referenced their duty to protect the public. Dr. J. Mehsen Joseph of the American Public Health Association (APHA) referred to another kind of control when he lamented that home testing would render testees unavailable for physicians' scrutiny (32). This rhetoric of control over technology revealed the paternalistic impulse of the FDA and other public health care officials.

Later that spring, the FDA held its first public meeting on blood collection kits. Officials from the FDA, CDC, National Institutes of Health (NIH), and College of American Pathologists reinforced the dominant theme of the Wyden hearing: skeptical, cautious evaluation and scientific validation. Several public health care officials expressed concern that private home testing might lead to less control over the testing process and might make public surveillance of HIV more difficult. Millenson of UHL also drew on the authority of science and technology, citing data from scientific studies and indicting his FDA opponents as political, self-interested, and unscientific in their refusal to consider UHL's application. "So long as politics, not science, guides the government action on AIDS," Millenson stated, "people will die endlessly" (9). Opponents and proponents of approval, then, accused each other of nonscientific motives; each side problematically separated science from the marketplace, politics, or other spheres in order to characterize science and scientists themselves as objective and credible.

Although the cautious consensus against immediate approval of home testing seemed to overpower the less organized efforts of UHL and other proponents, the issue was far from closed. In March 1990, UHL filed a lawsuit against the FDA for refusing to consider its application. Just a month later, the FDA changed its policy and agreed to review applications for home collection HIV tests. According to the FDA, the exigence for this change was not the lawsuit but biomedical advancements such as improved filter-paper tests and new HIV/ AIDS treatments and therapies. Media reports echoed the FDA's justification based on biomedical advancement and progress. A subhead in the *Washington Post*, for instance, read "Medical Advances Spur Policy Shift" (Gladwell). The FDA's decision, however, was to review applications, not necessarily to approve them.

In July 1990 the FDA held a Blood Products Advisory Committee (BPAC) meeting to review UHL's product AIDS Check. Dr. Jay Epstein and other FDA officials made it clear that the agency was still against approval. Their presentations, and much of the following discussion, revolved around a list of twenty-nine concerns about technical aspects of the tests as well as specimen collection, shipment, and counseling. The FDA's tour de force of concerns worked rhetorically to give presence to the risks of the product and to create a need for continued regulation and control.[3] After hearing the FDA's concerns, one committee member, Dr. Ross Eckert, joked that UHL's application had been sent to the "subdivision of non-approvability" (U.S. Public Health Service, 30th Meeting 107). The FDA was simply displaying the "absence of data that is needed by a scientific and technical committee in a scientific and technical agency," an agency official retorted (111). At another point in the meeting, Eckert questioned the FDA's disinterestedness by suggesting that the agency's objections were motivated by a desire to protect the financial interests of existing testing networks. As in the FDA hearing a year earlier, FDA officials and their biomedical allies framed much of their discussion with a theme of control— control over rapidly evolving testing technology, control over the testing process, and control over epidemiological surveillance through testing. Although Millenson attempted to meet the FDA's demand for scientific validation, citing studies in several prominent medical journals, he appeared to be no match for his opponents and for their rhetoric emphasizing the risk and need for control of home testing: a rhetoric that called for non-approval. At the conclusion of the meeting, the committee voted three to one against approval, citing a number of scientific-technical and public health concerns.

Little changed in the controversy until 1993, when the health care giant Johnson & Johnson bought what was left of the much smaller UHL and its test kit and renamed them Direct Access Diagnostics (DAD) and Confide, respectively. Millenson stayed on as head of the new subsidiary. Shortly after this takeover, the FDA granted an expedited review of DAD's application. The agency that had once stonewalled AIDS Check was now facilitating the approval of Confide, a move that was not so strange, given the agency's record of privileging big companies' products (such as Burroughes Wellcome's AZT).[4] This FDA approval pattern suggests that politics and big business had more to do with changes in the FDA's policy than did changes in the test's safety and efficacy. Johnson & Johnson began a three-year, deep-pocketed lobbying campaign for Confide: it hired former U.S. Surgeon General C. Everett Koop as its primary spokesperson; in December, it formed a fifty-plus-member Community Advisory Committee that included renowned AIDS scientists and biomedical experts such as Donald Francis, Marcus Conant, and Michael Gottlieb, AIDS activists and educators such as Project Inform's Martin Delaney, public-policy experts such as Bruce Decker, public-relations experts such as Sean Strub, and leaders of minority health organizations, such as Rene Rodriguez. Even before DAD's committee was formed, a number of its future members, as well as state government officials, sent letters to FDA Commissioner David Kessler, urging him to approve home testing. Several of the letters pleaded that certain groups of people desperately needed the increased access to testing and its benefits that home tests would provide (a claim I will interrogate more fully). In addition, several of the letters referenced discussions and meetings with DAD, which had been busy recruiting a range of new allies.

On 22 June 1994, the FDA held a third, more widely publicized meeting on home testing. This gathering of more than sixty speakers—the first forum dominated by proponents rather than skeptics and opponents of home testing— marked a major turning point in the controversy; indeed, one advisory committee member called the meeting a "stacked deck" (U.S. Public Health Service, 44th Meeting 311). In this meeting, DAD was able to tip the scales of the debate to the benefits rather than the risks of home collection testing, and to shift the primary terms of the debate from evaluative ones (e.g., "How effective and safe is the new test?") to procedural ones (e.g., "How can we ensure the effectiveness and safety of the test once it enters the marketplace?"). The burden of proof, in other words, shifted from the proponents to the opponents of home testing. In contrast to the conclusions of previous meetings, the advisory committee now decided that the benefits of home collection testing outweighed its risks; they recommended that Confide be approved, provided that the test underwent minor adjustments and post-market studies. The FDA would not follow this recommendation for some time, however.

The impressive network of Johnson & Johnson/DAD supporters attending the FDA meeting included many of the members of DAD's Community Advisory Committee whom I have named, along with additional scientists and biomedical experts, mental-health experts, counselors, educators, activists, and people with AIDS (PWAs). A few of these speakers were paid consultants of DAD, and almost all of them had their travel expenses to the meeting paid by DAD. Supporters of home testing argued, among other things, that testing was the best or only weapon in the war against AIDS; that home collection testing was needed to control and contain the AIDS epidemic; that home collection testing would give more people (especially high-risk, underserved people) access to testing and medical care; and that home collection testing would improve, extend, or save lives. These arguments, made by scientists and nonscientists alike, included a range of both "scientific" and "nonscientific" appeals. For example, Koop urged the FDA to approve home testing based on good science, sound ethics, and plain old common sense (U.S. Public Health Service, 44th Meeting 155–56)—appeals that paralleled his dual ethos as both a scientific-medical expert and the friendly doctor next door.

The group of health-care officials who had dominated earlier FDA meetings continued to advocate a cautious approach to home testing, although several of these officials, in their references to the inevitability of home testing and their emphasis on procedural concerns about approval, now seemed more willing to consider approval. One committee member, a Dr. Snyder, even suggested that home collection testing was part of an inevitable trend and paradigm shift toward self-diagnosis and home health care (363). This new willingness was probably at least partly a response to the changing cultural context of the debate, including the lobbying effort of Johnson & Johnson and its allies, continuing pressure from AIDS activist groups such as ACT UP, recent pressure from a Republican Congress to further deregulate and privatize health care, and a burgeoning market for home health care technologies. None of these exigencies was mentioned by government officials or advisers, however. Instead, the FDA's Epstein, who ran most of the meeting, announced that recent technological improvements and the availability of new drug treatments were the reasons for holding the meeting and reconsidering approval (U.S. Public Health Service, 44th Meeting 122). Once again, the complex exigencies that contributed to changes in policy were reduced to scientific developments.

A third and perhaps unlikely alliance came out of the 22 June meeting—an alliance that continued to publicly express its opposition to home testing after the meeting. Representatives from the National Association of Lesbian and Gay Health Clinics and the National Association of People with AIDS joined forces with Shepard Smith and his organization Americans for a Sound HIV/AIDS Policy, a conservative group that had lobbied for mandatory testing and contact tracing as well as for workplace restrictions on HIV-positive people (policies the other two groups clearly opposed). Speakers from these three different groups all argued that home testing was a risky technology that needed to be controlled, and that the risks of home testing far outweighed its potential benefits. Over the course of the controversy, home collection testing would be opposed by other groups as well, including the American Foundation for AIDS Research, the National AIDS Network, the AIDS Action Council, and several ACT UP chapters. Each group used the scales *topos* to frame arguments about approval; this *topos* was problematic in that it oversimplified complicated issues about the test and its possible uses and thus led to exaggerated epideictic arguments about risks or benefits rather than to careful deliberation. In fact, home testing is neither the best new scientific weapon for controlling AIDS nor a technology out of control. Rather, it is a complex product of technoscience that makes possible a range of beneficial *and* harmful effects for different people.

The 22 June meeting and the recommendation for approval sparked an explosion of discourse in popular media and biomedical journals. Before and after the date of the meeting, opinion-editorial essays and "informative" reports appeared in such popular forums as *USA Today*, the *New York Times*, the *Washington Post*, the *Los Angeles Times*, the *San Francisco Chronicle*, the *New Republic*, and *Forbes*. Many of these essays, including Koop's opinion piece in *USA Today*, explicitly supported home collection testing, mentioned the need for more access to HIV testing, and chided the FDA for holding up the approval process. In addition, Confide spokesperson Koop appeared on *CBS This Morning* and NBC's *Today Show* to promote Johnson & Johnson's test kit. Biomedical journals such as the *Lancet* and more popular scientific, medical, and health-related periodicals, such as *Scientific American* and *Health* (forums where Johnson & Johnson spends advertising dollars), were also reporting the promise of home collection testing. Several of these reports suggested that approval of the new technology was imminent, or at least inevitable. For example, a *Laboratory Medicine* piece was titled "Imminent Approval of HIV Home Test Stirs Debate" (Thomas); a *Nature* piece led with "Postal Tests on the Way" (Concar); and a report in the *Journal of the Physicians Association for AIDS Care* stated, "Both sides agree [that approval of home collection test kits] may not be imminent, but is likely inevitable" (Cimons 6).[5] Like most reports of the FDA's 1990 policy shift, some of the reports around the 1994 FDA meeting attributed the shift in the debate toward approval largely to advancements of science and technology. An article in *AIDS ALERT*, for example, began with the line "New Advances, New Attitudes"; it went on to quote FDA official Mary Pendergast to the effect that "science and technology have evolved considerably" ("Over-the-Counter" 105–6). Actually, the technical aspects of Confide and of testing in general had not changed much in the preceding few years. But such reports played into the problematic view of technoscience as some sort of self-determining and constantly and inevitably progressing entity that is ultimately beyond human control.

Opponents of home collection testing, including representatives of the National Lesbian and Gay Health Association (NLGHA), who feared losing government funding for testing programs if home tests were approved, were mobilizing their own campaign. On 26 October, NLGHA, the National Association of People with AIDS, and Americans for a Sound AIDS Policy sent a letter of complaint to FDA's Kessler and to Secretary of Health and Human Services Donna Shalala; it accused DAD of violating FDA regulations against pre-approval publicity, and it called for an investigation of DAD and a denial of its

Confide application (Portelli and Bayer). The eight alleged "unlawful" violations included direct mail campaigns in *POZ* (a magazine for HIV-positive readers) and Koop's television promotion of the test as safe and effective. In support of their allegations, the authors of the letter began to map out DAD's powerful promotional network, which by fall 1994 also included one of the most prominent names in American politics.

Speaker of the House Newt Gingrich, who once called the FDA "the leading job killer in America," on 2 September wrote to White House Chief of Staff Leon Panetta, asking him to look into the status of Confide at the FDA. "I hope as you review the issue in the next few days you will agree that the delay must end immediately and that the FDA should approve the home test without any qualifications," wrote Gingrich. Panetta subsequently sent a letter to Kessler, and he was reassured that approval was just around the corner (Simpson). Given the agenda of Gingrich and other Republicans to promote big business and to privatize, deregulate, and otherwise reform health care, Gingrich's advocacy of Confide may not be surprising. Home collection testing certainly has the potential to shift the cost and liability of HIV testing from the government to the private sector, where, according to one analyst, it would constitute a three-hundred-million-dollar market (Freundlich). A mapping of the links in Johnson & Johnson's network reveals a more concrete possible reason for Gingrich's advocacy: the company had recently contributed approximately thirty thousand dollars to Gingrich's Progress and Freedom Foundation (Simpson).

It was not until May 1996, nearly two years after the pivotal 1994 FDA meeting, that Confide was finally approved. After being pilot-marketed in Texas and Florida, Confide went on sale nationwide in January 1997, but its marketing campaign was limited because of a legal dispute between Johnson & Johnson and Millenson, the test's inventor, over the ownership of DAD and Confide. Still, ads for Confide and for Home Access Express, the second home collection test to receive approval, appeared in various national media forums, including television and magazines. Eventually an arbitrator and then a court ordered Johnson & Johnson to turn over the company and the test to Millenson, which partly explains why Confide was on the market for a little more than a year before Johnson & Johnson axed it, purportedly because of lower than expected sales (90,000 units).[6] The end of Confide was not the end of home collection testing, however. The FDA has approved at least two other home collection tests, including Home Access Health Corporation's Home Access and Home Access Express kits, 150,000 units of which have been sold. Several other home collection and home performance tests have been developed, and some are being illegally sold via the Internet.

My narrative overview of the history of Confide points to several noteworthy findings about the discourse and networks of technoscience. First, the development and approval of Confide were made possible by variety of exigencies, only some of which can be attributed to science and technology and their rhetorics. If one were to reconstruct the approval controversy only through media accounts or the texts produced by DAD and its allies, one might tell a story about the triumph of technoscience; one might thus attribute shifts in the approval debate to advancements in science and technology, such as new and improved tests and new treatments or therapies for people living with HIV/AIDS, and to powerful, authoritative scientific rhetors, like Koop and Francis, and their rhetoric. Such a story, however, would fail to account for several of the cultural conditions and constraints of the controversy. DAD's success depended on various cultural exigencies and factors, some of which could be considered extra-scientific and extra-rhetorical; these include lawsuits, economic power, public pressure, media pressure, political influence, and a larger cultural trend toward privatized, market-driven, and consumer-oriented health care.

This observation leads to a second one: the networks and rhetorics that helped shape the controversy over home collection HIV testing were heterogeneous and multifaceted, extending across scientific/technical and nonscientific/public/social spheres. The networks of home-testing skeptics, opponents, and proponents included medical and other scientific experts, as well as people who had various nonscientific backgrounds and types of expertise (e.g., politicians, activists, educators, and counselors). Although members of each group attempted to claim the authority of science and technology and to portray their opponents as motivated by politics, money, or paranoia, the rhetorics and other resources they themselves mobilized were not purely "scientific."

Certainly appeals to science and technology abounded in the rhetoric of the controversy; those for and against approval both cited scientific "facts" or "data," deployed Prelli's scientific *topoi* of skepticism and disinterestedness, and accused their opponents of being unscientific or extra-scientific. Public policy and other types of nonscientific appeals were also prevalent in the rhetoric about home testing, however, even in the arguments of some scientists. Koop, for example, in the 1994 FDA meeting simultaneously drew on the authority of science and on other cultural values such as common sense and individual empowerment. The networks and rhetorics of the controversy, then, begin to show technoscience is not a set of discourse communities and practices distinct from, or merely influenced by, or embedded in the rest of culture. Rather, as Donna Haraway puts it, the very "tissue of technoscience" is made up of "economic, technical, political, organic, historical, mythic, textual" and other cultural threads (62). While these first two findings or observations may not be surprising to some, they strike me as different from those articulated in much work on the rhetoric of science. That work often demarcates boundaries between science and other spheres/knowledges/rhetorics; and often, as Dilip Gaonkar has pointed out, it focuses on and attributes agency to the intentional rhetorical strategies of important scientists as these are revealed in their texts.

Conceptualizing technoscience more loosely as heterogeneous cultural practice or action, as Latour and Haraway do, can open up additional sites for rhetorical study and enrich the ways we think about technoscience.

A third finding, which I will discuss further in the next section, is that the different players and networks in the controversy often relied on reductive, problematic notions of technoscience, some of which can be summarized here. Several speakers from the FDA, CDC, and other government agencies, perhaps trying to protect the interests of established HIV testing networks and programs, suggested, somewhat paternalistically, that the new home collection testing technology needed to be evaluated cautiously, and that its applications needed to be regulated carefully. Groups that more strongly opposed approval, particularly the alliance of NAPWA, ASAP, and NALGHC (the last feared losing funding for its testing programs), depicted home testing technoscience as a threatening entity that should be controlled. Other contributors to the debate seemed to assume that approval of home testing was inevitable and even imminent, that technoscience was a constantly and inevitably self-progressing entity, and that society might as well accept the generally positive changes that technoscience makes possible. Representatives and allies of DAD argued, perhaps even more problematically, that home testing was an expedient, desperately needed tool for intervening in and controlling an epidemic that was out of control. This tool, many of the arguments went, would provide access, especially for those who really needed it, to knowledge and medical care that would prevent or contain transmission and improve, prolong, and save lives. These conceptions of home testing technology—all of which oversimplify our complex, interactive relationships with technoscience—were evident in various types of discourse (e.g., biomedical, public policy, or popular media) and were articulated by scientists and nonscientists alike. This last observation, then, reinforces Paula Treichler's assertion that there is a continuum, not a dichotomy, between biomedical and popular discourses and (mis)conceptions (37).

The *Kairos* of Technoscience

Carolyn Miller describes the classical concept of *kairos* as a central issue in the rhetorics of science and technology, given their respective emphases on progress and opportunity ("*Kairos*" 310; "Opportunity" 81). In the rhetoric of technology in particular, *kairos* can denote an opportune moment for action based partly on forecasting or projecting into an uncertain future (83). According to Miller, *kairos* as "technological forecasting" involves the twin themes of promise/benefit and threat/risk, as well as the twin ideologies of technology as progress and technology as out of control ("Opportunity" 89). Arguments for or against action or intervention in technoscientific discourse often rely on "kairotic" premises or assumptions about the benefits promised by science and technology or the threats or risks posed by them. As Miller explains, "The ideology of progress and the ideology of technology out-of-control are thus complementary kairotic constructions: they both read from a series of changing moments a trajectory into the future and a message about appropriate action at the present" (89). Yet both themes are problematic in their induction of science and technology and their effects as simply either good or bad. Miller's description of *kairos* in the rhetoric of technology can be related to the "scales *topos*." This trope, which framed the discussion of home collection testing at the Congressional hearing and at several FDA meetings, presents the balancing or weighing of potential benefits against risks and costs as a means of deciding on a course of action. As Debra Hawhee has noted, the classical figure of *kairos* personified was sometimes depicted holding scales and tipping them to create an advantage (61–62); Hawhee accordingly discusses normative measuring as one of the dimensions of *kairos* (71–72).

Kairos—here defined as opportune, timely action based partly on a future projection—was a central notion in the discourse surrounding Confide. This discourse emphasized the urgent need for the kairotic intervention of technoscience in both the social body and the individual body, especially the infected one. Many arguments for approval of home testing, particularly those made around and after the June 1994 FDA meeting, claimed that the benefits of home testing far outweighed the risks; proponents called for the intervention of new home testing technology as a better way to contain and control the HIV/AIDS epidemic. Famed AIDS scientist Donald Francis made this call in his testimony at the 1994 meeting, which he ended with a plea for urgent action: "Typical of the AIDS epidemic, we will deliberate and deliberate before we act. . . . I encourage you not to follow that path now. I suggest you feel the urgency, see the need, and approve home access HIV testing" (U.S. Public Health Service, 44th Meeting 190). The DAD Community Advisory Committee statement, written in 1995, ends with a similar call for kairotic action. After establishing the need and opportune moment for home testing with an incremental series of "facts," the writers urge the FDA to quickly approve this "important and timely service to American people." Post-approval discourse about home testing was similarly saturated with *kairos*-related appeals. The advertising campaign for Confide featured the slogans "It's time to know" and "Now is the time. This is the test." The Confide web site contained the line, "The need for Confide is now."

Arguments about the *kairos* for Confide often depended on a number of related claims and assumptions about home testing, technoscience, and HIV/ AIDS which were articulated or implied in various ways:

- AIDS is a public health and biomedical emergency that requires kairotic, timely intervention by technoscience.

- HIV infection is basically equivalent to AIDS, which is basically a death sentence: HIV = AIDS = death.
- Technoscience is an expedient tool that can be used to contain, control, and curb HIV/AIDS.
- Technoscience is constantly and inevitably progressing or advancing. Home testing must simply be accepted as part of this progression.
- In lieu of a cure or vaccine, testing is the best or only weapon at hand in the war against AIDS.
- Testing is technoscience's form of espionage or reconnaissance to detect the stealthy, stalking HIV agent, especially in the bodies of asymptomatic infected people who are spreading it to others.
- The more infected bodies we can identify, and the earlier we can identify them, the better.
- Existing HIV testing programs are not reaching enough high-risk, underserved people. Home testing will expand access to testing among these people.
- Home testing provides knowledge that will protect the mostly uninfected general public and lead to behavior change and life-saving health care for infected individuals.

In the last claim, we see the dual societal and individual trajectories of *kairos*. This complex body of persuasion, which I call the "knowledge enthymeme," can be diagrammed in the following way: home testing → knowledge or information → transmission-blocking action and/or access to health care → protection from infection and/or improved, prolonged, or saved lives.[7]

In my view, these *kairos*-related commonplaces—linguistic tags for shared beliefs—are idealistic at best and dangerous at worst. Too much faith in the power and progress of technoscience, for example, can lead to complacency about its possible harmful effects. Among other things, the inaccurate conflation of HIV and AIDS reifies the perception of the HIV-positive body as a dying AIDS victim. The assumption that the knowledge produced by testing is life-saving glosses over practical concerns about access and complex issues about how knowledge is constructed, interpreted, and used.

The logical first step in making a case for the *kairos* of home testing is establishing the need for its intervention. Proponents of approval did this in a number of ways. Often they depicted HIV/AIDS as a public health emergency, an epidemic spun out of control that was stalking particular groups and even the general public (this rhetorical move is common in calls for mandatory testing and other traditional public health control measures). Some rhetors, notably representatives of minority health organizations, attempted to create a heightened sense of need and an opportune moment for home testing in communities of color and other groups being disproportionately devastated by HIV/AIDS. Rene Rodriguez of the Interamerican College of Physicians and Surgeons, for example, lamented that AIDS was "now out of bounds and out of reach" in Hispanic communities (U.S. Public Health Service, 44th Meeting 271), and she ended her testimony with an injunction for approval: "Do it now, before more lives are lost" (272). Others took a more general approach, depicting HIV/AIDS as a national emergency, an "All-American Epidemic" (in U.S. Public Health Service, 44th Meeting 155). In the 1989 FDA public meeting about new testing technology, Millenson similarly emphasized the ongoing emergency of AIDS as a way to shame the FDA into action (a tactic commonly used by AIDS activist groups); he cited the CDC's estimate that as many as one and a half million people in the United States might unknowingly be infected with HIV and stated, "More than 35,000 cases of full-blown AIDS have been diagnosed in the U.S. since my company submitted its PMA. . . . Untold thousands have become infected simply because there is not a home AIDS test available" (U.S. Public Health Service, 30th Meeting, 94). Several speakers at the 1994 FDA hearing also took up this rhetoric of emergency and urgency. Koop, for example, described how "AIDS has moved relentlessly across the face of our nation, city by city, group by group" and is now "without limits" (U.S. Public Health Service, 44th Meeting 154). Thus the intervention of home testing was needed to protect the body politic from the stalker known as AIDS.

In addition to establishing the need for public health action, rhetors supporting home testing also referred to *kairos* in terms of the effects of HIV and AIDS on individual infected bodies; the home test was needed to detect and intervene in such bodies. Authors of an article in the *New England Journal of Medicine*, as well as several speakers at the 1994 FDA hearing, discussed the "missed opportunities" of people who do not know they are infected and who may not be tested until it is too late (U.S. Public Health Service, 44th Meeting 242). "Through testing," stated Koop, "we intervene in the life of an infected person to enhance the quality and quantity of life" (155). Scientific, biomedical advancements in HIV/AIDS treatments—pentamadine and other prophylaxis, AZT, and later protease inhibitors and the new cocktail therapies—were and are often cited in arguments for early diagnosis through testing. They are used as the exigence in the part of the knowledge enthymeme that argues that testing will provide infected individuals with knowledge that will lead to access to life-saving medical interventions. In addition, arguments about individual *kairos* often depended on an assumption that HIV leads to AIDS which leads to death, an assumption that works to conflate HIV and AIDS as a death sentence and to construct the HIV-infected body as a time bomb ticking away until it eventually explodes.

Calls for the kairotic intervention of home testing have often described the technology as a new tool for the expedient control of the AIDS epidemic. Some of these calls use military or war metaphors to figure the virus as a stealthy secret agent or spy, and home testing technology as a new weapon or reconnaissance tool for the epidemiological and biomedical war against HIV/AIDS.[8] In his testimony at the 1994 FDA hearing, Koop provides a colorful illustration:

> The weapons we wield against AIDS are both too few and too feeble. . . . The only effective weapon over the past decade has been our capacity for reconnaissance. We have a way to find it—testing. Testing is all we have, and therefore testing is what we must do. . . . And now comes the opportunity to radically increase our ability to find the virus by introducing a home access HIV test . . . the single most important weapon that we could employ to fight AIDS. And therefore I urge you to approve it. (U.S. Public Health Service, 44th Meeting 155)

Here Koop advocates home testing as a tool for counterattack or counter-espionage, as something akin to secret spy glasses for exposing the virus that lurks in the infected body and stalks the body politic. Furthermore, he and others in the debate assert, rather problematically, that in lieu of a vaccine or cure, home testing is the most effective or even the only effective weapon we have for intervention and control in the war against HIV/AIDS. An article previously published in the *Washington Post* had similarly claimed that HIV testing and counseling were the "only weapons we have" (Markman). Cory Gaber, the attorney for ViroTechnology, Inc., spoke to the same effect in the 1989 FDA meeting: home testing was the "single presently available instrument for successfully thwarting the AIDS epidemic" (U.S. Public Health Service, Transcript of Blood Collection Kits 158). Not everyone arguing about home testing put so much stock in the ability of testing to thwart the spreading epidemic, however. Members of the FDA's 1994 Blood Products Advisory Committee, particularly the bioethicist Karen Porter, questioned the dominant claims of Koop and others that "testing was the only weapon we have" and that "not approving home testing would be a mammoth sort of missed opportunity" (U.S. Public Health Service, 44th Meeting 319). The claims of Koop and other Confide allies reduced the complex technoscientific elements and practices associated with home testing to one simple, expedient tool. This move depends on a conceptualization of science and technology as a tool we can control and use to gain power—a view that privileges human agency and mastery, our ability to predict and control the functions and effects of technology. At the same time, it depends on a somewhat contradictory view of technology as a self-determining agent of instrumentality and progress, a view that emphasizes technology's agency: we need only approve home testing, and then we can step back and watch it save lives. Both these views are related to the ideology of technology-as-progress that Miller discusses—an ideology that facilitates a faith in the promise and power of technology to enact positive change.[9] Proponents of home testing drew on this ideology to shift the emphasis of the debate to the potential benefits of implementing home collection testing. Their faith in home testing and overreliance on it as the best or only weapon in the war against AIDS may have squelched a fuller, more critical discussion of home testing's functions and effects.

The Rhetoric of Access and Needy Bodies

Concerns about who would be targeted by home collection technology, who would use it, and who would benefit from it were raised early on, but they came to the forefront in the June 1994 FDA public meeting. Although some proponents of home testing (like Koop and Francis) advocated the widespread voluntary testing of all sexually active adults, most focused their arguments on certain "high-risk," underserved groups who especially needed access to HIV testing and its supposed benefits. These groups were variously described as less educated, poor, and living in ghettoized urban areas; as ethnic minorities (including African American, Hispanic, Latino, and Puerto Rican); as gay or bisexual men; or as "young nonwhite males," migrant workers, immigrants, single mothers, pregnant women, and intravenous drug users. While this list may seem fairly heterogeneous, most of the bodies here implied are linked as deviants or queers by what Cindy Patton calls the "queer paradigm." Referring to the historical association of risk with particular deviant groups in the United States, Patton explains, "Once perceptions of HIV risk were linked to social deviance, literally anyone or any category of people deemed epidemiologically significant could be converted into nominal queers" (*Last* 19). With the possible exception of some pregnant women, all the bodies mentioned above could be considered marginal to dominant U.S. culture. They are often rendered docile, insofar as their needs are defined for them and they are subject to public health intervention and regulation. For example, gay men and some groups of pregnant women have been targets of calls for mandatory testing.

The different categories of bodies in the list above sometimes overlap. Take, for example, the disturbingly familiar *construct* of the single, pregnant black woman on welfare who is addicted to sex and drugs. In *Disease and Representation*, Sander Gilman asserts that in the United States the quintessential AIDS patient is represented as "black, drug-using, homosexual, and urban" (266)— another construct one can easily form from the list just offered. It is not hard to see how these constructs function as deviant "others" who are defined against the norm of the low-risk, straight, middle-class, white "general public" (itself a constructed category).

Jay Epstein of the FDA asked at the outset of the June 1994 meeting if home test kits would likely expand testing among high-risk, infected people in hard-to-reach communities or, instead, among members of the low-risk "worried well," a term meant to refer to mostly white, middle-class heterosexuals in the "general public" who are considered to be at low risk but who are unnecessarily anxious about being infected with HIV (U.S. Public Health Service, 44th Meeting 130). Allies of Johnson & Johnson, most of whom had been flown to the meeting as members of DAD's Community Advisory Committee, offered a litany of responses to this question. Test inventor Millenson suggested that young people and people of color would benefit from home testing (150). Helen Miramontes of the California Nurses Association concurred that home testing would be particularly helpful to "vital young people" and "ethnic and racial minority communities," and added "gay communities" to the list (208). Speakers from HIV/AIDS clinics in southern California and South Florida suggested that home testing was needed by, and would be used by, young, high-risk minority people, or that it would at the very least free public resources for such people (184, 241). Several representatives of health care service providers to communities of color testified about the magnified need for home testing in the communities they serve, where HIV/AIDS is even more of an emergency; where many people are underserved by health care services; where barriers such as location prevent many people from obtaining health care services; and where many people are fearful or distrustful of public health care and current testing programs. The Hispanic community, because it is "inadequately served in terms of medical care and health awareness," must have more access to HIV testing, argued Rene Rodriguez of the Interamerican College of Physicians in her letter to FDA Commissioner Kessler; increased testing will lead to more awareness, which will lead to better medical care, her argument implied. In his letter, Louis Núñez, president of the National Puerto Rican Coalition, similarly implored, "Greater access to testing is imperative for Puerto Ricans in dire need of HIV/AIDS services."

In their letters and testimony at the 1994 public meeting, several representatives of minority health organizations charged the FDA with paternalism for denying home testing to communities in need. Rodriguez argued that the option of home testing would significantly increase access to testing and lifesaving health care for underserved Hispanic "special populations," including migrant farmworkers, homeless people, and substance abusers (U.S. Public Health Service, 44th Meeting 295). Lydia Valencia of the Puerto Rican Congress of New Jersey took a more extreme position, arguing that Hispanic Puerto Rican communities, especially women and children, are not just underserved by the testing status quo, but are in effect sentenced to die by it and by a paternalistic refusal to approve home testing (204).[10] The pleas of Rodriguez, Valencia, and other minority health advocates were understandable in view of the patterns of neglect by the public health system and the disproportionate devastation by HIV/AIDS in their communities. Yet their seemingly uncritical faith in the ability of home testing to intervene in the epidemic in their communities is a little disturbing. Not only does their faith posit a notion of technology as inherently beneficial and effective, it also creates an overreliance on testing at the expense of other, possibly more effective means of prevention, such as community-based education and needle exchange programs.

Claims about the need for more testing among minority and other underserved "high-risk" groups, and about the ability of home testing to break down barriers, create more access, and thus meet this health need, are problematic on several counts. First, these claims rely on uncritical, idealistic notions of technoscience and its power. Contrary to the rhetoric of Rodriguez and others, home testing (and HIV testing more generally) is not the magic bullet for fighting AIDS in minority communities; it is not the solution to problems of prevention and access to health care. The knowledge of serostatus that HIV testing provides is not necessarily empowering; it can, in fact, lead to numerous harmful effects, such as psychological distress, spousal abuse, and discrimination. Neither is this knowledge necessarily life-saving—it does not magically lead to behavior change or automatically connect people to health care.[11] The premise that testing will lead to life-saving medical treatment naively assumes that such treatment actually exists, that people will be referred to it, that they will have access to it, that they will use it, and that they will benefit from it. Each of these assumptions is challengeable. For example, many people who test positive are not insured, are underinsured, or lose their insurance as a result of taking the test. A recent article in the *New York Times* reported that minorities and women in New York have significantly less access to medical treatments and drugs for HIV/AIDS than do whites and men (Richardson).

In the 1994 public meeting about the approvability of Confide, one of the FDA's advisors, a Dr. Woodland, compared home testing to an ATM machine in the way it provides quick access to information and other "goods." This comparison only echoed earlier representations of home testing as an accessible, simple, easy-to-use tool. But while the ATM machine might be a commonly used technology for some people, it is certainly not so for others. Its use requires access to a physical machine, an ATM card, and a bank account with money. As my opening description of the Confide testing system was meant to illustrate, a person must have or have access to numerous things—forty or more expendable dollars, a telephone, a "home" and address, a certain level and type of literacy, and possibly a credit card and a computer networked to the Internet—in order even to obtain and use a home collection testing kit. It is obvious, but worth stating, that some members of the groups invoked as needing home testing—for example, migrant workers and some injecting drug users—would not be able to access the technology, much less the limited benefits it might make possible.

Second, arguments for home testing that draw on interpretations of certain groups' needs as exigence can reify reductive, harmful associations between these groups and risk. Paula Treichler, Cindy Patton, and a host of other AIDS theorists and activists have demonstrated how from the early 1980s risk for HIV/AIDS was defined through the epidemiological, identity-based categories of "risk groups," first gay men and later injecting drug users, sex workers, and others. More recently, women and ethnic minorities, particularly minority youths, have been targeted in national prevention efforts. As Treichler and others explain, such groups have been stigmatized in both popular and biomedical discourse as deviant, contaminated, and contaminating in homophobic, racist, and classist ways. For example, the prevalence of AIDS among gay men was explained by their deviant lifestyle, which included promiscuous sex and drug abuse. One does not have to look that closely to see the classist and racist undertones in arguments about the need for home testing. A related problem with risk-group categories is the way they homogenize populations, a factor that Foucault describes as a disciplinary function (*Discipline* 183). "Minorities," "the Hispanic community," "the Puerto Rican community," and "urban African Americans" are not actually homogeneous groups of poor people who live in ghettos.

Risk-group categories are problematic from a pedagogical standpoint in several ways. Because they essentially locate risk in fragmented, homogeneously defined groups, these categories may actually block some people's identification with risk, as Patton explains in *Last Served?* Many people engaging in risky practices might not recognize themselves in the typical risk-group categories. Instead, these categories might work to affirm boundaries between us and them, between normal and deviant. "I'm safe from risk because I'm not one of them," some people might infer. Foucault writes about this middle-class anxiety to maintain boundaries of subjectivity; and in his analysis of representations of AIDS in the United States, Gilman writes more specifically about the "need to see a clear boundary existing between the heterosexual, non-IV drug using, white community and those at risk" (266). In addition, beyond their limited epidemiological functions, risk groups simply misconstrue risk. As many HIV/AIDS educators have been stressing now for some time, it is not who one is or where one lives *per se* that puts one at risk, but rather specific activities in which one engages.

Finally, arguments for home testing that stress need and access participate in what Nancy Fraser, in *Unruly Practices*, calls the "political struggle over needs interpretation." Fraser calls for critiques of discourses about needs, critiques that interrogate the politics and power relations of need interpretations by asking "who interprets the needs in question and from what perspective and in the light of what interests" (164). In her analysis of the interpretation of needs regarding the welfare system, Fraser shows how women welfare recipients are constructed by those in power as needy, deviant, and without agency (152–53). As Fraser points out, those whose needs are so interpreted are often left out of this public interpretive struggle; their needs are constructed for them. She explains, "They are rendered passive, positioned as potential recipients of predefined services rather than as agents involved in interpreting their needs and shaping their life conditions" (174). In addition, the needs in question are located *in* the needy, making them the targets and objects of government policy and programs. Constructions of "minorities" and other underserved, high-risk groups, and interpretations of their need for home testing, were useful to DAD and its allies in their bid for approval. Constructions of "minorities" and other "needy" groups of subjects or bodies worked as rhetorical instruments to justify the need for home testing and its potential benefits. As I will show, this is about where DAD's interest in such groups ended. Along with government officials, DAD and its heavily recruited allies interpreted the needs of the "underserved" for them, in the process oversimplifying those needs and relying on a solution (approval of home testing) that fails to account fully for people's material conditions, such as their income or insurance coverage. While Confide's advocates often chided the FDA and other critics for being paternalistic, they too took a paternalistic stance in arguing what is best for certain groups. Consider the following remarks by Koop at the 1994 FDA meeting: "Through testing, we enable someone at risk, but not yet infected, to learn how to change behavior that might save his or her life. Through testing, we intervene in the life of an infected person to enhance the quality and quantity of life. Through testing, we equip people to stop transmitting this disease unwittingly to hundreds and thousands of others" (U.S. Public Health Service, 44th Meeting 155). Note that the testees are not the actors in this passage. The "Confide in DAD" (here the acronym seems particularly fitting) appeals of Koop and other public health experts often calls for allowing, enabling, permitting, directing, equipping, and intervening in the lives of (needy) people through home collection testing.

   To be sure, arguments about need and access were critiqued as soon as they were raised during the approval process. Skeptics and critics of home testing, including representatives of several testing clinics, argued that it would be the "worried well" rather than those "truly at risk" who would be targeted by DAD and who would actually use Confide if approved. Dennis Ouellet of the LA Free Clinic, for example, predicted that Johnson & Johnson would "capitalize by marketing to white middle-class fears, not to minorities or drug users in the inner city, where it's needed" (Rosin 12). In the June 1994 FDA hearing discussed above, Shepard Smith of Americans for a Sound HIV/AIDS Policy stated, "We think that this [Confide] is going to be used predominantly by the white 'worried well.' And again, when we look at the dynamics of the epidemic today, it's predominantly in communities of color" (U.S. Public Health Service, 44th Meeting 164). The director of Whitman-Walker Clinic stated that Johnson & Johnson would most like target middle- and upper-income areas of cit-

ies and suburbs (Freundlich and Hamilton 58). And Christopher Portelli, head
of the eleven-member National Alliance of Lesbian and Gay Health Clinics,
called the home test a "get-rich-quick scheme" (Portelli and Stryker 30) whose
buyers would be "middle- and upper-class, low-risk folks who just want to
'be sure'" (Portelli and Bayer). DAD, that is, would exploit and capitalize on
the widespread anxiety of healthy, wealthy people. Others claimed that DAD
would target young, white, well-off, sexually active women or "Cosmo girls,"
a group that already constitutes a market for home pregnancy tests and condoms (Freundlich and Hamilton 58; Smith in U.S. Public Health Service, 44th
Meeting 164). It is clear from their comments that opponents of Confide also
relied on the rhetoric of need and the paternalistic impulse to look out for the
best interest of those interpreted as needy and underserved, still stereotypically
portrayed as poor minority people.

One of the main elements of the opponents' critiques of home testing was
Confide's projected cost of forty to fifty dollars (earlier projections had been as
low as fifteen or twenty dollars), a cost described by Confide advocates as "reasonable" and "inexpensive." But although forty dollars might be the cost of
a fine dinner for these advocates, it might represent a sizable portion of some
people's entire monthly income. The neediest people simply could not afford
the new test, critics claimed. "Why pay $40 when you can get anonymous test-
ing for free?" asked Whitman-Walker's Marion Brown (U.S. Public Health
Service, 44th Meeting 222). Home testing might actually be a cheaper option
for many middle-class people, who are more likely to get tested in private physicians' offices than at free public clinics, as Rick Blake observed in a July 1996
AIDS ALERT article ("HIV Home Test" 80). Home testing will be cheaper and
easier for government as well, because the cost and liability of testing shifts to
the private consumer.

Bodies in the Market

The notion of access is also important in much of the post-approval advertising
discourse associated with home collecting testing kits: witness the very names
of the two major home testing companies, Direct Access Diagnostics and Home
Access Health Corporation. The Home Access Health Corporation web site
states, "Our company and our web site are dedicated to breaking down the barriers to health care access by bringing technology and people together." Similarly, the stated mission of DAD was to "expand consumer access to quality,
self-directed diagnostic products and services." It is easy to see a consumer-
driven *topos* of individual empowerment at work in these descriptions. Home
testing, the companies state or imply, empowers individual lay consumers by
bringing them closer to technology, expanding their options, and enabling them
to take charge of their own health assessment. The question raised by their lan-

guage is "Who, specifically, does home testing empower?" An examination of the bodies in the advertisements of Confide and Home Access, which have appeared on the major television networks and in mainstream and gay newspapers and magazines, can begin to reveal who is being targeted for the new products, who is using or will use them, and how they are being used or will be used.

A look at television, print, and web site advertisements largely confirms the predictions of critics of home testing in the approval debate; the new tests seem to be marketed primarily to those labeled the "worried well"—young, white, middle-class, mostly straight people (and some gay men) with buying power. The ads clearly try to tap into this group's anxiety about HIV/AIDS, offering them fast, accurate, convenient, private relief. One widely run Confide print and television ad features a young white single woman who declares, "I feel a lot better now that I know." A commercial for Home Access Express shows a similar young white single woman calling to get her test results, then sighing and exhaling, "I'm OK. I'm OK." The voice-over then states, "Home Access Express, making you feel right . . . at home." This woman's affirmation begs the question, "Are HIV-positive people not OK?" "I'm OK because I'm clean, because I'm not one of 'them,'" her words imply.

Several Home Access print ads also promise relief and peace of mind to anxious testees and their partners, but in more explicitly sexual terms. One ad, apparently targeting young straight men on the dating scene, depicts a young white man with long hair whispering the words, "I'm negative" into his lover's ears (figure 11.2). "Once women waited to hear three little words. Now it's just two," reads the ad's heading. The same ad tells readers that Home Access will allow you to "make love with your eyes open." This rhetoric dangerously suggests that home testing offers a convenient means to get a partner into bed.

Another ad, appearing in gay magazines and newspapers, shows a muscular, sweaty, shirtless man sitting and holding a basketball (figure 11.3). It leads with the words, "You used to worry you'd never have sex. Now you worry when you do." HIV is indeed an important thing to worry about, the ad later affirms. "You're taking an HIV test because you want to know if you're OK," a third ad reads, adding, "You can ease your worries and clear up any nagging questions. And if the woman in your life is having any doubts—don't worry. That little prick [the lancet used for collecting the blood sample] is sure to satisfy her." The Home Access test kit is being marketed as a way to achieve relief and offer assurance for both the testee and his or her partner.

In addition to relief, assurance, and accuracy, the major selling points of both test kits are their provisions of privacy (a concept that is often conflated in the discourse with anonymity and confidentiality), convenience, and sense of personal empowerment and autonomy, all of which could be considered middle-class values and privileges that come with a price tag only some can

ONCE WOMEN WAITED TO HEAR THREE LITTLE WORDS. NOW IT'S JUST TWO.

Oh, how times have changed. That's not to say romance is out of style, but ignorance certainly is. Because as much as things have changed, it still holds true that knowledge is power. Nowhere is this more evident than when it comes to HIV.

SOME THINGS ARE BEST DONE IN THE PRIVACY OF YOUR OWN HOME. If you decide to get tested for HIV, we invite you to consider the Home Access Express™ HIV test. It's the same laboratory test used by doctors and hospitals— with the decidedly big advantage that you have access to it in the safe, private environment of your own home. You'll also find it interesting to know that it's greater than 99.9% accurate.

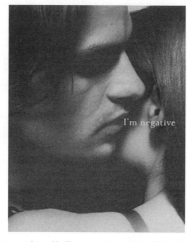

Here's how it works: when you call 1.800.HIV.TEST, we send you a kit complete with everything you need for testing*. You then call a separate toll-free number to activate a personal identification code. This anonymous code gives you exclusive access to your test result as well as pre and post-test counseling. Next, you follow the easy sample collection instructions,

return your sample to us and call three business days later for your test result.

CALL US IF YOU NEED TO TALK. As part of the testing process, we provide counseling 24 hours a day, seven days a week. We also offer helpful information about HIV, advice on treatment and referrals to health services in your area. Of course, everything is done anonymously because this entire system has been created with the protection of your privacy in mind.

MAKE LOVE WITH YOUR EYES OPEN. This test gives you the knowledge you need to make informed choices about sex in a day and age when even meaningless flings can have meaningful results. $49.95 plus shipping and handling is a small price to pay for the peace of mind it provides. Since all the answers you need are available when you call 1.800.HIV.TEST, the only question is, what are you waiting for?

1.800.HIV.TEST
THE HOME ACCESS HIV 1 TEST SYSTEM

Figure 11.2. Home Access print ad suggesting HIV testing as a seduction technique

Figure 11.3. Home Access print ad promising relief from testing

afford. Consider the Home Access television commercial that begins with heavy breathing and a dark screen: "1–800–HIV–TEST" quickly appears on the screen, accompanied by the pitch, "Now you can have an HIV test sent to your home." The camera pans out, and the screen becomes a television set in an upscale gym full of weights, Stairmasters, treadmills, and mostly white patrons. One by one the patrons stop working out to look up at the set as the commercial continues. Finally a white man and white woman glance at each other, smiling nervously, and then quickly look away. "If this isn't the right time to call, call when the time is right," the voice states; Home Access is "the best convenient alternative to testing at your doctor's office," the place where many middle-class people get tested. A print ad for Home Access Express—a kit that conveniently gives the consumer test results in just three business days—contains the lines, "This anonymous code gives you exclusive access to your test result," and "You'll have to pay a little extra for . . . delivery to your door." These lines and others, which depict the product as an exclusive, deluxe commodity like membership in an upscale gym or country club, were designed to appeal to the discriminating, discreet consumer of means.

Advertisements for Confide and Home Access also appeal to the American middle-class values of privacy, empowerment, and autonomy. A woman in a Confide commercial, for example, tells viewers that she doesn't want the whole world to know she's taking an HIV test. "I want to know. It's my life," the ad goes on. Two Confide print ads, one showing a young white man and the other a middle-aged Hispanic man, offer privacy as the main advantage of the new test kit: "I think some things are private. An HIV test is one of them." Privacy and anonymity have historically been important values to gay communities too, which were part of the target audience for several ads. The two men just described appear to be young, single, economically comfortable, and ambiguously either straight or gay, facilitating connection to both straight and gay viewers. Unlike the public bodies of the pre-approval discourse, bodies that are in need of and subject to public intervention, the bodies in the home testing advertisements enjoy both privacy and agency. They can assert their autonomy and take charge of their own health assessment. In the Confide commercial entitled "Man," we see scenes of a young, single, sexually ambiguous white man driving an expensive car, at work holding an expensive camera, sitting at home with Chinese take-out in a big chair below a nice print, and, finally, out having a good time with his friends. He is clearly a man who can afford to spend forty dollars for the relief he appears to get at the end of the commercial. The people in the upscale gym with the television set could also afford to test at home, even multiple times. Judging by the bodies it constructs, then, home collection advertising discourse appears to target mostly young, white, middle-class, health-conscious consumers from the "general public." The only person of color in a

Confide television commercial is a counselor, not a testee. Both Confide and Home Access have been marketed as private, convenient alternatives to testing at a physician's office, as ways to take charge of one's own health, as ways to achieve relief and assurance in the convenience and privacy of one's own home.

It would be a stretch to see the testee in the commercials just mentioned and read "homeless person," "migrant worker," "injecting drug user" (although many of these are white and middle-class), "poor person," or even "underserved person" or "person of color." Such bodies still play important roles in the commercials, however, as what the clean, "normal" subjects define and measure themselves against. As Julia Epstein explains, the "clearly white, middle-class, suburban, 'decent,' and, above all, heterosexual 'general population'" has historically been delimited against the "same-sex desire, racial difference, injection drug use, and illness" of "high-risk" groups (159). And Jennifer Terry, using Foucault to theorize deviant subject formation, explains how deviant and normal subjectivity rely on each other (58). The "normal-looking" people in most home test ads accordingly seem to be taking the test in order to affirm that they are still clean and within "normal" subjectivity. For example, the woman in the Home Access direct response ad, who calls in to get her result and then sighs, "I'm OK," is reassured that she is not one of those dirty, infected people who are presumably not OK. Home testing marketing discourse, then, functions in part to protect normal, middle-class subjectivity from its risky, deviant counterparts.[12]

The Material Effects of
Home Collection Testing and Its Discourse

My analysis of the discourses surrounding home collection HIV testing points to several implications and possible effects, including the disciplining of actual bodies. Home collection testing transforms HIV antibody testing insofar as it involves different "disembodied" technologies (e.g., mail and telephone) and different sites (the home), and thus it distributes bodies in space differently. In its extension into the home, home testing amplifies and differently distributes the panoptic power of testing, relying more on self-surveillance than on institutional surveillance. Although home collection testing systems include a centralized results center, their disciplinary power relies mainly on the self-surveillance of individuals who extract "knowledge" about themselves, assess their own risk, and determine their future course of action with little or no guidance. While this may seem empowering, it also restricts the opportunity to educate and counsel people. In addition, home collection testing further depersonalizes the individual testee, as she or he becomes less a documented "case" than a random code number. Such transformations make the new techniques of home testing, in Foucault's words, "much more efficient and much less wasteful (less costly economically, less risky in their results, less open to loopholes and resistances)" (*Power/Knowledge* 119). Home testing shifts some of the cost, legal liability, and responsibility of testing away from existing testing programs, many of which receive government funding.

Home collection testing expands the disciplinary gaze of the HIV examination, then, opening up new ways to "make" individuals, to extract knowledge about the "nature" of individuals, and to use this knowledge to measure, homogenize, classify, hierarchize, distribute, regulate, and even punish them (*Discipline* 2). Foucault asserts that the normalizing gaze and surveillance of the examination "makes it possible to qualify, to classify, to punish" (*Discipline* 184). The disciplinary biopower of home collection testing may work *on* actual bodies in punitive ways. What is to stop employers and insurance companies— notorious for denying, limiting, and canceling coverage to people with HIV/ AIDS—from screening without explicit written consent? What is to stop a person from coercing his or her lover, spouse, or child into being tested at home? What is to stop people from obtaining the code numbers of others and calling in to get their results? Indeed, some home test companies seem to encourage such practices, which open up possibilities for domestic abuse and other harmful effects, particularly for women and children. Several web sites of home collection and performance HIV test companies explicitly advocate that partners get tested together and share results. One even describes an 800 number that partners and others can call to check the testee's results. Other test kits are designed for parents to use to test their teen-agers. Home collection testing opens up a new set of contexts for potential public and private misuses and abuses.

As I have already discussed, DAD and Home Access have apparently marketed their tests to people who identify with the "normal" general public rather than with "deviant" high-risk groups. The disciplinary rhetoric of home testing can work to affirm these people's sense of normality and to limit their self-recognition of risk. According to Cindy Patton, the "general public" has been conditioned by a national HIV prevention pedagogy that teaches partner selection as a strategy for safer sex (*Fatal Advice*). Patton explains how approaching safer sex through partner selection can encourage people to view risk as remote (you won't get HIV if you have "ordinary sex with ordinary people") and to use avoidance tactics such as limiting partners and "choosing partners carefully" rather than actually practicing specific transmission-blocking techniques. As Patton explains, the HIV test lends a "veneer of scientific validity" to strategies of partner selection, serving as a "quick information stop" (*Inventing* 30), a means for people to "clear" themselves and perhaps their partners as "clean" before deciding whether or not they need to practice safer sex

(*Last* 31). "The test, erroneously and fatally enough," Patton writes, "was their mechanism for determining whether to use condoms with a specific partner or to discover whether past partner selection strategies had been adequate" (*Last* 33). Home test kits, then, can be seen as mechanisms that participate in and extend the dangerous safer-sex pedagogy Patton describes, which depends on self-surveillance and the normalization of risk and sex practices. Home test kits might help people define their sex practices and their own and others' bodies as healthy and safe (or not) in ways that can actually block their identification with risk. In this way the transformed disciplinary power of home colection testing works *in* or *through* people as well as on them, because it depends heavily on the initiative and self-surveillance of the testee. The home test user is given a general informational booklet (not required for taking the test) rather than being guided through culturally sensitive, client-centered pre-test education and counseling. While the person who tests positive gets to talk for the first time with another person, the person who tests negative is typically connected only to a brief, recorded message rather than being given post-test counseling and other services she or he might need. It is up to the testee, therefore, to read and listen to, make sense of, interpret, and contextualize the information provided. The information-giving model of education that DAD and Home Access call "counseling" depends on the commonplace belief in the magical power of knowledge to create behavior change, as well as on a construction of the testee as an isolated individual, unconnected to cultural contexts. Such a model fails to provide the culturally and linguistically sensitive counseling the CDC recommends, and thus it is less likely to subvert risky strategies of self-surveillance and normalization in regard to sex and other practices. I should point out here that the counseling and preventive education that I support, however personalized and contextualized, still works to shape, normalize, and otherwise discipline testees through confessional discourse and other means; I do not offer a way out of testing's disciplinary matrix of biopower, just a different way of disciplining that I hope produces more beneficial effects.

Unfortunately, it seems that some home testing companies are actually promoting precarious partner-selection approaches to safer sex; these approaches often involve testing at the beginning of a relationship or when a relationship is about to "move to the next level." The opening image of Home Access's web page is a crotch shot of a man in a pair of jeans with the words, "Know what you're getting into." According to *Business Week*, ChemTrak, another home test company, envisions new couples taking its test together before consummating their relationship. The company's web page states that it expects the product to be "regularly used for relationship wellness testing." When I called Confide's 800 number to order a test kit, one of the questions the salesperson asked was, "Do you need a test kit for your partner?" Another company's web page tells potential buyers, "You have the right to know if your partner carries the virus" (HIV Oral Test). Negative Only, Inc. even offers an 800 number that people can call to affirm their partner's results. Besides serving as a test for fidelity and facilitating partner-selection strategies, such language shatters any pretense of privacy or anonymity and practically invites abuse of spouses and partners. One advantage of such companies' promoting partner-selection strategies is that such strategies often involved repeated testing, with new "checkups" for new relationships—and repeated testing means selling more test kits.

On a larger scale, a shift toward home HIV testing in the private sector will probably affect larger testing patterns and the distribution of resources. A few proponents of home testing have claimed that it would free publicly funded testing resources often clogged by the "worried well." Pessimists, however—including the bioethicist Karen Porter and the gay/lesbian clinic spokesperson Portelli—have feared that the availability of home testing would cause just the opposite: the reduction of precious federal and state government funding from free public testing programs, many of which are designed to serve people at risk. "What is most likely to happen," predicted Porter, "is that rather than empower communities that are currently underserved, we will further create a situation where those communities are increasingly underserved and have less access to testing services" (U.S. Public Health Service, 44th Meeting 317). Indeed, this is a likely scenario, given the current health care trends of privatization, commercialization, managed competition, and government funding cutbacks. The people who can already afford to get tested at a physician's office will have another, possibly cheaper option, but those who rely on publicly funded health care services might, ironically, have less access to testing. Thus, home testing might widen the gap between the haves and the have-nots.

As I began my research on home collection testing, my stance toward the new technology was generally positive. More access to testing is a good thing, I reasoned, even if is used primarily by middle-class white people. After all, HIV is spreading among these people too. Furthermore, home testing makes possible some limited benefits for a limited group. The more I have looked at the rhetorics, practices, and effects of home testing, however, the more I have become ambivalent and even skeptical. Home collection testing also makes possible a number of harmful effects, and it may in the long run draw resources away from publicly funded programs of testing and counseling and preventive education. I am worried about home collection testing's limited accessibility (owing partly to its high cost), its lack of adequate counseling and education, and the ethic of expediency that seems to be driving its promotion. Rather than simply "let the market decide if it's a good thing, as DAD advocate Donald Francis suggested (quoted in Herscher), I think we need to deliberate carefully and thoroughly about home testing and its possible effects.

One postscript: although Confide is now off the market, home collection testing is not going away anytime soon. The Home Access test is still going strong, and oral fluid collection tests (such as SmithKline Beecham's OraSure), urine collection tests, and rapid-response performance tests (tests that will give on-the-spot results in a matter of minutes) have been developed and are now being considered for the home. Some of these tests, as yet unapproved for home use, are being illegally marketed over the Internet or sold outside the United States, mostly in developing countries in Southeast Asia (Stix). Much of the rhetoric surrounding the new crop of HIV testing products echoes the rhetoric in the controversy over Confide's approval. The new tests are touted as cutting-edge, as part of the inevitable evolution of testing technology. As one health care article observed, "Urine and Saliva Tests for HIV [Are] Gaining Momentum" (Karpen 21). And some have predicted that the new tests will expand access to testing for underserved groups. Some of the tests have certainly expanded access to insurance companies; within two days of OraSure's approval by the FDA for professional use, insurance companies had ordered approximately one million test units ("HIV Saliva Test"). It remains to be seen whether existing or new HIV home tests will increase access for, and meet the material needs of, the many people who were "represented" in the pre-approval rhetoric of home testing, but who have thus far been neglected in its post-approval rhetorics and practices.

Notes

1. In popular media and health-related texts, home collection testing systems have been described as simple, easy-to-use, do-it-yourself kits. An *AIDS ALERT* piece, for example, calls the Confide system a "simple, straightforward test" ("Home HIV Test Kits" 1). In addition, the test kits have been described mistakenly both as test kits for AIDS and as home performance kits that provide immediate results at home.

2. Take, for example, the following article titles: "Banned at Home: An FDA Ruling on AIDS Tests," "First Home Test for AIDS Stirs Old Controversies" (Herscher), "Controversial Home AIDS Test: Why It's Needed," "Home AIDS Testing Questioned" (Flannery), "Mail-Order AIDS Tests" (Weiss), "AIDS Testing Hits Home" (Welch), "A Do-It-Yourself AIDS Test" (Koop), "Should Home AIDS Testing Be Allowed?" (Markman), "Tug-of-War Over an AIDS Test" (Freundlich), "FDA May Allow AIDS Home Tests" (Gladwell), and "Home AIDS Test: Is it a Positive Step?" The conflation of HIV and AIDS often works in conjunction with the *topos* of AIDS as emergency in calls for increased HIV antibody testing.

3. In *The New Rhetoric*, Perelman and Olbrechts-Tyteca describe *presence* as the selection, presentation, and emphasis of elements of an argument (116).

4. Regarding the relationship between the FDA and big business, see Nussbaum's *Good Intentions* and Burkholz's *The FDA Follies*. On the approval of AZT, in particular, see parts one and two of Nussbaum, chapters eight and nine of Burkholz, and chapter one of Erni's *Unstable Frontiers*.

5. Further examples include "Over-the-Counter HIV Home Test Kits May Receive FDA Approval within a Year," "Home Testing Kits for HIV Apt to Get FDA Approval" (Marwick), and "Bad Blood" (Rosin).

6. Johnson & Johnson did not mention the two other contingencies that affected their decision: a court had ordered the company to turn over Confide to Millenson in the legal dispute over ownership; and the company was in trouble with the FDA for quality control measures and for not submitting mandatory reports regarding customer complaints (Canedy).

7. I use the term *enthymeme* in the Isocratean sense that Jeffrey Walker has discussed. Rather than as an informal syllogism consisting of a claim supported by a major and minor premise, Walker understands the enthymeme as a complex body of persuasion or web of arguments, some of which are emotively charged (53). Thus, an enthymeme can include a variety of claims, promises, and *topoi* working to motivate identification with a particular stance or argument.

8. Compare Treichler's analysis of HIV as 007.

9. The other ideology of technology to which Miller refers, the ideology of technology out of control, also undergirded arguments about *kairos* in the approval debate. Opponents of home collection testing argued that home testing was far too risky, and that approving home testing would potentially be disastrous or catastrophic. Representing the National Association of People with AIDS at the 1994 FDA meeting, Dr. Alberto Avendano used the metaphor of Pandora's box to highlight the "unanticipated consequences" and "potential harm" of the new technology (U.S. Public Health Service, 44th Meeting 234–35). This metaphor was also invoked in the organization's position statement on home collection testing and in the letter NAPWA cowrote to the FDA complaining about Johnson & Johnson's promotional campaign. In a magazine piece published later in 1994, Christopher Portelli of the National Association of Lesbian and Gay Health Clinics wrote that "the potential for catastrophic impact . . . outweighs the intended advantages" (Portelli and Stryker 25).

10. Echoing arguments made in the July 1994 meeting, reports and articles in health care and other periodicals, and in newspapers such as *USA Today*, the *Washington Post*, and the *Los Angeles Times*, hailed the promise of the new home collection test to expand testing in certain underserved groups. A 1995 article in the health care newsletter *AIDS ALERT*, for example, predicted that "minorities [would be] more likely to buy kits" and "home testing [would expand] access" ("Home-test"). Similarly, the public statement issued by DAD's Community Advisory Committee specifically mentioned minorities, people living in rural areas, single mothers, and other underserved populations as beneficiaries of home testing.

11. A meta-analysis by Donna Higgins et al. of more than fifty behavioral studies questions the premise that knowledge of serostatus leads to transmission-preventing behaviors.

12. According to a recent *USA Today* article, both Home Access and DAD have reported that their products are being used mostly by males whose primary risk for HIV was heterosexual contact, although the tests are also being used by large numbers of women and gay men. Very few testees report injecting drug use (Painter). This limited information about early uses of home testing, provided by the companies themselves,

further chips away at some of the claims made earlier by home testing advocates about increasing access to underserved members of high-risk groups.

Works Cited

"Banned at Home: An FDA Ruling on AIDS tests." *Time*, 18 April 1988: 26.

Bayer, Ronald, and Jeff Stryker. "Testing for HIV Infection at Home." *New England Journal of Medicine* 332 (1995): 1,296–1,299.

Beall, Douglas P., and John J. Whyte. "Now That We Can, Should We? Investigating the Wisdom of Home HIV Testing." *Maryland Medical Journal* 44 (1995): 355–57.

Burkholz, Herbert. *The FDA Follies*. New York: Basic Books, 1994.

Canedy, Dana. "F.D.A Warnings Preceded Withdrawal of H.I.V. Test." *New York Times*, 3 July 1997.

ChemTrak web page. http://www.chemtrak.com/ (1996).

Cimons, Marlene. "Debate Revived over Home Collection HIV Tests." *Journal of the Physicians Association for AIDS Care*, July 1994: 6–7, 31.

Concar, David. "Postal Tests on the Way." *Nature* 345 (3 May 1990): 6.

Conlan, Michael. "FDA Open to Home Test Kits for Detecting HIV Virus." *Drug Topics* 139.6 (20 March 1995): 60.

"Controversial Home AIDS Test: Why It's Needed." *Los Angeles Times*, 7 August 1994.

Delaney, Martin. "Access Should Be Our Primary Concern." *POZ*, August/Sept. 1994: 76.

Direct Access Diagnostics Community Advisory Committee. Public statement. 7 July 1994.

Epstein, Julia. *Altered Conditions: Disease, Medicine, and Storytelling*. New York: Routledge, 1995.

Erni, John Nguyet. *Unstable Frontiers: Technomedicine and the Cultural Politics of "Curing" AIDS*. Minneapolis: University of Minnesota Press, 1994.

EZ Med Test. Home Medical Test Kits web page.

Flannery, Mary. "Home AIDS Testing Questioned." *Philadelphia Daily News*, 2 May 1990.

Foucault, Michel. *Discipline and Punish: The Birth of the Prison*. Translated by Alan Sheridan. New York: Vintage, 1979.

Foucault, Michel. *The History of Sexuality*. Vol. 1. *An Introduction*. Translated by Robert Hurley. New York: Vintage, 1978.

Foucault, Michel. *Power/Knowledge: Selected Interviews and Other Writings 1972–1977*. Edited by Colin Gordon. Translated by Colin Gordon et al. New York: Pantheon, 1980.

Foulke, Judith, et al. "Sales Stopped on Unapproved AIDS Tests." *FDA Consumer* 25 (December 1991): 44.

Fraser, Nancy. *Unruly Practices: Power, Discourse, and Gender in Contemporary Social Theory*. Minneapolis: University of Minnesota Press, 1988.

Freundlich, Naomi. "Tug-of-War Over an AIDS Test." *Business Week*, 11 November 1996: 46.

Freundlich, Naomi, and Joan O'C. Hamilton. "The Trials of a Home HIV Test." *Business Week*, 18 March 1996: 56–58.

Gaonkar, Dilip Parameshwar. "The Idea of Rhetoric in the Rhetoric of Science." *Southern Communication Journal* 58 (1993): 258–94.

Gilman, Sander L. *Disease and Representation: Images of Illness from Madness to AIDS*. Ithaca: Cornell University Press, 1988.

Gladwell, Malcolm. "FDA May Allow AIDS Home Tests: Medical Advances Spur Policy Shift." *Washington Post*, 25 April 1990.

Grosz, Elizabeth. *Volatile Bodies: Towards a Corporeal Feminism*. Bloomington: Indiana University Press, 1994.

Haraway, Donna J. *Modestitness@Secondillennium.FemaleManeetsncoMouse: Feminism and Technoscience*. New York: Routledge, 1997.

Hawhee, Debra. "*Kairos* Revisited: The Rhetorical Situation and the Art of Becoming a Rhetor." M.A. thesis, University of Tennessee, 1994.

Herscher, Elaine. "First Home Test for AIDS Stirs Old Controversies." *San Francisco Chronicle*, 18 December 1994.

Higgins, Donna L., et al. "Evidence for the Effects of HIV Antibody Counseling and Testing on Risk Behaviors." *Journal of the American Medical Association* 266 (1991): 2419–29.

"HIV Home Test May Change Testing Patterns in US." *AIDS ALERT*, July 1996: 79–81.

HIV Oral Test. Web page. http://www.aidstesting.com/ (1997).

"HIV Saliva Test May Help Hard-to-Reach Populations." *AIDS ALERT*, February 1995: 29–30.

Home Access Health Corporation. Home Access web page. http://www.homeaccess.com/hahc/level12/general.html/ (1996).

"Home AIDS Test: Is it a Positive Step." *Muscle and Fitness*, October 1996: 135.

"Home HIV Test Kits Offer Privacy and Convenience." *AIDS ALERT* supplement, July 1996: 1–2.

"Home-Test Support Grows as More Questions Arise." *AIDS Alert*, July 1995: 94–95.

Huber, Peter "Blood Tests." *Forbes*, 1 August 1994: 97.

Karpen, Maxine. "There's No Place Like Home." *AIDS Patient Care*, December 1990: 20–22.

Koop, C. Everett. "A Do-It-Yourself AIDS Test." *USA Today*, 22 June 1994.

Latour, Bruno. *Science in Action: How to Follow Scientists and Engineers through Society*. Cambridge, Mass.: Harvard University Press, 1987.

Leary, Warren E. "U.S. Studies Home Testing for AIDS." *New York Times*, 26 April 1990.

Mail-in HIV Testing and Phone Counseling with Medical Referral Briefing Book. Los Angeles: Health Policy and Research Foundation, 1995.

Markman, Howard. "Should Home AIDS Testing Be Allowed?" *Washington Post*, 9 January 1990.

Marwick, Charles. "Home Testing Kits for HIV Apt to Get FDA Approval." *Journal of the American Medical Association* 273 (1995): 908–9.

Miller, Carolyn R. "*Kairos* in the Rhetoric of Science." In *A Rhetoric of Doing: Essays on Written Discourse in Honor of James L. Kinneavy*, edited by Roger Cherry et al., 310–37. Carbondale: Southern Illinois University Press, 1992.

Miller, Carolyn R. "Opportunity, Opportunism, and Progress: *Kairos* in the Rhetoric of Technology." *Argumentation* 8 (1994): 81–96.

Núñez, Louis. Letter to David Kessler, 7 October 1993. In *Mail-in HIV Testing and Phone Counseling with Referral Briefing Book*. N.d., n.p.

Nussbaum, Bruce. *Good Intentions: How Big Business and the Medical Establishment are Corrupting the Fight against AIDS*. New York: Atlantic Monthly Press, 1990.

"Over-the-Counter HIV Home Test Kits May Receive FDA Approval within a Year." *AIDS ALERT*, August 1994: 105–8.

Painter, Kim. "HIV Home Test Kits Catching on But Still Criticized." *USA Today*, 12 May 1997.

Patton, Cindy. *Fatal Advice: How Safe-Sex Education Went Wrong*. Durham: Duke University Press, 1996.

Patton, Cindy. *Inventing AIDS*. New York: Routledge, 1990.

Patton, Cindy. *Last Served? Gendering the HIV Pandemic*. London: Taylor and Francis, 1994.

Perelman, Chaim, and Lucy Olbrechts-Tyteca. *The New Rhetoric: A Treatise on Argumentation*. Translated by John Wilkinson and Purcell Weaver. Notre Dame: University of Notre Dame Press, 1969.

Phillips, Kathryn A., et al. "Potential Use of Home HIV Testing." *New England Journal of Medicine* 332 (1995): 1,308–10.

Portelli, Christopher, and Ronald Bayer. "Should the FDA Approve the Home HIV Test?" *Health* 9 (September 1995): 20.

Portelli, Christopher, and Jeff Stryker. "Should HIV Home Tests Be Approved?" *Priorities* 7.3 (1995): 26–30.

Portelli, Christopher J., et al. Letter to Donna Shalala, William Purvis, and David Kessler, 26 October 1994. Provided by National Lesbian and Gay Health Alliance.

Prelli, Lawrence J. *A Rhetoric of Science: Inventing Scientific Discourse*. Columbia: University of South Carolina Press, 1989.

Richardson, Lynda. "White Patients More Likely to Use AIDS Drugs, Study Says." *New York Times*, 27 July 1997.

Rodriguez, Rene F. Letter to David Kessler, 4 March 1994. In *Mail-In HIV Testing and Phone Counseling with Referral Briefing Book*. n.p.

Rosin, Hanna. "Bad Blood." *New Republic*, 27 June 1994: 12–13.

Simpson, Glenn R. "Gingrich Aided Pharmaceutical Firm That Later Contributed to Foundation." *Roll Call*, 5 January 1995: 26.

Sloan, Pat, and Emily DeNitto. "J&J Seeks Approval of HIV Self-Test Kit." *Advertising Age*, 23 May 1994: 1.

Stix, Gary. "Private Screening: At-Home HIV Tests Stir Up Controversy." *Scientific American*, July 1994: 99–100.

Taylor, Elizabeth. Letter to David A. Kessler, 1 August 1994. In *Mail-In HIV Testing and Phone Counseling with Referral Briefing Book*. n.p.

Terry, Jennifer. "Theorizing Deviant Historiography." *differences* 3.2 (1991): 55–74.

"Testing Position Paper." Los Angeles: Health Policy and Research Foundation, 1994.

Thomas, Jennifer. "Imminent Approval of HIV Home Test Stirs Debate." *Laboratory Medicine* 26.6 (June 1995): 373.

Treichler, Paula A. "AIDS, Homophobia, and Biomedical Discourse: An Epidemic of Signification." In *AIDS: Cultural Analysis/Cultural Criticism*, edited by Douglas Crimp, 31–70. Cambridge, Mass.: MIT Press, 1988.

United States Congress. House of Representatives. Subcommittee on Regulation, Business Opportunities, and Energy. *Transcript of Risks and Implications of AIDS-HIV Testing in Nontraditional Laboratories and in the Home.* 101st Cong., 1st sess., 23 March 1989.

United States Public Health Service. Food and Drug Administration. Center for Biologics Evaluation and Research. Blood Products Advisory Committee. Transcript of Blood Collection Kits Labeled for Human Immunodeficiency Virus Type 1 Antibody Testing. Bethesda, Md., 6 April 1989.

United States Public Health Service. Food and Drug Administration. Center for Biologics Evaluation and Research. Blood Products Advisory Committee. Transcript of the 44th Meeting. Gaithersberg, Md., 22 June 1994.

United States Public Health Service. Food and Drug Administration. Center for Biologics Evaluation and Research. Blood Products Advisory Committee. Transcript of the 30th Meeting. Rockville, Md., 18 July 1990.

United States Public Health Service. National Center for Health Statistics. *AIDS Knowledge and Attitudes for 1992: Data from the National Health Interview Survey. Advance Data from Vital and Health Statistics.* 1994.

Valencia, Lydia. Letter to David Kessler, 14 May 1993. In "Should the FDA Approve the Home HIV Test?" by Christopher Portelli and Ronald Bayer. *Health* 9 (September 1995): 20.

Walker, Jeffrey. "The Body of Persuasion: A Theory of the Enthymeme." *College English* 56 (1994): 46–65.

Weiss, Rick. "Mail-Order AIDS Tests." *Science News* 135 (1989): 268.

Welch, Dawn. "AIDS Testing Hits Home." *Health*, January 1988: 23–24.

12 *Melissa Jane Hardie*

Beard

Today I hear people say that I'm the toughest kind of man to make
into a good husband, a confirmed bachelor. The trouble is, I have yet
to experience that confirmation.

Liberace, Liberace: An Autobiography

Tangier: An Introduction

In late 1989, the U.S. media were briefly galvanized by Malcolm Forbes's sev-
entieth birthday party in Tangier. Forbes escorted Elizabeth Taylor and hosted
a large number of other luminaries to a spectacle on foreign shores, compre-
hensively covered by the national and international media. Writing about the
event in the *Village Voice*, Gary Indiana observed that the "guests looked ugly
and, beyond that, dead" (41). For Indiana, the party served to close the decade
with an ostentatious display of its social remnants, "tiresome relics" of its most
embarrassing aspects (41). They were, he wrote, "stale celebrity detritus from
the early Reagan Era lumbering through yet another sterile effusion of gloating
privilege on its way to richly deserved oblivion" (41). Indiana refers to the party
as "Malcolm Forbes's 70th birthday blowout in Tangier, *qua* glamorous media
event" (41) to register the signal asymmetry of the reputation of the party, its
ostensible occasion, and its own economy of reheated 1980s spectacle. Mapping a vitiated political and economic culture onto the birthday celebration, Indiana's description inverts it into an improbable and unintentional wake: the
spectacular withering of a cultural hegemony. The collapse of public with private identities structures his account of the ironically funereal birthday bash, its
"incipient ghoulishness" (41) captured by the "nearly uniform ickiness" (41) of
the press photographs. The extension of private landmarks—birthdays—into
the spectacularly public sphere is read by Indiana in terms of global as well as
media privilege. Forbes's Americanness, and his media ubiquity, translate the

275

private into a domain of privilege at the expense of the public life of others: "the Forbes party . . . confirmed the plain fact that certain expressions of privilege require abridgment of other people's rights" (41).

Indiana suggests the unwelcome intrusion of privilege in the space of rights, and the indexical relationship between abridgment and privilege calibrated by "certain expressions." But his story also alludes more obliquely to another set of "abridgments," another set of "privileges" and "certain expressions." Though manifestly writing a critique of Forbes's vulgar spectacle, Indiana locates a less spectacularly publicized aspect of Forbes's event—the reputed sexuality of Forbes himself. Indiana refers to Forbes's date as "the stuporous, drugged looking Liz Taylor, pointedly bussing the birthday boy" (41). Alluding to a friend's comment about Forbes's dubious antics in Tangier as "the rest of it," Indiana writes, "My friend did not mean the jokes about Malcolm Forbes ubiquitous in Tangier, jokes that lend a certain piquancy to Forbes's 'romance' with Liz" (41). To emphasize his point, Indiana writes that her role as date recalls "Liz's awesome role as the hapless travel buddy of Sebastian Venable in *Suddenly, Last Summer*" (41). In the same way that the party was an untimely revival of the aesthetic vulgarity of the early 1980s, Indiana's citation of this film installs a camp economy. Camp ironically revives or reprises outdated *modes de vie*, often locating the spectacular in the everyday. Indiana, mobilizing a rhetoric of displacement and exemplarity while never going so far as to exemplify precisely what his opaque critique criticizes, not coincidentally effects just this rhetoric through a reference to *Suddenly, Last Summer*, a film that portrays a set of cryptic exchanges on the vacation or retreat of Sebastian Venable and his cousin, played by Elizabeth Taylor. Told through a series of rather hysterical flashbacks, *Suddenly, Last Summer* never shows Sebastian Venable himself: Venable, dead by the time of the narrative, is the ghoul whose physical immateriality haunts this text's preteritive disclosure of homosexuality, a "condition" in *Suddenly, Last Summer* which, according to Vito Russo, "could be 'inferred but not shown'—by special permission of the Breen Office" (116).[1] Similarly, Indiana's use of the film as a historical counterpart to the party obeys the logic of what might be "inferred but not shown": the nature of Forbes's relationship to Taylor as beard. Taylor revives the everyday life of the beard, as "hapless travel buddy," locating a camp esthetic of life imitating art.

A beard is a woman or man who disguises the sexual interest of her or his partner. Beards offer the fiction of conjugal heterosexual identity. The beard—the term metaphorizes disguise and disclosure as corporeal manifestations—is a material signifier in a complex rhetoric of disclosure and orientation. The beard encourages us to take literally the visibility of sheer manifestation. Indiana's elliptical syntax never really describes what "the rest of it" is *not*; he prefers to relay that preterition to the "incipiently ghoulish" venue of cinematic realization and revival. The abridgment to which Indiana refers obliquely is the spectacle of the closet and its manifestation in the spectacular persona of Liz

Taylor as beard. The relay of signification from historical occasion to cinematic rehearsal figures the relay of closeting from a gay man to his beard; the beard becomes the attenuated point of connection between these competing domains of representation—reportage or cinematic relay. I am suggesting, in other words, that the beard is not merely an effect of the closet, but also a closeted subject, whose particular function is to articulate the phantasmic relationship between the "real" and the "cinematic."

Beards function as material signifiers of reputation: their own reputation and its translation to another. In this sense, beards configure a material reputation for their companions. Beards, though, must necessarily be circumspect. Their legitimation depends entirely on the discretion with which they perform their function: a beard can only be a beard insofar as he or she doesn't seem to be one. Like that of double agents, their work is performed best when it is simultaneously visible and invisible: they offer the sublime horizon of a seamless text. Beards, in this sense, are always potentially disclosing precisely what they are meant to conceal; they threaten to precipitate the publication of a partner's sexual identity. In this way, they operate with a logic congruent to the closet in Eve Kosofsky Sedgwick's terms, in that they offer both a viewpoint and a spectacle: the orientation of the closet, and the spectacle of closeting as bearding (222–23). Beards offer a perversely literal sense to the expression "sexual orientation," because they orient, in their persons, the public performance of a sexuality; beards are the material articulation of a presumed proclivity. Most commonly, they orient in terms of proximity, although a category of beard might be the absent spouse, whose absent presence also offers various guarantees.[2]

Hollywood has inculcated its particular culture of bearding as a consequence of the homophobic discourses that inform both the financial and textual economics of the movie industry. One way to consider the short history of the "outing" epidemic would be as a bi-coastal articulation of the question of how and how far the cinematic apparatus reaches in the lives of celebrities and the public.[3] If the arranged marriage has become part of the cinematic apparatus, that suggests the movie industry's power to articulate the public liabilities of the putatively private space of the star. The arranged marriage suggests a commensurability between spectator and star in the way in which film culture breaches the public/private divide. As Sharon Willis writes:

Even while offering the pleasures and the lure of an illusory highly privatized space, cinematic experience is, in many ways, the most eminently social form of consumption, [and] we must work on the contradictions common to the subject constructed through cinematic forms of address and to the apparatus itself; upon the crucial ideological formation that splits "public" from "private." (265)

Here we might also consider the spectacle's close relations to the cinematic, and the inscription of the vocabulary of cinema with the vocabulary of actions and sexuality in the private sphere. For example, if one of the preoccupations of a popular reception of cinema is the "authenticity" of sexual performance in cinema, that is precisely because cinematic spectacularity itself rides on this productive misrecognition, and because such a logic of misrecognition extends to the spectacular private lives of public identities. Actors, after all, are presumed to act.

Beards parody, then, the "naturalness" of the disguise: the beard, a natural growth on an uncultivated male face, is a figure for the unnatural natural effect. If we assume that what demarcates the private from the public in the life of the celebrity is the veil that he or she draws over certain aspects of his or her life, then the beard metonymizes that effect of veiling, that process of revelation which obscures. The figure of the beard is a form of disguise which alerts us to the practices of disguising: it is a *deviation* of the aim of disguise in *not* disguising disguise. Celebrity dates, for example, pivot on precisely this threshold location: celebrity couples at openings and previews, entering or leaving a cinema, gallery, or other hall of spectacle, simultaneously occupy the public space of celebrity and the threshold domain of the metaphoric opening.

The celebrity beard as actor was a role assumed by Elizabeth Taylor in her curious position as exemplary beard. Taylor's professional and personal associations with gay and closeted actors—most memorably, her couplings with Rock Hudson and Montgomery Clift—historicize her role as beard for Malcolm Forbes.[4] In a biography of Taylor that came out in 1990, shortly after Forbes's death, Alexander Walker writes that Forbes "hungered for publicity as much as she remained wary of it" (544); Walker suggests that the fact that Taylor was able to "take the heat at so many of his media-manipulating events signifies a bond between them of more-and-usual closeness and flexibility" (544). In a vocabulary that would seem to point obliquely to Taylor as beard, Walker suspends the usual logic of antithetical meaning (lover versus beard) to suggest that the bearding relationship marks a supplementary intimacy, rather than its pretext; he ascribes to the relationship a "flexibility" which signified, in the private domain, the drawing of "heat" in the public. Walker writes that Forbes "borrowed her fabulous life" (545); after his death, in a homophobic conjugation of the sexual choreographies implied by the unstated possibilities of the beard relationship, rumors would circulate that Taylor had contracted HIV/AIDS (545); not the least active factor in this rumor was the function of HIV/AIDS as a historical spectral double, the "incipiently ghoulish" precursor of the practice of outing through the 1980s, in the spectacular cases of Rock Hudson and Liberace.

What might it mean, though, for Taylor to be an exemplary beard, given that the function of the beard is indexical to its discretion, and given that Taylor was already known as the companion of gay men in films as well as in "real" life? Elizabeth Taylor's status as exemplary beard orients my critical conjunction of queer theory, popular discourses on sexuality and disclosure, and the practice of outing in the early 1990s. This chapter opened with the Forbes birthday bash at the end of the 1980s, and with the figure of Taylor as beard, to organize a number of questions that directly engage the problematic of a material rhetoric. The year 1990 marked the publication of Eve Sedgwick's *Epistemology of the Closet* and Judith Butler's *Gender Trouble*—two books that decisively recast gender and sexuality studies for the rest of the decade. Each postulated the interlacing of rhetoric and the material in the performative functions of bodies and texts, and their rhetoric of sexual orientation and disclosure has preoccupied critical theory in the past decade. The rise of "queer theory" in the early 1990s reoriented questions about the performative and citational aspects of sex/gender identity and orientation. An academic reinvestment of questions about sexual performativity and its discursive formations coincided with a reconstitution of these issues in popular media. The practice of outing, as a political as well as rhetorical intervention, became readable within the academic context as an "epistemology of the closet"; within popular media, outing became readable as the rhetoric of an engaged marginal practice of queer sexuality. The outing actions of Queer Nation and others, documented by Larry Gross and Michelangelo Signorile, intersected with mass-media disclosures of sexual orientation in tabloid publications such as the *National Enquirer*. If the practice of outing involved an ironic borrowing of the rhetoric of scandalous disclosure, this borrowing developed into a curious alliance between the practitioners of radical outing and tabloid journalism.

Public debates over the representation of sexualities in the public sphere and their articulation within various esthetic schemata had been initiated in the so-called "culture wars." Debates surrounding funding by the National Endowment for the Arts, and associated incidents, reconfigured the question of sexual disclosure through the contentious reappraisal of the relationship among sexuality, esthetics, and the state.[5] NEA funding, reconfigured as a form of state authorization, may be reread is a kind of outing, or putting into the public arena, of questions about the relationship between sexuality and performativity. Such contestations suggested a displaced analysis of sexuality as "citational." These "culture wars" reoriented popular discourses around sexuality through their reinvestment of the space of public life, whether that was the spatialized metaphor of the gallery or the space of public disclosure offered by mass-media outlets.

At the middle of the decade, these struggles over the proper demarcation of public and social spaces were recast as contests over the ideology and ethics of "outing" as a strategy within gay and lesbian media—a strategy that brought boutique, marginal, or subcultural media to intersect with mainstream tabloid culture. The birthday party of Malcolm Forbes, in late 1989, was quickly superseded as a media event by Forbes's death and outing by an activist journalist, Michelangelo Signorile. Forbes's outing was the first major move in a campaign executed by Signorile in *OutWeek*, and by the coalition known as Queer Nation in leaflets and posters distributed in Manhattan. The convergence of small-scale distribution and alternative press publications with the highest-volume print media—the *National Enquirer*, the *Globe*, *People*—was a modal registration of the outing polemic: to relocate the address of sexual disclosure from a narrow to a broad audience. Outing tied the question of reputation to the question of fame, establishing an indexical relationship between the visibility of particular persons and the "visibility" of their sexuality.

Indiana's scathing relation of Forbes's touristy privacy rehearses at one re-move the argument for outing that was to proceed through the next few years in the *Village Voice*, *OutWeek*, and elsewhere in the alternative as well as main-stream media: that the closeting of public figures has consequences for the public identity of private individuals; it is a "privilege" which constitutes an "abridgment" of the "rights" of citizens. For Indiana, the abridgment of the rights of the citizens of Morocco was also an abridgment of the rights of tour-ists other than Forbes and Taylor; he notes that Forbes's "birthday obsequies . . . succeeded in ruining more quotidian pleasures for hundreds" (41), including vacationing families who planned to stay at "the two large campsites outside Tangier" (41), which were closed for the duration of the event. Indiana cites the infringement of the rights of fellow tourists to locate a special category, the "tourist," whose particular activities are abridged precisely at their point of congruence with Forbes's spectacular hijinks: the everyday, rather than spec-tacular, exercise of tourist rights.

Writing of Henry James's preteritive maneuvers around homosexuality, Sedgwick suggests "that the rallying effect of periphrasis and preterition on this particular meaning is, if anything, more damaging than (though not sepa-rable from) its obliterative effect" (203–4). She continues to say that the de-coding of such preterition places the reader "in a discourse in which there was *a* homosexual meaning, in which all homosexual meaning meant a single thing" (204). This single meaning, in turn, promises that "the reassuring exhil-aration of knowingness is to buy into the specific formula 'We Know What That Means'" (204), a formula which "animates and perpetuates the mecha-nism of homophobic male self-ignorance" (204). For Sedgwick, then, part of the homophobic effect of not-saying is precisely the way in which it can be con-strued as a saying; it is the contingency of a strategy that orients its reference to the *singular* fact of male homosexuality—homosexuality as the (in this sense) natural and final point of preteritive relation.

Ironically, Indiana's broad hinting at the nature of Forbes's relationship with Taylor may be construed only retrospectively as an outing. As drag might be understood as a spectacular dissimulation, spectacles both hide and disclose; Indiana's thinly veiled reference to Forbes's gay identity was not explicitly un-derstood as an outing, and in fact Indiana was a vocal opponent of Signorile's practice.[6] Taylor's "pointedly bussing" Forbes is a beard, just as her hapless cinematic counterpart in *Suddenly, Last Summer* is a decoy for the gay acts of Venable. This relationship, "pointed" and "piquant" in Indiana's article, is alluded to but never made explicit; Indiana merely refers to the ubiquitous jokes as what "the rest of it" might not be.

The effects of outing were registered in diverse ways in mainstream media and elsewhere, as the practice polarized public debate over the ethics and politics of disclosure. In its polemical formation, outing disturbed traditional political ascription and locations; as Brownworth wrote, "In the still-as-apathetic-as-the-'80s '90s . . . [outing is] one of the few issues to goad liberals and conservatives alike" (249). The act of outing was a "goad," a rhetoric of perverse or repulsive persuasive power; outing was a performance which specifically attempted to elicit a response. In 1990, the practice of outing, which followed Forbes's party and his death soon after, displayed a logic antithetical to that of the clubbish practice of preteritive revelation: outing was a strategy that also exemplified a rhetoric of spectacle commensurate with the spectacular privacy of the closet.

Malcolm Forbes was outed by Michelangelo Signorile in *OutWeek* some months after his death. For Signorile, "Going over the top was the only way to get a lot of attention," and outing's "trademark was upper-case invective" (*Queer in America* 72). Signorile positioned outing as a direct response to the popular press and as an oblique one to "elitist" publications, precisely by not addressing his invective to them: he felt that "too much attention was given the *New York Times*," and that in fact "*People* magazine . . . was far more important than the *Times* in reaching vast numbers of Americans and changing their opinions about many issues" (*Queer In America* 71).

Signorile attacked the bearding of Forbes precisely because of the inferences that might be made from Taylor's "pointed bussing." Taylor's role as the beard of Forbes was the factor that precipitated his outing: Signorile was incensed over the *interpretability* of Taylor's presence. The spatial implications of outing are variously realized in these texts through tropes of "bussing," "closeness," and "flexibility"; for Signorile, the inflexible space of the columnist's text is demonized as a space of nondisclosure. In an early outing article on Forbes, he wrote:

These monster columnists are oppressing us each day in their spaces—and half the time they're gay or lesbian themselves! But that doesn't stop them from deeming us invisible, making homophobic remarks or schmoozing and worshipping the people who are killing us. When William Norwich [of the *Daily News*] tells us that Liz Taylor and Malcolm Forbes are "dating," millions of people get the wrong impression, though Norwich knows better. (*Queer In America* 72)

While demonstrating his own adeptness with preterition, Signorile continues to out Forbes, although unsurprisingly he has to reach to the metaphor (with all its preteritive potential) to do so. Titling his piece "The Other Side of Malcolm," Signorile describes the memorial service for Forbes as populated by "pretty boys, Hollywood agents, publishing magnates and celebrity beards" (208). He writes that while it may surprise some that "our big, macho, American publishing tycoon" was "a homo," "lots of others knew for a long time of Forbes' secret gay life and simply *excused* his being a fag" ("The Other Side of Malcolm" 208).

The "other side," then is the tolerant exercise of discretion, not the secret of sexuality per se but the secret of its nondisclosure, a secret materialized in the figure of the beard. If the rhetoric of closeting implies discretion, inhibition, or a failure to disclose, the beard may be understood as a false disclosure, or as a discreet ambivalence. As feint, beards are calculated to give the "wrong impression" by virtue, Signorile suggests, of giving no precise impression at all.

Signorile writes that "outing was a natural, inevitable outcome of the work that everyone in the larger lesbian and gay movement had done for over twenty years" (*Queer in America* 70). He sites the teleology of noting in an internalized history of community action, arguing that "something inside of me told me that it had to be done, that it was the right thing to do" (*Queer In America* 70). "Something inside" Signorile locates the impetus of outing in a curiously internal yet nonsubjective space. His impulse, which speaks to the *agency* of activism, is oriented in a supra-agency of impulse that has its own ethical logic: the *intensity* of Signorile's impulse provides the logic of its appropriateness, an unsurprising articulation of desire, as it productively mechanizes bodily organizations.[7] Outing must first of all come from within, supplanting the subjectivity of the "outed" with that of the "outer": one interior subject externalizes actions in terms of the process of outing; another is externalized in the process of being outed. For Signorile, the outing of Forbes, his first and most notorious, was to be as spectacular as Forbes himself—outing was to be a practice written as large and legibly as the closeting was by its nature public, and "the historical record had to be corrected quickly, before a slew of biographies came out falsely saying that Elizabeth Taylor had been Forbes' lover" (*Queer in America* 73).

In contrasting Indiana's protection with Signorile's invective, I want to reorient the "incipiently ghoulish" venue of the party as the departure point for two quite distinct structures of haunting: the ghoulish return of "it" (gay sexuality) in its preteritive double, "what it is not," and the ghoulish post-mortem outing of the "double life" of Malcolm Forbes, in which Signorile paired a putatively ghoulish gay sexuality with a haunted (bearded) heterosexuality. After all, ghouls are spectacular precisely in their evanescent or immaterial materiality. Like rhetorics, they effect material guises and affective change, while remaining precariously situated on the threshold between the discursive and nondiscursive.

This incipiently ghoulish realm of outing suggests another question: what if the target of Sedgwick's singular enunciation is not the "truth" (contingent, fleeting, ineffable) of the fact of male homosexuality but the truth of the beard (material and figurative, license and collateral)? Forbes's outing raises the question of the outing of the beard. How might the sexual identity of the beard be read within an epistemology of the closet which, in Sedgwick's much-repeated phrase, is not merely homophile but also anti-homophobic? Sedgwick locates the anti-homophobic as one subject position with which to articulate her expansive schemata of the closet; I wish to reorient the beard not as the signifier of homophobia but as a refuge from it—not as the betraying sign of heterosexuality presumption but as its extrapolation from the venue of celebrity spectacularity. Outing has elicited many responses, including some registration of its politics of visibility within the iconography of gay sexuality. Again in 1990, the ascendancy of the gay-porn actor Joey Stefano was tied to an erotics of outing: Stefano became a celebrity in gay porn as an openly gay man when, paradoxically enough, the upper reaches of gay-porn celebrity had been populated by men who identified as heterosexual (Isherwood 60–61). The conundrum of men who have public (broadcast) gay sex but who identify as heterosexual is a useful inversion of the rhetorical issue that I want to pursue in the rest of this chapter: the signification of the beard. In the context of outing and of the recasting of public and private identifies and cultures which outing premises, and of a theoretical revision of the relationship between discourse and bodies in their enunciative and citational capacities, how do we understand the position of a person who functions as a beard? How might a beard articulate crucial questions about manifest sexualities and sexual identifications?

In the rest of this chapter I explore the complex performativity of the beard through a number of key examples: the brief career of porn star Joey Stefano; the *mariage blanc* of Rock Hudson; and Liberace's autobiographical dilation on the question of marriage. From these three examples, I hope to reanimate the figure of the beard beyond the simple articulations of homophobia, the closet, and outing, and to draw it into a material rhetorical practice that theorizes the rhetoricity of bodies and the material effects of rhetorical acts. This chapter will offer an analysis of the rhetoric of sexual disclosure through the metaphoric of beards.

Joey

Elizabeth Taylor, as exemplary beard, appears again in the brief career of Joey Stefano (real name, Nicolas Iacona), as narrated by Charles Isherwood in *Wonder Bread and Ecstasy: The Life and Death of Joey Stefano*. Stefano, an actor in gay videos who died of a drug overdose in 1994, appeared in films directed and produced by Chi Chi LaRue, a drag queen who was required by the gay production house Catalina to adopt a more "masculine" name:

If Chi Chi LaRue the director was now considered Catalina material, Chi Chi LaRue the name was not. 'It wasn't masculine,' LaRue recalls. So a man named Taylor Hudson— culled from the surnames of Elizabeth and Rock (there's a masculine concept)— was credited with *Billboard* and indeed all of LaRue's Catalina releases for several years. (57)

"Taylor Hudson," the unlikely conjugation of Taylor and Hudson in the realm of porn, is a reminder of the ironic surplus of the performance of masculinity.[8] The pseudonym "Taylor Hudson" locates both the function of Taylor's name as conjugal beard and Hudson's career, in a reprisal of the parodic performance of heterosexual masculinity for which Hudson became renowned.

It is reminiscent too of the inverted logic by which Judith Butler calculates the temporality of "gender insubordination." Imitation takes on a perverse valence in Butler's work; for her, the relationship between imitation and origin is inverse. The imitation, in other words, offers a guarantee for the authenticity of origins; origins require imitation to guarantee their status *as* origin, and thus the authenticating *quality* of the imitation logically precedes the origin. "How can something operate as an origin," Butler asks, "if there are no secondary consequences which retrospectively confirm the originality of that origin? ("Gender Insubordination" 22). In fact, Butler suggests, *imitation* does not copy that which is prior, but produces and *inverts* the very qualities of priority and derivativeness ("Gender Insubordination" 22). "Taylor Hudson" becomes, then, a mnemonic for the function of "gay identities" in their "parodic or imitative effect":

The parodic or imitative effect of gay identities works neither to copy nor to emulate heterosexuality, but rather, to expose heterosexuality as an incessant and panicked imitation of its own naturalized idealization. That heterosexuality is always in the act of elaborating itself is evidence that it is perpetually at risk, that is, that it "knows" its own possibility of becoming undone: hence, its compulsion to repeat which is at once a foreclosure of that which threatens its coherence. ("Gender Insubordination" 22–23)

From this one might conclude that the term *beard* metonymically stages what homosexuality instantiates: the undoing of the logic of heterosexual priority. This *knownness* of heterosexuality can, in one sense, be seen as the inverse of the *knowingness* of preterition in the way that preterition gestures to the "known" status of homosexuality: heterosexuality is in danger of becoming "unknown" precisely when a discourse of "knowingness" ("I Know What That Means," in Sedgwick's terms) is circumvented in the articulation of gay identity. The beard might be understood as just such a circumvention, articulating the point of connection between the *known* and the *knowing* which crucially emplots the pivotal structure of the closet *as* an epistemology. In particular, as a "stage name" (though a name significantly sited behind the camera), "Taylor Hudson" figures the way in which the cinematic optic idealizes the "known" operations of heterosexuality (figurative and nominative) as they embed the representation of homosexuality—literally or erotically realized—in the gay porn video. The analysis of what is *known*, versus what is *knowing*, is staged in the ascription of stage names to the viewpoint that orients knowledge behind the camera. Just as the redubbing of Chi Chi LaRue as "Taylor Hudson" locates as supplementary adjunct a masculine gender ascription that has *already* been inverted as the stage name Chi Chi La Rue, situating what is knowing behind the camera relocates what can be known of the acting—the performance—that the camera records.

In 1990 Joey Stefano's ascendancy in porn could be understood as one result of the outing campaign of the early 1990s. According to Charles Isherwood, the 1980s saw the ascendancy of actors who identified as straight off screen but performed in gay videos; he argues that "the rise of the cult of heterosexual men in gay porn in the 1980s may be linked to circumstances specific to the times: the spread of AIDS" (60). Noting that closeting is de rigueur in mainstream cinema, Isherwood suggests that "porn stars, on a literal level, are thus the only gay movie stars" (84); yet he adds parenthetically, "(How sad an irony it is, therefore, that many of the biggest make public their private heterosexuality!)" (84).

Interestingly, Isherwood sees the manifestations of the cinematic as *literal*, when the cinematic is precisely that space most often demarcated as textual or figural. And it is precisely because the *acts* of cinematic space are understood as figural that the *identity* of heterosexual can notionally be maintained outside its particular localities. But here one might ask with Butler, "Is it not possible to maintain and pursue heterosexual identifications and aims within homosexual practices, and homosexual identifications and aims within heterosexual practices?" (Gender Insubordination" 17). The visibility of the gay sex actor in a porn film is in this sense still readable within the same logic of the closet: ironic in Isherwood's terms, but consistent in mine with the function of visible homosexuality as the authenticating imitation (textual, cinematic) of a "known" heterosexual identity, private, internal, and self-confirming. Heterosexuality, in Isherwood's terms, becomes a private truth; its privacy is ironically mimed in his text's use of parenthesis, and yet made spectacular as exclamation: (!). Maintaining a heterosexual identification in the face of a public homosexual practice is an intriguing inversion of the logic of the beard, under which the undisclosed realm of the private (the non-cinematic space) is invoked for its *qualities of privacy alone* to situate the sexuality of the actor. It is a kind of displaced binary in which public space is homosexualized. Like the beard, this assertion locates a subjectivity understood as passively, or privately, heterosexual.

Joey Stefano's career in the 1990s was contoured, according to Isherwood, by the outing campaign and HIV/AIDS-related activism. His identity as an actively gay man and as a receptive partner in anal sex suggests to Isherwood that the popularity of Stefano was "a by-product of this new wave of activism sweeping gay culture" (61). Situating erotic preferences in a reasonably unambiguous relation to the context of local political and cultural effects, Isherwood writes that "consumers of gay porn were expanding their sexual horizons, granting icon status for the first time to a star who was almost exclusively a bottom. The hegemony of the top was toppled; a new mood had arrived" (61). Such a contingency-oriented model of sexual orientation is hardly encompassed in the act of "granting icon status." And yet, in another sense, Isherwood locates another inversion of unusual consequence (to borrow Judith Butler's term) in that he sees the agency of activism translated as the iconicity of the "bottom." The "bottom," traditionally figured as a posture of compliance, becomes the site of activist self-representation.

For Butler, the question of gender most be understood to be addressed through an analysis of the function of category, once we address the question of avowing sexual preference. She writes:

> The question is not one of *avowing* or *disavowing* the category of lesbian or gay, but, rather, why it is that the category becomes the site of this "ethical" choice? What does it mean to *avow* a category that can only maintain its specificity and coherence by performing a prior set of *disavowals*? Does this make "coming out" into the avowal of disavowal, that is, a return to the closet in the guise of an escape? And it is not something like heterosexuality or bisexuality that is disavowed by the category, but a set of identificatory and practical crossings between these categories that renders the discreteness of each equally suspect. ("Gender Insubordination" 16–17)

In this sense, the avowal of homosexuality is an avowal of *known* categories rather than an avowal of *knowing* orientation. Butler's logic is perhaps nowhere better exemplified than in the "coming out" of the heterosexual gay porn star, who hopes that by simply asserting his sexual preference he will undo the visual and material manifestation of that crossing which the video provides: a crossing which also traverses the distinction between an immaterial and material signification of sexual preference; a crossing, into the public and audiovisual realm of the secret of homosexuality, which embeds the secret of heterosexual preference.

Shame

Nothing thrives like fear and uncertainty.
                                   Liberace, *Liberace: An Autobiography*

The deaths of Rock Hudson and Liberace from AIDS-related illnesses in the 1980s constituted a sadder form of outing. The demise of both stars became retrospectively iconic as the campaign for outing drew strength, in the early 1990s, from the indignity each man faced as his sexuality was publicly canvassed, through assumptions about seropositivity and through palimony actions which were brought during their illnesses.

Both men had chosen to be discreet about their personal lives, and both had recourse to beards on occasion. Hudson even married in 1955, in an arrangement possibly organized by his manager to quell the threats of *Confidential* magazine to out him (Hudson and Davidson 95). In his autobiography, Hudson chooses a curiously passive model—his tell-all is structured around the reminiscences of friends, while still maintaining an autobiographical cast—and so that text never accounts precisely for the nature of the relationship between Hudson and his wife, Phyllis Gates; it offers instead a number of alternative accounts of the marriage. In deliberating the status of this marriage as a beard, the autobiography summarizes, through the voice of Hudson's coauthor Sara Davidson, "I have come to conclude that the truth lies somewhere in the gray area between opposing views" (Hudson and Davidson 7). In her own autobiography, *My Husband, Rock Hudson*, Hudson's former wife supports the opacity of this arrangement, characterizing it as at least in part a romance, but acknowledging the expedient aspects of the marriage. One of Hudson's lovers spoke of Hudson's dissimulation, saying, "Rock was an actor and he played two roles—one in public and one at home. In public, he was guarded, but at home, he could be what he called 'a secret libertine'" (Hudson and Davidson 160). In a sense, then, professional life colonized the public space: guarded or bearded by both a professional demeanor and the facility his profession gave him, Hudson quarantined the "libertinism" of sexuality. In the circumstance of his marriage, Phyllis Gates suggested, "Rock charmed women. He acted from morning till night. I used to say he did better acting at home than at the Studio" (Hudson and Davidson 97). To her, this meant that Hudson was a "slave of the media" (Gates and Thomas 103) and that she was an "ornament" (180). Hudson, in short, extended his professional life into the domain of the marriage— a space that materialized as a contingency of publicity in the 1950s.

Traditional models of outing have followed the logic of the Hudson–Gates marriage to presume that the coupling of a gay man and beard is a kind of "passing," an act of bad faith insupportable within a discourse of liberation. According to Richard Meyer, Rock Hudson's marriage was sufficient to secure and emit the sign "heterosexuality" (274). He suggests that "though the marriage would last less than three years, the sign would remain publicly affixed to Rock Hudson's body for the following three decades" (274). In fact, the fixity of that "sign" seems moot; Hudson was dogged by rumors throughout his career—in particular, by a persistent rumor that he had "married" the singer and actor Jim Nabors. Susan St. James, his costar in *McMillan and Wife*, reported that when she was doing publicity tours, "everyone" asked whether Hudson was gay (Hudson and Davidson 177). It seems unlikely, then, that the fixity of the sign "heterosexual" is as permanent or even as feasible as Meyer suggests.

Locating heterosexual presumption in terms of discourses of marginal identity and subcultural identification, Larry Gross suggests that the "vicarious" association between gay fan and star "can provide the soil for the cultivation of a self-image that is less determined by the values of the dominant culture"

(117). He describes gay passing as a "relative invisibility" that "creates the possibility of passing, an option exercised by some people of color and Jews (and . . . often enforced by external institutions such as Hollywood studios)" (118). Rather than being a subterfuge or supplementary activity, for Gross passing is the degree zero of gay identity: "In fact, . . . all gay people start out by passing, first unconsciously, as we rarely think of ourselves as gay early on, and then consciously, before deciding to come out. And most gay people pass some of the time, because no one can come out over and over, day after day, in opposition to the universal assumption of heterosexuality" (118).

This unlikely identification of heterosexual passing as the initial formation of gay identity suggests that while homosexual identification postulates the priority of homosexual subjectivity, it does so within the framework of a temporal lag which inverts the priority of homosexuality: heterosexual performance precedes homosexual determination. Passing, the strategy of sexual dissimulation, is an unconscious but necessary precursor to homosexual "consciousness." Passing, then, becomes in Butler's terms the necessary precursor to homosexual identification in that it is an *imitation* which signifies the *originary* status of what it follows—except that, in this case, it is logically prior to what it is necessarily behind.[9]

This temporal inversion is reminiscent of Lee Edelman's analysis of the structuring logic of psychoanalysis. For Edelman, the narrative of psychoanalysis, with its refusal of "unidirectional understanding of the temporality of psychic development" (96), articulates its logic in terms of metalepsis, defined as "the rhetorical substitution of cause for effect or effect for cause, a substitution that affects the relationship of early and late, or before and behind" (96). Whereas Gross proposes a simple model of developmental sexuality, his terminology suggests the inversion of the very logic that model adduces. Unconscious passing stages the metaleptic reversal of cause and effect. Edelman reads Cleland's account of "preposterous pleasure" in *Memoirs of a Woman of Pleasure* as a "literalization" effected by sodomy in that "it signally condenses the disturbance of positionality that is located in and effected by the sodomitical scene" (104). According to him, the "sodomite . . . like the Moebius loop, represents and enacts a troubling resistance to the binary logic of before and behind, constituting himself as a single-sided surface whose front and back are never completely distinguishable as such" (105).[10] The Moebius loop, *qua* sodomitical body, resists the logic of before and behind as the beard may do by substituting cause (closeting) for effect ("Taylor Hudson"). Similarly, might the beard be regarded as a site in which an *imitative* heterosexuality can still be understood to further an *originary* homosexuality, precisely as the effect of homosexuality?

In *Gender Trouble*, Judith Butler's problematic invests in just such an (anti)-foundational logic, contoured through her rereading of the genealogy. She seeks to "expose the foundational categories of sex, gender, and desire as effects of a specific formation of power," a practice which "requires a form of critical enquiry that Foucault, reformulating Nietzsche, designates as 'genealogy'" (ix). In Butler's hands,

> genealogical critique refuses to search for the origins of gender, the inner truth of female desire, a genuine or authentic sexual identity that repression has kept from view; rather, genealogy investigates the political stakes in designating as an *origin* and *cause* those identity categories that are in fact the effects of institutions, practices, discourses with multiple and diffuse points of origin. (*Gender Trouble* ix)

The genealogy, Moebius-like in Edelman's terms, turns effect to cause and vice versa, enacting a resistance to the logic of what is before and what is behind. What disturbance might we bring to the category of the beard, once we examine its genealogical disruption of the inadequacies of a "passing" model? What are the consequences of an analysis that presupposes sexuality as the "origin" or "cause" of the beard, rather than as an "effect" of the discursive construction of the "identity" homosexual—in other words, an analysis that posits the beard as the "incipiently ghoulish" registration of potential acts of homosexuality encoded within the identity of the homosexual? In particular, this disruption effects a complication of the post-Foucauldian analysis of the recent transformation of the conceptualization of sexuality from acts (or practices) to identities—an emphasis on sexual object-choice ("preference") over sexual aim (the homosexual versus the sodomite). What effect does the act of bearding have on the "identity" of the gay man?

Bearding offers a means of insulation, or prophylaxis. The beard passively orients a presumptive heterosexuality. More vigorously, the beard signifies apotropaically: the beard figures repulsion and resistance. Gross reads passing, the beard's subterfuge, as a gesture of self-denial or shame. Significantly, one of the early texts of gay liberation to theorize self-oppression—shame—was titled *With Downward Gays: Aspects of Homosexual Self Oppression* (Gross 23); the title punned rather self-consciously on the bidirectionality of gays/ gaze, self-knowledge and internal vision punningly realized with outward demeanor. This gesture rehearsed the shame of language as an embarrassment of potential meanings, in the form of homophones. Homosexual bearding masks faciality at both a literal level and a figurative, punning level. On Edelman's logic, though, faciality, or more precisely *sidedness*, is the topos of identity most complexly refigured by the sodomitical body: rather than viewing the beard as constituting facelessness, we might think differently about the faciality of shame. The opacity of the beard, in this sense, might be related to a deferral of that problematic Butler isolates as central to her own "epistemology of the closet":

> Conventionally, one comes out of the closet (and yet, how often is it the case that we are "outed" when we are young and without resources?); so we are out of the closet, but into what? what new unbounded spatiality? . . . Curiously, it is the figure of the closet that

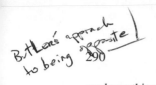
Butler's approach to being opposite!

produces this expectation, and which guarantees its dissatisfaction. For being "out" always depends to some extent on being "in"; it gains its meaning only within that polarity. Hence being "out" must produce the closet again and again in order to maintain itself as "out." In this sense, *outness* can only produce a new opacity; and *the closet* produces the promise of a disclosure that can, by definition, never come. Is this infinite postponement of the disclosure of "gayness," produced by the very act of "coming out," to be lamented? Or is this very deferral of the signified *to be valued*, a site for the production of values, precisely because the term now takes on a life that cannot be, can never be, permanently controlled? ("Gender Insubordination" 16)
Judith Butler

Wayne Koestenbaum, for instance, addresses the postcard as one such space of openness. Writing of Oscar Wilde's correspondence with Alfred Douglas, he notes that "Ronald Firbank composed his novels on postcards—an emblematic space for openly gay writing; unlike the closet of sealed envelopes, postcards preclude privacy" (179). Outing similarly took the premise that a whole series of new venues, including tabloids as well as emblematically gay spaces, could now be understood to preclude privacy. Whereas Koestenbaum writes of a putatively private correspondence that is redirected to an anonymous and unfamiliar audience, the posters of Queer Nation and gay and lesbian publications redirected their address specifically to a mainstream clientele. What the beard suggests, however, is that another model of being out—being public while not being out—may arrest that logic of the binarism which informs the metaphoric of closeting. Beards, after all, are meaningful *only* as public manifestations. The beard points not to the "truth" of an internalized knowledge of self but to the public spatiality of "out" as one in which public identity is always deferred. If we follow Butler in adducing as our problematic the category *itself* as the place of ethical self-determination, might the deferral of categorical definition offered by the beard be understood not as a passive assumption of the identity and perquisites of heterosexuality, but rather as a deferral of the problematic of the category per se? Might not the beard be understood as a resistance to the impersonation of heterosexual identity, as a refuge from heterosexual impersonation, as an *act* which does not merely reproduce metonymically the *identity* of the homosexual?

Writing of "shame," and following the work of Silvan Tomkins, Eve Sedgwick and Adam Frank suggest that if, according to Silvan Tomkins, "the lowering of the eyelids, the lowering of the eyes, the hanging of the head is the attitude of shame, it may also be that of reading" (20). Locating "sheer textual attention as a "force field-creating power" (20), they hypostatize "the kind of skin that sheer textual attention can weave around a reading body" (20). For Sedgwick and Frank, such prophylactic isolation is not congruent with a "pernicious" notion of reading as "escape." Instead they ask:

Escape from what? The "real world," ostensibly, the "responsibility" of "acting" or "performing" in that world—yet this reading posture registers as extroversion at least as much as introversion, as public as it does private: all a reader need do to transform this "inner life" experience to an audible performance is begin reading aloud. (20–21)

The mechanisms—facial, bodily, and performative—that can be understood to conceal the face—shame—can equally be understood as a productive diversion of attention and as a point of refuge from the requirements of the public sphere, even as this withdrawal may, like the beard, be understood as active "extroversion."

Beards

In his autobiography, Liberace writes of a number of romances that never led to marriage. He dilates on the apotropaic function of marriage itself, an ironic inversion of the intimacy marriage usually signifies. "Everytime I've come close to marriage," he writes, "some incident made me know, gave me a warning, that it wouldn't work" (299). Ironically, the fear of endangering his career was an impediment to Liberace's marrying; the efficacy of his potential bride as a beard was on a continuum with this apparently oxymoronic effect, as Bob Thomas suggests in his biography of the pianist. Writing of one entanglement, Thomas asks, "Did he really want to marry and thus endanger his career? More important, did he believe that he could play the role of husband? Or would Joanne become like the wife of Cole Porter and other public figures, providing disguise for a homosexual husband?" (100). For Liberace, a breach was effected in this engagement because of the publicity Joanne Rio brought to their relationship, and he writes that "our 'romance' got too much publicity" (300). Publicity turns Romance to "romance," and he writes:

I don't know why I put the word "romance" in quotation marks unless it is because there is the romance of infatuation, which doesn't last, and the Romance that is born of true love. Sometimes one can become the other. Neither Joanne nor I minded very much what was printed about us. Maybe Romance, with a capital "R," is more private than "romance" in quotation marks. Anyway, the serpent of publicity got into our temporary Garden of Eden. (300)

The distinction Liberace draws between Romance and "romance" traces the trajectory of bearding from this failed affair to the piquant "romance" (after Indiana) suggested by Elizabeth Taylor's dating of Malcolm Forbes, a "romance" itself bearded by the ironizing surplus of scare quotes. As it turned out, the mere contemplation of marriage was Liberace's beard. Never married, he addresses the question of why he was not married by narrating instead the humorous failures of his heterosexual romances. Of Sonja Henie, he writes:

As I recall, it was not unlike a scene from the Gloria Swanson picture *Sunset Boulevard*. The two of us sat in a darkened room watching Sonja. After each reel the lights would come up; she controlled them with a rheostat right on her chair. . . . Then we'd view the next reel of the film. I even recall some of the titles. There was *Once In A Million*, in which she starred with Adolphe Menjou and Don Ameche. I remember admiring Mr. Menjou's clothes. (302)

Henie's failure to disarticulate private passion from public identity allows Liberace to do precisely the same with his anecdote, orienting the performance of public identity as a camp revival. Substituting the Swanson–Holden relationship of *Sunset Boulevard* for his and Henie's, Liberace relays bearding to the field of cinematic realization, as Indiana did in describing Taylor's romance with Forbes. In each case, a beard articulates the connections of the non-romance to the romance of the textual *as* metaphor for the lives of cinema stars. Turning the erstwhile boudoir into a screening room, Henie defers the registration of romance by substituting the grammar of cinematic disclosure, repetition, and embellishment. Liberace's ironic admiration of Menjou's clothes offers a camp coda to the display.

Another romance, with Frances Goodrich, is arrested by a double entendre, the "strangest conflict of interest" (301). Liberace divulges that "Frances, influenced no doubt by her family, tried to talk me into doing something so completely opposite to what I would ever want to do that it amazes me" (301): that is, to leave show business to manage the family's orchards. Here the conjugal withdrawal into the private sphere is parodied as sun-kissed retirement, and Liberace returns to the trope of the domestic public space, the orchard of conjugal privacy, when he concludes, "Obviously that romance was not sun-kissed" (301). Again, in this ironic return to the cinematic space of bearded public conjugality—the orchard—the preteritive articulation of romance allows us to know simply what that romance "obviously" was not. The "complete opposite" of what Liberace is becomes a professional question; assuming familial obligations is situated as the antagonistic other at the heart of marital obligation.

Liberace's closeting is usually evidenced through reference to a lawsuit in which he sued a columnist for the imputation of homosexuality. Referring to the columnist's pseudonym "Cassandra" as a "nom de slur" (14), Liberace devotes considerable space to the narrative of his successful court action. Margaret Thompson Drewal writes:

Liberace masked his sexual preferences from his public, and indeed in 1959 he won a libel suit against a British critic who implied he was homosexual. Not that the critic was unable to prove Liberace's sexual preferences, but rather Liberace's lawyer was able to prove that the review defamed the star's character. (149)

Liberace's suit against "Cassandra" could be read as a closeting gesture; I suggest that his engagement with heterosexual discourse offered a more complex relay of the subtle potential of the beard. What Drewal might have added here is that the libel action also did not involve Liberace's denying his homosexuality. Similarly, a blunt denial of homosexuality is remarkably absent from Liberace's autobiography. In what sense, we might ask, *did* Liberace "mask" his sexual preference? Drewal suggests that Liberace's personae disarticulated "Camp performance" from "gay identity." Although it is hard to construe how Liberace can be understood to be distinct from discourses of gay identity in any sense, Drewal asks:

If gay signifying practices serve to critique dominant heterosexist and patriarchal ideology through inversion, parody, travesty, and the displacement of binary gender codes, then what happens when those practices are severed from their gay signifier and put into the service of the very patriarchal and heterosexist ideology of capitalism that Camp politics seek to disrupt and contest? (149)

An answer to this question might turn on what kind of "service" the "Camp performance" is understood to be doing. In a general sense, it seems that severing those practices from their "gay signifier" ought to be more rather than less disruptive of heterosexist ideology. The beard then might be understood as just such an untethered "Camp performance," loosened from the necessary association among camp, impersonation, and gay identity while never failing to shadow its presence precisely at the point at which it may be subsumed by that ideology which it more furtively critiques.

Liberace offers the analysis of his heterosexual romances as an answer to a tacit question; he writes, "I suppose that as long as I remain a bachelor people are going to ask me why I have never married" (299). Marriage is a deferred option, and its specter raises the prospect of an immaterial beard, a gesture toward a horizon of unrealized action. In a text full of digression and incompletion (of stories and historical sequences, as well as of "engagements"), deferral is a topos for the inadequacy of self-revelation. Liberace thematizes deferral as a textual effect, writing "Someone once said that 'repartee' is something clever you think of on the way home" (29). The return of deferment is a similarly biographical phenomenon; if the autobiography opens with this trope of delayed return, it closes with the specter of a second life: "With all the hard work, disappointments and struggles behind me," he writes, "I anticipate a sort of 'second' life, perhaps even a fuller and more rewarding one, of which I may write again (306).

If deferral of the "second life" of identity is one consequence of the beard, the example of Liberace suggests another: in his spectacular visibility, Liberace offers the paradox of spectacular dissimulation as a tropological enunciation of the figural investments signaled by the idea of the privacy of the star. It is a dissimulation that incites interest even when it cloaks. So Sedgwick and Frank write of shame or an "additional skin shimmering as if shrink-wrapped around a body-and-book, or body-and-playing/working environment" (20–21). The beard hinges that space between work and play that shadows the cinematic spectacle of the beard, similarly "making figural not escape or detachment but attention, interest" (20–21).

This chapter has attempted to read the rhetorical complexity of the beard as it marks shame and incites inspection, a double movement that recapitulates the inverse logic of a metaleptic retracing of the cause and effect of acts and identities. The specter of the beard haunts both current and historical accounts of the worldliness of the homosexual, not only in critics of his witting or ironic deployment of heterosexual deferral, but also in his discomfort with being put into a public space of inspection—a discomfort turned, like shame, to spectacular benefit as the evanescent spectacle of the bearded body.

Notes

1. The Breen Office was one manifestation of the Motion Picture Production Code, a self-regulatory industry standard which persisted until the late 1960s (Russo 31).

2. Dolly Parton is perhaps the best known of celebrities with an absent spouse who is sometimes rumored to be a beard; of her husband, Carl Dean, she writes: "He's very much a loner, and of course that suits my lifestyle perfectly. We see each other often, but we are not in each other's face all the time. I often sit up late at night writing, as I am with this book, while he's snoozing away. Then he'll be up and gone before I get up" (Parton 155). In other words, even when they are together, they are apart. Parton seems reluctant ever to invoke the conjugal intimacy of marriage.

3. Obviously, a more complete account of outing, such as Signorile's, locates a tripartite operation, including Washington, D.C., as another crucial axis of power and closeted site. His representation finds its fruit in the anonymous novel *Primary Colors* by Joe Klein, for example, in which the generic features of the *roman à clef* instantiate the thematic of homosexual secrets and an abiding nostalgia for past regimes: libertarian *and* homophobic.

4. See, for example, John Parker's *Five for Hollywood: Their Friendship, Their Fame, Their Tragedies* for a popular account of these relationships; and my "'I Embrace The Difference': Elizabeth Taylor and the Closet" for an analysis of the implications of these proximities.

5. For a comprehensive documentation of these complex responses to the Helms initiative, see Bolton.

6. See Signorile's account of his interaction with Indiana over the issue of outing: "I had also criticized Gary Indiana, another openly gay writer. . . . He fired back in one of the fiercest attacks on me ever, comparing me to a right-wing zealot, calling me a psychopath, and describing me as an 'infant crapping in his diapers'" (*Queer In America* 125). Another version of this chapter could focus more specifically on the practice of outing as a complex agonism between mainstream, subcultural, and alternative New York publications in the early 1990s.

7. In this sense, outing becomes congruent with an essentializing model of sexuality—sexuality as the mechanical responses of a body to its own desire.

8. See Meyer's meticulous analysis of the body of Rock Hudson as an unlikely anchor of heterosexuality. See also Steven Cohan for a complex analysis of the spectacle of bare-chested masculinity in Hollywood products of the 1950s.

9. Judith Butler's "Passing, Queering: Nella Larsen's Psychoanalytical Challenge" offers a strong, complicated analysis of the crossing of gender categories and race stud-

ies in the analysis of sexual difference. Her analysis articulates the relationship between race and sexuality as they "converge at and as the constitutive outside of a normative heterosexuality" (166). Gross maintains the identification of the closet as a type of passing at an analogical, rather than theoretical level.

10. This notion of the preposterous suggests also the figure of the "preposterous," or hysteron proteron. On this preposterous figure, see Patricia Parker and Richard Rand 51–56. For an explicit exploration of this trope and its relationship to the sodomitical body, see Jonathan Goldberg's *Sodometries: Renaissance Texts and Modern Sexualities*.

Works Cited

Bolton, Richard, ed. *Culture Wars: Documents from the Recent Controversies in the Arts.* New York: New Press, 1992.

Boone, Joseph A., and Michael Cadden, eds. *Engendering Men: The Question of Male Feminist Criticism.* New York and London: Routledge, 1990.

Brownworth, Victoria A. "Campus Queer Query." *OutWeek,* 16 May 1990. Reprinted in Gross, 249–53.

Butler, Judith. *Gender Trouble: Feminism and the Subversion of Identity.* New York: Routledge, 1990.

Butler, Judith. "Imitation and Gender Insubordination." In *Inside/Out: Lesbian Theories, Gay Theories,* edited by Diana Fuss, 13–31. New York: Routledge, 1991.

Butler, Judith. "Passing, Queering: Nella Larsen's Psychoanalytical Challenge." In *Bodies That Matter,* by Judith Butler, 167–85. New York: Routledge, 1993.

Cohan, Steven. "Masquerading As the American Male in the Fifties: *Picnic,* William Holden and the Spectacle of Masculinity in Hollywood Film." In *Male Trouble,* edited by Constance Penley and Sharon Willis, 203–32. Minneapolis: University of Minnesota Press, 1993.

Drewal, Margaret Thompson. "The Camp Trace in Corporate America: Liberace and the Rockettes at Radio City Music Hall." In *The Politics and Poetics of Camp,* edited by Moe Meyers, 149–81. London: Routledge, 1994.

Edelman, Lee. "Seeing Things: Representation, the Scene of Surveillance, and the Spectacle of Gay Male Sex." In *Inside/Out: Lesbian Theories, Gay Theories,* edited by Diana Fuss, 93–116. New York: Routledge, 1991.

Fuss, Diana, ed. *Inside/Out: Lesbian Theories, Gay Theories.* New York: Routledge, 1991.

Gates, Phyllis, and Bob Thomas. *My Husband, Rock Hudson: The Real Story of Rock Hudson's Marriage to Phyllis Gates.* London: Angus & Robertson, 1987.

Goldberg, Jonathan. *Sodometries: Renaissance Texts and Modern Sexualities.* Stanford: Stanford University Press, 1992.

Gross, Larry. *Contested Closets: The Politics and Ethics of Outing.* Minneapolis: University of Minnesota Press, 1993.

Hardie, Melissa Jane. "'I Embrace the Difference': Elizabeth Taylor and the Closet." In *Sexy Bodies: The Strange Carnalities of Feminism,* edited by Elizabeth Grosz and Elspeth Probyn, 155–71. London: Routledge, 1995.

Hudson, Rock, and Sara Davidson. *Rock Hudson: His Story.* London: Bantam, 1987.

Indiana, Gary. "Spectacle: The Glittering Swine." *Village Voice*, 19 September 1989.

Isherwood, Charles. *Wonder Bread and Ecstasy: The Life and Death of Joey Stefano.* Los Angeles: Alyson Publications, 1996.

Koestenbaum, Wayne. "Wilde's Hard Labor and the Birth of Gay Reading." In *Engendering Men: The Question of Male Feminist Criticism*, edited by Joseph A. Boone and Michael Cadden, 176–89. New York and London: Routledge, 1990.

Liberace [Wladziu Valentino Liberace]. *Liberace: An Autobiography.* London: Star Books, 1974.

Meyer, Richard. "Rock Hudson's Body." In *Inside/Out: Lesbian Theories, Gay Theories,* edited by Diana Fuss, 259–88. New York: Routledge, 1991.

Meyers, Moe, ed. *The Politics and Poetics of Camp.* London: Routledge, 1994.

Parker, John. *Five for Hollywood: Their Friendship, Their Fame, Their Tragedies.* London: Macmillan, 1989.

Parker, Patricia. *Literary Fat Ladies: Rhetoric, Gender, Property.* New York: Methuen, 1987.

Parton, Dolly. *My Life and Other Unfinished Business.* New York: Harper Collins, 1994.

Penley, Constance, and Sharon Willis, eds. *Male Trouble.* Minneapolis: University of Minnesota Press, 1993.

Rand, Richard. "Hysteron and Proteron." *Oxford Literary Review* 8 (1986): 51–56.

Russo, Vito. *The Celluloid Closet: Homosexuality in the Movies.* New York: Harper and Row, 1981.

Sedgwick, Eve Kosofsky. *Epistemology of the Closet.* Berkeley: University of California Press, 1990.

Sedgwick, Eve Kosofsky, and Adam Frank. "Shame in the Cybernetic Fold: Reading Silvan Tomkins." In *Shame and Its Sisters: A Silvan Tomkins Reader*, edited by E. K. Sedgwick and A. Frank, 1–31. Durham: Duke University Press, 1995.

Signorile, Michelangelo. "The Other Side of Malcolm." *OutWeek*, 18 Mar. 1990, 40–45; reprinted in Gross, 207–16.

Signorile, Michelangelo. *Queer in America: Sex, the Media and the Closets of Power.* London: Abacus, 1994.

Thomas, Bob. *Liberace.* New York: St. Martin's, 1987.

Walker, Alexander. *Elizabeth.* London: Fontana, 1990.

Willis, Sharon. "Disputed Territories: Masculinity and Social Space." In *Male Trouble*, edited by Constance Penley and Sharon Willis, 263–81. Minneapolis: University of Minnesota Press, 1993.

13 *Barbara Dickson*

Reading Maternity Materially
The Case of Demi Moore

In August 1991, *Vanity Fair* ran on its cover a photo of actor Demi Moore, seven months pregnant and wearing nothing but diamonds. That representation of the celebrity's body prompted a journalistic and marketing brouhaha, as numerous writers argued over possible readings of the cover, and commercial outlets around the country debated whether to display the magazine at checkstands or shelve it behind the counter. The magazine itself offered readings of the cover in a series of articles that competed to define the meaning of the visual text. Perhaps the most definitive claim for a reading of the cover is one that Moore herself makes: she claims the cover as a "feminist statement" (quoted in Conant 118).

Does that representation of the pregnant body in fact liberate the feminine body in some way? In this chapter I want to address that question in some detail, while I simultaneously (and perhaps more importantly) try to illuminate what kind of thing "material rhetoric" is, and what kind of work material rhetoric can do. In this way my essay cooperates with others in this collection in a sustained meditation on the nature and scope of material rhetoric.

As I understand it, material rhetoric is a mode of interpretation that takes as its object of study the significations of material things and corporal entities — objects that signify not through language but through their spatial organization, mobility, mass, utility, orality, and tactility.[1] Of primary interest to material rhetoric are material objects that represent the human body, because of the way these representations are then taken up by and inscribed on corporal bodies. This way of reading operates on the assumption that these significations are open to multiple interpretations, and so it examines how those significations are contained and constrained by language practices. It shares, in this, the assumption of discourse analysis that all meaning is produced intertextually and all knowledge consensually. That is, discourse analysis (as rhetoricians use it) is a way of reading that examines how a field or a discipline constitutes itself through textual practices that build toward a shared understanding of what can be taken for granted, what counts as evidence, and what is a community's proper object of study. As it has been most usefully practiced by scholars such as Charles Bazerman, Carol Berkenkotter and Thomas Huckin, Cheryl Geisler, and Jack Selzer, discourse analysis seeks to determine how these textual practices create enough stability to produce consensual knowledge within discourse communities. Material rhetoric examines instead how multiple discourses and material practices collude and collide with one another to produce an object that momentarily destabilizes common understandings and makes available multiple readings. It seeks to know how this object can be read as providing for or constraining agency, the ability of persons singly and collectively to produce change.

Material rhetoric also shares the assumption of cultural materialism that corporal bodies are socially produced—and therefore shares as well its interest in identifying how rhetorical and literary productions are potentially disruptive of the dominant structures which produce them. Cultural materialism, however, is closely aligned with the social body; it is primarily interested in identifying the interactions between cultural and material production, the contradictions between the two, and how those contradictions lead to changes in the relations between the two. Material rhetoric is instead closely aligned with the corporal body and seeks to know how texts are taken up by and inscribed on human bodies that inhabit a web of cultural relationships. In this differentiation from cultural materialism, material rhetoric does not seek to overthrow the notion that bodies are culturally produced; rather, it seeks to know better how ordinary bodies can act within that web. In sum, then, material rhetoric, as a mode of interpretation, reads for the ways persons inscribe on their corporal bodies the culture that produces them and that they mutually produce. It seeks invention in the improvisations of the bodily writings; agency, in the ways these improvisations resist hegemonic structurings of the body and so change the relationships between these corporal bodies and the structures they inhabit; and persuasion, in the ways these changed relationships more fully satisfy the desires of the acting body.

This undeniably partial description of material rhetoric will be elaborated through its practice, not by a definition that confines it nor by a set of normative prescriptions that determine at the outset what it can—and therefore cannot—

do. Let me return, then, to how I propose we might usefully read Demi Moore off the cover of *Vanity Fair*. First, we must consider that her photo operates as a textual event in itself, and so my initial task will be to offer a reading of that text. But since we must also understand the text as operating intertextually— so that its reading is contested by the texts that shape both its production and its reception—my second task here will be to provide a reading of three other kinds of texts that I understand to be wielding the most weight in this struggle for meaning: the broader popular discourse of pregnancy written in widely circulating magazines, the series of articles in *Vanity Fair* that attempt to recuperate the cover photo, and the letters from readers that offer multiple and sometimes disruptive readings of it. Finally, I will pursue a rereading of the cover shot that takes these various texts into account, and I will use that reading to further illuminate what kind of thing material rhetoric is and what it can do.

Conventionality and Subversion in the Cover Shot

The photograph under consideration here was composed by Annie Leibovitz, an accomplished veteran of magazine cover photography, a genre that requires both photographic skill and an understanding of the conventions that govern the form. Magazine covers are designed to arrest the attention of consumers and hold it long enough to persuade them to buy the magazine. As such, covers appeal to multiple desires for affiliation, for dominance, for security, and for escape. When a cover is dominated by a photograph of a celebrity, as this one is, it also participates in a tradition of artistic representation of women analyzed by John Berger in *Ways of Seeing*. More specifically, this picture of an undressed Demi Moore is a publicity shot designed to keep Demi Moore before the public as a desirable object that we consume through her films, and the magazine as an object that satisfies that desire to consume. Publicity, Berger claims, "is the process of manufacturing glamour," and "glamour" is "the state of being envied" (131). Further, the state of being envied "depends precisely upon not sharing your experience with those who envy you. You are observed with interest, but you do not observe with interest. If you do, you will be less enviable" (133). That Moore is constituted as an object of envy is most easily read in the way she and Leibovitz cooperate to structure her gaze. We look at Moore; Moore overlooks us. The gazes not chosen reinforce this interpretation. Moore could have looked her audience, through the lens of the camera, in the eye, a gaze that would have offered reciprocity. She could have rested her eyes on her abdomen, a conventional pose for madonnas, a gaze that would have represented conventional piety. She did neither.

Berger further claims that the persuasive force of the glamour shot lies in its ability to convince us that if we who envy buy the product being sold, we will ourselves be transformed by that product into objects of envy. But what is it that this photograph asks us to buy? The diamonds secured to Moore's earlobes? Possibly. The magazine? Even more possible. I would maintain, however, that this photograph, as produced cooperatively by Moore and Leibovitz, is invented to persuade us that Demi Moore when pregnant is still desirable. Let me make clear why I maintain this position (and what I mean by the word "still") through a further analysis of the picture.

As well as being a publicity glamour shot, this representation of Moore also participates in the long tradition of nudes, the painted or photographed representations of the unclothed woman. In discussing this tradition, Berger distinguishes between the naked woman and the nude:

> To be naked is to be oneself. To be nude is to be seen naked by others but not to be recognized for oneself. A naked body has to be seen as an object in order to become a nude. . . . The principal protagonist is never painted. He is the spectator in front of the picture and he is presumed to be a man. Everything is addressed to him. (54)

Berger further argues that this method of representation reinscribes the long patriarchal discourse which displays men as "doing," so that representations of a man "suggest what he is capable of doing to you or for you" (46). Women, conversely, are displayed as "being," as presence, so that a representation of a woman "defines what can and cannot be done to her. . . . Consequently, how a woman appears to a man can determine how she will be treated" (46). Women, then, constantly surveil themselves to exercise some control over how they will be treated by men. They develop an internal male monitor that allows them some agency in their relationships with men. The more their representations appeal to men, the more control women, as objects of male desire, can exercise over the performances of men. Appearing desirable becomes a means of agency, even if it is subordinated to the male gaze. From this point of view, Moore's and Leibovitz's representation might then be read as women working cooperatively to make Moore appeal to men's desire for her so that Moore can exercise some control in relationships with men who exert control over her performance—producers, directors, and ticket-buyers.

Although this answers in part my earlier query about what Moore is hoping to persuade spectators to buy, it does not explain my use of the word "still." I wrote that the cover shot was an effort to persuade that Moore was *still* desirable because the emphatic profiling of Moore's pregnancy disrupts current renderings of the feminine body beautiful. Traditional renderings of nudes, those mostly supine women who organize the paintings of Rubens, Botticelli, and Titian, are ambiguous about pregnancy. With their rounded shoulders, breasts, arms, thighs, and bellies, these women may or not be pregnant; pregnancy is illegible in these paintings. In photographic nudes of more recent years—and I refer here to the photographs composed for the centerfolds of men's magazines like *Playboy*, or the near-nudes featured on the covers of women's magazines like *Cosmopolitan*—the woman is represented as emphatically not pregnant. Indeed, the flatness or concavity of the female abdomen is repeatedly announced as one of the components of the beautiful, desirable female body. The emphatic profiling of Moore's pregnancy thus disrupts the conventionality of this cover and opens it to contested readings.

But the *Vanity Fair* photograph is disruptive in another way. In its depiction of Moore as at once pregnant and sexually desirable, it unites two discourses about women that are traditionally used to split her in half. Julia Kristeva, in *Tales of Love*, describes the cult of the Virgin as deployed by Western patriarchal language to remove bodily mothers from *jouissance*, from the semiotic drives that threaten the Symbolic and so render mothers as controlled by the Symbolic of the father. The only woman "loved by God" is the purely virginal, spiritual, sexless mother. Kristeva's telling of the story of the Virgin helps to account for a cult of motherhood, long cultivated in Western texts, which splits the feminine in two in order to control it. Either the woman can be the object of masculine desire, or she can be the mother purified of semiotic sexual drives. A sexually desiring and desirable pregnant woman, whose body is the seam between nature and culture, between mother and child, is deeply perverse and therefore as taboo as incest (258–60). This split between the sexually desirable woman and the sanctified mother is magnified in American texts informed by a puritanical code which suppresses sexuality in anxious attempts to rid the human body of physical desires that leave it vulnerable to temptations to act outside the narrow parameters it defines as holy. Unable to think both sexuality and sanctity at once, the woman's body is cut in two to better contain her. To display the pregnant body as sexually desirable undoes conventionality by proposing an unorthodox unity. A Bergerian analysis of this cover, then, brings us to a recognition of this disruption and of the invention performed by Leibovitz and Moore.

Moore's Body Language Intertextually: Popular Discourse

Designed primarily to read for artistic participation in the long commodification of women under patriarchal capitalism, the method is less persuasive when used to analyze the specifics of this disruption. Because my interest here is in investigating whether the *Vanity Fair* representation is somehow liberatory—somehow allows pregnant women to inscribe its text on their own bodies and mobilize it to enhance their ability to satisfy their desires—then this analysis must account for the rest of the textual language that both produces it and governs its reception. A material, rhetorical reading that seeks to examine how multiple discourses play in this text, and to know how this test provides for or constrains agency and enables changes that more nearly satisfy the desires of the acting bodies, must consider what Molefi Asante describes as the rhetorical condition, "the structure and power pattern, assumed or imposed, during a rhetorical situation by society" (22). Asante argues that the rhetorical condition operating in a given situation determines to a large extent what can and cannot be said, and in our culture these conditions are more often organized in a hierarchy that is self-perpetuating: "Since power finds its efficacy in acquiescence, messages structured in a hierarchical manner reduce the leverage of the audience to respond" (26).

The rhetorical condition in which this visual text is embedded is, to a great degree, established by the discourse of pregnancy that circulates in popular and women's magazines. A review of more than twenty articles that take sexuality and pregnancy as their primary topics, in *Redbook*, *Cosmopolitan*, *Essence*, and *Glamour* (magazines occupying different class and race niches from *Vanity Fair*), reveals a rather disconcerting consistency. Discourse analysis might be quite useful here and could consider how these texts reached such a point of stability, but it is more useful for my purpose to examine how a sample of these texts represents the pregnant body and its possibilities for sexual desirability and satisfaction. In the interest of economy, I will confine my analysis to three *Redbook* articles published within the same time period as the *Vanity Fair* cover and representative of the popular discourse of pregnancy; I will read the three articles after the example of Susan Wells, who has argued in *Sweet Reason* that the discourses of modernity (and I take the popular discourse of pregnancy to be one such discourse) can best be interpreted by reading them with an eye for the ways in which figurative language produces a subject, the ways narrative strategies temporally locate that subject, and the ways intersubjective mediation between reason and desire yields action.

In November 1993, *Redbook* published "Beauty Strategies for Pregnant Moms," an article whose title already suggests that beauty does not necessarily accompany pregnancy. The story's lead also makes precarious the position of the pregnant woman in the realm of the beautiful:

You're never more radiantly beautiful than when you're pregnant: Your skin glows; your hair shines. So goes the myth. But pregnancy can just as likely cause your skin to break out, puff up, or darken. And you may have more bad hair days than ever before. (Menter 74)

The article continues cataloging all the hazards likely to frustrate a pregnant woman's attempt to construct herself as desirable: pregnancy "can make some women's acne worse, especially if the pregnancy is emotionally stressful. . . . Women who feel positive about being pregnant are the ones most likely to look good" (74). The pregnant body is figured here as both prone to a lack of emotional control and responsible for its consequences. "Stretch marks are a pregnant woman's biggest beauty fear . . . and unfortunately, they're not preventable" (74). Here, the pregnant woman is relieved of responsibility, but only because she's both anxious and out of control. The problems the pregnant woman is likely to encounter with her hair—uneven dye jobs, lax perms, limp locks—consume several inches of text in which, again, the pregnant woman is constructed as out of control of her body, the hapless victim of "raging hormones." Before turning to tips for self-care, the article concludes with advice on how to manage unruly hair "in the beginning when you feel really lousy, and near the end, when you're big, bloated, and overwhelmed" (75). To "stressed-out," "fearful," and "out of control," the article adds both physical and emotional disability. Accompanying all this in a special section is a second article, "Dressing for Two." Written almost entirely in the imperative—a rhetorical practice, Asante notes, which structures a hierarchical situation effectively silencing the audience—this article lists dos and don'ts for pregnant women. "Look for darker shades of your best colors. They're more slimming," is followed by "Opt for tapered pants. They will be more flattering than full baggy ones because they accentuate your ankles—one of the few areas where you (hopefully) haven't gained weight" (Feldon G-3). The pregnant woman in these commands is marked as a body that falls out of the category of the beautiful owing to her excess bulk. Women are advised further and forcefully to stick to their present wardrobes for as long as possible, or to alter them slightly to delay having to wear clothes that signal pregnancy, and to wear light colors near their faces "to draw attention away from your tummy" (G-3). In this fashion piece the pregnant woman is precluded from normative standards of beauty and can retain desirability only through the tricks of optical illusion and distraction. Most notable in both accounts is that the pregnant woman is figured as needing expert advice in multiple areas. She is advised to seek her doctor's opinion before dyeing her hair, applying Retin-A to her skin, exposing her skin to sunlight, taking a bath, or starting a fitness program. She should also seek the expert advice and assistance of tailors, cosmetologists, hairdressers, and specialty retailers. These numerous experts are constructed as the subjects who know, in opposition to a pregnant woman who presumably does not.

These two articles are followed in April 1994 by "The Truth about Sex during Pregnancy." The story opens with this tag-line teaser: "Will you make love more, or less? Will he love or hate your growing body? How will you both get around that huge stomach? Learn the surprising sexual secrets of expectant couples" (Roberts 62). From these opening lines, the subject that will be formed in this article's language emerges not as a discrete body but as embodied in a relationship, as a subject inhabiting a tenuous space. The tentativeness of her position hinges on her heterosexual relationship and on her relationship to her fetus, a relationship this article marks multiple times as fraught with anxiety. "The number one concern is whether having sex is going to hurt the baby" (62–63). The pregnant woman is also marked as deviant: she is represented as seeking to "know what's normal" (62), as prone to either loss of sexual interest or insatiability, as "desperate to make love one day and sickened by the thought the next" (65), and again as the victim of "mood swings caused by raging hormones" (62). But even more important to our discussion here is that figuring the pregnant woman both as inhabiting a tenuous space and as deviant makes her desirability even more complex; it engages not only her desirability but also her desire. If the first two articles served to illustrate that the desirability of the pregnant woman depends on her ability to mask her pregnancy so that it can "pass" into normative categories of the beautiful, and on her submission to expert advice to do so, the third article figures the woman's desirability from three perspectives: the woman's surveillance of herself, the woman's surveillance of the man's surveillance of her, and the man's surveillance of her. "Some women bask in their expanding stomachs and fuller breasts, feeling more feminine and desirable. Others watch their bellies grow larger and feel anything but sexy" (67). The desirability of the pregnant woman is then not determinate, but local and uncertain. The pregnant woman also watches him watching her: "Will he love or hate my growing body?" is proposed as an abiding and open question (62). The surveillance of the man constructs the same uncertainty about the desirability of the pregnant woman. "Around the fourth or fifth month, though, the pregnancy begins to show, and while same men are uncomfortable with the physical changes, others are aroused" (67). The pregnant woman who is the subject of this article emerges as anxious, deviant, tenuously and tentatively located, and uncertainly desirable.

The narrative strategies of these three stories further construct the subject as temporally displaced. This displacement occurs through the solution to the problems pregnancy poses to the woman's desirability. In the article focusing on beauty strategies, the woman is reassured that after delivery her acne will clear up, her melasma will bleach, her stretch marks will fade, and her hair will bounce. The article on dressing offers all its advice so that the woman's "basic style doesn't have to change just because you're expecting" and recommends "designs you'll want to wear after you give birth, before you're back to your prepregnancy weight" (G-3). All these reassurances work together to render the changes of pregnancy insubstantial, without weight. The article that claims to tell the truth about sex and pregnancy concludes with these lines: "Within a few short months, they'll slip right back into the lovemaking patterns that helped make them the proud parents of a beautiful baby" (69). In each statement, the hope for the pregnant woman's desirability is pinned to a future moment which will bring the return of the past. The present moment the subject occupies, already tenuously between a man and a fetus's body, is now erased. This circular movement is reinscribed in the figure of the roller-coaster, used twice in these articles to describe the transitory time of pregnancy. A roller-coaster, of course, picks you up, takes you on a wild ride, and then returns you to your starting point. No substantial change is effected. The pregnant woman, so constructed, is also rendered static: a woman on a side trip from which she will return unchanged.

The ability of this subject to mediate between reason and desire is an ability tightly constrained in these texts. If we consider that the pregnant woman is here constructed as only uncertainly desirable, then we must consider that her ability to control others through their desire for her as uncertain, too. And if we consider that the pregnant woman is also subjected to the imperatives of expert advice, then her ability to mediate is doubly constrained. But most important, particularly in the last article, her ability to satisfy her own desires by mediating reason and desire intersubjectively is even more constrained by the submission of her desire to claims of obligation to satisfy the desires and needs of her fetus and her partner. The authority of medical discourse, as in the story of beauty strategies, permeates this text. Again and again, it is invoked to ensure that in seeking to satisfy her sexual desires, the pregnant woman does nothing that could possibly harm the baby. The front page of the article includes a subtext, set off in an outline and in bold print, that names six conditions under which a woman "should get medical advice about intercourse" (62). Four other sexual practices are made taboo. The pregnant woman can still negotiate to satisfy her sexual desire, but in an arena bound by imperatives and admonishments. And again and again, the woman's desire is made subordinate to the man's desire. A sexually desiring woman must first be desirable to that man— a desirability already uncertain, and associated here with yet more factors that render it still more uncertain. The man may find her bulk unattractive, her mood swings off-putting, her focus on the pregnancy unappealing, or her evident maternity uninviting. Her ability to satisfy her sexual desires is then subject to his decision. If she desires sex, he maintains the right to grant it or deny it. His device, conversely, is her responsibility. The article's author, recalling her own lack of desire during pregnancy, reveals her anxiety about this obligation: "And I worried. Is this normal? How long would my husband be satisfied with just a cuddle?" (62). Another woman, prohibited from intercourse because of an "incompetent cervix,"[2] nonetheless performs oral sex on her husband at his desire: "I felt cheated . . . I often felt heroic, but I was secretly thinking he owed me" (69). These articles, as I read them, reveal that the popular discourse about pregnancy sets the following conditions for the production and reception of texts about pregnancy, conditions that structure what can and cannot be said about the pregnant woman.

First, the pregnant woman is excluded from normative standards of beauty that circumscribe, for many, what is figured as desirable. Second, the woman is figured as out of control of both her body and her emotions, a subject at the mercy of an unstable body. Third, the woman is figured as subject to the authority of medicine. Fourth, the desires of the pregnant woman are figured as subordinate to the needs of her fetus and the desires of her male partner. Her body is figured as community property held by a medical discourse which exercises authority over it, a baby with higher claims to it, and a mate with claims that may override her desires. And finally, the pregnant woman as a subject is chronologically erased, rendering her unchanged by time.

Vanity Fair's Say: Recovering the Cover as Liberatory

These are the conditions under which the texts within *Vanity Fair* work to recuperate the visual text of the cover shot, and in the midst of which Moore makes her claim for the photo as a feminist statement. Headlined "More Demi Moore" on the cover, the photo is duplicated inside with a tag-line that encourages a reading of the featured body as healthy, as following the dictates of medical authority, and as caught in a family romance: "Demi Moore glows with great expectations" (8). The article inside, titled "Demi's Big Moment," tells a story only tangentially related to the cover shot—a tale of the actress's rise to fame in the cutthroat world of Hollywood moviemaking, a variation on the rags-to-riches American myth. Readers learn that Moore was born to a teenage mother, fathered by a man she met only once, raised by a man who later committed suicide, and subjected to the emotional overturning of roles common to children of alcoholic parents. She was "an unusually skinny little girl afflicted with a cantankerous right eye" who moved every six months until she finally left home at sixteen, then worked as a secretary, landed a modeling job, attracted attention with her modeling, and secured her first acting job. The article appeals to the pathos of the neglected child, the ugly duckling, the good kid down on her luck, in order to construct reader sympathy for a woman who is otherwise the object of envy. Embedded in this long, very American tale is the ethos of the self-made woman. Moore has overcome, we learn, deep insecurities about her self-worth, her body, and her beauty in order to pursue her passion for acting. She succeeds not by education and training but through determination, hard work, and keenly honed instincts. She quit taking acting classes, she claims, because she could not stand "being judged and failing," and so she succeeds through a unique talent. The article repeatedly represents Moore as a subject rather than an object, and a subject cut of a rare cloth: "'I'm ambitious and very driven,' Moore concedes. 'I want [stardom]. I'm not, like, Oh, yes, well, if it happens.' I really want this'" (106).

This difference from the common run is represented not only in her childhood hardships, her unique talent, and her extraordinary ambition, but also in her childbearing practices. Moving to Kentucky just three weeks short of her expected delivery to be with her husband when he is on location, Moore takes her childbirth experience into her own hands. After contacting a local doctor to ensure help with delivery, Moore reports, "I said, This is how I want it to be. Do you have a problem?" (144). This representation, as I read it, works in two ways. It again constructs Moore as unique, but it also illustrates her appropriation of the expert advice that in the broader discourse is used to construct pregnant women as the subjects who do not know. Her appropriation of that construction, while it does not allow Moore to escape expertise, does allow her agency in its exercise. Her appropriation is seen as successful, because the article continues to represent her throughout as a good mother, nursing her first child until she is two years old, bringing her to the movie set every day, and watching *Sesame Street* on television.

The subject that emerges from this narrative is in many ways oppositional to the subject that emerges from the popular discourse of pregnancy. Moore is represented as certainly beautiful and not as subject to medical advice, but rather as an agent able to appropriate that expertise to her own ends. Most important, her ability to satisfy her own desires—she's "passionate" about her work, "wild" about her child, and "deeply committed" to her husband—seems hardly constrained by her pregnancy. True, this representation does more to construct Moore as exotic than to open her subject position to occupancy by other pregnant women, but the initial article does succeed in rehabilitating the pregnant body as an object of desire—an object position long denied that body.

Recuperating the cover shot as a text that opens possibilities for even greater freedom continues in subsequent articles. An article appearing a year later takes "the shot that was seen round the world" as a central concern. Entitled "Demi's Body Language," it opens with this question: "How did Demi Moore transform herself from the nude madonna who graced the most talked-about magazine of the year into the sleek siren of these pages?" (112). In this opening sentence, Moore is represented as a mother, a sex goddess, and an active subject capable of transformation. The metonymic link of maternity and sexuality is extended both with photographs accompanying the text and within the text itself. One photograph shows Moore stretched across the floor, one knee raised to accentuate both her muscle tone and her waistline, and arms raised toward her head, allowing full exposure of her breasts and loose hair.

Particularly interesting are the different ways the two rhetors in this situation, Moore and writer Jennet Conant, interpret the change in Moore's body—a change that already works against the popular discourse that writes pregnancy as a movement that affects no substantial change.[3] A tag-line in the corner of the photo (headed "Naked Truth") quotes Moore: "I said I would get better with each baby and I have" (114). Moore thereby claims the change in her body as evidence of progress, as a good situation getting even better. Conant describes the change as from a "gamin," a "fresh, androgynous figure" who, "after nearly five years of marriage to actor Bruce Willis, and two babies . . . has grown up. . . . Moore looks lusher now"; this description is more ambiguous than Moore's about whether the change is truly progress or simply difference. The contest between Moore and Conant continues in their reading of the cover shot. Moore claims that the linkage between maternity and sexuality is a "feminist statement," and "says she's proud to have had a positive influence on America's uptight national character. 'The nicest surprise,' she says, 'is that people were moved by something I did that was very natural to me, and that in the process I could have done something to make other women look at themselves differently'" (118). In this declamation, Moore seeks to include readers in a construction of themselves as objects of desire, an inclusion more emphatically invited here than in the article that ran with the cover. Conant, however, troubles Moore's reading of her actions and that text. She precedes Moore's interpretation of the picture with comments on the widespread publicity it earned, which made it "the most controversial nude since Andrew Wyeth's Helga." She notes Moore's previous admission that she discussed with photographer Annie Leibovitz certain possibilities for the cover: "Wouldn't it be kind of quirky or goofy to put a pregnant woman in black lingerie?". And she follows this by writing that "it wasn't exhibitionism as much as a natural expression of the way she was feeling at the time." Conant thus raises the possibility that it *was* exhibitionism that prompted the cover photo. Conant flags for the reader, too, the recuperation Moore is exercising over the reading of the photo: "She has a pronounced ability to interpret events as meaningful experiences" (118).

Moore's attempt to claim the photo as a feminist statement that opens possibilities for greater freedom for more than just herself, troubled and contested here, is pursued in a third article, published in December 1993. Moore claims the cover again over a headline, "Demi's Big Wish." The visual texts here make noteworthy departures from those of the previous two articles. While the cover shot is a typical holiday piece with Moore perched on a Santa-suited David Letterman's lap, two inside shots accompanying the text emphasize not Moore's status as a sex goddess but her role as a mother. And both are photographic renderings of scenes from famous oil paintings. In one, a supine Moore turns her backside to the camera and gazes at the reflection of her face in a mirror while resting her arms on the edge of a couch draped in scarlet. On the couch lies an infant (though not one of Moore's), naked and sleeping, with a feather boa that suggests wings. A tag-line reads, "The Visitation—Demi Moore poses here in a photo inspired by Velazquez." A second photo shows Moore costumed in a nineteenth-century gown, one shoulder bared, gazing out heavily draped French doors. Its tag-line reads, "Woman at Window." The accompanying story, titled "Demi's State of Grace," spends more than half its column inches on Moore's role as mother, opening with a description of her normalcy as a mom waiting for afternoon kindergarten to end, a woman who "could pass for any other mom today." Her third pregnancy is becoming visible on her body "but not so much that her condition announces itself" (Bennett 178). It continues with a profile of the scheduling and staffing strategies that allow Moore in pursue both her career ambitions and her proclaimed dedication to her children.

This article positions Moore much more frequently in relationship to other mothers, both in its opening paragraph and in its later reports of the morning (and afternoon) sickness plaguing her third pregnancy. But once again, the article turns to the cover photo of Moore naked and pregnant. Writer Leslie Bennett characterizes the photo as a shrewd move by an ambitious actress: "She even figured out a way to turn pregnancy into a *cause célèbre* with the infamous nude *Vanity Fair* cover that was shot when she was hugely pregnant with Scout" (178). Moore never directly addresses that cover shot, but when the interviewing writer turns to a discussion of sexism in Hollywood, Moore resists being positioned by the writer as playing into an agenda that tends to "glamorize the premise of women being sold as sex objects." Instead, Moore interprets her position as that of an agent of change for greater liberation: "'I want to see great change take place for women, and I want to be part of the solution,' she says brightly. 'But it doesn't serve me to get caught up in any negativity about what isn't. Let's go in and see what we can do about what is'" (180). The rhetorical move of reinterpreting her actions as resistant, practiced in the earlier articles, is repeated even more frequently in this one. Moore deflects questions about how many staff persons she employs to care for her children and defends her right to do so. She emphatically claims her right to be both mother and movie star: "I have the passion and desire to not compromise any of my goals. If I had to choose, I'm clear on what it would be. But I'm being shown by the doing that I don't have to choose." The writer concedes the closing lines of the article to a quote from Moore, a declamation that once again Moore claims as resistant and progressive:

Having it all just means having the things that make you happy. . . . There isn't any reason why you shouldn't try. . . . When they say, 'Well, this is how it's always been,' I say, 'Well, why can't it be different?' If I see it as possible, it is possible. (215)

This series of articles, then, offers rhetorical confirmation that Demi Moore's pregnant body successfully rehabilitates that often-excluded body as an object of desire. It simultaneously contests Moore's proposition that her cover photo makes a feminist statement that is somehow liberatory, by countering that the photo represents a moment of exhibitionism, an opportunism that supports and so reinscribes voyeuristic control of the woman's body, and by continuing the construction of Moore as so exotic that her subject position is unique and cannot be occupied by others. But, particularly in Moore's rhetorical claims, it also reveals the play of interpretations available, the possibilities that may be open to women who interpret Moore's claims for agency as available for themselves.

Public Uptake

I now consider this interpretive play through a reading of the letters sent to and published by *Vanity Fair* in the October issue following the release of the contested cover, but I am fully aware that this interpretation is compromised in a couple of ways. First, all that I am reading are those letters the magazine chose to publish, a choice certainly governed by the magazine's self-interest and in no way representative of the full range of available responses. Second, I am aware that regarding reader response as an interpretation of multiple discourses is always troublesome because it leaves open a range of questions about the purposiveness of the reading. In any event, treating interpretation as if it were free of cultural constraints is naive at best and threatens to leave material rhetoric empty as a critical practice of interpretation. I merely consider these letters useful as a means of identifying a few of the interpretations made of the picture, and as a means of further investigating Moore's claim to have made a feminist statement that provides a possibility for greater agency and thus liberty. *Vanity Fair* published thirty-four readers' letters, introducing them with a paragraph claiming a "deluge" of letters and reporting the results of several media polls, including one "with opinion dividing right down the middle" (October 1994 28). The published letters include twenty-one applauding the cover, nine disparaging it, and four too ambivalent to categorize.

That interpretative play is never free of cultural constraints becomes evident if the letters are categorized by topical content. The sacred and the taboo occupy six of the writers. Three claim that exposing the pregnant body to public view violates it; one explicitly claims this photo as pornographic, and another claims she "felt categorized and violated" (Bowie 34). Two others simply report that they are offended and will no longer purchase the magazine. A sixth writer engages the photo from another perspective within the dualism: "We are so unused to seeing powerful images of women that Demi ignites like a cross before vampires" (Hogan 34). These letters thus serve as evidence both of the continuing power of the traditional splitting of the feminine body along the siren/sanctified divide, and of the power of the visual disruption. Seven writers engage the photo as a work of art, mostly applauding Leibovitz's mastery of composition. That for many readers this text operates as representation of the beautiful is evident in the connections made between it and canonized works: "Renoir and Bonnard would have applauded," writes one (Rogers 34); "A new Eve. Perfect," writes another (Thorson 34). A long letter applauding the photo as art compares it to Jacob Epstein's sculptures of nude pregnant women, claiming that Moore's pose "is almost exactly that" of Epstein's *Genesis* (Silber 34). Only one of the seven disparages it as art, claiming that it crosses the line between sophistication and bad taste. Three letters claim that the work serves an educational function—two specifically that it is instructional for women seeking a better body image. Three others claim it as a victory for freedom of the press. The remaining letters all read the photo as working within categories of mirror-imaging or memorialization, and these letters most directly engage Moore's proposition. Two women applaud it for representing the beauty of their own pregnant bodies; three men claim that it commemorates for them their wives' beauty during pregnancy. Another woman rejects it, claiming "most women don't want to look at their own abdomens enceinte" (Handley 34). An obstetrician suggests that pregnant women will see themselves reflected in Moore and will therefore be able to see themselves as beautiful (Berman 28).

A Material Re-reading

The readers' response to this photo serves as further evidence that this visual text is open to contestatory readings, but readings still shaped by the conditions of the popular discourse of pregnancy and by an artistic tradition that represents naked women as objects of beauty composed for men. It also points to the several ways women inscribe this visual text on their own bodies, and these ways suggest that Moore's and Leibovitz's rehabilitation of the pregnant body as an object of male desire does make that object position available to other women, in spite of the relentless rhetorical construction of Moore as an exotic.

It is still open and contested whether this cover photo is a feminist statement that operates to increase the ability of pregnant women to mediate reason and desire intersubjectively in order to satisfy their own desires. These letters reveal the rhetorical muscle of the popular discourse of pregnancy. Most letter-writers engage the text as saying something about pregnant woman as uncertainly desirable. Three explicitly invoke the authority of medicine in an effort to claim the photo as educational. But the letters also reveal that this photo makes the pregnant body present in the moment in a way that the popular discourse of pregnancy does not when it locates that body temporally as secured to a future moment that brings a return of the past, and spatially when it describes the pregnant body's movement as circular, returning unchanged.

What these letters reveal perhaps most clearly is the persuasive force of visual representation, a medium of representation often neglected by a more traditional rhetorical method. A number of these letters provide evidence of the ways the visual text is taken up as a commemoration of the corporal body, or as providing a possibility for new ways of representing a body often secreted away from representation. Not one of these letters even tangentially engages the written text, which runs more than four thousand words. The written contests between Moore and her interviewers may be erased by the power of the visual text. What a material rhetoric has done in this chapter is to read between these multiple inscriptions—bodily, visual, and textual—and to map the relationships among them. It has specified how the object of the cover shot disrupts the stable understanding of the de-eroticized pregnant body in popular American culture and identifies the possibilities for increased agency in it. It also furthers our understanding of the ways in which dominant discourses write our bodies, how those inscriptions are mobilized in material practices, and how the practices may be transformed through them. It has not sought to dissolve the object of study into itself—as Dillip Gaonkar claims a meta-discourse of interpretation is wont to do—nor to operate as a mediator of claims to truth. Instead, as a practice of material rhetoric, it has sought to keep the conversation open, the contest still running, because in that possibility of continued interpretive play lies the possibility for greater mediation and thus for greater change. A material rhetoric takes the disruption made by the picture of Demi Moore as, if only possibly, a feminist statement, but almost certainly as a rhetorical statement full of the promise of change. Whether that change is for the better, in allowing for greater agency by a pregnant woman, or for the worse, reinscribing yet another moment of a woman's life when she is vulnerable to scopic control, remains open to discussion.

Notes

1. My notion of how things and bodies signify arises from two sources. Walter Benjamin, in his theory of language, proposes that objects signify simply by their physical being, and that it is the obligation of persons to translate that "lamp-language" into the language of man. While I do not share Benjamin's ethical position that by so translating things we approach a universal language that will bring a return of a lost paradisiacal language, I do share his convictions that things indeed signify and that those significations are open to multiple and contested readings. Maxine Sheets-Johnstone claims that power begins in the inscriptions of corporal bodies that species members "read" for potentials of a "series of species-specific capabilities," and that those readings are the opening sallies in negotiations for group power and satisfactions.

2. Emily Martin provides an insightful discussion of the ways in which a woman's reproductive organs are designated as failures in numerous situations, and she provides compelling arguments that these labels have been used to subject women to the discipline of expert advice as well as to further constrict the arena within which a woman can be considered "normal."

3. A further area of study that material rhetoric might usefully pursue would be a method of reading that pays attention to the multiple rhetors competing for sway in numerous popular texts. In this chapter, I have restricted my analysis to the rhetorical moves deployed by Moore, Leibovitz, and the article-writers, but it might be expanded to include the magazine's editors, who finally determine what gets printed, the publishers who exercise veto capabilities, and the multiple advertisers who must be appeased by editorial content.

Works Cited

Asante, K. Molefi. *The Afrocentric Idea*. Philadephia: Temple University Press, 1987.

Bazerman, Charles. *Shaping Written Knowledge*. Madison: University of Wisconsin Press, 1988.

Benjamin, Walter. "On Language as Such and on the Language of Man." In *Reflections: Essays, Aphorisms, Autobiographical Writings*, by Walter Benjamin, edited by Peter Demetz, 314–33. New York: Schocken, 1986.

Bennetts, Leslie. "Demi's State of Grace." *Vanity Fair*, December 1993: 176–81, 208–15.

Berger, John. *Ways of Seeing*. London: BBC and Penguin Books, 1972.

Berkenkotter, Carol, and Thomas Huckin. *Genre Knowledge in Disciplinary Communication: Cognition/Culture/Power*. Hillsdale, N.J.: Lawrence Erlbaum, 1995.

Berman, Richard L. Letter. *Vanity Fair*, October 1991: 28.

Bowie, Martha F. Letter. *Vanity Fair*, October 1991: 34.

Collins, Nancy. "Demi's Big Moment." *Vanity Fair*, December 1993: 56.

Conant, Jennett. "Demi's Body Language." *Vanity Fair*, August 1992: 112–18, 188–90.

Feldon, Leah. "Dressing for Two." *Redbook*, November 1993: G-3.

Gaonkar, Dillip. "The Idea of Rhetoric in the Rhetoric of Science." In *Rhetorical Hermeneutics: Invention and Interpretation in the Age of Science*, edited by Alan Gross and William M. Keith, 25–85. Albany: SUNY Press, 1997.

Geisler, Cheryl. *Academic Literacy and the Nature of Expertise*. Hillsdale, N.J.: Lawrence Erlbaum, 1994.

Handley, Barbara W. Letter. *Vanity Fair*, October 1991: 34.

Hogan, Mary Ann. Letter. *Vanity Fair*, October 1991: 34.

Kristeva, Julia. *Tales of Love*. Translated by Leon Roudiez. New York: Columbia University Press, 1987.

Martin, Emily. *The Woman in the Body: A Cultural Analysis of Reproduction*. Boston: Beacon, 1990.

Menter, Marcia. "Beauty Strategies for Pregnant Moms." *Redbook*, November 1993: 74, 76.

Roberts, Roxanne. "The Truth about Sex during Pregnancy." *Redbook*, April 1994: 62.

Rogers, Dolores. Letter. *Redbook*, October 1991: 34.

Selzer, Jack, ed. *Understanding Scientific Prose*. Madison: University of Wisconsin Press, 1993.

Sheets-Johnstone, Maxine. *The Roots of Power: Animate Form and Gendered Bodies*. Chicago: Open Court, 1994.

Silber, Evelyn. Letter. *Vanity Fair*, October 1991: 34.

Thorson, James A. Letter. *Vanity Fair*, October 1991: 34.

Wells, Susan. *Sweet Reason: Rhetoric and the Discourses of Modernity*. Chicago: University of Chicago Press, 1996.

14 *Yameng Liu*

Dick Morris, Ideology, and Regulating the Flow of Rhetorical Resources

On 30 August 1996, just as the Democratic National Convention in Chicago was about to reach its celebratory climax, Dick Morris—President Clinton's chief political consultant, and a man who had been widely credited with everything from formulating winning strategies for the president to scripting the hugely successful convention itself—was suddenly forced to resign in the wake of a tabloid exposé of his year-long liaison with a Washington call girl. The revelation was as stunning as it was disturbing. Not only had Morris, a married man whose advice had led to the president's endorsement of "family values," associated with a prostitute over an extended period; he also had allegedly discussed White House business with her and even let her listen in on his private calls with Clinton. The scandal, however did not seem to change significantly the way Morris was perceived and represented in the mainstream media.

The pre-scandal journalistic coverage of Morris tended to single out two facts as the defining features of his professional life: he had worked for candidates of both parties; and he was responsible for Clinton's effort to appropriate issues and positions traditionally belonging to Republicans. A political analysis of the Clinton presidency in a May 1996 issue of the *New York Times Magazine* set the tone for other stories about Morris when it identified him as an "ambidextrous operator" and as the "part of Clinton that refuses to walk a clear ideological line." The "most controversial part of Morris," the analyst stated, was "his willingness to work for both Republicans and Democrats" (Purdum 39–40). Exactly the same focus and perspective are found in reports of and comments on Morris's fall and its aftermath. *Newsweek*, similarly characterizing Morris as "an ideologically ambidextrous strategist" ("Lives of the Party" 34), traced his career as a political consultant under the heading "Working Both Sides of the Aisle" (34); *Time* waxed indignant but reaffirmed the same perspective when it referred to the fallen strategist as a "highly paid political prostitute" guilty of "ideological promiscuity." The Morris case, writer Lance Morrow suggests, "opens a door" not on "Dick Morris' character (who cares?)," but on "a general atmosphere of sleaze" that "causes the agile politician to dance around repudiating things that he held sacred day before yesterday" said accounts for "the polymorphous con jobs on political display" (78). And in a more recent comment on Morris's new book *Behind the Oval Office*, *New York Times* columnist Maureen Dowd insists that "in this bodice ripper, the bodice doesn't belong to the call girl who caused Morris' expulsion from paradise." Morris "says he focuses on issues" rather than image, Dowd further points out, yet "what he really means is that you can choose issues to project image." As a result of trying to turn everything into an instrument of power, "the presidency has been corrupted and even ruined by quantitative thinking" about gains or losses in the polls (17).

For the mainstream media, then, Morris's most serious ethical lapse is neither his involvement in the sex scandal nor even his betrayal of trust, but his flagrant transgression of established political, ideological, and ultimately rhetorical boundaries. The public opinion-makers' outrage over Morris's conduct reminds us of their earlier frowning on David Gergen, a prominent Republican pundit who accepted Clinton's appointment as the White House communication director early in the Democratic president's first term. Both cases draw our attention to an unwritten rule of rhetorical behavior: a communication expert working in the domain of politics should commit herself only to one particular ideological stance and should work only to advance the interests and causes consistent with that commitment. To violate this rule and to offer services to clients regardless of their party affiliation is to court two serious consequences. First, the violator would turn her expertise into mere mercenary skills and would deprive herself of a vitally important axiological core. Second, should unscrupulous consults and politicians be locked, in Dowd's words, in an "unholy," "obsessive" relationship about "point spreads" (17), the political power concerned would be corrupted or even ruined. Dowd's dire prognosis shows the extent to which mainstream American political culture remains firmly convinced of the need to keep the employment of rhetorical skills under control. It explains the rather peculiar way in which Morris has been identified in mass media, as well as the reason that his case has been turned into a bald cautionary tale against working both sides of the two-party political formation. It betrays, more significantly, a deep-seated anxiety over an emerging free market of the kind of services Morris specializes in.

What bothers public opinion is not the political elite's unrestricted access to rhetorical resources, but its alliance with the *free-flowing* type of *embodied* rhetorical resources. Had Morris offered his services exclusively and consistently to the Democrats, his problem would most likely have been represented as yet another celebrity sex scandal, and few journalists would have paid attention to his tendency to think of everything—issue, value, and principle included—in terms of its political profitability to his client. Rhetorical savvy, in other words, is considered a legitimate commodity as long as it is circulated within, say, *either* a COMECON *or* an ECM. No restriction is placed on its movement inside the borders of the trading bloc to which it belongs. It becomes contraband, however, as soon as it starts to move in and out of the two competing markets freely, without due regard for the *ideologically constituted* line demarcating one from the other. Such an assumption points to a hitherto unrecognized feature of the complex relationship between ideology and rhetoric: ideology's function as a key mechanism in regulating the deployment and movement of human resources in contemporary rhetorical practices.

From a historical perspective, as Michael Billig observes, rhetoric and ideology might not seem to be connected at all: the "very concept of 'ideology' was a product of that new movement of thought which swept aside . . . the older, prescientific modes of thought, foremost amongst which was classical rhetoric" (3). Kenneth Burke's rhetorical analysis of ideology as a central Marxist concept changes this perception once and for all. Distinguishing among seven meanings of the term "ideology" (e.g., "a system of ideas, aiming at social or political action"; "any set of interrelated terms, having practical civic consequences"; "myth" designed for purposes of "government control"), Burke argues persuasively for seeing ideology as quintessentially rhetorical. Among the reasons he offers are the orientation of the concept toward the extralinguistic (e.g., "civic consequences"), its functioning as an inducement of social and political action, its mode of passing the factional for the universal (a well-established means of persuasion/argumentation), and conversely its utility as a tool of rhetorical criticism when the veiled, partisan, interested character of any system of ideas is exposed and the system's claim to universal validity is discredited (103–4). On the basis of Burke's original ideas, a new consensus is emerging among contemporary scholars that no ideologically free or neutral rhetorical practice ever exists, and that, Sharon Crowley's words, there is no way rhetoricians "can denounce partisanship and remain rhetoricians" (455). As a result of this consensus, a powerful ideological approach to rhetorical analysis has been developing. Known as "ideological criticism," this approach "focuses on how conflict, power, and material interests shape and influence social and symbolic interaction"; it takes a special interest in "the political dimensions of discourse in order to expose the underlying beliefs and assumptions at work in rhetorical theory and practice" (McPhail 340).

While ideology has thus become a key concept in contemporary rhetoric, redirecting the collective attention of rhetoricians back to the conflict of political interests and power relations that gave rise to rhetoric as a specialized study of discourse in the first place, the term is being employed mainly as a generative topic—an analytical tool, an argumentative device, and a focal point for clustering a group of otherwise dispersed and unrelated terms into a new functional set; in short, it has become a versatile *resource* for enabling and thematizing rhetorical practices. Yet the journalistic coverage of the Morris case throws light on another dimension of the role ideology has been playing in the current disciplinary formation of rhetoric. Perhaps unknown to many practicing rhetors affected by this dimension, ideology has been serving as a key component of what Foucault terms a "complex grid" of prohibitions. Foucault uses the metaphor of a prohibitive grid in order to defamiliarize the "order of discourse" to which we are all subject. In every society, he observes, the production of discourse is "at once controlled, selected, organized, and redistributed by a certain number of procedures whose role is to ward off its powers and dangers, to gain mastery over its chance events, to evade its ponderous, formidable materiality." He identifies three of the procedures as the most instrumental: the forbidden speech, the reason/madness division, and the will to truth. These three "intersect, reinforce, or compensate for each other," forming a network of prohibitions and ensuring that "we do not have the right to say everything" or that "we cannot speak of just anything in any circumstances whatever" ("Order of Discourse" 154–55).

Although Foucault's discussion is conducted at a level of generalization too high to bear directly on the interpretation of the Morris case per se, it nevertheless offers a perspective on two implications of the way the case has been reported and analyzed. By reissuing in no uncertain terms what appears to be a standing commandment against "working both sides of the aisle," or against transgressing an invisible yet all too real boundary, the journalistic representation partakes in a broad effort to control the powers and dangers of politically oriented rhetorical practices, or to contain the "ponderous, formidable materiality" of these practice—a materiality which, if left unchecked, is capable of asserting itself by corrupting or even ruining the powerful. And in identifying Morris's ideological ambidexterity as his single most unpardonable sin, this rhetoric not only pinpoints ideology as a key mechanism for containing the formidable power of materiality, but it also identifies regulation of the flow of embodied rhetorical resources as ideology's characteristic mode of operation. This regulatory operation is conducted through the imposition of a set of *normative*, ideology-related constraints on the behavior of the law-abiding practitioners of rhetoric, including its theorists. Foremost among the warrants by which the prohibitive function claims its normative status are the equation of the ideological with the ethical and the institutionalized principle of ideological consistency.

Constrained by a need to maintain ideological consistency, political consultants in general have to establish their party affiliation or define their basic political stance and then work within the confines of that carefully cultivated ethos. A political consultant is always identified with a specific brand of ideology; someone who is affiliated with the Democrats or who belongs to the liberal camp, for example, is expected to offer professional expertise only in the service of causes endorsed or promoted by that party or camp. To devise communication strategies for opposing camps or incompatible causes is to violate a taboo, and the violation is almost certain to cost the violator her rhetorical ethos and professional credibility. The same fate awaits any public commentator or opinion-maker in the journalistic domain. The circulation of rhetorical resources in this domain is similarly governed by the principle of ideological consistency. Rhetorically agile commentators who argue for, say, the pro-life cause one week and the pro-choice cause the next, are unlikely to get sympathy and understanding even from readers who are sophisticated enough to acknowledge, *in principle* or *in theory*, that there are always at least two (equally legitimate) sides to any case, and that it is reasonable for one's perspective, always in a dynamic process of being recontextualized, to change from situation to situation.

The same unwritten rule is obeyed even by theorists of rhetoric, who are supposedly more removed from the specific operational details of the public sphere. A probe into what accounts for the largely tacit and voluntary adherence to the principle leads us to identify the fusion of the ideological with the ethical as an even more pivotal underwriter of this prohibitive function. Many who practice ideological criticism, for example, deem it their moral duty to represent what Mark McPhail calls "those marginalized by hegemonic social and discursive structures." They adopt and maintain this stance out of the conviction that once the ideological character of discourse has been acknowledged, there are only two opposed courses of action available to any rhetorical critic: either "[participating] in the emancipation" of the non-dominant groups "by taking the ideological turn," or "[becoming] complicit in their oppression by invoking the analytical abstractions and objective approaches of traditional criticism" (McPhail 341). Despite their conceptual idealism, theorists like McPhail no doubt would find the rigorous structural and ethical dichotomy they have thus set up disturbingly suspect and titillatingly deconstructible, were they to be made aware of it. For power, as Foucault reminds us, is always "exercised from innumerable points," and "there is no binary and all-encompassing opposition between rulers and ruled at the root of power relations . . . extending from the top down and reacting on more and more limited groups to the very depths of the social body" (*History of Sexuality* 94).

These theorists, moreover, are certainly too conversant with established rhetorical interpretations of ideology not to understand that, in Burke's words, whoever gives "the word ['ideology'] a strong dyslogistic weighting" would too "be resoundingly dyslogized by it" (105). The rule of rhetorical invention is such that as Burke sees it, the ideology of ideological criticism itself is always a legitimate and productive object of analysis. An ideological analysis of those forms of ideological criticism that focus on examining the political motivation of the analyzed would no doubt raise questions about the critics' own motivation: are they motivated by the interests of the marginalized and the oppressed social groups they claim to represent, or rather by the need for "maintaining [their] practitioners, their preferred texts and their preferred methods in a dominant position within the academy" (Crowley 454)—or both? And yet the ethicalization of ideology has been so thorough that the reflexive instinct of the practitioners has largely been suppressed, and not much interest in a political self-anatomy has been shown even by those concerned primarily with the political. Both among the ideologically self-conscious practitioners, who are fully aware of the interested nature of their own practices, and among those who deny the necessary partisanship of their own stances, the general tendency is to stick to the stance that one has chosen as the only morally sound position, and to view any deviation from that position as an ethical lapse. As a result, the rhetorical resources or capital, once invested, tend to stay where they were put; they do not usually flow out of even those markets of received ideas that have already been theoretically saturated, and toward the emerging markets of new (if still *out(-)land*ish) perspectives in quest of higher rhetorical profits or dividends. The moral dichotomization within which ideological positions are defined and the law of ideological consistency, functioning powerfully and yet inconspicuously as a Foucauldian "procedure of prohibition," have together prevented the insiders from formulating (self-)critiques against what Billig terms "those vanguard ideologies, which seek to replace the contradictions of common sense by the coherent philosophy of the party" (26).

The ideological regime in rhetorical practices imposes all kinds of party lines within which a contemporary rhetor is *expected* to stake out her individual "homestead"—constituted usually of a more or less fixed combination of a specific area of investigation, a particular and clearly identifiable approach, a limited and coherent set of philosophical assumptions, and a consistently cultivated theoretical or professional persona. The procedure helps give practitioners in this field a reassuring sense of direction, order, security, and ethical propriety. Yet modern discursive economy is such that discouraging the human resources they represent from moving freely across all kinds of boundaries in search of newer and more interesting inventional possibilities may not be in the best interest of rhetorical production. For example, the need to remain committed to the ideologically specific position one has subscribed to (e.g., the "emancipatory" or the "critical"), and to avoid being perceived as switching to the opposing side (e.g., the "hegemonic" or the "conservative"), often tends to perpetuate old binary discursive formations and to prevent counterdiscourses from developing *within* what has emerged as the popular or dominant way of thinking. Keeping a lot of rhetorical capital within the narrow confines of one particular mode of practice also leads to scholarly inefficiency and "stagflation." The subtle pressure not to wander away from one's own homestead often results in pious repetition of the same set of tenets, or in meticulous reaffirmation of the same familiar posture. All this goes against what Richard Rorty describes as the trend of European linguistic practices since the end of the eighteenth century: "changing at a faster and faster rate," with "more people offering more radical redescriptions of more things than ever before," and with "young people going through half a dozen spiritual gestalt-switches before reaching adulthood" (7).

There is, moreover, nothing natural or permanent about either equating the ideological with the ethical, or using ideological consideration as a key mechanism for controlling the movement and distribution of resources in rhetorical practices. Synchronically, practicing rhetors in the domain of law, for instance, are not generally subject to ideological constraints. An attorney could provide legal counsel to clients across the entire political spectrum without being accused of becoming "ideologically ambidextrous." Compunction of conscience is seldom felt even by those who render service to unpopular causes or to known felons. Within the cultural framework of legal discourse, there is little expectation for contemporary practitioners of forensic rhetoric to identify with and stick to one particular ideological stance as a precondition for professional success. And diachronically, though the concept can be applied retroactively to rhetorical practices long before the term "ideology" was invented, there is no basis for assuming that classical rhetoricians attached the same importance to the principle of ideological consistency; rather, the principle gradually became institutionalized and universalized as a result of changing social and cultural conditions.

A sophistic education "required students to argue both sides of the thesis, as a way of helping them see the many facets of an issue." By their "immediate teaching," the sophists "obscured the traditional patterns of Greek morality and raised up a generation of skeptics prepared to argue for any action which seemed to their own interest" (Murphy et al. 22). Aristotle insists in *On Rhetoric* that persuasion through character (*ethos*) "should result from the speech, not from a previous opinion that the speaker is a certain kind of person" (1356a). For him, in other words, character is a context-specific construct rather than a consistently maintained stance deriving from the traits associated with a material speaker. And despite all his emphasis on ethical ideals in *De Oratore*, Cicero—as Michael Grant points out—"was frequently compelled or induced by circumstances to champion unworthy causes for short-term results, and his peculiar gifts often enabled him to guide them to success" (22). Grant's observation is heavily tinted by his own ideological commitment. The connotation of words such as *compelled*, *unworthy*, or *short-term* is indicative of his rather than Cicero's judgment. Cicero in fact declares it "the greatest possible mistake" to suppose that speeches made in court contain rhetors' "considered and certified opinions." All those speeches, he announces, merely "reflect the demands of some particular case or emergency." Although that claim is dismissed by Grant as "opportunistic inconsistency . . . elevated into a principle" (23), it shows nevertheless that at least until Cicero's time, it remained assumed that rhetorical resources did not have to be held hostage to the rhetor's personal opinion or ideology. Whether in Aristotle's delinking of *ethos* from the actual ideological stance the rhetor happens to espouse in real life, or in Cicero's more explicit declaration that the speech has nothing to do with the rhetor's "certified opinions," classical practitioners of the art of persuasion got a license to apply rhetorical skills freely, without being bothered by prior political or ideological considerations. Had Dick Morris worked as a practicing rhetor in Aristotle's or Cicero's time, it would have been very strange if his practice as an "ideologically ambidextrous strategist" had provoked ire and condemnation from the classical counterpart of what we now call "public opinion." He *was* expected to be ambidextrous in responding to the demands or exigencies of each "particular case and emergency."

The contrast of two diametrically opposed expectations helps to identify yet another difference between classical and modern rhetoric. More relevantly, it throws light on the historically contingent means by which ideology came to be used as a controlling mechanism. A heightened awareness of a causal relationship among changing cultural conditions, changing status and function of key concepts, and changing rhetorical behaviors makes us wonder if Morris's wanton transgression of traditional ideological lines may not in fact signify the decline of ideology's role as a means for (to paraphrase Foucault) denying rhetors their right to argue for every position they find interesting or to address any topic "in any circumstances whatever." And this awareness further makes us wonder if this situation may not be symptomatic of some profound ongoing cultural changes that, ironically, work toward restoring the classical norm of a freer movement of embodied rhetorical resources. In his National Public Radio commentary on the Morris scandal, James Fallows notes "how very important political 'consultants' have become" within the short time of one generation, and how both their power and their celebrity have soared as journalists, "bored with interviewing mere party officials, have grown fascinated with experts who can provide clever campaign 'spin'" ("A Dip in the Bathos Tub"). Without disputing the factual part of Fallow's observation, it ought to take something more than mere boredom on the journalists' part to explain why the rhetoric of *party* officials has lost its appeal, and why the more detached and fluid campaign spin generated by someone conceptually unrestricted by party line has become increasingly fascinating to the public. Even though mainstream journalists in general had distanced themselves dutifully from Morris's practice of bipartisan counseling even before the publication of the exposé, they could not help but marvel at the enormous influence he was able to exert over the political processes of this country. In Eric Pooley's detailed profile of Morris in *Time*, published on the eve of his fall from grace, awe of Morris's prowess and admiration for his savvy easily overwhelm a sense of uneasiness about his character and his ideologically incorrect mode of practice. Moreover, only seven or eight months after Morris's humiliation, the talk of the town had become his "rehabilitation" as a public figure. All this indicates that even if people still feel far from comfortable with the blurring of familiar ideological lines, they are becoming more and more indifferent or even accommodative toward the kind of illicit boundary-crossing Morris specializes in.

This increasingly blasé attitude accounts for the dramatic improvement in President Clinton's approval rate after he started practicing, at Morris's urging, a kind of flagrant political transvestism. From Clinton we are led to similar efforts to de-emphasize ideological differences in the party politics of other countries (e.g., Britain), and in an even broader context, to a post–Cold War, postmodern world where hard and fast walls have been crumbling, ideology has lost its importance as a key player in international politics, the identity of many nations becomes difficult to tell, and the concept of "nation" as a coherent political entity is itself being challenged. What we are facing is a brave new world definable more and more by hard-to-regulate movements of personnel, information, resources, and products across all kinds of boundaries in the name of globalization. The unfettered growth of a global finance market and the constant, huge flows of capital across borders in search of speculative opportunities, for instance, have posed a serious challenge to the sovereignty and autonomy of any self-contained political entity.

This relentless process of globalization is dominated, in Stuart Hall's words, "by the image which crosses and re-crosses linguistic frontiers much more rapidly and more easily, and which speaks across languages in a much more immediate way" (27). An "over-integrated, over-concentrated, and condensed form of economic power" is "[living] culturally through difference" and "constantly teasing itself with pleasures of the transgressive Other" (31). It is hardly surprising, therefore, that Frederic Jameson observes that pastiche, a "neutral practice" of mimicry devoid of "any conviction that alongside the abnormal tongue . . . some healthy linguistic normality still exists," has risen to displace parody as the dominant stylistic mode of this postmodern, post-literacy situation, and that the practice of "random cannibalization of all the styles of the past" or "the play of random stylistic allusion" has become the new norm (17–18). Today, crossing boundaries or frontiers is increasingly routine. Random, kaleidoscopic regrouping of disparate perspectives and concepts, in total disregard of existing rules or taboos, is only to be expected. Old divisions, categories, and differences are utilized more as targets than as guidelines. Against this cultural backdrop, Morris's case quivers with meaning for contemporary rhetoricians.

It urges us to re-examine our most fundamental assumptions and to find out what changes or new commitments we have to make so that the conceptualization of rhetoric can better adapt to and reflect changing cultural conditions. It forces us to rethink, in particular, the trend toward a more thoroughgoing ideologization or ethicalization in rhetoric; this does not seem to parallel the trend in the real world, and at its worst, it threatens to impose new party lines, to discourage unorthodox thinking, and to exclude all but one ideologically and hence morally correct position. Finally, the case calls for efforts to define the ideal orator anew for our time. If Clinton exemplifies a new generation of politicians, could Morris (minus the sexual scandal) foreshadow a new generation of practicing rhetors? While serving as Clinton's chief advisor, reports Eric Pooley, Morris would "[fret] at night, imagining that he's running Dole's campaign and plotting against his own best moves" (31). The same writer describes him as "an adviser with no core ideology to make Bill Clinton [or any other of his clients] search for his own," a "gleeful genius who preaches what he's paid to preach, who can teach it round or teach it flat" (24, 26). If this practice goes against the fundamental values of the American people, it is hard to explain why Morris became what *Time* called "the most influential private citizen in America," or why he was on the verge of becoming a "political millionaire" (Pooley 24, 31). His phenomenal ascendance to power can be explained only by a close fit between his unique style, stance, and approach and what actually underlies the present sociopolitical formation and the developing cultural ethos. Whether we acknowledge it or not, a foundational assumption responsible for the development of postmodernist discourse and culture is, as Rorty points out, the understanding that "anything could be made to look good or bad, important or unimportant, useful or useless, by being redescribed" (7).

Pooley's characterization of Morris as a strategist who forfeits his core ideology in order to make his clients search for their own is as inaccurate as it is illuminating. As an individual, as a social and political being, Morris cannot but possess a core ideology—whether that core is as fixed and monolithic as the term suggests is another matter. What is special about him is that unlike many other practitioners, he makes a clear distinction between his private core ideology, which is relatively coherent and stable, and what may be called his *professional ideology*, which is shaped by the contingencies and exigencies

of his changing contexts and circumstances, and which undergoes corresponding metamorphoses. Rather than letting his own *private* ideology determine the
scope of his professional services and set a limit to his rhetorical imagination
in order to maintain his personal ideological constancy, Morris "gleefully" hops
around different camps. Sizing things up from conflicting perspectives, he plots
against one ideology-specific position on behalf of another by deftly thinking
and arguing across ideologically imposed boundaries. His professional disregard for the established borders in no sense means a denial of the ideological or the political nature of any position, stance, policy, or action. Rather, his
disregard forces his clients themselves to become more ideologically self-
conscious. What results from the approach is often a more effective mobiliza-
tion, regrouping, or realliance of diverse interests and resources for the fulfillment of the clients' broadly defined agendas.

The Dick Morris case, trivial as it might appear *prima facie* to rhetorical
critics, thus touches on issues that are by no means only marginally relevant
to the development of contemporary oratory. Among the issues the case has
spotlighted are, first the very nature of the political interests to be identified
and anatomized in rhetorical analysis: Are they stable, clearcut, consistent, and
morally unambiguous, or are they instead combinative, complex, contingent,
context-dependent, and often morally baffling? The second is the relationship
between rhetoric and politics: Are political interests in general better served by
a rhetoric restricted by, or liberated from, the dominant political cartography of
the time? And third, what is the relationship between rhetoric and ethics: does
the ethicality of rhetorical practices reside in remaining committed to one particular stance and in maintaining coherence between one's private and professional ideology, or is it instead embodied in facilitating the mobility, engagement, and productive recombination of public interests? All these issues point
to possibilities for provocative new thinking in rhetorical studies in the long
run. A scholarly consensus may emerge in the future that sees both a genuine
"rhetorical turn" and the rise of rhetoric again as a *power* of great civic consequences (like the practice of legal discourse today) as contingent on the emancipation of pent-up energies and resources through the removal of many imposed or self-imposed constraints. Rhetorical practitioners and theorists alike
may see the need to reclaim their vital cultural right to "speak of just anything
in any circumstances whatever" with ideological or moral impunity—a right
similar to that enjoyed by their sophistic counterparts in the classical age.

More immediately, the issues occasioned inadvertently by the Morris case
put two questions squarely before rhetoricians of our time. Shall we try to foster a new rhetorical culture in which would-be rhetors are encouraged to acquire a genuine ability to see and think from *really* different perspectives, or
shall we instead endeavor to maintain the existing framework, in which rhetors
are warned against thinking and "working both sides of the aisle," or are made

to feel duty-bound to remain committed to one position and to see and argue everything from that position? Shall we work toward relaxing the prohibitive "procedures" and facilitating an ever freer flow of rhetorical resources, or shall we continue to impose a restrictive regime in the name of political commitment, ethical integrity, or ideological probity, even at the cost of a rhetorical study or theory divorced from what is going on rhetorically in the actual world, and unable to exert much material impact on it? For anyone who is concerned about the danger that contemporary rhetoric will lose its relevance, vitality, and power, there can be no escaping these questions.

Works Cited

Aristotle. *On Rhetoric*. Translated by George A. Kennedy. New York: Oxford University Press, 1991.

Billig, Michael. *Ideology and Opinions*. London: Sage, 1991.

Burke, Kenneth. *A Rhetoric of Motives*. 1950. Reprint, Berkeley: University of California Press, 1969.

Crowley, Sharon. "Reflections on an Argument That Won't Go Away: or, a Turn of the Ideological Screw." *Quarterly Journal of Speech* 78 (1992): 450–65.

Dowd, Maureen. "Leaders as Followers." *New York Times*, 12 January 1997.

Fallows, James. "A Dip in the Bathos Tub." *NPR Commentary*, 3 September 1996. Reprinted in *Atlantic Unbound*, http://www.theatlantic.com, 22 October 1997.

Foucault, Michel. *The History of Sexuality*. Vol. 1. Translated by Robert Hurley. New York: Vintage, 1980.

Foucault, Michel. "The Order of Discourse." In *The Rhetorical Tradition*, edited by Patricia Bizzell and Bruce Herzberg, 1,154–64. Boston: Bedford, 1990.

Grant, Michael. Introduction. In *Selected Political Speeches of Cicero*, 7–32. London: Penguin, 1969.

Hall, Stuart. "The Local and the Global: Globalization and Ethnicity." In *Culture, Globalization and the World System*, edited by Anthony D. Kind, 17–39. London: Macmillan, 1991.

Jameson, Frederic. *Postmodernism, or the Cultural Logic of Late Capitalism*. London: Verso, 1991.

"The Lives of the Party." *Newsweek*, 2 September 1996: 28–35.

McPhail, Mark Lawrence. "Ideological Criticism." In *Encyclopedia of Rhetoric and Composition*, edited by Theresa Enos, 340–41. New York: Garland, 1996.

Morrow, Lance. "Does the Morris Thing Matter?" *Time*, 9 September 1996: 78.

Murphy, James J., et al. *A Synoptic History of Classical Rhetoric*. 2d ed. Davis, Calif.: Hermagoras, 1995.

Pooley, Eric. "Who Is Dick Morris?" *Time*, 2 September 1996: 24–31.

Purdum, Todd S. "Facets of Clinton." *New York Times Magazine*, 19 May 1996: 36–41, 62, 77–78.

Rorty, Richard. *Contingency, Irony, and Solidarity*. Cambridge: Cambridge University Press, 1989.

"Working Both Sides of the Aisle." *Newsweek*, 9 September 1996: 34.

15 *Celeste Condit*

The Materiality of Coding
Rhetoric, Genetics, and the Matter of Life

> Man being generically a biological organism, the ideal terminology
> must present his symbolic behavior as grounded in biological
> conditions.
>
> Kenneth Burke, *Permanence and Change*

What Is a Materialist Rhetoric?

A suitably provocative beginning place for a reconsideration of the materiality of human discourse is that code which might arguably be identified as the
generative discourse of living being—the genetic code. Whatever the degree of
determinativeness one assigns to genes, their functioning as a discursive system is surely fascinating. Four nucleic acids—adenine, guanine, cytosine, and
thymine—form the letters of the code. They are arranged along the spiraling
double helix that is called DNA in triplet "words" called codons. When activated, the series of codons specify—by their physical shape and electrical
charges, and through the direct physical interactions of these physical features
with other chemicals—the construction of various series of the twenty amino
acids that are the building blocks of life. The further serializing of these amino
acid chains specifies a theoretically near-infinite series of enzymes or proteins, the "writing" of which constitutes the structural/material skeletons of all
known living things.

This stunningly metaphorical image of DNA as the basic code of life has
not, however, gone uncontested. Like that other major code-based entity fundamental to human life—rhetoric—the discourse of genetics has been viewed
and criticized as abstract and disembodied, that is, as a-material or immaterial.
One of the most popular refrains in science studies in this decade has been a
critique of scientists' use of metaphors about information, codes, communication, and blueprints to describe genetics (Hubbard and Wald; Fox Keller; Lipp-

326

materiality of language ? –MPL? (handwritten)

man; Nelkin and Lindee; Rosner and Johnson). Critics routinely emphasize that the discourse of modern genetics represents a "hegemonic bloc" that privileges the gene at the expense of a fuller organismic perspective (Kay 10); they dismiss DNA as a "dead molecule" (Lewontin; Fox Keller) and complain that it has been inappropriately elevated to the grand status of the "secret of life," when in fact that sacred label would be better assigned to the full organism, perhaps as it functions with and within its environment.

It is odd that the science critics' complaint about DNA would parallel the popular critique of rhetoric, because most of these science critics would claim to take language seriously. Yet the complaint that DNA is nothing but immaterial code is frustratingly similar to the "common-sense" dismissal of language by many people on the grounds that it is immaterial—mere words, nothing but air vibrating, the opposite of "deeds" or the real. The shared grounds of these complaints derive from the long-standing (and now well-analyzed, e.g. by Harding) Western dualism between the real and the ideal, appearance and reality, the word and the thing. This chapter seeks to drip a little more acid on that persistent dualism by juxtaposing a material perspective on DNA and life with a material perspective on rhetoric, thereby highlighting the materiality of coding in general. A byproduct will be a distinction among codes, communication, and rhetoric that parallels the distinctions among DNA, cell, and organism, a view within which all components are material and significant, rather than some components being ideal and some real. The chapter develops the perspective that it is appropriate to view DNA as part of a coding system, as long as that coding system is understood as a complex set of material processes rather than as a neutral site or conveyer of abstract information. Simultaneously, the chapter offers pointers for the construction of a more thoroughly material theory of rhetoric.

Toward a Material Perspective on "Coding"

Initially it seems unclear whether new-found knowledge of the material workings of the genetic code provides a contrast with or similarity to the more obtrusive codes of daily life and public discourse. Surely, speaking and writing are not material in the same sense as genetic coding is? Except in war and lovemaking, human beings do not use the physical conformations of their bodies and direct contact with other physical substances to communicate in the direct fashion used by amino acids and other molecules. Yet further reflection suggests that communication is every bit as material. Speaking is an act of breathing, of the physical vibration of air molecules, of hearts supplying blood for hand motions and body-lean. In a vacuum—where there is no matter (no air)—we could not hear each other. In darkness, we cannot read each other's lips or other nonverbal messages. Even in writing, though the body is less immediately present and though our communication seems more channeled through pure words, the process is physical nonetheless, as Lester Faigley makes abundantly clear in a chapter in this book. All known communication is a matter of physical contact among material particles.

Nevertheless, our theories of language have led us, by and large, to view these material features as irrelevant or secondary to communication. In a long lineage that stretches back to Plato but which has been revivified in different epistemes by Descartes, Kant, and Locke, Western philosophy has viewed language as constituted of two components: first and foremost, a non-material Idea that is then, second, translated or communicated via ancillary material apparatus, such as words on a printed page or spoken sentences. Theorists writing in the twentieth century have been highly critical of this dualism. Ludwig Wittgenstein, Alfred Korzybski, I. A. Richards, Mary Daly, Kenneth Burke, Jacques Derrida, and Michel Foucault have all launched attacks on the theory of reference, and these have been interpreted as direct challenges to the binary of language/object and the consequent privileging of "the real" over language that are featured in one fashion in the scientific revolution and in another in the Platonic/Christian tradition.

These attacks on the view of language as reference, well taken as they are, have not successfully fused the distinction between language and reality, the idea and the thing. They have not, therefore, foreclosed the sense that language is immaterial—something other than the material forces of the universe that we imagine as having real being. In most cases, theorists have succeeded merely in reversing the hierarchy—in elevating the sign over the referent, the ideal over the material (often by effacing the material). For example, Derrida, drawing on (if transcending in some ways) the structuralists, successfully points out that meaning (reinterpreted as sign function) exists only in language. He clearly decries the tendency of Western philosophy to dematerialize the signifier ("the sign is that ill-named thing, the only one, that escapes the instituting question of philosophy: 'What is . . . ?'" (*Of Grammatology* 19). He then shows that signs do not come after referents, but have their own form of being (one of constant deferral, to which one may or may not want to apply the label "being"). However, though he denies that his reversal of the classical sign/referent relationship implies the non-existence of material reality (*Limited Inc.* 150), Derrida never speculates about linkages between the material and the tracks and traces of the bivalent linguistic forces, called language, which create meaning (a.k.a. "linguistic function"). Moreover, he cannot theorize these relationships precisely because his theory of sign function carves out a singular sign (rather than intertextual discourses) and explicitly cuts off the sign's potential for meaning from specific contexts and specific addressees/receivers (*Limited Inc.* 9–12; also *Spurs* 129). Instead of locating meaning (or sign function) in the particular material contexts where it emerges, therefore, Derrida falls back to the structuralist position of identifying the functioning of the sign with an abstraction called the code: "The fundamental condition of its functioning is its delimitation with regard to a certain code" (*Limited Inc.* 10ff.). Signs cannot act materially if their sole linkage is to a code and if there is no linkage to the specific human usages of that code—and this is something that Derrida's theory explicitly describes as relatively unimportant, rather than as a fundamental aspect of communication (*Limited Inc.* 65). Derrida thus takes us a step out of the Western metaphysics of the sign–referent relationship, but only to replace this with a sign–code relationship.[1]

These arguments suggest that Derrida constructs a theory that is legitimately readable as an effacement of the material on two grounds. First, he ties the function/meaning of the sign to its code, which is an abstraction, not described as located anywhere; that is, it is not "present" and is thus heavily dependent on the idealist structuralism that he attacks in other ways (see, for example, his description of concepts as belonging to a "system," *Limited Inc.* 21). Second, and more simply, Derrida's theory does not take us to a sufficiently full materialism because there is no place for the material made explicit in it.[2]

This is not to say that Derrida's critics (see Graff, in Derrida, *Limited Inc.* 114–42) are correct when they argue that Derrida has erred by denying the existence of objective reality and by rejecting the concept of reference; in fact, Derrida is correct that the concept of "objective reality" is irreparably flawed by its confusion of ontology and epistemology, and the concept of reference is incomplete in ways that Derrida's notion of "tracks" repairs. Instead, these arguments indicate that Derrida's insufficiency lies in his inadequate attention to materiality and in his rejection of relationship as particularized contexts. Both these inadequacies, however, make it legitimate to identify Derrida's theory of language as still tarnished by components of the structuralist version of idealism. This is not to say that one cannot construct a materialist interpretation of much of the Derridean corpus. The identification of the code's being in "tracks" or "traces" opens the possibility of a materialist interpretation of signs. But that theoretical work remains to be done.[3] Thus Derrida, though he succeeds in trumping the concept of reference, does not specify what kind of material being language might have, or what the relationships might be among the sign, its physicality, and the other biosocial forces in humanity's universe.

As the references in other chapters in this book suggest, Michel Foucault has gone further toward a material rhetoric than Derrida. He is widely viewed as the central contemporary figure in proffering material views of discourse. Foucault, however, also takes us only part of the journey. Foucault provides a view of language as social and a view of the social as in some unspecified way material, but his theory also features a lacuna between language and the material (understood as the physical—i.e., as the recalcitrance that our language and our wills always encounter and interact with in the forms of both nature and institutions). Foucault argues that a text is material insofar as it features a repeatability that is limited by material conditions; he says that "a statement must have a substance, a support, a place, and a date" (101). Unlike Derrida, Foucault is quite clear about the delimitations of context, and he appropriately focuses on texts and their interrelationships rather than on isolated signs. But Foucault explicitly excludes from this definition of the materiality of a text its physical nature and material circulation by making distinctions between *enunciations* and *statements*. He concludes that "the materiality of the statement is not defined by the space occupied or the date of its formulation; but rather by its status as a thing or object"; moreover, the different copies of a book are the same set of statements, because "a book, however many copies or editions are made of it, however many different substances it may use, is a locus of exact equivalence for the statements—for them it is an authority that permits repetition without any change of identity" (102).[4] Thus, though he goes farther in incorporating an explicitly material orientation toward language than does Derrida, Foucault also effaces the material at the level of the physical (i.e., the space it occupies). This occurs even in his later works, where he focuses intensively on the material components of social institutions, without ever providing an explicit theory of the relationship among the discursive, the institutional, the behavioral, and the material. Foucault's massive, impressive, and informative works thereby stop short of telling us how it is that the materially signified, at the level of the social, has being in the world other than as an ideal. Foucault thus leaves work for us to do in specifying how it is that texts function in the world.

This argument about Foucault, Derrida, and those of us who have built on their work presumes, of course, that "the material" must be in some way related to the physical. This is not a widely held presumption in rhetorical studies. Literally for centuries, the rough functional effectiveness of idealist concepts like "mind" and "spirit" have enabled us to get by with a notion of words as immaterial ideas that get processed by the magic human mind—an immaterial idea processor. That trick no longer works, however, once one declares that the idea/material binary is a delusion, at least if one wants to account for the social effects of discourse (rather than viewing language as the rational processing of information). Once one begins to talk about the social circulation of signs rather than about the disembodied contemplation of ideas, one needs to account for how those signs have impact on the world. It is not enough to say that signs enter the human mind and then humans make impact on the world, because we are trying to account for the impact on the humans in the first place. A theory of the material in the social thus demands that another step be taken, so that this sociolinguistic materiality is theorized thoroughly, in relation to all the layers (forms) of materiality with which we come into contact. It is oddly perverse for a theory to take as its guiding metaphor "the material" but then to deny (sometimes vehemently) the underlying base of the guiding metaphor: physical matter.

Contemporary theorists who are widely identified as the wellsprings of post-structural perspectives have thus incompletely challenged the language/matter dualism. They have not theorized the linkage between language and other forms of materiality at all levels, including the physical. They therefore continue to be read not as merging the linguistic and the material but rather as reversing the classical privileging of the real over the linguistic, so that we may now privilege the linguistic over the real. Theorists such as Jean Baudrillard and Arthur Kroker have exercised this privilege with great flair. One might see these deficiencies either as grounds for "going beyond" post-structuralism, or merely as correcting one errant strand of the broad post-structuralist movement—call it "ultra-structuralism."[5] However we label (and thus shuffle, unify, and divide) the academic camps, additional steps need to be taken toward theorizing the materialistic characteristics of language, and hence rhetoric, if the general project opened up by post-structuralism is to be fulfilled.

One theorist useful in this endeavor is Kenneth Burke. Burke can be profitably identified as an idiosyncratic American post-structuralist (Brock). In his essay "What are the Signs of What" in *Language as Symbolic Action* (359–79), Burke describes the ways in which language creates "things" out of the diffuse material reality of the physical and social worlds through a process of "entitlement." The foundation of Burke's insight, of course, is shared with many other theorists. One of the major contributions of investigations into language in the twentieth century—made from different angles by Alfred Korzybski, Albert Einstein, Werner Heisenberg, Jacques Derrida, Ferdinand de Saussure, Peter Berger, and Thomas Luckman, among other physicists, theorists, and philosophers—has been the notion that what we understand as objects is not necessary essences. That is, what we see or understand as an "object" is usually not defined by an immutable pairing of form and matter in an integral and differentiable wholeness with a distinctive "essence" that constitutes its meaning. Burke, however, takes an additional step in constructing a material theory. He does not simply deny the priority of the object and discredit reference, nor does he leave the impression that the linguistic act is self-sufficient. Instead, he helps indicate that to identify something as an "object" is a linguistic act that, through the activity of naming, constitutes a set of form–matter–meaning relationships as being useful process relationships to identify within a given framework. The physical material of the universe, pre-deployed in socially specified forms, already exists and offers both substance for and recalcitrance against each naming activity; however, the linguistic act (always already operating in a pre-existing historicized and institutionalized network) also exerts a fundamental force of its own, one without which humans would not describe objects as discrete entities belonging to members of a class. Following Burke's lead, we might see "the electron" as offering a prime example of this relationship. To say that an electron is a "thing" or an "object" is extremely awkward: an electron is constituted of a charge often localizable around opposing charges. The continual "movement" of an electron, whereby it cannot be denoted as at a place but rather as probabilistically in a general region, and its constitution in energy rather than as the solid thing we have long envisioned as matter, models a new understanding of the relationships that prevail among substance, meaning, matter, and form. The electron is a field of shifting but constrained relationships. However, the electron is nonetheless a useful term, and its utility arises from the conjuncture of features in the linguistic, social, and physical planes.

The new relationship between language and physical material with which we need to come to terms is to see matter and form as non-discrete in essence, or, to put it another way, as lacking in essence where essence is understood as a permanent character. Instead of discrete objects, the universe—both human and natural—is constituted of matter/energy in constant motion, taking on shifting forms through shifting relationships. Meaning arises out of the matter/form configurations as they take on and move through specific relationships and relationship patterns that are specified by language; that is, they are abstracted and categorized as members of a set with similarities significant enough to name— to treat as sharing significance. "Essence" then appears as such only because language is an essence-making machine. Language carves out a specific set of relationships and simultaneously generalizes these relationships by naming them. The process of naming (generalization) eliminates the specificity of each relationship (which is always temporary) and thereby makes it appear that the world holds classes of objects—permanent material forms that have essential characteristics.

To say that language "creates" objects, however, in the ultra-structuralist fashion, is not sufficient; indeed, to say that is misleading. Ultra-structuralist metaphors treat "creation" as a godlike act—something is created out of nothing—rather than as an artistic act (e.g., the creation of a *David* from a specific block of marble with particular tensile strength, hued veins, and shape). This ultra-structuralist error arises because these theorists have worked energetically and appropriately to repudiate the notion of "objectivity"—to establish that the object is arbitrary. However, in the process, they have tended *to conflate objectivity with materiality,* and they have thus tended to repudiate, or at least to fail to account for, the material component of discursive action. Since language as used by human beings does not operate without regard to the material realm, it is better to say that language users constitute objects out of matter/form relationships, or, more technically, that language essentializes (by selection and identification) material/form patterns and relationships into perceived objects. This formulation, which respects the materiality of language—materiality that includes the history of uses of the community, the characteristics of human beings, and the form/matter relationships that pass through being in the universe—restricts one's sense that language can be merely a free play of *jouissance.* It does not, however, either eliminate the creativity of human language use or lessen its achievement and significance. To the contrary, by materializing discourse we appreciate much more fully the power and creativity involved in good language use. If any"thing" can be created from no"thing," then creation is hardly an impressive act of an impact; but if creation requires grappling with a social-material universe that resists our rearrangement of it, then creation is a full and demanding endeavor. (This view thus makes us appreciate the rhetoric of Lincoln or King or Cady Stanton more than the literature of Twain or Melville, except to the extent that we see Twain and Melville as rhetoricians.)

A materialist view of language and rhetoric, as opposed to either an objectivist or a relativist view, is advantageous precisely because it allows us to understand both the creativity of language and the substantiality of its limitations. A materialist view of language understands rhetoric as a constructive act, but it still leaves us with a relatively solid universe. Our natural-world analogies are again good touchstones. Atoms in metals defy our notion of "objects." As a consequence of our basic physics or chemistry classes, we understand an atom as an ordered set of protons and neutrons surrounded by a balancing set of electrons. However, in metals, especially when they are conducting electricity, the electrons lose their "belongingness" to individual sets of neutrons and protons; they move around in the network of the element. In the face of this movement, it becomes rather difficult to identify any individual atoms that constitute the mass. In a sense, there are no atoms there as objects as we have defined "atoms." They all lack the essence that our naming of "atom" gave them. There is only a soupy mass of rapidly shifting relationships within a lot of open space. And yet, one still cannot put one's hand through the metal. It is solid, and it can easily be distinguished from a pond of water. The process or functional relationships and interactions that exist are not dependent on having a named essence, but on the matter, energy, and relationships. Bringing these relationships into the social circle of human life through language, however, embeds them in new, particular (non-necessary) relationships. The work of language is therefore neither simply to reflect nor simply to create matter, but to *identify*, thereby reifying socially useful or esthetically compelling facets of the complex and shifting material/energy/relationships to fit within other human-scale frameworks of matter/relationships.

The same linguistic transformation of a material reality into an object occurs in the case of "the gene." Defining the gene as an object is impossible. The gene is a series of nucleic acids on a strip of DNA that code for particular proteins—but not exactly. Genes have irrelevant filler material in them—is that part of the gene? Some stretches of DNA participate in coding more than one gene product—is that stretch of DNA "one gene" or "two genes"? Genes function only when they have promoter sequences and termination sequences and other auxiliary components, but these components are not necessarily contiguous with the transcription unit, do not get translated, and are not part of the code that makes the gene products—so are these components part of the gene or not? *The gene*, in short, is a term that functions to identify a discrete object for the purposes of scientific communication, but no discrete object called "a gene" can be identified. Rather, "the gene" is a set of overlapping relationships between materials and forms that serve specific functions. *The gene* thus provides a paradigmatic example of the way in which language constructs an objectified essence where none exists in nature—but where that objectification is useful and is related to real material processes of undeniable significance—and thus provides a terministic screen that both enables and misleads. There is a genetic process that is materially real, having relationships of consequence in the matter of life, but "the gene" is also a linguistic construction operating in sociolinguistic frameworks that find its demarcation useful.

The reformulation I am urging here can be described as a move from "objectivism" to "materialism," and specifically to linguistic or structural materialism. This view sees objects as provisional but real and useful in two senses. First, objects are generally constituted out of matter, energy, and relationships that we can reasonably and profitably postulate to have an existence that exceeds human linguistic accountings of them. Second, although such objects are unified primarily by linguistic structuration (for human beings), they are usually unified in that fashion because thus to unify them serves useful purposes in a given context, more and less general in its scope in varying cases. Linguistic materialism thus escapes both the false permanence and naturalized essentialism of objectivist views, and also the pure indeterminacy and random meaninglessness of ungrounded relativism or structuralism. Instead it offers a semi-transitory/semi-stable substantiality that recognizes both the reality of forces in the universe and the way in which motivated human action objectifies those forces through language into more and less durable relationships with more and less intensive presence and visibility.

Why is it, then, that rhetoricians, who have so much at stake in taking the materiality of rhetoric seriously, have been so easily seduced by ultra-structuralist notions that efface the materiality of language? Why has Baudrillard been more popular among us than Burke? Perhaps it is merely because ultra-structuralism provides an attractive reversal that puts language "on top," even if the relationship is still a binary, hierarchical one. Perhaps it is because our recent focus on rhetoric-as-criticism in the place of rhetoric-as-performance has effaced the evident signs of physicality that exist in performance in favor of the more passive, less physically evident processes of watching and reading. Perhaps it is because the "physical world" has in this century been pervasively associated with the politically reactionary. Among the many reasons for these preferences, however, the most serious is that as lovers of art, we react quite rightly against anything that smacks of physical reductionism. When we are told that language, like genes, is a matter of physical action, we humanistic and post-humanistic types respond in dissonant chorus, "Is that all there is? Is meaning nothing more than protoplasm vibrating?"

Incorporating the physical into our understandings of coding need not, however, mean a *reduction* of meaning to the merely physical. An analysis of the vocabularies used to describe the gene can help to explore this reaction. Scientists have identified the functioning of DNA as being a "genetic code," and they speak comfortably of a stretch of DNA as containing "information." At other times, however, they speak (in language unintelligible to those not trained in the sciences) of hydrogen-bonding and phosphorylation, and of molecular shapes, weights, and sizes—an evidently material description. In other words, the scientists employ two vocabularies to describe different aspects of the same phenomenon. The physically descriptive vocabulary is about objects and their sizes, their forms of chemical and physical interaction. But the communication vocabulary they use is quite different. It is about the interactions, functions, and outcomes of the material processes that occur. But this communication vocabulary is not about a spirit or an idea that exists in some other realm from the material processes: the vocabulary is simply about different aspects of the same unique but material processes. The scientists would find it quite odd to say that DNA has an "idea" that is then transmitted by the cell's organic machinery (though popular science might make such a translation for the public). Instead, scientific vocabularies portray DNA's form and material substance as precisely *about* the information that it produces.[6] This does not "reduce" the information to meaningless physical process. Rather the reverse: the physical process of DNA is about producing the highly meaningful information that is the genetic code. Thus, the question "Is that all there is?" is itself shallow; rather, in specifying that the meaning of language is developed in the highly complicated material processes of speaking, writing, and broadcasting, we are locating a rich dynamic through which language, a process of making meaning, emerges out of forms and materials. We are not reducing language to matter but exploring how it is that meaning arises materially, and hence how meaning matters. We are not eliminating the need for a vocabulary that discusses meaning, but we are requiring ourselves to change that vocabulary so that it reflects its relationship to matter rather than places itself as an ideal in opposition to matter.

Clues for constructing such a vocabulary can be borrowed from contemporary natural scientists, who bifurcate their categories in a more productive manner than has the Western metaphysical tradition. In philosophical language about human discourse, Westerners have operated with an *object/idea* distinction. In contrast, good natural scientists employ an *object/process* dichotomy. One can examine the physiological *objects* of the body (thymine, cytosine, guanine, etc.) in a context of understanding the *process* with its functions (goals or purposes) and outcomes. On this model, both object and process are seen as material, and meaning is viewed as deriving from the object/process combination. Meaning literally could not come into being, could not exist, without the object, because the process is embodied in the object—though without process, objects themselves lack the essentialization that constitutes meaning. Even though (as Kay, Fox Keller, and others have pointed out) the object/process perspective has not come easily to many natural scientists and is not uniformly manifested in their discourse, it still provides a useful model.

Our theories of language would do well to adopt this way of viewing the relationship between meaning and matter.[7] The combination of object and process is necessary for understanding how it is that language has effects in the world—that is, for understanding how meaning is something real, something material, and not merely a function of disembodied spirit or mind. Fully integrating this perspective will require a huge overhaul of our view of language and rhetoric, but some of the groundwork for such a shift has already been laid by preliminary theories that take seriously language and rhetoric as material. Some of the key components of a materialist theory of rhetoric have been described by Kenneth Burke and Michael Calvin McGee. Burke's contribution can be summarized in the famous definition of humans as "bodies that learn language." This is not a formula that I understand Burke as having worked out very fully with regard to the characteristics of the body, but his work is suggestive when read as an alternative route for post-structuralism rather than as a failure to reach the ultra-structuralist position.[8]

As a companion piece to Burke's materialism of the body, McGee has specified some of the sociohistorical dimensions of a materialist rhetoric, arguing that we should "think of rhetoric as an object, as material and as omnipresent as air and water" ("Materialist's Conception" 26). McGee also suggests ("The 'Ideograph'") that the meaning of language is determined by the pattern of synchronic and diachronic usages of words and word sets within a culture (especially the socially key words he calls "ideographs"). McGee's theory is materialist in contrast to the view of the structuralists who saw meaning as determined by a set of structured binary relationships in a language net that was devoid of *particular* human actions (Eco; Saussure). The structuralist model portrayed meaning as inherent to a network of relationships that were essentially atemporal and overdetermined by the possibilities of structuration and language itself. Structuralists thus overcame the mind/body dualism or the idea/object split simply by effacing the body or matter. McGee's materialist model points to actual usages, not an imagined network or system, as the source of further meaning-uses. Although the writings of ultra-structuralists such as Baudrillard put the linguistic structure into action, making it part of a social process, they simultaneously heightened the a-materiality of the system by portraying language as a field of "free play" and by portraying "presence" as if it were an unmotivated choice (Derrida, *Spurs*). Thus, ultra-structuralism imagines once again, in the covertly neo-Platonic French philosophical tradition, that humans could live without the constraints of materiality in a zone of pure writing (see Condit, "Kenneth Burke"). As I have noted, the ultra-structuralists repeat the error of privileging the realm of idea over the realm of material being, this time by (covertly, implicitly) denying the existence of the latter.

In contrast, McGee's materialist theory explicitly accounts for the meaning of language as being derived from persuasive work done by the prior (and present) inhabitants of a culture. Language's meaning is identified with the entire constellation of social relationships and concrete and particular interchanges of symbols actually executed by any interacting set of human beings. From this perspective, culturally active symbols are not simply open to "play." While creative play may generate new possibilities, broad, culture-wide changes can occur only through sustained or highly amplified discursive work. In contrast to the sense of free play, work is a thoroughly material process, entailing not only access to media but also risk of attack by hostile audiences weaned on alternative codes and meaning structures. In McGee's theoretical framework, therefore, meaning derives from a history of usages of an interrelated set of vocabularies. In contrast to the structuralist claim that language was "arbitrary," language is instead described as *motivated*—by a history of experiences, needs, wants, desires, and relationships. The fact that no two languages can be precisely translated into each other is a sign of this lack of arbitrariness: specific cultural motives ground the relationships among the linguistic structures. (The fact that many relatively effective translations can be made is a sign of the existence of some broad similarities across human cultures; thus language systems share motivational structures to some extent—making specific sounds and signs somewhat arbitrary, but leaving the highly specific relationships of individual languages non-arbitrary, but rather culturally motivated, just as the larger, repeated relationships are motivated by general human needs.)[9]

The genetic model is again of interest as we seek to explore the relationship of arbitrariness and motivation in material code systems. To what extent can it be said that the use of thymine, cytosine, guanine, and adenine as the coding elements of life is an "arbitrary" choice? Or why should there be merely three codons per gene? Or why should some codons spell out specific amino acids, while others spell out various versions of "stop" codons? On the surface, the genetic code seems arbitrary. The ingredients could be shuffled. In fact, RNA life forms that are parasitic on the DNA of other living entities can exist by employing a code that substitutes uracil for thymine. Nonetheless, all nonparasitic life shares precisely the DNA code. While alternative forms of DNA are a theoretical possibility, they appear so far only in science fiction. In a strong sense, then, the particular code of DNA does not appear to be arbitrary.

To understand why, one must move out of the vocabulary of information (ideas) and into the vocabulary of physical objects. There are particular relations of size, bonding strength and type, and other chemical relationships that make the specific materials of DNA, in precisely the forms and components they take, particularly well suited to producing life in many forms within the material universe as we know it. Thus, in a materially based system, the forms that information takes are not arbitrary because they are constituted from the constricted options available in the material strata. This does not mean that the material substrate determines the forms taken; one can constitute amoebae or gorillas from the same basic materials. The physical properties of the materials do, however, constrain or delimit the forms that can be taken: *Star Trek*'s Q cannot be constructed from DNA as it is materially constituted.

Just as the physical conformation of the nucleic acids in DNA constitutes the code for heredity, the material relationships in a society—the precise temporal and geographical distributions of class, of demographics, of genders, of sexualities, of abilities, and so on—constitute the motivations—the material—that is language. Although the specific letters *c*, *a*, and *t* are "arbitrary," the existence of the category of "cat"—delimiting the range of entities and relationships that are cats—is not arbitrary but constructed (motivated) by a complex set of social relationships (e g., by the existence of four-legged animals that have specific characteristics and relationships to humans that are different from those of other four-legged animals, but also from the "lexical dogs" of the society: see Burke, "Language as Symbolic Action" 73–74). The category of "cat" is not, indeed, an objective fact that is tied to the existence of an ideal type of animal, because there is no term for "cat" in societies where there are no cats, and the range of animals that count within the category of "cat"-translatable terms varies according to social relationships with catlike creatures in other societies. But the term *cat* is material; that is, it both responds to and establishes sets of relationships among historically embedded substances, both linguistic and nonlinguistic.

To McGee's version of historical materialism, therefore, we might add a physical component. Human meanings arise from the specific histories of their cultures, but also from the specific material limitations of human bodies and human environments. We are, today, virtually without any academic knowledge of these relationships. In the human case, however, it is important to remember what sociobiologists dogmatically forget: that one must always combine awareness of historical and biological components. Animal species are simpler; perhaps in part because they do not use language extensively, they do not remake their environments extensively. Biologists thus can usually assume safely that the animal in a given environment is roughly the same animal in any environment (since animals tend to evolve rapidly into different forms when placed in different environments, or else they become extinct). Human animals, however, remake their environments extensively. As a consequence, the material structures that constitute human–environment interfaces change. Because of language, humans make their environments evolve faster than they themselves evolve in their environments. One cannot, therefore, study the material structures of human life in the ahistorical and nondiscursive manner in which one studies the material structures of animal life.

McGee's work recalls this situatedness of discourse in some detail. He insists that the constitution of the meaningfulness of a rhetoric lies in the specific configuration of "'speaker/speech/audience/occasion/change' operating in society through time" ("Materialist's Conception" 29). In his earlier work, he laid emphasis on the speaker; in his later work, he emphasizes the audience. In either case, however, a materialist rhetoric must emphasize the particular performance of a discourse. There are, no doubt, texts that travel well (for a variety of reasons) in many performances, but because the material conditions of the performance of a text are different in every situation, so too are important dimensions of its meaning. This does not mean that we cannot understand some things in a text in ways that others of different times and places might understand them, but it does mean that we cannot retrieve fully the same meaning from any text that others in different times and places would receive. Each performance of a code has different material relationships and therefore different material impacts. Each copy of a book, therefore, does make a different statement (in contradiction to Foucault)—and that is one reason why the number of copies printed of a given book matters.

Does DNA Do Rhetoric? Or: Purpose, Power, Identity, Life

What does all this have to do with the genetic code?

The code of a "gene" is likewise not independent of its context; it too gains its significance only in relationship to the cell/organism/environment in which it exists and with which it relates. Although it is built from four fundamental "bases" arranged in three codon sets, the genetic code speaks forth the enormous, striking, awesome variety that is life on Earth. The biological system of heredity produces both unimaginable difference and also the relatively reliable copying of species within species. Cats (almost) always produce kittens that look like their parents. But cats use the same basic DNA forms that are used by humans, alligators, and bacteria—perhaps even by bacteria on Mars. This system too is bound by its history, however. There are no dinosaurs now, even though DNA is capable of coding for dinosaurs. Even in a relatively simple coding system, therefore, a certain type of closedness is compatible with an immense openness of forms. Until we understand both these aspects of language as products of its materiality, we do not understand it well at all. In rhetorical studies, this implies the need to pursue somewhat more vigorously, albeit differently, the insight that it is as important to study what is not said as what has been said (Wander). If rhetoric as a locus of social formation is understood as the materialization of the possible, then a rhetorical analysis is about understanding how rhetorical sources make speakable what has otherwise been unsaid. The ways in which the resources of form, ideology, and experience interact in such creative efforts have thus far been explored only incidentally.

Can DNA and its relationships to the cell and the organism and the tribe offer us guidance here? Unfortunately, such interactions among elements can be understood either as communication or as rhetoric, but scientists uniformly speak about DNA with the vocabulary of "communication," not the vocabulary of rhetoric. So does DNA communicate, but not "do" rhetoric? And what implications does that have for using DNA as a further model of materiality for language (and vice versa)?

The first apparent sticking point for claiming that DNA does rhetoric is the concept of intent. Historically, definitions of rhetoric and accounts of rhetorical practice have presumed that a rhetor is one who seeks, at least somewhat consciously and intentionally, to craft a message that produces a particular set of results with a particular audience. Both materialists and post-structuralists have recently questioned the sense in which any individual can be said to execute an intent, however. So let us ask the simpler question of whether DNA can act with purpose.

The concept of purpose stands as a post-structuralist's substitute criterion for "intent" in rhetorical action because the term *purpose* presumes that there is a directionality to the (symbolic) movements made by a person. It does not, however, specify that those movements come from conscious intent, but merely from some set of regularizable relationships (which are codable because they are regularizable), within which there is a hierarchy (a set of preferences), established by some source. Employing this notion of purpose, the argument that I will put forward suggests that life is the movement of coded material that differentially favors the reproduction of its own code: life is the reproduction of identity. The purposiveness of this movement is established by the "preference" of the coded material for self-reproduction. The establishment of this "preference" may be a physical accident (the accidental creation of a physical entity that has this physical characteristic), but instantly as this self-preferring form happens into existence, a new order of being is created—one that exhibits self-preference. This is the first form of purpose, because it is the first hierarchy. Other purposes develop as the coding system expands.

Many steps are necessary to explore the propositions that life is the reproduction of identity, that such reproduction is, per se, coding, and that such coding is by definition purposive. First, one must identify DNA as the singular site of the emergent property that we call "life." That is, in DNA we must see a characteristic that is born of dead materials but that creates from those dead materials a new feature that transcends their characteristics in an important way. That is, the existence of DNA produces the possibility of motivated motion.[10] This is not to say that DNA is sufficient for life; DNA has only been able to evolve from presumably more primitive collections of acids into a complex and distinctive molecule because of a complex evolutionary history that includes the simultaneous creation of an ever more complex coding molecule via the creation of an ever more complex entity (the cell) of which it is a part. Moreover, DNA can code only as a cellular transactional process. That is, DNA cannot "initiate" its own replication nor its production of RNA (which enables the production of specific proteins for the cell's function). Neither, however, should we place the cell as primary, because the cell does not exist without DNA. The cell structure and DNA are rather fully interdependent and are therefore both determinative of life. Thus, DNA is not sufficient for life, nor does it "control" life, but it is correct to say that it is necessary for life, and distinctive of life, and as such, it is far more than a "dead molecule."

Next, think that unlike inert atoms, DNA has motion, and enables life, because it constitutes the possibility of reproducing an identity. I will leave aside for now the debate over whether the identity that the DNA is reproducing is itself or that of the organism (I believe that there is sense in saying that both are true, and that this establishes an important tension in the evolution and expression of life), for in either case, DNA can do so because to code should be understood as the creation of an identity (always imperfect, but more on that soon). What DNA does in reproducing (or being reproduced, if one wishes to keep the cell in mind) is to reproduce an identity, which it can do because it is a code, and our nations of code and identity are mutually dependent.[11]

The term *identity*, of course, is problematic in itself. Derrida has convincingly argued that there really is no such thing as identity because iteration is always both sameness and difference. For DNA this is at least half true, though the fact that the DNA must retain half of its material self to reproduce its formal self is a complication that probably ought not to be overlooked. If we operate with a Wittgensteinian notion of language, however, Derrida's argument should not discredit our use of the term *identity*.[12] Derrida merely makes us aware that our use of *identity*, perhaps somewhat paradoxically, must be as probabilistic and approximate as our use of any other term. That is, we recognize in "identity" a limit term that is approached in various degrees but never achieved. A greater difficulty is that this definition imports the concept of "form." That is, identity is the repetition of the same form with different molecules.

In employing the concept of form, we must be careful not to reproduce the standard form/matter split, because that would vitiate our attempt to construct a materialist theory. Instead, we need to understand form as a type or part of materiality. Form is *a set of relations,* and as such it is always material in its own right; also, therefore, forms are only analogous to one another, never perfectly identical. Form is material because, as a set of relations among material elements, it exists in space and time. That is, something can be said to have a form only to the extent that its atoms (its physical material) arrange in a particular way in space-time. The abstracting ability of language has deluded us, at least since Plato, into thinking that form could exist elsewhere than in the materiality of the world, because language can imagine for us something that is not in the material world (e.g., just as it can imagine the ideal of "identity" even though in practice identity is a non-existent limit that entities can approach but not achieve). Form, however, is not an abstraction from matter, but rather an arrangement of matter, and that arrangement is not separate from the matter itself but integral to it, having existence, particularly the existence of space and time. We have been deluded about this by the use of examples such as the "form" of a vase. We imagine a lump of clay being reformed into a vase, and thus we think that the form (vase) is independent of the matter (clay). But matter cannot be de-formed (except perhaps by becoming not-matter, i.e. energy); it can only be re-formed. The vase is both form and matter, as is the lump of clay before it is re-formed into a vase. Just as the existence of matter depends on having some range of forms, so each of those forms is absolutely dependent on the material characteristics of the matter and its environment. (One can't make a vase out of water unless the temperature is below freezing.) To produce a fully materialist view of rhetoric requires, therefore, that we no longer think of relationships as non-material (im-material), and thence that we stop thinking of form as immaterial. Form and relationships are intrinsic dimensions of materiality.[13]

Because relationships are material, they are capable of similitude and analogy, but never of pure identity. That is, two atoms are "the same" in that we can abstract an analogous form; they have the same number of protons, neutrons, and electrons. Hence we say they are the same, but they are never exactly the same, both because they are never made of precisely the same components and because they never have precisely the same configurations or exist in the same time and space. Hence, when we use the term *identity*, we don't really mean "exactly the same." We mean something like "having enough similitude to be abstracted as having closely analogous form" (closely analogous for some purpose of ours). A DNA molecule, then, is never exactly reproduced (even if it rejoins with its former "other half" after unzipping, things will have changed). Rather than creating strict identity, then, the DNA is replicating only in what Wittgenstein might all too appropriately identify as a "family resemblance."

That is, to the extent that the DNA allows replication of a form analogous in major ways to itself, then it has replicated and encouraged its future replication; but this "replication" is not of a self but of a relationship (or, it is a self only to the extent that we recognize selves as sets of relationships). In the case of living things, these relationships exist on two planes, both of which are important: the "relationship" of the old molecule to the new (offspring), and the pattern repetitions within the old molecule which constitute the self-code (see below for a specification of this in a third level). Unlike other codings, hereditary codings feature both these types of relationship between all molecules that are related, and this constitutes a distinctive feature of life. A code, then, identifies to the extent that this dual relationship exists. Life is thus the duality of relational forms in a coding—the forms in the self-coder are validated as a discrete identity by their replication to some substantial degree in the other (the offspring).

"Major ways" is a crucial weasel phrase. How do we know when a DNA molecule has replicated itself and when it has mutated? What counts as "major" in this case? Clearly, alternate phosphorylation or shifting from B to Z forms is not generally considered mutation (because these are merely temporary "markings" or "formations" a single sequence can take). I would suggest that a key feature of living entities is to stabilize identity by creating discrete coding units. It is precisely, then, because the cell/DNA is able to "discriminate" what is itself and what is not itself that it is able to reproduce itself (that is, to reproduce analogous relationships); and it is able to do that simply because it is constituted as a code having discrete parts that can be reliably reproduced. Each triplet codon of DNA specifies a discrete amino acid—a discrete form/material—and the order of the codons specifies the order (form) of the molecule being replicated. DNA thus constitutes a template that allows simultaneous coding of two elements of material being: the order, and the components in the order. The ability to code in this fashion—that is, the ability to "identify" discrete chunks of ordered form/matter—is what constitutes the possibility of what we recognize and categorize as life/identity.

This is very different from non-life. Non-life does not replicate itself because it does not constitute discrete chunks of form/matter that can be replicated in a duality of forms. Life is thus, distinctively, about coding. This does not mean that codes are perfect, perfectly stable, infallible, and so on. DNA often makes mistakes (though the organism has a "DNA-repair mechanism" specifically adapted to correct those mistakes and repair the code). DNA does mutate, and it produces faulty RNA and faulty proteins. That is, it changes identities, and in relatively rare cases those new identities go on to replicate themselves successfully. This is not an accidental feature of DNA; without such mutational failures, without the changes in identity, DNA could never have evolved to be what it is. Thus, as a Derridean perspective might urge us to note, the possibility of life/identity is bound up with both change and similitude: identity requires non/identity. However, with non-life there is neither identity nor non-identity. Where there is no code (with its inevitable failure of coding), there is no life.

This does not mean that life's *only* "secret" is its characteristic as an identifier/coder. My formulation does mean, however, that the codes of the living have a kind of material self-ratification, and that all living things have their own purposes.[14] We do not have to valorize those purposes, but they are "there" (in a material, but not objective sense) to be recognized; they are not simply created by our science. Whether we know the codes or not, and however we know them, they keep reproducing, and thereby they keep offering both the material of our lives and resistance to our wills. Thus, though we constitute discrete objects for ourselves through our language, all living organisms create their own codes and coding units that stand outside our language games (though we may recode them into our language games as well). Human life is thus a constant rhetorical engagement between the human linguistic coding process and the coding processes of all living things. Although this positing of "pre-social bodies" may be heresy for some post-humanists, and threatening for those of us who have long had our careers tied to the centrality of human language, it is essential to make this move in order to escape anthropocentrism. Extending Derrida's critique of Western philosophy's vision of language as self-presence (*Of Grammatology*), this account specifies that language use is no longer to be understood as the activity wherein humans in isolation construct meaning. Instead, language is a conversation with being(s).

If we thus say that organisms reproduce themselves by motivated motion in the world—specifically by the motivated motion of reproducing a code (that is, their analog-identity), where coding is the repetition of a discrete form in a duality of relational forms—we are also saying that coding and living must be identified as verbs, not nouns. Coding implies a construction, an activity; atoms are not codes, even though their forms occur millions of times in the universe. Thus, in thinking about language and life, our focus should not be on codes but on coding. This orientation introduces the inherent relationality of coding as a communication process that is always two-way. As the science critics have rightly observed (e.g., Fox Keller), some high-profile scientists have tended to treat the "communication" that goes on between DNA and other cell components as though it were a one-way transmission from DNA to RNA to proteins. They have thereby been led to speak of DNA as "commanding" or controlling the cell. But, as communication theorists have come to emphasize over the past two decades, communication is never one-way. Communication is a relationship, and to "communicate" successfully always requires that both parties share a code. Consequently, one must say that the other components of a cell "share" the code of the DNA. If they did not, then the DNA's form would not help to produce and reproduce the cell. Thus, it is not only wrong to speak as if the

DNA–cell communication were one-way; it is also wrong to speak as if the "code" of DNA rested solely within the DNA. That "code" is a shared entity of all the parts of the cell. The isolable materiality of the DNA draws our attention to it as "a code" or as "the codescript," but the "code" lies not in the configuration of the DNA but rather in the homology between the configuration of the DNA and the configuration of the cell. That is, the materiality of DNA's code is to be found not solely in the atoms of the DNA, but in the *relationship* (again, a material phenomenon) between the configuration of those atoms and the cell. This means that for life to exist there must be a third level of analogy in the coding system. Not only is there the discrete code of the "parent" DNA and its analog in the offspring (whose existence identifies the parent form as a code); in addition, the code of the DNA is a kind of complex formal analog-in-translation with the cell, and this formal analogy can only be recognized in process. Life's coding thus has a trilateral relationality built into its formal character: (1) repetitive patterns within DNA; (2) DNA/rest of the cell; and (3) offspring. Consequently, "code" as it is generally used is an unfortunate abstraction from the process of "coding," and it is the complex process of coding (i.e., communication) that should be our central focus.

We have thus elevated our sights from "codes" to "communication." The argument has indicated that DNA acts with purpose because it acts to code an identity. But that does not get us all the way to "rhetoric." As John Peters has suggested, an important feature of the scientific revolution was the suppression of the concept of "rhetoric" in favor of the concept of communication. That move simultaneously enshrined an objectivist epistemology over a social constructivist one and effaced the idea that discourse, because it was always addressed in a specific context to a specific audience, was always a matter of power. Taking DNA as our model of materiality, even with the cell around it, mires us in this model of communication rather than of rhetoric. DNA and the cell are communicators, but they are not rhetoricians because DNA always presumes the same (and self-same) audience. In the communication of DNA and the cell, the cell is invariant in the way it interprets the code of DNA. While cell conditions alter so that the cell uses different parts of the DNA and encourages more or less of certain messages from the DNA, the DNA and the cell are locked into a relatively static relationship with a relatively fixed code (in a given generation). There is no power struggle because there is a unity of purpose. The codes are internal, shared, and not themselves subject to dispute. One code is simultaneously the code to be reproduced and the code that reproduces (communicates).

Moving up the ladder a bit to the multicellular organism can help us move away from the communication model and toward a rhetorical one, but only slightly. Different cells in the same organism have different parts of the code "turned on" and hence feature some coding dissimilarities among themselves, but there is a shared underlying code (except in the case of cancers, where the consequences for communication are obvious). This shared code is not an accidental feature. Again, the homology of relationship between the organism and its DNA operates at two levels. There cannot be a zero-sum game between the elements of the organism. If the stomach dies, the brain cannot live. That shared interest is underwritten at the level of the coding process by a shared codescript. Thus, the power disparities in a multicellular organism, though not nonexistent, are severely bounded by the conditions of mutual survival. Even in a multicelled organism, in the most fundamental conditions, there is only one audience for the communicative processes of the lifecode, and that is the organism itself (and its offspring, which are other selves to the extent that they share the code): one code to communicate, one code to be communicated as the (next/self) identity.

Of course, the degree of possibility of different audiences, even within the organism, creates a profound shift in life because it constitutes a need to select among different relationships. To the extent that identity is always in part a relational quality, this creates the need to alternate identities. This in turn, combined with the need to select alternative codes, creates differentiality of purposes. The change to multiple addressees in a coding system thus changes the nature of life. It is striking that this shift is mirrored in the character of DNA itself. In single-celled organisms, the DNA is relatively simple—a circle or simple strand, albeit still a double helix. However, the process of evolution, which is generally understood as a process of making greater complexity and more options, is also a process of making the DNA ever more complex, so that in more complex organisms it folds up to make parts inaccessible and increases the number of regulative devices that direct the reading of its coded being. The constitution of mRNA as an intermediary for DNA probably also reflects this need.

This having been said, the coding processes of DNA within a single organism presume (relatively) the self-same audience with an identical code. The communicative interactions of DNA within an organism therefore do not mandate choices among competing purposes, and consequently they do not distribute power (that is, they do not distribute materials differentially between competing agents).[15] These are not, therefore, rhetorical interactions. Only when we shift to the level of analyzing codes existing between organisms does the possibility of a multiplicity of audiences with very imperfectly shared codescripts and unshared purposes become dominant. When one speaks of two different organisms, the code that communicates between the organisms is no longer the code that constitutes the identity of the individual organism and its self-replication. Communication becomes qualitatively different from mere self-coding. As the code becomes external to the self-code, the dimension of power (a lack of sharing of preferences; multiplicity in hierarchies) is intro-

duced. This does not mean that organisms lack substantial degrees of inter-
dependence, or that codes are radically uninterpretable between individuals
or even species. All organisms on the planet are to some extent interdependent and can to some extent understand one another—perhaps because they all
share something of the same DNA codescript, or only because, being alive,
they all share in common a dependence on coding. However, as we move from
the multicelled organism, to the hereditary family, to the tribe, to the nation-
state, to the species, to the interspecies nexus, we move progressively to greater
and greater variabilities in audiences and codes, and we operationalize with
ever greater significance the disparities of purpose that make power more operative than simple self-reference. That is, we move from the simple models of
communication to the more complex models of rhetoric. Thus, while DNA and
rhetoric may interanimate each other as models of material processes, that
interanimation is parallel at some points (communication) and contrasting at
others.

This chapter has surely led us to places we had not imagined traveling as
rhetoricians, all to say that we need a material theory of rhetoric, and to try to
use the coding of DNA as a model for how that material rhetoric might be understood to incorporate both gross physical materiality (biological and social,
both historicized) and the characteristics of the activity of coding as the approach to the limit of identity through the reproduction of discrete chunks (codons) of form/matter (codes). There is much work left for all of us to do. But
as a rhetorician, I am not fully happy with theory. If my theoretical perspective
is not useful in critical understandings of my universe, it is not compelling,
even if the arguments can be made tighter than I have had the space, time,
and intellect to make them. Therefore, I want to turn now to a case study that
considers briefly the rhetoric of public discourse about genetics, in the form of
a single speech by the director of the National Center for Human Genome
Research.

Toward a Material Critique of Gene Talk

Public discourse about genetics is strongly polarized. Advocates of the mir-
acles of genetic technologies paint glowing pictures: genetic medicines cure
debilitating disease, save lives, prevent handicaps, and even produce children
who are super-intelligent, strong, and musically talented. Opponents of genetic
technologies, in contrast, predict a dystopic genetic future in which women are
reduced to breeding machines, an elite core of physicians make decisions about
who will bear children and of what sort, and poor people with no access to genetic medicine labor at disfiguring menial jobs to support the expensive medical enhancements of the rich.

It is, of course, not surprising that something as new and powerful as genetics should generate rival camps with vehemently opposed discourses. The contradictory codes about genetics are not, however, merely produced by rival camps. They are also internal to the official discourse that supports genetic research. Consider the annual budget statement of Francis Collins, director of the National Center for Human Genome Research. On 13 May 1993, Collins argued for the Center's 152-million-dollar budget request for that year. He began by touting the "unparalleled contributions to our understanding of human disease" that the center had made in its short four-year "life." He then celebrated the increase in the number of disease genes being discovered. He explained the utility of these discoveries with an example:

Discovery of one of those genes, for a common form of inherited colon cancer, now makes it potentially possible to identify individuals predisposed to this often lethal cancer. Because colon cancer is often completely curable when it is detected early, this represents a prime example of how a gene discovery can lead directly to life-saving interventions. This gene was isolated within six months of when it was located on chromosome 2; in the past, such work would have taken several years.

After having set this encouraging motivational framework, Collins explained in some detail the technical goals of the program over the next five years. As he neared the conclusion of his statement, however, the director took back what his introduction had given. He announced that the National Advisory Council for Human Genome Research had taken a position against actually using the genetic information that has been generated in much clinical research. The statement, published in the *Journal of the American Medical Association*, was one "recommending that genetic testing for predisposition to certain cancers be delayed until we gain more knowledge about how to deliver these tests in a way that will insure the best health outcome and that is socially and psychologically responsible." Collins's speech is thus built on an aporetic stasis that both urges the scientific revolution forward on pragmatic grounds and simultaneously balks at enactment of its pragmatic byproducts.

Collins's contradictory discourse is typical of the still relatively sparse public discourse dealing with the genetic revolution. On the one hand, for example, the National Center for Human Genome Research spends the majority of its budget on research and technological developments to bring about the genetic revolution. On the other hand, it spends around 5 percent of its budget on "Ethical, Legal, and Social Implications" research, much of which constitutes arguments against implementation of genetic research, or against spending on such projects. The contradiction is vividly evident in *The Code of Codes* (Kevles and Hood), a book featuring many of the major players in the early years of the Human Genome Project. The first half of this volume celebrates the genetic revolution, and the second half castigates it. If genetics offers such clearly desirable and singular medical treatment, why is the discourse of genetics so self-contradictory? Why is implementation so complex that a moratorium is necessary on its usage? Why not simply screen everyone (or everyone "at risk") for colon cancer and treat them? Now that a gene for hereditary breast cancer has been located (accounting for 5 to 10 percent of all breast cancers), why not simply test all women and treat those with the allele that predisposes one to illness?

I wish to suggest that, from a materialist's perspective, this is not just an ideological contradiction—that is, not just words logically in conflict with themselves. Rather, these words are in conflict because these different words are tied to different features of the materiality of the physical and social formations of human beings involved in the discourse. A terse way of describing the problem is to say that what the medical and scientific community "wills" or "intends" to do is to control human genes, but that the way in which genes are embedded in human bodies, and the way in which human bodies are embedded in the social formation, create enormous and differentially distributed costs to that control.

I have elsewhere explored the constraints operating on the social formations with regard to the use of genetic technologies (Condit, "Bad Science"). Here I want to emphasize that it is not enough to note the factors in the social formation that are at issue. It is not enough to identify Collins's discourse as a hegemonic project that furthers the interests of scientists, biotechnical companies, and (perhaps) class elites. In fact, a large part of the problem constituted by the Human Genome Project is not simply that of class and partisan interests (though it is clearly also that). Rather, part of the Human Genome Project's difficulties arise from the biological impediments to the social implementation of genetic medicine, which are then experienced in a classed/gendered/raced way. These impediments arise from the fact that such diseases are not so easily controllable as the models of medicine in the era of antibiotics and surgery would lead us to expect. Genetic control, at least for the foreseeable future, and arguably in the long term, does not offer cures that entail little more than a shot or a pill. Because our genes are fundamentally entwined with our identity and development, and yet also have only a probabilistic nature rather than a deterministic one, doctors and scientists are not sure how to impose control on the whole individuals they treat without violating fundamental aspects of those individuals. Genetics is unlike the two major disease models of the past century—germ theories and cancer research—which have sought to eliminate components that are conceived of as "alien" to the body. Instead, genetics promises to diagnose portions of the body itself as defective, or to remake the body itself.

To understand the impact of this difference, consider the required factors with two of the diseases the Human Genome Center has focused on most heavily—colon and breast cancer. First, for these diseases the "cure" currently requires removal of the offending organ. Colon removal and radical mastectomy may be preferable to death from cancer, but they are not the kind of treatment that one recommends casually. This radical approach to cure is especially problematic because the genetic configuration associated with the disease gives only a predisposition to cancer, not a certain prediction. Though 85 percent of women from cancer-prone families with the BRCA1 gene will have breast cancer by age seventy, 15 percent will not. Moreover, mastectomy substantially reduces the risk of breast cancer, but it does not eliminate the possibility. Moreover, there are other treatments, such as close monitoring through self and clinical examination and mammography, that do not cure the disease but may not require such physically horrific treatment. Which does one choose? And when? No one knows at what age the diseases of colon cancer and breast cancer will strike. Do you remove the colon of a twelve-year-old to prevent a cancer that may strike at thirty?

A genetic "diagnosis" of the predisposition toward disease thus marks a body as fundamentally flawed, but the actual biological life-course of the individual is only indeterminately linked to this genetic flaw. Individuals cannot take such diagnoses lightly, dismissing them as mere probabilities, because the consequences of such dismissal may be too grave and are too probable. Yet the diagnosis does not prescribe a particular cure or even the need for a cure. The gap in probability is made enormously consequential by the fact that the treatments needed are (because the cause is fundamental) very radical in themselves.

Precisely because genetic medicine seeks to control something that is so fundamental to the human body, and because there are so many complex linkages among genes and the rest of the body's systems, that control entails fundamental difficulties. Those difficulties include not only the technical problems associated with manipulating genes, but also a host of biosocial factors. How do non-technically trained persons assimilate the complex risk factors, trade-offs, and consequences in order to make these decisions for themselves? How can technically trained persons make these decisions for others, when the decisions are so integrally related to one's cultural and personal values and one's socio-economic and personal situations? There is therefore no ideal decision, no ideal model of control of genes, and also no ideal controller for the exercise of genetic control. I would argue that this suggests that there are inherent limitations in any effort to control one's own identity, built from the limits of one's identity. Current public discourse about genetic medicine displays the material, social, and linguistic confluence of such limits.

The aporetic stasis of the public discourse about genetics has arisen, therefore, because scientists and medical personnel have been forced to recognize that rational, technical control of the fundamental being of the body is not separable from the biosocial limits of those bodies in their worlds. Unfortunately, the major critical discourse in response to this aporia has been no wiser. It has simply sought to deny the criticality of the role of genes in the body (e.g., Hubbard and Wald 158; Lippman 1,471). Both sides lead us to ignore the significance and problems raised by the interfaces of the gene and by knowledge of the gene in our lives, perhaps because both sides are underwritten by an understanding of codes that is immaterial and arhetorical. A better way to come to terms with ourselves (both our limits and our potentials) is to look through glasses that focus the materiality of codes and the central roles of materialized rhetorics and other codes (such as DNA) in human life. I fear that there is much work for a material rhetoric to do here in the next century.

General Implications of a Material Perspective on Code-Sharing

The proto-theory of linguistic materialism that I have offered seeks to bridge the gap between the "idea" and the "material" realm—between the mind and the body—by understanding ideas through the activity of coding, which is itself a material activity, incorporating forms based on the character of identity and relationship. It asks us to recognize that the materialism endorsed for the social formation is of a piece with the materialism of the body. It encourages rhetoricians to develop critical approaches that discount neither the social formation nor the body in favor of idealistic (Platonic, Cartesian, or ultra-structuralist) notions of codes.

I am aware that mine is not likely to be a popular agenda among (post)humanists. When scientists have yelled "Nature!" we humanists have always yelled "Nurture!" in return. Such exclamations are not only emotionally gratifying, but they also have served the laudable object of producing some (small) social balance against the forces of pure reductionist biologism and physicalism. Nonetheless, I cannot help but feel that the shout of "nurture" is insufficient to an account of our being and speaking. Rather than seeing all human behavior as reducible to biology, or rather than seeing all of biology as a flaccid, inactive product of social codes, I believe we can have the sophistication to view an active biology in conversation with an active social coding system. Viewing both forms of action as coding provides a bridge for this sort of discourse, and such a form of discourse can offer new visions, new usages, and new critical capacities to the repertoire of rhetoricians.

I have provided here only a "proto-theory" toward that end. I have, after all, critiqued Derrida and Foucault for refuting the concept of "reference" without specifying what kind of being language might have, and how it is related to the other biosocial forces in the world. This chapter has provided only the smallest of gestures toward that larger project. As I understand it, my achievements have been, first, simply to show that the materialist project is one that is not yet accomplished (some appearances in social theory to the contrary), and second, to indicate that this materiality must take account of language's physical manifestations and the way in which the material recalcitrance of other aspects of the biosocial sphere relate to it. In the face of these small contributions, I take consolation in the fact that it is the glory and the trial of material actions that, not being ideal concoctions safely ensconced in a dreamer's imagination, they require much labor, social interaction, and time's evolution to construct.

Notes

Thank you to Jack Selzer, Sharon Crowley, and the participants in the Penn State Conference on Rhetoric and Composition, 1997, for their feedback on various drafts of this chapter. Their critical challenges to my views have been enormously helpful to me in refining them.

1. The preferable, "rhetorical/material" alternative would be to replace the sign–referent relationship with the speaker–audience relationship. I see this as taking a further step in a direction plotted by Derrida, in two ways. First, it draws on Derrida's deconstruction of "being" as a relationship between a speaker/thinker and the sign that is the self-presence of the referent to the person (philosopher), though it doesn't accept Derrida's alternative. Derrida explicitly denies the receiver/speaker relationship as the site of the meaning (function) of the sign because he argues that contexts are never delimitable in a definitive (external, objective) fashion, and because he remains (albeit ironically, unwillingly) within one part of the Platonic tradition, which seeks to place the sign outside the control of "man as the measure of all things." He thus seeks to displace "intent" and does not realize that the alternative to speaker intent is not necessarily an eternally open/closed coded mark (a code that is both universal and not, both Platonic and not—as in *Spurs* 137), but instead in a relationship among persons and social systems (rather than between sign-code or sign-speaker). Derrida is in error on these moves because the nondelimitability of a context from the outside is a philosophical requirement, not a rhetorical one. A context is delimitable to the communicators employing sign sets in whatever ways they delimit it (whether consciously or not). Hence, delimitability is a philosophical and critical problem, not a functional problem—and not the basis for denying the reality of the specific actions of code-sharing, within their historical-social context, as the site of the source of the meaning of discourse. Moreover, the alternative of human relationships in place of sign-code relationships allows us to return to a notion of presence, not as the (static, permanent, fixed) presence of the sign/referent to the person (philosopher), but rather as the processual presence of the one and the other to each other in signification through the encrustations of social history (rhetoric = identification/consubstantiality: Burke, *Rhetoric of Motives* 19ff.). The move I propose is thus, second, methodologically in tune with Derrida's flight from philosophy.

2. This in spite of the fact that he posits a general writing to transcend a specific writing (e.g., *Limited Inc.* 10) that would be in some ways institutional and thus material. He points to such a concept but does not develop it.

3. The theory would run something like this: Tracks and traces are tracks and traces of previous social, personal, and relational usages evidenced both in the vocabulary and grammar learned by humans and in the other material social relationships, including de-

ployment of buildings, institutional structures, economic distributions, and so forth. The code thus constitutes both "deferred" meanings and also present meanings. The code, as the presence of the past, has a distinctive quality of materiality that, having been deferred, represents ranges of possibilities and interpretations rather than the material quality of a brick wall that has a sort of imminent recalcitrance. I don't know whether Derrida would embrace such a theoretical expansion.

4. The rhetorical alternative again draws on Wittgensteinian notions of meaning so that there need be no distinction between enunciation and statement. Instead, a statement is only quasi-unified, not fully unified, and it consists of a series of overlapping potentials, a shared repertoire, from which is drawn a range of possibilities, potentially infinite but not all-inclusive.

5. Richard Harlan has coined the term *super-structuralism* to represent some of these tendencies, but the overlap is not precise.

6. Fox Keller notices the disjunction between information theory and the use of the concepts of information in genetics discourse, but she does not seem to recognize the ways in which the relinkage of information with specific cell functions is a constructive interpretive move made routinely by many geneticists in practice, if not in their editorials to a broader audience.

7. Scientists have been able to adopt this approach only through a historical accident. Their philosophies of science valorized only objects to begin with, but when they discovered the genetic code, there had already developed a theory of language (information approaches) that specified the process orientation. In language theory, that process orientation was alloyed to the older spirit dimension, but scientists were able to adopt only the process portion of the model because they had the object model as an anchor.

8. I think it is possible to read Burke's notion of "substance" as consonant with a materialist epistemology, though I would hate to expend too much effort arguing for a particular interpretation of any language philosopher (see Condit, "Post-Burke"). I believe that Burke's discussion of action and motion seeks to get at some of this relationship, but ultimately Burke was blinkered by the idea/object distinction and unable quite to get to an object/process orientation. Responding to the behavioralists, he was still trying to emphasize what was distinctive about human beings as opposed to animals, and that led him to the ideational fallacy. His emphasis on the substantiality of language nonetheless laid important groundwork for the next move.

9. Compare this with Derrida's assertion that some meaning components are fully translatable between languages: "Such a stratum of readability could eventually be translated with no loss into any language which disposes of a certain material" (*Spurs* 129).

10. I here modify Burke's assignment of action to linguistically motivated motions; instead I offer a tripartite system—movement/motion/action—where movement is assigned to objects, motion is assigned to the purposive behaviors of all living things, and action is linguistically motivated motion.

11. Note that this usage does not require that intentionality means consciousness. DNA simply has a structure that tends to reproduce under the right conditions: with a given temperature and with particular amino acids in proximity and with the lack of other acids in proximity, etc., DNA unzips and, through purely physical and chemical forces, each half of the spiral helix attracts new elements to reconstruct its "other half" so that it is once again as it was. For DNA, reproduction is uniquely about retaining half

of its formal/material self and exchanging half of its material self so that it once again becomes its formal self. To that extent, it seems appropriate to say that DNA reproduces (or allows the reproduction of) its own identity. It thereby also and necessarily participates in the reproduction of the cell.

12. I believe that Derrida's deconstructive method, and the oppositional critical discourse that relies heavily on it epistemologically if not methodologically, offer an alternative, and less desirable, approach to language than that offered by Wittgenstein. As other critics have noted, Derrida's approach is to show that language does not, after all (i.e., as promised by the objectivists), offer us fixed and stable categories. Derrida attempts to respond to this attack in *Limited Inc.* (117), but there he ultimately concedes that he remains within the philosophic game of "all or nothing" as a necessity of the game. A rhetorical discourse, following the lines of Wittgenstein, does not have to play the "all or nothing" game (though it can do so when it wants to!). Therefore, though he intends to deny it, Derrida's discourse gives support to the conclusion that there is no fixity or stability—literally no "meaning" (see especially in Baudrillard 17)—to language. Wittgenstein's alternative is to say that language is not fixed, stable, and clear, but that it is not therefore meaningless. Between the absolute certainty and precision of the objectivists and the absolute untetheredness of the ultra-structuralists, Wittgenstein offers a sense of language which sees its categories as fuzzy agglomerations (family resemblances) operating within fixed parameters (games). These fuzzy characteristics and boundaries of application do not invalidate meaning but simply make it more complex. I advocate and (fallibly) try to operate with a Wittgensteinian notion here, and it is that orientation that I urge to the term *identity*.

13. You might perceive here an important route for further specification of the functioning of language as form in a material theory of rhetoric.

14. The fundamental purpose is to code identity, because purpose requires the recognition of the same/different that is intrinsic to coding. This formulation seems to solve the problem of providing a post-structural materialist accounting of intent. We need not understand intent as rational autonomy or independence from social circumstances. Rather, we can define intent as the production of codes through a highly complex interacting set of corporeally distinguished code/identity-producing entities. To make such a definition, let us view a human being as a corporeally delimited organism with linguistic abilities ("bodies that learn languages," in Burke's words). Each individual is absolutely unique. While each is shaped by both social and biological forces that are not unique, the particular intersection of the multiple forces on the particular body is unique. That unique identity is accumulated through a personal history (lived experience of pasts, not narrated accounts of those pasts). Thus, when any given (new) circumstance arises—that is, when any new social force impinges on an individual, inciting response or providing opportunity—then those social forces must play out through the material structure that is the encoded body of the individual. In the case of humans, an enormously significant part of that body is the particular language codes that form their personal equipment for living (the narratives of their life pasts, their ideologies, their vocabularies, and so on). Hence, individuals with similar backgrounds may, in a statistical sense, generally act in similar fashions (they may be statistically predictable), as post-Marxist, feminist, post-colonialist, and other theories dictate; but all individuals subject

to particular identity-making forces do not act uniformly, nor are their codings predictable with precision.

Thus, though one's intentions might be traceable in rather specific ways to social forces, it also makes sense to say that a particular action flows out of the particular person's intent. That is, each person's intention, though strongly directed by social (and bio logical) forces, is uniquely that person's because it is also a unique characteristic of the particular interstices of social factors in interaction with the particular corporal encoding of that particular human body (code-set) as it has developed through its own personal history or trajectory.

This linguistically material account has the advantage that it allows, perhaps requires, us for different research purposes to locate rhetoric both at the site of the individual and at the site of the social, and even in the relationships between the two.

15. Viruses are interesting exceptions. Their identity relationships are trickier because they presume a complex self/other code. The virus has its own DNA, but for it, the host cell's DNA is also the virus's "host"—which in turn must have a specificity that the virus identifies with and thus in a particular way is also its self as an addressee. However, there is also a disidentification between viral DNA and host DNA from the perspective of the host, a factor which constitutes a kind of asymmetrical power relationship.

Works Cited

Baudrillard, Jean. *Fatal Strategies*. Translated by Philip Beitchman and W. G. J. Niesluchowski. New York: Semiotext(e)/Pluto, 1990.

Brock, Bernard, ed. *Kenneth Burke and Contemporary European Thought*. University: University of Alabama Press, 1995.

Burke, Kenneth. *Language as Symbolic Action: Essays on Life, Literature, and Method*. Berkeley: University of California Press, 1966.

Burke, Kenneth. *Permanence and Change: An Anatomy of Purpose*. 3d ed. Berkeley: University of California Press, 1984.

Burke, Kenneth. *A Rhetoric of Motives*. 1950. Berkeley: University of California Press, 1969.

Collins, Francis. Statement of the Director, National Center for Human Genome Research. *Department of Labor, Health and Human Services. Education, and Related Agencies Appropriations for 1994. Part 4: National Institute of Health*. Washington, D.C.: Government Printing Office, 1994.

Condit, Celeste. "How Bad Science Stays That Way: Brain Sex, Demarcation, and the Status of Truth in the Rhetoric of Science." *Rhetoric Society Quarterly* 26 (1996): 82–109.

Condit, Celeste. "Kenneth Burke and Linguistic Reflexivity: Reflections on the Scene of the Philosophy of Communication in the Twentieth Century." In *Kenneth Burke and Contemporary European Thought*, edited by Bernard Brock, 207–62. University: University of Alabama Press, 1995.

Condit, Celeste. "Post-Burke. Transcending the Sub-stance of Dramatism." *Quarterly Journal of Speech* 78 (1992): 349–55.

Derrida, Jacques. *Limited Inc.* 1988. Reprint, Chicago: Northwestern University Press, 1995.

Derrida, Jacques. *Of Grammatology*. Translated by Gayatri Chakravorty Spivak. Baltimore: Johns Hopkins University Press, 1976.

Derrida, Jacques. *Spurs: Nietzsche's Styles*. Translated by Barbara Harlow. Chicago: University of Chicago Press, 1979.

Eco, Umberto. *A Theory of Semiotics*. Bloomington: Indiana University Press, 1979.

Foucault, Michel. *The Archaeology of Knowledge and The Discourse on Language*. Translated by A. M. Sheridan Smith. New York: Pantheon, 1972.

Harding, Sandra. *The Science Question in Feminism*. Ithaca: Cornell University Press, 1986.

Harlan, Richard. *Superstructuralism: The Philosophy of Structuralism and Post-Structuralism*. 1987. Reprint, London: Routledge, 1994.

Hubbard, Ruth, and Elijah Wald. *Exploding the Gene Myth: How Genetic Information Is Produced and Manipulated by Scientists, Physicians, Employers, Insurance Companies, Educators, and Law Enforcers*. Boston: Beacon, 1993.

Kay, Lily E. *The Molecular Vision of Life: Caltech, the Rockefeller Foundation, and the Rise of the New Biology*. New York: Oxford University Press, 1993.

Keller, Evelyn Fox. *Refiguring Life: Metaphors of Twentieth-Century Biology*. New York: Columbia University Press, 1995.

Kevles, Daniel J., and LeRoy Hood, eds. *The Code of Codes: Scientific and Social Issues in the Human Genome Project*. Cambridge, Mass.: Harvard University Press, 1992.

Kroker, Arthur. "The Arc of Dead Power: Margritte/Baudrillard/Augustine." *Canadian Journal of Political and Social Theory* 8 (1984): 53–69.

Lewontin, Richard C. "The Dream of the Human Genome." *New York Review of Books*, 28 May 1992: 31–40.

Lippman, Abby. "Led (Astray) by Genetic Maps: The Cartography of the Human Genome and Health Care." *Social Science and Medicine* 35 (1992): 1,469–76.

McGee, Michael Calvin. "The 'Ideograph': A Link Between Rhetoric and Ideology." *Quarterly Journal of Speech* 66 (1980): 1–17.

McGee, Michael Calvin. "A Materialist's Conception of Rhetoric." In *Explorations in Rhetoric: Studies in Honor of Douglas Ehninger*, edited by Ray E. McKerrow, 23–48. Glenview, Ill.: Scott, Foresman, 1982.

Nelkin, Dorothy, and Susan Lindee. *The DNA Mystique: The Gene as Cultural Icon*. New York: W. H. Freeman, 1995.

Peters, John Durham. "John Locke, the Individual, and the Origin of Communication." *Quarterly Journal of Speech* 75 (1989): 387–99.

Rosner, Mary, and T. R. Johnson. "Telling Stories: Metaphors of the Human Genome Project." *Hypatia* 10 (1995): 104–29.

Saussure, Ferdinand de. *Course in General Linguistics*. New York: McGraw-Hill, 1966.

Wander, Philip. "The Third Persona: An Ideological Turn in Rhetorical Theory." *Communication Studies* 35 (1984): 197–216.

Wittgenstein, Ludwig. *Philosophical Investigations*. Translated by G. E. M. Anscombe. Oxford: Basil Blackwell, 1963.

16 *Sharon Crowley*

Afterword
The Material of Rhetoric

I began writing this book by trying to consider the materiality of the
body only to find that the thought of materiality invariably moved me
into other domains. I tried to discipline myself to stay on the subject,
but found that I could not fix bodies as simple objects of thought. Not
only did bodies tend to indicate a world beyond themselves, but this
movement beyond their own boundaries, a movement of boundary itself, appeared to be quite central to what bodies "are."

Judith Butler, Bodies That Matter

In his introduction to this book Jack Selzer notes that we live in an era marked
by a so-called discursive turn, an era in which scholars have been preoccupied
with "the text" and the ways in which discourse is thought to play a role not only
in the invention of culture but in the construction of reality as well. If rhetorical theorists celebrated the discursive turn as a welcome return of scholarly interest in language and hence in rhetoric, they may now be dismayed to learn
of the interest in bodies and the material that is displayed in this book. What,
they might ask, does rhetoric have to do with bodies and matter? Rhetoric is
after all a verbal art, they might aver, and this is why the canon of delivery
has (justifiably) received only sporadic attention from rhetorical theorists since
ancient times (Urch). It is a fine irony, then, that at the very moment when post-
structuralist philosophers have legitimated the study of rhetoric, rhetoricians
are being urged to look at the human body and the material conditions and
practices associated with it. The chapters herein, most of them written by scholars who identify with rhetorical studies, manifest a great deal of interest in bodies—pregnant, queer, eaten, drugged, dissected, rustic, testable bodies. We
read too about the material conditions and practices—images, texts, monuments, institutional inertia—that produce such bodies. Where have such scholarly interests come from?

The scholarly focus on bodies and material practices owes much to the
second-wave American feminists who launched a thoroughgoing critique of re-

ceived attitudes about sex, gender, and the body during the 1970s. Susan Bordo eloquently makes the case that it was feminists who first cast their scholarly gaze on bodies: "Neither Foucault nor any other post-structuralist thinker discovered or invented the idea . . . that the 'definition and shaping' of the body is 'the focal point for struggles over the shape of power.' That was discovered by feminism, and long before it entered into its marriage with post-structuralist thought" (17). To bring her point home, Bordo quotes from a set of consciousness-raising exercises for men, developed by second-wave feminists in 1971:

> Sit down in a straight chair. Cross your legs at the ankles and keep your knees pressed together. Try to do this while you're having a conversation with someone, but pay attention at all times to keeping your knees pressed tightly together.
> Run a short distance, keeping your knees together. You'll find you have to take short, high steps if you run this way. Women have been taught it is unfeminine to run like a man with long, free strides. See how far you get running this way for thirty seconds.
> Walk down a city street. Pay a lot of attention to your clothing; make sure your pants are zipped, shirt tucked in, buttons done. Look straight ahead. Every time a man walks past you, avert your eyes and make your face expressionless. (19)

I quote this passage, in the age of Chamique Holdsclaw, not to make the point that "You've come a long way, baby." To the contrary, I suspect that even now many of my women readers will find their public behavior depicted in the last paragraph of the passage. I do want the passage to point up the fact that, in modern culture, women are particularly well placed to develop analyses and critiques of the body and of the regimes that govern bodily practices. Women's worth has been measured through and by their bodies: Are these virginal or not? Impregnable or not? "Attractive" or not? Negatively charged cultural constructions of women's bodies as both dangerous and fragile have forced women to become highly conscious of their bodies—the space they occupy in a room, on the street, in a crowd. As objects of the male gaze, women know what it means to occupy the position of "the other," even if they do not read the philosophical texts in which they are imagined as such.

The great contribution made to body studies by second-wave feminists was their articulation of the fact that bodies are intricately enmeshed in what Bordo calls "the 'micropractices' of everyday life"—eating, cooking, cleaning house, wearing clothes, going to the doctor, to the hospital, to church, or to school. Feminists from Mary Wollstonecraft to Mary Daly forcefully elaborated the ways in which everyday material practices are saturated with politics. As second-wave feminists claimed, the personal is the political.

The fact that public discourse typically assumes a male subject (and hence a male body) has made it necessary for feminists to interrogate the assumptions that inform public practices and rhetoric about them. The assumption that distinct public and private spheres exist, for example, animates much contemporary rhetorical criticism of public discourse. However, it is doubtful whether this theoretical distinction has ever applied to women; that is, it is doubtful that the "official" public sphere—conceptualized by bourgeois theorists like Adam Smith and Joseph Addison in the eighteenth century, and revived by Habermas in our own—was conceived as a place wherein women traffic. This is emphatically not to say that women did not participate in public practices, as they continue to do today.[1] But we should remember that the eighteenth-century coffeehouses on which Habermas models his notion of the public sphere denied access to women. Women's bodies were banned from public spaces during the nineteenth century, and women were denied access to public discourse both de facto and de jure until first-wave feminists during the late nineteenth century secured their rights to own property, legally represent their children, and vote. (The connection between their inability to own property and their inability to claim legal rights to their own and their children's bodies was not lost on first-wave feminists.) It is also doubtful that contemporary women can easily locate or inhabit a so-called "private space" that shields them from the effects of certain public discourses, such as those governing health care and reproduction. Christina Haas's chapter richly details the complex legal struggles required to create such spaces for some of the women who utilize health clinics where abortions are performed. If a secure realm of privacy exists for women, surely it ought to include sexual habits and birth-control practices.

Animated by both political and scholarly agendas, then, feminist scholars continue to investigate the material conditions of reproduction, women's health, the circulation of disease, the distribution of justice, and other crucial issues. (The chapters by Hollis, Sharer, and Wells are contributions to this effort.) Investigations such as these are profoundly rhetorical. Feminists practice rhetoric when they attempt to have a voice in policy-making and when they intervene in public practices. But feminists, including feminist scholars, also analyze the public rhetorics that affect women's lives, not only in the attempt to understand how these are deployed but also in order to intervene in the power relations that produce and sustain them.

Post-structuralist thought also laid some important theoretical groundwork for the development of scholarly interest in bodies and material practices. One needs to be careful here: as Celeste Condit rightly observes in her chapter, a radical version of post-structuralist thought—what Condit calls "ultrastructuralism"—can be read as hostile to materialism and the material. Nonetheless, it remains true that some post-structuralist thinkers, such as Michel Foucault and Pierre Bourdieu, must be credited with contributing to the development of the theoretical machinery that allows us to think the body and the practices that produce it. Indeed, Pasi Falk, author of *The Consuming Body*, argues that post-structuralists' relentless resolution of dualisms into continua opened the way for the dissolution of the body/mind distinction that has been embedded in Western thought at least since Plato (4). Jacques Derrida has taught us that all such inherited dualisms privilege one term over the other, and of course Western thought has always privileged minds over bodies. The post-structuralist displacement of body/mind onto a continuum

$$\text{BODY} \longleftrightarrow \text{MIND}$$

privileges neither of these terms. Rather, it opens up a space for thinking about the relations that obtain between body and mind, and for speculating about the difficulty of distinguishing the limits of either in relation to the other.

Falk and other writers attribute to Sigmund Freud an early instance of the habit of eliding the distinction between *psyche* and *soma*. In *The Ego and the Id*, Freud comments on the constructive relation of the body to the ego:

A person's own body, and above all its surface, is a place from which both external and internal perceptions spring. It is seen like any other object, but to the touch it yields two kinds of sensations, one of which may be equivalent to an internal perception. . . . Pain, too, seems to play a part in the process, and the way in which we gain new knowledge of our organs during painful illnesses is perhaps a model of the way by which in general we arrived at the idea of our body. The ego is first and foremost a bodily ego; it is not merely a surface entity, but is itself the projection of a surface. (19–20)

In this passage there is such play with the notion of "the surface" that it is difficult to draw any other conclusion than that drawn by Freud: egos are bodily entities. Because of the way human perception works, the ego does not just depend on the body for its formation but projects itself as an imagined body, as the surface it imagines itself "to inhabit." The surface is the interior, the outside is the inside, there is no sure way of telling which is which.

So much, then, for another inherited distinction on which the mind/body dualism depended: inside and outside. Freud's analysis of the embodiment of perception, and hence of ego, raises an interesting series of questions. How do we mark "the inside" of a human body as opposed to its "outside"? Where, for example, does the "outside" of the human eye end or begin? At the eyeball? The iris? The retina? But then where does the retina begin and end? Female genitalia raise further interesting questions about the confidence with which we can distinguish between bodily insides and outsides, as Luce Irigaray has convincingly demonstrated. And, to elaborate on Freud's example, when I place two parts of my body together, say, touching thumb to index finger, both digits experience the touch as both "inside" and "outside." To distinguish skin as the differentiating organ requires intense concentration, as well as my (learned) assumption that the "skin" of my thumb is the same "skin" that covers my finger. Is the mouth an "inside" or an "outside"? In her chapter on the Donner expedition, Christine De Vinne notes the grim fascination with which Americans contemplated the news that members of this group had practiced cannibalism. I suspect that fascination with the Donner story has to do, at least in part, with its challenge to the distinctions we like to make between bodily insides and out-sides, and our habit of attaching our sense of identity to the presumed limits of the body.[2] Once someone has consumed (parts of) someone else, who is she? Something of this same uneasiness apparently attends the practice of organ do-nation. Very few people sign up as organ donors when they are issued drivers' licenses, and the bodies of only about 10 percent of donors are made available to hospitals. Families, it seems, are loath to allow parts of their loved ones to become part of someone else.

Cultural anxiety about bodily boundaries exhibits itself in other ways as well. Scholars who study disability, as well as those who are interested in ex-ceptional bodies, are investigating the ways in which cultural-material prac-tices shape and maintain what is included in the category of "the normal body" and the cultural uses to which the category of the "not-normal" is put (Davis; Thomson). Our culture seems to do its most rigorous policing around the boundaries of the sexed body in an effort to maintain a rigid distinction between male and female. In her study of hermaphroditism, Elizabeth Grosz notes that even though the existence and formation of external genitalia are the criteria most often used to determine anatomical sex, there are at least six different combinations of additional factors—such as chromosomal sex, internal sex organs, and hormonal functions—that combine to produce beings whose sex might be said to be both female and male (59–60). The problem, says Grosz, is not with hermaphroditic bodies but with a restrictive system of sexual clas-sification that insists on a bipolar distinction between male and female. Within such a regime, we do not celebrate the multiplicity of sexes "given" us by "na-ture"; rather, we presume that people whose bodies do not clearly comply with our bipolar definition of "true sexuality" are inadequately or inappropriately sexed, and we urge or force them to become one or the other. If our presump-tion of bipolar sex is troubled by the range and variety of sexes found in nature, it becomes even more troubling when we discover, as we do when reading the work of Thomas Laquer and other historians of sexuality, that "male" and "fe-male" have not always been defined as they now are.

The body $\leftrightarrow$ mind continuum also complicates modern notions of iden-tity and the self. Bodies are sexed, raced, gendered, abled or disabled, whole or fragmented, aged or young, fat, thin, or anorexic. In other words, bodies are marked in ways that carry a great deal of cultural freight. Identities are also marked by cultural constructions of bodies, and hence cultural evaluations of bodies extend to the subjects who inhabit them and with whose limits they are supposedly coterminous. Certainly this is the point of Peter Mortensen's study of rusticity, included here. Students of the new field called "whiteness studies" take this insight as their motivation as well, assuming that the cultural privilege accorded to bodies marked as racially white produces something that can be called "white identity" (Dyer).

Freud's elision of body-mind also suggests that the private mental space accorded to "the self" on modern models of identity, the space of fantasy, is produced to some extent by the body's being-in-culture. Slavoj Zizek notes that "at its most fundamental, fantasy tells me what I am to others" (9). That is to say, our fantasies, those wonderful or terrifying stories we weave about ourselves in our supposedly most private moments, are actually extensions of culture into that space formerly and mistakenly called "mind." Zizek argues that fantasy has a "radically intersubjective character" insofar as it is "an attempt to provide an answer to the question 'What does society want from me,' to unearth the meaning of the murky events in which I am forced to participate." Hence the rabidly racist fantasies advanced by white supremacists, say, are not simply graphic projections of a mental force called "hatred" onto the bodies of others, as the traditional account would have it. Zizek reads such fantasies, rather, as the racist's attempt to cope with the realization that his identity is not in fact the founding center of the universe—that he inhabits a network of ideological and material relations that relate, at best, indifferently to his person.

So, fantasy is constructed, at least in part, by ideology. Does it at the same time construct ideology? In other words, is the body ↔ mind continuum repeated when human beings are considered as aggregates? Certainly, feminist thinkers have taken the psychoanalytic insight about the intersubjective nature of fantasy in overtly political directions. In her recent work Zillah Eisenstein reminds us that shared fantasies have physical impacts on real bodies. Arguing that ethnic hatreds are projections of "fear of the other," Eisenstein writes that "hatred is not only color-coded but inscribed on such body parts as noses, hair, vaginas, eyes. . . . Bodies are always in part psychic constructions of meaning symbolized through coloring hatred on sexualized sites" (22). This is one reason why the enactment of ethnic and racial hatreds in war or other violent episodes often involves rape and torture. The aim is not merely to inflict pain, but actually to eradicate the enemy's subjectivity by invading, harming, and even erasing his or her body (Scarry).

Jacqueline Rose argues further that fantasy "fuels . . . the forging of the collective will. . . . You don't have to buy into Freud's account of hidden guilt to recognize the force in the real world of the unconscious dreams of nations" (3). Rose's primary example is Israel, where, she says, "if you listen to one dominant rhetoric, it seems as if Israel cannot grant statehood to the Palestinians, not just because of felt real and present danger, but also because so great is the charge of fantasy against such a possibility, that, were it to be granted, the nation would lose all inner rationale and psychically collapse in on itself" (4). Rose's work causes me to speculate about the shared fantasies that motivate other nations' politics. The reunification of Germany seems to mark a triumph of national fantasy over impossible realities, while the American fantasy of superpowerhood rationalizes sending thousands of young bodies to Iraq, to Panama, to Rwanda, to Bosnia, either to make war or to keep the peace (which is which is not always clear).

And what has all this to do with rhetoric? Not much, certainly, if rhetoric is defined as "strategic, agent-centered discourse in the public realm" (Gross and Keith 2). Celeste Condit's theory of linguistic materialism, elaborated in this book, puts the notion of agency under severe strain—that is, if "agency" refers to a sovereign actor, fully aware of the discursive and practical constraints operating on discourse and able to embody persuasive intent in a spoken or written text. I do think, however, that rhetoric's traditional association with public discourse is still one of its defining characteristics. Contemporary claims that the *polis* has ceased to exist, it seems to me, overlook the multiple arenas in which such public discourse is staged and waged (King). The chapters in this book suggest a wide range of public arenas in which rhetoric is operative, from abortion clinics to memorial areas to media depictions of ideological loyalty. They demonstrate how discourses like those of AIDS prevention or the beautiful pregnancy actually produce practices that circumscribe or open new or other possibilities.

From my point of view, one of the most important contributions to rhetorical studies of analyses like these is that they point up the interestedness of boundary-drawing and distinction-making. Distinctions and boundaries are never disinterested: when someone is named as a witch, a factory worker, a rustic, or an illiterate, someone else profits from that distinction. When images are distinguished from texts, someone profits. What I learn from these chapters is that no body is disinterested. And that is why this work is central to rhetorical studies, which has always taken the study of partisanship as its province.

Notes

1. See Eley and Ryan for elaborations of this historical fact. My point is only that the "official" public sphere characterized in theory is a male or masculinized sphere. For arguments in support of this position, see Fraser and Pateman.

2. See Derrida and Falk for elaborations of this argument.

Works Cited

Bordo, Susan R. *Unbearable Weight: Feminism, Western Culture, and the Body.* Berkeley: University of California Press, 1993.

Butler, Judith. *Bodies that Matter: On the Discursive Limits of "Sex."* New York: Routledge, 1993.

Davis, Lennard J. "Constructing Normalcy: The Bell Curve, the Novel, and the Invention of the Disabled Body in the Nineteenth Century." In *The Disability Studies Reader*, edited by Lennard J. Davis, 9–28. New York: Routledge, 1997.

Derrida, Jacques. "'Eating Well,' or the Calculation of the Subject: An Interview with Jacques Derrida." In *Who Comes After the Subject?*, edited by Eduardo Cadava et al., 96–119. New York: Routledge, 1991.

Dyer, Richard. *White*. New York: Routledge, 1997.

Eisenstein, Zillah. *Hatreds: Racialized and Sexualized Conflicts in the 21st Century*. New York: Routledge, 1996.

Eley, Geoff. "Nations, Publics, and Political Cultures: Placing Habermas in the Nineteenth Century." In *Habermas and the Public Sphere*, edited by Craig Calhoun, 236–58. Cambridge, Mass.: MIT Press, 1997.

Falk, Pasi. *The Consuming Body*. London: Sage, 1994.

Fraser, Nancy. "Rethinking the Public Sphere: A Contribution to the Critique of Actually Existing Democracy." *Social Text* 25/26 (1990): 56–80.

Freud, Sigmund. *The Ego and the Id*. Translated by Joan Riviere. Edited by James Strachey. New York: Norton, 1960.

Gross, Alan G., and William M. Keith. Introduction. In *Rhetorical Hermeneutics: Invention and Interpretation in the Age of Science*, edited by Alan G. Gross and William M. Keith, 1–22. Albany: SUNY Press, 1997.

Grosz, Elizabeth. "Intolerable Ambiguity: Freaks as/at the Limit." In *Freakery: Cultural Spectacles of the Extraordinary Body*, edited by Rosemarie Garland Thomson, 55–66. New York: New York University Press, 1996.

Irigaray, Luce. *This Sex Which Is Not One*. Translated by Catherine Porter. Ithaca: Cornell University Press, 1985.

King, Andrew. "The Rhetorical Critic and the Invisible Polis." In *Rhetorical Hermeneutics: Invention and Interpretation in the Age of Science*, edited by Alan Gross and William M. Keith, 299–314. Albany: SUNY Press, 1997.

Laquer, Thomas. *Making Sex: Body and Gender from the Greeks to Freud*. Cambridge, Mass.: Harvard University Press, 1990.

Pateman, Carol. *The Sexual Contract*. Stanford: Stanford University Press, 1988.

Rose, Jacqueline. *States of Fantasy*. Oxford: Clarendon Press, 1996.

Ryan, Mary N. "Gender and Public Access: Women's Politics in Nineteenth-Century America." In *Habermas and the Public Sphere*, edited by Craig Calhoun, 259–88. Cambridge, Mass.: MIT Press, 1997.

Scarry, Elaine. *The Body in Pain: The Making and Unmaking of the World*. Oxford: Oxford University Press, 1985.

Thomson, Rosemarie Garland. "Introduction: From Wonder to Error—a Genealogy of Freak Discourse in Modernity." In *Freakery: Cultural Spectacles of the Extraordinary Body*, edited by Rosemarie Garland Thomson, 1–19. New York: New York University Press, 1996.

Urch, Kakie. "Big Gun: The Canon of Delivery, Rhetorical Production, and Power." Unpublished MS.

Zizek, Slavoj. *The Plague of Fantasies*. London: Verso, 1997.

Selected Bibliography on Material Rhetoric

Contributors

Index

Selected Bibliography on Material Rhetoric

Allen, Theodore W. *Racial Oppression and Social Control*. Vol. 1 of *The Invention of the White Race*. London: Verso/New Left, 1994.

Arendt, Hannah. *The Human Condition*. Chicago: University of Chicago Press, 1958.

Balsamo, Anne. *Technologies of the Gendered Body: Reading Cyborg Women*. Durham: Duke University Press, 1996.

Barthes, Roland. *The Fashion System*. Berkeley: University of California Press, 1990.

Barthes, Roland. *Mythologies*. Translated by Annette Lavers. New York: Hill and Wang, 1972.

Baudrillard, Jean. *Fatal Strategies*. Translated by Philip Beitchman and W. G. J. Niesluchowski. New York: Semiotext(e)/Pluto, 1990.

Beck, Ulrich. *Risk Society*. London: Sage, 1992.

Bell, Elizabeth, Lynda Haas, and Laura Sells, eds. *From Mouse to Mermaid: The Politics of Film, Gender, and Culture*. Bloomington: Indiana University Press, 1995.

Bell, Vikki. *Interrogating Incest: Feminism, Foucault, and the Law*. London: Routledge, 1993.

Berger, John. *About Looking*. New York: Pantheon, 1980.

Berger, John. *Ways of Seeing*. New York: Viking, 1973.

Berlin, James. "Revisionary Histories of Rhetoric: Politics, Power, and Plurality." In *Writing Histories of Rhetoric*, edited by Victor Vitanza, 112–27. Carbondale: Southern Illinois University Press, 1994.

Berlin, James. "Revisionary History: The Dialectical Method." In *Rethinking the History of Rhetoric*, edited by Takis Poulakos, 135–51. Boulder: Westview, 1993.

Bhaba, Homi. *Location of Culture*. New York: Routledge, 1994.

Biesecker, Barbara. "Coming to Terms with Recent Attempts to Write Women into the History of Rhetoric." *Philosophy and Rhetoric* 12:2 (1992): 140–61.

Bizzell, Patricia. "Opportunities for Feminist Research in the History of Rhetoric." *Rhetoric Review* 11 (Fall 1992): 50–58.

Blair, Carole. "Refiguring Systems of Rhetoric." *Pre/Text* 12:3–4 (1991): 180–89.

Blair, Karen J. *The History of American Women's Voluntary Organizations, 1810–1960. A Guide to Sources*. Boston: G. K. Hall, 1989.

Bolter, Jay David. "Ekphrasis, Virtual Reality, and the Future of Writing." In *The Future of the Book*, edited by Geoffrey Nunberg, 253–72. Berkeley: University of California Press, 1996.

Bordo, Susan R. "The Body and the Reproduction of Femininity: A Feminist Appropriation of Foucault." In *Gender/Body/Knowledge: Feminist Reconstructions of Being and Knowing*, edited by Alison M. Jaggar and Susan R. Bordo, 13–33. New Brunswick: Rutgers University Press, 1989.

Bordo, Susan R. "Reading the Male Body." *Michigan Quarterly Review* 32 (1993): 708–23.

Bordo, Susan R. *Twilight Zones: The Hidden Life of Cultural Images from Plato to O.J.* Berkeley: University of California Press, 1997.

Bordo, Susan R. *Unbearable Weight: Feminism, Western Culture, and the Body*. Berkeley: University of California Press, 1993.

Borst, Charlotte. *Catching Babies: The Professionalization of Childbirth, 1870–1920*. Cambridge, Mass.: Harvard University Press, 1995.

Bourdieu, Pierre. *The Logic of Practice*. Stanford: Stanford University Press, 1990.

Bourdieu, Pierre. *Outline of a Theory of Practice*. Cambridge: Cambridge University Press, 1977.

Boyle, T. Coraghessan. *World's End*. New York: Penguin, 1987.

Brandt, Deborah. *Literacy as Involvement: The Acts of Writers, Readers, and Texts*. Carbondale: Southern Illinois University Press, 1990.

Brodhead, Richard. *Cultures of Letters: Scenes of Reading and Writing in Nineteenth-Century America*. Chicago: University of Chicago Press, 1993.

Brodky, Linda, and Michelle Fine. "Presence of Mind in the Absence of the Body." In *Writing Permitted in Designated Areas Only*, edited by Linda Brodkey, 114–30. Minneapolis: University of Minnesota Press, 1996.

Brody, Miriam. *Manly Writing: Gender, Rhetoric, and the Rise of Composition*. Carbondale: Southern Illinois University Press, 1993.

Brumberg, Joan Jacobs. *The Body Project: An Intimate History of American Girls*. New York: Random House, 1997.

Bukatmin, Scott. *Terminal Identity: The Virtual Subject in Postmodern Science Fiction*. Durham: Duke University Press, 1993.

Burke, Kenneth. *Language as Symbolic Action: Essays on Life, Literature, and Method*. Berkeley: University of California Press, 1966.

Burke, Kenneth. *Permanence and Change: An Anatomy of Purpose*. 3d ed. Berkeley: University of California Press, 1984.

Burke, Kenneth. *A Rhetoric of Motives*. 1950. Reprint, Berkeley: University of California Press, 1969.

Butler, Judith. *Bodies that Matter: On the Discursive Limits of "Sex."* New York: Routledge, 1993.

Butler, Judith. *Excitable Speech: A Politics of the Performative.* New York: Routledge, 1997.

Butler, Judith. *Gender Trouble: Feminism and the Subversion of Identity.* New York: Routledge, 1990.

Butler, Judith. "Imitation and Gender Insubordination." In *Inside/Out: Lesbian Theories, Gay Theories,* edited by Diana Fuss, 13–31. New York: Routledge, 1991.

Calhoun, Craig, ed. *Habermas and the Public Sphere.* Cambridge, Mass.: MIT Press, 1993.

Carr, Stephen, Mark Francis, Leanne G. Rivlin, and Andrew M. Stone. *Public Space.* New York: Cambridge University Press, 1992.

Cloud, Dana L. "The Materiality of Discourse as Oxymoron: A Challenge to Critical Rhetoric." *Western Journal of Communication* 58 (1994): 141–63.

Comaroff, Jean. "Bodily Reform as Historical Practice." In *Ethnography and the Historical Imagination,* edited by John Comaroff and Jean Comaroff, 74–79. Boulder: Westview, 1992.

Conboy, Katie, Nadia Medina, and Sarah Stanburg, eds. *Writing on the Body: Female Embodiment and Feminist Theory.* New York: Columbia University Press, 1997.

Couser, G. Thomas. *Recovering Bodies: Illness, Disability, and Life Writing.* Madison: University of Wisconsin Press, 1997.

Crary, Jonathan, and Sanford Kwinter, eds. *Incorporations.* New York: Zone 6; distributed, Cambridge, Mass.: MIT Press, 1992.

Cravens, Hamilton. *The Triumph of Evolution: American Scientists and the Heredity–Environment Controversy, 1900–1941.* Philadelphia: University of Pennsylvania Press, 1978.

Davis, Lennard J. "Constructing Normalcy: The Bell Curve, the Novel, and the Invention of the Disabled Body in the Nineteenth Century." In *The Disability Studies Reader,* edited by Lennard J. Davis, 9–28. New York: Routledge, 1997.

Davis, Lennard J. *Enforcing Normalcy: Disability, Deafness, and the Body.* New York: Verse, 1995.

Dean, Tim. "Bodies That Matter: Rhetoric and Sexuality." *Pre/Text* 15 (1994): 80–92.

Dean-Jones, Lesley. *Women's Bodies in Classical Greek Science.* Oxford: Oxford University Press, 1994.

Degler, Carl N. *In Search of Human Nature: The Decline and Revival of Darwinism in American Social Thought.* New York: Oxford University Press, 1991.

Deleuze, Gilles. *Logic of the Sense.* Translated by Mark Lester. New York: Columbia University Press, 1990.

Deleuze, Gilles, and Felix Guattari. *Anti-Oedipus*. Vol. 1 of *Capitalism and Schizophrenia*. Translated R. Hurley et al. Minneapolis: University of Minnesota Press, 1983.

Deleuze, Gilles, and Felix Guattari. *A Thousand Plateaus*. Vol. 2 of *Capitalism and Schizophrenia*. Translated by Brian Masumi. Minneapolis: University of Minnesota Press, 1983.

Derrida, Jacques. *Limited Inc*. 1988. Reprint, Chicago: Northwestern University Press, 1995.

Derrida, Jacques. *Of Grammatology*. Translated by Gayatri Chakravorty Spivak. Baltimore: Johns Hopkins University Press, 1976.

Derrida, Jacques. *Spurs: Nietzsche's Styles*. Translated by Barbara Harlow. Chicago: University of Chicago Press, 1979.

Diamond, Irene, and Lee Quinby. *Feminism and Foucault: Reflections on Resistance*. Boston: Northeastern University Press, 1988.

Diprose, Rosalyn. *The Bodies of Women: Ethics, Embodiment, and Sexual Difference*. London: Routledge, 1994.

Diprose, Rosalyn, and Robyn Ferrell. *Cartographies: Poststructuralism and the Mapping of Bodies and Spaces*. North Sydney, Australia: Allen and Unwin, 1991.

Doyle, Laura. *Bordering on the Body: The Racial Matrix of Modern Fiction and Culture*. New York: Oxford University Press, 1994.

Doyle, Richard. *On Beyond Living: Rhetorical Transformations of the Life Sciences*. Stanford: Stanford University Press, 1997.

Duden, Barbara. *Disembodying Woman: Perspectives on Pregnancy and the Unborn*. Translated by Lee Hoinacki. Cambridge, Mass.: Harvard University Press, 1993.

Duden, Barbara. *The Woman beneath the Skin: A Doctor's Patients in Eighteenth-Century Germany*. Translated by Thomas Dunlap. Cambridge, Mass.: Harvard University Press, 1991.

Dyer, Richard. *White*. New York: Routledge, 1997.

Ebert, Teresa. *Ludic Feminism and After: Postmodernism, Desire, and Labor in Late Capitalism*. Ann Arbor: University of Michigan Press, 1996.

Elshtain, Jean Bethke. *Public Man, Private Woman: Women in Social and Political Thought*. Princeton: Princeton University Press, 1981.

Epstein, Julia. *Altered Conditions: Disease, Medicine, and Stoytelling*. New York: Routledge, 1995.

Epstein, Julia, and Kristina Straub, eds. *Body Guards: The Cultural Politics of Gender Ambiguity*. New York: Routledge, 1991.

Ewen, Stuart. *All Consuming Images*. New York: Basic Books, 1988.

Faigley, Lester, *Fragments of Rationality: Postmodernity and the Subject of Composition*. Pittsburgh: University of Pittsburgh Press, 1992.

Falk, Pasi. *The Consuming Body*. London: Sage, 1994.

Fanon, Franz. *Black Skin, White Masks*. Translated by Charles Markham. New York: Grove, 1967.

Fausto-Sterling, Anne. *Myths of Gender: Biological Theories about Women and Men*. 2d ed. New York: Basic Books, 1992.

Featherstone, Mike, Mike Hepworth, and Bryan Turner, eds. *The Body: Social Process and Cultural Theory*. Newberry Park, Calif.: Sage, 1991.

Finkelstein, Joanne. *The Fashioned Self*. Cambridge: Polity, 1991.

Foucault, Michel. *The Archaeology of Knowledge and The Discourse on Language*. 1971. Translated by A. M. Sheridan Smith. New York: Pantheon Books, 1972.

Foucault, Michel. *The Birth of the Clinic: An Archaeology of Medical Perception*. Translated by A. M. Sheridan Smith. New York: Pantheon, 1973.

Foucault, Michel. *Discipline and Punish: The Birth of the Prison*. Translated by Alan Sheridan. London: Penguin, 1975.

Foucault, Michel. *The History of Sexuality: An Introduction*. Vol. 1. Translated by Robert Hurley. New York: Vintage, 1980.

Foucault, Michel. "The Subject and Power." In *Michel Foucault: Beyond Structuralism and Hermeneutics*, edited by Hubert L. Dreyfus and Paul Rabinow, 208–26. 2d ed. Chicago: University of Chicago Press, 1983.

Fraser, Nancy. "Rethinking the Public Sphere: A Contribution to the Critique of Actually Existing Democracy." *Social Text* 25/26 (1990): 56–80.

Fraser, Nancy. *Unruly Practices: Power, Discourse, and Gender in Contemporary Social Theory*. Minneapolis: University of Minnesota Press, 1989.

Fuss, Diana, ed. *Essentially Speaking: Feminism, Nature, and Difference*. New York: Routledge, 1989.

Fuss, Diana, ed. *Inside/Out: Lesbian Theories, Gay Theories*. New York: Routledge, 1991.

Gallagher, Catherine, and Thomas Laqueur, eds. *The Making of the Modern Body: Sexuality and Society in the Nineteenth Century*. Berkeley: University of California Press, 1987.

Gallop, Jane. *Thinking through the Body*. New York: Columbia University Press, 1988.

Gatens, Moira. *Imagined Bodies: Ethics, Power, and Corporeality*. New York: Routledge, 1996.

Gates, Henry Louis. *The Signifying Monkey*. New York: Oxford, 1988.

Gere, Ann Ruggles. *Intimate Practices: Literacy and Cultural Work in US Women's Clubs, 1880–1920*. Champaign: University of Illinois Press, 1997.

Gere, Ann Ruggles. *Writing Groups: History, Theory and Implications*. Carbondale: Southern Illinois University Press, 1987.

Giddens, Anthony. *Modernity and Self-Identity: Self and Society in the Late Modern Age*. Cambridge: Polity, 1991.

Gilman, Sander. "Damaged Men: Thoughts on Kafka's Body." In *Constructing

Masculinity, edited by Maurice Berger et al., 176–89. New York: Routledge, 1995.

Gilmore, William J. *Reading Becomes a Necessity of Life: Material and Cultural Life in Rural New England, 1780–1835*. Knoxville: University of Tennessee Press, 1989.

Ginsberg, Faye D., and Rayna Rapp. *Conceiving the New World Order: The Global Politics of Reproduction*. Berkeley: University of California Press, 1995.

Giroux, Henry, ed. *Postmodernism, Feminism, and Cultural Politics: Redrawing the Educational Boundaries*. Albany: SUNY Press, 1991.

Glenn, Cheryl. *Rhetoric Retold: Regendering the Tradition from Antiquity to the Renaissance*. Carbondale: Southern Illinois University Press, 1997.

Gould, Stephen Jay. *The Mismeasure of Man*. New York: Norton, 1981.

Gray, Chris Habels, ed. *The Cyborg Handbook*. New York: Routledge, 1995.

Grosz, Elizabeth. "Bodies and Knowledges: Feminism and the Crisis of Reason." In *Feminist Epistemologies*, edited by Linda Alcoff and Elizabeth Potter, 187–216. New York: Routledge, 1993.

Grosz, Elizabeth. "Bodies–Cities." In *Sexuality and Space*, edited by Beatriz Colomina, 241–53. Princeton: Princeton University Press, 1992.

Grosz, Elizabeth. *Space, Time, and Perversion*. New York: Routledge, 1995.

Grosz, Elizabeth. *Volatile Bodies: Toward a Corporeal Feminism*. Bloomington: Indiana University Press, 1994.

Grosz, Elizabeth, and Elspeth Probyn. *Sexy Bodies: The Strange Carnalities of Feminism*. New York: Routledge, 1995.

Gullette, Margaret. *Declining to Decline: Cultural Combat and the Politics of the Midlife*. Charlottesville: University Press of Virginia, 1997.

Gumbrecht, Hans Ulrich, and K. Ludwig Pfeiffer, eds. *Materialists of Communication*. Translated by William Whobrey. Stanford: Stanford University Press, 1994.

Gurak, Laura. *Persuasion and Privacy in Cyberspace*. New Haven: Yale University Press, 1997.

Haas, Christina. *Writing Technology: Studies on the Materiality of Literacy*. Mahway, N.J.: Lawrence Erlbaum, 1996.

Habermas, Jürgen. *The Structural Transformation of the Public Sphere: An Inquiry into a Category of Bourgeois Society*. Translated by Thomas Burger. Cambridge, Mass.: MIT Press, 1989.

Haiken, Elizabeth. *Venus Envy: A History of Cosmetic Surgery*. Baltimore: Johns Hopkins University Press, 1997.

Haraway, Donna J. "A Manifesto for Cyborgs: Science, Technology, and Socialist Feminism in the 1980s." *Socialist Review* 80 (1985): 65–107.

Haraway, Donna J. *Modestitness@Secondillennium.FemaleManeetsncoMouse: Feminism and Technoscience*. New York: Routledge, 1997.

Haraway, Donna J. *Simians, Cyborgs, and Women: The Reinvention of Nature.* New York: Routledge, 1991.

Hardie, Melissa Jane. "'I Embrace the Difference': Elizabeth Taylor and the Closet." In *Sexy Bodies: The Strange Carnalities of Feminism,* edited by Elizabeth Grosz and Elspeth Probyn, 155–71. London: Routledge, 1995.

Harding, Sandra. *The Science Question in Feminism.* Ithaca: Cornell University Press, 1986.

Harlan, Richard. *Superstructuralism: The Philosophy of Structuralism and Post-Structuralism.* 1987. London: Routledge, 1994.

Haussman, Bernice. *Changing Sex: Transsexualism, Technology, and the Idea of Gender.* Durham: Duke University Press, 1995.

Hayden, Sara. "Re-Claiming Bodies of Knowledge: An Exploration of the Relationship between Feminist Theorizing and Feminine Style in the Rhetoric of the Boston Women's Health Book Collective." *Western Journal of Communication* 61.2 (Spring 1997): 127–63.

Hayles, N. Katherine. *Chaos Bound: Orderly Disorder in Contemporary Literature and Science.* Ithaca: Cornell University Press, 1990.

Hayles, N. Katherine. "The Materiality of Informatics." *Configurations* 1 (1993): 147–70.

Hayles, N. Katherine. "Virtual Bodies and Flickering Signifiers." *October* 66 (1993): 69–91.

Heywood, Leslie. *Bodymakers: A Cultural Anatomy of Women's Body Building.* New Brunswick: Rutgers University Press, 1998.

Hillman, David, and Carla Mazzio, eds. *The Body in Parts: Fantasies of Corporeality in Early Modern Europe.* New York: Routledge, 1997.

Hollis, Karyn L. "Autobiographical Writing at the Bryn Mawr Summer School for Women Workers." *College Composition and Communication* 45 (1994): 31–60.

hooks, bell. *Teaching to Transgress.* New York: Routledge, 1994.

Hubbard, Ruth, and Elijah Wald. *Exploding the Gene Myth: How Genetic Information Is Produced and Manipulated by Scientists, Physicians, Employers, Insurance Companies, Educators, and Law Enforcers.* Boston: Beacon, 1993.

Hyde, Alan. *Bodies of Law.* Princeton: Princeton University Press, 1997.

Irigaray, Luce. *This Sex Which Is Not One.* Translated by Catherine Porter. Ithaca: Cornell University Press, 1985.

Jacobus, Mary, Evelyn Fox Keller, and Sally Shuttlesworth, eds. *Body/Politics: Women and the Discourses of Science.* New York: Routledge, 1990.

Jaggar, Allison, and Susan Bordo, eds. *Gender/Body/Knowledge: Feminist Reconstructions of Being and Knowing.* New Brunswick: Rutgers University Press, 1989.

Jarratt, Susan. "Speaking to the Past: Feminist Historiography in Rhetoric." *Pre/Text* 11 (1990): 190–209.

Johnson, Mark. *The Body in the Mind: The Bodily Basis of Meaning, Imagination, and Reason.* Chicago: University of Chicago Press, 1987.

Jordonova, Ludmilla. *Sexual Visions: Images of Gender in Science and Medicine between the Eighteenth and Twentieth Centuries.* Madison: University of Wisconsin Press, 1989.

Kaufmann, Michael. *Textual Bodies: Modernism, Postmodernism, and Print.* Lewisburg: Bucknell University Press, 1994.

Keller, Evelyn Fox. *Refiguring Life: Metaphors of Twentieth-Century Biology.* New York: Columbia University Press, 1995.

Keller, Evelyn Fox. *Reflections on Gender and Science.* New Haven: Yale University Press, 1985.

Keller, Evelyn Fox. *Secrets of Life, Secrets of Death: Essays on Language, Gender, and Science.* New York: Routledge, 1992.

Keller, Evelyn Fox, and Helen Longino, eds. *Feminism and Science.* New York: Oxford University Press, 1996.

Kevles, Daniel J., and LeRoy Hood, eds. *The Code of Codes: Scientific and Social Issues in the Human Genome Project.* Cambridge, Mass.: Harvard University Press, 1992.

Kilgour, Maggie. *From Communion to Cannibalism: An Anatomy of Metaphors of Incorporation.* Princeton: Princeton University Press, 1990.

King, Stephen. *The Dead Zone.* New York: Viking, 1979.

Kirby, Katherine M. *Indifferent Boundaries: Spatial Concepts of Human Subjectivity.* New York: Guilford, 1996.

Komesaroff, Paul. *Troubled Bodies: Critical Perspectives on Postmodernism, Medical Ethics, and the Body.* Durham: Duke University Press, 1995.

Kristeva, Julia. *Powers of Horor: An Essay on Abjection.* New York: Columbia University Press, 1982.

Kroker, Arthur, and Marylouise Kroker. *Body Invaders: Sexuality and the Postmodern Condition.* New York: Macmillan, 1988.

Laqueur, Thomas. *Making Sex: Body and Gender from the Greeks to Freud.* Cambridge, Mass.: Harvard University Press, 1990.

Latour, Bruno, and Steve Woolgar. *Laboratory Life: The Construction of Scientific Facts.* Princeton: Princeton University Press, 1986.

Leder, Drew. *The Absent Body.* Chicago: University of Chicago Press, 1990.

Lefkovitz, Lori, ed. *Textual Bodies: Changing Boundaries of Literary Representation.* Albany: SUNY Press, 1997.

Livingston, Ira, and Judith Halberstam. *Posthuman Bodies.* Bloomington: Indiana University Press, 1995.

Locke, Margaret. *Encounters with Aging: Mythologies of Menopause in Japan and North America.* Berkeley: University of California Press, 1993.

Lowe, Donald. *The Body in Late-Capitalist USA.* Durham: Duke University Press, 1995.

Lu, Min-Zhan. "Reading and Writing Differences: The Problematic of 'Experience'." In *Feminism and Composition Studies: In Other Words,* edited by Susan Jarratt and Lynne Worsham, 239–51. New York: MLA, 1998.

Lykke, Nina, and Rosi Braidotti, eds. *Between Monsters, Goddesses, and Cyborgs: Feminist Confrontations with Science, Medicine, and Cyberspace.* Atlantic Highlands, N.J.: Zed Books, 1996.

MacCannell, Juliet, and Laura Zakarin, eds. *Thinking Bodies.* Stanford: Stanford University Press, 1994.

Mailloux, Steven. *Rhetorical Power.* Ithaca.: Cornell University Press, 1989.

Mailloux, Steven. *Rhetoric, Sophistry, Pragmatism.* London: Cambridge University Press, 1995.

Mann, Doug. "The Body as an 'Object' of Historical Knowledge." *Dialogue* 35 (1996): 753–76.

Martin, Emily. *Flexible Bodies: Tracking Immunity in American Culture from the Days of Polio to the Age of AIDS.* Boston: Beacon, 1994.

Martin, Emily. *The Woman in the Body: A Cultural Analysis of Reproduction.* 1987. Reprint, Boston: Beacon, 1992.

Marvin, Carolyn. "The Body of the Text: Literacy's Corporeal Constant." *Quarterly Journal of Speech* 80 (1994): 129–49.

Marvin, Carolyn. *When Old Technologies Were New: Thinking about Electronic Communication in the Late Nineteenth Century.* New York: Oxford University Press, 1988.

McGee, Michael Calvin. "A Materialist's Conception of Rhetoric." In *Explorations in Rhetoric: Studies in Honor of Douglas Ehninger,* edited by Ray E. McKerrow, 23–48. Glenview, Ill.: Scott, Foresman, 1982.

McGuire, Michael. "Materialism: Reductionist Dogma or Critical Rhetoric?" In *Rhetoric and Philosophy,* edited by Richard A. Cherwitz, 187–212. Hillsdale, N.J.: Lawrence Erlbaum, 1990.

McNay, Lois. *Foucault and Feminism: Power, Gender and the Self.* Boston: Northeastern University Press, 1992.

Medway, Peter. "Virtual and Material Buildings: Construction and Constructivism in Architecture and Writing." *Written Communication* 13 (1996): 473–514.

Merleau-Ponty, Maurice. *The Phenomenology of Perception.* Translated by Colin Smith. Boston: Routledge, 1962.

Merleau-Ponty, Maurice. *The Primacy of Perception.* Edited by James Edie. Evanston: Northwestern University Press, 1964.

Merleau-Ponty, Maurice. *The Visible and the Invisible.* Edited by Claud LeFort. Translated by Alphonso Lingis. Evanston: Northwestern University Press, 1968.

Miller, Thomas. *The Formation of College English: Rhetoric and Belles Let-tres in the British Cultural Provinces*. Pittsburgh: University of Pittsburgh Press, 1997.

Miller, Thomas. "Teaching the Histories of Rhetoric as Social Praxis." *Rhetoric Review* 12 (Fall 1993): 70–82.

Moore, Pamela L. *Building Bodies*. New Brunswick: Rutgers University Press, 1997.

Moore, Stephen. *God's Gym: Divine Male Bodies of the Body*. New York: Rout-ledge, 1997.

Murphy, Julien S. *The Constructed Body: AIDS, Reproductive Technology, and Ethics*. Albany: SUNY Press, 1995.

Nelkin, Dorothy, and Susan Lindee. *The DNA Mystique: The Gene as Cultural Icon*. New York: W. H. Freeman, 1995.

Nelson, Cary. *Repression and Recovery: Modern American Poetry and the Politics of Cultural Memory*. Madison: University of Wisconsin Press, 1989.

Newman, Karen. *Fetal Positions: Individualism, Science, Visuality*. Stanford: Stanford University Press, 1996.

Ong, Walter J. *Orality and Literacy: The Technologizing of the Word*. New York: Methuen, 1982.

Oudshoorn, Nelly. *Beyond the Natural Body: An Archaeology of Sex Hor-mones*. New York: Routledge, 1994.

Parker, Andrew, and Eve Kosofsky Sedgewick, eds. *Performativity and Per-formance*. New York: Routledge, 1995.

Parker, Patricia. *Literary Fat Ladies: Rhetoric, Gender, Property*. New York: Methuen, 1987.

Patterson, Randi, and Gail Corning. "Researching the Body: An Annotated Bibliography for Rhetoric." *Rhetoric Society Quarterly* 27 (1997): 5–30.

Piles, Steve, and Nigel Thrift, eds. *Mapping the Subject: Geographies of Cul-tural Transformation*. New York: Routledge, 1995.

Plant, Sadie. *Zero + Ones: Digital Women + the New Technoculture*. New York: Doubleday, 1997.

Proctor, Robert. *Racial Hygiene: Medicine under the Nazis*. Cambridge, Mass.: Harvard University Press, 1988.

Railsback, Celeste Condit. "Beyond Rhetorical Relativism: A Structural-Material Model of Truth and Objective Reality." *Quarterly Journal of Speech* 69 (1983): 351–63.

Rinaldi, Jacqueline. "Rhetoric and Healing: Revising Naratives about Disabil-ity." *College English* 58 (1996): 820–34.

Rony, Fatimah Tobing. *The Third Eye: Race, Cinema, and Ethnographic Spec-tacle*. Durham: Duke University Press, 1996.

Rothman, Sheila. *Living in the Shadow of Death: Tuberculosis and the Social Experience of Illness in American History*. New York: Basic Books, 1994.

Saussure, Ferdinand de. *Course in General Linguistics*. New York: McGraw-Hill, 1966.

Sawday, Jonathan. *The Body Emblazoned: Dissection and the Human Body in Renaissance Culture*. New York: Routledge, 1995.

Sawicki, Jana. *Disciplining Foucault: Feminism, Power, and the Body*. New York: Routledge, 1991.

Scarry, Elaine. *The Body in Pain: The Making and Unmaking of the World*. New York: Oxford University Press, 1985.

Schatzki, Theodore R., and Wolfgang Natter, eds. *The Social and Political Body*. New York: Guilford, 1996.

Schiebinger, Londa. *Nature's Body: Gender in the Making of Modern Science*. Boston: Beacon, 1993.

Schilb, John. "Future Historiographies of Rhetoric and the Present Age of Anxiety." In *Writing Histories of Rhetoric*, edited by Victor Vitanza, 128–38. Carbondale: Southern Illinois University Press, 1994.

Scott, Sue, and David Morgan, eds. *Body Matters: Essays on the Sociology of the Body*. London: Falmer, 1993.

Sedgwick, Eve Kosofsky. *Epistemology of the Closet*. Berkeley: University of California Press, 1990.

Seltzer, Mark. *Bodies and Machines*. New York: Routledge, 1992.

Seltzer, Mark. *Serial Killers*. New York: Routledge, 1997.

Sennett, Richard. *Flesh and Stone: The Body and the City in Western Civilization*. New York: Norton, 1994.

Shaviro, Steven. *The Cinematic Body*. Minneapolis: University of Minnesota Press, 1994.

Sheets-Johnstone, Maxine. *The Roots of Power: Animate Form and Gendered Bodies*. Chicago: Open Court, 1994.

Shilling, Chris. *The Body and Social Theory*. Newbury Park, Calif.: Sage, 1993.

Silverman, David, and Brian Torode. *The Material Word: Some Theories of Language and Its Limits*. London: Routledge and Kegan Paul, 1980.

Simpson, Mark. *Male Impersonators: Men Performing Masculinity*. New York: Routledge, 1994.

Spelman, Elizabeth. "Woman As Body: Ancient and Contemporary Views." *Feminist Studies* 8 (1982): 109–31.

Squier, Susan. *Babies in Bottles:Twentieth-Century Visions of Reproductive Technology*. New Brunswick: Rutgers University Press, 1994.

Stafford, Barbara. *Body Criticism: Imaging the Unseen in Enlightenment Art and Medicine*. Cambridge, Mass.: MIT Press, 1991.

Strathern, Andrew. *Body Thoughts*. Ann Arbor: University of Michigan Press, 1996.

Synnott, A. *The Body Social: Symbolism, Self, and Society*. London: Routledge, 1993.

Terry, Jennifer, ed. *Processed Lives: Gender and Technology in Everyday Life.* New York: Routledge, 1997.

Terry, Jennifer, and Jacqueline Urla, eds. *Deviant Bodies: Critical Pespectives on Difference in Science and Popular Culture.* Bloomington: Indiana University Press, 1995.

Trent, James W., Jr. *Inventing the Feeble Mind: A History of Mental Retardation in the United States.* Berkeley: University of California Press, 1994.

Tuana, Nancy. *The Less Noble Sex: Scientific, Religious, and Philosophical Conceptions of Women's Nature.* Bloomington: Indiana University Press, 1993.

Tuana, Nancy, ed. *Feminism and Science.* Bloomington: Indiana University Press, 1989.

Tuman, Myron, ed. *Literary Online: The Promise (and Peril) of Reading and Writing with Computers.* Pittsburgh: University of Pittsburgh Press, 1992.

Turkle, Sherry. *Life on the Screen: Identity in the Age of the Internet.* New York: Simon and Schuster, 1995.

Turner, Bryan S. *The Body and Society.* 2d ed. London: Sage, 1996.

Varela, Francisco. *The Embodied Mind: Cognitive Science and the Human Experience.* Cambridge, Mass.: MIT Press, 1991.

Villanueva, Victor. *Bootstraps: From an American Academic of Color.* Urbana, Ill.: NCTE, 1993.

Walker, Jeffrey. "Of Brains and Rhetorics." *College English* 52 (1990): 143–63.

Wexler, Alice. *Mapping Fate: A Memoir of Family, Risk, and Genetic Research.* New York: Times Books, 1995.

Wills, David. *Prosthesis.* Stanford: Stanford University Press, 1995.

Wittgenstein, Ludwig. *Philosophical Investigations.* Translated by G. E. M. Anscombe. Oxford: Basil Blackwell, 1963.

Woodmansee, Martha, and Peter Jaszi, eds. *The Construction of Authorship: Textual Appropriation in Law and Literature.* Durham: Duke University Press, 1994.

Woolf, Virginia. *A Room of One's Own.* New York: Harcourt, Brace, and World, 1929.

Young, Iris Marion. *Justice and the Politics of Difference.* Princeton: Princeton University Press, 1990.

Young, Iris Marion. *Throwing Like a Girl and Other Essays in Feminist Philosophy and Social Theory.* Bloomington: Indiana University Press, 1990.

Contributors

CAROLE BLAIR, professor of American studies at the University of California, Davis, is co-editor and co-translator of *Friedrich Nietzsche on Rhetoric and Language* (Oxford) and co-editor of *Critical Questions: Invention, Creativity, and the Criticism of Discourse and the Media* (St. Martin's); she has also contributed essays to many journals and books. Her research has focused on critical reconstructions of rhetorical scholarship and the material conditions of the academy that shape that scholarship. She is now completing, with Neil Michel, a rhetorical and cultural study of American commemorative art.

CELESTE CONDIT is a professor in the Department of Speech Communication at the University of Georgia. She is interested in the role of rhetoric in processes of social change and stability, especially with regard to issues of human reproduction. She is author of *Decoding Abortion Rhetoric: Communicating Social Change* (University of Illinois Press, 1990), co-author with Jon Louis Lucaites of *Crafting Equality: America's Anglo-American Word* (University of Chicago Press, 1993), and co-editor with Roxanne Parrott of *Evaluating Women's Health Messages* (Sage). She is currently working on a book entitled *The Meanings of the Gene: Public Debates about Human Heredity* (University of Wisconsin Press).

SHARON CROWLEY recently left Penn State to become professor of English at Arizona State University. She has recently completed *Composition in the University: Historical and Polemical Essays* (University of Pittsburgh Press, 1998). She is currently working on a critique of liberal rhetorical theory.

CHRISTINE DE VINNE is assistant professor of English at Ursuline College in Cleveland. Since completing her dissertation on confessional rhetoric in American autobiography, she has specialized in the study of life-writing, publishing essays on autobiographical fiction, hagiography, and the gender structure of American Sign Language.

BARBARA DICKSON is pursuing a doctorate in English at Wayne State University, with an emphasis on American rhetorics. Her dissertation project is an investigation of the construction of the pregnant body in American literature and in medical, legal, and popular discourses. Her "Leaving Science and Technology for Business and Management: Quality Control as a Discourse on the Move" (with Ellen Barton) appeared in 1996 in *Rhetoric Society Quarterly*.

LESTER FAIGLEY chairs the Division of Rhetoric and Composition at the University of Texas at Austin. His widely honored 1992 book *Fragments of Rationality* (University of Pittsburgh Press) examines the impacts on the teaching of writing brought about by changes in American culture since the 1960s, particularly the introduction of electronic technologies into the university.

CHRISTINA HAAS's interest in the embodied nature of writing grows out of her work on literacy and technology, some of it published in *Writing Technology: Studies in the Materiality of Literacy* (Erlbaum, 1996). Her contribution to this volume is part of a large-scale study of the discourse practices operating in an urban abortion clinic.

MELISSA JANE HARDIE teaches English and cultural studies in the English Department at the University of Sydney. She is currently completing a book, *Camp Quality: Women, Popular Culture, Queer Aesthetics*. Her most recent publications include "'I Embrace The Difference': Elizabeth Taylor and the Closet" (in Grosz and Probyn's *Sexy Bodies: The Strange Carnalities of Feminism*), "Restless: Paglia v Sontag" (in *Australian Feminist Studies*), and "Fluff and Granite: Ayn Rand's Feminist Camp Aesthetic" (in Gladstein and Sciabarra's *Feminist Interpretations of Ayn Rand*). In the future she plans to study liberation and nostalgia in popular fiction.

KARYN HOLLIS is assistant professor of English at Villanova University, where she directs the Writing Program. She is currently at work on a book-length study of writing at the Bryn Mawr Summer School for Women Workers.

YAMENG LIU, assistant professor of English and rhetoric at Carnegie Mellon University, works on comparative rhetoric and rhetorical theory. His articles have appeared in *College English, Philosophy and Rhetoric, Philosophy East and West, Argumentation, Rhetoric Review*, and other journals. With Richard Young, he has edited *Landmark Essays on Rhetorical Invention in Writing* (Hermagoras). He is currently working on book-length projects on historiographies of Chinese rhetoric and on the rhetoric of comparative studies.

PETER MORTENSEN is associate professor of English at the University of Kentucky. He recently co-edited (with Gesa E. Kirsch) *Ethics and Representation in Qualitative Studies of Literacy* (NCTE, 1996), and he is completing work on *Imagining Rhetoric: Women's Civic Rhetoric in Postrevolutionary America* (with Janet Carey Eldred), to appear in the Pittsburgh Series in Literacy, Composition, and Culture. Mortensen's work on illiteracy is part of a book project entitled *Illiterate Sorrows: The Uses of Illiteracy in Industrial America.*

JOHN SCHILB, recently of the University of Maryland, now holds the Culbertson Chair in the English Department at Indiana University. His most recent book is *Between the Lines: Relating Composition Theory and Literary Theory* (Boynton-Cook, 1996), and he is also the editor (with John Clifford) of *Writing Theory and Critical Theory* (MLA, 1994) and (with Patricia Harkin) of *Contending with Words: Composition and Rhetoric in a Postmodern Age* (MLA, 1991).

J. BLAKE SCOTT recently completed his dissertation at Penn State, a rhetorical and cultural study of HIV testing in the United States that is entitled "Disciplinary Diagnosis: Rhetoric, AIDS, and the Technoscience of HIV Testing." His chapter in this book is an abbreviated version of a chapter from the dissertation. Scott's other interests include classical rhetoric and technical writing, and he has published essays in *Rhetoric Review*, *Technical Communication Quarterly*, and elsewhere.

JACK SELZER, who teaches at Penn State, has published *Kenneth Burke in Greenwich Village: Conversing with the Moderns, 1915–1931* (University of Wisconsin Press, 1996). He is currently working on a sequel that will consider the relationships among Burke's writings and his intellectual affiliations during the 1930s.

WENDY B. SHARER teaches at Penn State, where she is a doctoral candidate in the English Department's program in rhetoric. Her interest in the preservation of historical materials stems from her dissertation research, which focuses on rhetorical practices and adult education in American women's civic, political, and philanthropic organizations in the late nineteenth and early twentieth centuries. Her article "'Going into Society' or 'Bringing Society In'?: Rhetoric and Problematic Philanthropy in *The Silent Partner*" was recently published in *ATQ: American Transcendental Quarterly.*

SUSAN WELLS is professor of English at Temple University; her most recent book is *Sweet Reason: Rhetoric and the Discourses of Modernity* (University of Chicago Press, 1995). Her chapter in this book derives from her study of nineteenth-century women physicians, forthcoming from the University of Wisconsin Press, tentatively entitled *Out of the Dead House.*

Index

abortion: and Permanent Injunction against Women's Choice Services, 219–25, 230, 233–34; and public-private, 12, 219–25, 229–33, 359; Supreme Court rulings about, 229–33

Absolute Impotence advertising campaign, 190, 191

access: to drugs, 208, 209; to historical materials, 122, 127–28, 129–30, 134–39; to home collection testing system, 242, 250, 252–59, 268, 269; to medical schools, 59

Adbusters magazine, 191–93

advertising: body in, 191–94; and growing interest in materiality, 10, 12; about home collection testing system, 12, 242, 248, 251, 260–65; and literacy, 188–94; of Prozac, 206, 207

aesthetics, 212–13, 279

African Americans, 8, 100, 109, 110–12, 144, 221

Agnew, D. Hayes, 60, 66

agriculture, 147–48, 179–80

AIDS: and beards, 278, 286–91; organizations concerned with, 244, 246–48, 250, 259. *See also* AIDS Memorial Quilt; home collection testing system

AIDS Memorial Quilt, 11, 23–24, 27, 34, 37–39, 44, 48

alphabet, 12, 176–81, 184, 186, 188

American Dream, 83–84

American West. *See* cannibalism; frontier; westward movement

ancient Greece. *See* Greece, ancient

Anglo-Americans: degeneration of, 12, 144, 150, 151, 157–59, 161, 162; superiority of, 147, 150

animals, language of, 338–39

anthropology, 4, 79

Appalachia, 150, 214–15

Arapesh people (New Guinea), 81

arbitrariness, 337, 338

archival research, 11–12. *See also* historical materials

Arendt, Hannah, 219, 225–27, 229

Aristotle, 70, 184, 320–21

art, 212–13, 276, 310

Arthur Mervyn (Charles Brockden Brown), 151–52

Astronauts Memorial (Cape Canaveral, Fla.), 23

audience, 10, 117, 339, 340, 346

authenticity, 278, 284, 285

authority, of medical profession, 305–7, 311

autobiography, 12, 77, 287; and access to health care system, 208–9; distribution of, 209; and historical materialism, 207–9, 210–11, 213, 215–16; McGlashan's mediation in, 91–92; production of, 209; after Prozac, 202–17; and psychological materialism, 202, 205–7, 211, 215, 216–17; and race, 214. *See also specific person*

"Ave Maria" (LaSota), 110–12

Baartman, Saartjie, 5, 6–7, 8

Barthes, Roland, 7

Baudrillard, Jean, 331, 334, 337

beards: and AIDS, 286–91; and authenticity, 278, 284, 285; and camp performance, 276, 292, 293; and closet, 276–77, 279, 280, 281, 289–90, 292–93; and culture, 12, 275, 286; definition/meanings of, 12, 276, 277–78, 282, 289–91; and gay porn, 283–86;

beards (*continue]d*)
  and gender, 279, 284, 286, 288–89, 293;
  and ghoulishness, 275, 276, 278, 283,
  289; and growing interest in materiality,
  12–13; and Hudson (Rock), 278, 283,
  286–87; and imitation, 284, 285, 288; and
  Liberace, 275, 278, 283, 286–87, 291–93;
  and outing, 277, 279–83, 286–87, 290; and
  politics, 281, 286, 289; and public-private,
  275–94; and reputation, 277, 280; and romance, 276, 291–92, 293; and self, 290;
  and shame, 286–91, 293, 294; and Stefano,
  283, 285–86; and Taylor as beard, 276–77,
  278–79, 280–82, 291, 292
beauty, 302–4, 305, 310, 311. *See also*
  glamour
Benét, Stephen Vincent, 101
Benhabib, Seyla, 218, 226
Benjamin, Walter, 70–71, 185
Berger, John, 185–86, 299, 300
Berlin, James, 120, 123, 128, 203, 204
bibliographies, 136–37
Biesecker, Barbara, 9, 123, 124
Binet, Alfred, 154–55, 157
biography, 84–85. *See also* autobiography
Blackmar, Frank, 148–50, 154
Blackmun, Harry, 231
Black Revolutionary War Patriots Memorial,
  36
"Black Swans" (Slater), 12, 209–15
Blair, Carole, 9, 11, 13, 39, 40, 120, 122, 174
Blair, Karen J., 130, 136
body/bodies: in advertising, 191–94; and
  African Americans, 109; boundaries of,
  361; and coding, 327–28, 351; as community property, 305–6; control of, 302–4,
  305; and culture, 298, 358, 361, 362; definitions of, 7; and Donne's self-analysis,
  4–5, 6, 8; erasing of, 362; fantasies about,
  362; and feminism, 7, 357–59; of Freytag-
  Loringhoven, 4, 6, 8; and growing interest in materiality, 9, 10, 12, 13, 357; and
  history, 7–8; of "Hottentot Venus," 5,
  6–7, 8; and identity, 13, 361; images of, 5,
  191–94; as information system, 216–17;
  inside and outside of, 360–61; and language theories, 351; and literacy, 174,
  191–94; and mascots, 5–6, 8; as means
  of liberation, 108–9; normal, 361; poetry
  about, 104–10; and politics, 358; and post-

structuralism, 358, 359–60; and power,
  358; and race/racism, 5, 7; and sex organs,
  361; as site of resistance, 108; of women,
  7, 8, 11, 13, 310, 358–59; and women's
  movement, 7; and working women's poetry,
  104–10, 114–16. *See also* abortion; advertising; dissection; home collection testing
  system; mind-body relationship; Moore,
  Demi; pregnancy
body language, 301–6
books, 184, 339. *See also* literacy
Bordo, Susan, 7, 108, 358
Boyle, Kay, 121
Brandeis, Louis, 230, 233
Breen, Patrick, diary of, 76–77, 78, 81,
  86–87
Breen family, 76–77, 81, 86, 87, 88, 90
Brown, Charles Brockden, 151–52
Brown, Thelma, 113–15
Brown v. Board of Education (1954), 26
Brushland (Darby), 153–54
Bryn Mawr Summer School: African Americans at, 100, 110–12; agency and voice in,
  116–17; curriculum at, 99–100; demise
  of, 100, 116–17; feminism at, 99; founding of, 99; and leftist ideology, 100, 102,
  116; legacy of, 101, 117; preservation of
  records and student works from, 101; re-
  cruitment of students for, 99; student-
  centered pedagogy at, 100–101, 102–3;
  support for, 99, 116–17. *See also* poetry,
  working women's
Burke, Kenneth, 3, 7, 9, 13, 316, 319, 326,
  328, 331–32, 334, 336, 338
Butler, Judith, 7, 9, 13, 279, 284, 285, 286,
  288–90, 357
"Buttons" (Feldman), 104

"camp performance," 276, 292, 293
cancer, 346, 348, 349–50
cannibalism: as distinguishing savagery
  from civilization, 79, 88; of Donner Party
  confessions into McGlashan's textual property, 90–92; exoneration for, 89; and growing interest in materiality, 11; homicidal,
  88; and inside/outside, 360–61; lack of
  language for communicating about, 85–8
  6; and manifestations of cannibal destiny,
  77–84; nineteenth century study of, 79;
  psychosocial aspects of, 80; purposes of,

79; and racism, 88; and scripting and con-
scripting the body, 84–92; and self-Other
relationship, 80; survival, 76, 79, 80–81; as
taboo, 80; taxonomy of, 79; and westering
culture, 76, 77, 82–83. *See also* Donner
Party
capitalism, 7, 70, 174, 176, 187, 204, 207,
216–17
Carter, Jean, 101, 102
cartoons/comic strips, 133, 187, 196, 198
Catholicism, 175, 184
Center for Disease Control (CDC), 240, 243,
250, 253
Certeau, Michel de, 17
Cheney, Lynn, 204
Chiapas, Mexico, Zapatistas in, 194–98
Cicero, 70, 321
Cigoli, Ludovico, 67
Civil Rights Memorial (Montgomery, Ala.),
11, 23, 24–26, 28, 29, 37, 39, 42, 44, 45,
46–47
Cixous, Helene, 7
class issue(s): and Bryn Mawr Summer
School, 116; and genetics, 349; and home
collection testing system, 258–60, 261,
264–65; and literacy, 150; poetry as, 98;
and Prozac, 208, 214, 215; among white
women, 113–14; and working women,
98, 100, 109–10, 112, 113–15
Clift, Montgomery, 278
Clinton, Bill, 48, 314, 315, 322, 323
closet, and beards, 276–77, 279, 280, 281,
289–90, 292–93
coding: closeness in, 339–40; as communication process, 344, 345; and DNA doing
rhetoric, 339–47; and growing interest in
materiality, 11, 13, 351–52; materiality
of, 327, 351; meaning of, 327; and motivation, 337–38; and reproduction of code,
340–41; toward material perspective on,
327–39. *See also* DNA
Colosio, Luis Donaldo, 194–95
comic strips. *See* cartoons/comic strips
Commission on Preservation and Access, 129,
136, 139
communication, 328, 340, 344–47
Community Advisory Committee. *See* Direct
Access Diagnostics (DAD)
computers, 188, 216. *See also* Internet; web
sites

Confederate Soldiers Monument (Montgomery, Ala.), 42, 43
confessions, of Donner Party, 85, 87, 90–92
Confide (HIV test kit): advertising for, 12,
248, 251, 260–65; development and approval of, 245–50, 257; elements in, 240,
241; end of, 248, 269; instructions for
using, 240; and *kairos* of technoscience,
250–55; ordering/cost of, 239–40, 260;
ownership of, 248. *See also* home collection testing system
cosmetic surgery, 8
cover photos, 299–301, 306–12
Cullen, Countee, 101
culture: and beards, 12, 275, 286; and body,
298, 358, 361, 362; and discourse, 357;
and dissection, 62–63; and Donner Party,
80–84, 88, 89–90, 92; and growing interest
in materiality, 9, 10, 11, 12, 298, 336; and
historical materials, 126–27, 128; histories
of, 338; and home collection testing system,
12, 242–50; and identity, 361; and ideology, 320, 323, 324–25; and language, 337;
and literacy, 147, 161; and meaning, 338;
and pregnancy, 298, 310, 312; and rhetoric,
320, 323, 324–25; and role of women, 133;
superiority of American, 147; and technoscience, 242–50; westering, 76, 77, 82–83;
and writing, 180
"Culture Jammers Toolbox" (web site),
193–94
"culture wars," 279–80

DAD. *See* Direct Access Diagnostics (DAD)
Daly, Mary, 328
Darby, John (pseud.). *See* Gerretson, James
Darwinism, 149–50
Dearstyne, Bruce, 128, 135, 137
Dees, Morris, 25
defects, and literacy, 150–51, 153–54. *See
also* heredity; race/racism, degeneration
of Anglo-American
degeneracy: and age, 149; of Anglo-American
race, 12, 144, 150, 151, 157–59, 161, 162;
and literacy, 12, 144, 148–49, 150, 151,
154, 157–59, 161, 162
Deleuze, Gilles, 7
depersonalization, 265–66
Derrida, Jacques, 13, 328–29, 330, 331, 337,
341, 343–44, 351

Descartes, René, 328
design, literacy as, 188–94. *See also* visual
  design
desirability, and pregnancy, 302–4, 305, 307,
  308, 309, 311
determinism, 8, 89, 150, 326
deviant, women as, 302–4. *See also* gay porn
Diderot, Denis, 176
Direct Access Diagnostics (DAD), 244, 245,
  247–51, 256, 259, 260, 266, 267
disabilities, 361
discourse, 298, 302, 339, 347–48, 350–51,
  357, 363
dissection: and artful arrangement of body,
  67; and body as house, 70–71; as cultural
  break, 62–63; demonstrator of, 60–61;
  directions for, 61; of female bodies, 60;
  gender reactions to, 60, 68–69; and grave
  robbers, 68; and growing interest in materiality, 11, 69–70; and "laws of health," 67;
  in medical schools, 60–62; as moral instruction, 65–66, 67, 68; and mysterious
  interior of body, 64–66; as pleasure, 64,
  68–69; as practice of seeing, 64, 66–67,
  68–69; and public-private, 63, 64–66, 67–
  68; and reading of fiction, 66, 67, 68, 69;
  as site of instruction, 67–68; and women
  physicians, 58–74; women's societies concerning, 65–66; and writing, 68
DNA: and cell, 344–45; as doing rhetoric,
  339–47; and growing interest in materiality, 11, 13; "information" in, 335; and language theories, 326–27, 334, 335, 337–38,
  351; and purpose, 345; and vocabulary of
  "communication," 340
Donne, John, 4–5, 6, 8
Donner family, 77, 81, 82, 84, 87, 88
Donner Party, 11, 360–61; and American
  culture, 80–84, 88, 89–90, 92; and confession, 85, 87, 90–92; discovery of cannibalism among, 78, 87; dissimilar memories
  about, 77–78, 85–86, 87; exoneration of,
  89; facts about, 77; first-person accounts
  about, 75–76, 77–78, 79, 81–82, 84–85,
  86–88, 90; McGlashan's account of, 76–
  77, 78, 84, 85, 86, 90–92; members of, 81–
  82; mythologization of, 89–90; noncannibal identity among, 75–76, 86–87; racism
  among, 88; remorse and guilt among, 87–
  88, 92; representative nature of, 81–82;

and rhetorical determinism, 89; scholarly
  interpretations about, 78–79; second- and
  third-hand accounts about, 78, 86; standards
  of, 83; textual artifacts of, 77–78
Douglas, William O., 231
Draper, Jessica, 173, 174, 188
drugs, 12, 208, 209. *See also* Prozac
Durito, Don (fictional character), 198

Eastman, George, 186
eating, psychosocial aspects of, 80. *See also*
  cannibalism
economy, and literacy, 146–47
education: Moore photograph as, 310–11;
  of physicians, 59–62; progressive, 100;
  of women, 117, 131; of workers, 100,
  101. *See also* Bryn Mawr Summer School;
  literacy
Eisenstein, Elizabeth, 183–84
Ejército Zapatista de Liberación Nacional,
  194–98
Eli Lilly Company, 203, 206, 207, 212
Eliot, George, 5
Eliot, T. S., 101
Enlightenment, 174, 184, 188
enunciations, 330
environment, 144, 150, 157–58, 159, 339
Epstein, Jay, 244, 246, 255–56
essence, 332
essentialism, 332–33
ethics, 10, 318, 319, 320–21, 323, 324, 325
ethnicity, 4, 8, 10, 362
eugenics, 149, 151
evolution, 12, 144, 341, 346, 352
exoticism, of Demi Moore, 307, 309, 311

"Factories" (Burgdorf), 106–7
Falk, Pasi, 359–60
Fallows, James, 321
fantasy, 362–63
farmhands, literacy of, 147, 148–49
Farnham, Eliza, 78, 86, 88
feeble-minded, 154–59, 160
feminine, in rhetoric, 9
feminism: and body, 7, 357–59; at Bryn
  Mawr Summer School, 99, 105–6; Chicana, 48; and fantasy, 362; and growing interest in materiality, 9, 10; and historical
  scholarship, 123–24, 130–31; and Marxism, 7; and Moore cover photo, 297, 306,

308, 309, 311, 312; and politics, 362; and public-private, 233–34, 359; and science/medicine, 58; and working women's poetry, 105–6. *See also specific person or organization*
film/film industry, 6, 187, 188, 309. *See also* beards
Food and Drug Administration (FDA), 239, 251, 253, 255–56, 257, 259, 269; and approval of home collection testing system, 242–50; Blood Products Advisory Committee (BPAC) of, 244, 254
Foot, Mirjam, 125, 134
Forbes, Malcolm, 12, 275–76, 278, 279–82, 283, 291, 292
form, 334, 335, 339–40, 342–43, 344–45, 346, 351
Foucault, Michel: on anxiety about materiality, 22–23; body definition of, 7, 358, 359; "centres of observation" of, 240; and class issues, 258; and genealogy, 289; and homogenization of populations, 258; and ideology, 317, 318–19, 321; language theory of, 328, 329–30, 339, 351; and materiality, 8, 17, 20, 22, 23; "order of things" of, 128; on politics and language, 20; as post-structuralist, 13, 358, 359; on power, 318–19; and situatedness of discourse, 339; and technoscience, 240, 242, 258, 265, 266; and working women's poetry, 105–6, 108, 114–15
Francis, Donald, 245, 249, 251, 255, 268
Fraser, Nancy, 8, 13, 218, 219, 225–26, 227–29, 233, 242, 258–59
Freedom Forum Journalists Memorial, 23
Freud, Sigmund, 80, 212–13, 360, 362
Freundlich, Naomi, 248, 260
Freytag-Loringhoven, Elsa von, 4, 6, 8
frontier, 83–84, 88, 322–23. *See also* westward movement
Futureworld (film), 188

gay porn, 283–86
gays, passing of, 288. *See also* beards; home collection testing system; *specific person*
gender: and beards, 279, 284, 286, 288–89, 293; and control, 300; and genetics, 349; and growing interest in materiality, 4, 7, 11; and identity, 11; and Prozac, 208; reactions to dissection by, 60, 68–69; and working

women's poetry, 105, 109–16. *See also* women
genealogy, 289
genes, 333–34, 335–36, 347–51
genetic code. *See* coding; DNA
genetics: advantages and disadvantages of research about, 347–48; and literacy, 156; mapping of, 203, 204; Mendelian, 156; and motivation, 337–38; public discourse about, 347–48, 350–51; testing, 348. *See also* coding; defects; genes; heredity
Gergen, David, 315
Gerretson, James (pseud. John Darby), 153–54, 158
ghoulishness, 275, 276, 278, 283, 289
Gingrich, Newt, 248
glamour, 191–93, *192*, 275, 299–300. *See also* beauty
globalization, and ideology, 322–23
Goddard, Henry Herbert, 154–57, 159–62
Gómez-Peña, Guillermo, 195
Goody, Jack, 176, 184
grave robbers, 68
Graves, Franklin (Donner Party), 88
Grayson, Donald K., 78, 89
Great Depression, 112–13
Great Men rhetorical canon, 123
Greece, ancient, 12, 177–80, 181, 226, 229, 320–22, 324
Greenaway, Peter, 6
Gross, Larry, 279, 287–88, 289
Grosz, Elizabeth, 7, 240, 361
"grounded theory approach" (GTA), 221–25
Guattari, Felix, 7
Gurría, José Angel, 196
Gutenberg, Johannes, 177, 179, 181, 182, 184, 185

Habermas, Jürgen, 219, 225–26, 227–28
Hahnemann Medical College (Homeopathic Medical College), 59, 60
Hall, Stuart, 322
Halpert, Herbert Norman, 160
Ham, Gerald, 127, 128
Handley, Barbara W., 311
"Hands" (Bowman), 109–10
Haraway, Donna, 8, 12, 249, 250
Hardkoop (Donner Party member), 87
Harvard University Library Task Group, 124–25, 126, 127, 129

Hassan, Ahmad Y. al-, 182
Havelock, Eric, 176
Hayles, Katherine, 8
health care system, 208–9
Heisenberg, Werner, 331
Henie, Sonja, 291–92
heredity, 150–51, 154–61
Herrnstein, Richard J., 162–63
Hirsch, E. D., 162–63
historical materialism, 203–4, 207–9, 210–
    11, 213, 215–17
historical materials: access to, 122, 127–28,
    129–30, 134–39; acquisition of, 121, 122,
    124, 125–27, 135, 138; availability of,
    120–21, 123–24, 134–39; disintegration
    and discarding of, 11, 121, 122, 124–27;
    expansion in number of, 124–27; and femi-
    nism, 123–24, 130–31; and growing in-
    terest in materiality, 9, 10, 11–12; and in-
    volvement imperative, 129–30, 135–39;
    organization of, 121–22, 128, 137–38;
    preservation of, 11–12, 101, 121, 122–23,
    124–27, 129–39; "primariness" of, 127;
    rarity or uniqueness of, 127; relevancy
    of, 120; and revisionist history, 120–21,
    122–24, 134, 139; selection of, 120, 124,
    134; use of, 126–27, 138; of women's
    associations, 121–22, 130–34, 136
history: and body, 7–8; Donner Party story
    as collective, 90; material aspects of, 4.
    See also historical materialism; historical
    materials
HIV, and beards, 278. *See also* Confide; home
    collection testing system
Holden, William, 291–92
Hollywood. *See* film/film industry
Home Access/Home Access Express, 242,
    248, 261, 264–65, 266, 267, 269
home collection testing system: access to, 242,
    250, 252–59, 268, 269; advertising about,
    12, 242, 248, 251, 260–65; approval of,
    242–50, 251, 252–53, 254, 257, 259; and
    class issues, 258–60, 261, 264–65; costs-
    benefits of, 243, 250–55; and culture, 12,
    242–50; functions of, 239–40; and grow-
    ing interest in materiality, 12; and *kairos* of
    technoscience, 250–55; material effects of,
    265–69; and needy bodies, 242, 250, 252–
    59, 268; and partner selection, 266–68; and
    politics, 243, 258–59; and public-private,

243, 261, 264, 266, 268; and race, 258–59,
    261, 264–65; and technoscience, 249–50,
    252; who would use, 255–59, 266–67.
    See also Confide; Home Access/Home
    Access Express
homogenization of populations, 258, 266
homosexuality. *See* beards; gay porn; gays;
    home collection testing system
hooks, bell, 104
Horace C. (literacy case study), 156–57
"Hottentot Venus," 5, 6–7, 8
Houghton, Eliza Poor Donner, 90–92
Howe, Edgar Watson, 144–45, 146, 147, 149,
    150, 153
Howells, William Dean, 145
Hubbard, Ruth, 326, 350–51
Hudson, Rock, 12, 278, 283, 286–87
Hudson, Taylor (pseud.), 284–85, 288
Hughes, Langston, 101
Human Genome Project, 11, 347, 348–50
humanism, 21–23, 351
humans, definition of, 336
"Hymn to God My God, in My Sickness"
    (Donne), 4–5

ideal orator, 323
idea(s), 328, 330, 336, 337, 338, 351
identity, 4, 11, 13, 339–47, 349, 351, 361–62
ideographs, 19–20
ideology: consistency in, 319–20; core,
    323–24; criticism of, 316–17, 318, 319;
    and culture, 320, 323, 324–25; and DNA
    doing rhetoric, 339–40; and ethics, 318,
    319, 320–21, 323, 324, 325; and globaliza-
    tion, 322–23; and growing interest in ma-
    teriality, 11; and law, 320; leftist, 100,
    102, 105–6, 112–13, 114, 116, 117; and
    Marxism, 316; meanings of, 316, 318–19;
    and Morris case, 314–16, 317–18; norma-
    tive constraints on, 317–18; professional,
    323–24; and public-private, 323–24
"Illustrated Books and Newspapers"
    (Wordsworth), 175
images: of angels, 212–13; attitudes to-
    ward, 174; of body, 5, 191–94; computer-
    generated, 188; criticisms of, 187; devel-
    opment of, 174, 176–77, 180, 186; distrust
    of, 185; and growing interest in materiality,
    12; mass-produced, 185; and pictographs,
    176–77, 180; and printing press, 177, 181–

83, 184; reproduction of, 182–83, 186; and technology, 175, 185–88; and texts, 363; true-to-life, 185–88; on web sites, 194–98. *See also* advertising; cover photos; photography
imitation, 284, 285, 288
immigrants, 144, 150
imperialism/colonialism, 11, 82, 147, 187. *See also* westward movement
Indiana, Gary, 275–77, 280, 281, 282, 292
individual. *See* public-private
individualism, and literacy, 176, 183
Innis, Harold, 176, 181
inside and outside, 360–61
insurance companies, 208, 209, 266, 269
intelligence, 143–44, 149–50, 151, 152, 153–54, 161, 162
intent. *See* purpose
Internet, 194–98. *See also* web sites
Irigaray, Luce, 7, 360
Isherwood, Charles, 283, 285–86

Jacobi, Mary Putnam, 63, 66
James, Henry, 280
Jameson, Frederic, 204, 322
Jefferson Memorial (Washington, D.C.), 36
Jews, passing by, 288
Johnson & Johnson, 239, 244, 245, 246, 247, 248, 256, 259–60
journey motif, 213–15
Jurassic Park (film), 188
"Just Do It!" slogan (Nike), 191, 193

The Kallikak Family (Goddard), 154–56, 157
Kant, Immanuel, 213, 328
Kaysen, Susanna, 12, 202, 206, 208, 210, 211
Keller, Evelyn Fox, 8, 13, 58, 326, 327, 336, 344
Kennedy, Caroline, 230
Kent State University May 4 Memorial (Ohio), 11, 23, 24, 26–27, 30, 31, 32, 40, 41, 42
Keseberg, Lewis, 81–82, 84–85, 87–88, 90
Kessler-Harris, Alice, 110, 247–48, 256
"kindling" theories, 205–6, 210
King, Martin Luther, Jr., 26, 333
King Memorial Baptist Church (Montgomery, Ala.), 42
Kite, Elizabeth S., 154, 157–62
"knowledge enthymeme," 252

Koop, C. Everett, 240, 245, 246, 247, 248, 249, 253, 254, 255, 259
Korean War Veterans Memorial (Washington, D.C.), 23, 36
Korzybski, Alfred, 328, 331
Kramer, Peter, 203, 204, 205–6, 209, 210
Kristeva, Julia, 301

labor movement, 99, 116
Lamarckianism, 150
language: of animals, 338–39; body, 301–6; and communication, 328; components of, 328; creativity of, 333; and culture, 337; Derrida's theory of, 328–29, 330, 331, 337, 341, 343, 344, 351; and environment, 339; as field of "free play," 337; Foucault's theory of, 328, 329–30, 339, 351; idea as component of, 328, 330, 336, 337, 338, 351; lack of, 85–86; limitations of, 333; materiality of, 8–14, 327, 328–52; and matter, 331–33; McGee's theory of, 336–37, 338, 339; and meaning, 337, 338; as motivation, 337–38; object as component of, 328–29, 331, 332, 333–34, 335, 336; as physical, 329–30, 331, 332, 335, 338, 351–52; post-structuralists' theories of, 331–32, 336; power of, 3–4; and "presence," 337; proto-theory of materiality of, 351–52, 363; and reality, 4; and reference theory, 328–29, 331, 351; sign function of, 328–29, 330; social aspects of, 329–31, 332, 333, 336–37, 339–40, 351; stereotypical attitudes toward, 3; structuralists' theories of, 328–29, 334, 336, 337; translation of, 337; ultra-structuralists' theories of, 331–35, 336, 337, 351
LaRue, Chi Chi, 283–84, 285
Laski, Harold, 100
LaSota, Kitty, 110–12
Latour, Bruno, 239, 240, 250
law, 8, 176, 177, 320
"Lawrence, Massachusetts" (Kiezulas), 115–16
leftist ideology, 100, 102, 105–6, 112–13, 114, 116, 117. *See also* Marxism
Leibovitz, Annie, 299, 300, 301, 308, 310, 311
Lévi-Strauss, Claude, 79, 80
Levy, Kate, 174, 188, 194
Lewis, Sinclair, 144

Lewontin, Richard C., 13, 327
Liberace, 12, 275, 278, 283, 286–87, 291–93
life, and DNA doing rhetoric, 339–47
Lin, Maya, 39
Lincoln Memorial (Washington, D.C.), 24, 47
Lippman, Abby, 326–27, 351
Listening to Prozac (Kramer), 203, 204,
  205–6, 209, 210
literacy: and advertising, 188–94; of African
  Americans, 144; and age, 149; and agriculture, 147–48, 179–80; and alphabet, 12,
  176–81, 184, 186, 188; in Appalachia, 150;
  and capitalism, 174, 175, 176, 187; and
  class, 150; community, 138; and culture,
  147, 161; and Darwinism, 149–50; and degeneracy, 12, 144, 148–49, 150, 151, 154,
  157–59, 161, 162; denial of materiality of,
  188; and economy, 146–47; and environment, 144, 150, 157–58, 159; of farmhands,
  147, 148–49; and growing interest in materiality, 9, 10, 12; and heredity, 150–51,
  154–61; of immigrants, 144, 150; and intelligence, 143–44, 149–50, 151, 152,
  153–54, 161, 162; limited, 147; and mass
  media, 186, 187–88; and morality, 145,
  147, 150, 151–52, 153, 162; as multimedia,
  175–76; and national aid for state education, 146; in New Jersey Pine Barrens, 151–
  62; in nineteenth century, 145–46; and oral
  and visual dichotomy, 176, 180; and perma-
  nency of illiteracy, 144, 154–61; as pluralistic and socially situated, 184; and poverty,
  145–46, 151, 153; and printing press, 177,
  181–83, 184; and racial degeneracy, 150,
  151, 157–59, 161, 162; and religion, 151–
  52, 160, 175, 176, 183, 184; as remediable,
  144; in rural America, 12, 143–70; and
  science, 175, 176, 177, 183–84; and social advancement, 163; and technology,
  181–83, 185–88; and texts, 174; in urban
  areas, 159, 162; as visual design, 188–94;
  and web sites, 171, 172, 173, 174, 175,
  188, 190, 192–98
"Little Girl, Be Careful What You Say" (Sandburg), 3
"Llanarth's lair" (web site), 173, 174
Locke, John, 328
Logan, Robert, 176–77, 181, 183, 184
Longshore, Hannah, 11, 60–61, 63, 65, 66
"Lost" (Kuhn), 108–9

Lukacs, Georg, 208
Lyotard, Jean-François, 17, 23

"Machine, The" (Kosovicz), 107–8
machines, 104–10, 113, 116
MacLeish, Archibald, 101
Mailloux, Steven, 9
Man-Eating Myth, The (Arens), 79–80
Marcuse, Herbert, 189
marriage, 277, 283, 287, 291–92, 293
Martin, Henri-Jean, 182, 183, 184
Marxism: capitalism of, 70; and feminism,
  7; and historical materialism, 204, 207–8,
  210, 211; and ideology, 316; materialism of, 8, 10, 70; and working women's
  poetry, 105, 114–15, 116. *See also* leftist
  ideology
Mary N. (literacy case study), 156
mascots, 5–6, 8
mass media, 186, 187–88
material rhetoric: anxiety about, 22–23; challenges to theorizing a, 17–23; characteristics of, 71, 336; consequences of, 19–20,
  22, 23, 34, 36; critics of, 38–39; growing
  interest in, 8–14; lack of idiom for referencing, 17–18; and liberal humanism, 21–23;
  meanings of, 297–98; and ordinary idiom,
  16; in practice, 298–99; questions concerning, 10–11; sociohistorical dimensions
  of, 336–37, 338, 339; and symbolicity, 18–
  20, 23, 50; what is, 13, 326–27. *See also*
  specific theorist or topic
maternity. *See* Moore, Demi; pregnancy
matter, 331–33, 342, 343, 346
Mayer, W. F., 153
McDougal, Frances H., 89–90
McGavran, Mary Theodora, 60
McGee, Michael Calvin, 13, 19, 336–37, 338,
  339
McGlashan, Charles F., 76–77, 78, 84, 85, 86,
  90–92
McLean Hospital (Boston), 202, 206, 208, 210
McPhee, John, 161–62
meaning, 38, 337, 338
Media Foundation, 191
medical profession, authority of, 305–7, 311
medical schools, 59–62
medicine: access of American women to "regular," 58–59; and development of medical
  profession, 59; and feminism, 58; in nine-

teenth century, 58–74; women in, 11, 58–74. *See also* dissection; medical schools
Melville, Herman, 333
memorials: appropriation of, 39–40; as challenges, 42, 44; characteristics of, 17; as communal spaces, 48, 50; competition among, 44; contextualizing of, 40; as destinations, 46; destruction and vulnerability of, 37–38; as exemplars of material rhetoric, 11, 17, 23–50; functions of, 34, 36; as means of correcting, 42; and Moore cover photo, 311; oral speech compared with, 17; as prescribing pathways, 47–48, 50; questions about material rhetoric and, 30–50; reactions to, 45–50; as silencing, 44–45; as summons, 46–47, 48, 50; supplementing of, 40, 42; surge in building of, 23–24, 36–37, 39; text on, 30–50. *See also specific memorial*
memory, 9, 10, 71, 77–78, 85–86, 87, 89
Merleau-Ponty, Maurice, 4, 7
Mexico, Zapatistas in, 194–98
Michel, Neil, 17, 39, 40
Middle East, archeological sites in, 178–80
Millenson, Elliot, 242, 243, 244, 248, 253, 256
Miller, Carolyn, 242, 250–51, 254
mind-body relationship, 7, 109–10, 336, 359–60, 361–62. *See also* Prozac
minorities. *See* African Americans; gays; home collection testing system
Miramontes, Helen, 256
modernism, 226
Modern Language and Literature Committee (Commission on Preservation and Access), 129, 136
Moonsammy, Rita Zorn, 161
Moore, Demi, 12, 297–98, 299, 300, 301, 306–9, 311, 312
moral instruction, dissection as, 65–66, 67, 68
morality, and literacy, 145, 147, 150, 151–52, 153, 162
Morris, Dick, 13, 314–16, 317–18, 321–22, 323–25
Morrow, Lance, 315
motherhood. *See* pregnancy
"Mother's Misery, A" (Ferrara), 112–13
motivation, 337–38, 341, 344
mutations, 343–44
Muybridge, Eadweard, 187

Nabors, Jim, 287
naked women, 300. *See also* Moore, Demi
NAMES Project. *See* AIDS Memorial Quilt
naming, process of, 332
National Abortion Rights Action League (NARAL), 222
National Association of Lesbian and Gay Health Clinics (NALGHC), 246, 250, 260
National Commemorative Works Act (1986), 36
National Endowment for the Arts, 279
National Endowment for the Humanities, 126
National Institutes of Health (NIH), 243
National Lesbian and Gay Health Associations (NLGHA), 247–48
National Women's Trade Union League, 99, 101, 131
nature, 351, 361
need interpretations, 258–59
"needy bodies," 12, 242, 250, 252–59, 268
neo-Marxism, 204, 207–9
New Deal, rhetoric of, 100, 117
Nietzsche, Friedrich, 16, 289
Nike, "Just Do It!" slogan of, 191
non-life, 343–44
North American Free Trade Agreement (NAFTA), 194–95, 198
nudes, 13, 300–301. *See also* Moore, Demi
Nuñez, Louis, 256
nurture, 351

object, 328–29, 331, 332, 333–34, 335, 336, 338, 345
Obsession, advertising about, 192, 193
O'Connor, Sandra Day, 231
Oklahoma City Murrah Federal Building, bombing of, 44
One-Way Street (Benjamin), 70–71
oral speech, memorials compared with, 17
organ donors, 361
Other, 80, 358, 362
outing, and beards, 277, 279–83, 286–87, 290
outside and inside, 360–61

partisanship, 20, 23, 363. *See also* ideology
partner selection, 266–68
passing, 288, 289, 304
Pathfinder (Time Warner web site), 173, 174
Patton, Cindy, 255, 258, 266–67

Phaedrus Media (web site), 171, 172
photography, 13, 185, 186–87. *See also* cover photos
physical: and growing interest in materiality, 9, 10, 11, 13; language as, 13, 329–30, 331, 332, 335, 338, 351–52; materiality as, 330–31; text as, 9, 10, 11
pictographs, 176–77, 180
Pillow Book, The (film), 6
Pine Barrens (N.J.): Goddard's writings about, 154–56, 159–61, 162; Kite's writings about, 154, 157–50, 160–61, 162; literacy in, 151–62; McPhee's writings about, 161–62; missionaries in, 151–52, 160
Plato, 328, 342, 351, 360
poetry: by African Americans, 110–12; as bridge between material and immaterial, 98–99; as class issue, 98; about literacy and images, 175; study at Bryn Mawr Summer School, 101–2. *See also* poetry, working women's; *specific poet*
poetry, working women's: authenticity of, 117; body in, 104–10, 114–16; and class issues, 109–10, 112, 113–15; and feminism, 105–6; function of, 101–2; and gender issues, 105, 109–16; and growing interest in materiality, 11; and leftist/Marxist ideology, 105–6, 112–13, 114–15, 117; about machines, 104–10, 113, 116; and mind-body relationship, 109–10; and race/racism, 105, 110–12; and Romanticism, 103; themes and style of, 102, 103–4
politics: and beards, 281, 286, 289; and body, 358; and fantasy, 362–63; and feminism, 362; and home collection testing system, 243, 258–59; and rhetoric, 11, 20, 324, 325. *See also* ideology; Morris, Dick
Portelli, Christopher, 248, 260, 268
Porter, Cole, 291
postcards, 290
postmodernism, 7, 9, 10
post-structuralism, 7, 9, 13, 331–32, 336, 340, 358, 359–60
Poulsen, Richard C., 79, 86
Pound, Ezra, 101
poverty, 145–46, 151, 153
power, 339–47, 358
pragmeme/pragmatics, 19–20
pregnancy: and authority of medical profession, 305–7, 311; and beauty, 302–4, 305,

310, 311; and body language, 302–6; and culture, 298, 310, 312; and desirability, 302–4, 305, 307, 308, 309, 311; and feminism, 297, 306, 308, 309, 311, 312; and growing interest in materiality, 13; and passing, 304; and sex, 304, 305, 307; as transitory, 304–5, 306. *See also* Moore, Demi
"presence," 337
Preston, Ann, 62, 65
printing/printing press, 177, 179, 181–83, 184
private/privacy, 218, 229–33, 261, 264, 290, 293, 324. *See also* public-private
privilege, 275–76, 280
Progressive Era, 99
provenance, of historical materials, 128
Prozac: access to, 208, 209; advertising of, 206, 207; and class issues, 208, 214, 215; and gender, 208; and growing interest in materiality, 12; and health care system, 208–9; and historical materialism, 207–9, 210–11, 213, 215–17; Kaysen's writings about, 202, 206, 208, 210, 211; Kramer's writings about, 203, 204, 205–6, 209, 210; and psychological materialism, 202, 205–7, 215, 216–17; Slater's writings about, 209–15
psychoanalysis, 288
psychological materiality, 12, 202, 205–7, 211, 215, 216–17
public, 10, 218, 225–29, 321. *See also* public-private
public-private: Arendt's views about, 219, 225–27, 229; and "culture wars," 279–80; and dissection, 63, 64–66, 67–68; distinguishing between, 218–19; extension of, 275–76; and feminism, 233–34, 359; Fraser's views about, 218, 219, 225–26, 227–29, 233, 242, 258–59; and growing interest in materiality, 9, 10, 12, 13; Habermas's views about, 219, 225–26, 227–28; historical contexts of, 225, 229–30; and home collection testing system, 243, 261, 264, 266, 268; and ideology, 323–24; and marriage, 277, 283, 287, 291–92, 293; and political action, 226, 229; and privacy issues, 225, 229–33; and privilege, 275–76, 280; spatial delineation of, 225–29; and "subaltern counterpublics," 228–29; and technoscience, 12. *See also* abortion;

beards; body/bodies; Moore, Demi; Morris, Dick; pregnancy
purpose, and DNA doing rhetoric, 339–47

Queer Nation, 279, 280, 290
"queer paradigm," 255
"queer theory," 8, 278, 279
Quintilian, 70

race/racism: and autobiography, 214; and body, 5, 7; and cannibalism, 88; degeneration of Anglo-American, 12, 144, 150, 151, 157–59, 161, 162; among Donner Party, 88; fantasies about, 362; and genetics, 349; and growing interest in materiality, 10; and guilt, 88; and home collection testing system, 258–59, 261, 264–65; and identity, 362; and literacy, 144, 150, 151, 157–59, 161, 162; superiority of Anglo-American, 147, 150; and working women, 100, 105, 110–12
reading, 66, 67, 68, 69, 183. *See also* literacy
reality, 4, 185–88, 357
Redbook magazine, 302–4
Reed family (Donner Party), 75–76, 78, 81, 85, 87
reference theory, 328–29, 331, 351
reification theory, 207–8
religion, 151–52, 160, 174–75, 176, 183, 184, 185
Renaissance, 185, 186
reproduction: of images, 182–83, 186; of text/memorials, 38–39, 50
reproductive freedom. *See* abortion
rhetoric: characteristics of, 363; and communication, 345–47; consequences of, 19–20, 22, 23; as criticism, 334–35; and culture, 320, 323, 324–25; definitions of, 18–19, 21, 363; difference between classical and modern, 320–22, 324; disciplinary formation of, 317–25; DNA as doing, 339–47; dualism of, 327; and ethics, 324; feminine in, 9; goal orientation of, 21–23, 50; and humanism, 21–23; legibility of, 20; motivation for using, 21, 22; partisanship character of, 20, 23; as performance, 334–35; and politics, 20, 324, 325; and public discourse, 363; rethinking, 23–50; revisionary histories of, 120–42; and social formation, 339–40; text as, 18;

vocabulary of, 340. *See also* material rhetoric
rhetorical analysis, 339–40
rhetorical condition, 301–2
Richards, I. A., 328
Richardson, Ida, 62, 63, 65, 66
RNA, 337–38, 341, 344
Rodriguez, Rene, 245, 253, 256, 257
romance, 276, 291–92, 293
Romanticism, 103
Roosevelt (Franklin Delano) Memorial (Washington, D.C.), 23, 36, 39
Rorty, Richard, 320, 323
Rosenberg, Charles E., 60, 69
Rosin, Hanna, 259
rural America: distinction between urban and, 159; and growing interest in materiality, 12; leaving of, 147, 148; literacy in, 12, 143–70; Pine Barrens as, 151–61; and revolt from village, 144–51
Russo, Vito, 276

Salinas, Carlos, 194–95
Sandburg, Carl, 3, 13, 101, 103
Sartre, Jean-Paul, 7
Saussure, Ferdinand de, 331
Scarry, Elaine, 85, 233, 362
Schmandt-Besserat, Denise, 176, 178–80
science/scientists: criticism about DNA by, 327; and feminism, 58; and growing interest in materiality, 4, 8, 10; and historical materialism, 215–16; and invention of printing press, 184; and literacy, 175, 176, 177, 183–84; use of metaphors by, 326; vocabulary of, 202–3, 335–36. *See also* coding; dissection; genetics; medicine; psychological materiality; technoscience
Scott-Levin (consulting firm), 209
Sedgwick, Eve Kosofsky, 8, 13, 277, 279, 280, 283, 284, 290–91, 293
self, 80, 206, 290, 361–62. *See also* autobiography
self-analysis, of Donne, 4–5, 6, 8
self-reproduction, 340–41
Selzer, Jack, 298, 357
sex, 61–62, 266–67, 304, 305, 307
sexism, 100, 133, 309
sex organs, 361
sexuality, 7, 11, 361. *See also* beards
Shalala, Donna, 247–48

shame, 286–91, 293, 294
sign function, of language, 328–29, 330
Signorile, Michelangelo, 279–80, 281–82
Simon, Theodore, 154–55, 157
Slater, Lauren, 12, 209–15
Slotkin, Richard, 82
Smith, Henry Nash, 82–83
Smith, Hilda Worthington, 99, 100, 101, 117
Smith, Shepard, 246, 259, 260
Smoky Pilgrim family (Blackmar study),
    148–50, 154
social issues: and coding, 13, 345; and grow-
    ing interest in materiality, 11, 13; and his-
    torical materials, 126–27, 128; and lan-
    guage theories, 329–31, 332, 333, 336–37,
    339–40, 351; and literacy, 163
sociology, 4, 150
sophists, 320–21, 324
Southern Poverty Law Center, 24–26
speech act, 19–20
spider's web, 3, 13–14
Stanton, Charles (Donner Party), 88
Star Wars (film), 188
statements, 330
Stefano, Joey, 283, 285–86
St. James, Susan, 287
Story of a Country Town, The (Howe), 144–
    45, 146, 147, 150, 153
structuralism, 328–29, 334, 336, 337. See also
    post-structuralism; ultra-structuralism
Styron, William, 12, 208, 209
"subaltern counterpublics," 228–29
Suddenly, Last Summer (film), 276, 281
Sunset Boulevard (film), 291–92
Supreme Court, U.S., privacy rulings of, 219,
    229–33
Swanson, Gloria, 291–92
symbolicity, 18–20, 23, 50

Taylor, Elizabeth, 275, 276–77, 278–79,
    280–82, 291, 292
technology, 9, 10, 175, 181–83, 185–88. See
    also technoscience
technoscience: access to, 242, 250, 252–59,
    268, 269; authority of, 249; boundary be-
    tween other worlds and, 249; and control,
    243; and culture, 249–50; faith in, 257;
    and growing interest in materiality, 12; and
    home collection testing system, 242–50,
    252; kairos of, 250–55; power of, 257

Terminator 2 (film), 188
text: and abortion, 12; access to, 38; act on
    person(s) of, 45–50; apparatuses and dura-
    bility of, 37–38, 50; body in, 7, 12; compar-
    ison to other texts of, 39–42; definitions
    of, 18; Foucault's views about, 330; func-
    tions of, 330; images in, 12, 363; kind of
    material for, 37–38, 50; and literacy, 174;
    and Moore photograph, 311–12; as physi-
    cal, 9, 10, 11; relationship to material rhe-
    toric of, 9, 10, 11, 16, 18, 30–50, 330; re-
    production or preservation of, 38–39, 50;
    significance of material existence of, 30–
    37; situatedness of, 339; transparent, 174.
    See also historical materials; memorials
Thornton, Jesse Quinn, 78, 86, 87, 88
"Thoughts" (Brown), 114–15
Three Fighting Men (Vietnam Veterans Me-
    morial), 24, 25, 47
Time magazine, Morris articles in, 315, 322,
    323
Time Warner, Pathfinder web site of, 173,
    174
Toy Story (film), 188
"transformation" of hurt, 212–13
Treichler, Paula, 250, 258
Tron (film), 188
True, A. C., 148, 149
Turner, Frederick Jackson, 83–84, 88
Twain, Mark, 68, 145, 333

ultra-structuralism, 331–35, 336, 337, 351,
    359
University Hospital Laboratories (UHL), 242,
    243–44
urban America, 159, 162
U.S. Bureau of Education, 143, 146
U.S. Department of Agriculture, 147–48
U.S. Holocaust Memorial Museum, 44
U.S. Law Enforcement Officers Memorial
    (Washington, D.C.), 23
U.S. Navy Memorial (Washington, D.C.), 23,
    39
U.S. Public Health Service, 244, 245, 246.
    See also Food and Drug Administration
utterances, 19–20

Vai people (Liberia), 184
Valencia, Lydia, 256
Van Doren, Carl, 144

Vanity Fair magazine, 13, 297, 299–301, 302, 306–11
"Venus Hottentot" (Alexander), 6–7
Vietnam Veterans Memorial (Washington, D.C.), 11, 23, 24, 25, 34, 36, 38, 39–40, 41, 42, 44, 47–48
Vietnam Women's Memorial (Washington, D.C.), 24, 26, 47–48
Vineland Training School, 151, 154, 155, 156, 158, 160
Virgin, cult of, 301
visual design: and alphabetic literacy narrative, 12, 176–85; literacy as, 8, 188–94; technologies of, 185–88; and web sites, 171, 174, 175, 185, 188, 194–98. *See also* cover photos; images
vocabulary, 202–3, 335–36, 337, 338, 340
Vuckovic, Alexander, 208, 210

Wald, Elijah, 326, 350–51
Watt, Ian, 184
WCS. *See* Women's Choice Services
web sites, 10, 171, 172, 173, 174, 175, 185, 188, 190, 192–98. *See also specific site*
westering culture, 76, 77, 82–83
westward movement, 82–84, 89, 90, 92
"whiteness studies," 361–62
Whitman, Walt, 101
Whitman-Walker Clinic, 243, 259–60
Wilde, Oscar, 290
Willard, Louis, 126, 138
Willis, Bruce, 307
Wilson, Edmund, Jr., 151
Wilson, Erasmus, 61–62
Wilson, Myoung Chung, 135
Wisconsin State Historical Records Advisory Board, 135–36
Witch Trials Tercentenary Memorial (Salem, Massachusetts), 11, 23, 24, 27, 30, 33, 34, 35, 36, 39, 42, 44–45, 47
Wittgenstein, Ludwig, 328, 341, 342

Woman's Medical College of Pennsylvania, 59–61, 62–63, 65, 66, 67–68
women: body of, 7, 8, 11, 13, 358–59; class issues among white, 113–15; cultural views of role of, 133; as deviant, 302–4; education of, 131; in medical schools, 59–61; naked and nude, 300; needs interpretations of, 258–59; and Other, 358; and practices of everyday life, 358–59; and public-private, 358–59; representation of, 300–301; working class, 11. *See also* abortion; feminism; gender; poetry, working women's; pregnancy; women physicians; women's associations
women physicians, 11, 58–74
women's associations, texts of, 121–22, 130–34, 136
Women's Choice Services (WCS): and "grounded theory approach," 221–25; Permanent Injunction against, 219–25, 229, 230, 233–34; and public-private materiality, 219–25, 229, 230, 233–34
wood blocks/engravings, 184, 186
Woolf, Virginia, 13–14
Wordsworth, William, 175
worker education movement, 100, 101
working women, 11, 98, 99–102, 109–12, 113–15, 117, 131. *See also* poetry, working women's
World War II Memorial (Washington, D.C.), 24, 36
writing, 68, 174, 176–80
Wurtzel, Elizabeth, 203, 207–8, 209, 210, 211

"¡Ya Basta!" (web site), 196
"Yellow Kid, The" (comic strip), 187
YWCA, 99, 101, 106, 107, 117, 131

Zakrzewska, Marie, 69
Zapatistas, 194–98
Zizek, Slavoj, 362